The **Rough Guide** to

Cambodia

written and researched by

Beverley Palmer

with additional contributions by

Charlotte Melville

www.roughguides.com

Contents

Festivals and ceremonies colour section following p.144

Temple architecture colour section following p.208

◄◄ Monks at Phnom Penh Independence Monument ◄ Morning market, Kratie

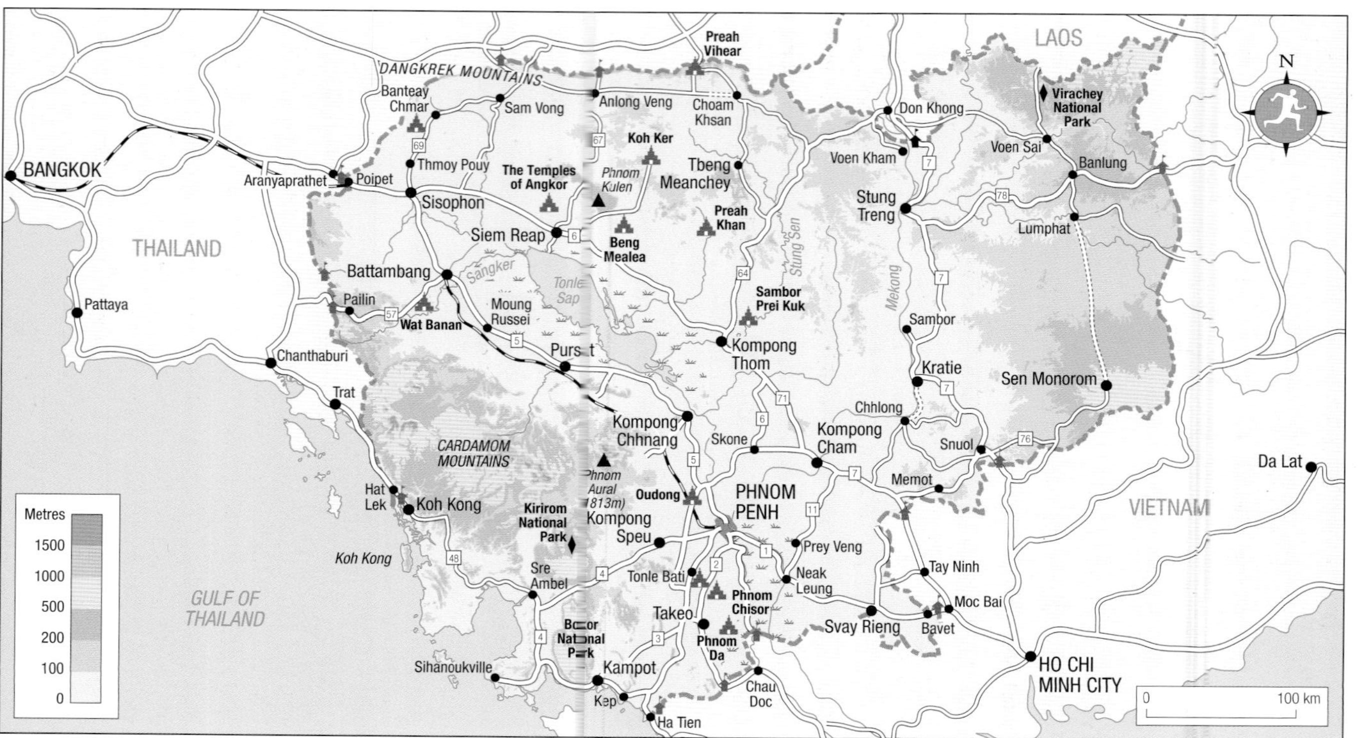
LAOS
THAILAND
VIETNAM
GULF OF THAILAND
DANGKREK MOUNTAINS
CARDAMOM MOUNTAINS
N
BANGKOK
Pattaya
Aranyaprathet
Poipet
Chanthaburi
Trat
Banteay Chmar
Sam Vong
Anlong Veng
Preah Vihear
Choam Khsan
Thmoy Pouy
Sisophon
The Temples of Angkor
Phnom Kulen
Koh Ker
Tbeng Meanchey
Preah Khan
Beng Mealea
Siem Reap
Battambang
Sangker
Tonle Sap
Pailin
Wat Banan
Moung Russei
Pursat
Stung Sen
Sambor Prei Kuk
Kompong Thom
Mekong
Don Khong
Voen Kham
Stung Treng
Virachey National Park
Voen Sai
Banlung
Lumphat
Sambor
Kratie
Sen Monorom
Chhlong
Snuol
Kompong Chhnang
Skone
Kompong Cham
Memot
Phnom Aural (1813m)
Oudong
PHNOM PENH
Hat Lek
Koh Kong
Kirirom National Park
Kompong Speu
Prey Veng
Tonle Bati
Neak Leung
Tay Ninh
Sre Ambel
Phnom Chisor
Moc Bai
Takeo
Svay Rieng
Bavet
Bokor National Park
Phnom Da
Sihanoukville
Kampot
Kep
Chau Doc
Ha Tien
HO CHI MINH CITY
Da Lat
Koh Kong
0
100 km
Metres
1500
1000
500
200
100
0
1
2
3
4
5
6
7
11
48
57
64
67
69
71
76
78

Introduction to

Cambodia

Thanks to the stunning temples of Angkor, Cambodia is now firmly established on the Southeast Asian tourist trail. Many visitors head straight to the temples, staying in the country just a few days, but those who delve deeper find that Cambodia, with its balmy climate and laid back attitude to life has much more to offer: white-sand beaches and relaxed off-shore islands, forest-clad hills and impenetrable jungle, a dynamic, yet beguiling, capital and sleepy provincial towns, in many of which colonial houses and shophouse terraces are now slowly being restored.

For a small country, Cambodia encompasses a surprisingly diverse range of terrain and scenery. Rice fields may be the quintessential feature of this predominantly flat and agricultural land, but there are also significant highland areas and 440km of coastline, as well as the massive Tonle Sap, Southeast Asia's largest freshwater lake, which dominates the heart of the country. In the east, the mighty Mekong River forms a natural divide, beyond which rise the mountains of Rattanakiri and Mondulkiri, where the last of Cambodia's jungle can be found. In the southwest, the heavily forested Cardamom Mountains run down to the sea, while parts of the southeast are regularly inundated, as the Mekong and its sister river, the Bassac, overflow their banks.

For all its natural beauty and rich heritage, Cambodia is still probably best known in the West for its suffering at the hands of the fanatical Khmer Rouge, who came to power in the 1970s with a programme of mass execution that resulted in the death of a fifth of the population. Their three-year terror was followed by a protracted guerrilla war that ended only in 1998 and left much of the country in ruins. Nowadays, however, Cambodia is at peace, and visitors will find it a safe place to travel.

Supported by Western aid, the infrastructure has at last improved; new roads now connect all but the most remote provincial centres, rendering most air and river routes redundant, and enterprise is booming, attested to in the capital, Phnom Penh, and major towns by thronging markets, restored colonial

Fact file

• Cambodia is about one and a half times the size of England – roughly the same area as Oklahoma. Around one twentieth of the country is covered by the waters of the Tonle Sap lake. The highest point is Phnom Aural (1771m) in the Cardamom Mountains.

• Cambodia's population is **around 15 million**, of which ninety percent is Khmer. The remainder consists of ethnic Chinese and Vietnamese (together around 6.5 percent), the Cham (2.5 percent) and the chunchiet (1 percent).

• **Theravada Buddhism** is practised by 95 percent of the population, alongside some animism and ancestor worship; the Cham are Muslim.

• Cambodia is a **constitutional monarchy**, with an elected government comprising two houses of parliament, the National Assembly and the Senate.

• Average **annual income** is just $610 per capita, putting Cambodia among the world's poorest countries. Average life expectancy, though improving, is just 61 years.

villas newly opened as boutique hotels and the re-emergence of a modest middle class. Cambodian food, influenced by the cuisines of both China and Thailand, is delicately flavoured and quite delicious; while the country's long tradition of artisanship has been revived, with weaving, stone-carving and silversmithing much in evidence. Temple sites, some dating back to the sixth century, dot the countryside – several have only recently become accessible and many are now being restored. The majority of the country's towns still retain some old-world charm, preserving quaint shophouse terraces and colonial architecture dating back to the period of French rule – though perhaps their most tangible colonial legacy is the piles of crusty baguettes heaped up in baskets and hawked around the streets in the early morning.

Though much still has to be done before Cambodia is properly back on its feet, and before most of the population see a substantial improvement in their standard of living, the recovery of the country is largely down to the Cambodians themselves, eternally optimistic, tenacious and tirelessly hospitable.

◀ Lights for the Buddha, Wat Phnom

Where to go

Most tourists make for the cosmopolitan capital, **Phnom Penh**, at some point during their visit. A pleasing, low-rise city graced with leafy boulevards, the capital offers the chance to take in the splendour of the Royal Palace and Silver Pagoda, while the cream of ancient Khmer art is housed a stone's throw away at the National Museum. The capital also boasts a vibrant riverside of pavement cafés and bars and is the best place in the country to shop, its colourful markets stocked with shimmering silks and intricate handicrafts.

Sugar palms

Peppering rice paddies with their distinctive mops of spiky leaves, sugar-palm trees are of great importance to the rural Cambodian economy, since every part of the tree can be put to good use. Arguably the most significant product is the **juice**, extracted by climbing a rickety ladder lashed to the trunk, cutting the stalk bearing the flowers and fixing in place a container to collect the juice. This tends to be a dry-season occupation, as high monsoon winds and wet trunks make the climb hazardous at other times of year. The cloudy liquid is cleared by first smoking the collection tube with burning palm fronds and then adding bark from the *popael* tree (of the honeysuckle family). Both the sweet, fresh juice and fermented, alcoholic **palm beer**, are sold by hawkers from containers suspended either from a shoulder pole or from bicycle or moto handlebars. These days a sanitized version, nicely packaged, can be found in tourist centres and supermarkets. **Palm sugar**, much used by sweet-toothed Cambodians for cooking, is made by thickening the juice in a cauldron and then pouring it into cylindrical tubes to set, after which it resembles grainy honey-coloured fudge. Nearly as important as the juice are the **leaves**, which are collected two or three times a year for use in thatch, wall panels, woven matting, baskets, fans and even packaging. Until quite recently, specially treated leaves were used to record religious teachings by **inscribing** them with a metal nib.

Palm **fruits**, slightly larger than a cricket ball, have a tough, fibrous black coating containing juicy, delicately flavoured kernels, which are translucent white and have the consistency of jelly; they're eaten either fresh or with syrup as a dessert. The **root** of the tree is used in traditional medicine as a cure for stomach ache and other ailments. Perhaps because the trees furnish so many other products, they are seldom cut for their **wood**, which is extremely durable. However, palm-wood souvenirs can be found in Phnom Penh and Siem Reap, easily identifiable by their distinctive light-and-dark striped grain. Palm-wood furniture has become à la mode in one or two of the country's trendy boutique hotels.

What's a wat – and what's not

Cambodia's wats are Buddhist monasteries, often generically referred to as pagodas, although they bear no resemblance to their Chinese namesakes. Wats are easily identified by the bright orange tiled roof of the principal building, the vihara, and can be vibrant, even wacky, affairs; the wealthier the foundation that runs the pagoda, the more extravagant the decoration, both inside and outside, with buildings painted in the most garish of primary colours, and courtyards featuring abundant and cartoonish statues of mythical beasts.

The term temple, on the other hand, is usually reserved for ancient Khmer monuments, dating from the sixth to the thirteenth centuries. Temples were generally built by kings to honour their ancestors or to serve as their state-temple – an image of the devaraja god associated with the king could be housed in a sanctuary tower (see the *Temple architecture* colour section). State-temples were seldom reused by successive kings, though occasionally they gained a new lease of life as monasteries.

The main reason that most people come to Cambodia, however, is to visit the world-famous **temples of Angkor**, just outside the engaging town of **Siem Reap**. Chief is the majestic **Angkor Wat**, but close by are the compact **Banteay Srei**, with enchanting bas-reliefs of demure divinities; **Ta Prohm**, clamped in the grip of giant kapok trees; and the intricately designed, slightly surreal, **Bayon**, carved with hundreds of faces. The pre-Angkorian temple **Sambor Prei Kuk** lies just to the northeast of the provincial town of Kompong Thom, while more intrepid travellers can escape the crowds and head for remote temples such as **Preah Vihear**, which clings dramatically to an escarpment on the Thai border, **Koh Ker** and **Beng Mealea**, all a day-trip northeast of Siem Reap.

▲ Elaborately decorated wat vihara

After seeing the temples of Angkor, many people head down to **Sihanoukville** to spend a few days lazing on

▲ Leading an ox to the fields, Siem Reap

pristine white-sand beaches lapped by the waters of the Gulf of Thailand. The coast is peppered with islands and there is a nascent diving industry. Just outside Sihanoukville is the **Ream National Park** where you can putter downstream as monkeys play in the mangroves and fishing eagles soar overhead. East of Sihanoukville, **Kampot** is a delightful town of mixed French and Chinese influences, with views to the brooding slopes of **Bokor Mountain**. Nearby is the beguiling seaside resort of **Kep**, with a minuscule beach and atmosphere of faded gentility. Its decrepit buildings are being restored, and the tiny town already hosts some of the country's most stylish accommodation. Inland from here is **Angkor Borei**, third-century capital of Cambodia, accessible only by water for much of the year.

Northeast of the capital, the Mekong at **Kratie** is home to a graceful population of Irrawaddy dolphins. Getting out to the remote northeastern provincial capitals of **Banlung** and **Sen Monorom** takes more time and effort, but the natural beauty of this part of the country is unrivalled, the hillsides brimming with wildlife, dotted with scenic waterfalls and home to villages of the minority chunchiet tribes, and where you can trek on foot or by elephant.

The northwestern border crossing from Thailand at **Poipet** is an increasingly popular point of entry to Cambodia, while nearby **Battambang** retains some of the country's most attractive colonial architecture and makes a convenient stopover on the way to Phnom Penh or an interesting side-trip from Siem Reap.

Fishing boats, Sihanoukville

When to go

A tropical country, Cambodia is warm all year round, though there are several distinct seasons. There is little rain between November and May, the so-called **dry season**, which itself divides into two distinct phases. The **cool season** (Nov–Feb) is the peak time for tourism, as it's cool enough to explore the temples in comfort and yet warm enough to sunbathe by the coast. The **hot season** (typically March–May) is when humidity and temperatures soar, with Phnom Penh and Battambang seeing peak daytime temperatures of 33–35°C. At this time, it's best to rise early to get out and about, returning for a snooze at midday and emerging again late in the afternoon. This is also when the dust thrown up from the country's dirt roads is at its worst, the billowing clouds ensuring that everything and everyone is coated in a fine film of grit. At Angkor, the unrelenting sun, allied to the lack of any breeze, makes for a baking visit, though this is an excellent time to hit the coast.

The **rainy season** lasts roughly from June to October. River levels rise dramatically, and in September and October the country's infrastructure is at its most stretched, with dirt roads reduced to deep slurry and a risk of flooding in provincial areas. Thankfully, the rains aren't unrelenting and fall mainly in the afternoon, so provided you don't want to get off the beaten track and don't mind doing most of your sightseeing in the mornings (which are normally dry), this isn't a bad time to visit. It's also the quietest time for tourism (at Angkor, you'll have the temples pretty much to yourself) and the countryside is at its lushest.

Average maximum daily temperatures (°C) and average monthly rainfall (mm)

	Jan	Feb	Mar	Apr	May	Jun	Jul	Aug	Sep	Oct	Nov	Dec
Phnom Penh												
°C	31	32	34	35	34	33	32	32	31	30	30	30
rainfall (mm)	10	10	45	80	120	150	165	160	215	240	135	55

20 things not to miss

It's not possible to see everything that Cambodia has to offer in one trip – and we don't suggest you try. What follows is a selective and subjective taste of the country's highlights: colourful festivals, serene beaches and nature reserves, and – of course – the finest of the temples at Angkor and elsewhere. They're all arranged in five colour-coded categories to help you find the very best things to see, do and experience. All entries have a page reference to take you straight into the Guide, where you can find out more.

01 **Angkor Thom** Page **191** • Expansive walled city, entered through a huge gateway decorated with enormous stone faces.

02 Apsara dance Page **175** • Elegantly stylized form of Khmer classical dance, evoking the apsaras – celestial goddesses of Hindu mythology.

03 Cambodian cuisine Page **34** • Richly flavoured with herbs and using only the freshest ingredients, the country's fragrant and distinctive cuisine offers plenty of culinary surprises, which you could learn to re-create yourself on a cookery course.

04 Sambor Prei Kuk Page **221** • These mellow, well-preserved brick ruins are among the very earliest surviving Khmer monuments.

05 Ream National Park Page **286** • Possibly Cambodia's most enchanting national park, with secluded, palm-fringed bays, a river lined with lush mangroves and abundant wildlife.

06 Banteay Srei Page **207** • This beautiful rose-pink temple is the most elaborately decorated of all Angkor's monuments.

07 Toul Sleng and Choeung Ek Pages **100 & 121** • Harrowing monuments to Cambodia's grisly past.

08 Yeak Laom lake Page **257** • Sparkling lake, set in an almost perfectly circular volcanic crater.

09 Tonle Sap lake Page **209** • Like an inland sea, this freshwater lake supports hundreds of floating villages in which life is lived entirely on the water.

10 Ta Prohm Page **198** • Nature holds this ruined temple in a vice-like grip, with gigantic tree roots wedged between massive stones.

11 Psar Toul Tom Poung Page **111** • One of Phnom Penh's most attractive markets, packed with vibrant silks and intriguing curios.

12 Elephants Page **261** • Take an elephant-back trek, or get close to Cambodia's remaining elephant population in Mondulkiri, where there's an elephant sanctuary.

13 Kep Page **298** • Once-deserted villas have been restored to luxurious accommodation in this tiny seaside resort, famous in Cambodia for its succulent crabs.

14 Sihanoukville Page **272** • Cambodia's liveliest resort, with tropical beaches, abundant seafood, a fledgling diving industry, busy nightlife, and tranquil off-shore islands where you can get away from it all.

15 Natural environment Pages **257** & **271** • Hang out with a local family in a rural homestay or in eco-lodges and experience Cambodia's fascinating natural environment at close hand.

16 A sunset trip on the Mekong Page **98** • Cruise along the river through Phnom Penh for spectacular views as the sun sinks behind the Royal Palace and Silver Pagoda.

17 Angkor Wat Page **185** • The zenith of Khmer architecture, this unforgettable temple, crowned with soaring towers and embellished with intricate bas-reliefs, is one of Cambodia's most memorable sights.

18 Royal Palace and Silver Pagoda Page **90** • The extravagant Royal Palace and Silver Pagoda, in the heart of Phnom Penh, are home to fabulous murals and a treasure-trove of Khmer sculpture.

19 Khmer art Pages **95** & **170** • Some of the country's most stunning ancient statues are on display in the National Museum in Phnom Penh and the Angkor National Museum in Siem Reap.

20 Irrawaddy dolphins Page **245** • These rare mammals live in small groups along a stretch of the Mekong in the northeast.

Basics

Basics

Getting there

There are no direct flights to Cambodia from Europe, North America, Australasia or South Africa, so if you plan to fly into the country you'll need to get a connecting flight from elsewhere in Southeast or East Asia. There are regular direct flights to Phnom Penh and Siem Reap from an increasing number of cities in the region; these include Bangkok, Hanoi, Ho Chi Minh City, Kuala Lumpur, Seoul, Singapore, Taipei and Vientiane. Airfares to Cambodia peak during the high season (July, August and the latter half of December) and are cheapest during the low season (roughly from mid-April to the end of May).

Flights from the UK and Ireland

There are plenty of daily flights, many nonstop, from **London Heathrow** to Southeast Asian cities, with some airlines offering connections to Phnom Penh. Flight times vary depending on routing; it takes 11–12 hours to fly nonstop from London to Bangkok, and another hour from there to Phnom Penh. Departing from elsewhere in the UK it may be more convenient to fly from a regional airport with a European carrier, such as Air France (who reintroduced flights to Phnom Penh via Bangkok in March 2011) and KLM, who offer flights to Southeast Asia via their respective hub cities. From **Ireland**, it's a matter of either getting a cheap connection to London Heathrow or flying to Cambodia via a different European hub city.

Thai Airways, Singapore Airlines and Malaysia Airlines offer some of the most competitive **fares** to Cambodia, with flights via **Bangkok**, **Singapore** and **Kuala Lumpur** respectively, from where there are regular connections on to Phnom Penh and Siem Reap. Return fares to Phnom Penh start at around £600 in low season, rising to £850 or more in high season.

Flights from the US and Canada

Flying from the **east coast** of North America to Cambodia it's quickest to travel via Europe. Conversely, from the **west coast** it may well be cheaper to fly westward via an Asian city such as Seoul or Taipei (the latter has direct connections to Phnom Penh on EVA Airways). There are daily flights from New York and Los Angeles to Bangkok, Hong Kong, Kuala Lumpur and Singapore, all of which have onward connections to Phnom Penh and Siem Reap. Fares from both the east and west coasts to Phnom Penh in low season are around $1000–1250, rising by $350 and more in high season. From Canada, low-season return fares from Toronto to Phnom Penh start at around Can$1180, and Can$1000 return from Vancouver.

Flights from Australia, New Zealand and South Africa

There's a wide selection of flights into Southeast Asia from Australia and New Zealand, to Bangkok, Kuala Lumpur, Singapore and Ho Chi Minh City with onward connections to Phnom Penh and Siem Reap. See p.21 for full details. Return **fares** from Australia to Phnom Penh start at around Aus$1000 in low season, rising to as much as Aus$2000 in high; from Auckland, Christchurch and Wellington expect to pay between NZ$2000 and NZ$3000, subject to seasonal variations.

In low season travelling to Phnom Penh via an Asian hub city from Cape Town you should expect to pay around ZAR12,000 return, while a return trip from Johannesburg will be about ZAR13,315.

Round-The-World flights

If Cambodia is only one stop on a longer journey, you might want to consider buying a **Round-The-World (RTW)** ticket. Cambodia can be added to itineraries offered by airline consortium Star Alliance (@www.staralliance.com) for example. Bangkok or Singapore are more common ports of call for many RTW tickets; from the UK, figure on around £1000 plus taxes for an RTW ticket including either of these destinations.

Getting there from neighbouring countries

If you're travelling overland to Cambodia, you can consider a number of border crossings open to foreigners, currently six from Thailand, six from Vietnam (with a further one in Mondulkiri due to open in 2011) and one from Laos.

Overland trips to Cambodia from Thailand are well publicized in Bangkok, particularly on Khao San Road, where travel agents sell their **Bangkok–Siem Reap** trips by alleging that doing the trip independently entails "problems" (dealing with Cambodian border officials, sorting out onward transport, and so on). In fact, it's straightforward to travel to Cambodia from Bangkok independently by public transport, and the convenience of travelling with one of these private firms is offset by the frustrations of their various scams: "we'll get your visa" (for 1200 baht); "you have to change ₿100 to riel" (you don't); "it's too late, you'll have to stay at this guest-house". Travelling independently, the trip from Bangkok to Siem Reap costs anything from $10 (train to Aranyaprathet, then a place on a public minibus) to $50 (bus to the border and then a taxi onwards) and takes around eight hours; using Khao San Road packages ($15–25) the journey can be considerably longer – twelve hours or more. Though some of the companies which run these packages are reputable, others aren't, and a significant number of travellers report the kinds of problems mentioned above. If you're intent on travelling with one of these outfits, it's worth asking fellow travellers about companies they would recommend or avoid. Check out @www.talesofasia.com for the latest.

All border crossings between Thailand and Cambodia are open daily (7am–8pm) and visas are issued on arrival at all points; however, **e-visas** (see p.60) are currently only accepted at Poipet and Koh Kong. The Aranyaprathet/**Poipet border crossing** is ideal if you want to start your visit to Cambodia in the north at Battambang and Siem Reap, but it is the most problematic. From Bangkok you can reach Aranyaprathet by train (2 daily; 5–7hr) or by a/c bus from either Suvarnabhumi, Bangkok's International airport (2 daily), or Bangkok's northern bus terminal, Morchit (frequent departures from 4am; 4–5hr). Once in Aranyaprathet take a tuk-tuk to the border (10min) and walk across, collecting your visa ($20) on the way. In Cambodia ignore all the touts and take a tuk-tuk or moto to either the taxi stand near the market or to one of the more reputable bus offices (Capitol, Phnom Penh Sorya Transport and Neak Krohorm) on the main road; a free shuttle bus runs from the border area to the transport stop where in theory you can take a bus – but they are infrequent. Onward transport on the Cambodian side of the border is readily available from Poipet to Sisophon, Siem Reap, Battambang and Phnom Penh; see p.153 for details. There is no train station at Poipet.

The Trat/**Koh Kong** crossing further south is good for Sihanoukville and Phnom Penh. From Bangkok there are a/c buses from Bangkok's eastern bus terminal to Trat (12 daily; 5hr). On the Cambodian side of the border, depending on when you arrive, you have the choice of continuing your journey straight away (the road linking Koh Kong through Sre Ambel to National Route 4 is good) or staying the night in Koh Kong; boats no longer run to Sihanoukville.

The other crossings are in the east at Ban Paakard/**Pailin (Psar Prom)** and Ban Leam/**Daun Lem**, from where you can head to Battambang (just over an hour on an excellent road) and in the north at Surin/**O'Smach**, and Chong Sa-Ngam/**Anlong Veng** (actually the border is about 25km north of Anlong Veng) – both 150km north of Siem Reap (2hr by taxi). These are not busy crossing points though, so your transport options on the Cambodian side will be limited.

There are currently six border crossings open to foreigners travelling overland from **Vietnam** (7am–5pm). These are: Moc Bai/**Bavet**, 200km southeast of Phnom Penh;

Six steps to a better kind of travel

At Rough Guides we are passionately committed to travel. We feel strongly that only through travelling do we truly come to understand the world we live in and the people we share it with – plus tourism has brought a great deal of **benefit** to developing economies around the world over the last few decades. But the extraordinary growth in tourism has also damaged some places irreparably, and of course **climate change** is exacerbated by most forms of transport, especially flying. This means that now more than ever it's important to **travel thoughtfully and responsibly**, with respect for the cultures you're visiting – not only to derive the most benefit from your trip but also to preserve the best bits of the planet for everyone to enjoy. At Rough Guides we feel there are six main areas in which you can make a difference:

- Consider what you're contributing to the **local economy**, and how much the services you use do the same, whether it's through employing local workers and guides or sourcing locally grown produce and local services.
- Consider the **environment** on holiday as well as at home. Water is scarce in many developing destinations, and the biodiversity of local flora and fauna can be adversely affected by tourism. Try to patronize businesses that take account of this.
- Travel with a purpose, not just to tick off experiences. Consider **spending longer** in a place, and getting to know it and its people.
- Give thought to how often you **fly**. Try to avoid short hops by air and more harmful night flights.
- Consider **alternatives to flying**, travelling instead by bus, train, boat and even by bike or on foot where possible.
- Make your trips "**climate neutral**" via a reputable carbon offset scheme. All Rough Guide flights are offset, and every year we donate money to a variety of charities devoted to combating the effects of climate change.

Chau Doc/**Kaoam Samnor** on the Bassac River; Tinh Bien/**Phnom Den** near Takeo; Hat Tien/**Prek Chak** east of Kep; **Trapeang Phlong** east of Snuol; O'Yadow, east of Banlung. Cambodian visas are issued on arrival at all points. From **Bavet**, it's easy to get shared taxis to Phnom Penh (around 2hr30min) on National Route 1. Phnom Penh Sorya Transport Company runs an international bus service between Ho Chi Minh City and Phnom Penh (4 daily). From **Chau Doc** there's an express boat (1 daily; around 5hr) up the Mekong River direct to Phnom Penh in the morning. *Sinh Café* in Ho Chi Minh City organizes a daily transfer by minibus and boat to Phnom Penh and the *Capitol Hotel* in Phnom Penh does the trip in the other direction. If you enter Cambodia at the other border crossings, transport options are at present more limited and you'll need to take a moto to the nearest town or a place in a shared taxi depending on your destination.

From **Laos** you enter at **Dong Khrolor** (7am–5pm), 56km north of the Cambodian town of **Stung Treng**. Cambodian visas are available on entry. From the border you can either get a bus to Stung Treng or Phnom Penh (2 daily in the early morning), or take any of the mini buses or taxis that wait at the border; alternatively, if you're not in a hurry, you could cross by land and then charter a private boat for the two-hour trip down the Mekong to Stung Treng, but expect to pay around $50.

Airlines, agents and operators

Airlines

Air Canada UK ⓣ0871/220 1111, Republic of Ireland ⓣ01/800 709900, US & Canada ⓣ1-888/247-2262, Australia ⓣ1300/655 767, New Zealand ⓣ0508/747 767, South Africa ⓣ021/422 3232; ⓦwww.aircanada.com.

Indochina Treasure: Vietnam, Cambodia and Laos in 16 days only from 1749 USD / person
Jewels of Indochina: Laos, Vietnam and Cambodia in 14 days only from 1609 USD / person

Free travel advice 

Contact for further enquiries email: info@asiapacifictravel.vn Call : +84 913224473 Fax : +844 37567862

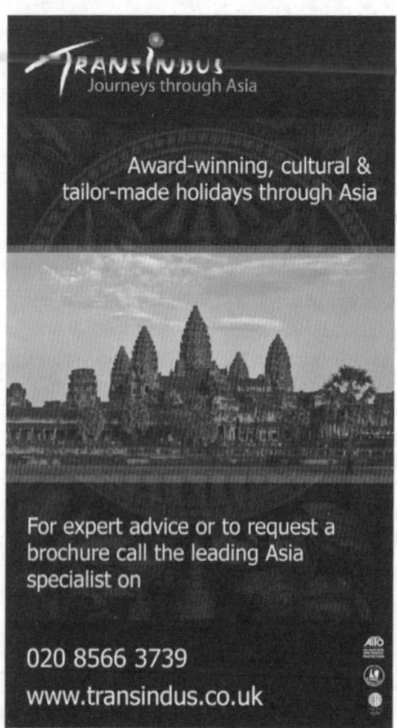

Air France UK ⓣ0871/663 3777, US ⓣ1-800/237-2747, Canada ⓣ1-800/667-2747, Australia ⓣ1300/390 190, New Zealand ⓣ09/921 6040, South Africa ⓣ0861/340 340; ⓦwww.airfrance.com.
Air New Zealand UK ⓣ0800/028 4149, US ⓣ1800-262/1234, Canada ⓣ1800-663/5494, Australia ⓣ13 24 76, New Zealand ⓣ0800/737 000; ⓦwww.airnewzealand.co.nz.
Asiana Airlines UK ⓣ0207/304 9900, US ⓣ213/365-4000 or 212/318-9200, Australia ⓣ02/9767 4343; ⓦwww.flyasiana.com.
Bangkok Airways UK ⓣ01293/596626, US & Canada ⓣ1-866-BANGKOK, Australia ⓣ02/8248 0050, New Zealand ⓣ09/969 7600; ⓦwww.bangkokair.com.
British Airways UK ⓣ0844/493 0787, Republic of Ireland ⓣ1890/626 747, US & Canada ⓣ1-800/AIRWAYS, Australia ⓣ1300/767 177, New Zealand ⓣ09/966 9777, South Africa ⓣ011/441 8600; ⓦwww.ba.com.
Cambodia Angkor Air ⓦwww.cambodiaangkorair.com.
Cathay Pacific UK ⓣ0208/834 8888, US ⓣ1-800/233-2742, Canada ⓣ1-800/2686-868, Australia ⓣ13 17 47, New Zealand ⓣ09/379 0861, South Africa ⓣ011/700 8900; ⓦwww.cathaypacific.com.
China Southern Airlines US ⓣ323/653 8088, Australia ⓣ03/867 60088; ⓦwww.flychinasouthern.com.
Delta US ⓣ0800/241-4141; ⓦwww.delta.com.
EVA Air UK ⓣ020/7380 8300, US & Canada ⓣ1-800/695-1188, Australia ⓣ02/9267 8872, New Zealand ⓣ09/358 8300; ⓦwww.evaair.com.
KLM (Royal Dutch Airlines) US ⓣ 1-800/241-4141, Canada ⓣ1-800/221-1212, UK ⓣ0871/231 0000, Republic of Ireland ⓣ0818/776 100, Australia ⓣ1300/392 192, New Zealand ⓣ09/921 6040, South Africa ⓣ0860/247 247; ⓦwww.klm.com.
Jetstar Australia ⓣ131 538, New Zealand ⓣ0800 800 995, US ⓣ1866-397-8170; ⓦwww.jetstar.com.
Korean Air UK ⓣ0800/413 000, Republic of Ireland ⓣ01/799 7990, US & Canada ⓣ1-800/438-5000, Australia ⓣ02/9262 6000, New Zealand ⓣ09/914 2000; ⓦwww.koreanair.com.
Malaysia Airlines UK ⓣ0871/423 9090, Republic of Ireland ⓣ01/6761 561, US ⓣ1-800/5529-264, Australia ⓣ13 26 27, New Zealand ⓣ0800/777 747, South Africa ⓣ11/8809 614; ⓦwww.malaysia-airlines.com.
Singapore Airlines UK ⓣ0844/800 2380, Republic of Ireland ⓣ01/671 0722, US ⓣ1-800/742-3333, Canada ⓣ1-800/663-3046, Australia ⓣ13 10 11, New Zealand ⓣ0800/808 909, South Africa ⓣ011/880 8560; ⓦwww.singaporeair.com.
South African Airways South Africa ⓣ011/978 1111, ⓦwww.flysaa.com.
Thai Airways UK ⓣ0844/561 0911, US ⓣ1-800/426-5204, Australia ⓣ1300/651 960, New Zealand ⓣ09/377 3886, South Africa ⓣ011/268 2580; ⓦwww.thaiairways.com.
Vietnam Airlines UK ⓣ0203/263 2062, US ⓣ1-415/677-9788, Canada ⓣ1-416/927-0275, Australia ⓣ02/92831355 and 03/9606 0214; ⓦwww.vietnamairlines.com.

Agents and operators

ebookers UK ⓣ0800/082 3000, ⓦwww.ebookers.com, Republic of Ireland ⓣ01/488 3507, ⓦwww.ebookers.ie. Low fares on an extensive selection of scheduled flights and package deals.
Flight Centre UK ⓣ0800/587 0058, ⓦwww.flightcentre.co.uk, US ⓣ1-877/922 4752, ⓦwww.flightcentre.us, Canada ⓣ1-877/967 5302, ⓦwww.flightcentre.ca, Australia ⓣ133 133, ⓦwww.flightcentre.com.au, New Zealand ⓣ0800/24 35 44, ⓦwww.flightcentre.co.nz, South Africa ⓣ0860/400 727, ⓦwww.flightcentre.co.za. Competitive choice of worldwide fares.
North South Travel UK ⓣ01245/608 291, ⓦwww.northsouthtravel.co.uk. Friendly, competitive travel agency, offering discounted fares worldwide. Profits are used to support projects in the developing world, especially the promotion of sustainable tourism.
STA Travel UK ⓣ0871/2300 040, US & Canada ⓣ1-800/781-4040, Australia ⓣ134 782, New Zealand ⓣ0800/474 400, South Africa ⓣ0861/781 781; ⓦwww.statravel.com. Worldwide specialists in independent travel; also student IDs, travel insurance, car rental, rail passes, and more. Good discounts for students and under-26s.
Trailfinders UK ⓣ0845/058 5858, Republic of Ireland ⓣ01/677 7888, Australia ⓣ1300/780 212; ⓦwww.trailfinders.com. One of the best-informed and most efficient agents for independent travellers.

Tour operators

If you want to avoid the hassle of making your own arrangements you might consider travelling with a **specialist tour operator**. However, although Cambodia is well covered, many tour companies still include it only as part of a visit to another Southeast Asian country. Tour prices start at around £500 for land-only options; those that include international flights tend to be £1200 to £1500, while choosing luxury accommodation and specialist activities, such as golfing, can set you back more than £4000. Single travellers,

Journey through lost kingdoms and discover the hidden history of Asia - let Asian Trails be your guide!

CAMBODIA
Asian Trails Ltd. (Phnom Penh Office)
No. 22, Street 294, Sangkat Boeng Keng Kong I
Khan Chamkarmorn, P.O. Box 621, Phnom Penh, Cambodia
Tel: (855 23) 216 555 Fax: (855 23) 216 591
E-mail: res@asiantrails.com.kh

CHINA
Asian Trails China
Rm. 1001, Scitech Tower, No. 22 Jianguomenwai Avenue
Beijing 100004, P.R. China
Tel: (86 10) 6515 9259 & 9279 & 9260 Fax: (86 10) 6515 9293
E-mail: kris.vangoethem@asiantrailschina.com

INDONESIA
P.T. Asian Trails Indonesia
Jl. By Pass Ngurah Rai No. 260 Sanur
Denpasar 80228, Bali, Indonesia
Tel: (62 361) 285 771 Fax: (62 361) 281 515
E-mail: info@asiantrailsbali.com

LAOS
Asian Trails Laos (AT Lao Co., Ltd.)
P.O. Box 5422, Unit 10, Ban Khounta Thong
Sikhottabong District, Vientiane, Lao P.D.R.
Tel: (856 21) 263 936 Fax: (856 21) 262 956
E-mail: vte@asiantrailslaos.com

MALAYSIA
Asian Trails (M) Sdn. Bhd.
11-2-B Jalan Manau off Jalan Kg. Attap 50460
Kuala Lumpur, Malaysia
Tel: (60 3) 2274 9488 Fax: (60 3) 2274 9588
E-mail: res@asiantrails.com.my

MYANMAR
Asian Trails Tour Ltd.
73 Pyay Road, Dagon Township, Yangon, Myanmar
Tel: (95 1) 211 212, 223 262 Fax: (95 1) 211 670
E-mail: res@asiantrails.com.mm

THAILAND
Asian Trails Ltd.
9th Floor, SG Tower, 161/1 Soi Mahadlek Luang 3, Rajdamri Road
Lumpini, Pathumwan, Bangkok 10330
Tel: (66 2) 626 2000 Fax: (66 2) 651 8111
E-mail: res@asiantrails.org

VIETNAM
Asian Trails Co., Ltd.
5th Floor, 21 Nguyen Trung Ngan Street, District 1
Ho Chi Minh City, Vietnam
Tel: (84 8) 3 910 2871 Fax: (84 8) 3 910 2874
E-mail: vietnam@asiantrails.com.vn

CONTACT
Contact us for our brochure or log into
www.asiantrails.info www.asiantrails.travel

or those nervous about travelling alone could consider the offerings from Explore or Intrepid. Plenty of small-group tours are available, some with an ethos of contributing to the local communities.

Adventure and activity tours

Adventure Center US ⓣ1-800/228-8747, ⓦwww.adventurecenter.com. This "soft adventure" specialist features Cambodia tours from a selection of operators.

Audley Travel UK ⓣ01993/838100, ⓦwww.audleytravel.com. An interesting choice of escorted group tours as well as tailor-made travel. Cambodia Discovered is a 14-day tour of Siem Reap and Phnom Penh before finishing with a few lazy days at the seaside resort of Kep. Audley supports Who Will, a charity for orphans and disadvantaged Cambodian children.

Explore! UK ⓣ0845/013 1537, Republic of Ireland ⓣ01/677 9479, US ⓣ1-800/486-9096, Canada ⓣ1-888/456-3522, Australia ⓣ08/913 0700, New Zealand ⓣ09/524 5118, South Africa ⓣ028/313 0526; ⓦwww.explore.co.uk. Highly regarded small-group operator that offers tours to Cambodia in various guises; its 16-day Heart of Cambodia trip covers everything including the dolphins at Kampie and a homestay, before finishing with the temples at Angkor.

Intrepid Travel UK ⓣ0203/147 7777, Ireland ⓣ01/524 0071, US ⓣ1-800/970-7299, Canada ⓣ1-866/360-1151, Australia ⓣ1300/364 512, New Zealand ⓣ0800/600 610, South Africa ⓣ27/1147 7400; ⓦwww.intrepidtravel.com. Southeast Asia specialist with an impressive choice of Cambodia offerings and an emphasis on low-impact tourism. Temples and beach aside, the 15-day Heart of Cambodia trip takes in a cookery course at Battambang, cycling around Kompong Cham and a speleological excursion at Kampot.

Peregrine UK & Republic of Ireland ⓣ0844/736 0170, Australia ⓣ1-300/791 485; ⓦwww.peregrineadventures.com. Cambodia is mostly offered with another Southeast Asian country: an interesting trip is the Saigon to Angkor Cycle; pedalling through Cambodia may be challenging, but not only will you get fit but you'll see plenty of local life along the way, and it is reasonably priced.

See Cambodia Differently ⓣ0208/150 5150, ⓦwww.seecambodiadifferently.com. Moderately priced, tailor-made and package tours to Cambodia. Its Cambodia Hotspots trip goes to the places most travellers want to see; online shop offers books and DVDs with a Cambodia theme.

Silk Steps UK ⓣ01278/722460, ⓦwww.silksteps.co.uk. Bespoke, reasonably priced tours to Cambodia with suggested itineraries to help you build your own trip.

Travel Indochina UK ⓣ01865/268 940, US ⓣ212/674-2887, Canada ⓣ416/345-9899, Australia ⓣ02/9244 2133; ⓦwww.travelindochina.co.uk. A wide range of mid-range Cambodia-specific tours lasting from five to 18 days. An adventurous 18-day Cambodia Encounter tour takes in Phnom Penh, Battambang and Angkor, plus the coast at Kep, Bokor and Kratie.

Eco- options

Cambodia Community Based Ecotourism Network ⓦwww.ccben.org, ⓔinfo@ccben.org. This Cambodian organization can help you find homestays and ecotourism sites throughout Cambodia.

Gecko's UK ⓣ0844/736 0175, Australia ⓣ03/8601 4444, ⓦwww.geckosadventures.com. Gecko's prides itself on "grassroots" trips using local guides; Cambodia in Depth is a 10-day temples-to-coast tour that includes a homestay and free time to make your own discoveries (land only).

Responsibletravel.com UK ⓣ01273/600030, ⓦwww.responsibletravel.com. An online travel agent with an extensive range of Cambodia tours from different companies; all tours have an ethical basis and there's an explanation with each one of how it benefits the local community.

Luxury travel

Abercrombie & Kent UK ⓣ0845/618 2204, ⓦwww.abercrombiekent.co.uk, US ⓣ1-800/554-7016, ⓦwww.abercrombiekent.com, Australia ⓣ1300/851 800, ⓦwww.abercrombiekent.com.au. Luxury tours to Asia include a nine-day Into the Heart of Cambodia which visits the temples of Angkor followed by a relaxing few days on the coast at Sihanoukville. A philanthropic project, Clean Water, provides wells for schools and communities in the Siem Reap area.

Absolute Asia US ⓣ1-800/736-8187, ⓦwww.absoluteasia.com. Deluxe private trips to Asia and Cambodia include a 16-day golfing tour of Vietnam and Cambodia (price on application).

Geographic Expeditions US ⓣ1-800/777-8183, ⓦwww.geoex.com. Luxury small-group tours to Asia include the expensive Heart of Cambodia option.

Kuoni UK ⓣ01306/747002, ⓦwww.kuoni.co.uk. Upmarket city breaks to Phnom Penh and Siem Reap can be combined with the coast at Sihanoukville; 4- and 5-star accommodation throughout.

Noble Caledonian UK ⓣ020/7752 0000, ⓦwww.noble-caledonian.co.uk. Cambodia by boat: boarding in the Vietnamese Delta, you cruise on the

Mekong to Phnom Penh and Kompong Cham, before exploring the Tonle Sap, finally disembarking at Siem Reap for the temples of Angkor (pricey).

Trans Indus UK ⓣ 0208/566 3739, ⓦ www.transindus.co.uk. Asia specialists with a choice of private tours; Cambodia Explorer is a deluxe trip of 14 days from Phnom Penh to Siem Reap; while Meeting the Hills is an inexpensive six-day visit including Sen Monorom.

Getting around

Getting around Cambodia is easier than it's ever been. Improvements to major roads have reduced the travel times between towns and given rise to a plethora of bus and mini bus services, making travel pretty cheap. Though towns lack any form of public transport, you'll find it simple to get around using the readily available tuk-tuks (a motorbike pulling a passenger carriage) and motos (motorbike taxis).

However, travelling can still be challenging, as many minor roads are no more than cart tracks which deteriorate further during the rainy season (June–Oct). Neither are Cambodian drivers known for their patience or safety-consciousness; though driving lessons and the need for a driving licence were introduced a few years ago, the instructor often has little more clue than the learner. Traffic in Phnom Penh is particularly chaotic and it's common for drivers to weave through impossibly small gaps in the opposite direction to the traffic flow – bad enough if you're closeted in the relative security of a Land Cruiser, but absolutely terrifying if you're perched on the back of a moto. However, there aren't nearly as many accidents as you might expect, as Cambodian road-users have evolved their own conventions for avoiding collisions.

Buses now run on most routes (including Phnom Penh to Stung Treng, Banlung and Sen Monorom), though be aware that you may still need to go through Phnom Penh to get from one side of the country to the other. Of most interest to travellers: **National Route 1** to the Vietnamese border is in great shape, and at Neak Leung the ferry crossing will soon be obsolete when a long-awaited bridge is built over the Mekong; from Poipet (the Thai border) the surfacing of National Route 5 to Siem Reap has reduced the journey time to just three hours. At the time of writing NR63 from NR7 to Banlung is the only major road still in poor condition; though it's fine from Banlung through to the Vietnamese border.

Note that travel to the provinces and within Phnom Penh can be difficult over **public holidays**, especially the Khmer New Year (mid-April; see p.63). On New Year's Eve everyone heads for their home village and all available transport heads out of town – even more packed than usual. Phnom Penh in particular becomes very quiet, with hardly a moto or tuk-tuk available, and the few that remain make a killing by doubling their fares.

Planes

Cambodia Angkor Air is Cambodia's semblance of a national airline. A joint venture with Vietnam Airlines, it flies between the capital and Siem Reap (4 daily) and from Siem Reap to Ho Chi Minh City (2 daily). Other than that, flights to the provinces have been the casualty of road improvements and at the time of writing there are no commercial flights to any of the country's provincial airports; even the airport at Sihanoukville, which re opened briefly in 2007, is now closed. Rumours that a couple of the provincial airstrips have been sold off for development mean it's improbable that flights will recommence in the foreseeable future.

If you want to fly you'll need to **buy your ticket** at least a day before you want to travel, either at one of the airline offices or at a travel agent in Phnom Penh or Siem Reap. A single **fare** costs $95, double that for a return.

Buses

Phnom Penh is Cambodia's transport hub with up to a dozen companies running air-conditioned buses and 15–20 seat VIP coaches (*laan destjow*) between the major centres. Phnom Penh Sorya Transport Company has the most extensive transport network serving most provincial and key international destinations, while Mekong Express operates non stop services from Phnom Penh to Sihanoukville and Siem Reap. However, there are few links between provincial centres (see "Travel details" at the end of each Guide chapter for more information) and some journeys will involve a change of bus and quite a bit of hanging around.

Buses (*laan tom*) run from Phnom Penh to the major towns, including Sihanoukville, Siem Reap, Battambang and Kompong Cham. These timetabled, a/c services offer a clean and pleasant enough way to travel, giving you a good view of the countryside. Fares are very reasonable at $4 to Sihanoukville and $6 to Siem Reap. To guarantee a place, buy your **ticket** the day before from the bus station; no standing passengers are allowed, and if all the seats have been sold you can't travel (see p.127 for frequencies).

There is also a recently introduced "night bus" running between Siem Reap and Sihanoukville leaving around 8pm each evening (via Phnom Penh); see p.178 for more details.

Small **city buses** (*laan kerong*) run regularly between **Phnom Penh** and the nearby towns of **Kompong Speu**, **Neak Leung** and **Takeo**. These are often packed to capacity, but they do more dropping off than taking on, so they get to be less of a squeeze as the journey progresses. Although slower than a shared taxi, and not as comfortable as the express buses, these are still a reasonable way to make local journeys: services run to a timetable and are cheap (8000 riel to Takeo, for example) and safe.

Buses display their destination in Cambodian and English. At bus stations you'll need to buy your **ticket** from the ticket office; if you get on a bus elsewhere, pay the conductor.

A number of private operators now run quite smart minibuses; the fares are about the same as buses and can be quite convenient (if you want to travel from Sen Monorom to Kratie for example). Your guesthouse or hotel can arrange a seat on these but make sure to book the day before you want to travel.

Tourist transport

There are plenty of private operations offering services by small bus – your guesthouse can arrange this for you, and they each have their preferred provider. Costs vary, but are typically a dollar or two more than in a shared taxi or public bus, and have the advantage that you'll be picked up from your guesthouse or hotel rather than having to traipse out to the nearest transport stop. Such buses are convenient, although not without their own problems – like having to trawl around town to other hotels and guesthouses to collect the rest of the passengers, but once you're on the way it's generally not too bad.

Travelling to Bangkok, Ho Chi Minh City and the Laos border can be arranged through guesthouses, but considerable delays have been reported by travellers, particularly on the Bangkok route. It might be worth comparing their offer with the service provided by Phnom Penh Sorya Transport (ⓦ www.ppsoryatransport.com) before you book. *Capitol Hotel* in Phnom Penh, which also has its own bus company, and *Sinh Café*, its associate organization in Ho Chi Minh City, also run a tourist boat service from Phnom Penh to Chau Doc for around $10 with connecting minibus through to Ho Chi Minh City.

Shared taxis, minibuses and pick-ups

Shared taxis – normally Toyota Camrys – operate a speedy if not necessarily comfortable service between provincial centres, while crowded, beaten-up minibuses and a few **pick-up trucks** cover some of the same routes. Pick-ups are rapidly becoming obsolete, victims of the better road conditions, but some continue to bump their way to remoter destinations and a place in the back is still the cheapest way to travel. The **minibuses** that gather around the transport stops and markets are best avoided; they are cramped, particularly badly maintained and sorely overloaded – accidents are frequent and can be fatal.

All these forms of transport are straightforward enough to use. Turn up at the local **transport stop** and state your destination, at which point you'll be swamped by touts trying to get you on their vehicle. Transport only leaves when full, so the fuller the vehicle, the sooner it's likely to leave. Once you've chosen a vehicle, agree the fare with the driver – most are honest, but a few have been known to hike their prices up for foreigners, so if in doubt ask other passengers what they are paying.

Breakdowns do happen, but Cambodian drivers are adept at roadside repairs and Cambodian passengers remain stoic in the face of delays; needless to say the worse the road the more likely there is to be a problem. You aren't expected to pay until you reach your destination, although occasionally the driver may ask for some money in advance for fuel – let the locals take care of this, and pay what you owe at the end.

Shared taxis

Shared taxis take four passengers in the back, plus two in front, which means that you are not necessarily going to be comfortable. You can improve things by **paying for two (or more) places**, and if you want to get away in a hurry you can buy up any remaining seats or even hire the whole vehicle. Shared taxis depart from transport stops in all provincial towns (though not to any schedule) throughout the day – the best time to turn up is between 7am and 8am; it's often more difficult to get away after lunch, as fewer people travel then. For less populous routes such as Phnom Penh to Sen Monorom, you may not have much choice as there may only be one or two taxis leaving per day. It pays to check at the transport stop the day before (mid- to late afternoon is usually good, as drivers are touting for the next day's fares) to reserve your place.

Shared taxis may not be the cheapest way to travel, but they do allow you a degree of flexibility in terms of departure time and are relatively quick; from Phnom Penh, typical fares are 25,000 riel to Battambang, 12,000 riel to Kampot, 40,000 riel to Sen Monorom. Though less prevalent these days, on some routes the driver shares his seat with a passenger, a practice which is accepted by the Khmers. If this bothers you, you might wish to pay for the place that would have been shared with the driver so it can be kept vacant.

Minibuses

Best avoided are the clapped-out **minibuses** that run between provincial destinations. The worst of Cambodia's transport options, they depart only when absolutely packed, with people, goods and livestock piled inside, on the roof and hanging out of the back – not only is this the most uncomfortable way to travel, but it is unsafe. The only thing going for them is their cheapness, with **fares** a few thousand riel less than the buses. Minibuses do not display their destination, so just ask around at the transport stop.

Pick-up trucks

Although a few Nissan and Toyota pick-up trucks still run, these days it's unlikely that you'll need to travel by them unless you're heading to the remotest of areas (north of Kompong Thom for example). When in the wet season you'll have no choice but to take a pick-up as it's the only thing that can take on the mud.

Seats in the cab – four in the rear, two in the front – cost roughly the same as in a shared taxi; as in taxis, you can pay for an extra seat if you want more comfort. The

back of a pick-up is the cheapest way to get around, costing around half the price of seats inside, though you'll have to sit on (or fit around) the goods being transported, and you risk being bounced around with nothing much to grab hold of. Take plenty of water and a sense of humour, and dust-proof your face by wrapping it in a scarf or *krama*.

Boats

For years, Cambodia's appalling roads meant travelling by boat was the principal means of getting between the capital and **Siem Reap**, but these days it's easier and quicker to travel by bus or taxi. Remarkably, one boat a day (wet season only) still forges up the Tonle Sap to Siem Reap at the thoroughly overpriced foreigners' fare of $35; it's not even a scenic trip as the Tonle Sap lake is so vast that it's more like being at sea.

Boats, seating about thirty people, operate daily between **Battambang** and **Siem Reap** taking up to eight hours to complete the trip. Though safer than the speedboats of old, movement is restricted; a cushion, plenty of water, food and a hat will make things more comfortable. In rough weather the Tonle Sap can whip up some fierce waves and travelling can be a little disconcerting.

An express boat service runs daily south along the Mekong between Phnom Penh and the Vietnamese border at **Chau Doc** ($21 for foreigners, 4hr); but the easiest and cheaper way is to book with the *Capitol Hotel* or Neak Krohorm Travel in Phnom Penh who can arrange a boat to Chau Doc and onward transport through to Ho Chi Minh City for around $10.

Boats between Sihanoukville for **Koh Kong** no longer run, though you can get to Koh S'dach.

The most scenic boat trip in Cambodia is up the Mekong from Kompong Cham to Kratie, but the only chance of doing this these days is by private cruise vessel.

Trains

Completed in 1932, Cambodia's rail network had become so decrepit that the trains stopped running in 2007. However, the lines are now being restored and the first train has recently run from Phnom Penh to Kampot. In due course the whole network will be refurbished and possibly extended with a link from Battambang to Poipet. Unfortunately, for the foreseeable future, the only use is going to be for freight.

City and town transport

There is no public transport in any Cambodian town; in Phnom Penh a trial bus service was abandoned due to lack of support. The usual mode of transport is the *romorque*, generally known as a tuk-tuk, a passenger carriage pulled by a motorbike; and the motorbike taxi, the moto, a small motorbike-cum-moped with a space in front of the driver for baggage. In Phnom Penh you'll also find **cyclos**, Cambodia's version of the pedicab. All these forms of transport are hailed from the side of the road and drop you at your destination. **Taxis** are available in Phnom Penh and Siem Reap, but elsewhere you'll only find cars, with driver, for hire by the day (or longer).

Motos

Motorbike taxis, or **motos**, are the staple means of travelling short (and sometimes long) distances in Cambodia, although riding on the back of a moto in the middle of anarchic traffic isn't everybody's idea of fun, and you may feel safer taking a tuk-tuk or taxi. Motos are identified by their drivers' baseball caps (although these days they wear a motorcycle helmet when on the move). You'll seldom need to flag down a moto – just stand by the road and moto drivers will usually come up and offer their services. Moto drivers indicate that they are available for hire by holding up a finger (usually the index one). Drivers come from a variety of backgrounds – you may find you are being driven by an off-duty policeman or a moonlighting government official.

If you have **bags**, the driver will squeeze them into the space between his knees and the handlebars – moto drivers are adept at balancing baggage, from rice sacks to backpacks, between their legs while negotiating chaotic traffic. Passengers sit behind the driver on a pillion seat – Cambodians typically squeeze as many passengers as possible onto this (three is common), although it's best not to follow their example and to stick to just one passenger per bike (in Siem Reap the police do not allow motos to take more than one foreigner). Although you'll see Cambodian women sitting side-saddle, it's safer if you sit astride and, if necessary, hang onto the driver.

Moto drivers have an image of foreigners as having bottomless pockets, so avoid misunderstandings by **agreeing the fare beforehand**; a typical journey around the capital will set you back 6000–8000 riel. If you want to hire a driver for longer periods, count on around 8000 riel per hour, or $8–10 per day. Curiosity and the remote chance of a fare will mean that even if you are already negotiating with someone, other moto drivers gather round. Etiquette dictates that you should go with the one you summoned, though in the unlikely event that someone offers you a cheaper fare you'll probably find "your" driver acquiesces. Fares go up during public holidays (sometimes to double the usual rate) when many drivers head home to their villages, which also makes it difficult to find transport.

Motos can be taken on quite long trips **out of town** – indeed it's the only way to get to some places, although it's not particularly comfortable. You'll probably have to pay for fuel in addition to the day hire. In the provinces drivers are sometimes irrationally fearful of bandits and can be reluctant to travel in remote areas late in the day, so bear their concerns in mind when planning your excursions.

Tuk-tuks

The introduction of tuk-tuks to Cambodia came about in 2001, when police in Siem Reap banned foreigners riding three-up on a moto (in spite of the fact that Cambodians are allowed to be three, four or even more up). Tuk-tuks have caught on in a big way and are now found in most provincial towns. Pulled by a motorbike, these covered passenger cabs seat four people (six with a squeeze) and have the advantage of affording some protection against the sun and rain as they have drop-down side-curtains. The motorbikes that pull them, however, are the same ones used as motos, and so are woefully underpowered, which makes for a slow trip. However, they are excellent for two or more travelling together and when you have baggage; if you've got the time they're also good for trips up to about 30km out of town. Expect to pay $10–15 for the day or long trips.

Cyclos

A dying breed, found only in Phnom Penh, the **cyclo** (pronounced *see-klo)* is Cambodia's version of the cycle trishaw; the word comes from the French – *cyclopousse*. Slower and more expensive than a moto, a trip across town by cyclo gives you time to take in the city and street scenes (although traffic fumes can be unpleasant). Cyclos take one passenger (or two at a squash) in a seat at the front, with the driver perched on a seat behind over the rear wheel.

Taxis

Both Phnom Penh and Siem Reap have **city taxis** (as opposed to shared taxis). These don't tout for fares on the streets, but instead congregate outside major hotels or on the riverfront in the capital. In Phnom Penh you can order one by phone (see p.115); fares are around $5 per journey.

In other towns you'll need to hire a **car and driver**. These can be hired for both short hops around town and long journeys (expect to pay around $35 per day for running around town, $40 plus for an out-of-town trip).

Self-drive car rental

Although Cambodia's roads and its signposting have improved, it's virtually impossible to rent a self-drive car in Cambodia. However, should you manage to do so, then you need to be aware of the headaches that driving yourself entails. Problems include finding appropriate documentation: a passport is required by the hire company and (oddly) a Cambodian licence by the police – although an international driving licence may now be accepted. Other problems are the lack of designated car parks (though there are now a few in Phnom Penh and Siem Reap); haphazard driving by other road users; and cursory insurance – any loss or damage to the vehicle is your responsibility. Whenever you park you should get someone to look after the vehicle; in town you'll usually find a parking attendant near markets and restaurants who will keep an eye on the vehicle for 1000 riel. It's normal to park as directed and leave the handbrake disengaged so that the car can be pushed out of the way to let other cars in or out. To prevent theft and damage when leaving the car overnight, you'll need to look for a hotel with parking or find a local with off-road space where they'll let you park for a nominal charge of $2–3. Given all this, it's far less hassle, and probably cheaper, to hire a **car and driver** (see under "Taxis", above).

Motorbikes and bicycles

Whether you ride a **motorbike** or **bicycle**, it's worth wearing sunglasses, long trousers and a long-sleeved shirt to protect you not only from the sun but also from the grit and gravel thrown up on the dusty roads.

When heading off into the countryside, remember that Cambodia (in spite of clearance programmes) has a huge problem with **land mines**, and no matter how tempting it may be to go cross-country, stick to well-used tracks and paths.

Motorbike hire

Renting a motorbike is a popular way to see Cambodia. Its **security** is your responsibility, so make sure you leave your motorbike somewhere secure when you stop – at night guesthouses will often bring it inside for you. Motorcycle helmets are now compulsory (for the driver only) and you risk being stopped by the police and issued with a spot fine ($5) if you're not wearing one. Note that road checks are particularly prevalent just before holidays and the weekend.

You can rent an **off-road 250cc bike** for around $10 per day or $60 a week from a number of companies, particularly in Phnom Penh (see the relevant city listings for details), although you'll have to leave your passport as security. Check the condition of the bike before heading off on a long trip – if it breaks down, it's your responsibility to get it repaired or returned to the owner. Away from the main highways take advice on local road conditions, as often even relatively short distances can take a long time.

Foreigners cannot rent motorbikes in either Siem Reap or Sihanoukville. Originally safety was given as the reason for the ban, but it's more likely to be a protectionist move to keep the moto "mafias" in business. In other towns it's easiest to use the **110cc run-arounds** available for rent from guesthouses and hire shops; rates are around $5 per day.

Even with the improvements in the road conditions, poor driving by other motorists makes it safer to travel only in daylight hours.

Cycling

Cycling in Cambodia can be a rewarding experience. In fact the Mekong Discovery Trail from Kratie to Stung Treng (see p.244) positively invites you to explore on two wheels. Bicycles are available for hire at many guesthouses and hire shops in towns for around $1.50–3 per day, although what you get varies considerably, from swish mountain bikes to sturdy but gearless affairs.

The main hazard is the manic traffic on the highways and you'd be advised to try to get to your destination by late afternoon since many Cambodian vehicles travel without lights and so won't see you as darkness falls. There are plenty of refreshment stalls along major roads, so you'll seldom go hungry, and the Cambodians will do their best if you're in need of help. If you get stuck between guesthouses you'll need to stop at a village (camping is technically illegal and

Addresses

Finding your way around towns is generally easy as most Cambodian towns are laid out on a grid plan. Nearly all towns now have street signs; usually a few main streets have names, with the majority being numbered. Despite that, most Cambodians have little idea of street numbers, so to locate a specific address you're best off heading for a nearby landmark and asking from there.

potentially dangerous because of the risk of land mines), where someone will give you space on their floor for a small consideration. It's essential to note that all motorized traffic takes precedence over bicycles, and you may find you have to veer onto the verge to get out of the way of speeding cars and trucks.

In Siem Reap and Sihanoukville a couple of places rent out electric bicycles, which can be a fun – if not necessarily faster – way to get around.

Organized tours

If you're short on time, or simply don't want to do it yourself, then taking an **organized tour** can get you around the country to the major sights with minimum effort. An increasing number of travel agencies and tour operators in Phnom Penh (see p.115) and Siem Reap (see p.179) arrange individual tours, so you don't need to conform to a fixed departure date or worry that a trip won't run if the group isn't large enough. Costs vary according to the type of accommodation you choose, where you go and what you do; allow upwards of $120 per person per day excluding food. Travel is by a/c vehicle, with guide, and includes accommodation and usually breakfast.

A cheaper alternative to such tours are the transport and accommodation deals arranged by some of the established **guesthouses** in Phnom Penh and Siem Reap. On these trips, a private bus takes a group of tourists between the capital and Siem Reap (or vice versa) or Sihanoukville, with accommodation and day-trips to major sights arranged through partner guesthouses in these towns (expect to pay up to $25–30 per person per day). Heading from Phnom Penh to Siem Reap, for example, you may get the option to stop at the temples of Sambor Preah Kuk en route.

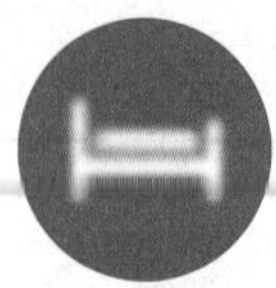

Accommodation

Finding accommodation is seldom a problem, and even provincial towns have a remarkable choice of guesthouses and modest hotels. Phnom Penh, Siem Reap and Sihanoukville have plenty of accommodation in all categories, and many other towns too have some classier hotels. Even off the beaten track you'll find a basic guesthouse or two.

Arriving anywhere by taxi or pick-up, the driver may well drop you at a guesthouse or at least point you in the right direction for one.

In most towns touts meet incoming transport and will take you free of charge to their favourite establishment; if you don't like it, feel free to go elsewhere. Sometimes tuk-tuk and moto drivers get a few thousand riel commission for dropping you off at a guesthouse if you don't specify one of your choice – this premium may be added to your room rate; but mostly they're just keen to introduce themselves and to secure work driving or guiding you for the duration of your stay.

In major towns and tourist centres accommodation in all price ranges can be booked in advance; sometimes this will get you a better room rate or a nicer room. Let them know the time you're coming and they will also meet you off a bus, boat or plane for no extra charge.

In basic accommodation, **rooms** are either *moi kreh* (one-bed) or *bpee kreh* (two-bed), meaning they come with one or two double beds respectively; having paid for the room it's up to you how many people share it. Mid-range accommodation tends to comprise conventional singles and doubles, but at the lower end they may

Accommodation price codes

Accommodation throughout the Guide has been categorized according to the following price codes, based on the cost of the cheapest **double room**, with en-suite facilities (but, in lower categories at least, not necessarily hot water) available at each particular establishment. Where **dormitory accommodation** is available, a riel or dollar price for a dorm bed (typically $1–2) is given in the text.

❶ $5 and under	❹ $16–25	❼ $81–140
❷ $6–10	❺ $26–50	❽ $141–200
❸ $11–15	❻ $51–80	❾ $201 and over

feature rooms with anything from one to four double beds, and one or two places are now even providing dormitories. Upmarket hotels typically play by international standards, with rates for single or double rooms. Even in budget establishments in the tourist centres, **breakfast** is increasingly included; ask when you book in. Off the tourist route, guesthouses probably won't have eating facilities and you'll need to go out for all meals.

Hotels often have **security boxes** in the rooms for guests' valuables, and guesthouses can usually lock things away for you at reception. Wherever you stay, it's customary **to pay** when you check out, not when you arrive.

Budget

Guesthouses are the mainstay of budget accommodation in Cambodia, but vary enormously. The least attractive are the single-storey establishments reminiscent of stables typically found around transport stops. These are the cheapest rooms you'll find and cost just $2–3 per night – though they're usually tiny, windowless affairs with paper-thin walls. In this range expect a single bed, nylon sheet, blanket and fan; bathrooms are usually shared. While the bottom sheet should be clean, the blanket is often not laundered between guests, so you may want to make sure you have a sarong or sheet with you.

Better **budget rooms** all over Cambodia cost $5–6 a night and are usually clean and tidy with cotton sheet, basic toiletries and a TV. In most towns you'll find the garish concrete blocks that Khmers love, and though clean, they lack atmosphere. Increasingly air conditioning is available for an extra $5–10 per night – electricity is pricey in Cambodia. From time to time you'll come across guesthouses in traditional wooden stilt-houses – they don't feature air conditioning or en-suite facilities, but compensate with masses of mellow wood and attractive balconies. Paying a few dollars more you'll get you a top sheet and, more will than not, a hot shower and fridge.

Note that the demarcation between a guesthouse and a cheap hotel can be a bit fuzzy; guesthouses in Siem Reap for example, charge rates bordering on those in the cheaper hotels. Rooms in the provinces should come with a mosquito net; if there isn't one when you arrive, make sure to ask for one.

Bathrooms, whether shared or en suite, vary considerably, but you'll mainly get Western-style toilets and at least a cold shower, although in out-of-the-way spots you may still come across squat toilets with cold *mandi* – a tub of cold water that you ladle over yourself (don't get into it as others will need to use the water too).

Tourism has caught on in a big way in Cambodia with the younger Cambodians taking leisure trips themselves. As a result, new guesthouses are springing up in most towns as everyone tries to get in on the act; clean, but plain, they typically cost $5 (fan) to $15 (a/c) per night, and have pretty much replaced the dark, dingy guesthouse of yesteryear. Another sign of the times is that some budget places are accepting payment by credit card – but don't rely on it quite yet. You'll find that guesthouses aimed at foreign tourists generally have internet access on the premises; although this may only be a communal computer or two, increasingly the savvier have wi-fi.

Mid-range

Mid-range accommodation covers a broad spectrum from around $16 to $80 and the choice has improved considerably in the last couple of years with so-called boutique hotels or resorts popping up in the most unexpected places. Hotels in this bracket usually have a variety of rooms, and you can ask to see a few before you make your choice. At the cheaper end, expect rooms to have a bathroom with hot shower, air conditioning, fridge and TV; going up in price brings coordinated decor and possibly an actual bathtub; breakfast will most likely be included too, along with internet access, often wi-fi.

Credit cards are increasingly accepted although there may be a surcharge of around four percent (the processing charge) to use it. It's worth checking whether government tax and service are included in the rack rate, as these can add up to twenty percent onto the bill.

A number of upmarket guesthouses feature in this mid-range price bracket. This is a deliberate choice by the owners, often because they don't provide all the services you'd expect in a hotel – such as 24-hour reception; alternatively it could be that by remaining a guesthouse the government's hotel tax can be avoided.

Luxury

Upmarket accommodation (priced above $80 a night for a double room) is widely available in Phnom Penh, Siem Reap, Battambang, Sihanoukville and Kep, with even a few places elsewhere. It's worth making a reservation if you want to stay somewhere particular, and to look out for any deals that are going. Besides opulent, supremely comfortable rooms, hotels in this price range rival those of the best hotels anywhere, often with a choice of restaurants and bars, a swimming pool, and other leisure facilities such as spa, fitness centre or tennis court; your room will probably also have wi-fi (or an alternative provision for internet access).

Food and drink

Cambodian food isn't particularly spicy, although it's often delicately flavoured with herbs such as lemon grass and coriander. Many dishes are variations on fare from other Asian countries, especially China, on which Khmer cuisine draws heavily.

Food is traditionally cooked in a single pot or wok over a charcoal stove; although gas burners are being introduced in the cities, many people prize the smoky flavour that food acquires when it's cooked over charcoal. A lot of dishes are fried in palm oil and aren't drained before serving, so food can be quite greasy; if you're vegetarian it's worth being aware that the pan is seldom washed out between the meat and vegetable dishes. Few Cambodians have refrigerators, and even if they do, they prefer to buy produce fresh from the markets as needed.

As in many countries where rice is the staple food, the most common way to refer to eating in Cambodia is *nyam bai*, literally "eat rice".

Where to eat

The cheapest food in Cambodia is available from **street hawkers** with handcarts or baskets dangling from a shoulder pole, who sell anything from fried noodles or baguettes, to fresh fruit and ice cream. Another source of cheap food is the country's **markets** – open both day and night, though often in separate locations – where stalls sell a variety of dishes and desserts at prices only slightly higher than those charged by street hawkers. Each stall usually has its own speciality, and you can order from any stall in the market irrespective of where you're sitting. When you've finished, you pay the stall closest to you for the whole lot and they'll sort out the money among themselves.

Noodle shops and cheap restaurants can be found all over town centres and are especially plentiful around markets and transport stops. **Noodle shops** (*haang geautieuv*) open around 5.30am for the breakfast trade, serving various noodle soups, along with dumplings and rice porridge in the larger establishments. By 9 or 10am they turn into **coffee shops**, serving hot and cold coffee and tea, as well as soft drinks and fresh coconuts, until they close at around 4 or 5pm.

Cheap restaurants (*haang bai*) are recognizable by a row of pots set out on a table out front, containing the day's fare, not dissimilar to Cambodian home cooking. To find out what's on offer, lift the lids and peer inside; the dishes you have chosen will be served to you in separate bowls along with a plate of rice. These are inexpensive places to fill up as the food is not only pretty decent but invariably good value at around 5000 riel per portion – similar in price to eating at a market stall – inclusive of rice and iced tea, a jug of which is kept replenished at the table.

For **international cuisine**, in Phnom Penh and Siem Reap there is a vast choice: French, Japanese, pizzas, burgers, Sunday roasts and so on. In Sihanoukville and Battambang there is also a decent – if slightly less eclectic – selection of international places, while these days even the smaller towns have Western options. At the other end of the scale, eating possibilities in rural areas can be quite restricted, and in the evenings you may be hard pushed to find anything more than a bowl of instant noodles.

Practically all restaurants are **open daily**, although some Western tourist-oriented places may close one day of the week, in which case this is stated in the reviews in the Guide. Khmers eat early by Western standards: breakfast is normally over by 8am, lunch by noon, while the dinner trade is relatively quiet and short-lived, as people (in the provinces, especially) prefer takeaway meals to eat at home. Thus Khmer restaurants are generally open from around 6am until 7 or 8pm in the provinces, or until around 9 or 10pm in Phnom Penh, Siem Reap and Sihanoukville. In general, there's no need to book in advance, even to eat at expensive restaurants – although we've given telephone numbers in the Guide for the few establishments where you might want to reserve for special events or where meals are packaged with a cultural performance (as in a handful of venues in Siem Reap).

How to eat

Most Cambodian meals are based around polished white **rice**, which is usually served either in a large bowl from which you help yourself, or as individual platefuls. The rice is eaten off a shallow bowl, like a soup plate, using a fork and spoon (Cambodians don't use knives), the spoon held in the right hand and used to eat from, the fork serving to break up the food and to push it onto the spoon. **Noodles**, eaten with chopsticks and a Chinese soup spoon, are also common, but tend to be consumed more as a snack than a meal in themselves. In Chinese restaurants you'll be given a small rice bowl and chopsticks, whether you're eating rice or noodles.

Diners typically order two or three dishes – fish or meat, vegetables and perhaps a soup – which are placed in the centre of the table; each person helps themselves from the communal fare in small amounts at a time. If not served with the meal, the soup follows at the end (though in Chinese restaurants it normally comes at the beginning of the meal), and is ladled into individual bowls from a much larger serving bowl.

Before eating, it's common for diners to wipe the bowls, eating implements and glasses with the tissues provided on every table. Although Cambodians typically do not eat with their fingers, it is acceptable to pick up pieces of meat or chicken with your right hand (the left hand is deemed unclean as it's used to clean yourself after going to the toilet). Toothpicks are provided on every

Cambodian delicacies

Cambodians eat just about everything, and nothing escapes a true gourmet, not even **insects**. In the markets you'll see big trays of grasshoppers, beetles and crickets, usually fried and sold by the bag, which are eaten like sweets. **Spiders** are a speciality of Skone, a town between Phnom Penh and Kompong Cham, where big black hairy tarantulas are skewered and fried.

Phnom Penh has a number of upmarket Chinese and seafood restaurants where, besides many varieties of shellfish and fish, **snake**, **turtle** and **game** such as deer, wild pig, rabbit and monitor lizard are served up. More mundanely, tiny sparrows, *jarb jeyan*, and other small birds can be found deep-fried in many Khmer restaurants. A few places also offer illegally hunted animals such as pangolin and bear, although a clampdown some years ago has reduced the practice.

restaurant table; etiquette dictates that you should hold the toothpick in one hand and cover your mouth with the other.

What to eat

Many Cambodian dishes are variations on Chinese equivalents and are stir-fried in a wok to order. Just about any combination of ingredients can be ordered: chicken, pork or frogs' legs might be stir-fried with ginger, spring onions and garlic; prawn or chicken with basil leaves. Rice or noodles can themselves be stir-fried with chopped pork, beef, crab or vegetables, with an egg scrambled in or fried and served on top. Stir-fried **sweet and sour** dishes are also available, usually made with fish or pork – though you can ask for a vegetarian version – and flavoured with a combination of ingredients including pineapple, onion and either green or red tomatoes.

Stews and curries are often available at market stalls and cheap restaurants. Cambodian **stews** are usually based on a light stock (with beef or fish), complemented by bitter gourd or field melon; it's not unusual for them to contain hard-boiled eggs either. **Curries**, usually made with beef, are only mildly spicy and generally quite dry.

Smoky, **charcoal-grilled** chicken and fish are available everywhere from roadside stalls to restaurants, the fish served with a dip of grated green mango, chilli, garlic and fish sauce, while the chicken comes with a salad garnish and a sweet chilli sauce.

Khmer cuisine features two kinds of soup: **sumlar**, freshly prepared to order and cooked quickly, and **sop**, based on a stock which has been simmering for a while. One of the commonest soups on restaurant menus is *sumlar sngouw jerooet*, made from either chicken or fish and cooked with onion, lemon and chives.

Breakfast

For **breakfast**, Cambodians often eat rice with either fried chicken or fried pork, served with sliced cucumber and pickled vegetables, and a side bowl of clear soup. Also popular in the mornings is **geautieuv sop**, rice noodles in a clear broth with chicken, pork or beef pieces; you might wish to decline the other ingredients, namely sliced-up intestines or gizzard and a chunk of congealed blood, which the Khmers slurp with relish, as it's said to make you strong. A dish of bean sprouts and a slice of lime will be provided on the side, which you can add to taste.

In the tourist centres **Western breakfasts** are available in guesthouses, hotels, cafés and restaurants catering for tourists and expat workers. In the provinces an occasional restaurant will cater for NGO workers and serve fried eggs or omelettes with bread, but otherwise it's difficult to find anything other than Khmer fare first thing in the morning.

Snacks

Cambodian snack foods are legion, the range varying with the time of day. Eaten with breakfast or as an afternoon snack, *noam bpaow* are steamed dumplings, originating from Chinese cuisine, made from white dough filled with a mix of minced pork, turnip, egg and chives. They're readily available from street vendors and at restaurants; there's a second, less common version, smaller and sweeter and filled with a green mung-bean paste.

In the afternoon and evening, crusty **baguettes**, filled with your choice of meat pâté or sardines and pickled vegetables, can be bought from street hawkers for around 2000 riel. At beer stalls in night markets, you'll find **grueng klaim**, fibrous strips of dried beef or pork served with pickles and generally eaten with alcoholic beverages.

Bany chaev are savoury wok-fried pancakes commonly available at market stalls; they're made from rice flour flecked with chives and coloured vivid yellow using turmeric. Filled with fried minced pork, onion, prawns and bean sprouts, they're eaten by wrapping pieces of the pancake in a lettuce leaf and dipping them in a fish sauce mixed with garlic, lemon and crushed peanuts.

Steamed or grilled eggs are incredibly popular and are available everywhere, most commonly from street vendors, night markets and at transport stops – where you'll often get a choice of eggs, with bite-sized quails' eggs easy to find. The black "thousand-year eggs" that you see at markets and food stalls are duck's eggs that have been stored in jars of salt until the shells turn black; by that time the whites and the yolks have turned into a jelly, not dissimilar in texture to soft-boiled eggs. They are eaten with rice or *borbor*, a soupçon of egg being taken with each spoonful of rice.

Often found at night markets or served up with beer is **pong dteer gowne**, literally ducks' eggs with duckling. Said to give strength and good health, it really does contain an unhatched duckling, boiled and served with some herbs and a sauce of salt, pepper and lemon juice – not too bad if you don't look too closely at what you're eating.

Cooked bananas are also much eaten as snacks, seasoned with salt and grilled over charcoal braziers, or wok-fried in a batter containing sesame seeds, which are at their most delicious when they're piping hot. Both are available in the markets, as are **noam ensaum jayk**, sweet sticky-rice parcels in different shapes, such as pyramids or rolls, containing a piece of banana and wrapped in banana leaves.

Among the more unusual snacks is the much-prized **grolan**, bamboo tubes containing a delicious mix of sticky rice, coconut milk and black beans, cooked over charcoal and sold bundled together by hawkers (usually in the provinces). The woody outer layer of the bamboo is removed after cooking, leaving a thin shell which you peel down to get at the contents. Seasonally available are **chook**, the cone-shaped, green seeds of the lotus flower, sold in bundles of three or five heads; to eat, pop the seeds out from the green rubbery pod, peel off their outer skins and consume the insides, which taste a bit like garden peas.

Accompaniments

No Cambodian meal is complete without a variety of accompaniments. One of the most prized of these is **prohok**, a salted, fermented fish paste which looks like a pinkish pâté and has an incredibly strong anchovy-like taste. A dollop of the paste is served on a plate with raw vegetables, *gee* and edible flowers; it's eaten either by adding a tiny amount to the accompanying vegetables or by taking a morsel with a spoonful of rice. *Prohok* isn't usually found on the menus of classy restaurants but is always available at market stalls and in Cambodian homes.

Though it's less pungent than *prohok*, **fish sauce** is still pretty smelly. Used as a dip with every type of food, it's made from both salt- and fresh-water fish, which are layered with salt in large vats; as the fish ferments the juice is extracted from the bottom and bottled.

Other accompaniments include **dips** of chilli sauce and soya sauce – to which you can add chopped-up chillies and garlic – which are either left in pots on the table or served in individual saucers.

Rice and noodles

Besides boiled rice, Cambodians enjoy rice cooked up as a porridge called **borbor**, usually available at market stalls, night markets and in some cheap restaurants, either as breakfast or an evening dish. *Borbor* can either be left unseasoned and used as a base to which you add your own ingredients – dried fish, pickles, salted egg or fried vegetables – or cooked in stock, with pieces of chicken, fish or pork and bean sprouts added before serving. Shredded ginger, a squeeze of lime and spicy soya bean paste from pots at the table can also be added to taste.

White rice-flour noodles, **geautiev** (pronounced *"goy teal"*), are available in different shapes and sizes – in fine threads for noodle soup, or wide and thick for use in *nom bany jowk*. The latter is sold by female street vendors from baskets dangling on shoulder poles and consists of noodles served cold with a lukewarm curry sauce over the top. Yellow egg noodles – **mee** – made from wheat flour are used in soups and stir-fries. Freshly made *mee* – called *mee kilo* because it's sold by weight – are available in the major towns, though elsewhere people make do with instant noodles imported in packets from Thailand and Vietnam. **Loat chat**, a hollow noodle similar to macaroni, is fried up by hawkers using hand-carts equipped with charcoal burners; a plate topped with a fried egg goes for 1000–1500 riel.

Meat

Meat is comparatively expensive and is invariably cut up into small pieces and mixed with plenty of vegetables. **Pork** is commonly available, attested to by the number of pigs wandering around even the smallest village, but **beef** is more difficult to obtain as cows are prized as work animals and not necessarily killed for food. The best beef is available in large towns; elsewhere it's often tough and chewy (in Western restaurants the beef is generally imported).

Not so much a soup as a meal in itself, **sop chhnang day** is a bit like a fondue: a clay pot of hot stock and meatballs is brought to the table and placed on a small burner in the middle. Once the soup is boiling you add a selection of ingredients to the pot according to taste, choosing from side plates featuring slices of raw beef (or venison), often mixed with raw egg prior to cooking; sprigs of herbs; various vegetables; yellow and white noodles; tofu; dried sheets of soya bean (which looks a bit like chicken skin); and mushrooms. Both the stock and the dishes are replenished as long as you keep on eating, and at the end of the meal the bill is calculated according to the number of side plates on the table. Restaurants specializing in *sop chhnang day* often display a sign outside depicting a steaming pan over a burner.

Another Cambodian favourite is **sait gow ang**, beef grilled over a small charcoal burner at the table. Nibbled with pickled vegetables and fresh herbs, it tends to be eaten as an evening snack to accompany drinking. Similar in style but more of a meal is **chhnang phnom pleung**, "volcano pot", so named because the burner is said to resemble a volcano in appearance; the beef (venison is also used) comes to the table ready sliced, with a raw egg stirred into the meat before cooking. It's accompanied by side dishes of raw vegetables such as green tomatoes, capsicum and salad greens. Once you've grilled the meat and vegetables to your taste, they're wrapped in a salad leaf and dipped in a sauce before being eaten.

Typically found at cheap restaurants, **kaar** is a stew usually made with pig's trotters and green cabbage (it can also be made with fish or bamboo shoots) and eaten with unseasoned rice porridge (*borbor*). Pork is the usual ingredient in **spring rolls** (though Vietnamese restaurants especially may do a vegetarian version as an appetizer); they're either steamed or fried and then rolled up in a lettuce leaf with sliced cucumber, bean sprouts and herbs, and eaten dipped in a sweet chilli sauce.

Chicken and duck

Chicken and duck in Cambodia often have a high bone-to-flesh ratio; except in tourist restaurants, the whole carcass is chopped up, which means you have to pick out the bones from each mouthful.

A refreshing option is *sumlar ngam ngouw*, a clear chicken broth made with pickled limes and herbs. Worth trying if you can find it is **baked chicken**, *sait mowan dot*, cooked in a metal pot in a wood-fired oven and really tasty. It's usually prepared to order, so there is quite a wait involved.

Fish

Fish is plentiful and the main source of protein for most Cambodians. Near the Tonle

Vegetarians and vegans

Although strict Buddhists do have a vegetarian meal once every two weeks on offering days, Cambodians in general can't understand why anyone who can afford meat or fish would not want to eat it, and even the monks aren't strictly vegetarian.

The best way to get a **vegetarian dish** is to ask for your order to be cooked without meat (*ot dak sait*) or fish (*ot dak trei*); in principle, most stir-fries and soups can be done this way. You might be told that the dish is "not delicious" without meat, and the waiter may also come back a couple of times just to check he's got it straight. However, to be sure that prawns, chicken, duck or even intestines aren't substituted, or that a meat stock isn't used, you'll need to specify a whole list of things to avoid, so some flexibility on your part wouldn't go amiss. **Vegans** will need to make sure that no eggs are used *(ot yoh pong mowan)* as these are widely used, but should have few problems avoiding dairy products, which are unlikely to be found outside Western restaurants.

In tourist centres one or two vegetarian restaurants have opened, while restaurants catering for foreigners will also have more choice and a better idea of what being a vegetarian means.

Sap there's a particularly good choice of **freshwater** varieties, and **sea fish** is plentiful along the coast, though inland it's only readily available in the specialist (and inevitably expensive) restaurants of Phnom Penh.

Fish is served up in all manner of ways – grilled, fried, in soups and stews. Popular in tourist areas is **amok**, a mild Cambodian-style fish curry (chicken is also used); the fish is mixed with coconut milk and seasonings and baked wrapped in banana leaves (a variation, offered by several Siem Reap restaurants, is to cook the fish in the shell of a young coconut).

Dried fish is a particular favourite. Much prized for sun-drying are large freshwater fish from the Tonle Sap, which are sliced lengthwise like kippers and grilled over charcoal, to be eaten with rice. When fish is cheap you'll see people drying their own in baskets outside their houses.

Vegetables

Cambodia's markets offer up a wide range of vegetables, some of which will be unfamiliar, all delivered fresh daily. Regrettably, you won't come across many of these on restaurant menus, though one unusual vegetable you will find in restaurants is the *trokooen*, **morning glory**, a water plant with a thick, hollow stem and elongated heart-shaped leaves, which are carefully removed prior to cooking; it's often served stir-fried with garlic and oyster sauce, and tastes a bit like spinach.

Fried mixed vegetables are ubiquitous in Khmer restaurants, the constituents varying according to what's available (in some establishments you may be able to choose from a selection). Green tomatoes, crisp and refreshing, are often added to this and other dishes; red ones are only available in limited quantities for special recipes. For a decent selection of vegetable dishes, though, you'll need to try the Chinese restaurants. At street stalls and in the markets you'll find *noam gachiey*, best described as chive burgers; made from rice flour, chives and herbs, they're steamed or fried, and dished up with either a sweet sauce (note that this is based on fish sauce) or soy sauce. Oddly enough, **French fries**, although not usually eaten by Cambodians, are available in many Cambodian restaurants, served with a variety of condiments and seasonings, including pepper with lemon juice, and bright-orange sweet chilli sauce.

Gee is the generic Cambodian term for all manner of herbs, used in cooking, served up by the plateful to be eaten on the side, or taken medicinally. You'll probably only recognize a few, such as mint and coriander; others include various types of water grass, vines, young tree leaves and weeds.

Pickles made with brine are frequently served in Cambodia as an appetizer or a side dish, and as a filling for baguettes.

There are many variations, made from combinations of cabbage, cucumber, ginger, turnip, bamboo shoots, onions and bean sprouts, often sculpted into shapes for extra visual appeal. Green mango salad, made from shredded green mango, dried shrimp, and fish paste topped with crushed peanut, is served up as a dish in restaurants, to be eaten as a starter or snack.

Desserts and sweetmeats

Specialist stalls, opening around lunchtime in the markets or in the late afternoon and evening along the street, serve Cambodian **desserts** in a vast range of colours and textures. Small custards, jellies and sticky-rice confections are displayed in large flat trays and cut or shaped into bite-sized pieces to be served in bowls, topped with grated ice and a slug of condensed milk; mixes of dried and crystallized fruits, beans and nuts are also on offer, served with ice and syrup. Other desserts include sweet sticky rice mixed with corn kernels, mung beans or lotus seed, poached pumpkin with syrup, and palm fruit with syrup, all of which are served up from large bowls by market stalls.

Khmer restaurants seldom serve desserts other than fresh fruit, though recently a few upmarket places are starting to offer them along with imported ice creams. Towns generally have a bakery or two producing a variety of **cakes**, many of which are approximations of familiar Western goodies, including custard-filled éclairs, small sponges and coconut tarts. Market stalls in all towns sell small, freshly baked sponge cakes. In Phnom Penh, Siem Reap and Sihanoukville you'll find Western-style cakes and pastries; elsewhere you may find cakes or tarts on the menu if the café has a link to Westerners.

Fruits

Colourful **fruit** stalls can be found everywhere in Cambodia, and the selection is enormous – stallholders will always let you try before you buy if you don't know what you're looking at. Imported apples, pears and grapes are also available, though comparatively expensive.

Bananas come in several varieties, some of which are seldom seen in the West; they're grown just about everywhere, and are sold in huge quantities – cheaply at around 1000 riel a hand – for snacking, cooking and as offerings for the pagoda. Quite easy to find are *jayk oumvong*, which is slender and stays green when ripe; *jayk numvar*, a medium-sized, plump, yellow banana, said to cool the body; and the finger-sized, very sweet *jayk pong mowan*, said to be warming, which is a little pricier than the other varieties. Relatively uncommon are the large, dry and fibrous red or green bananas, generally used for cooking.

The **durian** is a rugby-ball-sized fruit with a hard, spiky exterior. Much sought after by Khmers, it's an acquired taste for most Westerners as it has a rather fetid smell. Inside are several segments, each containing two or three stones surrounded by pale yellow, creamy textured flesh, which can be quite addictive once you've got over the odour.

Longans have a long season and are often sold still on the twig. The fruit are cherry-sized and have a hard brown skin; the flesh inside is similar to that of lychees in texture and flavour. Bright green and prickly skinned, **soursops** are pure white inside and have a tart but sweet taste. Hard, round and a bit like a bright green cricket ball, **guavas** have a crunchy, dry texture a bit like a hard pear. The flat brown pods of **tamarind** are simple to eat: split open the pods and discard the fibrous thread inside, then suck off the rich brown tangy flesh, but mind the hard seeds. The most picturesque of Khmer fruits, though, has to be the rosy pink **dragon fruit**, from a climbing cactus-like vine. Inside its waxy skin, the moist, pure-white flesh is dotted with black seeds and has quite a subtle taste, verging on bland.

Drinks

Bottled water is found everywhere, as Cambodian **tap water** isn't considered safe to drink. Be aware that the ice that is invariably added to cold drinks (unless you request otherwise) may not be hygienic except in Western restaurants; for more on this, see p.45.

Tea and coffee

Cambodians drink plenty of **green tea**, which is readily available in coffee shops and from market stalls; it's normally served free of charge with food in restaurants (other than in Siem Reap where foreigners are charged). If you like your tea strong, try *dtai grolab*, made by putting water and a mass of tea leaves into a small glass, placing a saucer on top, and turning the whole thing upside down to brew. When it's dark enough, the tea is decanted into another cup and plenty of sugar added, but no milk. **Lemon tea**, made with Chinese red dust tea and lemon juice, is refreshing both hot and iced, and is generally served with a hefty dose of sugar. **Indian tea**, sold locally under the Lipton brand, is served in hotels, guesthouses and restaurants that cater to foreigners.

Noodle shops, coffee shops and restaurants serve **coffee** from early morning to late afternoon, but in the evenings it can be difficult to find except at restaurants geared up for foreigners. The beans are generally imported from Laos and Vietnam – although domestically produced coffee from Rattanakiri and Mondulkiri can be found in some places. Each shop generally blends the coffee to its own particular recipe, adding wine, butter or chocolate powder during the roasting process, resulting in a thick, strong brew. White coffee is served with a slug of sweetened condensed milk already at the bottom of the glass, so don't stir it all in if you don't like your drink too sweet. Black coffee will often be served with sugar unless you specify otherwise.

Cambodians often have their coffee or tea **iced**, even for breakfast; if you want yours hot, ask for it to be served *ot dak tuk kork*, without ice. Most of the milk available is either sterilized, canned or sweetened condensed; when not added to coffee or tea, it's sometimes drunk iced, perhaps with a bright red or green cordial added.

Juices and fizzy soft drinks

For a drink on the hoof, iced **sugar-cane juice**, *tuk umpow*, is very refreshing and not actually that sweet. It costs around 1000 riel a glass and is sold everywhere from yellow carts equipped with a mangle through which the peeled canes are passed, sometimes with a piece of orange added for extra taste. Equally refreshing is the juice of a **green coconut** (1500–2500 riel): the top is cut off and you drink the juice before getting it cut in half so you can eat the soft, jelly-like flesh.

Fruit shakes, *tuk krolok*, are an important part of an evening's entertainment: juice stalls, recognizable by their fruit displays and blenders, set up in towns all over the country from the late afternoon. You can order a mixture of fruits to be juiced or just one or

Beer girls and taxi girls

Cambodia's **beer girls** will approach you almost before you've sat down in a Cambodian restaurant. Smartly dressed in uniforms colour-coded according to which brand of beer they're promoting, they rely on commissions based on the amount of beer they manage to sell, and will keep opening bottles or cans and topping up your glass, hoping to get you to drink more. You don't pay them for the beer, as the cost is added to your bill at the end by counting up the empties. Beer girls will often drink with Cambodian men to up their consumption, but that's generally as far as it goes, as the beer companies make sure the women get home safely afterwards.

Although things are more relaxed than they used to be, "decent" Cambodian women neither go to bars nor drink alcohol – indeed it's only relatively recently that they've begun to venture out to restaurants – so, while beer girls are somewhat looked down upon, the **taxi girls** who frequent the karaoke parlours and nightclubs are beyond the pale. Usually from very poor families, they have a role akin to that of hostess, dance partner and sometimes call girl rolled into one. If you invite them to join you at your table or dance with you, the charge will be added to your bill at the end of the evening, as will the cost of their drinks.

two; coconut milk, sugar syrup, condensed milk and shaved ice are also added, as is a raw egg (unless you specify otherwise – *ot yoh pong mowan*).

Freshly made **soya milk** is sold in the morning by street vendors; the green version is sweetened and thicker than the unsweetened white. Soya milk is also available canned, as is **winter-melon tea**, a juice made from the field melon which has a distinctive sweet, almost earthy taste. **Fizzy soft drinks** such as Coca-Cola, 7-Up and Sprite are widely available either in bottles or increasingly in cans; in many places you'll also be able to get Schweppes tonic and soda water.

Alcohol

Every Cambodian town has its **karaoke bar** where local men hang out of an evening; alcohol is readily available at these and also at the profusion of nightclubs and discos in Phnom Penh, Siem Reap and Sihanoukville.

Besides nightclubs and bars, most restaurants and night-market stalls serve **beer**. Cambodia's national beer is Angkor, brewed by an Australian/Cambodian joint venture in Sihanoukville; it's available in cans, large bottles and sometimes on draught, prices varying from around 4000 riel a can to 6000–8000 riel for a large bottle. Tiger, VB, Beer Lao and ABC Stout are also readily available, and there are many more local brews including beer from the newly opened Kingdom Brewery in Phnom Penh. Even if already chilled, beer is often drunk with ice.

Spirits are generally only found in larger restaurants, nightclubs and Western bars. Imported wines are available in smarter restaurants and Western-oriented places, and can be purchased in supermarkets and mini-markets. When not downing beer, Cambodians themselves usually prefer to stick to local, medicinal **rice wines**, which are available at stalls and shops where glasses of the stuff are ladled from large jars containing various plant or animal parts. Though quite sweet, they're strong and barely palatable, but cheap at a few hundred riel for a glass. Another local brew is sugar-palm beer, sold and brewed straight from the bamboo tubes in which the juice is collected (see p.7). It's quite refreshing and readily available in villages, and from vendors in the towns; it's also now available for tourists in nicely labelled bottles.

Health

Health care in Cambodia is poor. Even the best hospitals have inadequate facilities, low standards of cleanliness and appalling patient care, so use them only in the event of dire emergency. For anything serious, get to Bangkok if you are able to travel. Should you have no option but to go to a Cambodian hospital, try to get a friend – ideally, a Khmer-speaker – to accompany you for support.

In Phnom Penh a couple of private Western-oriented **clinics** offer slightly better care at increased cost. If you get ill outside Phnom Penh or Siem Reap, self-diagnosis and treatment is often better than visiting a clinic. Wherever you seek medical attention, you will be expected to pay upfront for treatment, medication and food.

Although every town has a number of **pharmacies** (typically open daily 7am–8pm) stocking an extensive range of medications, the staff aren't required to have a dispensing qualification, so you may want to check the product sheets (and even expiry dates) before you buy. Regrettably fake medicines abound and there's no easy way to determine if what you're buying is the real thing. Whenever possible buy only in Phnom Penh or Siem Reap which have a couple of reputable pharmacies (see p.115 & p.178) employing qualified personnel who can help with diagnosis and remedies for simple health problems.

Consider getting a pre-trip **dental check-up** if you're travelling for an extended period, as the only places to get dental treatment in Cambodia are in Phnom Penh and Siem Reap; elsewhere you'll have to grin and bear it. If you wear **glasses**, it's worth taking along a copy of your prescription (or a spare pair of glasses); you can get replacements made quite cheaply in Phnom Penh and Siem Reap.

Medical resources for travellers

UK and Ireland

Hospital for Tropical Diseases Travel Clinic ⓣ0207/388 9600, ⓦwww.thehtd.org.

MASTA (Medical Advisory Service for Travellers Abroad) ⓦwww.masta-travel-health.com. Enter your postcode to get details of your nearest clinic and its phone number; you can book an appointment online. Detailed country health advice sheets cost £3.99.

National Travel Health Network & Centre ⓦwww.nathnac.org. For detailed country-specific health information.

Tropical Medical Bureau Republic of Ireland ⓦwww.tmb.ie. Country-specific advice and list of travel clinics.

US and Canada

CDC (Centre for Disease Control) ⓣ800/232-4636, ⓦwww.cdc.gov/travel, ⓔcdcinfo@cdc.gov. Official US government travel health site for health alerts, travel health advice and travel clinic information.

International Society of Travel Medicine ⓣ1-404/373-8282, ⓦwww.istm.org, ⓔistm@istm.org. Has a full list of travel health clinics.

Canadian Society for International Health ⓦwww.csih.org. Extensive list of travel health centres.

Australia, New Zealand and South Africa

Travellers' Medical and Vaccination Centre ⓣ1300/658 844, ⓦwww.tmvc.com.au. Lists travel clinics in Australia, New Zealand and South Africa (ⓔinfo@traveldoctor.co.za).

Vaccinations and immunizations

It's worth checking before you leave that you are up to date with **routine immunizations**, such as tetanus and diphtheria. For Cambodia, you should consider immunizing yourself against hepatitis A, tuberculosis and typhoid; inoculations against hepatitis B, rabies and Japanese encephalitis are recommended if you are going to be at a particular risk (for example if you're working in a remote area). You'll need to produce proof that you've been vaccinated against yellow fever in the (admittedly unlikely) event of arriving from an infected area (West and Central Africa, or South America).

It is as well to consult your doctor or travel clinic as early as possible – even while you are planning your trip – since it can take anything up to eight weeks to complete a full course of immunizations (you may also need to take malaria prophylactics in advance; see p.45). All inoculations should be recorded on an **international travel vaccination card,** which is worth carrying with you in case you get sick or bitten by a dog.

Hepatitis

Hepatitis A, a viral infection of the liver, can be contracted from contaminated food and water – shellfish sold by hawkers and untreated water are particular risks in Cambodia – or by contact with an infected person. Symptoms include dark-coloured urine, aches and pains, nausea, general malaise and tiredness, with jaundice following after a few days. A blood test is needed for diagnosis, and rest, plenty of non-alcoholic fluids and a high carbohydrate diet are recommended for convalescence. A single shot of immunoglobulin offers short-term protection against hepatitis A.

Far more serious is **hepatitis B**, passed via contaminated body fluids; it can be contracted through non-sterile needles (including those used in tattooing and acupuncture), sexual contact or from a blood transfusion that hasn't been properly screened. Symptoms include non-specific abdominal pain, vomiting, loss of appetite, dark-coloured urine and jaundice. Immunization may be recommended if you are staying in Asia for longer than six months. In the event that you think you have contracted hepatitis B, it's especially important to seek medical attention.

A **combined vaccine** has recently become available offering ten years' protection against hepatitis A and five years' against hepatitis B; your doctor will be able to advise on its suitability.

Tuberculosis, rabies and tetanus

Tuberculosis, contracted from droplets coughed up by infected persons, is widespread in Cambodia and is a major cause of death in young children. You may have been inoculated against the disease in childhood, but if you're unsure, consider a skin (Heaf) test, which will determine if you already have immunity.

Rabies is contracted from the bite or saliva of an infected animal. Vaccinations are recommended if you're going to be spending a long time in rural areas; but even if you've been vaccinated, if you are bitten (or licked on an open wound) you will need to get two booster injections as quickly as possible, preferably within 24 to 48 hours.

Tetanus, a bacterial infection which causes muscular cramps and spasms, comes from spores in the earth and can enter the blood circulatory system through wounds and grazes. If left untreated it can cause breathing problems and sometimes death. It's worth checking if you've been vaccinated against tetanus in the last ten years and getting a booster if necessary.

Typhoid and cholera

Typhoid and cholera, bacterial infections that affect the digestive system, are spread by contaminated food and water, and outbreaks are thus usually associated with particularly unsanitary conditions.

Symptoms of **typhoid** include tiredness, dull headaches and spasmodic fevers, with spots appearing on the abdomen after about a week. Vaccination is suggested if you plan to stay in rural areas of Cambodia, but it doesn't confer complete immunity, so maintaining good standards of hygiene remains important.

Sudden, watery diarrhoea and rapid dehydration are among the symptoms of **cholera**, and medical advice is essential to treat the infection with antibiotics. Vaccination is no longer recommended for cholera due to its poor efficacy. From time to time there are outbreaks of cholera in Cambodia which are well publicized in the media.

General precautions

Cambodia is a hot and humid country, and **dehydration** is a potential problem, its onset indicated by headaches, dizziness, nausea and dark urine. **Cuts** and raw blisters can rapidly become infected and should be promptly treated by cleaning and disinfecting the wound and then applying an air-permeable dressing.

Bites and stings

Insects and **flies** are legion in Cambodia and are at their worst at the start of the dry season when there are stagnant pockets of water left from the rains. Even during the hot season (March–May) they come out in the evenings, swarming around light bulbs and warm flesh, though they are annoying rather than harmful (with the exception of mosquitoes, p.45).

On the coast, **sand flies** appear in the late afternoon and evening, delivering nasty bites which don't erupt until a few hours later, when they become incredibly red and itchy. Once you scratch, the bites become even more inflamed and can take up to a month to recede, leaving behind nasty scars. These little blighters have a limited range and mostly attack victims on the sand; if on or near the beach, it's probably best to use an insect repellent.

Sun and heat

Even when the sky is overcast the Cambodian sun is fierce, and you should take precautions against sunburn and heat stroke wherever you are. Cover up, use a high-protection-factor **sunscreen**, wear a hat and drink plenty of fluids throughout the day.

Hygiene and stomach complaints

Though catering facilities at many restaurants and food stalls can appear basic, the **food** you'll be served is usually absolutely fresh; all ingredients are bought daily and are mostly cooked to order. A good rule of thumb when selecting a place to eat is to pick one that is popular with local people, as the Khmers are fussy about their food and seldom give a place a second chance if they've found the food isn't fresh. Food from street hawkers is usually okay if it's cooked in front of you. Bottled water is available everywhere and it's best to stick to drinking that and to be cautious with ice, which is often cut up in the street from large blocks and handled by several people before it gets to your glass (though in Western restaurants it will probably come from an ice-maker).

Stomach complaints

The most common travellers' ailment is **upset tummy**. Travellers' **diarrhoea** often occurs in the early days of a trip as a result of a simple change in diet, though stomach cramps and vomiting may mean it's food poisoning. If symptoms persist for more than a couple of days, seek medical help as you may need antibiotics to clear up the problem.

Most diarrhoea is short-lived and can be handled by drinking plenty of fluids and avoiding rich or spicy food. Activated charcoal tablets sold across the counter at pharmacies help by absorbing the bad bugs in your gut and usually speed recovery. It's often a good idea to rest up for a day or two if your schedule allows. In the event of persistent diarrhoea or vomiting, it's worth taking **oral rehydration salts**, available at most pharmacies (or make your own from half a teaspoon of salt and eight teaspoons of sugar per litre of bottled water).

Unless you're going on a long journey, avoid taking Imodium and Lomotil. These bung you up by stopping gut movements and can extend the problem by preventing your body expelling the bugs that gave rise to the diarrhoea in the first place.

Dysentery and giardiasis

If there is blood or mucus in your faeces and you experience severe stomach cramps, you may have dysentery, which requires immediate medical attention. There are two forms of the disease, the more serious of which is **amoebic dysentery**. Even though the symptoms may well recede over a few days, the amoebae will remain in the gut and can go on to attack the liver; treatment with an antibiotic, metronidazole (Flagyl) is thus essential. Equally unpleasant is **bacillary dysentery**, also treated with antibiotics.

Giardiasis is caused by protozoa usually found in streams and rivers. Symptoms, typically watery diarrhoea and bad-smelling wind, appear around two weeks after the organism has entered the system and can last for up to two weeks. Giardiasis can be diagnosed from microscope analysis of stool samples, and is treated with metronidazole.

Mosquito-borne diseases

Given the prevalence in Cambodia of serious diseases spread by mosquitoes, including multi-resistant malaria, it is important to **avoid being bitten**. In the provinces and high-risk areas – in the jungle for example – most guesthouses provide **mosquito nets**; if there isn't one in your room, make sure to ask. Some guesthouses don't provide nets as they have installed window screens, but these are seldom completely effective as mosquitoes can also get in through ventilators or the gaps under doors. It's also worth asking for your room to be sprayed with insecticide when you go out in the evening; the disgusting stuff will have time to dissipate by the time you return.

Wearing long trousers, socks and a long-sleeved top will reduce the chances of being bitten. **Insect repellents** containing DEET are the most effective, although you may want to consider a natural alternative such as those based on citronella.

Malaria

Malaria is prevalent year-round, throughout the country – with the exception of Phnom Penh and the area closest to the Tonle Sap; in 2009, over 60,000 cases were reported, some resulting in death. It is a risk in Siem Reap and at Angkor Wat, and mefloquine resistance is reported on the western and northern borders from Koh Kong to Stung Treng. Malaria is contracted from the night-biting female *anopheles* mosquito, which injects a parasite into the bloodstream. Chills, fevers and sweating ensue after an incubation period of around twelve days, often along with aching joints, a cough and vomiting, and the symptoms repeat after a couple of days. In Cambodia the dangerous **falciparum** strain of the disease predominates; if untreated, it can be fatal.

Before you travel, it is important to take advice on a suitable **prophylaxis** regime, as a course of antimalarial medication needs to be started in advance of arriving in a risk area. **Mefloquine** (aka Larium) may be recommended, but has much-publicized side effects which should be discussed with your doctor. If you take it, you'll need to start a couple of weeks before you enter the malarial area and continue medication for at least four weeks after leaving, to cover the incubation period of the parasite. Where mefloquine-resistance is found alternatives are the antibiotic **doxycycline**, which should be taken a couple of days before you enter the malarial zone and continued for two weeks after you leave, or Malarone, an atovaquone/proguanil combination that has recently been approved. Note that taking antimalarials doesn't guarantee that you won't contract the disease, a fact which reinforces the need to avoid being bitten.

Emergency treatment for falciparum malaria is 600mg of quinine sulphate, taken three times a day for three days, followed by a single dose of three Fansidar tablets once the quinine course is completed. These tablets are available over the counter at pharmacies throughout Cambodia, but if you suspect malaria you should still see a doctor for a diagnostic blood test.

Dengue fever

Outbreaks of dengue fever occur annually in Cambodia with 37 deaths reported in 2009. Spread by the day-biting female *aedes* mosquito, this is a viral disease which takes about a week to develop following a bite. It resembles a bad case of flu; symptoms include high fever, aches and pains, headache and backache. After a couple of days a red rash appears on the torso, gradually spreading to the limbs. There may also be abnormal bleeding, which requires medical attention.

No vaccine is available at the time of writing, and there is no effective treatment, although paracetamol can be taken to relieve the symptoms (*not* aspirin, which can increase the potential for bleeding); you should also drink plenty of fluids and get lots of rest. Although the symptoms should improve after five or six days, lethargy and depression can last for a month or more – consult a doctor if symptoms persist. Those who have previously contracted dengue fever are at particular risk if they subsequently contract a different virus strain, which can result in **dengue haemorrhagic fever**. In this condition the usual symptoms of dengue fever are accompanied by abdominal pain and vomiting; immediate medical help should be sought, as this condition can be fatal.

Japanese encephalitis

Japanese encephalitis is a serious viral disease carried by night-biting mosquitoes which breed in the rice fields. The risk is highest between May and October. It's worth considering vaccination if you're going to be in rural areas of Cambodia for an extended period or are visiting during the high-risk period. Symptoms, which appear five to fifteen days after being bitten, include headaches, a stiff neck, flu-like aches and chills; there's no specific treatment, but it's wise to seek medical advice and take paracetamol or aspirin to ease the symptoms.

Sexually transmitted diseases

Cambodia is seriously at risk of an **HIV/AIDS** epidemic, with over one percent of the male population aged between 15 and 49 already infected. It isn't known how the virus first arrived in Cambodia, but a steep rise in the number of prostitutes during the UNTAC years certainly didn't help. A high proportion of Khmer men visit prostitutes and have a cultural aversion to the use of condoms, which sex-education programmes haven't resolved. This fact, allied to an increase in intravenous drug abuse, means that the virus is now running unchecked through the population.

Syphilis and **gonorrhoea** are rife, but while both are unpleasant and require a medical diagnosis, they can be treated effectively with antibiotics. Using reliable **condoms** – preferably Western brands – will reduce the chances of contracting an infection.

Other hazards

Avian flu (bird flu) was first identified in poultry in Southeast Asia in 2003. Occurring primarily in wild and domesticated birds (among which it is highly contagious and deadly), the virus is spread by contact with affected birds. At the time of writing, the WHO advises that there is no threat to health from the consumption of poultry or poultry products, including eggs. Although most reported cases of the virus have been contracted by bird-to-human contact, experts believe that human-to-human transmission is increasing, although currently only the closest family members of infected people have been contaminated. **Symptoms** are similar to influenza, with fever, sore throat and cough. Nine fatalities from the virus have been confirmed in Cambodia to date, the most recent in early 2010. However, the virus is not thought to pose a serious threat to tourists.

If you are at all concerned about swine flu, consider getting a general influenza vaccination before leaving home, as the latest vaccine may include the necessary antibodies to the H1N1 virus. Symptoms of swine flu are a general malaise, fever and headache, with flu-like aches and pains.

Crime and personal safety

Cambodia is now pretty safe to visit with the major danger being from explosives: it remains one of the world's most heavily mined countries and, furthermore, no one knows quite how much ordnance was dropped by the Americans over the country in the 1970s, or how much of it failed to explode. In the countryside, in spite of de-mining, it still pays to observe the simple rule of sticking to well-trodden paths.

Crime

On the whole, Cambodians are remarkably honest people (as attested by the money changers who sit unprotected on street corners surrounded by piles of notes), and crime is not a major problem. If you're using public transport, good care will be taken of your bags, and it's unusual to have anything go missing.

That said, **pickpockets** and petty thieves do operate, and it's advisable to take good care of your purse or wallet, especially in markets, on motos or tuk-tuks, at Poipet border area and on the beach at Sihanoukville. Incidents of **armed mugging** are not unknown either (some committed by robbers masquerading as police), so after dark, particularly in Phnom Penh, Siem Reap and Sihanoukville, it's wise to leave most of your money in the safe at your hotel or guesthouse, taking just enough cash for the evening.

If you are held up by muggers or armed robbers, don't resist and put yourself in danger, but do report the incident to the **police** as soon as possible – you'll need a signed, dated report from them to claim on your travel insurance – and, if you lose your passport, to your embassy as well. In Phnom Penh, Siem Reap and Sihanoukville, English-speaking **tourist police** will help, but in the provinces you'll have to deal with the local police, who are unlikely to have more than a smattering of English, so if possible take a Khmer-speaker with you.

Though the vast majority of Cambodian police will do their best to help in an emergency, a small minority are not averse to trying to elicit money from foreigners. If you're riding a motorbike or driving a motor vehicle, they may well deem that you've

Children at risk

Cambodia has an unfortunate reputation as a destination for paedophiles. Originally a side-product of the boom in prostitution during the UNTAC years, child sex tourism has grown in Cambodia as a result of crackdowns on child prostitution in other Southeast Asian countries, and remains a serious problem in spite of the hefty prison sentences which have been handed out to brothel owners and visitors involved in child sex tourism. Cambodia's highest-profile case involved Gary Glitter, who was deported in 2003, since when, dozens of other perpetrators have been jailed or deported to face trial in their home country.

The Ministry of the Interior (National Police) ask that anyone witnessing child prostitution in Cambodia immediately report it to the police **on their national "child-wise" hotline** (Ⓣ**023/997919** don't try to take matters into your own hands). ChildSafe (186 Street 13, Phnom Penh) has a 24-hour national hotline to report children at risk (Ⓣ012/311 112, Ⓦwww.childsafe-cambodia.org). The organization aims to protect Cambodian children from abuse. Their guidelines ask that tourists – tempting though it is to try to help – refrain from buying from children and giving money to children or to parents with young children; this is felt to keep them on the streets and in vulnerable situations. Instead, they ask that you help by supporting social workers or purchase products and services that sport the ChildSafe logo, which is now widely promoted in all provinces. You could also consider contacting **ECPAT** (End Child Prostitution, Abuse and Trafficking, Ⓦwww.ecpat.net).

Sex offenders who commit acts of paedophilia abroad can be prosecuted under the relevant national laws in their home country: in the UK contact Crimestoppers Ⓣ0800/555 111, Ⓦwww.crimestoppers-uk.org; in the US contact US Customs Immigration Enforcement on Ⓣ1-800/843 5678, Ⓦwww.cybertipline.org; in Canada contact NCECC (National Child Exploitation Coordination Centre) Ⓦwww.rcmp-grc.gc.ca; in Australia contact the Australian Federal Police Ⓣ1800/333 000, Ⓦwww.afp.gov.au. Be aware, however, that there are lots of mixed-race couples in Cambodia and, consequently, many sons and daughters (actual and adopted) of these relationships – so make sure of your facts before launching into any accusations.

Online abuse can be reported worldwide to the Virtual Global Taskforce (Ⓦwww.virtualglobaltaskforce.com). The site has links to relevant country-specific enforcement sites.

committed an offence. You can argue the "fine" down to a few dollars and may as well pay up, although if you can stand the hassle and don't mind wasting a lot more time you may feel it worth reporting such incidents to the police commissioner.

Road accidents usually attract vast crowds of curious onlookers, and if any damage to property or injury to a person or domestic animal has occurred, then you'll have to stay at the scene until the police arrive. It's the driver's responsibility to come to a financial arrangement with the other parties involved. In spite of their general amiability, it's not unknown for locals to try to coerce foreigners into coughing up money, even if they are the innocent party or merely a passenger.

Drugs offences

The possession and use of marijuana (called *ganja* locally), cocaine and heroin are illegal. Although the penalty for drugs offences does not include the death sentence as in some other Southeast Asian countries, it is likely to entail a lengthy prison sentence (from 5 year to life) which, in the absence of repatriation agreements with other countries, will have to be spent in full in a Cambodian jail.

Land mines and unexploded ordnance

The UN estimates that between four and six million **land mines** were laid in Cambodia between 1979 and 1991, but no one really knows. The Vietnamese and the government laid them as protection against Khmer Rouge guerrillas, who in turn laid them to intimidate local populations; neither side recorded the locations of the minefields. While over two thousand minefields have now been identified (usually through members of the local population being blown up), these are thought to represent just a fraction of the total number with new locations regularly being reported. Several organizations are actively working at de-mining the countryside, and at last the number of casualties is decreasing; but given the scale of the problem, it will be many years before the mines are cleared completely (see p.228 for more information).

The Angkor temple complexes are safe, but mines are still a risk in the countryside around Siem Reap. The border with Thailand, from Koh Kong to Preah Vihear, is particularly hazardous. In rural areas, take care not to leave well-used paths and don't take short cuts across rice fields without a local guide. Areas known to be badly contaminated are signed with a red skull and the words "Beware Mines".

As if this problem weren't enough, in the 1970s the United States dropped over half a million tonnes of bombs on Cambodia. This began as part of a secret and illicit plan to expose the Ho Chi Minh Trail used by communist North Vietnamese troops, and ended up in a massive countrywide bombing campaign to support the pro-American Lon Nol government against the Khmer Rouge. **Unexploded ordnance** (UXO), or explosive remnants of war (ERW), remains a risk in rural areas, with the southeast, centre and northeast of the country particularly affected; in the countryside it's foolish to pick up or kick any unidentified metal objects.

Money

Alongside the local currency, the riel, Cambodia has assimilated the US dollar into its economy, a situation that began with UNTAC in the early 1990s, when high-earning troops stationed in the country began spending their dollar salaries. Today you can use the dollar and riel interchangeably in all but a few cases.

Currency

Riel notes (there are no riel coins, nor is US coinage used in Cambodia) are available in denominations of 100, 500, 1000, 2000, 5000, 10,000, 20,000, 50,000 and 100,000. New notes were introduced in 2002, and now circulate alongside older notes and can be used interchangeably; you may also be passed an old 200 riel note, which is valid although no new notes of this denomination are being issued. The **exchange rate** is stable at around 4000 riel to the dollar; the best rates can be had in Phnom Penh, usually around Psar Thmei.

You can **pay** for most things solely in dollars, or solely in riel, or with a mixture of the two currencies; the larger the amount the more likely it is that the price will be quoted in dollars – note that the exchange rate when paying for dollar services in riel is inferior to the rate at the money changer by a few percent. Generally, you'll be charged in dollars for accommodation, when shopping in supermarkets and malls or eating in Western restaurants, and when paying for air tickets and boat fares. In markets, at noodle shops and food stalls, and when using local transport (such as motos, tuk-tuks, buses and pick-ups) prices are generally in riel (unless you wish to hire transport for the day, in which case you're likely to be quoted a dollar price). Things get a bit more confused near the Thai border, where people prefer to deal in **Thai baht**, or at Bavet, the Vietnamese border crossing where you may be quoted in dong. If you don't have baht you can generally pay in US dollars or riel, though you might end up paying fractionally more – you can change riel and dollars into baht at banks and local money changers. Throughout the Guide, prices are given in the currency in which you're most likely to be charged.

When paying in dollars, **change** will usually be given back in dollars for larger amounts, while for small sums and fractions of dollars you'll be given riel.

Bargaining

Prices at deluxe hotels, shops, and all food stalls, noodle shops and restaurants are fixed, as are fares for flights, bus journeys and boat trips. However, when shopping in markets, taking motos, tuk-tuks or cyclos and hiring a car, bargaining is pretty much expected. Mid-range hotel prices can often be negotiated, although at the budget end, guesthouse owners will seldom budge on price, preferring to leave the room empty.

Carrying your money

Old fashioned as it is, the safest way to carry your money is still as US-dollar **travellers' cheques**; with those from American Express the best known.

The usual fee for travellers'-cheque sales is one or two percent, though this may be waived if you buy the cheques through a bank where you have an account. It pays to get a selection of denominations. Make sure to keep the purchase agreement and a record of cheque serial numbers safe and separate from the cheques themselves. In the event that cheques are lost or stolen, the issuing company will expect you to report the loss forthwith, though none of the issuing companies is represented in Cambodia.

Instead of using a bank debit card you could consider a pre-paid **travel money card** from one of many providers, which can be loaded with an amount of money in a currency of your choice ($US), and then used in ATMs or to pay for services the same way as a credit or debit card; these have the security of not being associated with your bank account. Cards are usually issued free and are valid for a number of years (depending on the provider); many can be topped up by phone or internet while you are away. However, you will incur transaction charges when you use them, so check this with the issuer.

Arriving in Cambodia there are ATMs at both Phnom Penh and Siem Reap international airports and in the border areas at Poipet, Bavet and Koh Kong, so you can get $US cash as soon as you arrive. To change travellers' cheques, however, you'll need to get to a bank. Note also that unless you have obtained a **Cambodian visa** in advance, you'll need $20 in cash to buy one on arrival.

Credit cards, banks and ATMs

An increasing number of places accept **credit cards**, typically mid- and upper-range hotels and Western-oriented restaurants and shops in Phnom Penh, Siem Reap and Sihanoukville. While the use of credit cards is increasing it is not as prevalent as in the West; payment by card may attract a four-percent surcharge.

You can get a **cash advance** on Visa or MasterCard at banks and exchange bureaus in Phnom Penh, Battambang, Siem Reap and Sihanoukville, and at branches of the Canadia and ANZ Royal banks in most major towns. Acleda Bank (pronounced *A-See-Lay-Dah*) has branches all over the country but only accepts Visa. There are now ATMs in most major towns; note, though, that your money will be dispensed in US dollars. It's worth remembering that all cash advances are treated as loans, with interest accruing daily from the date of withdrawal; there may be a transaction fee (or two) on top of this.

Banking hours throughout Cambodia are generally Monday to Friday 8.30am to 3.30pm (often also Sat 8.30–11.30am).

Changing money

You can change dollars to riel at many banks, but it's generally more convenient to go to a **money changer**; they will usually also exchange Thai baht, pounds sterling and euros (it's difficult to exchange other currencies, although you'll possibly be able to do so at Psar Thmei in Phnom Penh and around the market in Siem Reap). Money changers are plentiful in all towns and are always found around markets, typically within goldsmiths' or jewellers' kiosks – look for the cabinets stacked with notes. When changing money, the dealer will do the sums on a calculator for you to agree, before counting out the notes in front of you; it is accepted practice that you then recount the money, as any discrepancy will not be considered once you've left the desk. Feel free to reject any notes in particularly dire condition. While riel are accepted regardless of condition, a dollar bill with even a minuscule blemish will be returned as unacceptable.

When changing money, it's better to opt for mid-value notes – 5000 or 10,000 riel for instance – which can be changed everywhere. Outside of market hours, you can still change dollars at shops, especially those selling phone cards; you'll need to ask around, and the rates will be worse to the tune of a few riel per dollar. You can change riel back into dollars at most money changers when leaving Cambodia, or into baht at money changers in Poipet. It's impossible to exchange riel once you've left the country.

Cashing travellers' cheques

Major banks will cash dollar travellers' cheques (into dollars only) for a two-percent commission; travellers' cheques in other currencies are sometimes viewed with suspicion and may be rejected. Don't rely on using travellers' cheques as payment for services or on cashing them other than at the banks, as they are accepted at few outlets.

Wiring money

Having money **wired from home** is fairly convenient these days with both the Acleda Bank and the Cambodia Asia Bank handling Western Union transfers, while the Canadia Bank is the agent for Moneygram. Fees vary however, and may be quite steep if you have to make an additional currency exchange, say from UK pounds to $US. It is also possible to have money wired directly from a bank in your home country to a bank account in Cambodia. If you choose this route, your home bank will need the name and address of the Cambodian bank, their bank code and the account name and number; money wired this way normally takes three to five working days to arrive and costs around £25/$35 per transaction (you'll also have to pay a handling fee in Cambodia).

Moneygram Ⓦ www.moneygram.com.
Western Union Ⓦ www.westernunion.com.

The media

Much of Cambodia's media is sponsored by the country's political parties, and though the prime minister has declared his support for press freedom, the media continues to be subject to the government's whims. There's a reasonable selection of English-language media, with two newspapers, a selection of magazines, plus satellite/cable TV and radio stations.

Newspapers and magazines

Cambodia has a surprisingly wide choice of **Khmer-language publications**, including around seven daily newspapers and a selection of monthly magazines, available in the capital and, in the main provincial towns. All the newspapers are pretty sensationalist, splashing graphic pictures of accidents and murders over their front pages. *Rasmei Kampuchea*, which at 18,000 copies per day has the largest circulation, and *Koh Santepheap* are both pro-government.

Cambodia's **English-language newspapers**, the *Cambodia Daily* (published daily except Sunday) and the *Phnom Penh Post* (Mon–Fri) can be found at newsstands around Phnom Penh, Battambang, Siem Reap and Sihanoukville. The *Cambodia Daily* carries a selection of foreign and domestic news, while the *Phnom Penh Post* contains Cambodian news and features. It's also worth looking out for the several English-language magazines. *Asia Life* (free from cafés and restaurants) is the *Time Out* of Phnom Penh with a host of articles related to new things happening in the city. *Southeast Asia Globe* ($4) is available in Western bars and restaurants; it takes a broader look at current affairs and economic events in the region, and includes items of consumer interest. *Bayon Pearnik*, a free satirical monthly, available in Western restaurants and bars in Phnom Penh, usually contains a travel feature on an unusual Cambodian destination and advertises bar and club launches. From time to time, new magazines come along; they are always worth checking out, although they often don't last long, as demand is limited.

Radio

Among the many **Khmer radio stations**, just a couple carry English programmes. The principal local station favoured by foreigners is Love FM on **97.5 FM**, featuring a mix of Western pop, news stories and phone-ins about the local entertainment scene. The BBC World Service is available 24 hours a day in the capital on 100 MHz FM; ABC Radio Australia also broadcasts 24 hours a day on 101.5 MHz FM in Phnom Penh, Siem Reap and Sihanoukville. On AM, Voice of Cambodia Radio International has programmes in English, French, Thai and Vietnamese.

English-language broadcasts can be heard throughout the country on short wave on the BBC World Service (visit Ⓦwww.bbc.co.uk/worldservice for frequencies and schedules), and on Voice of America (Ⓦwww.voa.gov), Radio Canada International (Ⓦwww.rcinet.ca) and ABC Radio Australia (Ⓦwww.abc.net.au). You can of course also listen online by accessing the radio pages of the respective broadcaster.

Asiawaves (Ⓦwww.asiawaves.net) lists Cambodian radio and television channels, gives the broadcasting frequency by town, and even has an archive of radio recordings.

Television

Cambodians are TV addicts and even in the remotest villages you'll find people ensconced around someone's (often battery-powered) TV. The country's seven **Khmer TV stations** broadcast a mix of political coverage, game shows, concerts, cartoons, sport – kick-boxing is a huge favourite – and Thai soaps dubbed into Khmer. The state broadcaster TVK, on Channel 7, is owned by the ruling CPP, who also have influence with most of the other channels, apart from Channel 9, which is loyal to FUNCINPEC.

Guesthouses and hotels usually offer **cable** and increasingly **satellite TV** stations, enabling you to watch a vast selection of foreign channels, typically including BBC World, CNN, CNBC, HBO, National Geographic and Star Sport.

Festivals

Cambodians are always celebrating a festival of some sort, heading out to a popular pagoda with family and friends or taking off for the provinces; unsurprisingly, festivals are the busiest times for shopping and travelling.

The major celebrations of the year are **Bonn Chaul Chhnam** (Khmer New Year; mid-April) and **Bonn Pchum Ben** (Festival of the Ancestors; mid-Sept to early Oct). These are festive occasions with everyone gathering at the family home and always involve lots of food and trips to the pagoda. The other big public holiday is **Bonn Om Tuk** (Water Festival; mid-Oct to late Nov), which occurs when the waters of the Tonle Sap reverse; activity is mainly centred on Phnom Penh with dragon-boat crews from around the country congregating to show off their prowess and massive crowds of supporters thronging the riverfront to cheer them on.

Buddhist **offering days** (exact dates vary from month to month according to the lunar calendar) are also colourful occasions: stalls do a roaring trade in bunches of flowers which are taken to pagodas and used to decorate shrines at home. Lotus buds – the traditional offering flower to the Buddha – are artistically folded to expose their pale-pink inner petals, while jasmine buds are threaded onto sticks and strings as fragrant tokens.

For more on festivals, see the *Festivals and ceremonies* colour section; for details of public holidays, see box on p.63.

Culture and etiquette

The traditional Cambodian form of greeting is the *sompeyar*, a gesture of extreme politeness as well as a sign of respect. Typically, the *sompeyar* is performed with hands placed palms together, fingers pointing up, in front of the body at chest level, and the head is inclined slightly forward as if about to bow. When greeting monks, however, the hands should be placed in front of the face, and when paying respects to Buddha (or the king), the hands are put in front of the forehead. The *sompeyar* is always used towards those older than yourself, and is taught to children at an early age. These days the handshake has become quite common, and is used between Cambodian men or when Cambodian men greet foreigners; generally women still greet foreigners using the *sompeyar*.

Cambodians are reserved people and find **public displays of affection** offensive; people in the provinces are particularly conservative, the chunchiet, Cambodia's minority hill-tribe people, even more so. Holding hands or linking arms in public, though quite a common sign of friendship between two men or two women, is considered unacceptable if it involves a member of the opposite sex; even married couples won't touch each other in public. Cambodian women who value their reputation do not go out drinking and dancing, and many will not want to be seen out with a man unless he is her fiancé (and even then she will be chaperoned). Things are, of course, different for Cambodian men, who are seen out and about drinking, eating and partying everywhere. However, times are changing, and a more cosmopolitan attitude is gaining ground in the towns, where you'll see groups of girls and boys out together, and women out with a group of friends.

Everywhere in Cambodia, travellers will gain more respect if they are **well dressed**. Cambodians themselves dress modestly, men usually wearing long trousers and a shirt. Women wear blouses rather than T-shirts, and sarongs or skirts to below the knee, though latterly women are starting to wear trousers or jeans and strappy tops. At formal events men will wear jacket and tie, women a traditional *sampot* – an ankle-length tube of material that you step into and then fold and tuck around the waist. For the tourist, all this means it's best to avoid skimpy clothes and shorts unless you're at the beach, and even there you will be stared at as Cambodians wouldn't dream of exposing any flesh, and even now usually go swimming in all their clothes. At Angkor Wat, where things are fairly relaxed due to the level of tourism, smart shorts are acceptable, although by preference shoulders should be covered.

When **visiting pagodas** it's important to wear clothes that keep your shoulders and legs covered. Hats should be removed when passing through the pagoda gate and shoes taken off before you go into any of the buildings (shoes are also removed before entering a Cambodian home). If you sit down on the floor inside the pagoda, do so with your feet to one side, not cross-legged, and don't point your finger or the soles of your feet towards the image of the Buddha (in fact, you should observe the same rule towards people generally, in any location). **Monks** are not allowed to touch women, so women should take care when walking near monks, and avoid sitting next to them on public transport.

Displaying anger won't get you far, as the Khmers find this embarrassing and will laugh, not to be provocative, but to hide their confusion. Being rational and calmly assertive will get you much further than getting annoyed. In fact, Cambodians can laugh at apparently inopportune moments, such as after an accident or if they can't understand you – again this is to cover their embarrassment.

Cambodians are intrigued at the **appearance of foreigners**, and it is not considered rude to stare quite intently at visitors. Local people will also giggle at men with earrings – in Cambodia boys are given an earring in the belief it will help an undescended testicle. It's hard to preserve your **personal space** in Cambodia, as Cambodians don't understand why anyone might want to be on their own; as a foreigner, you may find yourself being stared at, or notice that Cambodians deliberately sit near you. You needn't feel disconcerted by this, as it's just a friendly way of showing attention, and people will soon move on.

If you want to **beckon someone**, such as a waiter, don't wave your finger about, as this is considered rude. Instead hold your hand out with the palm facing down, and pull the fingers in towards the palm a few times, as if gripping something.

Shopping

Cambodia has a wide range of souvenirs and handicrafts: colourful textiles ranging from traditionally patterned silks to coarser chunchiet cloth; antiques and curios, such as wooden boxes for betel nut; and religious texts written on prepared palm leaves. Local handicrafts have been given a boost by various training schemes set up to help Cambodia's large disabled population, and there's now a phenomenal variety of quality products available. If you're shopping for items sold by length or weight, Cambodia uses the metric system.

Most shopping takes place in the **markets**, with those in Phnom Penh and Siem Reap offering a good selection of items. In the capital, Psar Toul Tom Poung (Russian Market) is the acknowledged place to buy souvenirs – and also motorcycle spares; while in Siem Reap, Psar Chas and the Siem Reap Night Market are up-coming places to look for crafts. Local children at the Angkor temples sell trinkets for a few thousand riel – bangles, hair slides made from coconut shell and handmade bamboo flutes in colourful woven straw sleeves. A relatively new phenomenon in Cambodia are shopping malls – though they're more akin to department stores. In Phnom Penh, Sorya, Sovanna and Paragon malls offer a vast range of consumer goods at fixed prices; Siem Reap has a couple of smaller enterprises and another is under construction in Battambang. In Phnom Penh and Siem Reap you'll also find plenty of specialist shops, galleries and hotel boutiques; though these are more expensive, their quality should be significantly better.

As a general rule, buy it when you see it: something unusual you chance upon in the provinces may not be available elsewhere.

Textiles

The ubiquitous chequered scarf, the *krama*, worn by Cambodian adults and children both male and female, is arguably the country's most popular tourist souvenir, and there are plenty to buy in markets everywhere. **Silk cloth** is widely available, woven in a variety of traditional designs and colours; now modern patterns have been created and can be found in the markets of Phnom Penh and Siem Reap. In Rattanakiri, you'll be able to find cloth produced by the **chunchiet**, normally cotton with some synthetic thread mixed in; it's coarser in texture than silk or pure cotton.

Kramas

Many *kramas* offered to tourists are woven from mixed synthetic threads; although the cloth feels soft, a *krama* of this sort is hot to wear and doesn't dry very well if you want to use it as a towel. The very best *kramas* come from Kompong Cham and Phnom Sarok and are made from cotton (*umbok*); those from Kompong Cham are often to be had from women pedlars in the markets, a large one costs around 12,000 riel.

Bargaining

Prices are fixed in shops and malls, but you're expected to bargain in markets and when buying from hawkers. Bargaining is seen as an amicable game, in which both parties aim to win. The seller usually starts at a moderately inflated price: for cheapish items, with a starting price below $10, expect to be able to knock around a third off; with pricey antiques and curios you'll be lucky to get a reduction of five percent. To keep a sense of perspective while bargaining, it's worth remembering that on items like a T-shirt or *krama*, the vendor's margin is often just 500–1000 riel.

Though cotton *kramas* feel stiff and thin at first, a few good scrubs in cold water will soften them up and increase the density of texture. They last for years and actually improve with wear, making a cool, dust-proof and absorbent fabric.

Silk

The weaving of **silk** in Cambodia can be traced back to the Angkor era, when the Khmer started to imitate imported cloth from India. Weaving skills learned over generations were lost with the Khmer Rouge, but the 1990s saw a resurgence of silk weaving in many Cambodian villages (the thread is usually imported from Vietnam, though a few Cambodian villages have again started to keep their own silkworms). Most of the cloth is produced to order for the dealers and silk-sellers of Phnom Penh, so if you visit a village where silk is woven, don't be surprised if they haven't any fabric for sale. Unpatterned silk is sometimes available by the metre in dark and pastel colours and modern designs are also becoming available.

Silk is produced in fixed widths – nearly always 800mm – and sold in two lengths: a **kabun** (3.6m), sufficient for a long straight skirt and short-sleeved top; and a **sampot** (half a *kabun*), which is enough for a long skirt. A *sampot* starts at around $15–20, but you can easily pay double this, depending on quality and design. Sometimes the silk will have been washed, which makes it softer in both texture and hue – and slightly more expensive. **Silk scarves** are inexpensive (around $5–6) and readily available. They come in a range of colours and are usually pre-washed, with the ends finished in hand-tied knots.

There are several different styles of fabric, with villages specializing in particular types of weaving. **Hol** is a time-honoured cloth decorated with small patterns symbolizing flowers, butterflies and diamonds, and traditionally produced with threads of five basic colours – yellow, red, black, green and blue (modern variations use pastel shades). The vibrant, shimmering hues change depending on the direction from which they are viewed. **Parmoong** is a lustrous ceremonial fabric, made by weaving a motif or border of gold or silver thread onto plain silk. Some *parmoong* is woven exclusively for men in checks or stripes of cream, green or red, to be worn in sarongs. Traditional wall-hangings, **pedan**, come in classical designs often featuring stylized temples and animals such as elephants and lions; they're inexpensive ($5–10) and easily transportable.

Chunchiet cloth

The **chunchiet** weave a range of cloth, employing generally simple designs based on a range of stripes woven with a motif – a bird and animal or even perhaps a helicopter. Traditionally the colours would have been from natural dyes in muted black, dark blue, red or cream, with a fairly loose weave, giving a rather coarse but quite durable fabric. Increasingly though, textiles are made from mixed-fibre thread and colourfast dyes; this gives a wider range of colours, although some can be startlingly bright.

Wood and marble carvings

Wood carvings are available in a wide range of sizes, from small heads of Jayavarman VII, modelled on the bust in the National Museum and costing just a couple of dollars, to almost life-sized dancing apsaras at $100 or more. In Phnom Penh you'll find a good selection along Street 178 near the National Museum, or in Psar Toul Tom Poung, though the fact that they're mass-produced means that they lack a certain finesse; to find something really fine you're better off at the workshop of the Artisans d'Angkor in Siem Reap (see p.177).

Marble carvings, varnished to a glossy finish, can be bought in the capital, Siem Reap or directly from workshops in Pursat (see p.137), where they are produced. Although some pieces – the replicas of Angkor Wat towers are an obvious example – are rather tacky, there are plenty of other items to choose from, including Buddha and animal statues.

Antiques and curios

Antiques and curios can be found at specialist stalls in and around Psar Toul Tom Poung in Phnom Penh, and at the Siem Reap Night Market. Look out for the partitioned **wooden boxes** used to store betel-chewing equipment (see *Festivals and ceremonies* colour section); you'll also find elegant silver boxes for the nuts, phials for the leaves and paste, and cutters – a bit like shears – for slicing the betel nuts. There are plenty of **religious artefacts** available too, ranging from wooden Buddha images and other carvings, to brass bowls and offering plates.

You may occasionally find antiquated traditional **musical instruments**, such as the *chapei*, a stringed instrument with a long neck and a round sound-box; and the *chhing*, two small brass plates similar to castanets in appearance, played by brushing them against each other.

Compasses used in the ancient Chinese art of feng shui can be bought for just a few dollars; they indicate compass directions related to the five elements – wood, fire, earth, metal and water. You might also be able to search out **opium weights**, used to weigh out the drug and often formed in the shape of small human figures or animals.

Cambodia's ancient temples have suffered massively from looting, and although it's unlikely that you'll be offered ancient figurines (most of the trade goes to Bangkok or Singapore), many other stolen artefacts – such as chunchiet funerary statues from Rattanakiri – are finding their way onto the market. To export anything purporting to be an antique you'll need the correct paperwork, so check the dealer can provide this before agreeing a deal. Also be aware that Cambodians are expert at artificially ageing their wares and be sure that you want the item for its own sake rather than because it's verifiably authentic.

Woven baskets, rattan and bamboo

A versatile fibre, **rattan** is used to produce furniture, popular with Cambodia's expats, and household items such as baskets, bowls and place-mats, which are sold in the markets of Phnom Penh and Siem Reap. Appealing purchases are the small, fine baskets produced around Oudong from the *kunung* vine; the best place to buy them is the hill at the site itself, where there's a good selection of pieces for a few thousand riel each. In Rattanakiri you can find *khapa*, deep, conical rattan-and-bamboo baskets fitted with shoulder straps so that they can be worn on the back; they cost around $10 and are still used by the chunchiet to carry produce to market. Everyday items made from rattan and bamboo and available in the markets can also make interesting souvenirs, including noodle ladles and nested baskets; the latter are used to measure out portions of rice but are also useful back home for storing fruit and vegetables.

Due to over-harvesting and massive de forestation, rattan is now in short supply; the best products are exported to Vietnam and China with the poorer quality kept for the home market.

Silver and gold

Most of the **silverware** in Cambodia is sold in Phnom Penh and produced in villages nearby, particularly at Kompong Luong, which can easily be visited as part of a trip to Oudong. The price will give you an indication of whether an item is solid silver or silver-plated copper – a few dollars for the silver-plated items; more than double that for a comparable item in solid silver.

Small silver or silver-plated boxes in the shape of fruits or animals are delightful and make terrific, inexpensive gifts. Considerably more expensive are ceremonial plates and offering bowls, usually made of solid silver and intricately decorated with leaf motifs. Silver necklaces, bracelets and earrings, mostly imported from Indonesia, are sold only for the tourist market (Khmers don't rate the metal for jewellery) and go for just a few dollars in the markets; modern silver designer jewellery is also available in the NGO-run shops and boutiques of Phnom Penh and Siem Reap.

There's nothing sentimental or romantic about the Khmer obsession with **gold jewellery** – which is considered a means of investment. This in part explains the hundreds of gold dealers in and around the markets all over the country, where it's not unusual to see local people negotiating to trade in their jewellery for more expensive pieces. Gold is good value and items can be made up quickly and quite cheaply to your own design, and even set with gems from the mines of Pailin and Rattanakiri.

Travelling with children

While travelling through Cambodia with your children is not for the nervous or over-protective parent, many families are now enjoying holidays here. Cambodians love children, although they do have a habit of greeting them with an affectionate pinch, which can be disconcerting; but the protectiveness of the West is non existent and there are no special facilities or particular concessions made for them. On public transport, children travel free if they share your seat; otherwise expect to pay the adult fare. If you need an extra bed for your child in your room, hotels will charge around \$10–15 per night. Under-11's are admitted free to the Angkor Heritage Park (passport required as proof) otherwise they are charged at the adult fee. To travel around it's worth considering hiring a car and driver – not only will this mean you can stop when you want for food and comfort breaks, but it'll be more comfortable – although note that child car seats are not available in Cambodia. Staying in guesthouses or hotels with a swimming pool is a big hit with children; alternatively many hotels with pools will let you use it for a daily fee (of around \$5).

In the main towns you'll be able to buy disposable nappies, formula milk and tins or jars of baby food at the supermarkets and mini-markets, but elsewhere you need to take your own supplies. Many Western children now take rice and noodle dishes in their stride, so eating out should be relatively simple (fussy eaters excepted) with stir-fries, simple chicken dishes and fried potatoes universally available.

There are no real activities designed for children, but with a little ingenuity resourceful parents should get by. In Phnom Penh and Siem Reap, Monument Books sells children's books and a limited supply of Western games and toys; while the markets have plenty of cheap plastic toys that you can pass on to a Cambodian child when you leave. Riding an elephant is a wonderful experience – crossing the causeway at Angkor Thom or making a circuit of the Bayon is not something you're likely to forget quickly (see p.192 for details). Provided it's done in short bursts – consider too, hiring a guide – children seem to adore the temples; clambering up temple steps, listening to tales of gods and demons, having their photo taken with the dancers at Angkor Wat and checking out the vast trees at Ta Prohm with enthusiasm. Horseriding and quad biking through the rice paddies are available at Siem Reap (see p.171); while fishing, picnics and badminton can be done pretty much anywhere. Cambodian children are always playing games – the flip-flop game and marbles for boys, skipping for girls only; a Western child is always welcomed and somehow language is never a problem. Consider finishing your visit to Cambodia at Sihanoukville, where the gently shelving beaches of Ochheuteal or Sokha are pretty safe and a nice wind-down before the long flight home.

Travel essentials

Costs

On the whole, Cambodia is an inexpensive place to visit; though, like everywhere, prices are starting to creep up. Most tourists won't notice the difference, but for Cambodians, many of whom have difficulty in eking out a living, it's a problem. Outside the upmarket hotels tipping is not expected, but a few hundred riel extra for a meal or a tuk-tuk or moto ride is appreciated.

Budget **rooms** are available for $5–6 across the country, and eating is also cheap – you'll pay around $2 for a breakfast of noodles and a coffee at a Khmer restaurant or noodle shop, and around the same for a lunch or dinner of two dishes with rice (although a meal in a Western-oriented restaurant will set you back around $6–7). Drinking water costs a fairly constant 1000 riel for a small bottle pretty much everywhere, while cans retail at 2000 riel for Coke and $1 for Angkor beer, $2.5 for a large bottle.

The most economical form of **transport** is in the back of a pick-up truck, the price of a trip varying according to the distance involved and the state of the road – during the rainy season (June–Oct) fares can rise by around twenty percent. Fares also rise over holidays, particularly the Khmer New Year. Speed comes at a price: Phnom Penh–Siem Reap by plane is $95 ($6 by bus), but this option don't exist on other routes.

Staying in guesthouses, eating at noodle shops and cheap restaurants and travelling on public transport can be done on just $15–20 a day. But if you want to stay in mid-range hotels, eat three Western-oriented meals per day and get around by hiring a car with a driver you'll need around $90 per day. And if you want to sample the best in luxury accommodation and top-notch food that Phnom Penh and Siem Reap have to offer, you can spend three hundred dollars a day or more.

Although it doesn't happen as blatantly as in Vietnam, foreigners in Cambodia are charged a **premium** in a number of situations. For example, a Cambodian pays $10 less than a foreigner to use the express boat between Phnom Penh and Chau Doc, and sights targeted at foreign tourists also have a dual-pricing policy, most notably Angkor, which is free for Cambodians but costs foreigners $20 for a day-pass.

A **sales tax** (comprising a ten percent government tax and ten percent service) is often charged in mid-range hotels. Where this applies, it should be advertised on a sign (in English) at reception.

Customs

You will need to fill out a **customs declaration** on arrival in Cambodia, although customs requirements are fairly loose and baggage checks are rare. On entry, you're allowed four hundred cigarettes (or the equivalent in cigars or tobacco), one bottle of spirits and a "reasonable" amount of perfume. You cannot bring in more than US$10,000 in cash, or take out more than 100,000 riel.

Electricity

The electrical supply is 220 volts AC, 50Hz. Cambodian sockets take two-pin, flat-pronged plugs. These days the electricity supply in towns is pretty reliable, although during the night some hotels do switch to generators which can be noisy. However, some areas, Banlung for example, still experience power cuts from time to time; in rural areas most villages still survive on a generator and batteries. Electricity is expensive (in Phnom Penh most of it is imported from Vietnam) and if you're taking a room with air conditioning you will be charged more. Note that if you buy electrical goods in Cambodia, you might need a transformer or to adjust their voltage setting before use abroad.

Entry and exit requirements

Visas for Cambodia are required by everyone other than nationals of Laos, Malaysia, the

Philippines and Singapore. These are issued on arrival at Phnom Penh and Siem Reap international airports, at Sihanoukville port, at all overland crossings from Thailand and Vietnam, and at Voen Kham from Laos. Arriving overland, make sure that the officials at the border put an entry stamp in your passport, as not having one is likely to cause hassle when you eventually leave the country. Single-entry, 30-day tourist **e-visas** are available on line, but they are only supported if you enter through the airports at Phnom Penh or Siem Reap, or overland at Koh Kong and Poipet (Ⓦwww.mfaic.gov.kh; payment is by PayPal). They are valid for three months from the date of issue and there's a $5 processing charge.

A single-entry **tourist visa** obtained on arrival ($20; one passport photograph required) is valid for thirty days, including the day of issue, and can be extended once only, for one month. Note that at the Thai border Cambodian officials may ask for 1000 baht (around $25–30), though if you ask for a receipt this does usually get reduced to $20 (see p.289 for more on this). You can also buy a **business visa** ($25; one passport photo) on arrival. Like the tourist visa this is valid for thirty days, but can be extended in a variety of ways (ranging from one-month single-entry extension, three months' single-entry, six months' multiple-entry and twelve months' multiple-entry; costs range from $42 to $270). Multiple entries are only available on a business visa.

Both tourist and business visas can only be **extended** in Phnom Penh at the inconveniently located Department for Immigration (Mon–Fri 8–11am & 2–4pm; Ⓣ012/581558, Ⓔinfo@immigration.gov.kh), 8km out of town opposite Pochentong airport. A tourist visa extension ($40) takes 28 days to process and takes effect from the date you submit your passport – an absurd situation which means you'll only get a few extra days' use out of the extension. As few people can afford to be without their passport for that length of time, they are forced into taking the **three-day service** at $45 for a one-month extension. Even then, applying for the extension is a time-consuming exercise involving at least two trips out to the airport. A far easier option is to use the **visa-extension services** offered by travel agents and guesthouses in town, who will do all the running around for just a few dollars' commission. If you **overstay** your visa you'll be charged $5 per day. From Phnom Penh and Siem Reap the departure tax is $25 for international flights and $6 for domestic departures (at Phnom Penh you can pay by credit card). There is no departure tax when leaving by land.

At the time of writing a temporary visa waiver had been introduced between Cambodia and Vietnam and Cambodia and Thailand, allowing nationals of the respective countries 14 days' visa-free stay.

Embassies and consulates

Australia 5 Canterbury Crescent, Deakin, ACT 2600 Ⓣ02/6273 1259, Ⓔcambodianembassy@ozemail.com.au, Ⓦwww.embassyofcambodia.org.nz/au.

France 4 rue Adolphe Yvon, 75116 Paris Ⓣ01/4503 4720, Ⓔambcambodgeparis@mangoosta.fr.

Germany Benjamin-Vogelsdorf Str., 213187 Berlin Ⓣ30/4863 7901, ⒺREC-Berlin@t-online.de.

Hong Kong Room 3606, Sigga CC 144–151 Connaught Rd West Ⓣ2546 0718, Ⓔcacghk@netvigator.com.

Laos Thadeua Rd, KM2 Vientiane, BP 34 Ⓣ02/131 4950, Ⓔrecamlao@laotel.com.

Malaysia 46 Jalan U-Than, 55000 Kuala Lumpur Ⓣ03/4257 1150, Ⓔreckl@tm.net.my.

Singapore 152 Beach Rd, #11-05 Gateway East, Singapore 189721 Ⓣ299 3028, Ⓔcambodiaembassy@pacific.net.sg.

Thailand 185 Rajdamri Rd, Lumphini Patumwan, Bangkok 10330 Ⓣ02/254 6630, Ⓔrecbkk@cscoms.com.

UK Wellington Building, Wellington Rd, St John's Wood, London NW8 9SP Ⓣ0207/483 9063, Ⓔcambodianembassy@btconnect.com, Ⓦwww.cambodiaembassy.org.uk; also covers Ireland.

US 4530 16th St, Washington DC 20011 Ⓣ202/726-7742, Ⓦwww.embassy.org/cambodia.

Vietnam 71A Tran Hung Dao St, Hanoi Ⓣ04/942 4788, Ⓔarch@fpt.vn; 41 Phung Khac Khoan, Ho Chi Minh City Ⓣ08/829 2751, Ⓔcambocg@hcm.vnn.vn.

Gay and lesbian Cambodia

Gay and lesbian travellers shouldn't experience any problems when travelling in

Cambodia – homosexuality is not illegal, although neither is it recognized and talked about. It's acceptable for two men or two women to link hands or arms in public, which would be unacceptable for straight couples. Cambodians find overt displays of affection offensive, however, so it's as well to be discreet. Be that as it may, there's an emerging gay scene (Ⓦwww.cambodia-gay.com) with gay-friendly establishments in Phnom Penh, Siem Reap (which has the country's only male-exclusive resort) and Sihanoukville.

Insurance

Before travelling to Cambodia you'd do well to take out an insurance policy to cover against theft, loss of personal items and documentation, illness and injury. However, before you pay for a new policy, it's worth checking whether you are already covered: some all-risks home insurance policies may cover your possessions when overseas, and many private medical schemes include cover when abroad – check that they cover Cambodia. Students will often find that their student health coverage extends during the vacations and for one term beyond the date of last enrolment.

A typical **travel insurance policy** usually provides cover for the loss of baggage, tickets and – up to a certain limit – cash or cheques, as well as cancellation or curtailment of your journey. Most of them exclude so-called "dangerous" activities unless an extra premium is paid: in Cambodia this can mean scuba diving, riding a motorbike and trekking.

Internet access

Getting online in Cambodia is effortless with internet shops and cafés almost everywhere and wi-fi available at hotels, guesthouses, cafés and bars, especially in the tourist areas (in the provinces connections may be slow, and costs a little higher than in the major towns). Connectivity for enabled laptops and smart phones is fairly good. Access is typically $1 per hour and connections are generally reliable. Although equipment may not be up-to-the-minute, you'll be able to use your memory stick, burn photographs to discs and email them at most places. In the countryside it's unlikely you'll get any internet access.

Laundry

You can get laundry done practically everywhere, at both hotels and guesthouses or at private laundries in all towns – look for the signs in English. Prices are pretty uniform, at 500–1000 riel per item or $2 per kilogram. In Phnom Penh and Siem Reap there are a number of places with driers, giving a speedy turn-around (3hr) even in the wet season.

Living in Cambodia

It's hard to get paid work in Cambodia, and even finding a post teaching English is pretty difficult. The UK charity Voluntary Service Overseas (Ⓦwww.vso.org.uk) and Australian Volunteers International (Ⓦwww.ozvol.org.au) both recruit volunteers to work on projects in Cambodia paid at local rates. If you want to do voluntary work (all be it that

Rough Guides travel insurance

Rough Guides has teamed up with WorldNomads.com to offer great **travel insurance** deals. Policies are available to residents of over 150 countries, with cover for a wide range of **adventure sports**, 24hr emergency assistance, high levels of medical and evacuation cover and a stream of **travel safety information**. Roughguides.com users can take advantage of their policies online 24/7, from anywhere in the world – even if you're already travelling. And since plans often change when you're on the road, you can extend your policy and even claim online. Roughguides.com users who buy travel insurance with WorldNomads.com can also leave a positive footprint and donate to a community development project. For more information go to Ⓦ**www.roughguides.com/shop**.

you may have to pay to do it) there are plenty of opportunities. Frontier (Ⓦwww.frontier.ac.uk) have projects teaching English or helping with wildlife conservation (from £995 for 4 weeks); Greenforce (Ⓦwww.greenforce.org) offers volunteering opportunities in schools and hospitals (around £1400 for 4 weeks); while Coral Cay Conservation (Ⓦwww.coralcay.org) has an ongoing project on Koh Rong (cheaper if you have diving experience). When you're in Cambodia keep your eye out in cafés and bars where organizations post their projects and ask for volunteers. The services of teachers, doctors and vets will be much appreciated even if it's only for a day or so.

Mail

Cambodia's **mail** is all consolidated in Phnom Penh. Sending mail from provincial cities is as reliable as posting from the capital, though it costs a little more. Within the capital itself, only the main post office is geared up to accept mail bound for abroad.

Mail to Europe, Australasia and North America takes between five and ten days, leaving Phnom Penh for major international destinations around twice a week – the specific days can be checked at the main post office. Stamps for **postcards** sent from the capital cost 2800–3000 riel (add 200 riel if posting from the provinces).

Parcels posted in Phnom Penh cost a whopping $17 for a one-kilogram package going abroad, so it's worth deferring the task if you're heading to Thailand, where postage is cheaper. You'll be charged 3000 riel for the obligatory customs form, detailing the contents and their value, but it isn't necessary to leave the package open for checking. Post offices sell mailing boxes if you need them.

Poste restante mail can be received at the main post offices in Phnom Penh, Sihanoukville and Siem Reap, at a cost of 500 riel per item. When collecting mail, bring your passport as proof of identity and ask them to check under both your first name and your family name.

Overcharging used to be quite a problem. Things are now better, but the post office in Siem Reap does seem to charge more than others in the country. **Rates** are displayed on a notice board inside Phnom Penh's main post office, so you can make your own calculations.

Maps

Understandably, Cambodia was poorly surveyed for many years and, thus, some older maps show roads and villages inaccurately. Many maps have now been updated, but it's worth bearing in mind that just because a road is marked on a map it doesn't mean it will be in decent condition. (In any case, Cambodia remains heavily contaminated with land mines, so it pays to stick to well-defined roads and tracks; see p.228 for more on this.)

Above and beyond the maps given in this guide, you might consider one of the Cambodia-only maps from Periplus, Nelles Verlag and Gecko Maps, which should get most travellers around with minimal problems. If you're only travelling between the main cities and tourist sites, the Rough Guide map of Vietnam, Cambodia and Laos should suffice.

Within Cambodia, bookstalls at Psar Thmei and Psar Toul Tom Poung in Phnom Penh and the Siem Reap Bookshop in Siem Reap sell a selection of maps. American military survey maps are among the most detailed available, but you may have to check out a lot of stalls to find the map for the sector of the country you want, as nobody stocks the whole range; expect to pay around $5-plus for one of these maps. These bookstalls also sell the country maps published by the Ministry of Tourism; these show the country in detail on one side and city plans of Phnom Penh, Siem Reap and Sihanoukville on the reverse; they cost a couple of dollars each.

If you're only going to Siem Reap, Travelfish (Ⓦwww.travelfish.com) has an iPhone app covering the town and temples of Angkor.

Opening hours and public holidays

In theory, government offices work Monday to Friday between 7.30 and 11.30am, and 2 and 5pm. In practice, though, you'll be lucky to find anyone at their desks before 8am and they'll probably be gone by 11am,

Public holidays

Dates for Buddhist religious holidays are variable, changing each year with the lunar calendar.

January 1 International New Year's Day.

January 7 Victory Day over the Genocide Regime. Celebrates the liberation of Phnom Penh from the Khmer Rouge in 1979.

Late January/February (variable) Meak Bochea Day. Buddhist festival commemorating and worshipping the Dhamma.

March 8 International Women's Day.

April 13–15 Bonn Chaul Chhnam – Khmer New Year.

Late April/May (variable) Visak Bochea Day. Buddhist festival celebrating the birth, enlightenment and passing to Nirvana of the Buddha.

May 1 International Labour Day.

May 13–15 Birthday of King Norodom Sihamoni.

May (variable) Visakha Bochea. Commemorates the birth of Buddha.

May (variable) Bonn Chroat Preah Nongkoal, the Royal Ploughing Ceremony. Celebrated just before the rains begin, this marks the start of the rice-planting season, and a ceremonial furrow is ploughed on the grounds in front of the National Museum in Phnom Penh.

June 18 Birthday of King-Mother Norodom Monineath Sihanouk.

September 24 Constitution Day.

September/October (2–3 days, variable) Bonn Pchum Ben, the Feast of the Ancestors. Celebrated on the day of the new moon, when families head out to the pagoda to make offerings to the dead.

October 29 Coronation Day of King Norodom Sihamoni.

October 31 Birthday of King-Father Norodom Sihanouk.

October/November (variable) Bonn Om Tuk, the Water Festival. Held at a variable time from late October to mid-November, it marks the end of the rains and the time when the water again starts to flow out of the Tonle Sap. A busy and colourful three-day event ensues, with boat races on the river near the Royal Palace in Phnom Penh and on the moat around Angkor Wat.

November 9 Independence Day. Marks independence from the French in 1953.

December 10 International Human Rights Day.

Any public holidays that fall on a Saturday or Sunday are taken the following Monday.

returning – or not – for an hour or two in the afternoon. Positions in the public service aren't well paid, but carry quite a bit of prestige, so officials ensure they show their faces in the office a few times each week, while moonlighting to earn a living wage. Public holidays can also be "stretched" particularly at Khmer New Year, Bonn Pchum Benn and for the Water Festival.

Post offices are open daily, excluding a few public holidays such as the Khmer New Year and Bonn Pchum Ben. The main office in Phnom Penh is open daily from 7am to 6pm; in the provinces, post office hours are 8 to 11am and 2 to 5.30pm, though they may close early on Saturday and Sunday if they're not busy or if the staff have other commitments. **Banks** are open Monday to Friday from 8.30am to 3.30pm, and sometimes on Saturday as well between 8.30 and 11.30am. **Markets** open daily from around 6am until 5pm, **shops** between 7am and 7pm (later in tourist areas).

Key **tourist sights**, such as the National Museum, the Royal Palace Silver Pagoda and Toul Sleng Genocide Museum in Phnom Penh, are open every day including most public holidays. In the provinces museums open on an ad hoc basis; the best bet is on a weekday morning between 9 and 10am (indeed they'll probably shut once you've left). The temples at Angkor, Tonle Bati and Sambor Prei Kuk and the country's national parks are open daily from dawn to dusk.

Phones

Nearly all of Cambodia's phone lines were destroyed during the Khmer Rouge era and have yet to be replaced; most people get by with a mobile phone only.

If you are going to need to make or receive a number of domestic calls consider buying a **Cambodian SIM card**. These can be purchased for a few dollars at most mobile phone shops; you'll need to show your passport as proof of identity. It's worth checking deals from a few providers before choosing; for example some networks throw in free SMSs (texts) when you register, while others have cheap off-peak international rates ($0.25 per minute). Expect to be charged 300–500 riel per minute for domestic calls. Mobile top-up cards start from $1 depending on the network, but be aware that the SIM card will be deactivated if you don't have money on your account or you haven't used it for a period of time – this varies with the provider but it's usually between one and six months. If your number is deactivated and you want to carry on using it you'll need to visit the network provider's office to get it reinstated; note though that telephone numbers get reissued after about a year. At the time of writing Cambodia has nine mobile phone service providers, the most popular being Mobitel (Ⓣ012 & 092) which has transmitters throughout the country giving pretty much universal reception. Other providers include Hello Axiata (code Ⓣ015 & 016), Smart (Ⓣ010, 069, 070 & 093), Mfone (Ⓣ085) and Star Cell (Ⓣ086 & 098). As you'd expect the smaller operators have fewer transmitters meaning you may not have reception in remote locations, so you may want to check coverage before purchasing a SIM card. If you're staying in Cambodia for a while a pre-paid mobile broadband account costs around $28 per month.

You can make **domestic** and **international phone calls** at the post offices and telecom offices in most towns. These services are invariably run by the government telecommunications network, **Camintel** (Ⓦwww.camintel.com), which also runs **public call boxes** in Phnom Penh and Siem Reap; to use these, you'll need a pre-paid phone card, available in denominations ranging from $5 to $50. Buying an "easy card" phone card, means you can make international calls from any call box. Depending on the access code you use (check when you buy your card) international calling rates can be as low as $0.15 per minute. To use the card insert it in the slot, dial the access code (Ⓣ177 is currently the cheapest), followed by the country code and number as usual. It's worth checking out options with your own telecommunications service provider before you travel to see if they have any arrangement for calling home from Cambodia, though it's likely to be fairly expensive. If you know you will be wanting to make lots of calls home, it's well worth signing up for an account with **Skype** before you go, which allows you to make free computer-to-computer calls and very cheap computer-to-telephone calls. Internet cafés

Calling home from Cambodia

There is no international directory enquiries service in Cambodia. To access the international services dial Ⓣ001 or 007 followed by the country code, then the city/area code without the initial zero.

To the UK: Ⓣ001 or 007 + 44 + area code

To the Republic of Ireland: Ⓣ001 or 007 + 353 + city code

To the US and Canada: Ⓣ001 or 007 + 1 + city code

To Australia: Ⓣ001 or 007 + 61+ city code

To New Zealand: Ⓣ001 or 007 + 64 + city code

To South Africa: Ⓣ001 or 007 + 27 + city code

often have headphones with a microphone so that you can use Skype with some privacy; all you pay is the posted fee for use of the internet.

For **domestic calls** only, the cut-price **glass-sided booths** found in all major towns are a cheap option at around 500 riel per minute, payable to the attendant. The booths vary in their coverage of Cambodia's various networks: accessible numbers will be written on the side of the booths.

In the unlikely event that you have to send a fax, the hotel business centres and internet shops are the most reliable places to do so.

To call Cambodia from abroad, dial your international access code, followed by ⓣ855, then the local area code (minus the initial 0), then the number. Note that phone companies may charge slightly more to call Cambodian mobile numbers.

If you want to use your home mobile phone, you'll need to check with your phone service provider whether it will work abroad, and what the call charges are to use it in Cambodia. It's unlikely that a mobile bought for use inside North America will work outside the US and Canada, unless it's a tri-band phone. However, most mobiles in the UK, Australia and New Zealand use GSM, which works well in Southeast Asia.

Photography

Cambodians (other than the chunchiet) generally love being photographed – although it is common courtesy to ask first; they also take a lot of photos themselves and may well ask you to stand in theirs. It's best to avoid taking photographs of anything with a military connotation, just in case.

While most people now have digital cameras, film can still be obtained (more easily than at home), with a 36-exposure roll of print film costing around $3 and slide film around $6. Developing and printing cost around $4 per roll of 36, though quality is variable.

You can get your digital shots transferred to CD or printed at most photographic shops in Phnom Penh and Siem Reap, although, as for film, the quality of the prints may not be as good as you'd get at home.

Time

Cambodia is 7hr ahead of GMT; 12hr ahead of New York and Montréal; 15hr ahead of Los Angeles and Vancouver; 1hr behind Perth; 4hr behind Sydney and 5hr behind Auckland; 5hr ahead of South Africa.

Toilets

Apart from places used to catering for foreigners, squat toilets are the rule. In general there are no public toilets, although there are now facilities throughout the Angkor Heritage Park, and in some places enterprising individuals have set up private facilities which you can use for a few hundred riel. It is fine to ask to use the loo at restaurants, even if you're not eating there, although you may sometimes wish you hadn't as they are often unsavoury. At transport stops there are usually toilets out at the back, but you'll need to provide your own toilet paper, sold in the markets and worth carrying with you. Sometimes you may have to do as the locals do and take to the bushes – but remember there is still a risk of mines, so don't stray off well-trodden paths.

Tourist information

There is a wealth of information on the temples of Angkor, which you can access both in Cambodia and outside the country; information on the rest of Cambodia is obtainable via the internet and the increasingly documented experiences of other travellers; supplementary information to that given in the Guide can also be obtained from local guesthouse owners.

Tourist offices

Most provincial towns have a **tourist office** (*destjow montepiak*). Although their opening hours are generally quite loose (typically Mon–Fri 8–11am & 2–4pm), someone at the office will usually speak a little English or French. Thanks to a recent grant from the Asian Development Bank (ADB) their facilities have improved and, for the time being at least, there are some quite nice leaflets available, though street plans remain elusive.

There are no Cambodian tourist offices abroad, and Cambodian embassies aren't equipped to handle tourist enquiries.

Travellers with disabilities

Cambodia has the unhappy distinction of having the highest proportion of disabled people per capita in the world (1 in 236 people) – due to land mines and the incidence of polio and other wasting diseases. There is no special provision for the disabled, so travellers with disabilities will need to be especially self-reliant, though Cambodians will be only too pleased to help out where they can.

Before travelling to Cambodia, disabled visitors should check out the airline facilities for both long-haul and domestic services. Stock up on any medication, get any essential equipment serviced and take a selection of spares and accoutrements (wet-wipes, spanners, Allen keys and bungee cords are particularly useful). It's worth checking that your travel insurance covers you for most eventualities, such as the loss of a wheelchair. Ask about hotel facilities as well, as lifts are still not as

Cambodia online

Online representation of Cambodia has improved greatly, with an increasing amount of information from government departments, private companies (particularly tour operators) and individuals.

Travel advisory services

Australian Department of Foreign Affairs and Trade ⓦwww.smartraveller.gov.au. Provides up-to-date advice and reports by country and region.

British Foreign and Commonwealth Office ⓦwww.fco.gov.uk/travel. Country profiles and constantly updated advice for travellers on circumstances affecting safety and security, health, and general issues.

Canada Department of Foreign Affairs and International Trade ⓦwww.voyage.gc.ca. Country information, covering warnings with recent updates, health, safety and general travel information.

Ireland Department of Foreign Affairs ⓦforeignaffairs.gov.ie. General travel information by country.

New Zealand Ministry of Foreign Affairs and Trade ⓦsafetravel.govt.nz. Country-specific advice and regional reports on safety and security, plus consular information.

South Africa Department of Foreign Affairs ⓦwww.dfa.gov.za/consular/travel-advice.htm. Allows nationals to register their travel plans.

US Department of State ⓦtravel.state.gov. Provides country-specific information for travellers, including warnings and risks.

General Cambodia information

Beauty and Darkness ⓦwww.mekong.net/cambodia. Documents the dark side of Cambodia's recent history, and contains a photo gallery and biographies of some of those who survived the Khmer Rouge atrocities; also some travelogues.

Cambodia Daily ⓦwww.cambodiadaily.com. Carries selected features and supplements from recent editions of the newspaper.

Cambodian Embassy in Washington DC ⓦwww.embassyofcambodia.org. Government reports and some tourist information.

Cambodian Information Centre ⓦwww.cambodia.org. Varied site offering information on everything from clubs and organizations to the legal system and even e-cards.

Cambodia Tribunal Monitor ⓦwww.cambodiatribunal.org. Up-to-the-minute information on the Genocide Tribunal.

common in Cambodia as you might hope. Rather than using buses for getting around, consider hiring a car and driver which will give you more comfort and flexibility.

Getting around pagodas and temples can be a problem, as even at relatively lowly pagodas there are flights of steps and entrance kerbs to negotiate. The temples at Angkor are particularly difficult, with steps up most entrance pavilions and the central sanctuaries. However, you can hire a helper cheaply at $15–20 a day, and locals will do all they can too, but in any case you don't need to reach every nook and cranny to find visiting a temple hugely rewarding.

Women travellers

The Cambodians are respectful to and protective of women, so travelling around the country shouldn't pose any problems for foreign women. All the same, it's as well to dress modestly and to avoid over-familiarity, which can be misconstrued, particularly after men have had a few beers. If someone does

Go Cambodia Ⓦ www.gocambodia.com. Easy to navigate, general-purpose site featuring articles on all aspects of Cambodian life – from sport to music to women's rights and recipes – with links to other sites.

His Majesty King Norodom Sihamoni Ⓦ www.norodomsihamoni.org. The king's official website, including his biography, news and diary.

Library of Congress Ⓦ www.loc.gov. Cambodia country study dating from the 1980s, but containing much historical, economic and political information that's still of relevance.

King-Father Norodom Sihanouk Ⓦ www.norodomsihanouk.info. Website of the king-father (and queen-mother) featuring biographies and the daily documents issued by this prolific scribe (mostly in French).

Phnom Penh Post Ⓦ www.phnompenhpost.com. Key articles from the daily English-language newspaper.

Royal Government of Cambodia Ⓦ www.cambodia.gov.kh. Official website of the Cambodian government, with profiles of the king, premier, information about the senate and constitution, with links to ministry and department pages.

Travel and tourism

Andy Brouwer Ⓦ www.andybrouwer.co.uk. This Cambodiaphile's site is full of travelogues, interviews with eminent Cambodian experts and links to associated sites.

Bayon Pearnik Ⓦ www.bayonpearnik.com. Online version of the free magazine, particularly big on biking excursions to remote areas.

Cambodian Ministry of Tourism Ⓦ www.mot.gov.kh. Features the country's highlights, province by province, plus information on accommodation, history and Khmer culture.

Canby Publications Ⓦ www.canbypublications.com. Convenient online extracts from their Cambodian city guides.

City of Phnom Penh Ⓦ www.phnompenh.gov.kh. Covers points of interest around Cambodia's capital and also features a detailed city history.

Tales of Asia Ⓦ www.talesofasia.com. In-depth look at Cambodia by long-term Siem Reap resident, Gordon Sharpless, with plenty of tales and practical information on the vagaries of the country; check here for the latest on crossing to Cambodia through Poipet.

overstep the mark, a firm "no" will normally suffice to ward them off. A good ruse used by Khmer women is to subtly put yourself in a position of superiority, by referring to yourself as the older sister (*bpong serey*) or aunt (*minq*) or by addressing the man as nephew (*kmaoy bprohs*). If this doesn't work, then kick up a huge fuss so that everyone in the vicinity knows that you're being harassed, which should shame the man into backing off.

Guide

Guide

Phnom Penh and around

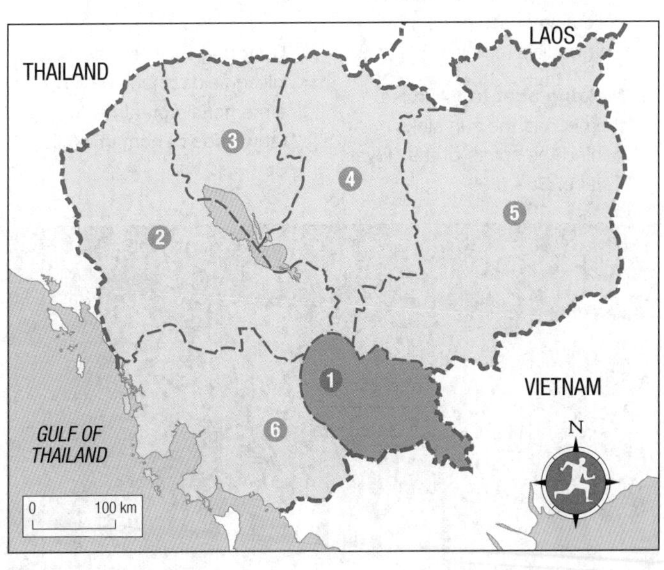

CHAPTER 1

Highlights

* **Cyclo rides** Enjoy an unhurried spin through the old French quarter. See p.84
* **Royal Palace** The soaring golden spires of the ceremonial Throne Room are Phnom Penh's most memorable sight. See p.91
* **Silver Pagoda** Home to a sacred emerald Buddha and a vast mural. See p.92
* **National Museum** A superb collection of sculpture from Cambodia's temples. See p.95
* **Mekong boat trips** Cruise the river as the sun sinks behind the spires of the Royal Palace. See p.98
* **Toul Sleng** Former torture chamber, now a grim museum to Khmer Rouge atrocities. See p.100
* **Wat Phnom** On a leafy hill, Wat Phnom affords a view that has changed little in half a century. See p.101
* **Psar Toul Tom Poung** Bargain for fine silks, antiques and curios at Phnom Penh's most enjoyable market. See p.111
* **Choeung Ek** The macabre killing fields, marked with a memorial containing thousands of human skulls. See p.121

▲ Royal Palace, Phnom Penh

Phnom Penh and around

A city of white buildings, where spires of gold and stupas of stone rocket out of the greenery into the vivid blue sky.

Such was American visitor Robert Casey's description of **Phnom Penh** in 1929, in which he also noted the shady, wide streets and pretty parks. His account bears a remarkable resemblance to the Phnom Penh of today, and life then seems to have been much as it is now, the open-fronted shops and shophouses bustling with haggling traders, and roadsides teeming with food vendors and colourful, busy markets.

Indeed, the capital of Cambodia and the heart of government is a captivating city of great charm and vitality, crisscrossed by broad tree-lined boulevards and dotted with old colonial villas. Situated in a virtually flat area at the confluence of the Tonle Sap, Bassac and Mekong rivers, the compact city hasn't yet been overwhelmed by towering high-rise developments, and imparts a sense of openness and light. Phnom Penh throbs with enterprise and energy, which makes it difficult to comprehend that a generation ago it was forcibly evacuated and left to ruin by the Khmer Rouge. Inevitably, and in spite of many improvements, some of the scars are still evident: side roads are pot-holed and strewn with rubble, some of the elegant villas are ruined beyond repair, and when it rains the antiquated drainage system backs up, flooding the roads.

It is testimony to the unflappable good nature and stoicism of the city's inhabitants that, despite past adversity, they remain upbeat and determined to improve their lot. Many people do two jobs to get by, keeping government offices ticking over for a few hours each day and then moonlighting as moto drivers or tutors; furthermore, the Cambodian belief in **education** is particularly strong here, and anyone who can afford to sends their children to supplementary classes outside school hours. This dynamism constantly attracts people from the provinces, who find it impossible to believe that Phnom Penh's streets aren't paved with metaphorical gold. Newcomers soon discover that it's tougher being poor in the city than in the country, and are often forced to rent tiny rooms for themselves and their families in one of the many shanties on the city's outskirts, ripped off for the privilege by affluent landlords.

For tourists and locals alike, the lively **riverfront** – a wide grassy promenade that runs beside the Tonle Sap for nearly 2km – is the city's focal point. In the evenings,

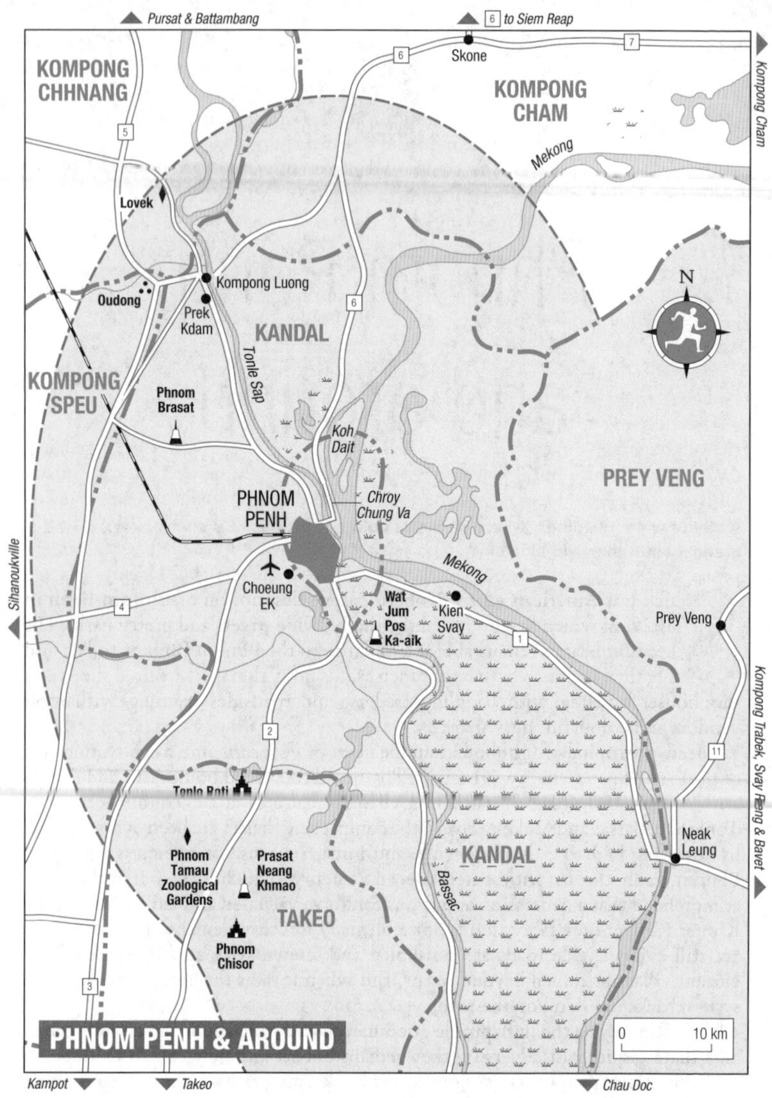

Phnom Penh residents come here to take the air, snack on hawker food and enjoy the impromptu waterside entertainment; the strip also shows the city at its most cosmopolitan, lined with Western restaurants, cafés and bars. Three key tourist sights lie close by. Arguably the most impressive of the city's attractions is the elegant complex housing the **Royal Palace** and **Silver Pagoda**. The palace's distinctive four-faced spire towers above the pitched golden roofs of its Throne Hall, while the adjacent Silver Pagoda is home to a stunning collection of Buddha statues. A block north of the palace is the **National Museum**, a dark-red building set in leafy surroundings housing a fabulous collection of ancient Cambodian sculpture dating back to as early as the sixth century. Also near the river are a number of lesser attractions, including **Wat Ounalom**, one of five pagodas founded during Phnom Penh's first spell as the capital, and bustling hilltop **Wat Phnom**, one of the city's prime pleasure spots, whose foundation is said to predate that of the city. The old French administrative area surrounds the hill on which Wat Phnom sits, with many fine **colonial buildings**, some restored. Also on many tourist itineraries, though for completely different reasons, is the **Toul Sleng Genocide Museum** south of the centre; a one-time school that became a centre for the torture of cadres who fell foul of the Pol Pot regime.

Many visitors stay just a couple of days in Phnom Penh before hopping on to Siem Reap and Angkor, or to the Vietnamese border crossings at Bavet and Chau Doc. There are, however, plenty of reasons to linger longer. The capital has the best **shopping** in the country, with a vast selection of souvenirs and crafts, and an excellent range of **cuisines** in its many restaurants. In addition, Phnom Penh offers a rare opportunity to get a glimpse of the **traditional culture** which the Khmer Rouge tried to wipe out, including classical dance and shadow puppetry.

If you do linger, there are several rewarding **day-trips** from the capital out into the surrounding countryside. The most obvious is an excursion to the Angkor-era temples of **Tonle Bati**, featuring well-preserved wall carvings, and **Phnom Chisor**, stunningly located on top of a hill. Especially poignant if you've visited the Genocide Museum is a trip to the killing fields at **Choeung Ek**, where a memorial stupa contains the remains of some of those murdered here. Among other possible day-trips are the old capitals of **Oudong** and **Lovek**, while a smattering of **rural villages** and **riverside pleasure spots** make a striking contrast to the historical treasures and bustle of Phnom Penh.

Some history

Cambodian legend – passed down through so many generations that the Khmers regard it as fact – has it that in 1372 a wealthy widow, **Daun Penh** (Grandmother Penh), was strolling along the Chrap Chheam River (now the Tonle Sap), when she came across the hollow trunk of a *koki* tree washed up on the banks. Inside it she discovered five Buddha statues, four cast in bronze and one carved in stone. As a mark of respect, she created a sanctuary for the statues on the top of a low mound, which became known as **Phnom Penh**, literally the hill of Penh; in due course, the hill gave its name to the city that grew up around it.

Phnom Penh began its first stint as a **capital** in 1432, when King **Ponhea Yat** fled south from Angkor and the invading Siamese. He set up a royal palace, increased the height of Daun Penh's hill and founded five **monasteries** – Wat Botum, Wat Koh, Wat Lanka, Wat Ounalom and Wat Phnom – all of which survive today. When Ponhea Yat died, his sons variously took succession, but for reasons that remain unclear, in the sixteenth century the court had moved out to Lovek, and later Oudong, and Phnom Penh reverted to being a fishing village.

Little is known of the subsequent three hundred years in Phnom Penh, though records left by missionaries indicate that by the seventeenth century a multicultural community of Asian and European traders had grown up along the banks of the Tonle Sap, and that Phnom Penh, with easy access by river to the ocean, had developed into a prosperous **port**, trading in gold, silk, incense, and in hides, bones, ivory and horn from elephants, rhinoceros and buffalo. Phnom Penh's prosperity declined in the later part of the century, when the Vietnamese invaded the Mekong delta, and cut off Phnom Penh's access to the sea.

The eighteenth century was a period of **dynastic squabbles** between pro-Thai and pro-Vietnamese factions of the royal family, and in 1770, Phnom Penh was actually burnt down by the Siamese, who proceeded to install a new king and take control of the country.

The Bonn Om Tuk Tragedy

The most important festival in the Cambodian calendar, Bonn Om Tuk, attracts more than two million visitors to the capital from the provinces each year to celebrate the reversing of the flow of the Tonle Sap river (variable, late Oct to mid Nov). Although the official attraction is the boat racing (see *Festivals and ceremonies* colour section) most of the attendees come to simply soak up the atmosphere with their families, eat copiously from the myriad street vendors and scoop up bargains from the sellers who lay their wares out along the riverfront. Those who have spent all their hard-earned money just on the journey meander through the animated streets by day and enjoy the free concerts and fireworks once the sun has set.

The sheer volume of people weaving a fragile dance along the riverfront is a spectacle in itself. Given the volatile mixture of millions of exuberant people and zero crowd control, it was almost inevitable that at some point something would go wrong.

On the final evening of the 2010 celebrations, disaster struck. After three glorious days that culminated in an extravagant closing ceremony and fabulous fireworks, panic broke out as the several-thousand-strong crowd poured onto a narrow footbridge. There was a stampede as people rushed to get off, resulting in the deaths of hundreds of people, mostly women. (The official figure stands at 351, although local reports at the time claimed more.) Almost as many again were injured and dozens forced to jump into the river. Most of the victims were visitors from the surrounding provinces. Several images appeared in the local press of the charred bodies of people electrocuted by the cables powering the neon lighting on the bridge. These promptly disappeared, however, as officials insisted that no such incidences had occurred.

Prime Minister Hun Sen called a day of mourning for the victims and described the tragedy as the country's largest since the Khmer Rouge era. He has since accepted that the government's careless attitude to crowd numbers was to blame, but was careful not to point the finger beyond this.

The festival is expected to continue as planned in 2011.

Late in the eighteenth century, the Vietnamese assumed suzerainty over Cambodia, and from 1808 all visits to Phnom Penh had to be approved by them. In 1812 Phnom Penh became the capital once again, though the court retreated to Oudong twice over the next fifty years amid continuing power-struggles between the Thais and Vietnamese.

In 1863, King Norodom (great-great-grandfather of the current king, Norodom Sihamoni), fearful of another Vietnamese invasion, signed a treaty for Cambodia to become a **French protectorate**. At the behest of the French, he uprooted the court from Oudong and the role of capital returned decisively to Phnom Penh, a place which the recently arrived French described as "an unsophisticated settlement made up of a string of thatched huts clustered along a single muddy track, the river banks crowded with the houseboats of fisher-folk". In fact, an estimate of its population at the time put it at around 25,000. Despite Phnom Penh regaining its access to the sea (the Mekong delta was now under French control) it remained very much an outpost, with the French far more concerned with the development of Saigon.

In 1889, a new Senior Resident, **Hyun de Verneville**, was appointed to the protectorate. Wanting to make Phnom Penh a place fit to be the French administrative centre in Cambodia, he created a chic colonial town. By 1900, roads had been laid out on a grid plan, a law court, public works and telegraph offices set up, and banks and schools built. A French quarter grew up in the area north of Wat Phnom, where imposing villas were built for the city's French administrators and traders; Wat Phnom itself gained landscaped gardens and a zoo.

In the 1920s and 1930s, Phnom Penh grew prosperous. The road network was extended, facilitated by the infilling of drainage canals; the Mekong was dredged, making the city accessible to seagoing vessels; parks were created and communications improved. In 1932, the city's **train station** was built and the railway line linking the capital to Battambang was completed. Foreign travellers were lured to Cambodia by exotic tales of hidden cities in the jungle.

The country's first **secondary school**, Lycée Sisowath, opened in Phnom Penh in 1936, and slowly an educated elite developed, laying the foundations for later political changes. During **World War II**, the occupying Japanese allowed the French to continue running things and their impact on the city was relatively benign; in October 1941, after the Japanese had arrived, the coronation of Norodom Sihanouk went ahead pretty much as normal in Phnom Penh.

With **independence** from the French in 1954, Phnom Penh at last became a true seat of government and an educated middle class began to gain prominence; café society began to blossom, cinemas and theatres thrived, and motorbikes and cars took to the boulevards. In the mid-1960s a national sports venue, the Olympic Stadium, was built and world celebrities began to visit – *Le Royal*, the city's premier hotel, played host to Jacqueline Kennedy.

The period of optimism was short-lived. Phnom Penh started to feel the effects of the Vietnam War in the late 1960s, when refugees began to flee the heavily-bombed border areas for the capital. The **civil war** of the early 1970s turned this exodus into a flood. **Lon Nol**'s forces (see p.319) fought a losing battle against the **Khmer Roug**e and, as the city came under siege, food became scarce despite US efforts to fly in supplies.

On **April 17, 1975**, the Khmer Rouge entered Phnom Penh. At first they were welcomed as harbingers of peace, but within hours the soldiers had ordered the population out of the capital. Reassurances that it was "just for a few days" were soon discredited, and as the people – the elderly, infirm and the dying among them – left carrying such possessions as they were able, the Khmer Rouge set about destroying the city. Buildings were ransacked, roofs blown off; even the National Bank was blown up in the Khmer Rouge's contempt for money. For three years, eight months and twenty days Phnom Penh was a ghost town.

With the **Vietnamese entry** into Phnom Penh on January 7, 1979, both returnees and new settlers began to arrive – although many former inhabitants either could not or would not return, having lost everything and everyone. Those arriving in the city took up residence in the vacant buildings, and to this day many still live in these same properties. During the Vietnamese era, the capital remained impoverished and decrepit, with much of the incoming aid from the Soviet Union and India finding its way into the pockets of senior officials. By 1987, Vietnamese interest was waning, and by 1989 they had withdrawn from Cambodia.

The UN subsequently took charge of Cambodia, and by 1992 the country was flooded with highly paid **UNTAC** forces. The atmosphere in Phnom Penh became surreal: its infrastructure was still in tatters, electricity and water were spasmodic, telecommunications nonexistent and evening curfews were put in force, but the city boomed as hotels, restaurants and bars sprang up to keep the troops entertained. Many Phnom Penh residents got rich quick on the back of this – supplying prostitutes and drugs played a part – and the capital gained a reputation for being a free-rolling, lawless city, one which it is still trying to lay to rest.

The city of today is slowly **repairing** the dereliction caused nearly three decades ago; roads are being rebuilt, the electricity is reliable and many of the charming colonial buildings are being restored. Alongside them, an increasing number of skyscrapers, high-rise apartment blocks and shopping malls are steadily peppering the horizon, particularly along Monivong and Sihanouk boulevards. With tourism

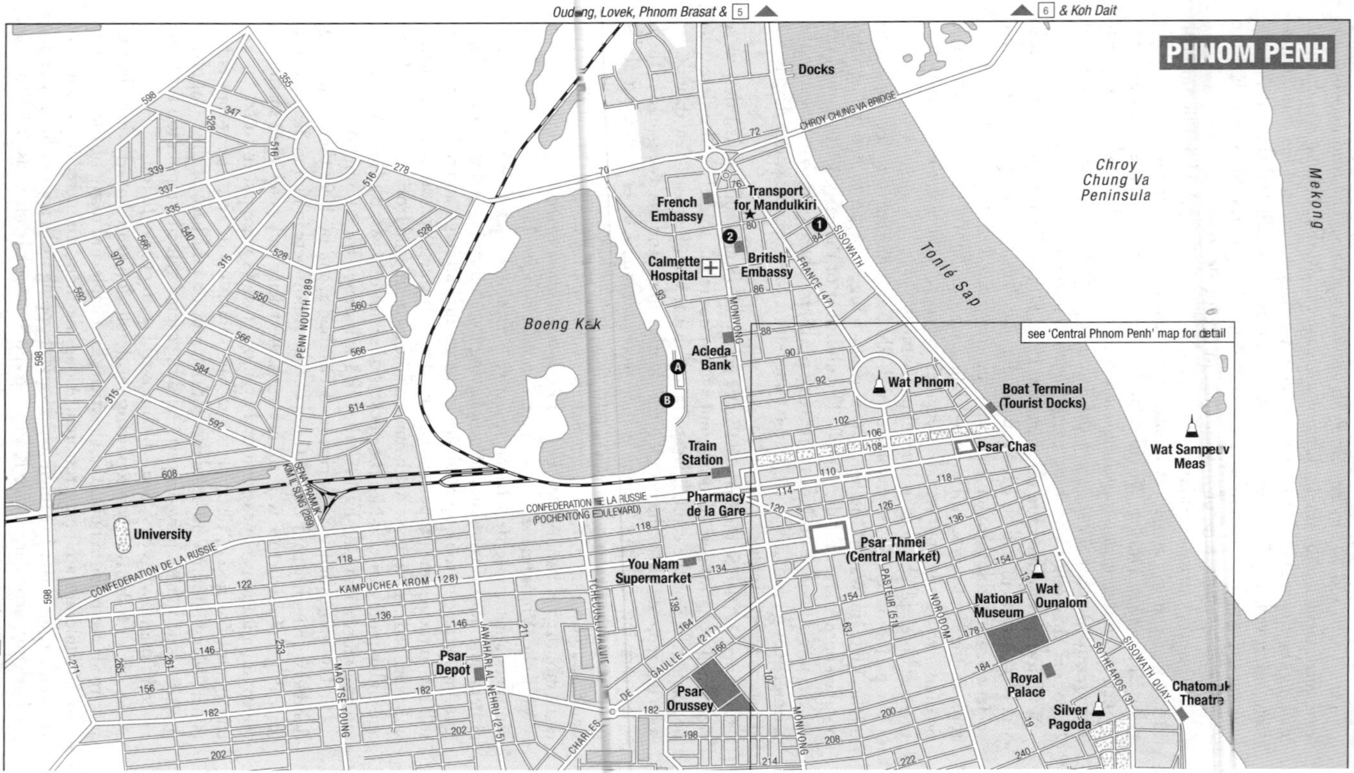

PHNOM PENH

Oudong, Lovek, Phnom Brasat & 5

6 & Koh Dait

4 & Airport

see 'Central Phnom Penh' map for detail

Mekong
Chroy Chung Va Peninsula
Tonlé Sap
Boeng Kak
Docks
Chroy Chung Va Bridge
Transport for Mandulkiri
French Embassy
British Embassy
Calmette Hospital
Acleda Bank
Train Station
Pharmacy de la Gare
Wat Phnom
Boat Terminal (Tourist Docks)
Psar Chas
Wat Sampeuv Meas
Psar Thmei (Central Market)
You Nam Supermarket
National Museum
Wat Ounalom
Royal Palace
Silver Pagoda
Chatomuk Theatre
Psar Orussey
Psar Depot
University
Sisowath
Sisowath Quay
Sothearos (3)
France (47)
Monivong
Norodom
Pasteur (51)
Confederation de la Russie (Pochentong Boulevard)
Confederation de la Russie
Kampuchea Krom (128)
Tchecoslovaquie
Charles de Gaulle (217)
Jawaharlal Nehru (215)
Mao Tse Toung
Penn Nouth 289
Sena Pramuk Kim Il Sung (289)

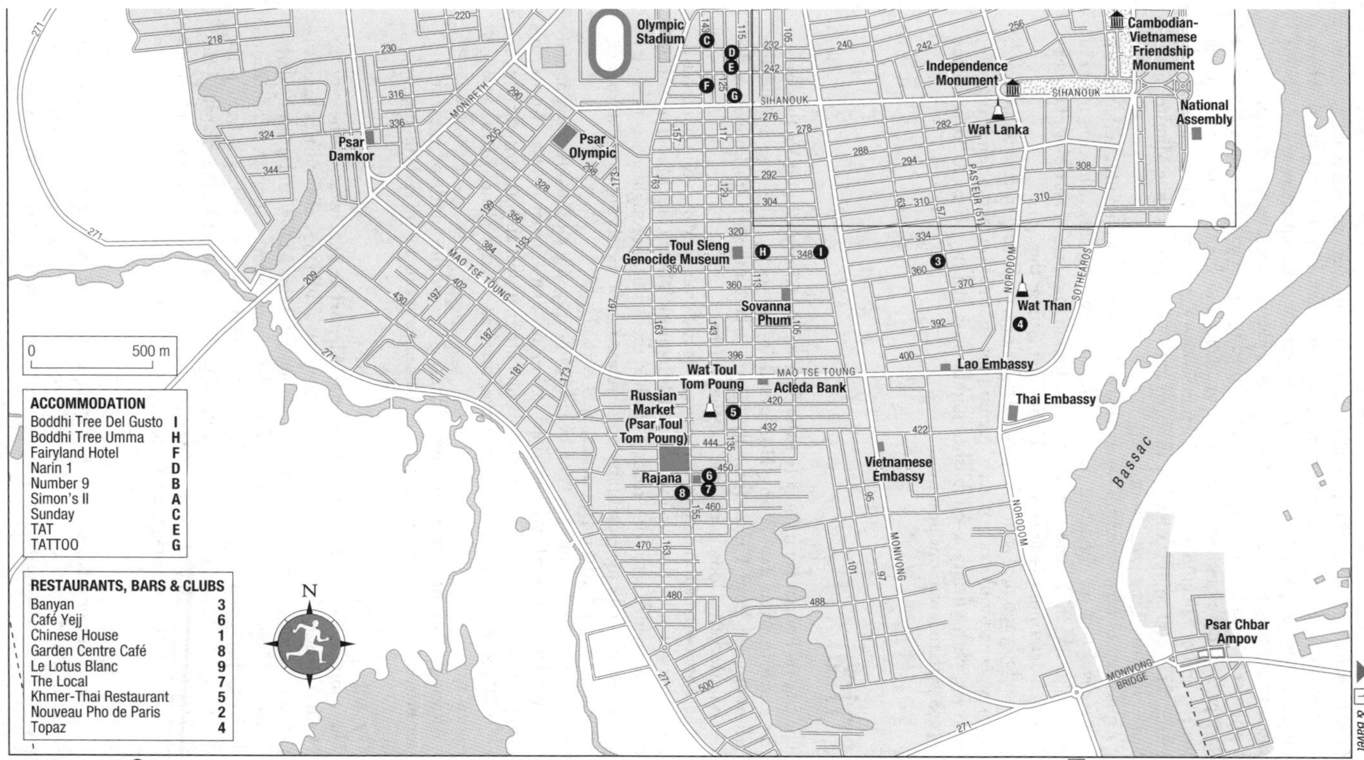
Olympic Stadium
Psar Olympic
Psar Damkor
Independence Monument
Cambodian-Vietnamese Friendship Monument
National Assembly
Wat Lanka
Wat Than
Toul Sleng Genocide Museum
Sovanna Phum
Wat Toul Tom Poung
Acleda Bank
Russian Market (Psar Toul Tom Poung)
Rajana
Lao Embassy
Thai Embassy
Vietnamese Embassy
Psar Chbar Ampov
Bassac
MONIVONG BRIDGE
SIHANOUK
MONIRETH
MAO TSE TOUNG
NORODOM
MONIVONG
PASTEUR (51)
SOTHEAROS
0 500 m
N
ACCOMMODATION
Boddhi Tree Del Gusto I
Boddhi Tree Umma H
Fairyland Hotel F
Narin 1 D
Number 9 B
Simon's II A
Sunday C
TAT E
TATTOO G
RESTAURANTS, BARS & CLUBS
Banyan 3
Café Yejj 6
Chinese House 1
Garden Centre Café 8
Le Lotus Blanc 9
The Local 7
Khmer-Thai Restaurant 5
Nouveau Pho de Paris 2
Topaz 4
1 & Bavet
Choeung Ek & 9
Takeo, Tonle Bati, Phnom Chisor & 2
Wat Jum Pos Ka-Aik

firmly in its sights, the municipal government has set out elaborate plans to continue smartening up the city, ranging from dictating the colour in which buildings will be painted – creamy yellow – to evicting squatters and makeshift shops from areas designated for development. Boeng Kak lake, for example, once a popular backpacker area, is now all but filled in and deserted to make way for a vast private development of hotels, apartments and luxury amenities. On the eastern end of Sihanouk Boulevard, Hun Sen Park and NagaWorld – a sprawling casino and hotel complex heavily invested in by Cambodia's Prime Minister, Hun Sen – dominates the waterfront.

Aspirations of car-ownership are attested to by the increase in traffic, and **exercise** – or *hat prahn* – is an important part of daily life now for many, who congregate in the city's parks in the late afternoon sun to join in impromptu **aerobics classes** or to march determinedly in laps, stretching their arms as they go.

Not so long ago the Cambodians abhorred banks, preferring instead to buy gold, but now even monks can be seen queuing for the ATM. Corruption is still rife; however, with a firmly re-established middle class, the city seems to be facing the future with renewed optimism.

Arrival

The city of Phnom Penh roughly extends from the **Chroy Chung Va Bridge** in the north to **Mao Tse Toung Boulevard** in the south. The area around the yellow-domed **Psar Thmei** (literally New Market, although it's known as the Central Market) is loosely regarded as the **centre**.

There are two major north–south routes, **Norodom** and **Monivong** boulevards, both intersected by the two great arcs of **Sihanouk/Nehru** and **Mao Tse Toung** boulevards, which act as ring roads; together, these four thoroughfares cut the city into segments and can be useful points of reference for specifying locations to taxi, tuk-tuk and moto drivers (see Basics, p.29 & p.30).

If you're heading to Phnom Penh by road or boat, you'll most likely arrive at one of several terminals that lie within 1.5km of Psar Thmei. Most visitors to Cambodia, however, arrive at Phnom Penh's international airport, just outside the city. Wherever and whenever you arrive, there are always plenty of tuk-tuks or motos available.

Although **freight trains** are now trundling across the south of the country (see box, p.81), it will be a while before passenger trains are up and running.

By air

The compact **Pochentong International Airport** is 8km west of the city on National Route 4. The main airport building has a full range of **facilities** based in the international arrivals hall, including several 24hr ATMs, and a bank (daily 7.30am–7.30pm), phones, a post office (daily 8am–6pm), a tourist information desk (see p.81) and an efficient **tuk-tuk and taxi** booth operating a fixed-price ($7 tuk-tuk; $9 taxi) service to the city. Motos are not allowed to hang around the airport terminal, but there are always plenty waiting on the main road, about 200m across the car park; the fare into town is between $3-5.

By road

Each bus company has its own respective depot, but two or three use the **bus station**, 200m southwest of Psar Thmei. Most shared taxis, minibuses and pick-ups use the **transport stop** (and the streets around it) 100m northwest of Psar

Getting back on track

There are currently no passenger trains in Cambodia, but work is in progress to change that. The French introduced train travel to the country in the 1930s, building a line that ran between Phnom Penh and Battambang and all the way up to the Thai border at Poipet. In the 1960s a line was built down to Sihanoukville with funds from France, China and West Germany. But the Khmer Rouge's lust for destruction extended to the travel infrastructure, and when the service resumed after the civil war, trains were forced to run with an empty flatbed carriage in front that would activate any mines planted by the Khmer Rouge the night before, a practice that continued well into the 1990s. Years of neglect led to disrepair and degradation. The service to Sihanoukville ended, and the trains between Poipet and Battambang dried up completely. The daily service between Battambang and Phnom Penh finally ground to a halt in 2009.

The Australian rail company, Toll Holdings, began a massive reconstruction programme on the track between Phnom Penh and Kampot in June 2009. The track was reopened for freight transport in October 2010, the first phase of a $141-million project that will one day connect Cambodia with Thailand, Singapore and Malaysia. Lines should be running south as far as Sihanoukville and its port by mid-2011, and a northern line resuming the Phnom Penh–Battambang–Poipet link in 2012. Once freight is being transported safely along these routes, there are high hopes for the service to be made public, although this will take a few years yet.

Thmei (see map, p.86). If you're arriving from Kampot, Sihanoukville or Takeo you'll be dropped at **Psar Damkor** on Mao Tse Toung Boulevard in the southwest of the city, while transport from Sre Ambel stops a bit nearer the centre, at **Psar Depot** on Nehru Boulevard. Transport from Bavet arrives at **Psar Olympic** near the stadium, or at **Chbar Ampov**, east of the Monivong Bridge in the far south of the city. All of these are inundated with moto and tuk-tuk drivers, although they often won't speak much English so it's useful to carry a map. Private minibuses (see "Listings", p.115) are increasingly running between provincial destinations and the capital. On request, they might drop you at your hotel or guesthouse if it's not too far from the depot.

By boat

Boats arrive at the **tourist docks** on the riverfront near the post office. Guesthouse touts meet the boats, though there are also plenty of tuk-tuk and moto drivers on hand; a moto ride into the centre will cost you about 3000 riel. Note that there is no longer a boat service from Battambang, Kompong Cham and Kratie.

Information and city transport

The **tourist information desk** at the airport's international arrivals hall (Mon–Fri 8am–4pm) has a 3D map of the city and a free booklet on Cambodia that contains useful general information. It's also worth getting hold of the *Phnom Penh Visitors Guide*, a free quarterly English-language booklet that contains details of places to stay, restaurants and sights, a map and a bit of history. You'll find copies in most guesthouses, restaurants and western cafés; extracts of the guide are available online at Ⓦwww.canbypublications.com. *Asia Life* (Ⓦwww.asialifecambodia.com), a free "What's On" guide to Phnom Penh, is published monthly; it has features and useful accounts of new openings and exhibitions. **Online** Ⓦwww.talesofasia.com takes a

Moving on from Phnom Penh

Most towns and cities in Cambodia can be reached directly from Phnom Penh. Siem Reap is particularly easy to get to, served by regular flights, by a daily boat up the Tonle Sap and by road transport along National Route 6; for Sihanoukville, there are efficient air-conditioned coaches which run from early morning to early afternoon.

By bus

As is the case at all bus stations, it's a good idea to keep a close eye on your bags. All buses out of Phnom Penh operate scheduled departures from the bus station (or their depots). Several companies, including Phnom Penh Sorya Transport Company, Mekong Express and GST, operate air-conditioned express coaches on the popular **Siem Reap** ($5–7) and **Sihanoukville** ($4) routes. Phnom Penh Sorya covers every other provincial town, using smaller twenty to thirty-seat coaches, for the less popular, more distant destinations. Destinations closer to the city, including Kompong Chhnang, Kompong Cham, Kompong Speu, Neak Leung, Oudong, Tonle Bati and Takeo, are served by small city buses also run by Phnom Penh Sorya.

Though not necessarily the quickest or cheapest option, the **Capitol Hotel** (tour line ⓣ023/217627), **Neak Krorhorm Travel** and several other guesthouses and travel companies, operate their own tourist buses to Siem Reap, Sihanoukville, Ho Chi Minh City (HCMC) and Bangkok, and to the Laos and Vietnam borders. A great development is that journeys to Bangkok and HCMC, which is still often referred to as Saigon, can be made without joining a new bus across the border, and your official dealings are done with the assistance of the bus operators (although you still have to get your visa at least 24 hours in advance from your guesthouse).

Guesthouse bus prices vary a bit, so it's worth comparing before you buy. For Laos, check if your ticket is just to the border or through to Don Det, 4000 Islands, in Laos. Phnom Penh Sorya have **comfortable air-conditioned coaches**, which run daily to Bangkok, to the border with Laos and to HCMC for $9–12.

By shared taxi, minibus and pick-up

From the transport stop at the northwest corner of Psar Thmei, plenty of shared taxis, minibuses and pick-up trucks head throughout the day for destinations north of Phnom Penh: **Kompong Thom**, **Siem Reap**, **Kompong Cham**, **Battambang**, **Sisophon** and **Poipet**. If you're going a long way, it's worth getting there by 6am or 7am. Later in the day when fewer people travel, you can have a long wait while the drivers gather up enough customers to make the trip worthwhile. For destinations closer to town you'll easily be able to get a shared taxi until mid-afternoon, after which departures become less frequent. Dramatic improvements in the roads mean that

refreshingly opinionated look at the local tourist scene. For **listings** of film screenings, theatre performances and other entertainment, the *Cambodia Daily* has a "What's On" section on Fridays, with classified ads for restaurants and bars on Tuesdays and Thursdays; the daily *Phnom Penh Post* is another useful source of information.

City transport

Although it's possible to see many of the sights on foot, Cambodia's heat and humidity, allied with the city's traffic and dust, don't make walking a particularly pleasant experience. **Motos**, **cyclos** and **tuk-tuks** are the workhorses of local transport, readily available all over town, picking you up from the kerb and dropping you right outside your destination. Phnom Penh has no public transport system – some years ago an experimental bus service was launched and lasted just taxis and minibuses now run to Kratie, Stung Treng, Rattanakiri and Mondulkiri. The once arduous roads between Rattanakiri and Mondulkiri (30,000 to 50,000 riel) are now mostly paved, with graded dirt for the last 100km to Rattanakiri; to Mondulkiri it's fully graded (5hr throughout the year). The bus, however, can take up to three hours longer, the drivers inexplicably aiming for 3pm arrival, stopping several times.

Key provincial destinations are also served by several private companies who run VIP express minibuses, seating 12–15 people (see "Listings", p.115); these are a good way to travel, quicker than the large buses and safer than taxis.

For the southern provinces of **Takeo**, **Sihanoukville, Kampot and Kep**, shared transport leaves from Psar Damkor; fares to the coast are 16,000 to 20,000 riel. Shared taxis for **Sre Ambel** and Koh Kong for the Thai border leave from Psar Depot and cost 50,000 riel. Destinations southeast of Phnom Penh, **Neak Leung** (for **Prey Veng** and the boat to **Chau Doc** in Vietnam), **Svay Rieng** and the border town of **Bavet** (commonly called Moc Bai after the town on the Vietnamese side of the border) are served by transport leaving from both Psar Olympic and Psar Chbar Ampov, the latter across the Monivong Bridge. Dramatic improvements to National Route 1, and the fact that the Monivong Bridge has recently doubled in size with a new identical arm for eastbound traffic that has greatly relieved the previously inevitable congestion, means that the journey to Bavet is now quicker, taking approximately three hours. The taxi fare to Bavet is around 18,000 riel.

By boat

Boats for Siem Reap and Chau Doc (foreigners' fare $35 and $25 respectively) leave from the passenger boat terminal (also known as the tourist docks) on the river near the main post office. **Express boats** take around five hours to power up the Tonle Sap to Siem Reap, subject to variations in the river's flow; they leave at 7am and have reserved seating; you can buy your ticket the day before or at the docks on the morning of departure. Both Delta Adventure (Ⓦwww.deltaadventuretours.com) and Blue Cruiser (Ⓦwww.bluecruiser.com) have offices along the riverfront.

By plane

The airport can be reached in under half an hour by moto or tuk-tuk ($4 and $7) or taxi ($9). All domestic carriers operate flights on the profitable route to Siem Reap; however, carriers in Cambodia come and go with alarming frequency and schedules change regularly, so it's best to check with a travel agent for the latest timetable. Flights to Rattanakiri and Stung Treng are currently suspended; it's not known if, or when, they will be reinstated.

two months, Cambodians being too used to the convenience of door-to-door transport.

Taxis can be hired at any of the major hotels, or by calling one of the firms recommended in "Listings" (p.115); expect to pay $4–5 for a single daytime journey within the city, or $5–8 at night, and a few taxis now operate on a meter system (advertised by the lit signs on their roofs). Taxis for hire by the day can be found lined up on the east side of Monivong Boulevard, near the intersection with Kampuchea Krom; the going rate is $25–30 per day around the city, $40–60 per day out of town. Taxis don't cruise for fares, although a few enterprising drivers meet incoming boats along the riverfront.

Due to the chaotic driving, the shameless speed traps and the police checks, the vast majority of visitors to Phnom Penh find hiring a ride better than driving, although motorbikes are a great way of exploring the surrounding countryside. If you do intend to **drive yourself** or rent a motorcycle you should be aware that, even compared to the impatient standards of Cambodian driving, the people of Phnom Penh take the biscuit. Cambodian drivers can also be rather hot-headed, so if you are driving, it's best not to insist on claiming your right of way or to be too heavy on the horn – incidents of road rage here can be violent. More an annoyance than a danger are the policemen who stop foreigners out of the blue and blatantly demand a $5 "fine" (ie bribe), usually with the phrase "beer money". It's unlikely you'll get away without paying, so it's easier to simply pay up rather than bravely protesting your innocence; you can usually bargain them down to a dollar or two. **Pedestrians** *never* have the right of way in Cambodia, and Phnom Penh is a place to exercise 360-degree vision, even at traffic lights and the striped, so-called pedestrian crossings.

Motos, tuk-tuks and cyclos

Fares around the city are creeping up: expect to pay around $1–2 per trip for a moto, but note that you will have to pay more if you are going out of the central area, or travelling in the rain or after dark, when prices go up to around $3–4 per trip. Some moto drivers speak a little English, especially the ones who hang out around the riverfront and other places where foreigners congregate. Away from these places you'll find English-speaking drivers few and far between, so it's useful to learn some landmarks, such as markets and monuments, and have a map handy.

Exercise a bit of caution when riding motos **at night**. While Phnom Penh is no longer the Wild West town it once was, robberies are not unknown, and moto passengers have recently been the target of bag-snatchers. It's certainly not worth being paranoid, but taking a tuk-tuk at night may be a safer option, keeping your bag on the inside and out of sight of passing motorbikes.

A fairly recent introduction to the capital, but now integral, tuk-tuks are more comfortable than motos, especially when two or more people are travelling together, or in the rain – as they have roll-down side-curtains; journeys around town cost $2–4. Don't expect a speedy trip though; tuk-tuks are powered by titchy motorbikes and progress can be painfully slow, particularly if there are a few people and their bags aboard.

Unique to the capital, cyclos (see Basics, p.30) remain popular and offer a leisurely way to get around, although they do cost slightly more than motos. The Cyclo Centre Phnom Penh is an NGO set up to help cyclo drivers. They offer showers, medical care and education, and can be found at 9 Street 158, not far from Sorya Mall (Ⓣ023/991178; Mon–Fri 8–11am & 1–5pm, Sat 1–5pm). You can't book for a trip, but if you turn up here there are usually cyclos around and starting

Phnom Penh addresses

Thanks to the French, who laid out the city on a **grid system**, Phnom Penh is remarkably easy to navigate. The **major streets** all have little-used official names, which have been changed periodically to honour particular regimes or sponsoring countries; the current names have been around since the mid-1990s. The rest of the streets are **numbered** and generally pretty easy to find. North–south streets have the odd numbers, with the low numbers nearest the river; even-numbered streets run east–west, with the low numbers in the north of the city. Signage is improving though, and areas of town are even acquiring district names that are posted above the road.

Individual **buildings** are numbered, but are almost without exception difficult to locate, as the numbering doesn't run consecutively, with the same number often being used more than once on the same street – Street 76, for example, boasted three no. 25s on the last count. Cruising until you spot your destination may be the only option unless you can call ahead for directions.

your ride from here is a good way to support the drivers, who rank among the poorest people in the capital. Alternatively you could contact Khmer Architecture Tours who organize a cyclo trip around the key post-1953 architectural sights on the second Sunday of each month (Ⓦwww.ka-tours.org); tours cost $12 and last two to three hours.

Accommodation

There's no shortage of accommodation in Phnom Penh, with an increasing number of guesthouses and hotels across the city catering for all pockets and tastes, from basic rooms to opulent colonial-era suites. No matter when you arrive, you should have no difficulty **finding a room**, although the very cheapest rooms fill up quickly. If you intend to stay for more than a couple of nights, it's worth asking for a discount at guesthouses and mid-range places. With deluxe accommodation you'll often get a better deal by booking through a travel agent or taking a two to three-night package.

The former backpacker area around **Boeng Kak lake** has now all but disappeared along with the water. The lake has been gradually filled by private developers and at the time of writing a small sliver to the east remained, along which a few guesthouses and homes still cling. But filling the lake with sand has led to flooding along the bank, leaving the area forlorn and increasingly abandoned. At the time of writing, **Number 9 Guesthouse** (Ⓔnumber9-guesthouse@hotmail.com; ❶) and *Simon's II* (Ⓣ012/608892; ❷–❸) were still operating a reasonable service, but for how long is anyone's guess (see map, p.79). Most of the budget accommodation is now in little clusters to the south of **Psar Orussey**, and on **Street 258** in the centre of town. There are also several cheap places with coveted locations close to the riverside. Recent years have seen increased competition in the **mid-range** bracket, with plenty of centrally located hotels along Monivong Boulevard and in Boeng Keng Kang, broadly around **Street 278**, near the NGO residential area. This is now the hottest location in town, with cosmopolitan restaurants, cafés, spas and boutique shops springing up all around it. **Deluxe hotels** in Phnom Penh rival those of any country, with the pride of place going to *Raffles Hotel Le Royal*; even if you're not staying there, it's worth a visit to admire the stunning colonial building or to enjoy a cocktail in its famous *Elephant Bar*.

If you are staying for a month or more, you could consider one of the **serviced apartments** offered by several hotels around town. Comprising bedroom, sitting room, bathroom and kitchenette, these go for around $700–1000 per month.

Psar Thmei (Central Market) and east to the riverfront

The following places are shown on the map on p.86.

Blue Lime 42 Street 19Z Ⓣ023/222260, Ⓦwww.bluelime.asia. This boutique hotel, tucked away down a little alley behind the National Museum, has the understated, contemporary style and service ethos to rival anything in Paris or New York. An exclusive haven from the hustle and bustle of town, the rooms are minimalistic and fresh, equipped with all mod cons, and some have their own completely private plunge-pool and terrace. The day-beds around the main pool itself are the perfect place to unwind, and the restaurant serves dishes from the Continent. ❺–❻

Fancy Guest House 169b Street 15 Ⓣ023/211829, Ⓦwww.thefancyguesthouse.com. In a great location just a block from the riverfront, this new hotel ticks all the boxes: sparkling rooms with a/c and hot water showers. The more expensive ones come with private balcony. ❸–❹

Last Home 21 Street 172 Ⓣ012/831702, Ⓦwww.lasthomecambodia.com. This friendly family-run

RESTAURANTS & CAFÉS

- Alley Cat Café 31
- Beef Soup Restaurant 34
- Boat Noodle 2 48
- Bopha Phnom Penh (Titanic) 4
- Le Café du Centre 32
- Café Fresco J
- Cantina 17
- Chi Cha 5
- Comme à la Maison 47
- East India Curry 9
- Ebony Apsara 28
- Friends 21
- Frizz 39
- Garden Centre 2 56
- Happy Herbs Pizza 19
- Java 44
- Khmer Borane 24
- Khmer Kitchen 51
- K'nyay 42
- Magnolia 41
- Malis 49
- Mama's 33
- Mamak's 10
- La Marmite 6
- La P'tite France 8
- Le Lotus Blanc 50
- Nature and Sea 52
- New Maharaja 54
- Nouveau Pho de Paris 29
- Origami 40
- Peking Canteen 14
- P+K 16
- Pop Café da Giorgio 23
- Rabbit Café 45
- Romdeng 30
- Royal India 35
- Sam Doo 15
- Shiva Shakti 43
- Tamarind 37
- The Shop 38
- Van's 3
- La Volpaia 1
- Le Wok 20

guesthouse close to Wat Ounalom is a little dingy but good value and has spacious rooms. 2–3

Pacific 234 Monivong Blvd ⓣ023/218592, ⓦwww.pacifichotel.com.kh. The fifty or so rooms here are large, bright and nicely furnished, with sturdy Cambodian wood furniture. The service is excellent, carried out with great pride and attention to detail. Breakfast included. 5

Royal 91 Street 154 ⓣ023/218026 or 012/854806, ⓔhou_leng@yahoo.com. Enduring family-run guesthouse, with a good selection of clean, comfortable accommodation and a café-bar that shows films on Cambodia's recent history most evenings. Brilliantly located within a couple of blocks of both the Central Market and the riverfront, they can also arrange onward transport, tickets and exchange. The lack of space has been solved by building up; the new rooms at the top have tiny balconies and great views of the city. 2–3

The riverfront

The following places are shown on the map on p.86.

Boddhi Tree Aram 70 Street 244 ⓣ011/854430, ⓦwww.boddhitree.com. The most recent of the Boddhi Tree group, this charming boutique hotel is just a few minutes' walk from the Royal Palace and riverfront. Booking is essential to secure one of the eight individual rooms with their crisp white linen and marble tiles. Pot plants abound and the atmosphere is serene with a hint of the luxurious. The terrace restaurant is open for breakfast, lunch and dinner. 6

Bougainvillier 272g Sisowath Quay ⓣ023/220528, ⓦwww.bougainvillierhotel.com. Well-appointed, spacious hotel rooms gain an ethnic touch through the use of Cambodian textiles and furnishings in muted tones. It has a terrific location and great rooms, with several brand-new ones in the recently acquired next-door building. Also boasts a fine French restaurant. Wi-fi and breakfast included. 6

Cambodiana 313 Sisowath Quay ⓣ023/426288, ⓦwww.hotelcambodiana.com. Set on the river, the colossal *Cambodiana* hasn't quite accepted that its days as the city's premier hotel have long gone. The rooms are large and comfy enough, the views are great and the casino gives the hotel just the slightest air of the illicit. Amenities include a choice of Asian and Western restaurants, a selection of bars, bakery, spa, gym, tennis courts, swimming pool and grounds running down to the river. However, you'll find far more charm and contemporary style for your money elsewhere. 8

Dara Raeng Sey Street 118 ⓣ023/428181. Functional rooms in a rambling corner building, conveniently located for both the riverfront and the old French quarter, come with either fan or a/c, as well as TV. The staff are very friendly and helpful, and can help organize day-trips and onwards travel, and as a result the hotel gets a lot of repeat custom. 2–3

FCC Phnom Penh (formerly known as the Foreign Correspondents Club of Cambodia) 363 Sisowath Quay ⓣ023/724014, ⓦwww.fcccambodia.com. Booking is essential to secure one of the seven individual rooms (all named after Angkorian temples) at this legendary restaurant and bar. Comfortable, modern accommodation is equipped to satisfy the needs of the visiting journo crowd, with writing desk, high-speed wi-fi, cable TV and bathrooms. Breakfast included. 6

Lazy Gecko 1 Street 258 ⓣ017/912935 or 012/619924. Recently moved from the banks of Boeng Kak, this Aussie-run guesthouse stands out along this backpacker street for great-value rooms with decent beds, a cool café and cocktail bar, board games and a popular quiz night. 1–3

Okay 38 Street 258 ⓣ023/986534 or 012/300804. This long-standing backpacker favourite, a little way south along the riverfront, has a good range of cheap rooms, some a little faded, and a busy restaurant where travellers congregate to use the free wi-fi, watch films and swap stories. They can arrange visa extensions, onward travel and laundry. 1–3

Paragon 219b Sisowath Quay ⓣ023/222607, ⓔinfo_paragonhotel@yahoo.com. This is a no-frills place, but for the price and location it's a real bargain, and they've recently installed a lift. Rooms are plain but spotless, and those with a river view and private balcony can be had for $25. 4

The Quay Sisowath Quay ⓣ023/992284, ⓦwww.thequayhotel.com. A new addition to the FCC group, this hotel blends soft cushions and carpets with cutting-edge design to produce a really luxurious setting. The staff are delightful, and the hotel has an excellent restaurant, *Chow*, as well as roof terrace complete with jacuzzi; perfect for happy-hour drinks overlooking the river. 7

River 108 2 Street 108 ⓣ023/218785, ⓦwww.river108.com. A new, luxurious Art Deco-styled boutique hotel, in shades of muted silver and gold with tinkling fountains, just a stone's throw from the water. 7

Around Wat Phnom

See map on p.86.

Raffles Hotel Le Royal Street 92, off Monivong Blvd ⓣ023/981888, ⓦwww.raffles.com. Dating from 1929, this impressive Art Deco hotel, set in lush gardens, was completely renovated in 1997 and restored to its original understated elegance, with the bonus of every modern convenience. Engravings of old Cambodia grace the corridors, and the luxurious guest rooms are individually decorated with specially commissioned prints and Cambodian artefacts. Amenities include a choice of restaurants and bars plus a patisserie, shop, spa and swimming pool. Happy-hour (daily 5–7pm) cocktails in the *Elephant Bar* are one of the capital's must-dos (although sadly a pool table has been installed). ⑨

From Psar Thmei to the Olympic Stadium

The following places are shown on either the map on p.86 or that on p.79.

Capitol 14 Street 182 ⓣ023/707299 or 217627 for buses, ⓦwww.capitolkh.com. This is the original Phnom Penh backpackers' guesthouse, which also runs its own buses to most popular destinations including Bangkok and Ho Chi Minh; travellers' cheques accepted and changed, and an in-house ATM has recently been installed. Rooms have no frills, though some have a/c and hot-water bathrooms. The restaurant serves inexpensive food, mostly stir-fries. ②

Dragon 238 Street 107 ⓣ012/239066, ⓔvireakcambodian@yahoo.com. This tidy, first-floor guesthouse offers a welcome respite from the bustle at street level with unpretentious, clean rooms; its balcony restaurant is great for a drink and a snack above the mayhem below. ②–③

Fairyland Hotel 99 Street 141 ⓣ023/214510 ⓔfairylandhotel@yahoo.com. A brand-new guesthouse built in a marble-floored tower with immaculate rooms – definitely more hotel than budget guesthouse, but a little soulless. Free wi-fi. ③

Narin 1 50 Street 125 ⓣ023/991955 or 012/852426. Another of Phnom Penh's early guest-houses, this old wooden house was undergoing extensive renovations at the time of writing, so expect brand-new and improved versions of the previous facilities (cheap food and traveller services) but possibly a higher price bracket. ②

Narin 2 20 Street 111 ⓣ023/986131 or 012/555568, ⓔtouchnarrin@hotmail.com. Subsidiary guesthouse of the original *Narin* with decent basic rooms in a modern purpose-built block. The large, airy restaurant is a great place to meet fellow travellers; all the usual travellers' services. ②–③

Sambath Phal 133 Street 150 ⓣ023/883466 ⓦwww.sambathphal.com. There isn't much English spoken here, but the welcome is still extremely warm and the rooms are in excellent condition in a brand-new building with a/c, private bathrooms, and free wi-fi. Just a few metres from the Central Market. ③

Sunday 97 Street 141 ⓣ023/211623, ⓔsundayguesthouse@hotmail.com. Welcoming guesthouse on a quiet street with comfortable rooms, a small restaurant, breezy terrace and a friendly atmosphere. Internet access and traveller services, including mini buses to Choeng Ek. ②–③

TAT 52 Street 125 ⓣ0129 21211, ⓔtatguesthouse@hotmail.com. This cheerful guesthouse run by Mama Tat is an old favourite with brightly decorated rooms and good furniture, internet access, a communal TV and video, and a rooftop restaurant serving decent Cambodian and Chinese food. They have recently opened *TATTOO* just a block south, which makes for a decent and similarly priced alternative when *TAT* is fully booked. ②

Boeng Keng Kang and around the Independence Monument

The following places are shown on the map on p.86.

Anise 2 Street 278 off Street 57 ⓣ023/222522, ⓦwww.anisehotel.com.kh. A sparkling addition to the city's mid-range hotels, *Anise* has twenty stylishly decorated rooms, all with a/c, minibar, tea- and coffee-making equipment, flat-screen TV and safety box. The best rooms have balconies and DVD players. Its bakery produces fresh croissants, while the indoor restaurant serves smallish, but delicious portions of Southeast Asian cuisine; the *Terrace Café* is a relaxed place for a coffee or cocktail. ⑤–⑥

Goldiana 10–12 Street 282 ⓣ023/219558, ⓦwww.goldiana.com. Popular with NGOs, this hotel may have rather dated decor, but the rooms are comfy and come with private bathroom, satellite TV, minibar, a/c, and spare phone lines for internet access. There's also a lovely rooftop swimming pool and a restaurant serving Khmer, Chinese and Western food. ❺–❻

Goldie Boutique 6 Street 57 ⓣ023/996670, ⓦwww.goldieguesthouse.com. All the rooms in this trendy little hotel are well appointed and tastefully decorated, with free wi-fi, and some with a sweet balcony. The management are on hand to answer all travel queries. ❹–❺

Manor House 21 Street 262 ⓣ023/992566, ⓦwww.manorhousecambodia.com. The Australian-Khmer owner has created a relaxed villa-style guesthouse, with a leafy garden and swimming pool. Once the home of a Japanese diplomat, the spacious rooms have capacious bathrooms and still have some of the original owner's furniture. Breakfast is included, as is wi-fi. ❺–❻

The Pavilion 227 Street 19, behind the Wat Botum ⓣ023/222280, ⓦwww.pavillion-cambodia.com. This eighteen-room guesthouse has been created by the impeccable conversion of two colonial mansions. No expense has been spared to present the very best of accommodation with an eco friendly ethos. With a swimming pool (guests and members only, no kids allowed), sunbeds, verdant gardens, jacuzzi, wi-fi and a restaurant and bar, it's almost too hard to leave. Advance reservations required by email only. ❻

Top Banana Corner of streets 51 & 278 ⓣ012/885572, ⓦwww.topbanana.biz. Two floors of simple budget rooms with a/c or fan in a prime location. Services include a top-notch balcony restaurant and bar (almost) overlooking Wat Lanka that hosts impromptu parties most nights. Free collection from bus, port and airport; communal TV and DVDs; laundry; onward transport and tours (although a little pricey). The *Mini Banana*, their new, less party-orientated sister guesthouse (same price range), is just 2 blocks to the south along Street 51 – enquire at the *Top Banana*. ❶–❸

South of the centre

The following places are shown on the map on p.79.

Boddhi Tree del Gusto 43 Street 98 ⓣ011/854430, ⓦwww.boddhitree.com. Tranquil guesthouse with accommodation in one of several adjoining 1930s colonial houses. The cream-coloured walls, shuttered windows and billowing white muslin create a colonial atmosphere, while outside you can relax in one of the shady courtyards. Restaurant and bar. ❹

Boddhi Tree Umma Street 113 ⓣ011/854430, ⓦwww.boddhitree.com. Set in a luxuriant, secluded courtyard garden this intimate guesthouse looks out over the S-21 genocide museum. Its twelve rooms are individually decorated using traditional Cambodian materials and are very attractive, although they can get a little stuffy and suffer from the road noise at times. The restaurant makes creative use of local produce in its excellent Continental menu. ❷–❹

You Khin 13a Street 830 ⓣ023/224843, ⓦwww.youkhinhouse.com. This charming new guesthouse is closely linked to the neighbouring school and allows the pupils to use the pool during the week. It is a wonderfully serene spot only a few blocks from the action in town. Seven smart rooms radiate off an airy central staircase, each one tastefully decorated in the Cambodian colours for the days of the week, all with enclosed shower cubicles (as opposed to the usual wet rooms) and a small area to relax. The intimate restaurant showcases the owner's late husband's art and a collection of guitars for guests to strum on, and they will soon be showing classic films on a projector over the pool in the evenings. A very calm and welcoming environment. ❺

The City

Most of the sights are located between the Tonle Sap and Monivong Boulevard, in an area bordered by Sihanouk Boulevard in the south and Wat Phnom in the north. The fabulous **Royal Palace** and **Silver Pagoda** dominate the southern riverfront, the shimmering golden roofs and towering spires glinting in the tropical glare. A block to the north is the dramatic, hybrid building of the **National Museum**, housing a rich collection of Khmer sculpture. **Wat Ounalom**, one of Cambodia's principal pagodas, sits two hundred metres to the north along the riverfront, its austere grey stupa housing the ashes of many prominent Khmers. The **riverside** along the Tonle Sap is a sight in itself, a pleasant walkway lined with restaurants.

Set back from the riverfront, at the northern end of Norodom Boulevard, the imposing white chedi of **Wat Phnom** sits atop the hill that gave the city its name. The area around contains several delightful French colonial buildings, including the main post office, the National Library, *Raffles Hotel Le Royal* and the rather grand train station.

South of the centre, the area around **Independence Monument** is a plush residential district and contains further monuments and a restful park. Two disparate attractions lie in the far south of the city: a short moto ride from the centre is the disturbing **Toul Sleng Genocide Museum**, with its sobering evidence of the paranoia and inhumanity of Pol Pot and his followers; fifteen minutes' walk further south, **Psar Toul Tom Poung** has the best souvenir-shopping in the country.

Royal Palace and Silver Pagoda

Behind the crenellated outer wall, the roofs of the **Royal Palace** and **Silver Pagoda**, adorned with soaring golden nagas and spires, glint enticingly against the sky. Built in traditional Khmer style, the surrounding wall is painted pale yellow and white, the two colours representing respectively the Buddhist and Hindu faiths.

The **entrance** to the complex (daily 8–11am & 2.30–5pm; $6 or 24,000 riel, inclusive of camera fee) is located on Sisowath Boulevard. English-speaking **guides** can be hired by the ticket office for a whopping $8, but they provide a wealth of information, not just on the palace and pagoda, but also Buddhist and Khmer culture. You must dress appropriately to be admitted: knees and elbows must be covered, and you are not allowed to wear hats or carry a backpack. To do the complex justice you'll need at least two hours, but note that the staff start to close up a half hour before the actual closing time. **Photography** isn't permitted inside the Throne Hall or the Silver Pagoda. On occasions the Throne Hall is closed for

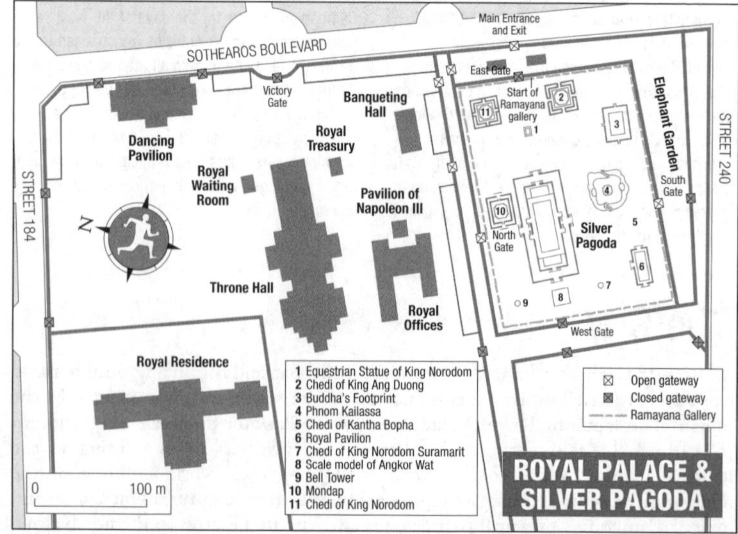

royal receptions and when the king has a meeting with his ministers. The royal residence itself, northwest of the Throne Hall, is always closed to the public. The complex is still worth a visit, although with short opening hours, steep entrance fee and the fact that many of the most impressive highlights are either covered up, cordoned off or no longer on display there's a definite sense of exploitation.

A **shop** on the site sells expensive silk, postcards and silver pieces, and there are a couple of pricey refreshment stalls.

Royal Palace

The current palace is less than one hundred years old, most of the buildings having been reconstructed in concrete in the early part of the twentieth century. The palace of King Norodom once stood here – the great-great-grandfather of the current king – he moved his capital here from Oudong in 1863; originally, it was also the site of the palace of King Ponhea Yat in 1434, of which nothing now remains.

Entering the pristine gardens dotted with topiaried trees you'll be close to the **Victory Gate**, which opens onto Sothearos Boulevard and faces the entrance steps to the Throne Hall. This was traditionally only used by the king and queen, though it's now used to admit visiting dignitaries. Just to the north of the gate, the **Dancing Pavilion** (Preah Tineang Chan Chhaya) was built for moonlit performances of classical Cambodian dance.

The Throne Hall

The present **Throne Hall** (Preah Tineang Tevea Vinicchay) was built by King Bat Sisowath in 1919 as a faithful reproduction of Norodom's wooden palace. As befits a building used for coronations and ceremonies, it's the most impressive building in the royal compound, topped by a much-photographed four-faced tower. The roof has seven tiers (counted from the lowest level up to the base of the spire) tiled in orange, sapphire and green, representing, respectively, prosperity, nature and freedom. Golden nagas at the corners of each level protect against evil spirits.

The hall's broad entrance staircase, its banisters formed by seven-headed nagas, leads up to a colonnaded veranda, each column of which is topped by a garuda with wings outstretched, appearing to support the overhanging roof. Entering the **Throne Room** by the east door, you'll find a ceiling painted with finely detailed scenes from the *Reamker* (Ramayana, see box, p.94) in muted colours, and walls stencilled with pastel leaf motifs and images of celestial beings, hands together in *sompeyar*. Down the centre of the hall runs a 35-metre-long, deep-pile carpet, its pattern and colours matching the surrounding tiles flanked by rows of gilt standard **lamps**, the lampshades supported by ceremonial nagas. The north and south entrance doors are protected by large mirrors, which are believed to deflect bad spirits. Unfortunately a velvet rope makes it impossible to get a proper view of the two elaborate golden **coronation thrones** ahead. They occupy a dais in the centre of the hall, above which a nine-tiered white and gold parasol, symbolizing peacefulness, heaven and ambition, is suspended; two large garudas guard the thrones from their position on the ceiling.

At the rear of the hall is an area where the king holds audiences with visiting VIPs and where the busts of six royal ancestors are displayed. **Anterooms** off the hall are used for different purposes: there are separate bedrooms for the king and the queen, to be used during the seven nights after the coronation, during which the royal couple have to sleep apart; another room serves as the king's prayer room; the last room is used to store the king's ashes after his death, while his chedi is being built.

Around the Throne Hall

On either side of the Throne Hall are two small but elaborate buildings. To the north, the **Royal Waiting Room** (Hor Samranphirum) is used on coronation day, from which king and queen mount ceremonial elephants from the platform attached to the east side of the building for the coronation procession. A room at ground level serves to store the royal musical instruments and coronation paraphernalia. The pavilion is now a museum for the king-father (the former King Sihanouk). To the south is the **Royal Treasury** (Hor Samritvimean), housing regalia vital to the coronation ceremony, including the Great Crown of Victory, the Sacred Sword and the Victory Spear.

The incongruous grey cast-iron building with a domed clock tower and observation gallery is the **Pavilion of Napoleon III**, used by Empress Eugénie during the inauguration of the Suez Canal in 1869. Presented to King Norodom by Napoleon III in 1876, the pavilion was re-erected here and now serves as a museum of **royal memorabilia**. Downstairs, glass cases contain a collection of royal silver and china tableware. There's also an anteroom housing a motley collection of paintings on subjects ranging from Venetian canals to Chinese landscapes, and a room glinting with gleaming medals resting on blue velvet cushions. At the top of the stairs, the austerity of the building is relieved by a collection of silk costumes elaborately embroidered in gold thread; these were made by Queen Kossomak, the present king's grandmother, for the Royal Ballet. A collection of royal portraits on display upstairs includes various pictures of the former King Sihanouk as a dashing young man.

Back outside, the building west of the pavilion houses the **Royal Offices** (Preah Reach Damnakchan). Dating from the 1950s, this is now part museum (housing a collection of gifts to the royal family) and part office for the Ministry of the Royal Palace. The rather plain building to the east is **Preah Tineang Phochani**, the Banqueting Hall; it is used to host banquets and royal orations, as well as performances of classical dance and music.

Leaving the royal complex by the south gate, you cross the alleyway to enter the courtyard of the Silver Pagoda by its north gate.

Silver Pagoda

Constructed in 1962 by former King Sihanouk to replace the wooden pagoda built by his grandfather in 1902, the **Silver Pagoda** is so named because of its 5329 silver floor tiles, each around 20cm square and weighing more than a kilogram. It's also known as **Wat Preah Keo Morokot**, the Pagoda of the Emerald Buddha, after the green Baccarat crystal Buddha within. The pagoda itself is clearly influenced by Bangkok's Wat Phra Kaeo, also home to a precious crystal Buddha to which the one in Phnom Penh bears an uncanny resemblance. Although more than half its contents were stolen during the Khmer Rouge years, the pagoda itself survived pretty much unscathed, and was used to demonstrate to the few international visitors that the regime was caring for Cambodia's cultural history. A rich collection of artefacts and Buddha images remains, making the pagoda more a museum than place of worship.

The vihara is approached by a stairway of specially imported Italian grey marble. On the veranda you'll need to leave your **shoes** in the racks and check in your **camera** with the security guards. Upon entering the pagoda, the silver tiles are almost entirely covered with a protective red carpet now, but a few can be spotted around the edges, some delicately engraved with leaf motifs. Atop a five-tiered dais in the centre of the pagoda is the **Emerald Buddha**, seated in meditation. Some sources say this is a modern reproduction, though others date it from the seventeenth century; whatever the case, at just 50cm in height it's put in the shade by the magnificence of the images surrounding it. One of the most dazzling is the life-sized **solid gold Buddha** at ground level, in the centre of the dais; produced

King Sihamoni

Dancer, teacher, artistic director and United Nations representative, **Norodom Sihamoni** was elected to be Cambodia's next king by the Throne Council in October 2004 on the surprise abdication of his father. The son of **Norodom Sihanouk** and his seventh wife Monineath, Sihamoni's name is made up from the first four letters of Sihanouk and the first four letters of Monineath. Born on May 14, 1953, most of his life was spent out of Cambodia: from the age of 9 he was educated in Prague where he learnt dance, music and theatre; he later studied cinematography in Korea.

In fact, other than his early childhood, the three years he spent **imprisoned** with his family in Phnom Penh during the Khmer Rouge years was the longest he spent in the country until becoming king in October 2004. On the arrival of the Vietnamese, the royal family went into **exile** and for a year Sihamoni acted as private secretary to his father, but from 1980 he was in France (where he spent the next twenty years) as a professor of classical dance in Paris.

From 1992, Sihamoni was Cambodia's permanent representative at the United Nations, and in 1993 he became its **UNESCO ambassador** – resigning both positions on becoming king. Sharing his father's love of cinema, Sihamoni was also director general of Khemara Pictures and has a couple of ballet films to his credit (*Dream* and *4 Elements*).

King Sihamoni keeps a lower profile than his father and as yet hasn't done anything to excite the media, though he is seen around the country and seems well regarded by his subjects. He holds regular meetings with the government and apparently isn't averse to bawling out his ministers, to keep them on their toes.

in Phnom Penh in 1907 for King Sisowath, it weighs ninety kilograms and is encrusted with 2086 diamonds and precious stones taken from royal jewellery. To its left, a silver seated Buddha is perched on top of a display case, while to the right is a case containing some delightful gold **statuettes** depicting key events from the life of Buddha. The tiny, highly detailed representations show him taking his first steps as a child on seven lotus pads, meditating under a bodhi tree and reclining on reaching nirvana.

Tucked away behind the dais is a serene life-sized standing Buddha from Burma, the elegance of its aged, cream marble not diminished by the brash red of the wooden pedestal. A haphazard, though nonetheless interesting, collection of Buddhas and other artefacts lines the back wall. The weighty gilded-wood **ceremonial litter**, over two metres long, and complete with throne, was used to transport the king on coronation day and required twelve men to carry it.

Display cases containing a diverse collection of objects line the pagoda walls, which include daggers, cigarette cases, headdresses and masks used for performances of the *Reamker* by the Royal Ballet. Recently, many of the most impressive and precious exhibits have been replaced by a motley selection of frankly not very exciting items. It's not known if they are away for restoration or have been removed permanently. Before leaving, check out the unusual **stained-glass windows**: one shows Hanuman (see p.94) astride a winged tiger.

The courtyard

Quiet and verdant, the pagoda courtyard is full of monuments, around which runs a fabulous 642-metre-long **mural**. Telling the epic tale of the *Ramayana* in minute detail, the mythical scenes were painted in vibrant colours by forty artisans working in 1903–04. The gallery cover has not protected the panels from water damage and despite a partial restoration in 1985, more work will be needed to

The Ramayana

The famous Hindu epic poem, the *Ramayana*, addresses the moral themes of good versus evil, duty, suffering and karma through the story of **Rama**, the seventh avatar of **Vishnu** (see p.328). A popular theme in Cambodian art and culture, its many episodes are depicted in temple carvings, pagoda art, classical dance and shadow puppetry. A simplified Cambodian version, the *Reamker*, also exists, more often portrayed in dance than in visual art.

At the outset of the story, ten-headed, twenty-armed **Ravana**, king of the *rakasa* demons, is terrorizing the world. As only a human can kill him, Vishnu agrees to appear on earth in human form to re-establish peace, and is duly born as Rama, one of the sons of Emperor Dasaratha. In due course, a sage teaches Rama mystical skills which come in handy in defeating the demons which crop up in the tale and in stringing Shiva's bow, by which feat Rama wins the hand of a princess, **Sita**.

The emperor plans to name Rama as his heir, but the mother of one of Rama's half-brothers tricks her husband into **banishing** Rama to the forest; he is accompanied there by Sita and another of his half-brothers, the loyal **Lakshmana**. After Rama cuts off the ears and nose of a witch who attacks Sita, Ravana gets his revenge by luring Rama away using a demon disguised as a golden deer; Lakshmana is despatched to find Rama, whereupon Ravana abducts Sita and takes her to his island kingdom of **Lanka**. While Rama enlists the help of Sugriva, the monkey king, Sita's whereabouts are discovered by **Hanuman**, son of the wind god. Rama and the monkey army rush to Lanka, where a mighty battle ensues; ultimately Rama looses the golden arrow of Brahma at Ravana who, pierced in the heart, dies ignominiously.

Although the tale as told in Cambodia often ends here, there are two standard denouements. In one, Sita steps into fire and emerges unscathed, proving she has not been defiled by Ravana, after which the couple return home to a joyous welcome and Rama is crowned king. In the alternative, sad, ending, Sita is exiled back to the forest, where she gives birth to twins. When they are 12, the twins are taken to court and Rama is persuaded that he is really their father. He begs forgiveness from Sita and she calls on Mother Earth to bear witness to her good faith. In a moment she is swallowed up by the earth, leaving Rama to mourn on earth for 11,000 years, until he is recalled by death to Brahma.

preserve what remains. Running **clockwise**, from the east entrance gate, the depiction begins with the **birth of Rama** and covers his marriage to **Sita**, her abduction and her rescue by the **monkey army**. Two of the most delightful scenes, both in good condition, show the monkey army setting out for Lanka (south gallery) and crossing to the island (north gallery).

Just east of the Silver Pagoda you'll see the monument of a **horseman**. Now bearing a head of Norodom, it began life as an equestrian statue of Napoleon III, a typically megalomaniac gift from the French emperor.

To either side of the statue are heavily embellished twin **chedi** – Norodom's to the north, Ang Duong's to the south (the latter also has a chedi at Oudong). In the east corner of the compound, a small plain pavilion contains a **footprint of the Buddha** (Buddhapada), a representation of the Buddha dating from the time before images were permitted to be made. There are also ancient manuscripts written on palm leaves, rare survivors of Cambodia's humid climate. Another stylized Buddha's footprint, this one a gift from Sri Lanka, can be found nearby in the pavilion atop the artificial hill, Phnom Kailassa.

To the southwest of Phnom Kailassa lies the open-sided chedi of the daughter of King Norodom Sihanouk, Kantha Bopha, who died as an infant in 1952 of leukaemia and whose name has been given to children's hospitals in both Phnom Penh and Siem Reap. Behind the Silver Pagoda is a **scale model** of Angkor Wat

– incongruous amid the religious and funerary relics. In the west corner of the compound is a **bell tower**, the pealing of whose bell used to signal the opening and closing of the gates to the compound. By the north gate is the **Mondap**, once housing palm-leaf texts, though now it houses a statue of Nandin, the bull ridden by Shiva.

Leaving the courtyard by the south gate, there is a jumble of buildings and a small garden where elephants were tied up when not at work: look out for the display of elephant-shaped boxes and a pavilion of howdahs and cow carts. Another building houses an exhibition related to the coronation of King Sihamoni.

National Museum

The impressive dark-red sandstone building of the **National Museum of Cambodia** houses a rich collection of sculpture, relics and artefacts, dating from prehistoric times to the present. The collection had to be abandoned in 1975 when the city was emptied by the Khmer Rouge; it was subsequently looted and the museum's director murdered. By 1979, when the population returned, the roof had collapsed and the galleries and courtyard had succumbed to the advances of nature – for a time the museum had to battle constantly to protect its exhibits from the guano produced by the millions of **bats** which had colonized the roof; these were finally driven out in 2002.

The museum opened in 1918, and, designed by the French archeologist, George Groslier, comprises four linked **galleries** that form a rectangle around a leafy courtyard, its roof topped with protective nagas.

Practicalities

The **entrance** to the museum (daily 8am–5pm; $3, photography – courtyard only – $1) is via the central flight of steps leading to the East Gallery. The massive wooden doors here, dating from 1918, and each weighing over a tonne, have carvings reminiscent of those at Banteay Srei. Inside, there's a place to leave your bags (free) and a stall with a good range of books, including the useful guidebook *Khmer Art in Stone* ($2), or the more comprehensive *New Guide to the National Museum Phnom Penh* ($10), as well as postcards and reproductions of some of the exhibits. English-speaking guides can be hired here ($5); they'll give you information on the archeological styles in the collection and an insight into life during the different periods of Cambodian history. The collection is arranged broadly chronologically, going clockwise from the southeast corner. If you visit the museum after you've seen Cambodia's temples, you'll be able to visualize how the museum's sculptures would have looked in their original surroundings.

East Gallery

The most striking piece in the East Gallery is a massive sandstone **Garuda** – over two metres tall, its wings outstretched – which dates from the tenth-century Koh Ker period. The rest of the gallery contains a collection of bronze artefacts, some dating back to the Funan period. To the left, the displays comprise mainly sculpture, including an interesting combination of Buddhist and Hindu images; some from the fifteenth to seventeenth centuries are of gilded copper and lacquer. The case closest to the entrance houses a fine statuette of Shiva and Uma on Nandin, while another case contains an intricate Buddha atop a naga and framed within a separate arcature; just beyond is a miscellaneous collection of hands and feet from long-disintegrated statues.

Display cases to the right (north) of the gallery contain an assortment of elaborate candleholders, heavy elephant bells, religious water vessels and the paraphernalia for **betel-nut** preparation, including betel-nut containers in the shape of peacocks. The corner chamber hosts the museum's collection of **wooden Buddha statues** in various states of gentle decay, all post-Angkor and showing signs of the gilt paints in which they were once decorated.

South Gallery

The gracious head and shoulders of a vast, hollow reclining **Shiva**, with two of his four arms remaining, takes pride of place in the southeast corner of the museum, behind which sits a small temporary exhibition space. Through into the South Gallery, a small but intricate collection of Sanskrit inscriptions on stones dating back to the fifth and sixth centuries are on display, many from the southern province of Takeo, supporting evidence of the region's political and religious importance during the pre-Angkor period.

Pre-Angkor

Further into the South Gallery, the focus is still on the pre-Angkor period, with slim, shapely sixth-century Buddhas in relaxed postures, their hair piled on top of their heads in tight ringlets. These early sculptors, though dextrous – the carved garments cleverly give an impression of the contours of the bodies underneath – had yet to master carving in the round, so these statues are carved in **high relief**, with stone remaining between the legs and arms.

Occupying pride of place is a massive, three-metre-tall, eight-armed image of **Vishnu** dating from the Phnom Da era (sixth century). The figure wears a plain, pleated loincloth low at the front and pulled up between the legs; the hands variously hold a flame, a conch and a staff, all symbols of Vishnu. A stone arc supports the figure, but in a step towards carving in the round, the stone has been chipped away between the arc and the limbs. Close by, on the south wall, is a sixth-century high relief of **Krishna**, standing left arm aloft, holding up Mount Govardhara.

Tucked in the corner by the doorway to the courtyard is a fine and varied collection of **linga** in excellent condition; nearby, a fine Vishnu from the ninth century (in Kulen style), unusually for Khmer sculpture, displays good muscle definition. A series of voluptuous female statues of Durga and female divinities, wearing elegantly draped *sampot*s, line the wall by the courtyard; the lady near the centre of the gallery is particularly elegant, her ear lobes elongated as though from wearing heavy jewellery, symbolizing wealth.

Angkor

A ninth-century, Kulen-style **Vishnu** in the portico of the South Gallery marks the shift to the more formal Angkor period – notice how the sculptors stabilized the statue's bulk, carving the right leg slightly forward of the body and supporting the arms with a staff and sword. The late ninth-century **Preah Ko period** is characterized by comely figures, epitomized by the shapely statue of Queen Rajendradevi in the west corner of the central section of the South Gallery. Also here is a contemporaneous image of a stocky Shiva.

Passing between a pair of delicately carved sandstone columns you enter the west section of the South Gallery and move into the **Bakheng period** (late ninth to early tenth century). This period is exemplified by a two-metre-tall Shiva from Phnom Krom, whose head was stolen from the Angkor Conservation Department in 1993 and illicitly traded. Through the *Missing Objects: Looting in Angkor* list it was discovered in the Metropolitan Museum of Art in New York, from where it was returned and is now reunited with its body. During the **Koh Ker period** (early to mid-tenth century) sculpture became more dynamic, as illustrated by the athletic torsos of two wrestlers entwined in a throw (in the courtyard window). It's worth stepping outside here to see some of the original heads from the divinities of the causeway to Angkor Thom, and also an unusual ablutions bowl made from polished schist, the spout in the shape of a buffalo head.

This section also contains some particularly fine statues from the tenth-century temple of **Banteay Srei**, regarded by many scholars as one of the high points of Khmer art. On a central plinth, a smiling **Shiva** and his (sadly headless) wife Uma face the south. He is unadorned save for a carved necklace, but in situ they would both have been draped with precious jewellery. On the wall a striking pediment from Banteay Srei illustrates a scene from the *Mahabharata*, the Hindu epic of two warring families, showing two cousins, Bhima and Duryodhana, in mortal combat.

West Gallery

Dating from the late tenth century on, the sculpture here is more formal than in earlier periods. An elegant example of a graceful female statue of the eleventh-century **Baphuon period** is the slender, small-breasted Lakshmi, consort of Vishnu; her *sampot* dips at the front to reveal her navel and rises above the waist at the back. The museum's pre-Angkor Wat collection contains only a few Buddha images as the kings of the time were mostly adherents of Hinduism, but by the eleventh century, Buddhism was gaining in influence, illustrated here by the Baphuon-era seated Buddhas, some showing a faint smile and sheltered by the seven-headed naga.

The **Angkor Wat period** is lightly represented, freestanding sculptures having been largely replaced by the mighty bas-reliefs carved in situ at the temples. One of the few noteworthy examples, by the west wall, is a pediment from the west entrance of Angkor Wat, depicting part of the *Jataka*, the stories describing the previous incarnations of the Buddha.

Towards the far end of the gallery is the museum's most famous statue, the image of **Jayavarman VII**, from the **Bayon period** (late twelfth century). Sitting cross-legged in meditation, the king is portrayed as a clean-shaven, slightly rotund middle-aged man, the expression peaceful. The head of Jayavarman VII is much reproduced as a tourist souvenir. The Buddhist theme resumes in the Bayon-period exhibits at the north end of the gallery, where a thirteenth-century pediment from Prah Palilay shows a seated Buddha in the earth-witnessing *mudra*.

North Gallery

Leaving the stone statuary behind, you skip forward a few centuries to the miscellany of the North Gallery. By far the most impressive exhibit here is the cabin of a nineteenth-century **royal boat**, made of elaborately carved *koki* wood. Inside, the floorboards are smooth and polished, while leaves, flowers and dragons decorate the exterior; the cabin would have been lavishly furnished, ensuring that the king could travel in relative comfort.

The massive funerary **urn** in the centre of the gallery, nearly three metres tall and made of wood, silver and copper overlaid with gilt, was used for the ashes of King Sisowath in 1927 and again for those of King Norodom Suramarit, the grandfather of the present king in 1960.

Not to be missed, just outside under the eaves behind the refreshment stand, is a magnificent **wall panel**, one of a pair looted from Banteay Chhmar temple in 1998 by the military personnel who were supposed to be guarding it. The blocks were cut out from the enclosing wall using machinery, loaded onto lorries and smuggled across the Thai border en route for sale in Bangkok, but were seized by Thai police on the way. Both were returned to Cambodia in 2000. Another panel reassembled here depicts a larger-than-life, multi-armed image of Lokesvara.

The riverfront

Sisowath Quay, hugging the river for nearly 4km from the Chroy Chung Va Bridge to Chatomuk Theatre, is the heart of the tourist scene in Phnom Penh, with a weekend night market and a plethora of Western bars and restaurants close to the Royal Palace and National Museum. From Street 106, midway along, the quay forms a broad promenade extending almost 2km south, and there are plans to extend this walkway by a further 4km, all the way to the bridge at Chbar Ampov. Every autumn, the river thrums with crowds flocking to the boat races and festivities of **Bonn Om Tuk**, the water festival (see *Festivals and ceremonies* colour section). For the rest of the year, the riverfront is fairly quiet by day, when it's a pleasant place to walk, and gets busier in the late afternoon when the inhabitants of Phnom Penh come out to *dah'leng*, a term that means anything from a short stroll to an all-day trip out of town. At about 5pm, the pavements around the public garden by the Royal Palace turn into a huge picnic-ground as mats are spread out, food and drink vendors appear and impromptu entertainment springs up. Many will also head across the road to the shrine with the statue of a four-armed Buddha. The story goes that many years ago a crocodile-shaped flag appeared in the river and on Buddhist holidays it would miraculously appear on a flag pole. Now, the spirit of the flag, Preah Ang Dong Kar, has a permanent home here and people make offerings asking for wealth and happiness – at the same time helping the flower and incense vendors to make a living. Boats and their captains can be hired for a late afternoon **cruise** on the Mekong ($10 per hour; look out for the signs at the north end of the promenade), where you can sup a beer (bring your own) and watch the sun set behind the Royal Palace.

Wat Ounalom

The rather sombre concrete chedi that fronts Sisowath Quay belies the fact that **Wat Ounalom** is one of Phnom Penh's oldest and most important pagodas, dating all the way back to the reign of Ponhea Yat in the fifteenth century – though there's little evidence now of its age. In the early 1970s, over five hundred monks lived at the pagoda, which also housed the library of the Institut Bouddhique, subsequently destroyed, along with many of the buildings, by the Khmer Rouge.

The pagoda gets its name from its role as repository for an *ounalom*, a hair from the **Buddha's eyebrow**, contained in the large chedi behind the vihara; you can gain access if you ask at the small bookshop near the entrance on Street 13. Within the chedi are four sanctuaries, the most revered being the one facing east, where there's a fine bronze Buddha. The monks use the **vihara**, which dates from 1952, in the early morning, after which time visitors can enter. Unusually, it's built on three floors, and houses a commemorative statue of Samdech Huot Tat, the venerable fourth patriarch of Cambodian Buddhism, who was murdered by the Khmer Rouge. Despite its unappealing exterior, the dark-grey chedi is worth a quick look for its **crypt**, in which hundreds of small cubicles hold the funerary urns of Cambodian notables, most of which are adorned with bright plastic flowers and a photograph of the deceased.

The Independence Monument and around

The riverfront south of the Royal Palace is home to the Chatomuk Theatre; while beyond the *Cambodiana* hotel is Hun Sen Park, now home to **Naga World**, a gaudy casino, hotel and restaurant complex, and Koh Pich, or Diamond Island, as it has been named since its transformation from quaint offshore farming village to an extension of the Hun Sen Park complex, comprising a children's park, ornamental gardens and the foundations of a vast exhibition centre. It was on the footbridge linking Diamond Island to the mainland that the **stampede** occurred during the water festival, Bonn Om Tuk, in November 2010 (see box, p.76).

The **Buddhist Institute** is a little further south and just around the corner is the enormous, new **National Assembly** building. This stretch of road is popular with the city's rich boys who come here to road-race their powerful SUVs in full sight of the police on guard at the Assembly building.

Alternatively, cut **inland** through a peaceful park to the Independence Monument, at the intersection of Sihanouk and Norodom boulevards. A golden stupa in the park commemorates the sixteen people killed outside the old National Assembly (corner of Street 240 and Sothearos Blvd) building on March 30, 1997, when grenades were thrown into a rally led by Sam Rainsy. Beyond it is the **Cambodian–Vietnamese Friendship Monument**, commemorating the Vietnamese liberation of Phnom Penh from the Khmer Rouge in January 1979; it features massive sandstone figures of a Khmer woman holding a baby, flanked by two armed Vietnamese liberation soldiers. It is a lovely place to stroll just before sunset, when a handful of trainers set up boom boxes and Cambodians pay 1000 riel to join them in a rigorously choreographed, unofficial aerobics class. You will see others taking a gentler, but equally serious, approach to exercise by walking determined laps around the park.

Across the park, **Wat Botum** is another of the five original pagodas founded by Ponhea Yat in 1442. The present structure was built by King Sisowath Monivong and dates from 1937; fortunately, it escaped damage by the Khmer Rouge. The grounds are crammed with elaborate and picturesque chedis, many of which hold the ashes of rich politicians and important monks; enormous, gaudy statues of giants, lions and tigers pepper the grounds.

From here, there's a good view west past the fountains to the recently refurbished **Independence Monument** (aka Victory Monument), commemorating independence from the French in 1953, and now also serving as a cenotaph to the country's war dead. The distinctive, dark-red sandstone tower, completed in 1958, is reminiscent of an Angkorian sanctuary tower, its multi-tiered roofs embellished with over a hundred nagas. At night it makes a dramatic sight when the fountains are floodlit in red, blue and white, the primary colours of the national flag.

Like Wat Botum, sprawling **Wat Lanka**, across from the monument, was also founded in 1442 and gets its name from its historic ties with monks in Sri Lanka. The pagoda vies with Wat Ounalom for importance, and many of the monks here are highly regarded teachers. Within the vihara there are scenes from the Buddha's life featuring an idiosyncratic local touch – one shows Angkor Wat, while another depicts tourists climbing Wat Phnom. Meditation classes for the public are held in the vihara three times a week (see "Listings", p.114).

The alleys around Wat Prayuvong, a couple of hundred metres south on Norodom Boulevard, are the city's centre for the manufacture of **spirit houses** (see p.332) and religious statuary in the capital – you can't miss the brightly painted displays on the roadside. Although everything is now made in concrete, the artistry remains elaborate and the variety of statues and statuettes fascinating; a number of artists here also do religious paintings, some on an impressive scale.

Southwest of the centre

The main reason to venture out towards the southern districts of the city is to visit the **Toul Sleng Genocide Museum**, an inevitably harrowing and heart-rending experience, but one which puts into context the suffering of the Cambodian people and country. More history from 1975 crops up 1500m east, at the site of the **former US Embassy** (now belonging to the Ministry of Fisheries and bearing no outward clues to its past), on the northeast corner of the intersection of Norodom and Mao Tse Toung boulevards. Under threat from advancing Khmer Rouge troops, US marines airlifted 276 Americans, other foreigners and Cambodians to safety – the last to leave, with the "Stars and Stripes" clutched under his arm, was the ambassador, John Gunter Dean. The evacuation was completed just five days before the Khmer Rouge entered Phnom Penh, and the Khmer Rouge subsequently used the premises as a place of execution, slaughtering senior officers of Lon Nol's army in the grounds.

Toul Sleng Genocide Museum

Originally the Toul Svay High School, from 1975 to 1979 the **Toul Sleng Genocide Museum** (daily 7.30–5.30am; $2; English-speaking guide $6; entrance off Street 113) was the notorious Khmer Rouge prison known as **S-21**, through whose gates more than thirteen thousand people (up to twenty thousand according to some estimates) passed to their deaths. S-21 was an interrogation centre designed for the educated and elite: here doctors, teachers, military personnel and government officials all passed through Khmer Rouge hands. The regime was indiscriminate in its choice of victims; even babies and children were among those detained, and subsequently slaughtered, to eliminate the possibility of them one day seeking to avenge their parents' deaths.

Through the gates, still surrounded by high walls and ringed by barbed wire, an eerie silence descends on the complex of three main buildings juxtaposing harshly against the palm and frangipani trees in the former high school playground.

Up to 1500 prisoners were housed here at any one time, either confined in tiny cells or chained to the floor or each other in the former classrooms. The most southern block A (to the left of the ticket booth) comprises three floors of cells that still contain **iron bedsteads** and the shackles used to chain the prisoners to the beds. Chilling photos in each room depict the unrecognizable corpse of the bed's final inhabitant.

Walking across the garden past school gym apparatus used by the Khmer Rouge as a grotesque torture device, you come to Block B. On the ground floor there is a display of thousands of black-and-white **photographs** of the victims, their eyes expressing a variety of emotions, from fear through defiance to emptiness. Each one of them holds a number; the Khmer Rouge were meticulous in documenting their prisoners and sometimes photographed victims following torture, also on display.

The **balconies** on the upper floors are still enclosed with the wire mesh that prevented the prisoners jumping to a premature death. The partition cells on these floors, of wood or brick, are so small that there is hardly room for someone to lie down. When the Vietnamese army entered the prison in January 1979, they found just seven prisoners alive; the corpses of some prisoners who had died shortly before were discovered in the cells and buried in graves in the courtyard. Although the majority murdered here were Cambodian, foreigners, both Western and Asian, were also interrogated and tortured.

Things get no easier emotionally as you progress into Block C where methods of **torture** are outlined, some of which are unflinchingly depicted in paintings by the artist Van Nath, one of the survivors. Prominent is a **water chamber** where prisoners were systematically drowned until they confessed. Worth reading are the sombre extracts in the exhibition area from forced "confessions", and the exchanges of letters between the cadres, who sadistically continued to victimize prisoners until their declarations conformed to the guards' own version of the truth. Newer exhibitions detail the ongoing criminal tribunals against the surviving Khmer Rouge leaders, the faces in many of the pictures so covered in graffiti that they now sit behind glass.

Every day at 10am and 3pm a made-for-television docu drama, *Bophana*, by Rithy Panh, traces the tangled, tragic romance between two Cambodians caught up with the Khmer Rouge. It's shown upstairs in the Documentation Centre of Cambodia in the same block.

Wat Phnom

In the northeast of the city, just a few hundred metres from the riverfront, **Wat Phnom** (daily dawn–dusk; foreigners $1), where the hilltop sanctuary from which the capital got its name once stood, is one of the principal pleasure spots for the inhabitants of Phnom Penh, drawing the crowds especially at weekends and on public holidays. Before climbing the hill (which, even at a mere 27m high, is sufficient to dwarf anything else in the capital), you'll be directed to one of the payment booths to buy your **ticket**. The nicest way up the hill is by the **naga staircase** on the east side, passing some bronze friezes (depicting scenes of battle) and dancing apsaras (reproductions of bas-reliefs at Angkor Wat) on the way. The sanctuary on the summit has been rebuilt many times, most recently in 1926, and nothing remains of the original structures; the surrounding gardens were originally landscaped in the late nineteenth century by the French, who also installed a zoo (of which nothing remains) and the clock on the south side of the hill, restored for the Millennium, now sports a dial that glows in fluorescent colours as night draws in.

This taste for the luminous bizarrely continues inside the **vihara** (which, before entering, you must take off your shoes) where a neon disc revolves behind the sitting Buddha, visible through the haze of burning incense. Over the years, the smoke has darkened the wall paintings, making it hard to make out the depictions of the *Jataka* stories. A constant stream of Khmer pass through the pagoda, paying their respects and trying to discover their fortunes by holding a palm-leaf book above their heads and, without looking, inserting a small pointer between the pages; the page thus picked out contains the prediction, although sometimes it takes three attempts to get an acceptable fortune.

Behind the vihara is a small shrine to **Daun Penh**, the woman credited with founding the sanctuary here (see p.75); the shrine contains her genial image, much revered. The large white chedi contains the ashes of King Ponhea Yat. On the north side of the hill just below the summit is a busy shrine to **Preah Chao**, a Taoist goddess whom people come to ask for good luck, health or success with their business; her helpers, Thien Ly Than (who can see for 1000 miles) and Thuan Phong Nhi (who can hear sounds 1000 miles away), stand close by. Judging by the elaborate **offerings** on the altar, requests are obviously granted – it's not unusual to see whole cooked chickens, surrounded by their cooked innards and unlaid eggs offered on plates. Resident **monkeys** are very good at stealing the offerings, and feeding them is said to be a good way of acquiring merit for the next life, as is releasing the tiny birds which hawkers sell from cages all around the hill – you may spot a Cambodian buying up the entire cage – although it is rumoured that the birds are trained to fly back to their cages once released.

For thirty years, **Sam Bo**, the much loved 50-year-old elephant at Wat Phnom, gave rides around the base of the hill, was fed endless bananas and posed placidly for countless photos. However, at the time of writing, the authorities announced that Sam Bo was a disruption to the traffic, and had to move elsewhere. For now she is lodging by Naga World complex, but where she will end up is uncertain.

Around Wat Phnom

During the colonial era, Wat Phnom was at the heart of the **French quarter**, its leafy boulevards graced by public buildings, offices and villas for the administrators. Many of these structures survive today and the immediate area is worth exploring to get a taste of their historic grandeur.

Phnom Penh's **main post office** is housed in a fine colonial building to the east of Wat Phnom, on Street 13. Dating from the early twentieth century, it occupies one side of a colonial square just off the river which in pre-Khmer Rouge years bustled with cafés and restaurants; an attempt is being made to resurrect the area, but there's a little way to go yet. The post office itself was restored in 2001; an old photograph of the interior hangs on the wall inside, the counters shown still recognizable today, though in other respects the building has had numerous makeovers.

West along Street 92 from Wat Phnom, the **National Library** (daily 8am–5pm) is a fine colonial building dating from 1924. During Pol Pot's regime, books from the library's collection were either destroyed or tossed out onto the pavement, and the building was turned into a stable. In the 1980s, the Vietnamese filled up the

Hello, what-is-your-name?

Alhough you may be approached by older people who learnt French at school, they represent the fortunate few who survived the murder of the educated during the Pol Pot era, when the number of French-speakers in Cambodia was drastically reduced. In the aftermath, the emphasis began to switch to English, as the arrival of UNTAC and the NGOs gave rise to a demand for English-speaking interpreters. Nowadays computers, tourism and Cambodia's membership of the Association of Southeast Asian Nations (ASEAN), whose working language is English, are driving the rush to learn the language.

English is now taught in **state schools**, though cursorily at best, so parents who can afford it send their children to supplementary English-language classes at private institutions immediately after school hours, with adults piling in to take courses after the children leave at 5pm. At 1000–1500 riel an hour, these lessons are an expensive business for many, but the outlay is regarded as a good investment, comprehension of English being perceived as essential to getting a decent job. Thanks to massive demand, any establishment with a few desks and chairs can set itself up as a language school, and the shortage of qualified teachers means that the instructor is often only a couple of study books ahead of their students. Classes are advertised on signs and banners in Phnom Penh and all major towns; the place to glimpse them being conducted in the capital is **Street 164**, parallel to and just north of Charles de Gaulle Boulevard, near Psar Orussey.

Although learning by rote is the norm in Cambodia, many students in the cities now have a reasonable understanding of English; elsewhere though, teaching is at best rudimentary and it is still possible that you'll encounter giggling children rattling off the well-worn phrase "Hello, what is your name?" before running off, without any expectation of a reply.

shelves with their own books, though barely a decade later these were bound with string and sold by the kilo. It's now the French who are helping to gradually re-stock the still rather bare library (though again with titles in their own language). The ground floor is busy with students hard at work in term time. A room off the ground-floor reading room contains a collection of rare palm-leaf manuscripts, the colour of parchment, and the walls are decorated with some nice etchings and photos of the country from the early twentieth century. The Archive Centre, in a building behind the library, sometimes has exhibitions of newly restored material. A few minutes' walk from here, at the western end of Street 92, the **Raffles Hotel Le Royal** is a fabulous blend of colonial, Khmer and Art Deco styles, set in lush tropical gardens; its conservatory is a delightful spot to take morning coffee or afternoon tea.

The **train station**, a little way to the southwest, occupies a commanding position facing the boulevard which runs between streets 106 and 108 all the way to the river. Built in the early 1930s, it has an impressive Art Deco facade, but there's little activity here aside from the freight trains running to and from Kampot (see box, p.81). The unmistakeable blue chedi in front of the station, **Preah Sakyamoni**, contains a sliver of a bone of Buddha, while behind the station, an old 1929 steam train has been restored and put on permanent display. The train was used until the early 1990s when diesel locomotives were introduced.

Traditional healers can be seen at work in front of the station, treating patients either by "coining", scraping the flesh of arms, back or chest with a copper disc to cause raised blood vessels; or "cupping", the alternative therapy championed in the West by Gwyneth Paltrow, where a heated glass jar is applied to the back, chest or forehead, causing raised red circles of flesh. Headaches, cold and flu symptoms, general aches and pains – indeed, just about any ailment – are claimed to be treatable by these methods.

Around Chroy Chung Va Bridge

Despite a smattering of colonial buildings, the area **north of Wat Phnom** is not an especially attractive part of the city, but it's worth a short detour for historical reasons. The **Chroy Chung Va Bridge** spanning the Tonle Sap was blown up in 1973 either by (depending on who you believe) Lon Nol forces attempting to hold off the Khmer Rouge from entering the city, or by the advancing Khmer Rouge forces. Known thenceforth as *spean bak*, "broken bridge", locals often now refer to it as *chuowa chuoul hauwy*, "not broken anymore". To expats it is the "Japanese Bridge", as it was rebuilt with funds from Japan in 1993.

The traffic island at the northern end of Monivong Boulevard, just before the bridge, contains the city's most bizarre monument. In 1999, the government, concerned about the proliferation of firearms, seized all the guns it could lay its hands on and, amid great political fanfare, had them crushed. The remains were melted down and a sculpture of a **revolver** with a knot tied in its barrel was cast; however, cynics say that only the broken guns were smashed and that the good ones were handed out to the police and military.

Screened by high white walls, you'll see the **French Embassy** on the western side of Monivong, just south of the traffic circle. In April 1975, eight hundred foreigners and six hundred Cambodians took refuge here from the Khmer Rouge, whereupon they were held hostage and denied diplomatic privileges. Eventually, foreigners and Cambodian women married to foreign men were released and escorted to the airport. Cambodian men married to foreign women had to remain, never to be seen again.

Eating

Phnom Penh has a vast range of places to eat, from noodle shops and market stalls, where you can fill up for a few thousand riel, to sophisticated Western places where prices for a main course rise to $15–20. In addition many guesthouses have small, if usually undistinguished, restaurants.

Restaurants

On the whole, the food in Phnom Penh is of a reasonable standard, so you're unlikely to go far wrong if you pick somewhere to eat at random. The bustling **riverfront and Sisowath Quay** are lined with cafés, restaurants and bars serving cuisine from all corners of the world. The attractive location means you need to pick carefully if you're on a budget, with the cheapest single-course meals going for $4–5. **Boeng Keng Kang**, broadly Street 278 from streets 51 to 63, is packed with swish cafés, refined but reasonably priced restaurants and bars, and the atmosphere is more laidback than the riverfront (where the myriad of vendors and beggars can get a little wearing). For fine-dining on imported meat and wine, there are some noteworthy **French restaurants** as well as some fancy fusion establishments; even though they're expensive in Cambodian terms they cost a fraction of what you would pay in the West.

A great place to fill up and try a selection of **traditional Khmer dishes** is at one of the **markets**; try the Central Market and Psar Kabkoh; the latter is a few blocks southeast of Independence Monument and dozens of sellers cook into the early evening. Most Cambodians come here to buy takeaway meals, but small plastic stools are ubiquitous and should suffice as a dining room. For *sop chhnang day*, where you cook meat and vegetables in a pot of stock at your table, there are plenty of establishments to try on Monivong and Sihanouk boulevards.

Phnom Penh has lots of good **Chinese** restaurants. **Street 136**, west of Psar Thmei, is home to a cluster of inexpensive – and roaringly popular – Chinese places. For a slap-up meal, several of the deluxe hotels have excellent Chinese restaurants. There are plenty of **Indian**, **Pakistani** and **Bangladeshi** places to eat in town, which are especially popular with the expat community. The city boasts a staggering variety of **Western restaurants**, and it's easy to eat something different every night, from pizza and pasta to grilled steaks and crunchy salads. Unsurprisingly, French food is particularly good.

In addition to sit-down meals, stalls and roadside vendors sell simple noodle and rice dishes for roughly 3000 riel to take away, while fresh baguettes and rolls are sold in the markets in the morning and are available all day around the city from

Prices

Eating **inexpensively** is not difficult in Phnom Penh if you stick to market stalls, simple Cambodian restaurants and some of the Indian and Chinese places listed in this guide. Using these you can eat for $2.50 to $5. In backpacker guesthouses you'll be able to eat for about $3–4, but once you venture into tourist-centred and Western-oriented establishments prices rise and you'll be looking at around $4–6 for a simple main course. In slightly plusher places, and those with a prestigious location, expect to pay upwards of $6–10 for a main course, maybe slightly more depending on what you choose. The **most expensive** places to eat are in the restaurants of the premier hotels and in a few French restaurants around town, where you should expect to pay $15–20 and above for a main course, with extra for vegetables and accompaniments.

Eating with a conscience

There are several cafés and restaurants around town that either train the underprivileged in the hospitality trade or donate profits to helping those in need. These establishments are moderately priced, so expect to pay around $10 for a starter and main course. All places listed here are shown on the maps on p.79 or p.86.

Café Yejj 170 Street 450, across the road from Psar Toul Tom Poung. Serving Siem Reap coffee, with free refills, along with Western bistro-style food, panini and wraps. The café helps women at risk by providing them with training and support. Daily 7am–6pm.

Friends (Mith Samlanh) 215 Street 13, near the National Museum. Trains street-youths in the restaurant and catering trade; tapas, Western and Cambodian snacks, shakes, iced coffees and great cocktails. Daily 11am–11pm.

Le Café du Centre Street 184, in the grounds of the French Cultural Centre. Serving sandwiches, daily specials, cakes and ice creams, this is another project of the street children's NGO Mith Samlanh. Daily 8am–9pm.

Le Lotus Blanc 152 Street 51. This vocational training restaurant, run by the charity Pour un Sourire d'Enfant, serves an extensive range of French and Asian dishes from $5, and has a good quality all-you-can-eat weekend buffet. Profits support the children from former Stung Meanchey rubbish dump, where the original centre still runs a restaurant (7min from the *Intercontinental Hotel*). Call ⓣ012/508537 for more information.

Rabbit Café Street 278. A lively little café open during the day, where you will be served delicious drinks and cakes by disabled Cambodian children who have been rescued and trained by the organization. Sells T-shirts and pictures.

Romdeng 47 Street 174, near Monivong Blvd. This non profit training school for former street-youths serves up Cambodian fare in a colonial villa. Lunch and dinner Monday–Saturday.

hawkers with handcarts. Fresh fruit can be bought from markets and at the specialist stalls on Monivong Boulevard south of Sihanouk, and on Sihanouk Boulevard itself southwest of the Olympic Stadium. To **self-cater**, it's easy enough to buy fresh produce and tinned goods from the markets; to buy Western provisions such as cheese, yoghurt, chocolate, and even brown bread, you'll have to go to one of the supermarkets listed on p.115.

Around Psar Thmei

East India Curry 9 Street 114. Extensive range of moderately priced dishes, all enticingly presented on banana leaves; excellent vegetarian options too, including a generous vegetarian thali.

Mamak's 18 Street 114. Since opening in 1992, this inexpensive halal Malaysian restaurant has become something of a Phnom Penh institution. *Roti chanai*, a paper-thin bread cooked on a griddle and eaten with curry sauce, is a popular breakfast dish, washed down with *teh tarek*, a sweet, milky-red tea, or *teh thomada*, the same but without the sweet milk. At midday they lay out an array of dishes to choose from, including spicy fish steaks, crispy fried chicken and plenty of vegetable dishes.

Peking Canteen 93 Street 136. The modest setting is more than made up for by the food, with divine steamed spring rolls and excellent beef with green peppers. Veggies should try their noodles with "special sauce" – a tasty soy and peanut dressing. Portions are plentiful and cheap.

Sam Doo 56–58 Kampuchea Krom Blvd. The basic surroundings bely the delicious fare, including juicy Szechuan prawns with a spicy dressing, Peking duck and renowned dim sum. Depending on your choice of food, and hunger level, it's an inexpensive to moderately priced establishment.

The riverfront

Bopha Phnom Penh (Titanic) Sisowath Quay, just south of the Tourist Boat Dock. A huge, decadent restaurant and lounge bar with an open front looking over the Tonle Sap. Gilt furnishings, wide wicker chairs and ornamental water features abound, and the food is perfectly good, but the main reason to go is the nightly apsara performance between 7 and 9pm.

Chi Cha 27 Street 110, near Psar Chas. Excellent budget Indian restaurant: for $3.50

you get a meat curry and a vegetable dish, roti, rice, dhal and salad, plus free second helpings of roti or rice.

Happy Herbs Pizza 345 Sisowath Quay ⓣ023/362349. This place has been running for years and still serves up the best pizza in town (and good vegetarian choices). Pizza can be made "happy" – with a marijuana-infused butter baste – for $1. Also does tasty pasta dishes, plus omelettes, pork chops and steak for a moderate price. Call for free delivery.

Khmer Borane 389 Sisowath Quay, near the corner with Street 184. In a prime riverfront spot this unpretentious restaurant serves up great Khmer food. The staff are attentive, the food well prepared (the fish *amok* is superb) and the prices economical.

La Marmite 80 Street 108. A sweet little corner bistro not far from the night market, with a fine, mostly French menu, wine list and the best *crème brûlée* in town. The staff are affable and efficient; main courses will set you back $6–8.

La P'tite France 8 Street 118. A quaint Parisian-style bistro just off the main quayside that will entice you to return. The chef, Didier, is proud of his entirely home-made menu, boasting beautifully prepared French classics and some fabulous desserts and pastries.

P + K 319 Sisowath Quay. Reasonably priced Khmer food with some concessions to the Western palette, but still popular with the local crowd. The picture menu is a big help. The stir-fried pork with ginger and sweet-and-sour fish are firm favourites.

Pop Café da Giorgio 371 Sisowath Quay, near the *FCC*. This tiny Italian restaurant is where the expats come to eat authentic pasta and other Italian dishes. What it lacks in size, it more than makes up for in atmosphere and the quality of its moderately priced food. Open 11am–2.30pm & 6–11pm.

Around the National Museum and Royal Palace

Alley Cat Café Street 19Z. At the end of a quiet alleyway behind the National Museum, this rocking café dishes up enormous breakfasts and Mexican dishes, and has recently started a steak night with beef imported from New Zealand. A great place to hang out for a few happy-hour beers.

Ebony Apsara 42 Street 178. A charming little café/bar serving a selection of local dishes and fresh juices. The back of the café is taken over by a small shop that sells a beautiful collection of handmade clothes and accessories. Well worth a look.

Frizz 67 Street 240. The menu at this small but excellent, moderately priced restaurant helpfully includes an accurate English translation of Cambodian dishes. The *chhnang phnom pleung*, "volcano pot", a table-top charcoal brazier, on which you can cook your own meat and vegetables is worth trying. Also does cookery courses (see p.114 for details).

Le Wok 33 Street 178. Chic French fusion restaurant connected with the Silk & Pepper boutique next door. Impeccable service and dishes like the sautéed chicken cooked with cashew nuts make it a real fine-dining experience. Also has reasonably priced lunch menus, with two courses and a drink for $10.

Tamarind 31 Street 240. This breezy restaurant done up in the colours and tiles of North Africa serves excellent tagines and a mouthwatering selection of tapas dishes and meze platters. The baklava with rum and raisin ice cream is heaven. Try and get a table on the upper terrace and enjoy a cocktail looking over the street.

Around Wat Phnom

La Volpaia Place de la Poste. Opposite the post office and *Van's*, this no-frills family Italian keeps it simple and delicious, and boasts a great French and Italian wine list to accompany the pasta and pizza dishes.

Van's Place de la Poste. In a beautiful, restored colonial property opposite the post office, this is French cuisine at its best in the city (with a price tag to match). Service has the kind of high-brow flair you'd expect in Paris and the food is traditional, rich and extravagant, a good example being the fois gras and truffle *crème brûlée*.

Around Psar Orussey and the Olympic Stadium

Beef Soup Restaurant *Favour Hotel*, Monivong Blvd. Locals reckon this is the best place for *sop chhnang day* in town; the beef version – as the restaurant's name suggests – is the house speciality and will set you back around $6 per person for one plate each of all the accompaniments, which include thinly sliced meat, several plates of vegetables – including mushrooms, noodles, tofu and a bubbling pot of stock. The waitresses will help you with the protocol, or just copy the locals.

Mama's 10 Street 111. Between *Capitol* and *Narin* guesthouses, *Mama's* has become a bit of an institution – the expansive Cambodian landlady dishes up traditional Khmer and French food from a French-language menu. Great place for breakfast before catching the early bus.

Nouveau Pho de Paris 258 Monivong Blvd. An enduring favourite, this popular Chinese, Cambodian and Vietnamese restaurant serves up huge steaming bowls of tasty *pho*, spring rolls with a dipping sauce of chilli and ground peanuts, and succulent crispy duck, to name but a few for around $3–4 each. There's a picture menu, and the waiters also speak English.
Origami 84 Sothearos Blvd, just north of the Vietnamese Friendship Memorial. The delicious sashimi platters at this smart, minimalist Japanese restaurant go for around $20 each, and should feed two people comfortably. There is a varied à la carte menu to join it. It's not cheap, but the fish is first rate if you feel like splashing out.
Royal India 21 Street 111. This simple, friendly restaurant dishes up consistently good and reasonably priced Indian food. The comprehensive menu includes chicken and mutton curries, freshly made samosas and good sweet lassis.

Around the Independence Monument

Boat Noodle 2 8 Street 294. Smart Khmer and Thai restaurant set out across endless levels, one table lets you view your friends on the other side through a tropical fish tank. Good Thai green curry and formal service.
Garden Centre 2 4 Street 57. Soothing water fountains relax the mind while plates of moderately priced salads and tasty toasted panini satisfy the stomach. Closed Tues.
Khmer Kitchen 25 Street 310 ⓣ012/712541. The best-value food in a rather expensive district. In an attractive garden courtyard, this traditional Khmer restaurant offers an extensive range of soups, stir-fries and curries, plus one-dish rice meals from as little as $2.50. A real find.
K'nyay 25 Street 268. This place does one of the best sweet potato, pumpkin and coconut curries in the city, and the vegetarian delicacies don't stop there; indeed almost the entire menu is dedicated to finding exciting ways to present vegan and vegetarian diners with delicious results. Closed Sundays.
Magnolia 55 Street 51. Served with style at this breezy courtyard restaurant, the mouth watering menu of Vietnamese and Thai delicacies offers real value for money. The $6 tom *yam soup* is excellent and will feed two with rice. Breakfast *pho ha noi* costs a bargain $2.50.
Malis 136 Norodom Blvd ⓣ023/221022. This trendy, upmarket Cambodian restaurant is unique in Phnom Penh, with its stylish modern building and tables around a raised pond in the courtyard. Popular with wealthier Khmers and the city's expat business and NGO workers, it serves traditional and modern Khmer food, such as scallops cooked in banana blossom, from 7am–11pm. It's not cheap though; a breakfast of *geautieuv sop* and coffee will set you back around $4, while dinner dishes start at $8 and rise steadily.
Nature and Sea Corner of streets 51 and 278, above *Herb Café*. A pale green oasis of calm at the top of two steep flights of stairs. The terrace restaurant is always balmy and peaceful above the roar of the street, with a first-rate view of Wat Lanka and delicious fruit shakes from $2. Crêpes, sandwiches and salads, all organic, make up the rest of the menu.
New Maharaja 11 Street 278. An impeccable Indian, Pakistani and Bangladeshi restaurant serving big portions of very good curries, soups and many of the traditional starters such as delicious vegetable samosas. One curry, rice and naan bread is enough for two.
Shiva Shakti 70 Sihanouk Blvd, near the Independence Monument. Classical Indian-Mogul cuisine in an upmarket setting, with specialities including tender kebabs and tandoori dishes. Expect to pay upwards of $8 for a single dish with rice and chapati or naan bread. Closed Mon.

South of the centre

Banyan 245 Street 51, next to *Tabitha* (see p.112). The $2 Thai buffet at lunchtime in a garden setting takes some beating; at night you can dine on more expensive, though still moderately priced Thai food under the stars. (This used to be the *Baan Thai* and has a loyal following among NGO workers.)
Khmer-Thai Restaurant 26 Street 135, near Wat Toul Tom Poung. Out on a limb in terms of location, this classy restaurant doesn't advertise, but is still packed out every night by locals in the know. Inexpensive Khmer and Thai food ($3–4 per dish) is served efficiently and in good-sized portions; the fish cakes with chilli dip are enough for two as a starter.
The Local 39 Street 454, southwest of the Russian Market. Recently picked up by an Australian owner, this is fast becoming a kid-friendly expat hangout and is a great place to recuperate after a hot afternoon at the market. Great BBQs, live music and a roof terrace. Its sister bar, the *Local 2*, is on Street 144 just off the riverfront.
Topaz 182 Norodom Blvd, next to Wat Than. Arguably the best French food in Phnom Penh, served in a startlingly modern building, with fine wines and succulent steaks that are exceptional. Expensive, but worth it.

Cafés and coffee shops

Phnom Penh's busy **café** society of the 1950s and 1960s vanished during the war years, but there has now been a massive revival and wherever you are in town you're pretty sure to find a place to have a break. Many are attached to galleries, shops or internet centres and new ones are opening every week, so this is just a selection of what's on offer.

Café Fresco 361 Sisowath Quay, under the *FCC*. Whether you want breakfast pastries, a mid-morning coffee, a smoothie or to create your own lunchtime sandwich (including a choice of breads) you'll be satisfied here. Not the cheapest place in town but given the quality and the location you're unlikely to be disappointed. New branch on corner of streets 51 and 306; daily 7am–8pm.

Comme à la Maison 13 Street 57. Adored by expats and visitors alike, the café is set off the road in a quiet garden and does a roaring trade in fresh bread and pastry. Perfect spot for coffee and a croissant while you read the paper.

Garden Centre Café 23 Street 57 ⓣ023/363002. As befits the name, the potted plants amid the tables in the shady courtyard are for sale, and there's also an extensive daytime menu of moderately priced Western and Asian food, and some excellent vegetarian dishes including appetizing quiches and freshly made salads. Closed Mon.

Java Sihanouk Blvd, east of Independence Monument. As well as full breakfasts with a choice of coffees, this café-gallery does light meals and a delightful range of home-made bagels, muffins and desserts. Changing exhibitions in the gallery feature works by local and foreign artists. The bakery at the back has delicious pastries to take away. *Java* also runs the coffee shop in Monument Books.

The Shop 39 Street 240. More London than Phnom Penh, you'll be hard-pressed to remember where you are. Not only does *The Shop* offer a fantastic café atmosphere, but it has great deli sandwiches and pastries and coffee too. Open 7am–7pm Mon–Sat, 7am–3pm Sun.

Drinking, entertainment and nightlife

Drinking for foreign visitors and expats in Phnom Penh falls loosely into three categories: the seedy, smoky girly bars that proliferate off the Sisowath Quay and along Street 51; the sophisticated, trendy cocktail **bars**, either with a river view or in a prime location in downtown Boeng Keng Kang (BKK); and the lively, more low-key hangouts that often have live music and may double up as pick-up joints, but with an easygoing attitude. The rest of Phnom Penh's **nightlife** is geared to Khmer men only and revolves around girlie bars, karaoke, dance halls and local discos. Under the strobe lights, you'll hear a deafening mix of Thai, Filipino and Western *popas* well as traditional Khmer music and songs – such as those by Cambodia's pop idol, Sin Sisamouth. Ask locals for the most popular spots of the moment; it makes for a fun night especially if, after a few drinks, you want to have a go at the elegantly flowing **rhom vong**, in which the men and women dance side by side, couples one behind the other, a bit like a double conga; the chain slowly progresses around the floor, hands gracefully weaving in and out. These venues are at their best after 10pm; entrance is usually free. Beer girls (see box, p.41) will be on hand to pour the drinks and for pay-as-you-go dances. These places are usually OK for foreigners, as long as you don't get too drunk or obnoxious. Bear in mind too that there is sometimes a thuggish element in places frequented by the rich, bored sons of the Cambodian nouveaux riches. Step on their feet while dancing or stare at their female companions and you may have a real incident on your hands.

Bars and clubs

The bars on and around Sisowath Quay could keep you busy for weeks, but with new nightspots opening across the town, catering for all tastes in ambience, liquor and music, the discerning bar-fly will look beyond the river, particularly around streets 278 and 51. Phnom Penh has an emerging and increasingly blooming **gay scene**, with a few great venues and more appearing.

Black Cat On the corner of Streets 51 and 172. An intimate little bar opposite the *Walkabout* (a girlie bar long since past its heyday) and open past midnight. A few friendly hostesses serve drinks on the leafy terrace, and you may get some live local bands playing for good measure.

Blue Cat Lounge Street 110. Busy from happy hour onwards, this classy bar brings in a happy and raucous crowd. A pool table and a Khmer and Western menu, plus a few nice tables out the front, make it a good place to start your night before moving to the club upstairs.

Blue Chilli 36 Street 178. Extravagant decor and handsome barmen at this all-welcoming gay bar. Now puts on artistic, and very funny, drag shows on Friday and Saturday nights.

Cantina Sisowath Quay. Run by well-known Phnom Penh expat Hurley Scroggins, this no-frills bar and eatery on the riverfront stands out from its immediate neighbours thanks to its cheerful staff, while the crowds sitting outside on the pavement at weekends give the place a party atmosphere.

Chinese House 45 Sisowath Quay, opposite the container dock. A long way up the riverfront, this restored colonial mansion is one of the most exclusive drinking addresses in town. Enjoy expensive but delicious dim sum in the upstairs lounge bar (open from 6pm), washed down with a bottle of good wine. It hosts regular live music in the art gallery below for a discerning clientele. Closed Monday.

Dodo Rhum House 42 Street 178. A brilliant bar that makes its own flavoured rum, open late for a lively crowd.

Elephant Bar *Raffles Hotel Le Royal*, Street 92. Splash out on a cocktail and soak up the 1930s elegance, with ambience and service to match, plus live music from the resident pianist. Happy hour 5–7pm.

Elsewhere 2 Street 278. This bar-restaurant with boutique shop above is definitely worth a mention as, at the time of writing, it was the only bar in town with a pool. The food is awful and the drinks are a little pricey, but they do have a happy hour, and it's a balmy spot to escape the heat of the city. Except on Sundays, when it gets overrun with ex pat families.

Equinox Street 278, just off Street 51. Popular with the young and beautiful, this bar-restaurant in the heart of BKK is currently the hottest address in town, and poses as an impressive small art gallery and live music venue as well.

FCC Phnom Penh Sisowath Quay ⓣ023/210142. Possibly the most atmospheric bar-cum-restaurant in the region (imagine a Southeast Asian version of the bar in *Casablanca*). The balmy air, whirring ceiling fans and spacious armchairs invite one to spend a hot afternoon getting slowly smashed. Relatively pricey; the drinks are worth it, the food is probably not.

Fish Bar On the corner of Sisowath Quay and Street 108. Cool cocktail bar popular with both wealthy Khmers and ex pats, with a good international wine list and fantastic fish and chips.

Green Vespa 95 Sisowath Quay (opposite the Tourist Dock). Popular Irish-owned bar has a huge drinks menu, with icy beers and spicy Bloody Marys; it runs regular promotions and has recently started serving an authentic Sunday roast.

Heart of Darkness 26 Street 51. This overrated bar has been here for ages and is one of those places everybody has to visit once. The gothic decor and eclectic music made it the hipster hangout of Phnom Penh a decade ago, but these days it is frequented by gangs of aggressive, affluent young Khmers. Getting progressively seedier from 7pm onwards, it's not uncommon for fights to break out among the different national factions; don't become another statistic.

Herb Café Corner of streets 51 and 278. Laid back bar/restaurant with a good atmosphere. Even reticent single travellers will be at ease here whiling away a few hours in their comfy chairs while sipping a draught beer or cocktail.

Mary & Jas 59 Street 172. A low-key and extremely cool bar and restaurant, which doubles up as small bookshop and boutique of extravagant dresses. The mood is relaxed, the beats chilled and the spring rolls to die for.

Metro Corner of Sisowath Blvd and Street 148. Another smart, western cocktail bar, with a no-smoking policy before 10pm. Cool ambience, attractive bar staff and delicious, but minimalist, food attract wealthy Khmers and the NGO crowd.

Rubies Corner of streets 19 and 240. Cracking corner bar focussing almost exclusively on good wine and reggae music. An ideal place for an appetizer before, or nightcap after, a slap-up meal along Street 240.

Salt Lounge 217 Street 136. Gay bar and club, just off the waterfront, with an edgy, industrial interior that draws a mixed party bag.

Sharky's 126 Street 130 ⓦwww.sharkysofcambodia.com. Cambodia's longest-running rock-and-roll bar and low-key pick-up spot is a great, lively hangout and serves decent Mexican, Thai and American food. Daily drink specials from 5pm.

Talkin' to a Stranger 21b Street 29. Beer garden, with a great selection of wines and imported beer. Regular live music events. Closed Mon.

Arts and culture

After being virtually obliterated by the Khmer Rouge, Cambodia's artistic and cultural traditions have seen a revival in recent years, thanks largely to the few performers and instructors who survived the regime. **Cultural shows** take place at **Sovanna Phum** (http://shadowpuppets.org), a performing arts society at the corner of streets 99 and 484 that stages performances of classical and folk dance, and shadow puppetry (see p.171) at 7.30pm on weekends ($7). From time to time there are performances of classical dance and shadow puppetry at the **Chatomuk Theatre**, on the riverfront near the *Cambodiana*. See the *Phnom Penh Post* and Friday's *Cambodia Daily* for details of what's on.

The former king Norodom Sihanouk was once an avid film-maker, and after the years of cultural repression, Phnom Penh is taking up the mantle again: October 2010 saw the launch of the first annual **Cambodian International Film Festival** (ⓦwww.cambodia-iff.com), with screenings of 120 films from 30 countries at theatres and outdoor arenas throughout the city. There are high hopes that subsequent years will be even bigger and better attended. There are several **cinemas** in the city – one on the fifth floor of Sorya Mall, Street 63, near Psar Thmei, has screenings throughout the day, from 9am to 8pm. Regular free screenings of French films, usually subtitled in English, take place at the **French Cultural Centre** at 214 Street 184. *The Flicks* on Street 95 next to *Boddhi Tree Del Gusto* has a large screen and bar, and shows Western films nightly.

Galleries, hosting changing exhibitions of art and sculpture, proliferate, and the magazine *Asia Life* is a good place to find out what is coming up. The **Chinese House** (ⓦwww.chinesehouse.asia) at 45 Sisowath Quay has permanent and temporary exhibitions by Asian artists in a beautifully restored colonial villa, and also hosts live music evenings. **Meta House** at 6 Street 264 (ⓦwww.meta-house.com) is unique as a night gallery and is open Friday and Saturday night (from 6pm until late) with exhibitions of contemporary Asian fine arts, multimedia and light installations. **Reyum** at 47 Street 178, near the National Museum (ⓦwww.reyum.org), in conjunction with the **Institute of Fine Arts and Culture**, puts on exhibitions of work by Cambodian students; these could be art or a display based on someone's research project. Also on the corner of streets 178 and 13, opposite the park in front of the National Museum is **Asasax Art**, which showcases collections by local modern artists and sells some attractive prints.

Shopping

Phnom Penh is the best place to shop in Cambodia, with **traditional markets** selling everything from beautiful **silk** *sampots* – the word for both the traditional Khmer skirt and a sufficient length of fabric to make one – which a **tailor** can then make up into garments of your own design, to myriad hand-crafted wooden, stone and silver-crafted trinkets. Contemporary woodcarvings and marble statues make bulky souvenirs, but are so evocative of Cambodia that it's hard not to pick up one or two, and you will see hundreds of intricate (usually low-grade) silver pots in the shape of animals on sale, which tuck more neatly into backpack or suitcase.

Jewellery is sold in abundance too, gold and silver, set with stones and gems in all imaginable designs and colours, and there are wonderful **antiques and curios** to be discovered, both originals and replicas of old wooden pagoda statues and a huge assortment of decorative boxes and trunks. **Haggling** is an essential part of market shopping, with prices starting ludicrously high, and it's worth checking around a few stalls as they will often sell identical pieces.

If you can't bear the hassle of the market, there are an increasing number of classy **boutiques** selling clothes, jewellery and soft furnishings particularly around BKK and Street 240, and Sihanouk Boulevard, near Lucky Supermarket, has several designer stores, including Lacoste, and a branch of the high-street store Mango will be opening there soon. Street 178 is known as "Art Street", as dozens of little warehouses sell an array of **paintings and small sculptures**, created for the tourist market. Alternatively, head to Sorya, Golden Sorya or Paragon **malls**, where you can find everything from underwear to sportswear.

Psar Toul Tom Poung

This is also known as the **Russian Market**, because all its goods used to come from Russia, one of the few countries to provide aid to Cambodia during the Vietnam occupation. The collapse of the USSR put paid to cheap imports, but ramshackle, stuffy and tremendous, this market retains its reputation as *the* place to buy textiles, antiques and silver – not to mention motorbike parts. It is a haven bursting with stalls selling bootleg DVDs, fake designer bags, silver jewellery, Chinese-style furniture, photocopied books, handicrafts and piles of multicoloured silks that can be bought for a few dollars and taken to a tailor to be transformed into dresses and jackets. You'll find these stalls at the south end of the market; book sellers along the west, while the north is taken over with hardware stalls, a small food quarter and mechanics workshops, where men fix up motorbikes in tiny cubicles, revving the engines and filling the stalls around them with smoke. The market is old and crumbling, but a government plan to rebuild it has been shelved for the time being. It is charming in its dilapidation, though a very unsafe place to work with a high fire risk and narrow exit routes.

Psar Thmei

The Central Market, as it is also known, is currently in the final stages of reconstruction following a devastating fire that all but destroyed it three years ago. The original architectural design has been maintained; painted daffodil yellow, it comprises a circular central hall where brightly-lit jewellery stalls have been reinstated and display sunglasses and row upon row of watches (look out for the one with the King's face on), gold and silver necklaces, rings and pendants, most of them set with glittering gem stones. The four arms that radiate off the main hall specialize mainly in T-shirts, caps, shoes and electrical goods, with the eastern wall largely devoted to plants and flowers. It is a smelly and eye-opening experience to stroll through the food market here, where every type of meat, fish, fruit and vegetable can be bought. There are some small stands selling dishes for a few thousand riel.

Local markets

A new **night market** along the riverfront between streets 106 and 108 opens on Friday and Saturday nights, popular mainly with local youngsters selling clothes, such as the ubiquitous *krama*, the traditional Cambodian scarf. This is a good place to go native, and enjoy a **meal** on the mats laid out by street hawkers at the western end as the sun goes down.

The most easily accessible of the local daily markets are **Psar Chas**, on the corner of Street 13 and Ang Duong, and **Psar Kandal**, near Wat Ounalom. where you

Shopping with a conscience

Numerous NGOs, other organizations and some private individuals have shops and outlets that directly help street children, women at risk and/or the disabled and other disadvantaged groups.

Cambodian Craft (aka **Chamber of Professional and Micro-Enterprises of Cambodia**) Wat Phnom (just off Norodom Boulevard). This co-operative provides training and support to rural villagers. Their Phnom Penh premises, housed in a beautiful 70-year-old traditional building on the south side of Wat Phnom traffic circle, host regular exhibitions and occasional demonstrations by artisans. The outlet has recently been given a face-lift and is well stocked with quality silverware, baskets, ceramics and textiles.

Daughters 65 Street 178 (opposite National Museum). This little boutique sells interesting jewellery and other accessories and doubles up as a spa and boutique and occasionally hosts temporary **art exhibitions**. The shop is run by women who have been rescued from the sex trafficking industry, and profits go towards saving other victims. You can sponsor a girl and or donate directly to the foundation.

Friends N' Stuff 213 Street 13 (two doors up from *Friends* restaurant). A new branch of the Friends family, the shop sells clothes, bags, jewellery and secondhand books, and also has a nail salon.

Mekong Quilts 49 Street 240 (one block west of *Silver Pagoda*). Brightly coloured quilts, cushions and throws in every pattern imaginable, made by impoverished women from the provinces who receive the profits of their work. Mekong Plus, the NGO behind the outlet, provides scholarships and promotes health initiatives in remote villages of the Svay Rieng province.

NCDP (National Centre of Disabled Persons) Compound of the Ministry for Women's Affairs, Norodom Boulevard, just south of junction with Kramuon Sar. A retail outlet for quality products made by disabled (primarily land-mine-disabled) people throughout the country. Especially worth visiting for the silk bags, purses and hanging mobiles.

Nyemo Stall 14, Psar Toul Tom Poung (south side). Unique designs of soft furnishings, accessories, bags and toys, with profits helping to train and support vulnerable women.

Peace Handicrafts 39c Street 155, near Psar Toul Tom Poung. Land-mine- and polio-disabled people produce carefully crafted silk items for sale in their co-operative shop.

Rajana Street 450, near Psar Toul Tom Poung. Sales of silk and bamboo crafts and jewellery help to support the NGOs' Fair Trade training programmes.

Rehab Craft 1 Street 278, Women with disabilities and victims of land mines sell a variety of high-quality silver, wood and stone items here, as well as some silk scarves and attractive leather goods,

Tabitha-Cambodia Corner of streets 51 and 360. This not-for-profit NGO-run outlet sells super silks made into garments and soft furnishings, cards, packed coffee and more. It operates by training disadvantaged women to sew. They then work from home and Tabitha purchases their output.

Tooït Tooït Stall 312, Psar Toul Tom Poung (main aisle, west side of the market). Supporting parents so that their children can go to school, the items on sale include shopping bags, beads and toys made from recycled materials such as newspapers, plastic bags and rice sacks.

Watthan Artisans Cambodia (WAC) Wat Than, 180 Norodom Blvd. A co-operative of disabled artisans who produce a range of handicrafts: silk scarves, home furnishings, woodcarvings and basketwork are just some of the items available for purchase.

can buy basics, fruit and vegetables and get a cheap meal; **Psar Kabkoh**, south of Sihanouk Boulevard on Street 9 is much the same, with a number of good food vendors. **Psar Olympic**, off Street 199 southwest of the Olympic Stadium, is visited by people from all over the country who make wholesale purchases here for resale elsewhere. Vendors from all over Cambodia, selling just about anything from dried fish to televisions, trade at the newly constructed **Psar Orussey** on Street 182, a sprawling place on two floors and a mezzanine. The stalls are crammed together and it can be confusing to find your way around, but the merchandise here is a good bit cheaper than at other markets. The adjacent Street 166 is big on traditional Khmer medicine shops, where leaves, tree bark and various animal parts are sold as tonics, the commodities usually boiled in water or soaked in wine.

Malls and Boutiques

For a more relaxed shopping experience, there are a growing number of smart boutiques and shops across the town, particularly on and around streets 240 and 278. Bliss, 29 Street 240, is a boutique specializing in fashionable women's wear. Tabitha, 26 Street 294, produces Western-style clothes from Cambodian textiles – it particularly prides itself on the range of scarves and shawls. Kabas Boutique at 18 Street 282 has a range of clothing in Cambodian fabrics with an on-site tailor who can adjust clothes to fit with a two-day turnaround. It also sells silk accessories and cushions. The shop at the back of Ebony Apsara on Street 178 sells some of the most fashionable clothes and jewellery in town, with only one or two of each piece on sale. For something a little more distinctive, head to one of the city's many privately owned shops and galleries: Northeast Cambodia Souvenir Shop, 52 Street 240, sells goods made with textiles from Rattanakiri, while across the road at 87 Street 240, Art Steel has rather cute, hand-painted pressed-steel geckos, for mounting on the wall (or ceiling).

The malls, Paragon and Sorya, are more like huge department stores, selling sportswear, electrical equipment; Sorya also has a cinema and a roller skating rink. The new Golden Sorya Shopping Centre on Street 51 also sells clothes and electrical goods and has a couple of mini-marts; all the above make good places to witness the local teen culture of flirting over a hamburger.

Listings

Airlines Angkor Airways, 32 Norodom Blvd ⓣ023/222056, ⓦwww.angkorairways.com; Bangkok Airways, 61 Street 214 ⓣ023/722545, ⓦwww.bangkokair.com; China Southern Airlines, A3 Regency Square, 168 Monireth Blvd ⓣ023/424588, ⓦwww.cs-air.com; Dragon Air, A4–A5 Regency Square, 168 Monireth Blvd ⓣ023/424300, ⓦwww.dragonair.com; EVA Air, Suite 11, 14b Street 205 ⓣ023/219911, ⓦwww.evaair.com; Jet Star Asia Airlines, 333b Monivong Blvd ⓣ023/220909, ⓦwww.jetstaraisa.com; Lao Airlines, 58c Sihanouk Blvd ⓣ023/222956, ⓦwww.laoairlines.com; Malaysia Airlines, 1st Floor, *Diamond Hotel*, 172–84 Monivong Blvd ⓣ023/218923, ⓦwww.malaysiaairlines.com; PMTair, Suite 9B, 294 Mao Tse Toung Blvd ⓣ023/224714, ⓦwww.pmtair.com; Royal Khmer Airlines 36B, 245 Mao Tse Toung Blvd ⓣ023/994502, ⓦwww.royalkhmerairlines.com; SilkAir, *Himawari Hotel*, 219b Monivong Blvd, ⓣ023/426808, ⓦwww.silkair.net; Thai Airways, 294 Mao Tse Toung Blvd ⓣ023/214359, ⓦwww.thaiair.com; Vietnam Airlines, 41 Street 214 ⓣ023/363396, ⓦwww.vietnamair.com.

Banks and exchange Acleda Bank, 61 Monivong Blvd and 28 Mao Tse Toung Blvd; ANZ Royal, corner Street 114 (Kramoun Sar) with branches around town; Canadia Bank, 265–269 Street 114 (Ang Duong St); Foreign Trade Bank of Cambodia, 3 Street 114 (Kramoun Sar). There are 24hr ATMs at the Acleda, ANZ and Cambodian Asia (branches around town) banks but they charge $4 handling fee for international cards. At the time of writing, Canadia Bank had the only ATM that didn't charge a handling fee. Western Union has branches all over town where you can exchange travellers' cheques, receive/make money transfers and get money on Visa and MasterCard (US dollars only). Exchange booths around town display their rates for dollars into riel; some of the best rates are to be had at Psar Thmei.

Books Monument Books, 111 Norodom Blvd (near Street 240) and 53 Street, for full range of subjects including Cambodia and Southeast Asia; D's Books, branches at 79 Street 240, 12 Street 178 (near the *FCC*) and on Street 93 (BKK) for secondhand books in many languages. Bound photocopies of all varieties of books can be found at Psar Thmei and Psar Toul Tom Poung.

Car rental The Car Rental Co., 49 Street 592 (ⓣ012/950950), has a selection of vehicles available with or without driver.

Cookery courses Learn to prepare traditional Khmer food with a choice of courses at Cambodia Cooking Class, 14 Street 285 (ⓣ023/882314), or book through *Frizz* restaurant, 67 Street 240 (ⓣ023/220953).

Dentists International SOS Medical & Dental Clinic, 161 Street 51 (ⓣ023/216911), has English-speaking staff. European Dental Clinic, 160a Norodom Blvd (ⓣ023/211363, emergency 012/854408), Mon–Sat 8am–noon & 2–7pm, has French, Thai and Khmer dentists.

Doctors English is spoken at the excellent but expensive International SOS Medical & Dental Clinic, 161 Street 51 (ⓣ023/216911, ⓦwww.internationalsos.com), 8am–5.30pm Mon–Fri, 8am–noon Sat; Naga Medical Centre, 11 Street 254 (ⓣ023/211360 or 011/811 1175, ⓦwww.nagaclinic.com; 24hr); Tropical and Travellers Medical Clinic, near Wat Phnom at 88 Street 108 (ⓣ023/366802).

Embassies and consulates Australia, 16B National Assembly ⓣ023/213470, ⓦwww.cambodia.embassy.gov.au; Canada, ⓦwww.phnompenh.gc.ca; Great Britain, 29 Street 75 ⓣ023/427124, ⓦhttp://ukincambodia.fco.gov.uk/en/; Laos, 15–17 Mao Tse Toung Blvd ⓣ023/982632; Thailand, 196 Norodom Blvd ⓣ023/726306, ⓦhttp://www.thaiembassy.org; US, corner of streets 96 and 51 ⓣ023/728000, ⓦwww.cambodia.usembassy.gov; Vietnam, 426 Monivong Blvd ⓣ023/362531.

Emergencies Ambulance ⓣ119 (from an 023 phone) or 023/724891; fire ⓣ118 (from an 023 phone) or 023/786693; police ⓣ117 (from an 023 phone) or 023/724793; hotline for the police to report child exploitation (national and in Phnom Penh) ⓣ023/997919 – English is spoken on all these numbers.

Hospitals American Medical, 7 Street 282 ⓣ012/891613; Calmette, north end of Monivong Blvd ⓣ023/426948.

Internet access There are internet cafés all over town. Rates are typically around $1 per hour.

Kick boxing Reproduced on the bas-reliefs of Angkor Wat, the ancient tradition of kick boxing is now enjoying a revival. Bouts start with loud music and much posturing by the contestants – though watching the animated antics of the crowd, for whom betting on the fight is the main attraction, can be as fascinating as the fights. Ask at your hotel or guesthouse for details of forthcoming bouts, which are advertised in the Khmer press.

Mail and courier services The main post office, on Street 13, between streets 98 and 102 (Mon–Sat 7am–6pm), provides the full range of services, including parcel post, fax, telephones and poste restante. There's a booth inside where you can buy aerogrammes, postcards, envelopes, writing paper and stamps. You can courier material abroad using EMS, Ministry of Posts and Telecommunications, corner of streets 13 and 102 (ⓣ023/427428), which offers an efficient and cost-effective service. Alternatively, try TNT (ⓣ023/430923), DHL (ⓣ023/427726), UPS (ⓣ023/427511) or Fedex (ⓣ023/216712).

Massage and spa Many massage parlours double as brothels, but there are now a number of reputable private spas where you can get a massage, aromatherapy, body scrubs and other treatments. Amret Spa, 3 Street 57 (ⓣ023/727997994), and Aziadée, 16a Street 282 (ⓣ023/996921), both have jacuzzis and offer a range of treatments. Slightly more expensive is Sayana Rumdul, 1 Street 282 (ⓣ023/727158), with waxing, steam rooms, and all styles of massage. Seeing Hands, set up with the help of an NGO which works with the blind in Cambodia, offer anma, Thai and shiatsu massage and reflexology; they're at 6 Street 178, just around the corner from the *FCC* (ⓣ012/234519; daily 8am–10pm; $7 per hour), and at 12 Street 13, opposite the post office (ⓣ012/680934; same times and price).

Meditation and yoga One-hour silent meditation sessions are held at Wat Lanka (Mon & Thurs at 6pm, Sun at 8.30am), supervised by English-speaking monks. Some wats have more yoga-orientated meditation classes, and NataRaj Yoga at 52 Street 302 has yoga and pilates classes for $9 per session.

Motorbike rental Adventure Moto, 16 Street 136 (ⓣ012/1896729, ⓦwww.adventure-moto.com), a

Western-run outfit with smart new bikes, from $8 per day for a city runabout to $50 per day for a powerful off-roader; 24/7 support; tours organized. Lucky! Lucky!, 413 Monivong Blvd (Ⓣ012/939601), charges $5 per day for a 110cc moped and $9 per day for a 250cc off-road bike, with discounts on rentals of a week or longer. Helmets are provided, but no insurance.

Opticians Opticians cluster along Sihanouk Boulevard near Lucky Supermarket, and in general offer a speedy and proficient service. Modern Optics, corner of Sihanouk Blvd and Street 63, has a good reputation, or try I Care Optical, 166 Norodom Blvd Ⓣ023/215778.

Pharmacies Pharmacie de la Gare, corner of Monivong and Pochentong boulevards (daily 8.30am–6pm), has English-speaking pharmacists and a good selection of Western drugs; they accept credit cards. U-Care has two branches with English-speaking pharmacists: corner Sothearos Blvd and Street 178, and corner of Sihanouk Blvd and Street 55.

Photography and film There are outlets all over town, with some of the better ones on Monivong Blvd, near Psar Thmei.

Police For foreigners and tourists Ⓣ012/942484.

Private bus companies A couple of reliable private companies operate 12 or 15-seater VIP express buses to destinations around the country including Sihanoukville, Poipet (via Siem Reap) and Rattanakiri. Contact Hua Lian on Charles de Gaulle Blvd, just north of the Olympic Stadium (Ⓣ023/880761 or 012/376807), or Ly Heng Express (and Mekong Tours), corner of Street 106 and Sisowath Quay (Ⓣ023/991726).

Running The Hash House Harriers meet on Sundays at 2.15pm outside the train station (Ⓦwww.p2h3.com).

Supermarkets Lucky, on Sihanouk Boulevard near the corner of Monivong (daily 8am–9pm) also has a branch on the ground floor of Sorya Mall, good for toiletries and delicatessen food. Slightly lower prices at You Nam (daily 8am–8pm), 400m southwest of the train station on Kampuchea Krom Boulevard on Monivong Boulevard between streets 178 and 184 (daily 8am–9pm), has a good choice of wines and spirits. Bayon Supermarket, 133–35 Monivong Blvd, near the intersection with Kampuchea Krom (daily 7am–8pm), does a good selection of cheeses and other chilled products. Total and Caltex Star petrol stations have mini-markets.

Swimming The *Blue Lime*, *Cambodiana*, *Goldiana* and *Phnom Penh* hotels have pools open to non-residents for around $5 per visit. *Elsewhere* bar has pools, minimum spend $5 on food and drink. The Phnom Penh Water Park on the airport road has water slides and swimming pools.

Taxis Expect to pay $4–5 for a daytime single fare, $5–8 at night, plus waiting time if you ask them to hang around for you. Some now operate a meter system. Bailey's (Ⓣ012/890000) offers reliable 24hr service; Taxi Vantha (Ⓣ023/993433 and 012/855000, Ⓦwww.taxivantha.com) has been operating since 1996; it has an on-call service 24/7 and is also available for long-distance trips; check its website for prices.

Travel agents The following well-established firms employ English-speaking staff and act as both travel agents and domestic tour operators: KU Travel & Tours, 77 Street 240 Ⓣ023/723456, Ⓦwww.kucambodia.com; Mittapheap, 262 Monivong Blvd Ⓣ023/222801, Ⓦwww.mittapheap.com; Neak Krorhom Travel & Tours, 127 Street 108 Ⓣ023/219496, Ⓔnkhtours@hotmail.com.

Visa extensions At the Department for Immigration near the airport; see p.58 for more. Almost all hotels and guesthouses can do this for you for $5–10 commission.

Around Phnom Penh

If you tire of Phnom Penh, a short journey will get you out of town and into a landscape of rice paddies and sugar palms, scattered with small villages and isolated pagodas. The **Chroy Chung Va peninsula**, the tip of land facing the city centre at the confluence of the Tonle Sap and Mekong rivers, is home to a collection of villages and feels very removed from the bustle of central Phnom Penh; its western side, facing the Royal Palace, is being transformed into a riverside park. The southernmost tip is now the property of the Sokha Resort group, where vast concrete foundations are being installed at the time of writing. A short way further northeast, reached by a short ferry trip from Phnom Penh, lies **Koh Dait**, a lush green island in the Mekong, whose inhabitants weave silk and grow a wide variety of produce on the fertile alluvial soil. **Wat Jum Pos Ka-aik**, east of town off National Route 1, has a remarkable collection of ten thousand Buddhas and can be tied in with a trip to **Kien Svay**, a popular riverside village about 12km from the city.

Phnom Brasat, some 27km northwest of town off National Route 5, is home to a kitsch collection of pagodas which are more reminiscent of the work of Salvador Dalí than of classical Khmer architecture – the experience is definitely more theme park than religious. Further north rise the distinctive hills of the old capital **Oudong**, dotted with the chedi of various kings; Khmerophiles might want to combine a trip here with a visit to the scant remains of nearby **Lovek**, its predecessor as capital.

A short moto-ride southwest of the city, the killing fields and memorial at **Choeung Ek** make a logical, if macabre, progression from a visit to the Toul Sleng Genocide Museum. Also south of the city, off National Route 2, the compact Angkorian temple of **Tonle Bati** enjoys a riverside location, and is a good place for a picnic and a swim. Further south, there are spectacular views from the ancient hilltop temple of **Phnom Chisor**. Both sites could be combined as a day-trip, although this means missing out on the tigers and bears at **Phnom Tamau**, Cambodia's only state-run zoo and wildlife rescue centre.

Chroy Chung Va peninsula

The three-kilometre spit of land that makes up the **Chroy Chung Va peninsula** used to be a farming area, though the Phnom Penh municipality has now controversially cleared out the villagers from the western side of the peninsula and turned it into a riverside park, facing the promenade on the city side. It's worth a visit to sip a coconut at one of the refreshment stalls while watching the sunset over the city, along with young lovers who come to spend some illicit time together out of sight of ever-watchful family eyes. If you make your way northeast along the banks of the Mekong you'll pass through several friendly villages inhabited by the **Cham**, Cambodia's Muslim minority.

The peninsula can easily be **reached** by moto ($2 one way); once across the Chroy Chung Va Bridge, take the first right, which heads right around the headland.

Koh Dait

Set in the middle of the Mekong 15km from Phnom Penh, **Koh Dait** is an oasis of calm and tranquillity. Primarily an agricultural community (peanuts are an important cash crop), the ten-kilometre-long island is home to a number of stilt-house villages, and you'll get to see a good cross-section of rural life as you meander along its leafy tracks. The island is noted for its **weaving** of *sampots*, and in the dry season looms clack away beneath the houses. As the river level falls after the rainy season, a wide sandy **beach** (entry $1 for tourists) is exposed at the northern end of the island, where food stalls and picnic huts serve traditional dishes and tasty fried chicken.

The island is easily reached from Phnom Penh by catching a moto, followed by any one of the several **ferries** whose jetties are signposted off National Route 6, about 14km from the city. The ferries run regularly throughout the day, departing when full; motorbikes and bicycles all go aboard with no problem (moto and driver 1500 riel, foot passengers 1000 riel), although most guesthouses also organize group tours ($10 per person) and private cruises run from the tourist dock ($20 per hour).

Wat Jum Pos Ka-aik and Kien Svay beach

The ten thousand Buddha statues at **Wat Jum Pos Ka-aik**, fashioned in just about every possible shape, size and material, were donated by wealthy patrons, from whose gifts the pagoda derives its conspicuous affluence. Indeed, the monks of Wat Jum Pos Ka-aik are much respected and well connected – it's not unusual to find them performing elaborate ceremonies for the dignitaries and well-heeled Cambodians who wish to gain merit in the next life or to receive blessings in this one.

The pagoda is entered through an avenue lined with *devas* (gods) on one side and *asuras* (demons) on the other; the modern-looking **hall** across the compound is where the Buddhas are arrayed in air-conditioned splendour, ranged in tiers from floor to ceiling, and illustrating every one of the forty *mudras* along the way. One of the most sublime images – a life-size standing bronze Buddha – is at the centre of the display towards the front; it wears a benign smile, while its lifelike eyes seem to follow you around the hall. The hands are held out in front of the body, palms facing out with fingers pointed up in *abhaya mudra*, the position of giving protection; a diamond is embedded in the centre of each palm.

If the **vihara** is open, it's worth putting your head inside to see the unusually decorated walls – by Cambodian standards these are stark, painted pale yellow and stencilled with golden Buddha images. A small white stupa nearby, in front of the bathing pool, contains bones found in the pagoda grounds of people murdered by the Khmer Rouge.

Kien Svay

Optimistically hailed by some locals as "the new Kep", **Kien Svay** (or Koki Beach, as it's also known) is really more of a muddy river bank. That said, it positively throngs at weekends with people venturing out from Phnom Penh to picnic at the rows of stilt-huts on the banks of the Mekong. The village is particularly noted for its crispy **fried bugs** – different sorts of beetle, cricket, silkworm and a variety of pupas. Hawkers and food stalls here also sell all sorts of other edibles, the idea being to buy your food and then laze around at the huts (it costs just a few thousand riel to rent one for a few hours or the day). To top it all, small boats ply the river with fish and lobsters for sale, cooking your choice of food on the spot using their on-board braziers.

The villages around Kien Svay are well known for their **weaving**, traditionally done by the women, though it's a family business these days and more men are joining in; silk and mixed-thread scarves and *kramas* are produced here for the markets in Phnom Penh.

Practicalities

Both Wat Jum Pos Ka-aik and Kien Svay are reached off **National Route 1**, across the Monivong Bridge. For the Wat Jum Pos Ka-aik, take the first right after the bridge (Street 369) along the Bassac River. The road is in good condition, passing through longan orchards. The pagoda is on the left after 7km, its entrance flanked by statues of *niek* and *yeak*, gods and giants, a favourite Cambodian theme. To reach **Kien Svay**, stay on National Route 1 until, 8km from the bridge, you pass the *L'Imprevu* resort; the turning for the beach is 1km beyond, to the left (north), through an ornate portico which looks like a pagoda gateway lined with food vendors. The beach can also be reached by taking a bus to Psar Koki, the town market, then a moto for the half-kilometre ride to the beach.

Just before the Kien Svay turn-off, and opposite the Cambodia Brewery hoarding, there's a good lunchtime Khmer **restaurant**, 777, overlooking paddy fields and a fishing lake. The speciality here is huge, succulent freshwater crayfish, *bong kong*, priced by weight – expect to pay around $10 for a dish to feed two.

Phnom Brasat

The complex of pagodas at **Phnom Brasat**, 27 km northwest of Phnom Penh, originally comprised just two hilltop sites, but now sprawls over four locations.

Preah Vessandaa

A popular theme at Cambodian pagodas is the tale of Preah Vessandaa – one of the previous **incarnations of the Buddha** – which is often told in tableaux, the figures usually life-sized and garishly coloured. According to the story, an old man, Chuchuk, was given a young woman, Amita, to be his wife in repayment of a debt. The couple were unable to have children, and Amita was snubbed by the other women. Knowing of King Vessandaa's generosity, Amita persuaded her husband to go to ask Vessandaa for two of his children. When depicted in temples, the story, usually told in a series of ten or so scenes, tells of Chuchuk's adventures on the way to the palace. One scene at Phnom Brasat shows Chuchuk dangling in a tree where he has been chased by the hunter Chetabut and his dogs; to escape, the old man lies that he is one of the king's messengers. As Chuchuk approaches the palace, the king's children run off, only to be discovered hiding under lily pads by the king, who grants them to the old man. After getting lost on his way home, Chuchuk ends up in the kingdom of the children's grandfather, who pays a ransom to buy them back. As told in Cambodia, the story ends when Chuchuk spends the money on a feast at which he gorges himself to death – a graphic injunction against the vice of gluttony.

The monks and nuns here have a vision of developing the site to Angkorian proportions, and the programme of construction seems never-ending, with the latest being a futuristic glass-domed edifice. As the building of new sanctuaries is seen as gaining particular merit, it's not unusual for wealthy patrons to make sizeable financial contributions.

Phnom Brasat is readily accessible by **moto** ($6–10 return) and tuk-tuk ($15); you'll probably want some transport to get around the sites anyway, as they're spread over a distance of about 5km.

The site

The most popular of the sites is **Wat Phnom Reap**, reached through a Bayon-style gateway of enormous faces flanked by elephants. The track is lined with *asuras* and *devas* tugging on two nagas, there to protect the city's wealth in an impressive attempt at re-creating the southern gate of Angkor Thom in Siem Reap. Dominating the compound is the amazing carmine-red concrete reproduction of Angkor Wat, **Prasat Mahar Nokor Vitmean Sooer**; it was completed in 1998, after just two years' work. A colonnaded gallery runs around the outside, sheltering elaborately decorated walls; apsaras nestle in niches, while bas-reliefs illustrate scenes from the life of Buddha and commemorate the construction of the temple by depicting the people who donated either money or labour, with a nearly life-size brass statue of the principal benefactor, Rohs Sarouen.

In the same complex, the entrance to **Prasat Pik Vongkot Boreay Brom Mlop** is guarded by two imposing statues of Hanuman, each standing on one leg with sword raised. Inside, an enormous seated Buddha dominates the hall; behind it and curling around it, a cheerful mural of the bodhi tree is dotted with birds and animals, rather like a child's pop-up book. The grounds around the temples currently resemble a building site, with two new temples under construction.

A few kilometres up the road, on the first hill you come to with its entrance portico on the right-hand side, is a much-restored, fifteen-metre-long reclining Buddha, carved out of the hillside. It's reputedly quite ancient – to quote one of the *achars*, "here 1400 years already" – and may conceivably be the only surviving part of the sixth-century pre-Angkorian ruins known to have been here. Steps lead up to the summit and vihara, where a series of **tableaux** illustrate scenes from the story of Preah Vessandaa. Bizarrely, Cambodia's gun culture pervades even here; in a painting of Angkor Wat, a man – presumably the benefactor – proudly displays his pistol holster.

Oudong and around

Oudong was the capital of Cambodia for 248 years, playing host to the crowning of several monarchs, including Norodom, great-great-grandfather of the current king, Norodom Sihamoni. However, in 1866, King Norodom was persuaded by the French to relocate the capital from here to the more strategically positioned Phnom Penh; the court, totalling more than ten thousand people, moved en masse and Oudong was abandoned. The old wooden city has long since rotted away, but the site, scattered with shrines and chedi, remains an important site for pilgrimage and has been recently designated a tourist spot, thus filling up with Cambodians on weekends and national holidays.

Oudong is 37km from the capital and can be reached by the Kompong Chhnang **bus**; state where you're going and get off at the billboard with the picture of the hill then hop on a moto for the final 3km. You can also get to Oudong on a guesthouse-run bus – the *Capitol* (see box, p.82) for instance, runs a trip there daily. With your own transport – a tuk-tuk would cost around $15 – you could also take in several villages en route to get a glimpse of the traditional Cambodian rural lifestyle, and combine Oudong with visits to Phnom Brasat or Lovek.

En route to the site

Heading north out of the capital, **National Route 5** follows the Tonle Sap most of the way to Oudong, passing Cham villages and newly built mosques (most mosques having been destroyed – and Cham religious leaders murdered – by the Khmer Rouge). This area is important for the production of *prohok*, fermented fish paste, in January and February, when the air is pungent with the odour of drying fish. The only village of any size on the way is **PREAK G'DAM** (literally, Crab Creek), where a busy ferry still crosses the Tonle Sap (this was the only crossing point for twenty years until the Chroy Chung Va Bridge was repaired in 1993). Good Khmer food is served up at the **restaurants** opposite the ferry entrance, with the bonus of terrific views across the rice fields to Oudong from their terraces at the back. Along the road, two more Khmer delicacies are on offer: **steamed turtle**, a village speciality proudly displayed on trays by the roadside, and *chook*, the seed pods of the lotus flower which Khmers eat as a snack.

A few kilometres beyond Preak G'dam, just off the highway on the right, is the village of **KOMPONG LUONG**. Once the royal port for Oudong, the village has for centuries been famous for its **silverwork**, and several generations of silversmiths still work together here to craft cups, bowls and all manner of small boxes in animal and fruit designs, shaping and decorating them by hand. Visitors are welcome to watch and purchase, though there's not much difference in price from the markets of Phnom Penh. Back on the road, it's just a few kilometres further to the two hills of Oudong, reached by turning left at the billboard for Angkor Beer, which also shows the chedi.

Oudong

Visible from afar, the multiple chedi on the larger of the two hills at **OUDONG** are something of a landmark. Approaching from National Route 5, you'll arrive at the foot of the larger hill, sometimes called **Phnom Preah Reach Troap**, the Hill of Royal Fortune, as the royal treasure was hidden here during the war with the Siamese in the sixteenth century. As you approach the hill you'll pass a small building on the left which contains human remains collected from another Khmer Rouge execution site nearby. To explore the site you'll need to make a circuit around the hills, but the following account takes the route starting at the furthest, less steep, set of steps.

The once ruined columns and rotten roof beams of **Preah Atharas** (*atharas* being an ancient unit of measure equal to eighteen cubits), the vihara at the top, were being restored or replaced at the time of writing. It was built by the Chinese in the thirteenth century to seal the cave – so legend has it – of a mythical sea monster, which had to be contained to stop the Chinese losing their dominance over the Khmer. The vihara was heavily damaged during fighting between Lon Nol and Khmer Rouge forces in 1973–74, and received further attacks from the Khmer Rouge post-1975, and for many years only a shoulder and part of the right side of the thirteenth-century eleven-metre-high seated Buddha remained; its resplendent restoration is now complete.

The ridge has an increasing number of shrines and several of the older ones are worth seeking out as you walk north. One of the first you'll come to is **Preah Ko**, featuring a particularly appealing statue of Nandin, the sacred mount of Shiva. Worshippers pour water over the bull's head, rendering the water holy, to then take home. Further north, **Preah Neak** contains a Buddha seated on a coiled naga, its multiple heads curved over to afford him protection. Easily recognized by the four faces that cap its spire, the pale-yellow chedi of **Chet Dey Mak Prohm** contains the ashes of King Sisowath Monivong (reigned 1927–41). Higher up the hill is the crumbling chedi **Tray Troeng**, built in 1891 by King Norodom for the ashes of his father, King Ang Duong (though there's some dispute as to whether the ashes are really here or in the Silver Pagoda in Phnom Penh). Some of the glazed ceramic flowers that once covered the chedi can still be seen, but the local children used to sell them to tourists when they "fell off", and now they have been replaced with modern alternatives.

The oldest chedi on the hill is **Damrei Sam Poan**, built in 1623 by Preah Bat Chey Cheta for the ashes of his uncle and predecessor, King Soriyopor. Surrounded by charmingly decayed elephant statues, the chedi is badly overgrown and the inner brick is starting to crumble. Until recently it had the tallest spire on the hill; today the chedi is dwarfed by the spire of the adjacent new pagoda, which has a gleaming marble terrace with stunning views over the countryside to the Tonle Sap. From here, a staircase of 509 steps leads to the foot of the hill.

At the base of the hill to the northwest, the sparkling golden temple in the new **Vipassana Dhura Buddhist Centre** complex is eye-catching from the summit, and worth a quick visit to marvel at its imposing jade Buddha and beautifully painted walls. Another vast reclining Buddha can be seen in the smaller shrine to the southeast of the complex, and in the centre of the large basin to the north stands a golden statue of **Preah Neang Kong Hing**, goddess of the Earth who draws water from the end of her long plaited hair.

The smaller hill can be reached by a separate stairway, at the top of which is a small, damaged mosque, **Vihara Ta Sann**. Close by are the ruins of a large reclining Buddha and, dating from 1567, a chedi built by King Bat Boromintho Reachea – for whom, no one seems to know.

Lovek

Little is known about **LOVEK**, the capital of Cambodia during the reign of King An Chan in the sixteenth century. It was captured by the Siamese in the latter part of the century, and the name has been passed down through a well-known local legend (see box, p.121) as much as anything else. Today a sparse village stretches

The legend of Lovek

When Lovek was capital, it was said to house two statues of Preah Ko and Preah Kaew which contained **sacred texts**, written in gold, recording "all the knowledge and wisdom in the world". During one of the periodic conflicts between the Thai and Khmer, the Thai army was encamped outside Lovek, which it had repeatedly failed to capture, and it was about to make its seasonal retreat in advance of the rains. The story goes that the Thai fired a cannon loaded with silver coins into the bamboo thickets that afforded the city some natural protection. During the rainy season, the Khmer gradually cleared the bamboo in their search for the coins, such that the Thai were easily able to capture the city in the following dry season. Removing the statues to Ayutthaya, the Thai were able to read the sacred texts and so became more knowledgeable than the Khmer. The legend has it that the statues are still hidden in Bangkok and that when they are returned to Cambodia the country will once again have ascendancy over Thailand.

across the site, consisting of a few houses, a school and two fine **shrines** at the farthest reaches: the larger Wat Preah Kaew (Pagoda of the Emerald Buddha) and Wat Preah Ko (Pagoda of the Sacred Cow) a little further beyond on the same site. In both wats, every inch of wall is painted with colourful murals of the legend. To the south of Wat Preah Ko is a two-metre, smiling green-marble Buddha surrounded by bowls of water that worshippers use to bathe him.

Finding Lovek is a bit of a challenge; to reach the village by moto, head north from Oudong on National Route 5 in the direction of Kompong Chhnang; after 12km take the turning at the small blue sign on the right for **Traleng Keng Pagoda site**. Beyond the concrete portico flanked by golden lions, the village stretches along a 5km straight track, before it bends at a right angle towards the shrines. You could get as far as the main road turning on the Phnom Penh–Kompong Chhnang bus, but the driver will need clear instructions.

Choeung Ek

Just 12km southwest of Phnom Penh is the notorious site of **CHOEUNG EK** (daily 7am–5pm; $2), where prisoners from Toul Sleng were brought for execution. As graphically portrayed in the film *The Killing Fields*, certain sites around the country – Choeung Ek is the best known – became places of **mass murder**, where the genocidal Khmer Rouge disposed of its enemies: men, women and children who had allegedly betrayed the state. Early on, the regime's victims were shot; later, to save on valuable bullets, they were bludgeoned or stabbed to death, and babies killed by being savagely thrown against trees. As fuel became scarce, victims were dragged out of the city and killed en route, their bodies dumped in the rice paddies closer to town.

Set amid peaceful fields and pleasant countryside, in what was once a Chinese burial ground, the **Choeung Ek Memorial** now contains the remains of 8985 bodies exhumed here in 1980, when 86 of the burial pits were excavated. Anecdotal estimates suggest that over 17,000 people may have been slaughtered here, and a further 43 mass graves under the lake at the site remain untouched; there are no plans for these to be investigated since there is nowhere sufficient to house the remains to Buddhist standards as yet. Inside the memorial, a gleaming glass-fronted chedi, skulls and bones are piled on shelves, arranged by age and gender, their tattered clothes below. Around the stupa, a pavilion houses a small exhibition describing the history of the site as well as a dated but informative short video, while an emotional (if ungrammatical) declaration close by states, "We are absolutely determined no [sic] to let this genocidal regime to reoccur in Kampuchea". It is a good idea to get a guide to take you round the site of grassy mounds and excavated sites for a "fixed donation" of $2. Be sure to wander around the eerily beautiful lake beyond, but beware of begging children who ask for a dollar once you've taken their picture.

The site is easily accessible by moto and tuk-tuk or on excursions run by various Phnom Penh guesthouses (some of which also include side-trips to Tonle Bati); you could even cycle there if you're prepared to brave the traffic. To drive here, find Monireth Boulevard and follow it south, forking left at the large petrol station, from where it's about 5km to Choeung Ek.

Tonle Bati and Phnom Chisor

Some 35km south of the capital down National Route 2 are the two small but appealing temples at **Tonle Bati**, while another crumbling, peaceful temple lies some 30km further south off the same road at **Phnom Chisor**. Tonle Bati can be easily reached on the bus for Takeo: buy your ticket directly from the bus operator for the best price, and get off by the Sokimex petrol station – where there's a large hoarding showing the temple – and take a moto the final 2.5km to the temple; alternatively, you can do the whole journey from the capital by moto and tuk-tuk ($8–12 return). To see Phnom Chisor, the Takeo bus also stops along the main road where enterprising moto drivers are on-hand to take you the final 2km for around $1. Alternatively, take an excursion operated by one of the capital's travel agents or guesthouses.

Tonle Bati

The peaceful site of **Tonle Bati** (daily 7am–6pm; $3) is set on the banks of the Bati River in a well-tended grove of coconut and mango trees, where you can

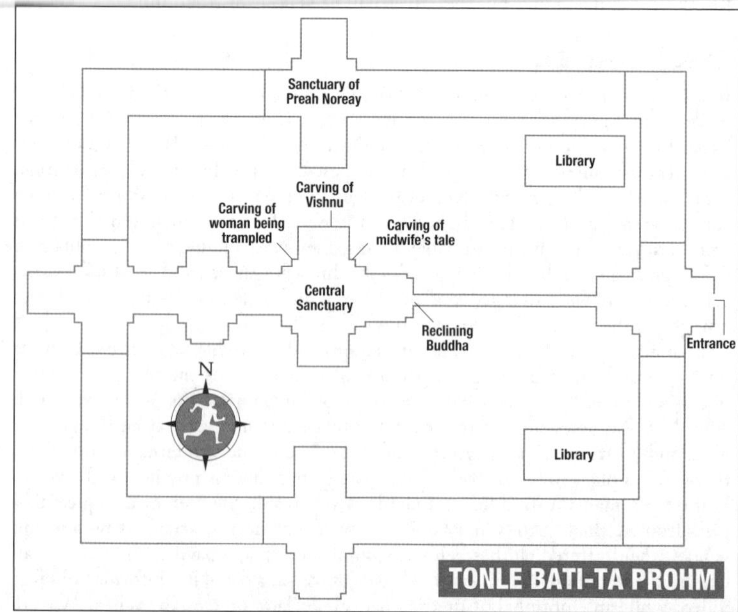

swim and picnic as well as seeing the two temples. You will be met immediately by a gaggle of young girls selling flowers, who will most likely follow you around until you leave, even if you're adamant about not buying. The first temple you come to on entering the site is the larger of the two, **Ta Prohm**. Constructed by Jayavarman VII – creator of the magnificent Angkor Thom – on the site of a sixth-century shrine, it's dedicated to the Hindu god Shiva (though Jayavarman eventually adopted Theravada Buddhism). The main entrance is from the east along a short laterite causeway, edged by flowers and shrubs; piled up to the side at the entrance are broken chunks of masonry, some elaborately carved with scenes from the Churning of the Ocean of Milk (see p.188) or the *Ramayana* (see box, p.94).

At the centre of the inner enclosure are the temple's five **sanctuaries**, its antechambers built in a cruciform shape, with shrines to the cardinal directions. Above the entrance, a carved stone image of a reclining Buddha has been colourfully coated in paint. The **main sanctuary**, of sandstone, contains an upright Buddha image, while the antechambers house damaged stone linga. Another image of Buddha, over the north arm of the cruciform, has been superimposed with a carving of a six-armed Vishnu, a change probably made when the Angkorian kingdom reverted to Hinduism after the death of Jayavarman VII.

Well-preserved **carvings** decorate the outside of the sanctuary and several tell unusual tales. High up on the northeast corner is a scene of two women and a kneeling man: one woman carries a basket on her head, containing the afterbirth from her recent confinement; the midwife, shown standing, was not given sufficient respect during the birth and has condemned the new mother to carry the basket for the rest of her life; her husband is shown begging for forgiveness. The corresponding spot on the northwest corner shows a king sitting next to his wife, who is said to have been unfaithful; below she is put to death by being trampled by a horse.

The north gopura used to contain a statue of **Preah Noreay**, a Hindu deity who is said to bestow fertility upon childless women; although the statue is still undergoing restoration at the National Museum, women continue to arrive here to seek his help.

Yeah Peau

Some 100m north of Ta Prohm in the grounds of the modern Wat Tonle Bati, lies the single, sandstone twelfth-century temple of **Yeah Peau**. Various legends surround the temple. One tale tells how King Preah Ket Mealea fell in love with a young girl named Peau, who gave birth to his son, whom she named Prohm. The king returned to his court but left behind a ring and sacred dagger so that in years to come Prohm would be able to prove his regal descent. Prohm duly went to his father's court and stayed many years, presumably forgetting his mother, for when he finally returned home he fell in love with her, refusing to believe her when she said he was her son. To resolve the matter, it was agreed that Peau and Prohm would each build a temple; if he finished first she would marry him, and if she finished first he would acknowledge her as his mother. The contest took place at night with the women helping Peau and the men assisting Prohm. In the middle of the night, the women raised a lighted candle into the sky. The men, thinking this was the morning star, settled down to sleep in the belief that they could not be beaten, leaving the women to carry on working and complete their temple first. (This rivalry between women and men is a common theme in Cambodian pagodas, cropping up many times in different guises.)

Wat Tonle Bati was badly damaged by the Khmer Rouge and some pieces of gnarled metal behind the main Buddha are all that is left of the original statue. Beside the Buddha is a statue of Peau, while outside in the courtyard are five large seated Buddhas, each with their hands in a different *mudra*.

Some 300m northwest of the temples are dozens of **picnic huts** built on stilts over the river (5000 riel per day rental, plus $3 site entrance fee). Once you've made your choice, the owners provide floor mats and cushions, plus a tray of drinks and snacks, and even inflated inner tubes for swimming. You pay for anything you use or consume, although as prices are higher than in restaurants, you might want to bring your own provisions.

Phnom Chisor and around

Originally known as Suryadri ("Sun Mountain"), **Phnom Chisor** (daily; $2 for foreigners) was built early in the eleventh century by Suryavarman I and was once a site of some significance, housing one of four sacred linga installed by the king in temples at the boundaries of his kingdom. A hot and tiring flight of 412 steps ascends the hill from the south, though there is a shady pavilion halfway up in which to rest, and refreshment-sellers on hand at the top and bottom. A modern pagoda is established at the summit and there are a burgeoning number of sanctuaries scattered about. One of the more interesting, to the right from the top of the steps, is **Prasat Preah Ko Preah Kaew**, containing images of the cow and small boy from which it gets its name: according to one far-fetched legend, also repeated at the Preah Ko shrine in Lovek, despite having been warned not to, a pregnant woman climbed a mango tree to eat some fruit, and fell; the shock induced labour, and from her womb emerged a baby boy and a cow.

At the far, northern, end of the hill, the ancient temple of **Prasat Boran** still retains some well-preserved carved sandstone lintels. The temple was built opening to the east, from which side you get a good view across the plains to Angkor Borei. From the eastern doorway, the old entrance road leads straight to the foot of the hill and still retains its two gatehouses. In the entrance, two stone **basins** are filled with water, which is ladled out for blessings using a couple of large seashells. The *achars* say the basins used to fill naturally – presumably from a spring – but after a US bomb came through the roof of the central sanctuary in the 1970s (thankfully it didn't explode) this stopped; to this day the roof remains covered with corrugated iron. The internal doors to the central sanctuary are very fine and decorated with images of Shiva standing on the back of a pig – although no one knows why. To the east a path leads around the hill to a small **cave shrine**, really more a collection of rocks, but containing enough room for two or three people to squeeze inside the crevice. An *achar* here dispenses blessings for a consideration, and will sell you one of his handkerchiefs decorated with holy symbols for protection and prosperity.

Around Phnom Chisor

Prasat Neang Khmao, 5km to the west of Phnom Chisor, is much visited by local people and features on guesthouse tours, but after the delights of Tonle Bati and Phnom Chisor there's relatively little to see. Just two ruined towers remain on a low mound, surrounded by a modern pagoda, during whose construction three other towers were removed.

The villages east of Phnom Chisor weave very fine traditional *hol* patterned **silk**. It's worth buying a piece if you can find someone with a finished length, although this isn't easy as most is produced to order. UNESCO is helping the weavers here re-learn the use of natural dyes, a skill that was lost during the Pol Pot years.

Phnom Tamau

The **Phnom Tamau Zoological Gardens and Wildlife Rescue Centre** is more of a safari park, set in an area of regenerating scrub forest between Tonle Bati and Phnom Chisor. Most animals in the zoo here were rescued from desperate situations: some as they were being taken out of the country to satisfy demand for exotic foods and medicine in China and Thailand; others were found for sale in the markets, were being kept as pets in tiny cages or were destined for the restaurant tables of Phnom Penh. Although many of the animals still have far from adequate facilities, the team of dedicated keepers do their best with limited finances. With an annual feeding bill alone of over $100,000, the centre relies on private donations and sponsorship for funding, so your entrance fee is going to a good cause.

The star attractions are undoubtedly the **tigers**, which by day prowl around a purpose-built deluxe enclosure; at night they are secured indoors and protected by armed keepers – poachers are still a cause for concern and a dead tiger can net thousands of dollars. **Sun bears** and **black bears** lodge nearby, while further enclosures contain other indigenous species – elephants, crocodiles, pangolins and various wild cats and fairly tame **cranes** among others. The zoo is also home to a 5-year-old baby elephant who lost a foot in a snare; he'll be in the zoo for life and goes by the name Lucky.

Practicalities

The zoo is 50km south of Phnom Penh off National Route 2. Look out for the **billboard** of animals 10km beyond Tonle Bati, from where it's a further 5km up the side road to the zoo entrance (daily 8.30am–4.30pm; foreigners $5, car 2000 riel, motorbike 1000 riel). The **Takeo bus** passes the turning, but the zoo is best visited with your own transport as the site stretches over several kilometres. On the way from the main road you'll have to run the gamut of elderly beggars who line the road; having no one to care for them, they walk daily from their villages to ask for alms, so you may wish to take a bundle of small notes that you can dispense as you feel appropriate. The layout plan at the entrance is worth studying as the zoo's set up budget was largely squandered on a grandiose scheme of roads meant to emulate Singapore Zoo, as a result of which there are now a lot of overgrown tracks going nowhere.

Prey Veng, Svay Rieng and the Bavet border crossing

The desperately poor southeastern provinces of **Prey Veng** and **Svay Rieng** are little visited by Khmer from other parts of the country, let alone foreign tourists, other than to make the journey along National Route 1 to the **Vietnamese border** crossings at Bavet and Chau Doc. The inhabitants here eke out an existence which is often below subsistence level: their rice crops are frequently washed away when the Mekong floods in the rainy season, and in the dry season the land bakes as hard as stone.

Neak Leung is the jumping-off point to both gateways into Vietnam: its ferries form a crucial link between Phnom Penh and the border at **Bavet**, while boats set off down the Mekong for the alternative crossing at **Chau Doc**. If you need somewhere to stay en route to the border, the pleasant provincial town of **Svay**

Rieng has guesthouses and restaurants, while Bavet has really improved its image and even has a decent guesthouse and restaurant, making it a useful place to stay if you want to cross to Vietnam first thing in the morning.

Neak Leung

Divided by the Mekong, the dusty transit town of **NEAK LEUNG** still lacks a bridge, and is consequently inevitably congested with vehicles revving up in semi-orderly queues to board the ferries that crisscross the Mekong. The bus from Phnom Penh arrives at the west bank; the town's restaurants and market are all on the east bank. Ferry tickets can be bought at the ticket office by the traffic barrier at the end of the road (200 riel per person). Neak Leung is known for its great river lobster (*bong kong*), served in the **restaurants** close by the east-bank ferry terminal. The town's other culinary speciality is sparrow; you'll see plucked birds strung up and ready for cooking.

Most people heading for **Chau Doc** in Vietnam go on organized trips from Phnom Penh (about $10), in which case your guide will arrange transfers between the various different forms of transport. If you're going solo, you need to get off the bus on the west bank, from where it is a 350m walk south along the road adjacent to the riverfront. Ask for a boat to **K'am Samnar** if you get lost (20,000 riel; 1hr 30min). People will point you in the right direction, but the boat leaves from behind a blue-roofed warehouse which isn't signposted. If you reach the bridge you've gone too far. The various immigration and customs buildings at the border post (open daily 7am–8pm) are quite scattered, so you'll need to hire a moto (about 4000 riel). After entering Vietnam at Vinh Xuong, you need to take a *xe om* (moto in Vietnamese; about $5) to get to Chau Doc, a journey of around an hour. For $8 the boat operator in Neak Leung will get you the whole way to Chau Doc.

Svay Rieng

The spread-out town of **SVAY RIENG** lies just off National Route 1, and chances are you'll see very little of it if you're rushing between the Vietnamese border and Phnom Penh. Other than the riverfront area near the landmark *Tonle Waikor Hotel*, named after the river which flows behind it, the nearest that the town gets to a sight is **Preah Bassac**, a tree-clad mound of rubble about 8km from town reached by moto in the dry season and by boat in the rainy. All that can be seen of the prasat is a single brick wall, which the locals will make sure that you find, but it has a delightful shady setting by the river, overlooking rice fields in the dry season and ringed by tiny hidden hamlets.

Transport to and from Phnom Penh and Bavet arrives and departs from the **market**, 1km or so northeast of the centre, where you can get a moto to the guesthouses on the main street near the river.

Refurbished in 1999, the massive *Tonle Waikor Hotel* is undoubtedly the best place to **stay** (Ⓣ044/945718; ❷–❸), featuring plain but spacious en-suite rooms with TV, fridge and air conditioning. There are several guesthouses clustered on the main road with similar, slightly worn rooms. The pick of these – as much for the friendliness of the management as the rooms themselves – is the corner house *Santapheap* (Ⓣ012/670499; ❶), a bargain with clean rooms, TVs and private bathrooms. Airier rooms are on the first floor.

There's decent Khmer **food** at the *Thunthean Sathea Restaurant*, 100m east of the guesthouses; their *sumlar ngam ngouw* (lemon chicken soup) is very tasty. About 200m beyond the *Tonle Waikor*, on the road towards Bavet, the *Boueng Meas Restaurant* serves up acceptable Khmer fare.

Other than enjoying a *tuk kralok* (fruit shake) on the riverfront, the only other thing to do in the evening is enjoy a Khmer film in the smart new cinema just west of the *Tonle Waikor Hotel*.

Bavet

The town of **BAVET** is often referred to as **Moc Bai** – the name of the adjacent town on the Vietnamese side. The formerly atrocious National Route 1 here was slowly disintegrating, until in early 2001 Prime Minister Hun Sen loaded his ministers onto a coach and took them along the road to the border, then left them to return the same way (he flew back by helicopter); work commenced on upgrading the road soon after, and is now complete. It's a pretty dull ride as the province was heavily bombed by the US during the Vietnam War, and has never quite recovered.

Practicalities

With a smart new border crossing (daily 7am–8pm) and decent road Bavet has improved out of all recognition. If you're arriving in Cambodia here, you can get a **shared taxi** to **Phnom Penh** (20,000 riel). A new and brilliant improvement to proceedings is that you no longer have to change bus at the border if you are booked on a bus in either direction; the bus operator will handle everything, although you will need to get your visa beforehand in Phnom Penh, as with all crossings into Vietnam. If you are going it alone and haven't booked through-transport to HCMC, you can get a motorbike taxi or minibus for the ten-kilometre ride to **Go Dau** once you get into **Moc Bai**, where you can get direct onward transport to HCMC – the whole trip takes under two hours.

If you cross to Cambodia late at night, or want to get over to Vietnam first thing in the morning, *Nouveau Pho de Paris* (Ⓣ044/946055; ❷–❸) is a smart new guest-house and restaurant about 100m from the border. In the evening you could visit one of the town's seven casinos, maybe not to gamble, but to have a meal and take in a show (check the hoardings for what's on). Internet access is available next door to *Nouveau Pho de Paris*.

Travel details

Buses

Bavet to: Phnom Penh (10 daily; 3hr 30min).
Neak Leung to: Phnom Penh (10 daily; 2hr).
Phnom Penh to: Bangkok, Thailand (daily; 10–12hr); Banlung (daily; 10–12hr); Battambang (5 daily; 5hr); Bavet (10 daily; 3hr 30min); Ho Chi Minh City, Vietnam (twice daily; around 6hr); Kampot (twice daily; 4–5hr); Kep (twice daily; 4–5 hr); Kompong Cham (10 daily; 2hr); Kompong Chhnang (10 daily; 2hr); Kompong Speu (9 daily; 1hr 30min); Kratie (daily; 7hr); Neak Leung (10 daily; 2hr); Oudong (10 daily; 1hr); Poipet (5 daily; 8hr); Pursat (5 daily; 3hr); Sen Monorom (daily; 7hr); Siem Reap (10 daily; 8hr); Sihanoukville (6 daily; 3hr 30min); Sisophon (4 daily; 7hr); Stung Treng (daily; 8hr); Takeo (4 daily; 2hr; 30min) Voen Kham, Laos border (daily; 8–10hr).

Shared taxis, minibuses and pick-up trucks

Bavet to: Neak Leung (10 daily; 1hr 30min); Phnom Penh (10 daily; 3hr 30min); Svay Rieng (10 daily; 30min).
Neak Leung to: Bavet (10 daily; 1hr 30min); Phnom Penh (10 daily; 1hr 30min); Prey Veng (4 daily; 2hr); Svay Rieng (10 daily; 1hr).
Phnom Penh to: Banlung (several daily; at least 10hr); Battambang (12 daily; 6hr); Bavet (20 daily; 3hr); Kampot (12 daily; 3hr); Koh Kong (several daily; 6hr); Kompong Cham (20 daily; 2hr 30min); Kompong Chhnang (4 daily; 2hr 30min); Kompong Thom (12 daily; 3hr); Neak Leung (20 daily; 1hr 30min); Pailin (10 daily; 6hr); Poipet (10 daily; 8hr); Pursat (10 daily; 4hr); Sen Monorom (several daily; at least 8hr); Siem Reap (hourly; 6–8hr);

Sihanoukville (20 daily; 3hr 30min); Sisophon (10 daily; 7hr); Svay Rieng (10 daily; 2hr 30min); Takeo (12 daily; 2hr 30min).
Prey Veng to: Kompong Cham (4 daily; 2hr); Neak Leung (4 daily; 2hr).
Svay Rieng to: Bavet (10 daily; 30min); Neak Leung (10 daily; 1hr); Phnom Penh (10 daily; 2hr 30min).

Boats

Phnom Penh to: Siem Reap (daily; 5hr); Chau Doc, Vietnam (daily; 5hr).

Flights

Phnom Penh to: Siem Reap (at least 6 daily; 45min).

Battambang and the northwest

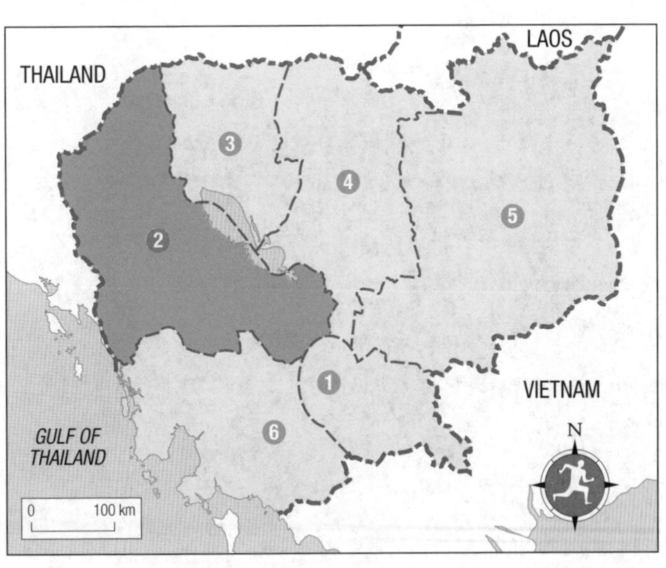

CHAPTER 2

Highlights

* **Floating villages** Take a boat out to explore the floating villages on the Tonle Sap near Kompong Chhnang. See p.135
* **Battambang** Laidback town with colonial architecture, a lazy riverside and a fledgling Western bar scene. See p.138
* **Wat Banan** Well-preserved ancient hilltop pagoda near Battambang, with superb views from the summit. See p.146
* **Banteay Chhmar** Remote, ruined, fabulously carved temple. See p.151
* **Ang Trapaeng Thmor** Wonderful wetlands, with a chance to see the elegant, endangered Sarus crane. See p.152

▲ Floating village, Tonle Sap

2

Battambang and the northwest

Strike north from Phnom Penh along National Route 5, west of the Tonle Sap, and you'll be following the route along which the Khmer Rouge retreated from Phnom Penh in 1979, ahead of the liberating Vietnamese forces. This is also the route that the invading Thai armies used in the opposite direction, as they repeatedly headed south to sack and pillage. Much of the northwest still shows clear Thai influence, especially in the style of the houses – not surprising given that the area came under Thai control at the end of the eighteenth century, and was only finally returned to Cambodia in 1946. These days the road is a busy transit corridor linking the capital to the Thai border and a trade route along which rice is transported from the sparsely populated but fertile plains to the more populous south. National Route 5 is in good condition, and the journey all the way to the border is about six hours. The train from Phnom Penh stopped some years ago, but the rails are being re-laid and freight trains are expected to run to Battambang in the not too distant future; it's muted that the line will be eventually extended to Poipet on the Thai border.

The first two towns of any size along National Route 5 out of Phnom Penh are Kompong Chhnang and Pursat. A busy river fishing port, **Kompong Chhnang** takes its name from the terracotta pots (*chhnang*) which are produced here and used all over Cambodia, while quiet **Pursat** is home to marble workshops where you might see craftsmen at work. From both towns you can get out to visit the **floating villages** on the Tonle Sap.

North of Pursat is laidback **Battambang**, one of Cambodia's largest towns with a lazy riverside ambience, colonial-era villas, shophouses and an Art Deco market. The surrounding province once had more temples than Siem Reap, although none was on the scale of Angkor Wat and most have long disappeared. The couple that remain are worth a visit, however, especially the hilltop site of **Wat Banan**, which you can see in a day-trip from Battambang.

On the Thai border in the far northwest, **Poipet** is increasingly used as a place to make a quick stop and change vehicles on the way between Bangkok and the temples at Siem Reap. If you're travelling along this route it's well worth breaking your journey at **Sisophon**, the crossroads town at the junction of national routes 5 and 6, to visit the rarely visited **Banteay Chhmar**, a ruined Angkorian temple which is still completely unrestored and overgrown by jungle.

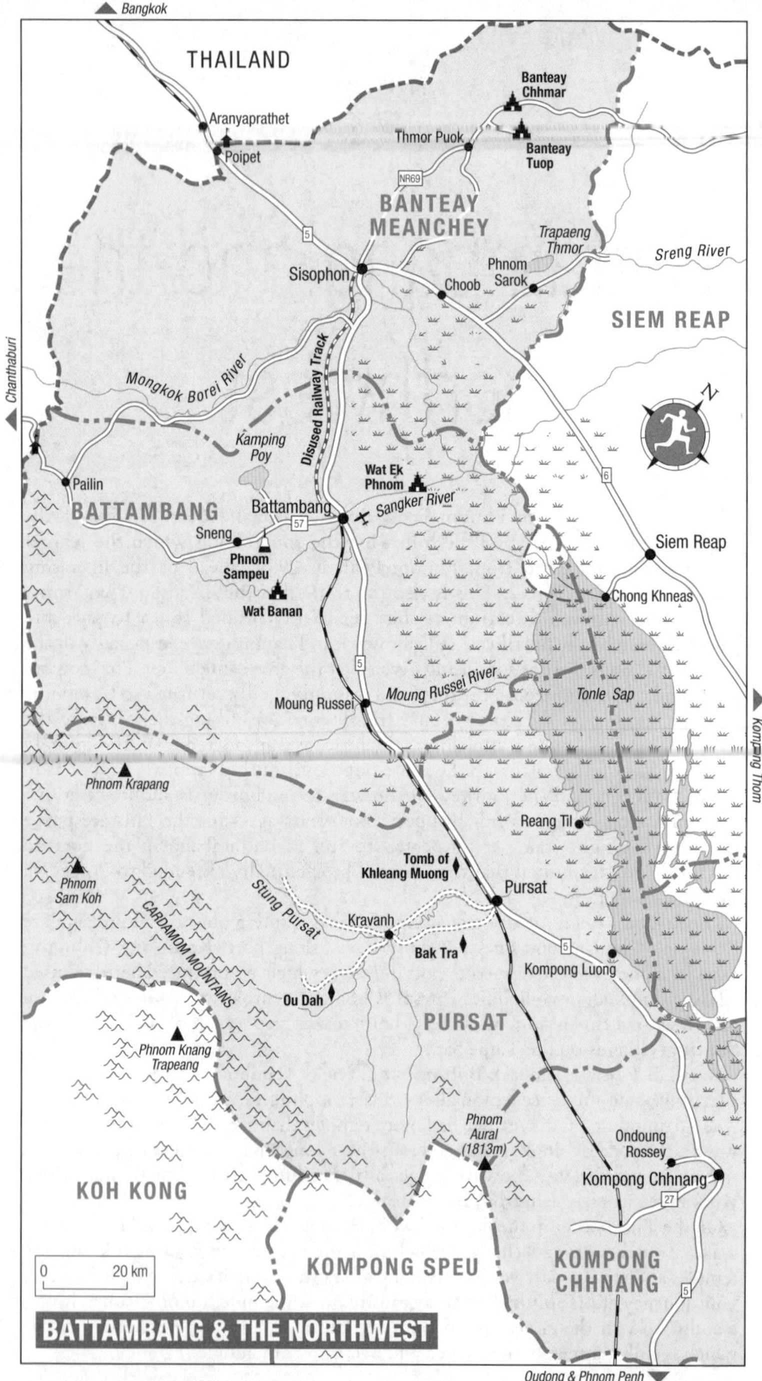
Bangkok
THAILAND
Aranyaprathet
Poipet
Thmor Puok
Banteay Chhmar
Banteay Tuop
NR69
BANTEAY MEANCHEY
5
Trapaeng Thmor
Sreng River
Sisophon
Phnom Sarok
Choob
SIEM REAP
Chanthaburi
Mongkok Borei River
Disused Railway Track
Kamping Poy
Wat Ek Phnom
Pailin
BATTAMBANG
Battambang
Sangker River
57
Sneng
Phnom Sampeu
Wat Banan
6
Siem Reap
Chong Khneas
5
Moung Russei
Moung Russei River
Tonle Sap
Kompong Thom
Phnom Krapang
Reang Til
Tomb of Khleang Muong
Phnom Sam Koh
Pursat
Stung Pursat
CARDAMOM MOUNTAINS
Kravanh
Bak Tra
Kompong Luong
Ou Dah
PURSAT
Phnom Knang Trapeang
Phnom Aural (1813m)
Ondoung Rossey
Kompong Chhnang
27
KOH KONG
0 20 km
KOMPONG SPEU
KOMPONG CHHNANG
BATTAMBANG & THE NORTHWEST
Oudong & Phnom Penh

It was to the mountainous border that the Khmer Rouge fled after their defeat, and from here that they waged a disruptive guerrilla war until 1996; in the far north, the remote Dangkrek Escarpment remained their foothold until the death of Pol Pot in 1998. The war was vicious and both the government and the Khmer Rouge laid **land mines**; the border is the most heavily mined area of the country and under no circumstances should you wander from defined tracks.

Kompong Chhnang and around

The old colonial town of **KOMPONG CHHNANG**, 83km north of Phnom Penh on National Route 5, is a quiet place to stop over for a day or to take a weekend break from Phnom Penh. Elsewhere in Cambodia you'll often see ox carts laden with the *chhnang* (terracotta pots) produced here – a slow and smooth method of transport that reduces the risk of damage to the fragile cargo (though increasingly ancient motorbike remorques are used). Several villages where the **pottery** is made can be visited nearby. Relaxing atmosphere apart, the chief attraction here is a trip to the **floating villages** on the Tonle Sap, where you'll get an authentic flavour of life on the water.

Practicalities

Taxis to and from Phnom Penh use the **transport stop**, northwest of the Independence Monument in the old part of town. Transport from Battambang and the north arrives at (and leaves from) the road just north of Psar Leu. There are plenty of **motos** around town during the day, but they can be hard to find at night; if you're staying far from the centre ask your guesthouse to arrange for you to be picked up after dinner. There are no bus stations in town, instead you'll be put off on the main road, either near the taxi stop or close to the Independence Monument; it's quite in order to ask the driver to stop where you want to get off. Leaving Kompong Chhnang you'll have to flag down a bus – it's best to do this in a prime location so they can see you (by the Independence Monument for example).

The **post** and **telephone offices** are 200m west of the transport stop, and the **tourist information** office 200m further on. **Internet shops** can be found around Psar Leu. Acleda Bank, in the centre of town, will change travellers' cheques and advance money on Visa cards; while Canadia Bank, 100m south of the Independence Monument on NR5, has an ATM (Visa and MasterCard). The **hospital** is nearby, just east of the monument. There's a mini-mart at the Tela petrol station northwest of the transport stop.

Accommodation

The town's newest hotel is the *Samrongsen Hotel* (ⓣ026/989011; ❸) about half a kilometre northeast of Psar Leu towards the waterfront. Rooms are spacious and clean and have all the expected amenities, but being away from the bustle of both the town and the waterfront makes it a little dull. Most NGO staff head for *Sokha's Guesthouse* (ⓣ012/762988; ❷), with a range of rooms and bungalows set in a lovely courtyard garden on a leafy back street near the Independence Monument. Right next to the monument, the *Mittapheap Guest House* (ⓣ012/949297; ❶) has some bright, clean rooms above its restaurant, while the *Sovann Phum Hotel* (ⓣ026/989333; ❷), a little way south on NR5, touts itself as a business hotel and has wi-fi.

The Town

From the town centre around the Psar Leu market, it's a short walk southwest to the old **French quarter** (roughly the area around *Sokha*'s *Guesthouse*), where shady tree-lined streets and overgrown parks surround faded colonial villas. Northeast of the centre, a broad causeway crosses a marshy flood plain and connects the town to its port, 2km away on the Tonle Sap. The houses which line the causeway balance precariously on high stilts, though even these are scarcely tall enough to prevent river water lapping at the doors during the rains. At the far end of the causeway, there's a good view across the river from **Wat Yeah Tep**.

The ethnic Vietnamese

The first Vietnamese settlers in Cambodia were **rice farmers**, many of whose ancestors migrated across disputed borders as long ago as the late seventeenth century; over generations they moved north along the Mekong and today mostly farm in the southeast provinces. The educated, predominantly Christian Vietnamese population of Phnom Penh has its origins in the **civil servants** brought over during Vietnamese rule and the French protectorate. Indeed, records of the time suggest Phnom Penh was more Vietnamese than Khmer. These days the majority of Cambodia's commercial fishing is accounted for by impoverished ethnic Vietnamese **fishing families**; predominantly Buddhist, they live in floating villages on the Tonle Sap and Mekong River, moving around with the annual inundation. Government estimates put the number of ethnic Vietnamese living in Cambodia at around 100,000, but given the difficulty of monitoring the large number who live in floating villages, the true figure is thought to be much higher.

Historically, Cambodians have long entertained feelings of hostility towards the Vietnamese, who are all too often referred to using the derogatory Khmer term, **Yuan**. The roots of this resentment go back to the Vietnamese annexation of the Mekong delta in the seventeenth century. Tensions were exacerbated during the brief period of Vietnamese rule over the whole country, during which time they tried to impose their language, names and mores on the Khmer. The situation was further aggravated during the French protectorate, when Vietnamese clerks were installed in Cambodia's administration, and matters were not helped when the French redrew the Cambodia–Vietnam border in favour of the Vietnamese after World War II.

Although you're unlikely to witness any racism against the Vietnamese today, it's as well to note that no Cambodian would be seen dead in the pointed hats worn by Vietnamese rice farmers, and that no provincial Cambodian woman would dream of wearing trousers, for fear of being mistaken for a Vietnamese. The country's current leader, Hun Sen, is often accused by his opponents of being a "Vietnamese puppet", while Vietnamese town-dwellers and rice farmers are accused of taking Cambodian jobs.

Kompong Chhnang is the principal fishing port for Phnom Penh, and throughout the year supplies of fresh fish are packed with ice and loaded daily onto a fleet of trucks to drip their way towards the city. The fishing families, primarily ethnic Vietnamese, live on the river in **floating villages**, their houses built on pontoons which bob on the waters of the Tonle Sap. The villages are served by floating markets and coffee shops, and though facilities can be basic (their water, for example, comes from the river itself), most homes have TV and many have small floating gardens, while pens between the pontoons house farmed fish.

If you want to get out on the river and around the floating villages, **boats** can be hired from the riverfront near the boat dock (around 20,000 riel per hour for a small boat). Taking to the water offers an interesting insight into the daily life of these unusual communities and is a more relaxing experience than visiting the commercialized floating villages on the Tonle Sap at Siem Reap (see p.209).

Local legend has it that the hill across the river is the corpse of the lady **Neing Kong Ray**, her hair flowing across the ground to the southeast, her feet to the northwest. The tale begins with twelve sisters who are wed *en masse* to a king. Things go wrong when the king takes a thirteenth wife, Santema, an evil giantess in disguise. Santema blinds the sisters and plots to kill Pothy Sen, one of their sons, to stop him becoming king. Pothy Sen promptly falls in love with and marries Santema's own daughter, Neing Kong Ray. When he subsequently discovers his mother-in-law's treachery, in his disgust he uses a magical potion to escape from his wife, creating a river between them. There's a statue of them near the Independence Monument.

Eating

A decent place to eat is the *Mittapheap Restaurant* (6am–2pm & 6–8pm), by the Independence Monument, which has an English menu and serves good Khmer soups and fish dishes, plus excellent fried noodles. Just across from the taxi stop, the friendly "*no name restaurant*" does excellent Khmer/Chinese food, and can rustle up omelettes, chips and simple Western dishes if you ask. During the daytime, noodle stalls and coffee shops open up around both Psar Leu and Psar Chhnang markets, but at night all you'll find are stalls selling fresh fruit and fruit shakes.

Around Kompong Chhnang

The roads in Kompong Chhnang are lined with stalls selling unglazed terracotta ware, ranging from plates indented with round dimples (used to bake tiny coconut cakes over charcoal fires) to elephant money boxes – they only take notes and you'll have to break them to get at your savings. Most of these pots are crafted in villages around Kompong Chhnang, and you can ride into the country to see the potters at work.

One potting village is **ONDOUNG ROSSEY**, about 7km northwest of town, where locals work at preparing clay and spinning the potting wheel in the shade of their houses; a small **Cambodian Crafts Federation** shop here sells a range of pottery. To get to Ondoung Rossey, either hire a moto (about $5 round trip) or, if you have your own transport, follow the Battambang road about 5km north from Kompong Chhnang and look for a small sign for the village on the left. Turn left here through a gateway onto a sealed road, then right through another gateway after about 1km onto a dirt road that leads to the village.

Three kilometres west from the centre of Kompong Chhnang, **Phnom Santuk** is a mound of huge boulders in the grounds of the wat of the same name; climb to the top for views over rice paddies dotted with sugar-palm trees and the Tonle Sap. It's worth hiring a moto for the trip as they can weave their way across the rice paddies to the pot-making villages afterwards – a route you'd never find on your own.

Pursat

Named after a tree that used to grow along its river banks, **PURSAT** is a pleasant rural town, 174km from Phnom Penh and 106km from Battambang. Pursat is little visited by tourists, and most of the foreigners who do come are NGO workers. Apart from some **floating villages** 35km away, there's not a lot to see, but it's a pleasant place to overnight or rest up for a day.

Practicalities

Arriving by taxi, ask to be dropped by the **main bridge** (*spean thmor*), from where it's a couple of hundred metres to the hotels and guesthouse. Buses stop on NR5 west of the main bridge, at (or opposite) their respective ticket offices. Pursat's **train station** is 2km west of town – though at the time of writing no trains are running. All road transport leaves from the **transport stop** a few hundred metres west of the bridge on National Route 5.

You'll find most facilities in Pursat to the north of NR5 along the west bank of the river, including the **post office**, **tourist information** office, a handful of **internet** outlets and the **hospital**. There are branches of Canadia and Acleda banks in town; both are on the main road west of the bridge. You can convert dollars to riel at the market; nearby you'll find cheap-rate **phone** booths for domestic calls and a couple of shops where international calls can be made.

Accommodation

Phnom Pich Hotel 200m north of the main bridge on the west bank of the river ⓣ052/951515. This hotel has the best-value accommodation in town, with large, bright and airy en-suite rooms with either fan or a/c [illegible] will get you hot water, internet and restaurant. Unfortunately rooms facing the river can be noisy. ❷

Pursat Century Hotel Set back from the main road, next to Acleda Bank ⓣ052/9888322, ⓔpursatcenturyhotel@yahoo.com. This newish place is popular with tour groups and the business trade, though it's a little grubby; its rooms have all the usual facilities – the cheapest with one bed, fan, cold water only and TV. The VIP suite has comfy sofas and two bathrooms. Free internet and on-site restaurant. ❷

Pursat Guesthouse On the main road next 100m from the bridge. Slightly shabby and showing signs of age, simple, unpretentious rooms are off a large balcony, with everything you need for a night. ❶

Thmey Thansour Hotel One block west of the river, 100m north of NR5 ⓣ052/951506. Long-standing, popular guesthouse with a range of rooms, the cheapest with fan and cold water only are in the wooden annexe; rooms in the main building have hot water, a/c and TV; free internet. The excellent restaurant is open all day serving Khmer food; the menu's in English. ❶–❸

The Town

Pursat Town straddles the **Stung Pursat**, which flows northeast into the Tonle Sap. The **market**, west of the river and north of the main road (National Route 5), is centrally located and a useful point of reference; the other helpful landmark is the **bridge** that carries the National Route 5 across the Stung Pursat. Sights in town are decidedly low-key, the main attraction being the island in the river overlooking the weir, 500m or so north of the market. Once a lovely sand bank, this is now **Koh Sampovmeas**, a concrete theme-park in the shape of a ship. Needless to say legend purports that a boat became stuck here, and eventually became overgrown and turned into an island. It's decidedly whacky, with statues and a small shrine. A pedestrian bridge crosses the river close by and you can take a pleasant stroll along a shady track that runs downstream

The Legend of Khleang Muong

An attraction for locals hereabouts is the small, well-tended tomb of **Khleang Muong**, one of Cambodia's national heroes. The story goes that in 1605, the Khmer were losing the war against the Thais, when Khleang Muong ordered his soldiers to dig a pit and to cast their weapons into it; he then committed suicide by throwing himself into the pit. Seven days later the Khmer army defeated the Thais with help from the ghosts of Khleang Muong and his army of soldiers. The victory is marked by an offering ceremony here in April or May each year, at the start of the planting season and just before the rains. The pavilion at the tomb contains a life-size bronze statue of Khleang Muong, and a matching one of his wife, who, according to legend, also killed herself. The site is at the village of **Banteay Chei**, a few kilometres west of town off National Route 5. It is easily reached by moto from Pursat, but it's probably only worth a visit if you're at a completely loose end.

along the river bank – though you'll need to return the same way as there are no bridges further north.

Pursat is the main centre in Cambodia for **marble carving**, the marble coming from the rocky outcrops of the nearby Cardamom Mountains. Popular subjects include Buddhas and dancing apsaras, as well as bangles and animal statues, and the quality is high, though so are the prices. The workshops are on the somnolent south bank of the river, east of NR5.

Eating

Outside of the guesthouses and hotels the choice for eating is limited; also don't leave it too late to eat in the evening, as places tend to close quite early. For a really inexpensive meal, there's the usual assortment of noodle shops by the market and cheap restaurants on National Route 5 near the bridge.

Community Villa Restaurant 1km south of town on NR5 ⓦwww.knkscambodia.org). This NGO-run restaurant serves Khmer and Western dishes and acts as a training centre with profits helping to support children's rights, people with HIV and a reproductive health project. Being this far out of town has really hit their trade and they're currently looking for premises in town.

Tepmachha (aka The Magic Fish) Restaurant Standing alone in a yellow building on the west bank of the river, 500m north of the market. Inexpensive Khmer and Chinese food, and a great setting for a late-afternoon drink.

Around Pursat: the floating villages and the Cardamom Mountains

KOMPONG LUONG is the closest of the Tonle Sap's floating villages to Pursat, though its precise distance from town varies, ranging from around 40km in the dry season to 35km in the rainy. Populated by a mixed community of Cham and Vietnamese families, the village has its own shops, restaurants, farms and even petrol stations.

Kompong Luong can be reached by **moto** from Pursat (around $10 return), or by **car** (about $30); both can be arranged through hotels in Pursat. To drive to Kompong Luong, head east out of Pursat on National Route 5 for 30km, where there's a turning north at Krakor to the Tonle Sap. Once you arrive at the lake, boatmen will offer to take you out to look around the village for around $10, depending on how long you want to stay out on the water.

Still mostly inaccessible and unexplored, the **Cardamom Mountain range** is an area of outstanding natural beauty, its primary jungle rich in flora and fauna.

A biodiversity study in 2000 established the presence of nearly 400 different species of animal, including tiger, Asian elephant, gaur and a population of critically endangered Siamese crocodiles, previously considered extinct in the wild. It's setting itself up to be an eco tourist destination but for now things are still a bit disorganized.

A trip into the hills is best done with a local guide – ask at the tourist office in Pursat – as the roads are not well signposted and there can be problems with collapsed bridges. It's a pretty journey as the road climbs steeply through the forest, crossing tiny gorges and streams. **Ou Dah**, 56km from Pursat, is an attractive spot with rapids and a small waterfall in the jungle-clad hills. Alternatively, at **Chrok La Eing**, 73km southeast of Pursat, there's a cascade and river for a swim. Bear in mind though there's also a high risk of malaria in the mountains, so take precautions against mosquito bites.

Battambang and around

Just 291km by road from the capital, **BATTAMBANG** is the only major town on National Route 5. Once a rather somnolent place – much of its allure deriving from the rows of endangered colonial-era shophouses around the centre of town and a handful of French-style villas in the leafy streets to the south – in recent years it became popular with visitors come to ride the flat-bedded bogie **bamboo train** (see box below). However, this will have ceased operation by the time you read this, and the effect on Battambang remains to be seen. The town itself has enough minor attractions to fill a gentle half-day, including a couple of tranquil **pagodas**, Wat Phephittam and Wat Dhum Rey Sor, and a **museum**, overlooking the meandering Sangker River, which houses a small collection of statuary from some of the province's temples.

Out of town, **Wat Banan** has well-preserved Angkor Wat-style sanctuary towers built on a low hill overlooking the river, while **Phnom Sampeu** features hilltop pagodas and cave shrines with a fine view over the rice fields from the summit. The two sites can be combined into an enjoyable day-trip.

Some history

The history of Battambang is quite separate from the rest of Cambodia, because for much of its existence it fell under **Thai**, rather than Khmer jurisdiction. Founded in the eleventh century, Battambang first came under Thai influence after the fall of Angkor in the fifteenth century. Due to the town's location on the primary route between Thailand and Cambodia's capitals (variously Lovek, Oudong and Phnom Penh), the Thai army was perpetually passing through in order to intervene in squabbles within the Cambodian royal family.

In 1795, a Cambodian named **Baen**, in return for his help in returning the pro-Thai King Ang Eng to the Cambodian throne, became lord governor of **Battambang province** (which at the time incorporated territory as far away as

Off the rails

Never the most salubrious place, Battambang's 1920s train station declined further when the train from Phnom Penh stopped; now the destitute who made their homes on the disused platforms have been moved on and it is being cleaned up in the expectation that goods trains will be running by early 2011. Sadly this means the end of the **bamboo train**.

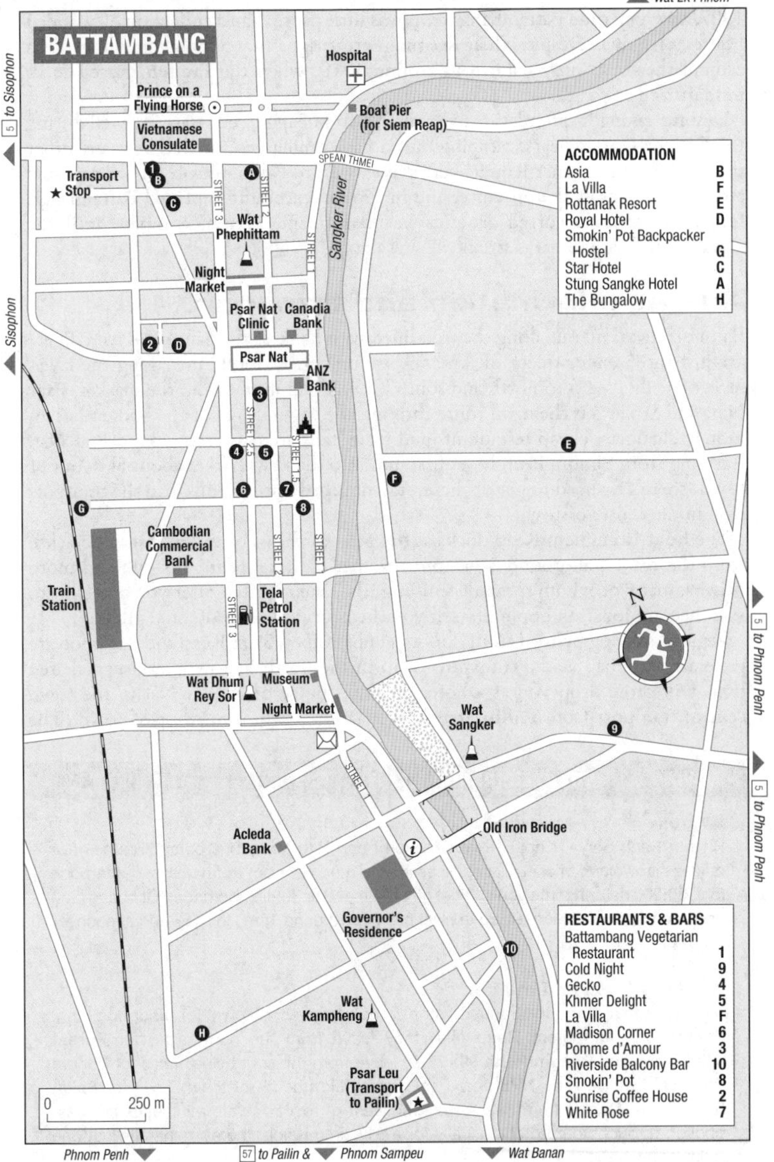

Siem Reap). Baen showed his loyalty to Thailand by paying tribute to the king in Bangkok, which effectively moved Battambang from Cambodian rule into Thai dominion.

Throughout the **nineteenth century** the province, although nominally under Thai jurisdiction, was largely left to its own affairs under a succession of all-powerful governors from the Baen family – a self-sufficient fiefdom, isolated from both Thailand and Cambodia. The province was returned to Cambodia in

1907, at which time Battambang town was little more than a collection of wooden houses on stilts. Despite their seeming great age, the colonial buildings seen around the town only date from around 1910, when the **French** moved in to modernize it.

Despite having its population evacuated, Battambang fared relatively well during the **Khmer Rouge** years, escaping the damage which was suffered by many other towns. After the Khmer Rouge were driven west to Pailin, they launched repeated attacks throughout the province, and in 1994 even briefly captured Battambang; ferocious battles occurred around Wat Banan and Phnom Sampeu until the amnesty deal of 1996 was struck.

Arrival, information and transport

Battambang is laid out along the tree-lined west bank of the Sangker River. There are just three main streets, all known by number. Street 1 runs along the river, Street 2 is divided into north and south by Wat Phephittam and the market, **Psar Nat**, and Street 3 is the main route through the town. Most of the budget hotels, money changers, cheap restaurants and fruit stalls are clustered around Psar Nat. Arriving from Phnom Penh buses first pull into the new market about 5km out of town; there's no need to get off here, stay onboard until it pulls into the transport stop in the centre of town.

The **boat** from Siem Reap docks at the pier northeast of town, just under 1km from the centre, at around 3 or 4pm; it's met by hotel touts, tuk-tuk and moto drivers, many of whom speak decent English – they'll often offer you a free lift to your accommodation hoping to sell you their services as a potential guide.

Visitors arriving by road from Phnom Penh, Poipet, Siem Reap and Sisophon are generally dropped at the **transport stop** in the north of town, although shared taxis will often drop you at a hotel of your choice or at Psar Nat in the town centre; transport from **Pailin** arrives at Psar Leu, 1km southwest of town. The

Moving on from Battambang

By bus

Phnom Penh Sorya, Capitol, Neak Krohorm and Rith Mony bus companies all have offices in town and offer similar services. Buses run to **Phnom Penh** until mid-afternoon (5hr; 30,000 riel); en route you can get off at Pursat (1hr 30min), Kompong Chhnang (3hr) or Oudong (4hr); for **Siem Reap** the last bus goes around 1pm (3hr; $5), and at noon for **Poipet** (3hr; $5).

By shared taxi and minibus

Most taxis leave from the transport stop in the northwest of town: for **Sisophon** (2hr), **Poipet** (3hr) and **Siem Reap** (4hr) they leave from the north side; for **Pursat** (1hr 30min) and **Phnom Penh** (4hr) they leave from the south side. Taxis for Phnom Penh also wait on the NR5 near Psar Thmei, 5km south of town. Taxis for **Pailin** (20,000 riel; 1hr) go from Psar Leu, southwest of town. Private minibuses are best booked through your hotel – usually for a $1 commission; there's generally just one a day early in the morning.

By boat

The boat trip down the Sangker River and across the Tonle Sap to **Siem Reap** continues to be popular with tourists, although it's now quicker and cheaper to get there by road. The boat pier is on the east bank of the river just north of Spean Thmei; one 30-seater boat a day leaves at 8am ($17; 6–8hr). It's far from comfortable, movement is restricted and you'd be advised to take food, plenty of water and a cushion.

now defunct **airport** is just south of town – but it's unlikely that passenger flights will ever resume.

The **tourist office** (Mon–Fri 8–11am & 2–5pm) is south of the centre in the compound of a lovely colonial house near the area of government offices, with several free-range turkeys strutting through the grounds. The friendly staff are happy to chat, and have a few leaflets (but no street map); best of all there's free internet access. **Moto** fares around the town are around 2000 riel, a bit more after dark or if you're going across the river.

Accommodation

Asia North of the market, towards the transport stop ⓣ053/953523, ⓦwww.asrhotel.com.kh. A good budget option, this modern hotel has small, but pleasantly furnished en-suite rooms with TV and fan or a/c; wi-fi. ❷

La Villa 185 Pom Romchek ⓣ053/730151, ⓦwww.lavilla-battambang.com. In a renovated 1930s merchant's house, on the river opposite Psar Nat, *La Villa* has only seven rooms and booking is essential. Rooms have colonial ambience (albeit slightly musty) and are furnished in period style; all with TV and DVD player, a/c and fan, hot shower, tea- and coffee- making facilities, wi-fi and safety box. In the orangery, the restaurant serves the best French food in Battambang. ❻

Rottanak Resort East of the river, 300m towards NR5 ⓣ053/953255, ⓦwww.rottanakresort.com. An inviting swimming pool surrounded by ten well-furnished, en-suite bungalows, all with hot water, a/c, TV, wi-fi and their own small seating areas, make this a relaxing choice; continental breakfast included. ❺

Royal Hotel 100m west of Psar Nat ⓣ053/953524, ⓦwww.asrhotel.com.kh. Long-standing, and one of the best-value hotels in town, the *Royal* for all its pushiness is a family-run place. Clean, en-suite rooms, most with TV, fan and fridge, are set around an atrium; a/c and hot water are available for a small premium. Rooftop bar and restaurant, internet, local trips and transport arranged. ❷

Smokin Pot Backpacker Hostel Near the railway station, west off Street 3 ⓣ012/821400, ⓔvannaksmokinpot@yahoo.com. A bed in this clean, new hostel is just $2.50 per night; bunk rooms are air-conditioned, and you get a proper locker for your kit. Balcony bar with great sunset views, and simple restaurant. ❶

Star Hotel Just north of the town centre ⓣ053/953522, ⓦwww.asrhotel.com.kh. Popular with tour groups, this charming small hotel has the same owners as the *Royal*. Its opulent rooms are heavy on Khmer wood; en-suite bathrooms with hot water, TV, a/c, fridge are standard. ❸

Stung Sangke Hotel North of NR5, one block from the river ⓣ053/953495, ⓦwww.stungsangkehotel.com. A great addition to the town's accommodation; its spacious, well-appointed rooms have TV, mini-bar, bathtubs, safety box and tea/coffee making facilities. Other facilities include restaurant, secure parking, wi-fi, lift, gym and swimming pool. ❺

The Bungalow South of town one block west of the Governor's residence ⓣ012/916123, ⓦwww.thebungalow.us. Run by a charming Khmer family, this a relaxing a low-key place to chill out for a few days. Choose from one of the three bungalows with private balconies, surrounded by lush gardens, or a vast, palatial room in the main house; all rooms have hot water, a/c, TV, internet access and work desk. On-site thatch-roofed restaurant. ❸–❹

The Town

Sleepy Battambang lacks both the traffic of Phnom Penh and the tourists of Siem Reap, making it a pleasant, if sprawling, town to stroll around. At the centre of town, the 1930s **Psar Nat**, is a faded Art Deco building, its white clock-towers at both ends lending a certain charm. The streets just south of the market are lined with colonial **shophouses**, more and more of which are being "restored" with bathroom-tile facades, mirror glass and garish plastic advertising signs. More appealing are the faded, shabby buildings still awaiting restoration, most of which retain their original wrought-iron balustrades on overhanging balconies. In the south of town the restored Governor's Residence is a stunning example of Battambang's French architecture.

Colonial architecture

An enduring legacy of the French protectorate is the European colonial architecture which still graces Phnom Penh and many of Cambodia's provincial towns. Particularly evocative of the period are the colonial **shophouses**, open-fronted shops at ground level set back under a wide colonnaded walkway created by an overhanging upper storey – often with balconies. Also characteristic of the period are the country's colonial **villas**, typically adorned with shuttered windows, balconies and turrets. Some of the best examples of shophouses can be found in Battambang, clustered along the main street leading to the market and, close by, on the riverfront. There are also good examples of colonial architecture around the river and old market area in Kampot (see p.294), and around the main post office in Phnom Penh (see p.90). Sadly, many of these old gems – especially the shophouses – are being renovated in a style popularized in modern China: glazed tiles are fixed to the facades (to save having to paint) and old shuttered windows are being sealed with mirror glass to keep in the air conditioning. Sadly the trend seems irreversible, as very few Cambodians see any reason to preserve their colonial past.

The picturesque **riverfront** with its wide grassy banks and paved walkway is a great place for a stroll. Originally the Sangker River was just 5m wide here, but when the Dambang River, south of town, was dammed by sinking a boat filled with earth across it, the Sangker gradually widened. Nowadays its banks lie at least 30m apart. In the late afternoon fruit-shake and food stalls set up near the post office; while across the bridge the park turns into a vast gymnasium as folk come to exercise after work. Disappointingly, the riverside road itself is dreary, lined with print shops and mobile-phone outlets.

While you're in Battambang seek out its oranges – sweet, juicy and green skinned even when ripe – this fruit is prized all over Cambodia.

One treasure to be found along the riverfront is a small sixteenth- or seventeenth-century **Chinese temple**, a one-storey structure restored in 1921 whose dark-red doors and heavily ridged roof tiles edged with ceremonial dragons look quite incongruous amid the area's colonial architecture. Inside the temple, the rather ferocious-looking god, Kwan Tai, is worshipped at a small altar; despite his looks he's revered for his loyalty and integrity.

Further south on Street 1 is the town's **museum** (Mon–Fri 8–11am & 2–5pm; $1; no photography), with a small but interesting collection of statues and temple carvings from the surrounding area. There are some wonderfully detailed sandstone lintels outside the building, and shiny linga and impressive carvings inside. Two particularly interesting pieces are a thirteenth-century statue of a Bodhisattva "tattooed" with a thousand Buddhas, and a well-worn depiction of Yama on a buffalo. The two oldest **pagodas** in Battambang, Wat Dhum Rey Sor and Wat Phephittam, have both been restored several times since their construction in 1848. Behind the museum lies **Wat Dhum Rey Sor** (Pagoda of the White Elephant) – named for a statue of a white elephant adorning the western steps up to the vihara. Outside the vihara are fine murals depicting scenes from the *Ramayana*; look out for Hanuman riding a steam engine on the east wall. The pagoda's stained-glass windows are delightful when the sun catches their brightly coloured panes. While you're here, look out for a section of high stone wall on the road running down to Psar Leu; this is all that remains of the **Kamphaeng**, the town's fort, demolished by the French.

Back at Psar Nat, the most interesting approach to **Wat Phephittam** is from the south, where the gates are guarded by two *yeaks* (giants); the monks claim that these used to sport threatening expressions, though now they wear a benign look

– a strange example of the Khmer belief in metamorphosis. Many of the monks here speak English and will give you a tour of the vihara (in exchange for letting them practise their language skills), which features some elaborate modern murals illustrating the life of Buddha. While you're in town you may see two distinctive **statues** relating to a bizarre legend surrounding Battambang, a name which literally translates as "lost stick". According to the tale, a man named Dambang Krognuing turned black after eating rice stirred with a black stick; he then deposed the king and assumed the throne. The erstwhile king's son subsequently defeated Dambang Krognuing with the aid of a magical flying horse, despite a vain attempt by the interloper to hurl his black stick at the prince's steed. A massive statue of Dambang Krognuing decorates the traffic circle on the way out of town towards the airport, while a statue of the prince on his flying horse sits at the north end of Street 3.

Eating

Food in Battambang is good and cheap, with a selection of **restaurants** within walking distance of the centre that serve decent Khmer and Chinese food and have English-language menus. There is also an increasing number of places geared to Westerners. For an authentic Khmer eating experience, check out the inexpensive **food stalls** in and around Psar Nat. Late afternoons, a busy night market sets up on the street south of Wat Phephittam, an excellent place to try out **Cambodian home cooking** – tasty pork with green beans and chilli and beef in a dry curry are standard, but it's very much a case of what the cook feels like making on the day, so the way to choose is to lift the lids on the pots and see what's on offer. More stalls set up at about 4pm on the riverfront near the post office; this is the place to come for savoury chicken *borbor*, baguettes, Khmer desserts and fruit shakes. The sweet-toothed can find cakes, cookies and pastries at the Ponleu Reaksmey Bakery on Street 3.

Restaurants

Battambang Vegetarian Restaurant Just north of the *Asia Hotel*. Open only for breakfast, though you can get a takeaway picnic lunch. The delicious vegetarian food is primarily soya based, with noodle soups, rice and dumplings being the main fare; fresh soya milk is available every day.

Cold Night East of the river across the old bridge. This used to be the only place in town to get Western food, now it's one of many. The burgers, steaks and spaghetti are still good – if you don't mind the hike out of town.

Gecko Street 3, 200m south of Psar Nat. In a terrific location this first-floor bar and restaurant occupies a corner spot overlooking Street 3. Staff are from underprivileged backgrounds and come here to train. They are paid a bonus for happy customers – you'll be asked to fill out a survey before you leave. Burritos, tacos, bagels, and pasta dishes are the main fare.

Khmer Delight One block south of Psar Nat, between sts 2 and 3. By day *Khmer Delight* is just another café, but by nightfall it's morphed into a bustling foreigners' restaurant with tablecloths and intimate table lights. The menu is extensive, and inexpensive with Khmer and Western food – British fish and chips and pork chops and mash for example, along with a choice of beers or wines. Try Phnom Banon brandy from Battambang to finish – one will probably be enough.

La Villa 185 Pom Romchek ⓣ012/991801, ⓦwww.lavilla-battambang.com. In the hotel of the same name, *La Villa* is Battambang's classiest restaurant. The dining room is in the orangery and it serves a wide range of dishes with style and flair. This is also the place to come for an atmospheric cocktail.

Pomme d'Amour Street 2.5. More akin to a Cuban *paladore* (or one of London's new underground restaurants) this centrally located restaurant opens only for dinner, and is the cosiest place in town for dining *à deux*, mains about $7. Grilled steak and prawn cocktail feature, though the style is French/Khmer fusion, food with a local twist.

Smokin' Pot Two blocks south of Psar Nat. This attractive café-restaurant features great-value food with an emphasis on Thai cuisine, but there are Khmer and Western dishes on the menu as well. Cookery classes run daily (see p.144).

Sunrise Coffee House Just west of the *Royal Hotel* (closed Sunday). The first stop in town for caffeine addicts, it also has a good range of filling breakfasts and teas. If you can't stomach rice or noodles for breakfast, try the burrito instead.

White Rose Street 2. Long-running, friendly restaurant, juice bar and ice-cream parlour, with a lengthy menu of economically priced Khmer and Chinese dishes ($2/dish), including spring rolls, and shrimp and vegetable dishes. Excellent, great-value food.

Drinking and nightlife

Nightlife for locals in Battambang mainly revolves around the seedy karaoke restaurants and bars on the streets near the train station. For tourists, Battambang has a burgeoning bar scene. *Madison Corner* (two blocks south of the market on Street 2.5) is a great little spot for early evening G&T or a few late evening beers, wi-fi, pool table, darts, wide-screen TV and scrumptious crêpes. Upstairs in an old wooden house in the south of town, on a curve of the river near Psar Leu, the atmospheric *Riverside Balcony Bar* (Tues–Sun 4–11pm) has soft lighting, good music and a range of cocktails. Evocative of French Indochina, the bar of *La Villa* (daily 5–9.30pm) is the place to sip a cocktail or after-dinner brandy – the downside is its early closing.

Listings

Banks and exchange All the banks in town change travellers' cheques at the usual two-percent commission. ANZ and Canadia banks, both near the market, advance cash on Visa and MasterCard and have ATMs. For Western Union money transfers, go to Acleda Bank or Cambodia Asia Bank (CAB), both on Street 3.
Bicycle hire It's harder than you'd think to hire a bicycle in Battambang; try Gecko ($2 per day) on Street 3 or Today Tours on Street 1.5.
Books The Smiling Book Shop, on Street 2 just south of Psar Nat, has an extensive range of clean, used books and a decent selection on Cambodia.
Circus North of town on NR5 towards Sisophon, the Phare Ponleu Selpak organization (Ⓦ www.phareps.org) has shows a couple of times a week (children $4, adults $8).
Consulate Vietnam, north of Psar Nat on Street 2 (Mon–Fri 8–11am & 2–5pm).
Cookery school Vannak at the *Smokin' Pot* was the first person to arrange cookery classes in Cambodia (daily, $8 per person); contact him by phone (Ⓣ 12/821400) or at Smokin' Pot to book.
Hospital and clinics Avoid the provincial hospital near the river, where facilities are basic and conditions none too clean. You'll be better off at a private clinic; try the Psar Nat Clinic, north of the market; English spoken.
Internet access In addition to hotels and guesthouses there are internet cafés all over town for 4000 riel/hour; the tourist information office has free access.
Massage Seeing Hands (massage by the blind) is on two blocks south of Psar Nat just west of Madison Corner ($5/hr).
Motorbike rental Gecko on Street 3 rents out motorbikes ($6 per day).
Pharmacies There are plenty of pharmacies near Psar Nat, though English-speakers are limited.
Phones There are cheap-rate phone booths near the market for domestic calls, and a couple of Camintel booths on the south side of the market for international calls, though it's cheaper and more reliable to use Skype at one of the many internet cafés.
Post office On Street 1 in the south of town (Mon–Fri 7–11am & 2–5pm).
Shopping Gecko on Street 3 has a small boutique selling scarves, jewellery and other small items. At the time of writing a couple of other tourist-oriented shops were opening.
Swimming pools Some hotels allow non-residents to use their swimming pools for a small daily fee: *Rottanak Resort* ($3), *Stung Sangke* ($5).
Supermarkets Chea Neing, west of Psar Nat, has a pretty good selection of imported luxuries, and there's a mini-mart at Tela petrol station, south on Street 3. A shopping mall is due to open in the south of town on Street 3 – no doubt this will include a branch of the Phnom Penh chain, Lucky.

Around Battambang

Phnom Sampeu, the main tourist sight close to town, has several active pagodas, a number of atmospheric caves (for which you'll need a torch) and a fine view of the

Festivals and ceremonies

You are unlikely to be in Cambodia for long before coming across a vibrant festival or noisy religious ceremony. Most Cambodians like nothing more than to don their glad-rags, pack up a picnic and head off to a pagoda, where after lighting some incense sticks and making an offering of flowers or food to the Buddha, they throw an impromptu party. As Theravada Buddhism follows the lunar calendar, the dates of most festivals and ceremonies vary with the phases of the moon.

Cambodians celebrate the Khmer New Year ▲

Prayers and offerings for Bonn Pchum Ben ▼

Castanets and talcum powder

Bonn Chaul Chhnam (Khmer New Year) is celebrated in mid-April. The festivities usually continue for a week, providing an opportunity for young people to get together and play various games – all of them barely disguised excuses for eyeing up a potential marriage partner. These include a version of skittles using the disc-like seed of the *angkunh*, a forest vine. The winner gets to smack two *angkunh* seeds against the loser's knee, holding them in one hand like castanets; if they fail to produce the required clacking sound, the "loser" gets to do it back at them. In the provinces, it's common to throw talcum powder and water at passers-by as part of the festivities, so watch out.

Hungry ghosts

Bonn Pchum Ben takes place between mid-September and early October. Families are supposed to visit seven different pagodas to pay their respects to their ancestors, risking a year of bad luck if they do not. Cambodians believe that at this time the doors to hell are opened and the "hungry ghosts" – those who have no families to make offerings for them – come out to feed, so rice is cast for them into dark corners of the pagoda.

Water festival

During the rainy season (June–Oct), so much water pours down the Mekong that the water flows back up the Tonle Sap river forming the massive Tonle Sap lake. Come October or November, the flow returns to its usual direction, an event marked by **Bonn Om Tuk**, the **Water Festival**. Celebrations focus on three days of boat races on the river at Phnom surrounding countryside. Combining a visit to Phnom Sampeu with **Wat Banan**, its Angkor-style towers sitting atop a small hill, makes for an excellent day out. Other places of interest near town are **Kamping Poy**, a vast reservoir created using forced labour during the Pol Pot era, and **Wat Ek Phnom**, an eleventh-century Hindu temple to the north of town. All these sites are covered by a single-entry **ticket** ($2), valid for one day and available at each of the sites – although it's not really practical to see all four places in a day. The best way around is by hiring a **tuk-tuk** or **moto** in Battambang for the round trip to Phnom Sampeu and Wat Banan (around $10 by tuk-tuk or $6 by moto). An excursion to the countryside north of Battambang is a wonderful way to pass a day (or half-day); tuk-tuk and moto drivers will ferry you around and act as your guide for just $8, arranging visits to Wat Ek Phnom, and to villages producing sticky rice, rice noodles, rice paper, fish paste and, at the appropriate time of the year, rice planting or harvesting.

Phnom Sampeu

The elongated rocky outcrop of **Phnom Sampeu** (Boat Mountain), about 15km southwest of Battambang on National Route 10, consists of two peaks connected by a narrow pathway. Local legend says that the outcrop is the broken hull of a ship, sunk by a crocodile whose love for a girl was unrequited; when she and her fiancé took to sea, they were attacked by the crocodile and drowned. Some distance away to the northwest, another quite separate small hill, **Phnom Kropeu** (Crocodile Mountain), continues the tale: the local population, scared of the crocodile, drained all the water from the area so that he couldn't swim away; eventually the poor croc died and turned into a hill.

On arrival, you'll be dropped at the foot of the **steps** leading steeply up the larger hill, near a cluster of refreshment stalls. You'll first need to buy a ticket ($2) at a small kiosk by the steps. At the foot of the steps is a gateway topped by a sculpture of a boat, and a large red chedi nearby, which holds the ashes of people who die with no next of kin.

If you have your own transport it's possible to drive to the top by following the track along the foot of the hill for a few hundred metres, then taking the cemented road on the right where the road forks (you could also walk up this route, and walk back down the main path). If you don't have a **guide**, there are plenty of local children who will accompany you up the hill and show you how to find the caves. They'll expect a small tip, but it's a good idea to let them tag along as there are unmarked forks in the paths, and they'll probably have a torch as well. **Don't stray from the defined paths** here as most of the hills hereabouts are thought to be mined.

The **main path** up the hill is a steep and tiring walk of around thirty to forty-five minutes. A right fork about halfway up makes a detour to the so-called **wind cave** (*leahng kshal*). The cave is approached through a pagoda-style gateway, beyond which steps lead down to a shady, rocky platform where a number of shrines have been placed. The cave itself is open at two ends, and a light, cool breeze usually blows through it (hence its name). The mouth of the cave is marked by a square wooden doorframe set into the cliff face. You can walk through the cave to the other side of the hill in about fifteen minutes – the cave floor is dry but uneven – though without your own torch you'll have to buy a candle from the guardian here, as the locals do, and hope it doesn't go out in the breeze.

Retrace your steps from the cave and then, just after the pagoda-style gateway, take the small path straight ahead which leads back to the main track up the hill. Turn right and walk for a few minutes to the **Chinese pagoda**, from where the path carries on climbing for another couple of hundred metres to reach a **Buddhist pagoda**. In 1994–95 Phnom Sampeu was at the front line of fighting between government forces and the Pailin faction of the Khmer Rouge. Remnants of the conflict can be seen in two abandoned Russian-built **anti-aircraft guns** by the Buddhist pagoda; signs warn against approaching the guns as the area around may be mined.

Beyond the pagoda it's just a hundred metres to the summit of the hill and the **Preah Jan** vihara. From here, there are panoramic views over the surrounding rice fields and countryside to Battambang. During the Khmer Rouge era, the pagoda buildings were used as a prison and **interrogation centre** – victims were pushed through a hole in the roof of a cave to fall to their deaths. A narrow rocky path behind the pagoda leads to the **Theatre Cave** (*leahng lacaun*). Although theatrical productions were once staged here, it's hard to imagine that this sinister cave was ever a place of enjoyment: a host of bats chirp in the roof crannies, and in the dim light it's easy to think you see the outlines of haunted faces on the cave walls. A reclining Buddha keeps watch, while a small metal cage contains the skulls and bones of bodies which were found all over the cave floor. A second cave, further down the hill, was the theatrical dressing room, and a cage here also contains human bones.

From here, the easiest way down is to follow the cemented road back down to the foot of the hill and the refreshment stands. Alternatively, you could take the narrow path off to the left just below the steps and cross to the other peak, then make your way down from there.

Wat Banan

The best preserved of the temples around Battambang, **Wat Banan** can be reached from Battambang by following Street 1 south out of town for 20km until you see some distinctive Angkor Wat-like towers; the temple lies immediately at the top of a steep laterite stairway which ascends a seventy-metre-high hill. Alternatively, you can get here directly from Phnom Sampeu via a narrow dirt road which passes through some delightful countryside.

It's known that Wat Banan was consecrated as a Buddhist temple, but scholars are uncertain who built the temple or exactly when it was completed – estimates put this between the tenth and thirteenth centuries. Five corn-on-the-cob towers remain, all in a somewhat collapsed state, and several of the carvings have lost their heads to vandals, though there are a few still in reasonable condition. You will likely be accompanied on the climb by young kids who hope for a tip by telling you a bit about the temple. It's certainly worth the steep clamber up to see the detailed lintels, beheaded apsaras and views out over endless paddies, with Phnom Sampeu clearly visible to the north.

Kamping Poy

The prettiness of the lake at **Kamping Poy** belies the fact that it was created by the Pol Pot regime using slave labour – over ten thousand people died during the construction of the eight-kilometre **dam** which bounds the lake. The dam lay at the heart of an extensive irrigation system, now sadly silted up and collapsed, which transported water to the surrounding fields, to allow dry-season rice cultivation and boost foreign income for the regime. From the lakeside there are fabulous views across the plains and lake to the distant hills; at weekends and holidays the lake is packed with Cambodians frolicking in the water, but during the week you'll have the place to yourself. **Boats** can generally be hired for around 4000 riel per hour. The rim of the dam is navigable by moto or on foot for several kilometres, which means that even at busy times you can get away for a quiet swim. Kamping Poy is 15km west of National Route 57; the turning is south of Phnom Sampeu.

Wat Ek Phnom

The ruined eleventh-century Hindu temple at **Wat Ek Phnom**, 12km north of Battambang on the river road, now sits in the grounds of a modern pagoda,

Penh, manned by teams from all over the country. People from the provinces pour in to support their local boat crews as they race from the Chroy Chung Va Bridge to the Royal Palace.

▲ Bonn Om Tuk, Phnom Penh

The divining of the Royal Bulls

Marking the start of the planting season in May, the ceremony of **Bonn Chroat Preah Nongkoal (Royal Ploughing Ceremony)**, held at Lean Preah Sre park in Phnom Penh, combines animism, Buddhism and plenty of pomp. It begins with chanting monks asking the earth spirits for permission to plough. Then ceremonial furrows are drawn, rice is scattered and offerings are made to the divinities. The most important part of the ceremony, however, is what the Royal Bulls choose when offered rice, grain, grass, water and wine. Rice or grain augur well; water signifies rain; grass is a sign that crops will be devastated by insects; and wine, that there will be drought.

▼ Royal Ploughing Ceremony, Phnom Penh

Enter bridegroom…with pig's head

Most **marriages** in Cambodia are arranged, with the couple given the chance to get to know each other on several occasions before the union is finalized. Then a propitious day for the wedding is decided, usually with the help of a fortune-teller. The day begins with the bridegroom and his party processing through the streets to the bride's house, bearing presents and trays of food, including an obligatory **pig's head**.

Most brides have at least six changes of costume for the day, ranging from ceremonial silk *sampots* to an often garishly coloured Western-style wedding gown.

▼ Wedding ceremony

Receptions often take over the whole road, as each family member will have invited practically everyone they know. This began as an opportunity to find partners for unmarried sons and daughters, but these days the aim is to make a profit, and guests are required to give cash, not presents.

Offering-day flowers in a Cambodian market ▲

Flower sculpture and ripe bananas

Buddhism is an intrinsic part of Khmer life, and **Buddhist observance days** occur on the days of the full, new and both quarter moons. On such days, old ladies make early morning visits to the pagoda, and everyone else tries at least to make an **offering of flowers or fruit** at home, so market stalls do a roaring trade in bunches of bananas and flowers. Lotus buds, the traditional offering flower to the Buddha, are folded artistically to expose their pale-pink inner petals, jasmine buds are threaded onto sticks and strings, and other flowers are bunched into vivid posies, to be taken to pagodas or used to decorate domestic shrines.

Nun with betel-stained lips, Angkor Wat ▼

Betel

Betel plays a central role in many Cambodian **ceremonies**: at weddings, it is central to the religious proceedings, with a plate of leaves and ornate containers of nut slivers and paste taking pride of place among the offerings. It has a mild narcotic effect, which becomes addictive, and nowadays is more or less the preserve of old women, easily spotted by their eroded, red-stained teeth and lips. A betel wad is a large flat **leaf** from a vine of the pepper family, smeared with **quicklime paste** and wrapped around a chunk of **betel nut**. Chewing causes a mass of red juices to be produced, which is spat out.

surrounded by lotus ponds, small streams and rivers, giving the feeling of being on an island. The temple itself is enclosed by a crumbling laterite wall, and the sandstone buildings of the main sanctuary are lined up in a row, joined by an enclosed walkway. The temple would originally have been reached via a couple of two-metre-high terraces, though these have collapsed, and you'll now have to scramble up a small hill. To enter the sanctuary itself, you'll have to climb through a window or a broken section of wall, or walk round to the slightly better-preserved south side, where a crumbling doorway survives, along with some carvings.

Pailin and around

Ringed by hills on the border with Thailand, **PAILIN**, once the gem-mining centre of Cambodia, is a down-beat town with not a lot going for it. After being ousted from power in 1979, the Khmer Rouge were easily able to hole up here, supporting their campaigns against the government by tapping into the area's rich natural resources – **gemstones and untouched forests**; it's said that gem-mining alone earned them a monthly revenue of $10 million. They held out until August 1996 when, in a move that marked the beginning of the end for the Khmer Rouge, Ieng Sary, the local commander, struck a deal with the Cambodian government, gaining immunity from prosecution for himself and taking three thousand defectors over to the government side. Even now though, older Pailin residents still reminisce about the Khmer Rouge years, when education and health care were available and food was given to the old and needy – these days, reliance on the free market means there are few public services.

It's 80km from Battambang to Pailin along National Route 57. On this recently upgraded road the journey from Battambang now takes just an hour, with the bone-jarring trips that left Pailin in isolation for so many years a distant memory. The road passes a couple of sites of interest including, after 15km, Phnom Sampeu (see p.145) and then, about 10km further on in the village of **SNENG**, the remains of a tenth-century temple, **Prasat Yeah Ten**. Three of the temple's entrances retain beautifully carved lintels, while behind the modern temple are three extremely old brick sanctuaries, perhaps also dating back to the tenth century.

The main reason for coming here, however, unless you're interested in Khmer Rouge history, is to **cross the border** into Thailand. At the border there are a couple of casinos popular with Thais and a scruffy border market, but no other attractions as such.

Practicalities

Pailin can be reached by bus (Rith Mony) or taxi from Battambang, a smooth, eighty-kilometre trip on National Route 57 that takes just over an hour. Once the road starts to climb, rice paddies give way to plantations. Not long ago it was jungle all the way to Pailin, but in the past few years private concerns have paid for the land to be cleared of mines (though it isn't as "clear" as you'd hope) and have grubbed out the jungle to plant cash crops. You'll also see the odd factory. As you near town, the road climbs steeply to Phnom Yat, where it executes a ninety-degree turn. From here it's a kilometre along the ridge to the traffic circle; go straight ahead and the market is downhill on your left, or follow the sharp turn downhill to the left and the **market** will be on your right. Around the market you'll find the town's **transport stop**, food stalls and money changers.

Although dollars and riel are both accepted in town, the Thai **baht** is the currency of choice; change dollars here and you'll be given baht unless you specifically ask

To the border

The **Thai border** (open daily 7am–8pm), 20km from Pailin, can be reached in about twenty minutes by shared taxi ($5) or half an hour by moto ($2.50). At the border itself there's a small market and a couple of **casinos**, which entertain an almost exclusively Thai clientele. Now and again there are hassles here, with Thai border guards insisting that you have a ticket for your onward journey out of Thailand before being admitted to the country – ask around in Battambang before setting off to assess the situation. Once across you can take a minibus to Chanthaburi (100 baht), then another bus to Bangkok, or Trat for Koh Chang.

for riel. There are branches of the Canadia and Acleda banks on the main road near the traffic circle.

The **post office** is east of the traffic circle behind the **hospital** and the **tourist office** is just opposite. **Phone** calls can be made from a couple of shops opposite the market; there's internet access at the *Pailin Ruby Hotel* (2000riel per hr).

Accommodation

The best and least unruly (Pailin attracts a lot of truckers) place to stay in town is the *Pailin Ruby* (Ⓣ055/6363603; ❷), west of the traffic circle on the main road through town. Rooms here are clean and pleasant enough, with en-suite bathrooms, TV and chunky wood furniture; hot water and a/c are available for an extra charge. Just uphill from the market the *Kim Young Heng Guest House* (Ⓣ016/939841; ❶), has a range of fan and a/c rooms, though most are windowless cells. Out of town, 4km towards the border, the very pleasant *Bamboo Guesthouse* (Ⓣ012/405818) has a range of wooden bungalows in a pleasant garden, with hot water, a/c or fan; TV is available. The restaurant and bar here are a bonus.

The town and around

Pailin is a sprawling and haphazard frontier town; only the few government buildings and the bank give it any feeling of permanence. In the south of town, on the road in from Battambang, is a small but unmistakeable hill, **Phnom Yat**, the summit dominated by mobile-telephone transmitters and a modern stupa. A peaceful vantage point from which to watch the sunset, the hill was named after a Buddhist pilgrim couple who arrived in Pailin at the end of the nineteenth century. Hunting and gem mining had already begun to destroy the countryside, and Yeah Yat and her husband set up a meditation centre on the hill where they could be close to nature and the mountain spirits. Yat began to receive messages from the spirits that there would continue to be a plentiful supply of gems in the soil as long as the miners respected the land, built pagodas and made appropriate offerings. As word of this prediction spread, superstitious miners did as they were told and continued to find gems; today, however, their luck is growing thin (although you might see visitors vainly scratching about in the soil around the temple). Locals say that to prevent bad luck, before you leave Pailin you should make a small offering here and thank the spirits for letting you use their water and air. Gory **tableaux** at the pagoda illustrate the fate that befalls those destined for hell, including a man having his tongue pulled out and another being boiled in oil. Tucked away behind the modern vihara is all that's left of the previous pagoda – wall paintings, floor tiles and a cracked stupa – after it was destroyed by the Khmer Rouge.

Close by, on the bend of the road, is **Wat Ratanasaoporn**, its enclosing wall covered in a bas-relief depicting the Churning of the Ocean of Milk (see p.188). The pagoda hit the headlines in 2000 when it emerged that the monks had been entertaining "ladies of the night" and eighty monks were defrocked following the scandal.

From here, the road runs down a ridge into town. Go straight on at the roundabout and the market is downhill on your left; following the sharp turn to the left, the road runs downhill to the **market** on the right. Here there are a few **gem dealers** hawking their wares alongside vendors of vegetables and household goods.

The gem mines

Pailin has been a gem-mining centre for nearly a hundred years, and it's said that sapphires, rubies and garnets once lay everywhere on the surface. Now much of the land is mined out, and fortune-seekers have to dig deep into the rocky ground in search of the stones, which in their raw state resemble fragments of broken glass. It's hard toil for the prospectors, and for most, hope turns to wistfulness as they sift painstakingly through mounds of red dirt, sorting earth from rocks; piles of spoil scar the landscape, creating an almost lunar scene. Most of the claims are now abandoned, and those prospectors still at work are pretty secretive about their diggings; but if you're interested to see them ask at *Bamboo Guesthouse* for information about where the current workings are, though there's little to see apart from a hole in the ground and a pile of earth. Typical finds today are small garnets and topazes; rubies and sapphires are now rare.

The Phnom Ching Chok Reservoir and O Chrah Waterfall

Phnom Ching Chok Reservoir (5 baht), about 5km southwest of town, used to be a popular weekend spot among locals, but it's currently closed due to a couple of unfortunate accidents. But if you fancy a hike, continue 400m past the entrance to the reservoir until you reach a fork in the road, then go straight on for another 3.5km, crossing a couple of streams, to **O Chrah Waterfall** on the left; there is a **risk of land mines**, so don't stray from the path. A moto should charge about 200 baht to take you out there and pick you up later; take a picnic from the town as there's nowhere to get refreshments.

Eating and drinking

Eating in Pailin is no gastronomic delight, but there are plenty of stalls in the market and cheap restaurants nearby. Near the top of the ridge road, the *Phkay Proek* is not bad. But for better ambience and a reliable meal head to *Bamboo Guesthouse* which serves Khmer and Thai food and can manage a few Western options too. **Nightlife** in Pailin revolves around numerous karaoke/dining places – though few foreigners venture inside.

Sisophon and around

SISOPHON, called *Svay* (mango) by the locals in these parts (no one seems to know why), and *Banteay Meanchey* by the bus companies, is the jumping-off point for a day-trip to the massive Angkorian temple ruins of **Banteay Chhmar** and **Banteay Tuop**. Though there's nothing much to do in the scruffy, dusty town, it's something of a diamond in the rough, being one of the friendliest places in Cambodia.

Banteay Chhmar apart, you can also use the town as the base to visit a few minor attractions on the border with Siem Reap province: the stone-carving village of **Choob**; **Phnom Sarok**, a traditional weaving village where they produce their own silkworms; and **Ang Trapaeng Thmor**, a reservoir rebuilt by forced labour under the Khmer Rouge and now designated a nature reserve for rare Sarus cranes.

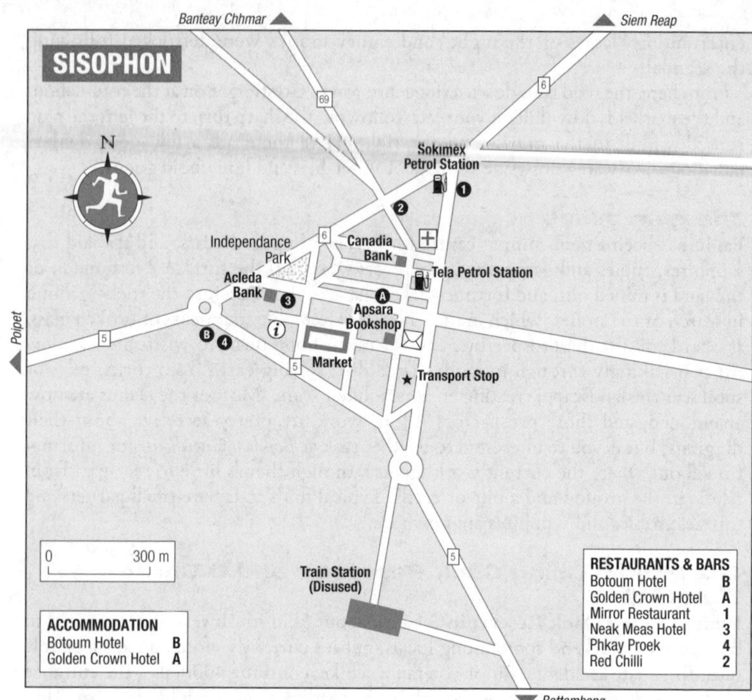

Practicalities

Arriving by road, you'll be dropped at the busy **transport stop** just east of the market, where moto drivers are readily available; this is also where you'll need to come for onward transport when leaving Sisophon. The **tourist office**, on a backstreet northwest of the market, is usually closed. You can cash travellers' cheques, change money and get an advance on cards at Acleda (Visa only) and Canadia banks; the latter also has an ATM. You can change money (dollars, riel and baht) at the market. You can make **phone calls** at cheap-rate booths around town. The provincial **hospital** is just east of Independence Park, and there are pharmacies near the market. Apsara Bookshop, northwest of the transport stop, has a small selection of maps.

Accommodation

An excellent place to stay, its courtyard crowded with well-tended plants, is the distinctive, red-painted *Botoum Hotel and Restaurant* (Ⓣ012/687858, Ⓔbotoumhotel@gmail.com; ❷) in the northwest of town, just off the roundabout to Poipet at the junction of NR5 and NR6. Rooms have hot showers, fan and TV (a/c available at extra cost), and as well as serving inexpensive, wholesome food the restaurant has an espresso machine. In the centre of town, just north of the market, the *Golden Crown Hotel* (Ⓣ054/958444; ❷) has clean, en-suite rooms all with TV and fridge, a decent Khmer/Chinese restaurant, and is popular with NGO workers. Staff at both hotels will help you arrange transport for Banteay Chhmar and other sites.

Eating and drinking

As well as the restaurants at the *Botoum* and *Golden Crown* hotels, the *Phkay Proek Restaurant*, next door to the *Botoum*, has an extensive menu in English, of Khmer,

Thai and Western food including a good choice of Western breakfast dishes. The newly opened *Mirror Restaurant*, just off NR6 in the east of town, is Sisophon's answer to a fast-food joint, serving ice cream, burgers and pizza. Just off the Independence Park, the pleasant *Red Chilli Restaurant* has a good choice of Khmer and Chinese food. In the late afternoon and early evening, stalls selling basic Khmer food, desserts and fruit shakes open on the south side of Independence Park.

Other than the seedy bar-brothels on the backstreets, and karaoke clubs such as the one at the *Neak Meas Hotel*, Sisophon has little to offer in the way of nightlife.

Banteay Chhmar and Banteay Tuop

Some 60km north of Sisophon, the huge temple of **Banteay Chhmar**, covering an area of around three square kilometres, was built by Jayavarman VII as a memorial to soldiers killed while defending his son in a battle against the Chams. Approaching the site you'll catch a glimpse of the temple's lotus-choked moat and laterite enclosing wall before entering via the causeway to the east, once edged by rows of gods and demons. Generally, everyone reaches the central complex through the multiple collapsed doorways of the eastern entrance. Some of the **carvings** hereabouts are in great condition, but require a little searching to find; look out for a lintel carved with bearded musicians, one playing a harp, and another carved with dancing cranes.

The inner enclosure is surrounded by a **gallery**, mostly filled in by accumulated dust, dirt and rubble; you'll have to scale huge piles of masonry and climb through what's left of the enclosing wall to approach the centre, so make sure you wear sturdy shoes. Tiny Buddha images remain perched in some of the niches along the gallery roof, but many more have been crudely hacked out, either when the state religion switched from Buddhism back to Hinduism in the thirteenth century or as a result of looting. The **faces** of the Bodhisattva Srindradeva look down from the remaining towers, while part of an eight-armed relief of Vishnu remains on the west face of the central tower, though sadly, like so many carvings here, it's missing its head – probably removed and sold for just a few dollars to a middleman, to be sold on for big money internationally.

Some of the magnificently carved **bas-reliefs** that once rivalled those at the Bayon can still be seen on the western exterior of the enclosing wall; one of the most spectacular features is a 32-armed god with his hands in two different *mudras*. Close by, you can see a fresh breach in the wall, the stone unweathered; this is where two massive panels were stripped out by the military in 1998 and trucked across the border en route for sale in Bangkok. Confiscated by the Thai police and returned to Cambodia, the panels are now in the National Museum in Phnom Penh (see p.97). To the north, another section of wall illustrates tales from the *Ramayana* and bears a good image of a *yeak* swallowing a horse.

The paths around the outer walls are kept reasonably clear, and you can return to the entrance either by walking around the outside of the enclosing wall or by scrambling over more rubble, heading back roughly the way you came in. Just across from the southwest corner of the moat is a French-run **silk-weaving project**, where you can watch local women weaving silk and buy a colourful scarf.

Practicalities

It's possible to visit Banteay Chhmar by moto ($12–15) from Sisophon, but it's an all-day expedition and you'll be better served by hiring a taxi ($30–35). National Route 69 heads directly north from Sisophon to **THMOR PUOK**, where there are a couple of restaurants and a small guesthouse. From here the road deteriorates for the final 17km to Banteay Chhmar (entrance fee $5). There are some food stalls near the entrance and although there's no formal **accommodation**, homestays are usually possible ($7 per night, food $4 per meal) – visit the Banteay

Chhmar CBT Office opposite the temple entrance for details (ⓣ012/237605, ⓔtsophal@globalheritagefund.org).

Banteay Tuop

Nine kilometres before reaching Banteay Chhmar (look for a stone sign with gold lettering beside the turn) a minor road branches off to the right from National Route 69. Following this road for about 10km brings you to **Banteay Tuop** (Army Fortress). The site was probably constructed at the same time as Banteay Chhmar, and though there are fewer carvings here than at Banteay Chhmar, the towers are taller. The ride there takes you through some classic rural scenery – when the road goes up onto the rim of a reservoir, look for a turning on the right that leads towards the towers.

Choob, Phnom Sarok and Ang Trapaeng Thmor

Heading east from Sisophon, there are a few places worth a look along the way to Siem Reap. The easiest to get to is the village of **CHOOB**, about 20km along National Route 6 from Sisophon. You'll know when you've arrived as the roadside is lined with sandstone carvings of Buddhas and apsaras, from the tiny to the enormous. The village's carving has a high reputation throughout the country, and even if you don't plan to buy, it's worth stopping to admire the intricacy of the statues and watch the carvers at work: some of the larger pieces take months to complete, and many are commissioned by temples or government offices. For those prepared to lug a statue home, prices can be very reasonable, after a bit of bargaining. The most prized types of sandstone have delicate veined markings and command a higher price. A **moto** to Choob from Sisophon costs $5–7 return; there's no public transport.

Though silkworms are bred by a couple of NGO projects, **PHNOM SAROK** is one of the few villages in the country where **sericulture** has been properly revived after the Khmer Rouge. Comprising just four streets and a crossroads, the place is also reputed throughout Cambodia for its thick cotton *kramas*, seldom sold outside Sisophon and Siem Reap, which are much sought after and command a premium price. Weaving looms clack away under the stilt-houses along the village's north street, and you'll see tree branches flecked with furry silkworm cocoons, looking like yellow balls. The families will be only too pleased to give you a little tour.

The village is 60km from Sisophon, close to the boundary between the provinces of Banteay Meanchey and Siem Reap. From Sisophon, you can get a **moto** all the way to the village (about $10); from Siem Reap you'll need to get a taxi to the turning on National Route 6 – marked by a statue 34km from Sisophon showing a woman spinning – and a moto the rest of the way; allow a full day to get there and back from either town. The only place to get **food** is a stall by the village crossroads which sells noodles and *borbor*, so it's worth bringing your own provisions.

A few kilometres west of Phnom Sarok, the **Sarus Crane Conservation Area** at **Ang Trapaeng Thmor** is a dry-season refuge for the globally endangered **Sarus crane** (*kriel*), and other water birds (about 200 species have been spotted here). In the early morning and late afternoon you may also see great and little egrets, purple and pond herons, and spotted and milky storks when they come out to feed along the banks of the reservoir. You can only visit on an organized trip which can be arranged through the Sam Veasna Centre; see p.179 for details.

Poipet

The border town of **POIPET** is a poor advertisement for Cambodia, lacking both charm and friendliness. The pushy transport touts who ply the border do it no

Crossing the border

The border crossing at Poipet is popular with travellers going overland in both directions between Siem Reap and Bangkok. Once across the border and into Thailand you'll need to make for **Aranyaprathet** – a four-kilometre journey by tuk-tuk – to head on to Bangkok by **train** (departures at 6.30am and 1.55pm; 5–6hr) or **bus** (regularly throughout the day until around 6pm; 5hr); there are also two buses a day direct to Bangkok's international airport, Suvarnabhumi (departing at 8.30am and 12.30pm; 5hr). If you're on private transport to Bangkok organized by a local travel agent, you'll be dropped on the Cambodian side of the border to make your own way across and meet sister transport on the Thai side for travel onwards. Keep in mind that these packages are fraught with scams and frustrations – the use of inferior transport and waiting around for hours for the transport to fill up are the main grouses – and in the end most travellers find it cheaper and quicker to do the trip on their own.

Crossing into Cambodia from Thailand

Arriving from Thailand, while a far from pleasant experience and not without its irritations, is slightly less of a hassle than it used to be and most scams are a thing of the past. Once you're stamped out of Thailand, walk across the footbridge, ignoring any touts who offer to get your visa. It is extremely easy to do this yourself, and all they will do is pass your passport through the window of the visa office and try to charge you for their efforts. A visa costs $20, plus one passport photo. The visa office is currently on the left before the casinos, but it's only a temporary affair while a new one is built. If you've got a Cambodian e-visa (ⓦevisa.mfaic.gov.kh) you can walk straight through. You may (or may not) need to fill out a health form, but there's no charge for this and it just takes a few moments. Ignore all the beggars, kids (who will offer to shelter you with an umbrella) and touts (who will tell you have to change dollars to riel – at inferior rates – you don't, baht and dollars are accepted everywhere), and make sure to look after your belongings as pick pockets are rife. After passing all the casinos, you'll come to the immigration office, just near the roundabout. Here there are a couple of simple forms to complete and you're in Cambodia. If you need money there are ATMs near the casinos, and on the main road in Sisophon.

favours, while the clouds of dust kicked up by trucks and garbage strewn along the roadside add little to its attractions. Unless you need refreshments, have missed the **border opening times** (daily 7am–8pm) or have a yen to gamble at the casinos, there's no reason to pause. Buses and shared taxis for Sisophon, Siem Reap, Battambang and Phnom Penh depart until early afternoon, with taxis to Sisophon and Siem Reap being available until around 5pm.

Onward transport from Sisophon is run by the "Poipet transport association" – for "association" read "mafia" – who have organized it so that tourists have to pay as much as possible to move on. It is all a bit iffy, but the best way of travelling on from Poipet is by free-market shared taxi ($5–10 for a place to Siem Reap, or take the whole taxi for $30–35). Some free-market taxis hang around at the traffic circle outside the immigration office or further down the main road towards the market – despite anything you may be told, **it is perfectly legal** to take a place in one of these, **you do not have to go to the transport stop**. But **do not pay in advance** and note that you may have to change taxis at Sisophon – you do not have to pay here, leave it to the taxi drivers to sort out; but to reiterate, **DO NOT PAY IN ADVANCE**.

If there's nothing at the traffic circle and you're not too burdened down by luggage, hop on a moto and get them to take you to a taxi for your chosen destination. If you take the free shuttle bus from the immigration office, it will ferry you to the "association" transport stop near the market where buses and "association" taxis wait. One of these taxis to Siem Reap is a fixed $45, but if you can get a few travellers together it's not too bad a price to pay to get away promptly for the three-hour journey to Siem Reap – again do not pay in advance. Alternatively, you can take a bus from here ($10 to Siem Reap, $5 to Battambang, $7.50 to Phnom Penh), but be aware that the last departure is at around 12.30pm. If you're on pre-paid transport from Bangkok your tour guide will shepherd you along, often just to the bus office, where you'll have to hang around (sometimes for several hours) to wait for transport to fill up. Don't expect any of this to be a civilized experience. Try to arrive in Poipet early in the morning, or before noon at the latest, which will give you time to sort out the inevitable problems. Crossing after 5pm may find you stuck in town until the first bus of the morning (6.30am).

If you need to stay, the best option, down a quiet side-street, 200m west of the market, is *Good Luck Hotel and Restaurant* (❷). Run by a kindly family, it has clean, simple, en-suite rooms all with air conditioning and TV; across the street its pleasant restaurant serves tasty Thai and Khmer food. Otherwise, near the traffic circle as you emerge from the immigration office, both *Holiday Palace Hotel* (❸) and its neighbour, *Orkiday Angkor Hotel* (❸), have well-appointed rooms with all facilities and reasonable decor. As for **eating**, the *Hope and Health Restaurant*, 1km from the traffic circle on the main road, offers Western dishes like spaghetti and hamburgers and gives its profits to the needy. Khmer staples can also be found at the fairly ghastly places along the main road or near the market.

Travel details

Shared taxis leave to no set schedule from early morning until late afternoon, though the earlier you get there the less you'll have to hang around, as most vehicles leave between 7 and 8am. Note that the frequencies given below are only approximate and it's generally easier to find transport in the mornings.

Buses

Battambang to: Kompong Chhnang (6 daily; 4hr); Pailin (daily; 1hr 30min); Phnom Penh (at least 6 daily; 6hr); Poipet (4 daily; 3hr); Pursat (6 daily; 4hr); Siem Reap (2 daily; 3hr).
Kompong Chhnang to: Battambang (6 daily; 4hr); Phnom Penh (6 daily; 2hr 30min); Pursat (6 daily; 2hr).
Pailin to: Battambang (daily; 1hr 30min).
Poipet to: Battambang (4 daily; 3hr); Kompong Cham (1 daily; 6hr); Phnom Penh (4 daily; 8hr); Siem Reap (4 daily; 3hr).
Pursat to: Battambang (6 daily; 2hr); Phnom Penh (6 daily; 4hr).

Shared taxis

Battambang to: Kompong Chhnang (4 daily; 4hr); Pailin (6 daily; 4–5hr); Phnom Penh (12 daily; 6hr); Poipet (12 daily; 3hr); Pursat (6 daily; 1hr 30min); Siem Reap (10 daily; 3hr); Sisophon (6 daily; 2hr).
Kompong Chhnang to: Battambang (4 daily; 4hr); Phnom Penh (8 daily; 2hr 30min); Pursat (4 daily; 2hr).
Pailin to: Battambang (6 daily; 1hr).
Poipet to: Battambang (12 daily; 3hr); Phnom Penh (10 daily; 8hr); Siem Reap (20 daily; 3hr); Sisophon (20 daily; 1hr).
Pursat to: Battambang (6 daily; 1hr 30min); Kompong Chhnang (4 daily; 2hr); Phnom Penh (10 daily; 4hr).
Sisophon to: Battambang (6 daily; 2hr); Phnom Penh (10 daily; 7hr); Poipet (20 daily; 1hr); Siem Reap (20 daily; 2hr).

Boats

Battambang to: Siem Reap (1 daily; 6–8hr).

Siem Reap and the temples of Angkor

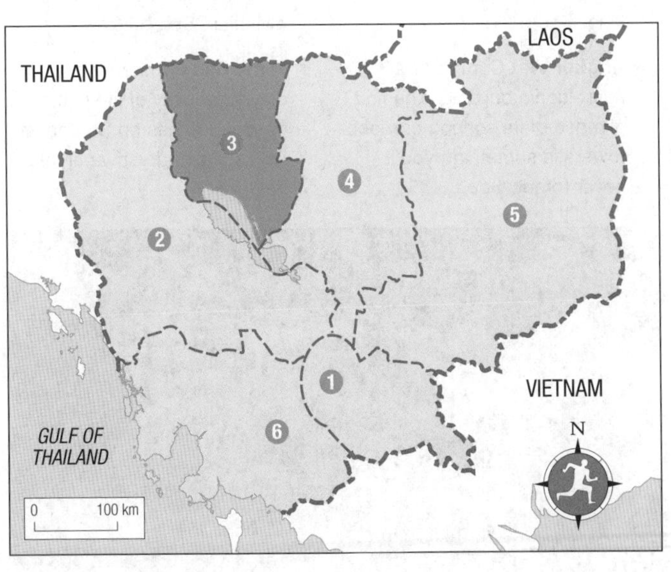

CHAPTER 3

Highlights

* **Siem Reap** Bustling pavement cafés, elegant restaurants and buzzing bars in Cambodia's most tourist-friendly town. See p.159

* **Bird's-eye view of Angkor** Take to the sky in a tethered helium balloon for an aerial view of the temples. See p.159

* **Apsara dance** Cambodia's ancient dance-form was once performed exclusively for the king. See p.175

* **Angkor Wat** Cambodia's most iconic building. The first glimpse of its soaring corncob towers is something you'll never forget. See p.185

* **Angkor Thom** Expansive, ancient walled city enclosing two fabulous royal terraces and the sacred Bayon temple with its forest of carved faces. See p.191

* **Ta Prohm** Atmospheric temple held in the clutch of giant trees. See p.198

* **Banteay Srei** Rosy-red sandstone temple with delightful carvings of female divinities. See p.207

* **Tonle Sap** Glimpse the distinctive way of life in the floating villages on Southeast Asia's largest freshwater lake. See p.209

▲ Market, Siem Reap

3

Siem Reap and the temples of Angkor

...Angkar...is of such extraordinary construction that it is not possible to describe it with a pen, particularly as it is like no other building in the world. It has towers and decoration and all the refinements that human genius can conceive of. There are many smaller towers of similar style, in the same stone, which are gilded. The temple is surrounded by a moat, and access is by a stone bridge, protected by two stone tigers so grand and fearsome as to strike terror into the visitor

Antonio da Magdalena, 1586

For six hundred years the area around the provincial town of Siem Reap, 310km northwest of Phnom Penh, was the heart of the Khmer Empire. Its rise to importance began in 802 with Jayavarman II's move to Phnom Kulen and ended when the Thais sacked Angkor Thom in 1431. A ready supply of water and the fertility of the land meant that the area could support large populations, and successive Angkorian kings constructed their royal cities and state-temples here. The empire reached its apogee in the twelfth century under the leadership of Jayavarman VII – the greatest temple-builder of all – when it stretched from the coast of Vietnam to the Malay peninsula, to Pagan in Burma and north to Laos. However, once abandoned, this part of Cambodia sank into obscurity until, at the end of the eighteenth century, as part of Battambang province, it came under Thai rule, a state of affairs that lasted until 1907, when the French negotiated its return.

For most visitors, **Angkor Wat**, an iconic temple of soaring towers and intricate carvings just a short drive from Siem Reap, is the chief reason to visit Cambodia. The first glimpse of its breathtaking sanctuaries lingers in the memory forever, while its gallery of bas-reliefs – exceptional in both detail and quality of execution – is a delight for novices and experts alike. Running it a close second is the nearby walled city of **Angkor Thom**, its gateways famously topped with four huge stone faces. The motif is continued at the very centre of Angkor Thom in the **Bayon**, Jayavarman VII's state-temple, which has two galleries of bas-reliefs.

There's much more to Angkor than just these main sights, however. The site is vast, covering an area of some four hundred square kilometres, and diverse, with buildings ranging in scale from early, tiny brick towers like **Prasat Kravan** to the massive and stark sandstone edifice of **Ta Keo**. You could easily spend two full weeks at Angkor and still have more to see, but most people find three days is

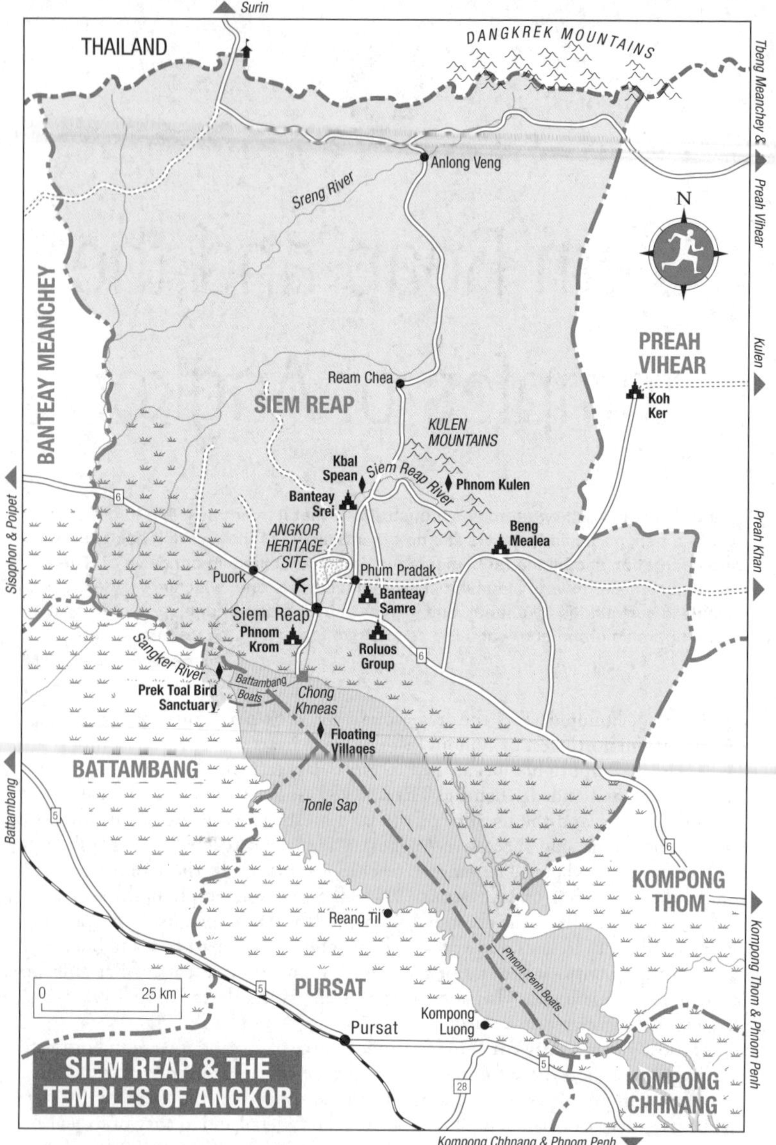

enough to take in the principal sites, albeit in a bit of a rush; four to five days is better. Many of the most important temple sites are within a few minutes' drive of **Siem Reap**, but a few are scattered much further afield; transport is easily hired in Siem Reap and access roads are now in decent condition.

The government's active promotion of Angkor Wat as a tourist destination has seen visitor figures soar, turning the once sleepy **Siem Reap** into a tourist hot spot. The **local airport** is linked with a number of Asian cities as well as Phnom

Penh; National Route 6 south to the capital and north to Thailand is in excellent condition; and boats from Phnom Penh and Battambang remain popular with tourists. Surprisingly, given the explosion of new hotels, restaurants and bars, Siem Reap retains its small-town atmosphere.

If you tire of temples, the floating villages of **Tonle Sap**, the massive freshwater lake that dominates central Cambodia, are worth exploring. The land south of Siem Reap is part of the lake's flood plain, and is inundated from June to November. North of town, the rice fields stretch out to the natural boundary formed by the Kulen Mountains which divide the lush lowland from the province's more barren north; here, at **Phnom Kulen** is Cambodia's largest reclining Buddha, carved out of a massive rock, while at two spots on the Siem Reap River (which rises in these mountains and flows south to drain into the great lake) the river bed itself has been carved with intricate linga and religious scenes. The far north of the province is worth visiting only if you are curious to see **Anlong Veng**, the site of Pol Pot's death.

Siem Reap

SIEM REAP (pronounced See-um Ree-up) manages to be simultaneously both a somnolent town and tourist honey-pot. By day, with most tourists at the temples, the town is a peaceful place; come dusk, the roads bustle with returning tuk-tuks packed with temple-weary sightseers, who descend on the restaurants and bars in the colonial area around Psar Chas. By mid-evening a party atmosphere pervades.

You're unlikely to want for anything in Siem Reap, and plenty of folk hang around much longer than they intended. The town offers the best selection of **accommodation** in the country, as well as an abundance of restaurants specializing in all manner of cuisine, including exceptional **Cambodian food**; at a handful of places you can also watch a fascinating Khmer **cultural performance** while you dine. There are plenty of opportunities to **shop** in numerous quality galleries, craft shops and souvenir stalls. Car and tuk-tuk hire for the temples is straightforward, and if you don't feel like arranging it yourself, one of any number of tour companies (or your hotel or guesthouse) will do it for you, picking you up from your door at sunrise and returning you after sunset.

Angkor from the air

An exhilarating way to see the Angkor area is from the air. Although over-flying of the temples is not permitted, you can still get a wonderful overview by balloon, helicopter or microlight. Angkor passes are not required for any of these aerial excursions.

If you're on a restricted budget the cheapest option is from the gondola of a tethered **helium balloon** ($15 per person, children $7.50, for 10min) located between the airport and Angkor Wat (ⓣ011/886789 or 012/520810, ⓔangkorballoon@citylink.com.kh). Weather permitting the balloon ascends to 200 metres around 30 times per day carrying 30 passengers at a time, from where there's a bird's-eye view of Angkor Wat and nearby temples. **Helicopter** trips start at $90 per person for a thrilling eight minutes viewing the Angkor Wat area with Helistar Cambodia (ⓣ088/888 0017 or 012/449555, ⓦwww.helistarcambodia.com) who fly from Siem Reap's airport. Longer (more expensive) flights can be arranged over the Tonle Sap, Kulen hills and so on. Most exciting of all though are SkyVenture's **microlight** trips (ⓣ077/602912 or 017/678533, ⓦwww.skyventure.org); flights start at $45 per person for 15 minutes around the areas of Roluos and Bakong temples, or consider a $145 "see it all" hour's trip.

Temples aside, Siem Reap has plenty more to occupy you, be it a **boat trip** out on the massive Tonle Sap lake (see p.210), where communities live on the water in floating villages, **quad biking** (see p.171) or **horseriding** (see p.171) through the paddy fields. You can also take to the sky by fixed balloon, microlight or helicopter for an awe-inspiring **aerial view** (see p.159) of the temples. Tours of the area can be arranged with specialist companies in town, although they don't come cheap (see p.179).

Arrival

Registered taxis ($7) and tuk-tuks ($5) for the six-kilometre ride from the **airport** into town can be hired at a booth just outside the exit from the arrival lounge. Minibuses from certain hotels meet planes, so look out for them if you've booked accommodation in advance, or intend to stay at one of them. A road from the airport runs directly to the temples and makes a day-trip from Bangkok to Angkor Wat viable if you arrive early in the morning; you can hire a car and driver at the airport. Prices vary according to how much you want to see. There are rumours that a second airport is in the pipeline, some 60 kilometres from Siem Reap.

Buses from all destinations arrive at Chong Kov Sou bus station and transport stop 3km east of town. There are always tuk-tuks available and plenty of guest-house touts, who you can quiz for information if you haven't decided where to stay. If you've pre-booked then make sure to let your accommodation know which bus you are arriving on so they can pick you up. A tuk-tuk trip from the bus station to town costs $2–3. Shared taxis also stop at the transport stop, although many (especially those coming in from the west) will drop you off in town if you ask.

Boats dock south of town at the newly built **port** at Chong Khneas on the Tonle Sap about 15km from Phnom Penh; the boat gets in between noon and early afternoon, while from Battambang it arrives mid- to late afternoon. Hotels will

Moving on from Siem Reap

Leaving Siem Reap by road, boat or plane is straightforward, with good transport connections to other parts of the country, as well as Thailand.

By bus

A number of companies run long-distance buses to **Phnom Penh** and **Bangkok**; these can be booked at their offices in town (see p.178), through guesthouses and hotels, or with the town's travel agents (see p.180). Note that on buses to **Bangkok** you must change vehicles at the border. In Poipet buses arrive at the transport stop near the market about 1km from the border – from where you can take the free shuttle bus to the border. From the border it's a further 4km to Aranyaprathet, a tuk-tuk costing around 100 baht. Getting an early ride on shared transport to Poipet will give you the option of choosing your onward transport in Thailand – you'll arrive in time to take the lunchtime train for the (approximately) five-hour trip to Bangkok. Some guest-houses in Siem Reap organize their own minibuses to **Phnom Penh** and Bangkok via Poipet – where they link up with onward transport operated by their Thai associates – but given the countless scams and delays associated with minibuses going in both directions, it's better sticking with shared taxis or reputable bus companies.

By shared taxi

Shared taxis to **Phnom Penh** and **Kompong Thom**, **Sisophon** (for **Battambang**), **Poipet** and **Anlong Veng** run from the roadside at the junction of National Route 6 and the turning to Siem Reap's Chong Kov Sou transport stop about 2km east of arrange for you to be collected from the port if you're staying with them; otherwise there's no shortage of tuk-tuks to take you into town ($4), not to mention guesthouse touts.

Many budget travellers now arrive overland from Thailand via **Poipet** (see p.153), and the road on the Cambodian side is now so good that the journey all the way from **Bangkok** can be done in a single day. If you're on a through ticket bought from one of the many travel agents on Bangkok's Khao San Road, the going may be fairly slow, and you'll be dropped at one of their affiliated guesthouses in Siem Reap.

Information

There are two **tourist offices** in town, one in the southwest corner of the Royal Gardens, the other on Sivatha Boulevard near Psar Chas. They're not particularly helpful as they assume that you'll have obtained information from your hotel or guesthouse – which you probably have, though they can find you a guide and a car if needed.

It is well worth considering **hiring a guide** for the temples ($30–50 per day per group, the price depends on the language required). You can hire a guide through hotels and guesthouses, travel agents or direct with the **Khmer Angkor Tour Guide Association** – KATGA (see p.178). All guides are KATGA-licensed and have to pass an examination on the history of the temples. As well as speaking at least one foreign language most are genuinely knowledgeable about the temples. Licensed guides can be identified by their uniform: brown trousers, beige shirt and name badge. Given how easy it is to meet other travellers in Siem Reap, it shouldn't be hard to get together to share the cost of guide hire, transport or both.

The useful free quarterly *Siem Reap Angkor Visitors Guide*, put out by Canby Publications, is available around town at hotels, guesthouses and restaurants. Besides the usual temple information, it contains up-to-the-minute news of places

town. When going from Siem Reap to Poipet on the Thai border, a shared taxi is your best bet; to hire a shared taxi outright costs $30–40, or about $10 per seat. The road to the Thai border is in excellent condition, and transport runs in that direction until late afternoon (3hr).

By boat

A boat leaves from the Chong Kneas **port** daily at 7am for **Phnom Penh** ($35; 5hr) and at 8am for **Battambang** ($17; 8hr). You'll need to book your ticket at least a day ahead – two days ahead between March and November. If you buy through your guesthouse or hotel, a minibus will collect you from the door, which may mean setting out as early as 5.30am, as the vehicle will pick up passengers from various locations before heading down to the port; if you choose to make your own way to the port, allow 30min by tuk-tuk.

By plane

As well as flights to Phnom Penh, there are an increasing number of departures to **international destinations** including **Bangkok**, **Hanoi**, **Ho Chi Minh City**, **Pakse** and **Vientiane**, and further afield to **Seoul**, **Kuala Lumpur, Singapore** and **Hong Kong.** You can buy plane tickets from the airline offices or from travel agents in town. If you're staying at a hotel they'll generally drive you to the airport free of charge. Departure tax must be paid by all passengers; it can be paid in cash or by credit card, domestic ($6) and international ($25).

to stay, eat and drink (though note that establishments pay for an entry); extracts of the guide are available online at Ⓦwww.canbypublications.com.

Town transport

Siem Reap is laid out on a grid sprawling a couple of kilometres north and south of National Route 6, and east and west of the Siem Reap River. Although a bit spread out, the centre is easily negotiable on foot, with most travellers facilities lying to the south of NR6, and particularly within 500m of Psar Chas. Tourists are not allowed to rent self-drive motorcycles or cars, although it is possible to hire a car with driver.

For visitors, the most popular way to get around town and out to the temples is the tuk-tuk, or romorque, a motorbike-drawn carriage see p.30. These are without a doubt the most pleasant and comfortable way to get around, seating two passengers in comfort (though you can squeeze in three or four). They can be hailed on the street or hired from outside any of the hotels, guesthouses and markets; count on $2 for a journey across town. To the temples they can be rented by the day for $13–15.

Motorcycle taxis, motos (see p.29), though less common these days, are great for short hops across town, especially when you're in a hurry; expect to pay 4000 riel, or $1, per trip. While you'll see Cambodians two, three and even more up on a moto, the provincial government has decreed that they can only carry one foreign passenger.

Transport to the temples

As there's no public transport to Angkor Wat and the temples are spread out over a fair area, it's best to hire your own transport to make the most of your time and entrance ticket. **Hiring a moto or tuk-tuk** is easy; many guesthouses have a selection of drivers who look after their guests, and there are many more around town, plenty of whom speak good English. A moto costs $8–10 from 8am to 5.30pm, while a tuk-tuk will be around $15 for the same period; for sunrise-to-sunset hire you'll need to add on a few dollars – negotiate this with your driver in advance. The fact that tuk-tuks are covered and provide protection from the sun and rain, as well as having a soft seat to lean back into, makes them well worth the extra expense when touring the temples. If you want to go to Banteay Srei and Kbal Spean, it's sensible to do both sites on the same day and you'll again need to negotiate the additional price with your driver (allow a full day for getting there, seeing the sites and tootling back). Although **cycling** is a wonderful way to see the

Siem Reap addresses

Although these days most of the roads in town have names or numbers, they are not commonly used by the locals, so when travelling around it's better to choose a **landmark**, such as a market or a hotel, when giving directions or negotiating a fare with a tuk-tuk driver. Along National Route 6, we refer to places west of the junction with Sivatha Boulevard as being on the "Airport Road", a commonly used local name. The road north past the *Grand Hotel d' Angkor*, officially Vithei Charles de Gaulle, is more commonly called "Angkor Wat Road" or "Road to Angkor Wat", while the road south past the hospital, 2 Thanou Street, is locally referred to as "Hospital Street". Along the east side of the river Achasvar Street is also called "River Road", and the road through the Psar Chas area, where you'll find most of Siem Reap's nightlife venues, is known both as "Pub Street" and "Bar Street".

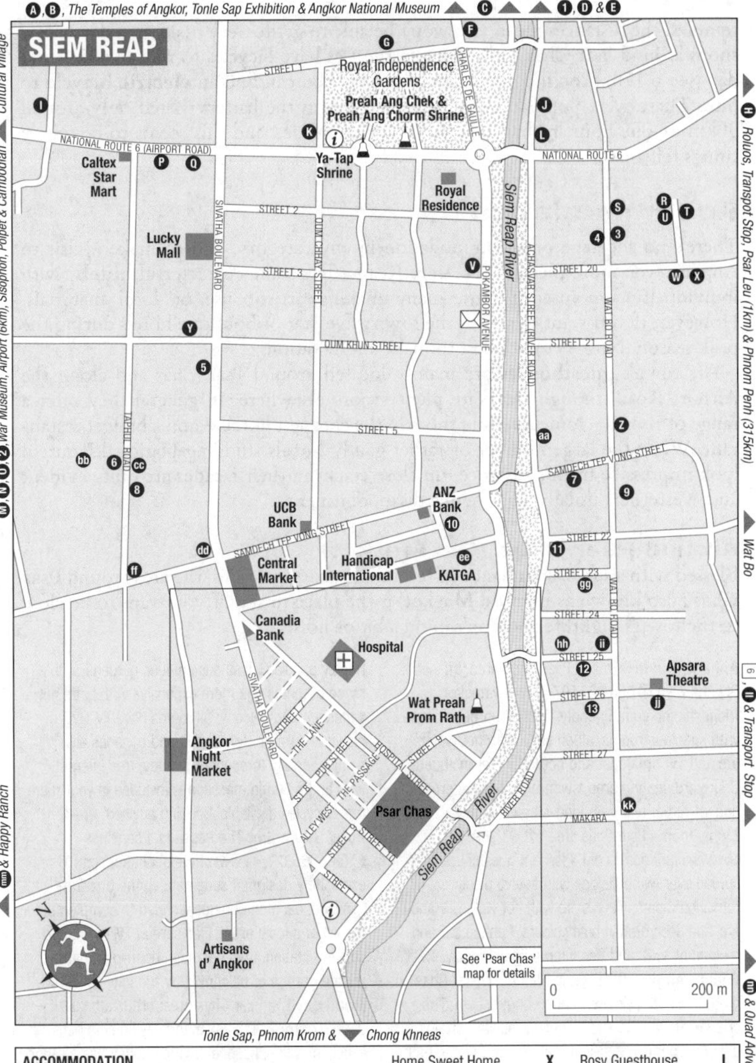

ACCOMMODATION

- Amansara — F
- Angkor Village — jj
- Angkor Village Resort — A
- Babel — U
- Baca Villa — cc
- Borann l'Auberge des Temples — E
- Bou Savy — I
- Bunnath — Q
- Chenla — P
- Earthwalkers — N
- European — T
- FCC Angkor — V
- Frangipani Villa — Z
- Garden Village — mm
- Grand Hotel d'Angkor — G
- Green Garden Home Villa — Y
- Green Village Palace — nn
- Heritage Suites — D
- Home Sweet Home — X
- Hotel de la Paix — dd
- Ivy 2 — ee
- Jasmine Lodge — O
- Karavansara Retreat — hh
- La Maison d'Angkor — M
- La Noria — J
- La Résidence d'Angkor — aa
- Les Orientalistes — kk
- Mom's — S
- Pavillon d'Orient — H
- Rosy Guesthouse — L
- Samnark Preahriem — R
- Shadow of Angkor II — ii
- Smiley's — bb
- Tara — B
- The Backpacker Hostel — ll
- The River Garden — C
- The Villa Siem Reap — ff
- Two Dragons — W
- Victoria Angkor — K
- Viroth's Hotel — gg

RESTAURANTS & CAFÉS

- Butterflies Garden — 12
- Café de la Paix — dd
- Café Indochine — 5
- Chivit Thai — 4
- Common Ground — 10
- FCC Angkor — V
- L'Oasi Italiana — 1
- Madame Butterfly — 2
- Moloppor — 11
- Peace Café — 13
- Queen BBQ — 7
- Restaurant Le Grand — G
- Rosy Guesthouse — L
- Sala Bai — 8
- Star Rise — 3
- Sugar Palm — 6
- Viroth's — 9

BARS

- FCC Angkor — V
- L'Explorateur Bar — K

temples, the distances mean you won't be able to get to very many in a day; a few shops around Psar Chas and most guesthouses have bicycles to rent for $2–4 per day (see p.178). You'll cover more ground if you can find an **electric bicycle** to hire. These were popular a few years ago but as the battery lasted only around 30km or one hour, recharging stations were needed and this seems to be where things fell apart.

Accommodation

There's no shortage of accommodation in any category, and to make a visit to Angkor even more memorable, Siem Reap offers some characterful **hotels**, with individually appointed rooms, many making artistic use of local materials. However, if you want to stay at the town's five-star or boutique hotels during the peak season (Nov–Feb), it's best to make a reservation.

The town's **guesthouses** are mainly located around Psar Chas and along the Airport Road, though there are plenty more elsewhere. In general they offer a range of rooms – some rivalling those in the cheapest hotels – and a budget restaurant. While the large number of rather gaudy **hotels** studding National Route 6 look impressive from a distance, up close cracks in their facades are quite evident and Westerners usually find them a disappointment.

Around Psar Chas (Old Market)

Blessed with a super-abundance of restaurants, bars and cafés, the area around **Psar Chas** (also known as the **Old Market**) is the place to stay if you want to be close to the town's nightlife and don't mind a bit of noise.

Angkor Friendship Inn Psar Chas area, off Sivatha Blvd ⓣ063/965197, ⓦwww.angkorfriendshipinn.com. Friendly, family-run guesthouse with spacious rooms, all en suite with hot water, a/c and TV; breakfast and bottled water included. Courtyard seating area, swimming pool, internet and wi-fi; popular with long-stay visitors. ❸

Ei8ht Rooms Psar Chas area ⓣ063/969788, ⓦwww.ei8htrooms.com. Pleasant guesthouse spread over two buildings with twelve nicely furnished rooms, all en suite with hot water, TV and a/c, and decorated in bold colours. Rooftop bar and restaurant, wi-fi and free internet; gay friendly. ❸–❹

Encore Angkor Off Sivatha Blvd near Psar Chas ⓣ063/969400, ⓦwww.encoreangkor.com. The crisp white sheets and billowing muslin curtains give the rooms a Zen-like feel; a/c, hot water, baths and safety boxes are standard; wi-fi, internet restaurant and swimming pool. ❹

Garden Village 500m from Psar Chas ⓣ012/217373, ⓦwww.gardenvillageguesthouse.com. Sprawling budget guesthouse with a range of rooms; the cheapest are rustic, no-frills affairs, with shared bathrooms and bamboo screen walls. Paying a bit more will get you solid walls and TV, while the top of the range are with hot water showers and a/c. Basic dorm beds $1 per night. ❶–❸

Golden Temple Villa Psar Chas area, off Sivatha Blvd ⓣ012/943459, ⓦwww.goldentemplevilla.com. Hugely popular guesthouse in lush gardens, with a range of rooms, the more expensive with bath, hot water, a/c and balcony; all rooms have TV, DVD player and fridge. Tea, coffee and bananas are complimentary throughout the day; free internet, wi-fi and a 20min massage is included in your room rate; bicycles available. Booking advised. ❷–❹

Hotel Be Angkor The Passage, Psar Chas ⓣ063/965321, ⓦwww.hotelbeangkor.com. Three exquisitely designed suites above the buzzing Passage, each one uniquely styled to complement the art of a local artist. Flat-screen TV, wi-fi, iPod docking station, mini bar, safe, open-plan bath, private garden or balcony. Gay friendly. ❼–❽

Mandalay Inn Psar Chas area, off Sivatha Blvd ⓣ063/761662, ⓦwww.mandalayinn.com. This excellent-value, hospitable guesthouse has a range of inexpensive rooms in two adjoining buildings that come with fan or a/c, hot water, TV and fridge. Rooftop gym, internet, wi-fi and a great restaurant serving Khmer and Burmese dishes. ❷

Shadow of Angkor Pokambor Av, 20m north of Psar Chas ⓣ063964774, ⓦwww.shadowofangkor.com. Basic rooms upstairs in an old colonial shophouse by the river, but the owners are caring and the location can't be faulted. For a/c go to its sister hotel on Wat Bo Road (see p.169). ❸

Steung Siemreap Street 9, Psar Chas ⓣ063/965167, ⓦwww.steungsiemreaphotel.com.

ACCOMMODATION			
Angkor Friendship Inn	G	Mandalay Inn	I
Ei8ht Rooms	F	Shadow of Angkor	C
Encore Angkor	D	Steung Siemreap	A
Golden Banana Boutique Resort	H	The One Hotel	B
Golden Temple Villa	E		
Hotel Be Angkor	B		

RESTAURANTS & CAFÉS			
AHA	20	Singing Tree	22
Angkor Palm	9	Soup Dragon	8
Champey	17	The Blue Pumpkin	7
Happy Herbs Pizza	1	The Coffee House	6
Khmer Kitchen	19	Viva	12
Le Grand Café	13		
Maharajah	3		

On a quiet street in the heart of town, this modern, colonial-influenced hotel has bright, airy rooms to international standards; swimming pool, restaurant and wi-fi; baby-sitting service. 7–8

The One Hotel The Passage, Psar Chas ⓣ063/965321, ⓦwww.theonehotelangkor.com. Private, luxury retreat tucked away above the bustling Psar Chas scene; this sole suite is equipped to the highest standard with tasteful modern decoration, state-of-the-art electrical equipment and rooftop lounge with jacuzzi; mobile phone while in residence, and a member of staff always available. 9

The Royal Gardens and beyond

Amansara Angkor Wat Rd ⓣ063/760333, ⓦwww.amanresorts.com. This low-rise resort in the tropical gardens of an old royal palace has everything the reclusive visitor needs in a hideaway; pool suites even have their own five-by-six-metre pools in their private courtyard. 9

Angkor Village Resort Apsara Rd ⓣ063/963361, ⓦwww.angkorvillage.com. Abundant use has been made of polished wood for these delightful, bright cottages in luxuriant gardens; 200m river-shaped swimming pool, restaurant and bar, spa, wi-fi. The downside is that you can't walk anywhere from here and that it's 10min by tuk-tuk to town. You may be better off at its sister hotel, the original *Angkor Village*, in the Wat Bo area of town. ❼

Grand Hotel d'Angkor 1 Vithei Charles de Gaulle ⓣ063/963888, ⓦwww.raffles.com/siemreap. Since 1932 *Grand Hotel d'Angkor* has offered visitors to Siem Reap opulent colonial elegance. Rooms, suites and villas are furnished in period style, decorated with Khmer artefacts and provided with every modern amenity. Service is attentive but unobtrusive. High tea and cocktails can be taken in the conservatory; there's a choice of restaurants and bars, bakery, swanky boutique, business centre, gym, tennis court, spa, theatre and a decent-length swimming pool. The exhibition area hosts changing displays of art relevant to Angkor. Rates include breakfast. ❾

Tara Angkor Wat Rd, 500m north of the Royal Gardens ⓣ63/966601, ⓦwww.taraandkorhotel.com. Smart, Art Deco-influenced hotel with Khmer/Western restaurant, choice of bars, shop, business centre, spa, fitness centre and swimming pool. Rooms are tastefully decorated with natural materials and many have balconies. ❻

The River Garden On the river road, north of NR6, west of the river ⓣ063/963400, ⓦwww.therivergarden.info. The most popular room here is the stand-alone, Khmer Cottage, great for families. The deluxe suite with masses of mellow wood, was once the home of the naive artist, Michel Delacroix. Verdant garden setting, swimming pool, restaurant (daily specials $4–5) and bar; popular cooking classes (see p.173). ❺–❼

Victoria Angkor Central Park, west side of the Royal Gardens ⓣ063/760428, ⓦwww.victoriahotels-asia.com. 1930s style with plenty of polished wood; choice of restaurants and bars, spa, sauna, boutique and swimming pool, transfer from the airport by vintage Citroen (at extra cost). The *L'Explorateur* bar is the perfect place for cocktails or after-dinner coffee, either in a/c comfort or on the sultry terrace (board games available). ❼

Airport Road

Most noticeable along **Airport Road** are the massive Angkor-this and Angkor-that hotels that vie for Asian package tourists, but among these are a handful of inexpensive guesthouses and a delightful boutique hotel. The drawback is that there aren't many eating places – although, that said, it's only a short tuk-tuk ride to the town centre.

Bou Savy Down a side road north of Airport Rd ⓣ063/964967, ⓦwww.bousavyguesthouse.com. Delightful, family-run guesthouse on a quiet street. En-suite rooms, most with hot water, TV, fridge and fan or a/c, breakfast and water included. Wi-fi, restaurant, plenty of seats in a plant-strewn courtyard. This is a popular home-from-home place and gets lots of volunteer groups staying – make sure to book. ❷

Bunnath 446 Airport Rd ⓣ063/963293, ⓦwww.bunnathguesthouse.hostel.com. Friendly, busy guesthouse run by a caring family; clean, simple en-suite rooms and the choice of cold or hot water, fan or a/c. ❷

Chenla 260 Airport Rd ⓣ063/963233, ⓦwww.chenlakh.com. Long-running, efficient guesthouse (popular with young Japanese tourists) with a range of rooms, hot water and a/c at extra cost; breakfast included. Dorm beds $2. ❷

Earthwalkers Down a side road south off Airport Rd ⓣ063/760107, ⓦwww.earthwalkers.no. This Scandinavian-managed guesthouse is well run, friendly and popular; the rooms (en suite, with fan or a/c) are quiet and comfortable. Dormitory beds $5. Breakfast included; bar, restaurant and footprint-shaped swimming pool. ❷

Jasmine Lodge 307 Airport Rd ⓣ012/784980, ⓦwww.jasminelodge.com. One of the better budget guesthouses; rooms come with attached bath, choice of a/c or fan and cable TV. The rooftop restaurant is a definite plus; wi-fi, movies. They can arrange for a homestay or for you to help out on a local charitable project. ❷

La Maison d'Angkor 71 Airport Rd, south side ⓣ063/965045, ⓦwww.lamaisondangkor.com. Relaxing boutique hotel with bungalows dotted through the garden; each room has private outdoor seating, TV, safety box, mini bar, fan and a/c; wi-fi throughout. Communal facilities include swimming pool, spa, library and French/Khmer restaurant (3-course set menu from $14). ❼

Sivatha Boulevard and around

Baca Villa 26 Taphul Rd ⓣ063/965328, ⓦwww.baca-villa.com. Scrupulously clean and reasonably sized, these are comfortable en-suite rooms in a family-run guesthouse. Just $10 will get you a/c and a hot water shower; internet, restaurant and bar, safety lockers. ❷

Green Garden Home Villa 51 Sivatha Blvd, just off the main road ⓣ063/96342, ⓦwww.greengardenhome.com. Quiet guesthouse in a picturesque garden, with swimming pool and breakfast area. The cheapest rooms are in the original old house opening off reception, with cold showers and fan; better rooms are in the new building with hot water and a/c available. ❸–❹

Hotel de la Paix Sivatha Blvd ⓣ063/966000, ⓦwww.hoteldelapaixangkor.com. Unmissable; this whitewashed, centrally located hotel is designed inside and out by the renowned Bill Bensley, with templesque portico (by night flames from its vase-topped columns lick the sky) and a skyline-dominating belvedere; inside serene 2m-tall apsaras welcome you at each entrance, their fingers gracefully pointing to the exits. The rooms and suites, of varying shapes, are meticulously furnished in black, grey and white; iPods are pre-loaded with mood-inducing music for you to take to the temples. Restaurant, bar, café, wi-fi, internet, boutique, spa, swimming pool, fitness centre and welfare programme supporting several local concerns complete the picture. ❾

Smiley's Off Taphul Rd ⓣ012/686060, ⓦwww.smileyguesthouse.com. From humble beginnings this guesthouse has grown to a palace of a-place; though it's no longer the cheapest in town (or the most smiling), the en-suite rooms are a decent size, with hot water and a/c available for a reasonable $12. ❷

The Villa Siem Reap Taphul Rd ⓣ063/761036, ⓦwww.thevillasiemreap.com. Clean, brightly-decorated en-suite rooms, all with hot water, a/c, TV, mini bar and room safe; wi-fi and restaurant with weekly BBQ – with Australian owners. Just 5min walk from Psar Chas. ❹

East of the river

The area on and around **Wat Bo Street** is a good bit quieter than staying on a major thoroughfare such as the Airport Road or Sivatha Boulevard. Apart from guesthouses, it also boasts a sprinkling of mid-range hotels, some decent restaurants and a few bars.

North of National Route 6

Borann l'Auberge des Temples On a leafy lane north of NR6 ⓣ063/964740, ⓦwww.borann.com. Tastefully decorated with local artefacts, the simply furnished bungalows have their own terraces in a leafy garden setting. Restaurant and pool, no TVs. ❹

Heritage Suites Near Wat Po Lanka, 500m north of NR6 ⓣ063/969100, ⓦwww.heritagesuiteshotel.com. Secluded Relais & Chateaux hotel with 26 rooms and suites in a mix of colonial and contemporary styles; all with a/c, internet, safe, and bath, some with private gardens, and open-air shower or jacuzzi. Decorated with a changing display of artwork, a traditionally-built wooded hall houses the lounge, bar and a gallery restaurant with Western/Khmer fusion food – including an innovative Khmer burger. Swimming pool and poolside bar, spa, picnic baskets, airport pick-up by 1962 Mercedes. ❽–❾

La Noria Achasvar St ⓣ063/964242, ⓦwww.lanoriaangkor.com. Housed in bungalows around a lush garden with a swimming pool. Rooms, furnished with traditional Khmer materials, are cool and tranquil, and have their own bathrooms, as well as individual terraces and sitting areas. The French restaurant hosts regular shadow-puppet shows (see p.177). ❹

Pavillon d'Orient Road 60, north of NR6 from Psar Leu ⓣ063/760646, ⓦwww.pavillon-orient-hotel.com. Charming boutique hotel tucked away on the outskirts of Siem Reap. Rooms in two-storey bungalows are cool and tasteful, with modern bathrooms, flat-screen TV, and balcony or terrace. Open-air restaurant, swimming pool, spa, wi-fi, and personal use of a tuk-tuk for the duration of your stay. ❼

Rosy Guesthouse Achasvar St, north of NR6 ⓣ063/ 965059, ⓦwww.rosyguesthouse.com. Welcoming guesthouse, with attractive, though not necessarily spacious, rooms; traditional artefacts are dotted through the communal areas, and there are views of the river from the first-floor balcony. Cheaper rooms have fans and shared bathroom – though with hot water shower; dearer ones are more spacious with en-suite bathrooms, hot water, fridge and a/c. TV and DVD players in all rooms. Great travellers' bar and restaurant, book exchange, DVDs to borrow, wi-fi and internet. Outlet for White Bicycles (see "Listings", p.178). The expat family owners live on-site with their children and pets. ❷–❹

Wat Bo area, between National Route 6 and Samdech Tep Vong Street

Babel On the cul-de-sac parallel to Wat Bo St ⓣ063/965474, ⓔBabelSiemReap @gmail.com. Breakfast is included in the room rate at this Western-run guesthouse on a quiet backstreet. Large, clean rooms with a/c and hot water, some with bath; restaurant and bar, seating in the verdant garden, great staff. ❷

European Up a dead-end street parallel to Wat Bo St ⓣ012/582237, ⓦwww.european-guesthouse .com. Quiet and friendly guesthouse with its own garden and large rooms, all with en-suite bathrooms; hot water and a/c available. ❷

Frangipani Villa Wat Bo St ⓣ067/999930, ⓦwww.frangipanihotel.com. Sparkling, new boutique hotel screened from the road. Room rate includes breakfast, free tea, coffee and water, and two pieces of laundry per day; some rooms have balconies. Wi-fi, internet, swimming pool, restaurant with a rooftop bar planned.

Home Sweet Home Off Wat Bo St ⓣ063/760279, ⓦwww.homesweethomeangkor.com. Modern, family-run guesthouse whose rooms feature attached bathrooms, TV and a/c, restaurant, wi-fi and internet. It does what it says in the name. ❷

Karavansara Retreat Street 25 ⓣ063/760678, ⓦwww.karavansara.com. Superbly renovated, French colonial villa with a choice of rooms all with modern decor and flat-screen TVs, bathrooms with marble basins and rainfall showers; some rooms have private terraces. Captivating photographs are a particular feature of the hotel. A traditional Khmer wooden house hold the restaurant and bar; wi-fi, swimming pool and attentive, cheerful staff. ❼

La Résidence d'Angkor Achasvar St ⓣ063/963390, ⓦwww.residencedangkor .com. Top-notch establishment, now part of the Orient Express group, with sympathetically designed accommodation making the best use of local materials. All rooms are luxuriously appointed with teak furniture, Khmer cotton and silk furnishings, and bamboo screens to mask the massive free-form bathtubs. Facilities include restaurant, bar, spa, gym, internet and wi-fi, souvenir shop and swimming pool fed by water bubbling from a lion and a linga. Meditation with English-speaking monks, and the chance to talk with them afterwards is organized one or two mornings per week. ❾

Mom's Wat Bo St ⓣ063/964037, ⓦwww .momguesthouse.com. Siem Reap's Old Faithful; a rather gaudy concrete house has replaced the old wooden one, but it's owned by the same friendly family. Rooms have TV, a/c and attached bathrooms; wi-fi and breakfast room. The swimming pool is a great addition. ❸

Samnark Preahriem Off Wat Bo St, behind *Mom's* ⓣ063/760378, ⓔpreahriem@camnet.com.kh. Rustic guesthouse in a tranquil courtyard at the end of a cul-de-sac, with a choice of rooms, some en suite. At the end of the day, put your feet up and listen to the cicadas buzz in the trees; guests can use the swimming pool at *Mom*'s (just through the fence). ❷

Two Dragons Off Wat Bo St ⓣ063/965107, ⓦwww.talesofasia.com/cambodia-twodragons .htm. Well-run guesthouse with lots of great information for the asking, popular with local expats. Rooms are in a two-storey house behind the small Thai restaurant and feature attached bathrooms, cable TV and a/c; there's wi-fi access throughout. ❸

South of Samdech Tep Vong Street

Angkor Village Street 26, off Wat Bo St ⓣ063/963361, ⓦwww.angkorvillage.com. Much copied, *Angkor Village* is the originator of bungalow accommodation in Siem Reap. Its bungalows have recently been refurbished bringing its facilities up-to-the-minute, and polished wood and crisp white linen complete the scene. A pavilion in the leafy grounds houses the French–Asian restaurant, and the swimming pool is picturesquely set among banana trees. ❼

Golden Banana Boutique Resort Phum Wat Damnak ⓣ063/766655, ⓦwww.goldenbanana .info. At the end of the alleyway west of Wat Damnak; note that due to a fall-out between partners, the other *Golden Banana* establishments hereabouts are quite separate. The resort has a number of pleasant bungalows around an inviting pool, which come with a/c, TV and DVD player, and there is wi-fi access throughout. Breakfast included. ❼

Green Village Palace On the street behind Wat Damnak ⓣ063/760623, ⓦwww.greenvillage cambodia.com. On a quiet leafy backstreet just 5min walk to Psar Chas, the rooms here are vast and clean, if plain; hot water, a/c, breakfast, tea and coffee throughout the day; internet and wi-fi. Garden with hammocks, restaurant and swimming pool. ❸

Les Orientalistes Wat Bo St ⓣ063/760278, ⓦwww.les-orientalistes.com. Shabby chic at its best, the five rooms in the traditional wooden house are crammed with antiques and artefacts. Bathrooms are a bit rudimentary, but the quirkiness is appealing. Well-regarded restaurant, though it helps if you speak French. ❹

Shadow of Angkor II Wat Bo St ⓣ063/760363, ⓦwww.shadowofangkor.com. Modern hotel with well-sized rooms furnished with traditional Khmer wood furniture, TV, hot water, a/c and wi-fi. Internet, swimming pool and restaurant. ❹

The Backpacker Hostel 7 Makara ⓣ012/313239, ⓦwww.angkorbackpacker.com. Rooms here are no cheaper than most of the other guesthouses in town, but a bed in the fan-cooled dorm will set you back just $2, with $5 for a/c; note though that the dorms fill up quickly and beds can't be booked. ❷

Viroth's Hotel St 23 ⓣ012/778096, ⓦwww.viroth-hotel.com. Stylish boutique hotel, its modernistic rooms have all the mod cons, and the tranquil grounds include a cosy swimming pool and even a jacuzzi. ❻

West of the River

There are just a couple of places to stay in the faded French quarter west of the Stung Siem Reap on the tree-lined roads between the river and Sivatha Boulevard.

FCC Angkor Pokambor Av ⓣ063/760280, ⓦwww.fcccambodia.com. Surrounded by trees in a picturesque riverfront location, this branch of the *Foreign Correspondents Club* (*FCC*) was built in colonial style in the grounds of the old governor's residence. Stylish rooms with all the amenities you'd expect of a modern, boutique hotel. There's also a terrific restaurant, bar, and adjoining shopping complex of tasteful boutiques. ❽

Ivy 2 Just off Pokambor Av, 300m north of Psar Chas ⓣ012/380516, ⓔivyasia@hotmail.com. Simple, en-suite rooms with fans, in a invy-clad, two-storey house. Friendly staff, laid back backpackers' restaurant – with daily specials – and bar, pool table, movies and hammocks in the shady courtyard. This is a Siem Reap guesthouse as they all used to be. ❶–❷

The Town

Said to mean "Siam defeated" in commemoration of a battle that possibly never happened, little is known about the **history** of Siem Reap, which sprawls to east and west of the river of the same name. Largely overshadowed by the Angkor temples, the town has only recently grown large enough to acquire its own identity. A traveller who visited in 1935, Geoffrey Gorer, described Siem Reap as "a charming little village, hardly touched by European influence, built along a winding river; the native houses are insignificant little structures in wood, hidden behind the vegetation that grows so lushly… along the river banks." The only hotels at the time were the *Grand Hotel d'Angkor*, now well inside the ever-expanding town, but then "a mile out of town" according to Norman Lewis, who stayed here in 1951, and its sister establishment, the *Bungalow des Ruines*, which was opposite Angkor Wat. Siem Reap remained relatively undeveloped during the first tourist rush of the 1950s and 1960s, and much was destroyed when the town was emptied under the Khmer Rouge, although the *Grand*, the shophouses of the Old Market, Psar Chas, and the occasional colonial villa escaped unscathed.

So far Siem Reap has managed to cash in on Angkor's burgeoning popularity without losing too many of its rustic charms, and though there's not a great deal of specific interest, a stroll around the town centre reveals a number of colourful shrines and a few minor attractions. As good a way to do this as any is to use the smart paved **walkway** that has been laid along the riverside south of National Route 6 to Psar Chas.

At the northern end of the walkway, opposite the *Grand Hotel d'Angkor*, are the formal Royal Gardens, one of the most restful spots in town. On the south side of the gardens, a **shrine** to the sister deities Preah Ang Chek and Preah Ang Chom houses figurines of the two – thought to have been Angkorian princesses – in brass and bronze, originally situated in the Gallery of a Thousand Buddhas at Angkor

Wat. The statues were hidden from the eyes of invaders and treasure hunters by successive generations of monks, who moved them repeatedly to stop their whereabouts becoming known. Moved to the current shrine in 1990, the statues are heaped daily with offerings; the taller, more slender of the two figures is Ang Chek, whose palm faces outward to show a Sanskrit inscription of protection. A third statue, discovered in 1995, is not on public view. Just to the west, surrounded by a traffic circle and marked by a huge tree in the middle of the road, is a shrine to **Ya Tep**, a local spirit said to bring protection and luck to the Siem Reap area. The offerings left at the shrine are sometimes quite extravagant – it's common to find whole cooked chickens.

A one-kilometre stroll south along the river brings you to the bustling **Psar Chas**, also known as the Old Market; souvenir stalls pack the section of the market facing the river, while further back a fresh-produce area takes over. Many of the surrounding colonial-era shophouses have been converted into vibrant restaurants and bars, the tables spilling out from shaded balconies onto the pavement.

Around 200m east of the river, **Wat Bo** is the oldest and most appealing of Siem Reap's Buddhist monasteries, dating back to the eighteenth century. The interior walls of the vihara, still in good condition, were decorated in the nineteenth century with scenes from the life of Buddha. Unusually, the paintings incorporate scenes of everyday life, including a Chinese man smoking opium and French soldiers watching a traditional dance performance. The pagoda is also home to a collection of old Buddha statues. Further south, the Life & Hope Association in the grounds of **Wat Damnak** is a sewing school for local women where you can talk to the students and buy a few items; help from clothes designers with time to spare would be greatly appreciated. Wat Damnak is also home to the Center for Khmer Studies – the largest library outside Phnom Penh.

Out from the centre

Siem Reap's **Angkor National Museum** (1.5km north of town on the Angkor Wat Road; daily 9am–8pm; $12 per person, students and children under 1.2m tall $6, audioguide $3, camera $2; online reservation may get you a discount; Ⓦwww.angkornationalmuseum.com; café, souvenir shop and shopping mall) is, despite its name, actually a private venture between the Ministry of Fine Arts and Culture, the APSARA Authority (see p.181) and a Thai management company. Choice pieces of ancient Khmer sculpture, once kept under lock and key at the Angkor Conservatory and off limits to all but VIPs, are now beautifully exhibited in vast galleries complete with explanatory signboards. Introductory and multimedia presentations provide orientation, explain the wealth of statuary on display, and give background to Cambodian history, heritage and religion. The fabulous gallery of 1,000 Buddha Images should not be missed. In fact the only downside is the extortionate entrance fee.

West of town the **War Museum** (daily 8am–5.30pm; $3) lies 500m north of National Route 6, just before the airport turn-off. Its collection of rusting tanks and anti-aircraft guns is no doubt stimulating if you get turned on by model designations and numbers. Near by, south of NR6, is one of those "see the whole country in an hour" theme parks that every country in Southeast Asia seems to have, the **Cambodian Cultural Village** (Ⓦwww.cambodianculturalvillage.com). As well as miniatures of many of Cambodia's temples and monuments, there are tableaux of wax figures portraying events from history. However, with an admission price of $11 for foreigners, very few overseas visitors bother (Cambodians get in for $1).

On the Angkor Wat Road, dominated by a massive head of Jayavarman VII, the Kantha Bopha **children's hospital** is one of Cambodia's unsung wonders; here all treatment is free and charitable donations allow staff to be paid a livi… Every Saturday (7.15pm; Ⓦwww.beatocello.com) a free concert is staged … persuade you to part with a few dollars or an armful of blood. While … further north, off the same road, is the engaging **Tonle Sap Exhibition** … 8am–6pm; free), covering all aspects of life on the lake. Put together by Kr… Thmei, a foundation which looks after deprived children (and helps revive Cambodia's lost traditions, such as shadow puppetry – see p.177), the exhibits include photographic displays of traditional fishing practices and maps of the lake's seasonal variation.

Activities

You don't need to be a skilled equestrian to enjoy The Happy Ranch (prices start at $19 for an hour; ⓣ012/920002, Ⓦwww.thehappyranch.com), where Sary Pann – a returning Khmer – has acquired a unique farm to home his increasing collection of well-cared-for horses and ponies. **Horseriding** or excursions by pony and trap take place early in the morning or late in the afternoon to avoid the hottest part of the day. Many of the horses have been rescued and brought back to health by Sary's love and care, but with veterinarians a rarity in Cambodia, any visiting professionals who can donate a day, or even just a few hours, would be warmly welcomed. The best ride is a two-hour hack ($36) through the countryside to the little-visited Wat Atvea.

But if travelling by single horse power isn't your thing, then Quad Adventure Cambodia (ⓣ017/784727, Ⓦwww.quad-adventure-cambodia.com from $25 for 1hr) may be, with guided **quad bike** excursions for children and adults through paddy fields and villages, though they do not enter the archaeological park. If you're considering riding or quad biking during your stay you'd be advised to check your travel insurance as you'll need to be covered by your own insurance, and will be asked to sign a liability waiver when you sign in.

There's no shortage of places in Siem Reap offering relaxing **massages** of every possible style from Khmer to Swedish, and from reflexology to full-body. Massage shops abound on Sihanouk Blvd, Hospital Street, around Psar Chas and at the Angkor Night Market. While these are all bona fide establishments, the cheapest places, though usually clean, will probably give your massage on a reclining chair or in a room with several massage couches; paying more you'll get relaxing surroundings, a nice robe and a massage in a separate room. All the upmarket hotels have reputable **spas**; the Amrita Spa at *Grand Hotel d'Angkor* (ⓣ063/963888), Spa Indochine at *Hotel de la Paix* (ⓣ063/966000) and the Kong Kea Spa (ranked on the Conde Nast 2010 Hot Spas list) at *La Résidence d'Angkor* (ⓣ063/963390) are especially recommended for their professionalism, range of treatments and atmosphere. Another highly recommended place is Body Tune Spa (Pokambor Ave near Psar Chas ⓣ063/764141); **traditional Khmer massage** is offered at Islands (Hospital Street near Psar Chas ⓣ012/757120).

After a few days at the temples a day lazing by a **swimming pool** can be a real treat. Many hotels and even guesthouses now have pools; but if yours doesn't, you can often pay to use one at another hotel for around $5 per day. Provided you buy some food and drink, you can use the pool for free at *Aqua Sydney Bar and Café* (9am to late), on 7 Makara. Alternatively, do as the Khmers do and head to the Western Baray where you can swim, picnic and lounge about all day for nothing.

Meditation, **pilates** and **yoga** are available at *Peace Café* (ⓣ092/177127, Ⓦwww.peacecafeangkor.com); "**monk chat**" is an opportunity to have an interesting discussion with an English-speaking, Cambodian monk.

If clambering over temples isn't enough exercise, the **running** club, Siem Reap Hash House Harriers, meets about once a month to no specific schedule; contact *Victoria Angkor Hotel* for the latest details (ⓣ063/760428).

A bizarre, private **museum** on a plot of land near Banteay Srei temple is crammed full of rusting war scrap and **land mines** (daily 8am–5pm; $2). The owner, Aki Ra, a self-taught de-miner who was once forced to lay mines as a Vietnamese conscript, has amassed a vast collection of mines, bomb casings, fuses and the like. It started off well, but unfortunately, these days feels more like a seedy tourist trap. More interestingly perhaps, behind the Central Market in town, Handicap International has an information centre in the grounds of its rehabilitation centre (Mon–Fri 8am–noon & 2–5pm; Ⓦwww.handicapinternational.be) where visitors can learn about land mines, their effect on Cambodia, the process of making prostheses, and see rehabilitation for those affected by mines.

Eating

As well as having plenty of Western fare, Siem Reap is also one of the best places in the country to sample **Cambodian cuisine**, with many restaurants serving a good range of skilfully prepared local specialities (and the bonus of menus in English). Cuisines from elsewhere in Asia are also well represented, in particular Thai and Indian, while Korean and Japanese places along Airport Road cater to tour groups.

Inexpensive wholesome dishes with helpings of rice are served up from early morning until late at night at the Khmer **restaurants** on the west side of Psar Chas. In the late afternoon food stalls selling every kind of Cambodian food set up on the pavements just off Sivatha Boulevard; they're open until activity dies down in the late evening or early hours of the morning; noodle dishes from $1.

Around Psar Chas

AHA The Passage, Psar Chas (11.30am–2.30pm & 6–10pm). Pricey, tapas-style, Khmer food and fine wines in air-conditioned, chic surroundings with superb service; delightful.

Angkor Palm Hospital St, near Psar Chas. Waiters here offer kindly advice on what and how to eat Khmer food; the platter for one is a veritable feast comprising eight dishes including spring rolls, spare ribs, *amok*, rice, mango salad and Khmer dessert for just $6.

Champey Psar Chas. Succulent *amok* and spicy mango salads are just two of the favourite dishes at this moderately priced French/Khmer restaurant with a reputation for excellent food and service.

Happy Herbs Pizza Hospital St, opposite the hospital ⓣ012/838134. Long-standing place that still serves up the best pizza ($4–6 depending on size) in town, along with consistently good pasta. Takeaways and deliveries can be ordered by phone.

Khmer Kitchen The Passage, Psar Chas. Outstanding, inexpensive, family-run restaurant that provides great Khmer home cooking with the occasional modern twist.

Le Grand Café Corner of Hospital St and Street 9. This restored French-colonial building is a great place for lunch, afternoon coffee or dinner with mixed menu of French, Italian, Cambodian and other international cuisine. It's not a budget option though, with the cheapest main course costing $6.

Maharajah Street 7, west of Psar Chas. Away from the tourist drag, this economically priced restaurant attracts plenty of repeat trade from those in the know. Freshly cooked, authentic Indian halal food, served with a smile by the kindly owner.

Singing Tree Alley West. Predominantly vegetarian café with seating on the alley; great salads, sandwiches and quiches all freshly prepared at around $5 per dish; their speciality is fruit shakes.

Soup Dragon Hospital St. Spread over three floors of a street-corner building, this popular restaurant is open from early morning, serving economical food from breakfast to dinner; its upper floor is a great spot for "happy hour" cocktails, while watching the world pass by on the street below.

The Blue Pumpkin Hospital St, near Psar Chas. When *The Blue Pumpkin* opened a few years ago it caused a huge stir – Cambodians had seen nothing like it; now it has branches all over town, including at Angkor Wat. The original bakery, with pavement café and a/c lounge upstairs, is packed from opening to closing (6am–10pm) and sells a wide selection of breads, sandwiches, pastries, shakes, ice creams and beverages. It's as cheap or as expensive as you make it here; pastries start at $1 and ice creams are $1 per scoop.

Cookery courses

Taking a Khmer cookery course is a useful and informative way to unders[...] about Cambodian cuisine. The most exclusive course in town is on R[...] Cuisine at the *Grand Hotel d'Angkor* ($75; ⓣ063/963888); after a market visi[...] chef, you'll learn about ingredients and how to combine them, before cooking a number of dishes which will be served at lunch with a complimentary glass of wine; a cookbook, certificate and Raffles apron complete the day. A cheaper option, Cooks in TukTuks at *The River Garden* ($25, ⓣ063/963400) also includes a market visit, before cooking up a lunchtime feast with the produce you've purchased; after eating lunch you can take a dip in the pool. Le Tigre de Papier ($12; ⓣ012/265811) runs two or three classes a day, which include a market visit to buy ingredients for a three-course meal which you prepare and then eat; proceeds from the purchase of a cookery book helps to support students at Sala Bai Hotel School in Siem Reap.

The Coffee House The Lane. Trendy coffee house, with all profits going to the Cambodia Orphan Fund, has a simple menu of reasonably priced food, Illy coffee, wi-fi, smiling staff and loyal expat following. More like someone's front room than a café.

Viva Hospital St near Psar Chas. Bright Mexican restaurant with loyal following serving all the hot favourites such as burritos and fajitas from $4 per dish; some Asian options.

Sivatha Boulevard and around

Café de la Paix *Hotel de la Paix*, Sivatha Blvd. Freshly baked bread, sandwiches, pastries, quiches and cakes to be enjoyed inside this stylish a/c café, on its terrace, or packed up to take away. They also have wi-fi and newspapers. The coffee is the best in town and it's all affordable ($5 for a good-sized sandwich with fresh-baked bread).

Café Indochine Sivatha Blvd. Moderately expensive French-run restaurant with a good reputation and Khmer/Western menu, which includes steaks; food can be a little bland.

Common Ground Street 14. Trendy coffee shop and bakery with free wi-fi on a quiet street near the old French quarter; profits go to support humanitarian projects. Coffee and cake will set you back a few dollars.

Sala Bai Taphul St (Mon–Fri 7–9am & noon–2pm). Hospitality school which opens to customers for training purposes; the inexpensive menu varies according to what the students are learning to cook.

Sugar Palm Taphul St (closed Sunday). Upstairs in a wooden house this is perfect for a candlelit dinner *à deux*; its inventive menu includes dishes such as chicken livers with ginger and the excellent, squid with black Kampot pepper, with mains costing around $7.

The Royal Gardens and around

FCC Angkor Pokambor Av ⓣ063/760280, ⓦwww.fcccambodia.com. Western dishes with an Asian twist in a relaxed setting that will ensure that you linger long after your meal is finished. Count on around $15–20 for dinner without drinks. The terrace bar is a great spot for sipping a cocktail after a long day sightseeing; wi-fi.

Madame Butterfly West on National Route 6. Fine Khmer cuisine in a French-run restaurant with tables in a charming, old wooden house or outside in the garden. Expect to spend $20 per person without drinks. A downside is that it can be busy with tour groups.

Restaurant Le Grand *Grand Hotel d'Angkor* ⓣ063/963888, ⓔdining.grandhotel@raffles.com. The classiest of the restaurants in this famous hotel, with a fine à la carte menu of Royal Khmer dishes, some of them donated by King Sihanouk. Backed up with a fine wine cellar and impeccable service, this is dining for foodies. Booking advised, dress code smart casual; allow $40–50 per person excluding drinks.

East of the river

North of National Route 6

L'Oasi Italiana On River Rd, east of the river, 2km north of NR6. A bit of a stretch, but worth it for the home-made pasta and the setting – tables are in thatched bungalows in the garden; pasta (around $7 a dish), pizza and crisp salads are the specialities. Not the best place if you're eating alone, but great for couples, groups and families. If you're eating in the evening it'd be best to get your tuk-tuk driver to come back for you.

Rosy Guesthouse Achasvar St, north of NR6 and east of the river. Terrific home-cooked dishes that include pasties, pies and jacket potatoes for around each; generous portions. Popular bar, regular charity quiz nights and other events; also book exchange, board games and wi-fi.

Between National Route 6 and Samdech Tep Vong Street

Chivit Thai Wat Bo St. Thai-style dining in a traditional wooden house where can you eat at low tables, seated on cushions or in the fairy-light-lit gardens. Besides excellent *tom yam* soup, they do a range of delicious stir-fries and of course, *pad Thai*, at very reasonable prices.

Star Rise Wat Bo St. Simple food, freshly cooked when you order (so it can take a little while) in a quirky, family-run, Khmer café. Does a good *amok*, and tasty grilled chicken baguettes; cheap.

South of Samdech Tep Vong Street

Butterflies Garden Street 25. Nice spot to while away a couple of hours out of the midday heat while enjoying a pomelo salad with chicken (or shrimps). Though it's more a lush courtyard than garden, with plenty of shade and tiny pools; the area is netted to keep in the colourful butterflies that are bought from local children and released every few days. Service can be a bit hit-and miss. Main dishes are around $4–6.

Moloppor Achasvar St. Hugely popular eatery with Japanese tempura, Chinese stir-fry, *dim sum* and some excellent noodle dishes for less than $3 each.

Peace Café Street 26. Vegetarian café and bakery; salads, quiches, cakes, cafetière coffee and cookies; prices are reasonable, expect to pay $3–5 for breakfast. Also food for the soul by way of yoga and meditation classes (see p.171). Wi-fi.

Queen BBQ Samdech Tep Vong St (from 6pm). This is a traditional Khmer barbecue restaurant where locals eat. Bag a table, then select your meal by choosing from the trays of meat, seafood and vegetables on offer. Place your uncooked food on the side plates provided (one side plate per type of food), and cook it on the table-top brazier. At the end of the night the number of side plates is added up to calculate your bill. Allow $5–10 per person including a few beers.

Viroth's Wat Bo St. A leisurely place to enjoy authentic Khmer food (some dishes with a French influence) in an elegant, minimalist open-air restaurant; recommended is the juicy and spicy papaya salad and the succulent lemon pork. Service can be slow, but the food is always worth the wait; main courses start at around $5.

Drinking, nightlife and entertainment

There's no shortage of watering holes in Siem Reap, so much so that the Cambodians refer to the road north of Psar Chas as "Bar Street" or "Pub Street". New **bars** are opening up all the time, and plenty stay open until the wee hours; many have happy hour (or two), and some bars do special deals (draft beer for 50¢ all day) in the low season. Also worth looking out for are happy hours at the more upmarket establishments when cocktails become more affordable.

Angkor Special The Passage. This simple restaurant-bar is a welcoming spot from which to watch the world go by and sup a cocktail at happy hour (buy one, get one free).

Angkor What? Pub St. Long-running pub with pool table and satellite TV. Basic food options.

Dead Fish Tower Sivatha Blvd. The wacky decor here – meandering stairways to the various different levels as well as a crocodile pit with real crocs – makes this place a world-class challenge to navigate while drunk. Live music (days vary) and excellent food.

FCC Angkor Pokambor Av. The place for drinks after a day at the ruins; fans of the *Foreign Correspondents Club* (*FCC*) in Phnom Penh will find this branch more modern but with just as much character, with comfortable, low-slung chairs and high ceilings. Sipping a drink on the terrace, listening to the cicadas as night falls and the candles are lit, is spellbinding.

Island Bar Angkor Night Market. Relaxed bar at the heart of the night market, opens in the late afternoon with cheap draft beer and, if you're lucky, a stylish display of bottle-twirling cocktail mixology.

Laundry Bar Northwest of Psar Chas. Cozy, laidback bar, with a cosmopolitan vibe; pool table. Stays open very late.

L'Explorateur Bar *Victoria Angkor*. The bar's terrace is especially recommended for cocktails; Kompong Speu, a mix of vodka, palm sugar and lime juice served icy cold in a pottery "glass" is moreish. Look out for happy hours.

Linga Bar North of Psar Chas. Welcoming gay bar that gets going late in the evening. It serves great cocktails and staff are happy to chat when they're not too busy.

Miss Wong The Lane. Sensual, gay-friendly bar that gets going late; more 1930s Shanghai than 21st-century Cambodia.

Red Piano Street 10, 50m northwest of Psar Chas. Attractive bar-restaurant and a great spot to chat over a beer or one of their "Tomb Raider" cocktails – still going strong, even after 10 years.

The Warehouse Hospital St, near Psar Chas. Two-storey, relaxed bar opens at 10.30am and closes around 3am when the last punter leaves. Great spot to while away a few hours in the heat of the day, or to people-watch late at night; free wi-fi.

X Bar Sivatha Blvd, 200m west of Psar Chas. Thriving roof top bar that pounds out rock and indie music until late; big-screen sports when there's a match.

Entertainment

Outside Phnom Penh, Siem Reap is the only place in Cambodia where you can watch **traditional dance** being performed. Indeed, it's actually easier to catch a performance here than in the capital, as several Siem Reap hotels and restaurants package a **cultural show**, featuring several dance styles, with a meal. Although touristy, these performances are professionally staged, have been going on at Angkor since the 1920s and are well worth booking to see. Shows usually open with the elegant apsara dance, often followed by a light-hearted item or two

Apsara dance

No visit to Cambodia is complete without at least a quick glimpse of women performing the ancient art of apsara dance, as depicted on the walls of Angkor's temples. Wearing glittering silk tunics, sequinned tops (into which they are sewn before each performance to achieve the requisite tight fit) and elaborate golden headdresses, they execute their movements with great deftness and deliberation, knees bent in plié, heels touching the floor first at each step, coy smiles on their faces. Every position has its own particular **symbolism** – a finger pointing to the sky, for instance, indicates "today", while standing sideways to the audience with the sole of the foot facing upwards represents flying.

In the reign of Jayavarman VII there were over three thousand apsara dancers at court – the dances were performed exclusively for the king – and so prized was their skill that when the Thais sacked Angkor in the fifteenth century, they took a troupe of dancers back home with them. Historically, the art form was taught only at the **royal court**, but so few exponents survived the ravages of the Khmer Rouge that the genre was very nearly extinguished. Subsequently, when Princess Boppha Devi – who had been a principal dancer with the royal troupe – wished to revive it, she found it helpful to study temple panels to establish the movements. It was not until 1995, a full sixteen years after the fall of the Khmer Rouge, that Cambodians once again witnessed a public performance of apsara dance, at Angkor Wat.

These days, the **Royal University of Fine Arts** in Phnom Penh takes much of the responsibility for training dancers, who are chosen not only for aptitude and youth (they start as young as 7), but for the flexibility and elegance of their hands. It takes six years for students to learn the 1500 intricate positions, and a further three to six years for them to attain the required level of artistic maturity. Also taught is the other principal Cambodian dance genre, *tontay*, in which the emphasis is on depicting folk tales and episodes from the **Reamker**.

The Royal University of Fine Arts mounts **performances** of apsara dance on special occasions (such as the Khmer New Year or the king's birthday) in front of Angkor Wat and sometimes in Phnom Penh. But more commonly, you'll be able to watch both styles of Cambodian dance in the cultural performances put on by hotels and restaurants in Phnom Penh and Siem Reap.

depicting popular folk tales, such as the fisherman's dance, which takes a comic look at rural courtship. The finale is a vibrant dance retelling part of the *Reamker*, the Khmer version of the Hindu epic *Ramayana* (see box, p.94), involving four roles – male, female, giant and monkey – with the dancers wearing intricate masks associated with their character. If the costumes for apsara dance are lavish, then those for the *Reamker* dances are positively opulent, heavily embroidered and embellished with tails, epaulettes and wings.

To make an evening out of a cultural show you could opt for the regular buffet dinner and cultural performance at the Apsara Terrace of the *Grand Hotel d'Angkor* (ⓣ063/963888). Similar in quality are the shows at the *Sofitel Angkor Phokeethra* (ⓣ63/964600), and the *Angkor Village*, which stages performances with dinner at its air-conditioned Apsara Theatre (Street 26 ⓣ063/963561). Performance times, frequency and price of admission change with the seasons, so call in advance for information and reservations. Free shows of lesser quality are put on by many of the restaurants around town; the *Temple Bar* balcony for example is packed in the early evening for dinner and the dance performance, but as soon as the show ends the balcony empties and the bar girls arrive.

A Cambodian folk art going all the way back to Angkorian times, shadow puppetry was all but lost during the Khmer Rouge era, but has since been revived, with performances both in Siem Reap and the capital. Entertaining shadow-puppet shows by street children looked after by Krousar Thmei are staged twice a week over dinner at *La Noria* (ⓣ063/964242, phone for prices and to reserve a table). Only a few puppets are used at each performance, changes of character being effected by dressing them in different *kramas*. For more on the puppets themselves, see box on p.177.

Cambodia-themed **movies** are shown nightly at Movie Zone ($3) in the Angkor Night Market.

Shopping

Shopping in Siem Reap is second only to the capital for variety and quality, and in some ways it's much easier to shop here since the various outlets are much closer together. **Psar Chas**, sometimes referred to as "Old Market", abounds in inexpensive souvenir stalls selling all manner of goods, including T-shirts, silk tops and trousers, and traditional Khmer **sampots** in Western sizes. Beware though as many of the textiles here, such as the fabric used to make the cotton **sarongs** with elephant motifs, are imported from Indonesia. Also at Psar Chas on the stall near the river are several selling English-language books, including some prominently displayed publications on Angkor. Look out also for a speciality of Siem Reap, woven **rattan**, made into baskets, place mats and plates – the ones with holes in are for serving dried fish. Remarkably, some great shopping can be had at the Angkor Night Market (ⓦwww.angkornightmarket.com), but walk past the stalls selling imported tack to the back (west side) where you'll find **Khmer Boutique** (stall C9) which is a great place to pick up authentic Khmer artefacts (all paperwork provided if your chosen item proves to be ancient). The Night Market is also the best place in Siem Reap to pick up a traditional cotton *krama* or throw – a great stall is the one south of the *Island Bar*; they'll be more expensive than the synthetic mixed thread ones at Psar Chas and the temples, but well worth the extra for the better quality and workmanship; especially prized are those woven at Phnom Sarok (see p.152). For additional shopping, see "Listings", p.178.

Craft shops and galleries

Until recently the quality of souvenirs in Siem Reap was something of a let-down, but a handful of **international artists** have now set up shop in Siem Reap and are offering their Asia-inspired works to visitors. In addition, Cambodian artists are

Shadow puppets

Shadow puppets are made of stretched, dried **cowhide**, the required outline drawn freehand onto the leather and pared out, after which holes are carefully punched in designated areas to allow back light (traditionally from a burning coconut shell) to shine through onto a plain screen. Once cut and punched, the figures are painstakingly **painted** using natural black and red dyes under the strict supervision of the puppet master. Two different sorts of puppet are produced, *sbaek thom* and *sbaek toich* (literally "large skin" and "small skin"). The *sbaek thom*, used to tell stories from the *Reamker*, are the larger of the two, around 1–2m tall and lack moving parts. By contrast, *sbaek toich* puppets have moveable arms and legs, and are commonly used to tell folk tales and stories of everyday life, usually humorous and with a moral ending. Both types of puppet are manipulated from below using sticks attached to strategic points. To see puppets being made, and to buy examples, you can visit the workshop at House of Peace, north side of National Route 6 about 2km from town.

now finding their feet and increasingly offering original works in stalls and shops around town.

Silk-weaving skills, lost during the Khmer Rouge era, have now been revived; Artisans d'Angkor, west off the southern end of Sivatha Boulevard (Mon–Sat 8am–noon & 2–4pm; free), has a crafts training school. English-speaking guides meet visitors for a tour of the workshops, where you can see students – selected from deprived local families – following an extensive curriculum in wood carving, stone carving and lacquer-work. The school also operates the **Angkor Silk Farm** at Puok, 16km west of Siem Reap off National Route 6 (daily 7–11.30am & 2–5.30pm; free), where guides are on hand to explain the intricacies of silk production and weaving. There are free bus services from Artisans d'Angkor in Siem Reap to the silk farm daily at 9.30am and 1.30pm.

Artisans d'Angkor Chantiers École, off Sivatha Blvd. The school's retail outlet sells an outstanding collection of premium-quality goods, including glossy lacquer-work, exquisite carvings, stunning fabrics and garments from their silk workshops at Puok.

House of Peace 3km from town towards the airport on Airport Rd. This workshop trains artisans to produce traditional Khmer shadow puppets; visitors can watch the process and buy the results.

Bambou Company Alley West & Lucky Mall. Boutique offering original designs of 100 percent cotton clothing for men, women and children.

Green Mango Alley West. Bohemian, boutique clothing at reasonable prices (dresses from $22).

McDermott Gallery 1 FCC Complex, Pokambor Av ⓦwww.mcdermottgallery.com. Upmarket gallery of fine-art photography of Angkor by the internationally acclaimed photographer, John McDermott .

McDermott Gallery 2 The Passage, Psar Chas ⓦwww.mcdermottgallery.com. Housed in a 1930s Khmer shophouse, renovated by French–Khmer architects, the gallery shows fine-art photography of Asia by photographers from Cambodia and around the world.

Mekong Quilts Sivatha Blvd, near Psar Chas ⓦwww.mekongquilts.org. Cotton and silk handcrafted quilts are made in rural villages in Vietnam (for now most are made here) and Cambodia – more will come from Cambodia as skills are developed within this non profit organization.

Rajana Hospital St, just southeast of Sivatha Blvd ⓦwww.rajanacrafts.org. Fair-trade organization, selling a variety of products including silver jewellery, original paintings on silk, paper products, baskets and bags.

Rehab Craft Pokambor Av, 50m north of Psar Chas ⓦwww.rehabcraftcambodia.com. Not-for-profit organization offering a range of crafts made by Cambodians with disabilities. Unfortunately products lack modern design, but this is being addressed by a volunteer designer.

Senteurs d'Angkor Hospital St, opposite Psar Chas. French chic is combined with the imaginative use of traditional Khmer materials to produce tasteful, original products including spices, candles, soaps and flavoured teas. You can also visit their workshops (free), south side of National Route 6 about 1.5km from town.

Wanderlust Alley West. Original, American designed, locally made clothing in bright colours and prints – ideal for Cambodia's hot climate.

Listings

Airlines Bangkok Airways, 571 Airport Rd ⓣ063/380191; Cambodia Angkor Air, Sivatha Blvd (near Central Market) ⓣ063/969268; Jetstar, 50 Sivatha Blvd ⓣ063/964388; Malaysia Airlines, Siem Reap Airport ⓣ063/964135–137; Vietnam Airlines, 342 National Route 6 (Airport Rd) ⓣ063/964488.

Angkor tour guides Licensed, foreign-language guides to the Angkor temples can be booked through the Khmer Angkor Tour Guide Association (KATGA) ⓣ063/964347, ⓦwww.khmerangkortourguide.com; from $25 per day (8am–5.30pm) for English-speaking guide. Note that guides do not drive tuk-tuks and tuk-tuk drivers do not guide.

Banks, ATMs and exchange There are plenty of places to obtain money in Siem Reap with ATMs at the airport, in the shopping malls, scattered across town (particularly around Psar Chas) as well as at banks. Acleda Bank, National Route 6 (towards the airport), Sivatha Blvd and National Route 6 (near Psar Leu); ANZ Royal, National Route 6 (near Psar Leu) and Samdech Tep Vong St; Canadia Bank, Sivatha Blvd northwest of Psar Chas and National Route 6 (near Psar Leu); UCB, Samdech Tep Vong St.

Bicycle rental White bicycles (a non profit organization that supports teenagers, with 50 cents per hire going to training) can be hired from a number of outlets around town including the *Rosy* and *Babel* guesthouses, and Peace of Angkor Tours, $2 per day, $5 for 3 days.

Books and newspapers Secondhand English-language books are available at Blue Apsara next to the Old Market and D's Books on Hospital St. Books on Cambodia and Angkor-related subjects can be found at Monument Books, on the riverside south of Psar Chas. Siem Reap Book Centre, on Hospital St, and the shop at the *Grand Hotel d'Angkor* both sell foreign-language newspapers and magazines; the former also stocks a range of books. The stalls at Psar Chas sell a selection of temple guides and books on Khmer history (though they are probably photocopies). The *Cambodia Daily* and the *Phnom Penh Post* can be purchased at Lucky Supermarket and at hotel newsstands.

Buses Siem Reap has a plethora of bus companies which all serve the most travelled Siem Reap-to-Phnom Penh route; most also provide services to Poipet, but only a few operate buses on the less travelled routes to Battambang and Kompong Cham (for Kampie, Rattanakiri and Mondulkiri) for example. Capitol (corner of St 7 and St 11); Neak Krorhorm (Pokambor Av 100m southwest of Psar Chas); Phnom Penh Sorya Transport (Sivatha Blvd, 200m west of Psar Chas; ⓦwww.ppsoryatransport.com). All the bus companies have ticket offices at Chong Kov Sou transport stop, 2km east of town.

Car hire A car and driver can be hired from most hotels, travel agents or from KATGA (see "Angkor tour guides" above); $30 per day around Angkor, $50 to Banteay Srei and $50–60 to Phnom Kulen. For Koh Ker and Beng Mealea, and Preah Vihear expect to pay $90–100 per day.

Dentists Pachem Dental Clinic, Angkor Wat Rd, just north of Angkor National Museum ⓣ063/965333, ⓦwww.pachemdental.com.

Emergencies Fire service, Sivatha Blvd ⓣ063/784464, 012/784464. For police, see p.179.

Golf For golf aficionados, there's an 18-hole course designed by Nick Faldo at the Angkor Golf Resort, 5km from town south off National Route 6 (ⓦwww.angkor-golf.com).

Hospitals and clinics The Royal Angkor International Hospital, National Route 6 (2km from the airport) (ⓣ063/761888, emergency ⓣ012/235888, ⓦwww.royalangkorhospital.com) has some of the better medical services including call-out service, 24-hour emergency care, ambulance, translation and evacuation to Bangkok. The government-run Siem Reap Provincial Hospital, 500m north of Psar Chas (ⓣ063/963111), is basic and to be used only as a last resort.

Internet access Wi-fi is almost universally available at hotels, guesthouses, restaurants and bars; otherwise expect to pay around $1 per hour at one of the many internet cafés around town.

Laundry Other than using your hotel or guesthouse's services, there are laundries all over town, charging 800–1000 riel per item. A few places on or near Sivatha Blvd now offer quick turnaround, which includes tumble drying (essential during the rainy season) for a bit more money.

Motorbike rental Foreign tourists – as distinct from expatriates – are banned from riding motorbikes around Siem Reap and the temples, ostensibly to safeguard them from having their bikes stolen by agents of the rental companies in order to elicit a replacement fee (it's also been claimed that tourists can't safely negotiate the chaotic traffic).

Opticians There are several opticians on Sivatha Blvd; AngkOOptic (ⓣ063/761237) near the Canadia Bank seems reliable.

Pharmacies The best of the town's pharmacies is U-Care. Its main branch, with trained, English-speaking pharmacists, is on Hospital St near *The Blue Pumpkin*; branches also at Lucky and the

Tour and specialist operators

Siem Reap's tour operators can not only customize tours to remoter areas, including distant parts of the Tonle Sap and northern Cambodia, but they can organize trips with specialist interest such as bird watching, cycling or motor biking, photography and visits to community based projects.

Beyond Unique Escapes, Alley West ⓣ063/969269, ⓦwww.beyonduniqueescapes .com. Specialists in small group cycling tours around the Siem Reap area from a 3 hour sunrise cycle to Angkor (Angkor pass required) to a full-day, 35km ride.

Diethelm Travel 470 Krous Village, off Airport Rd ⓣ063/963524, ⓦwww.diethelmtravel .com/cambodia. A range of tours around Siem Reap and Cambodia including soft adventures such as a camping safari to Koh Ker.

Exotissimo Travel Cambodia Street 60m, Off Angkor Wat Rd ⓣ063/964323, ⓦcambodia.exotissimo.com. This long-standing operator has a range of soft adventure tours including cycling, trekking and camping excursions in the Siem Reap area and around Cambodia.

Hidden Cambodia Adventure Tours Just off Angkor Wat Rd, near Jayavarman VII Hospital T012/655201, Wwww.hiddencambodia.com. Adventurous travel on foot, by dirt bike or 4WD around Siem Reap and throughout Cambodia; also with bike repair facilities.

Osmose Nature Tours Street 27 ⓣ012/832812, ⓦwww.osmosetonlesap.net. Specialist operator of Tonle Sap excursions from $55/day, including trips to the flooded reaches of the lake's flood plain and the bird sanctuary at Prek Toal.

Peace of Angkor Tours 435 Street 20 ⓣ063/760475, ⓦwww.peaceofangkor.com. Organizes tours to remoter areas of Cambodia, with a particular emphasis on photography; The Spirit of Cambodia is a day trip visiting five community projects in the Siem Reap area and 30 percent of the tour price is donated to them. Overnight trips, to Preah Vihear for example, can be arranged.

Sam Veasna Centre Street 26 T063/963710, Wwww.samveasna.org. Specialists in ornithological and wildlife trips around Siem Reap and the north of Cambodia; Sam Veasna works in conjunction with World Conservation Society (WCS) on projects to involve local communities in conserving nature.

Terre Cambodge Hup Guan St (behind ANZ Bank) ⓣ092/476682, ⓦwww.terre cambodge.com & ⓦwww.bikingcambodia.com. Trekking and mountain bike expeditions with village accommodation around Siem Reap; sampan cruises on the Tonle Sap; they also have a house to rent (ⓦwww.naryhouse.com).

Angkor National Museum malls. For minor matters there are plenty of pharmacies around Psar Chas and east of the river on National Route 6.

Phones You can make domestic calls from the booths around the markets and international calls at the main post office on Pokambor Av (daily 7am–5.30pm). Cheap international calls can be made at Siem Reap's internet cafés. Tourist SIM cards can be purchased from one of the many mobile telephone service providers, most of whom have offices on Sivatha Blvd.

Photography You'll find a handful of photographic studios along National Route 6, east of the river, that stock batteries, film and so on. Most of the photo shops in town can also make prints from your SD card or CD.

Police The tourist police office is opposite the main entrance to the Angkor Archaeological Park (ⓣ012/402424). To report sex offenders contact the police nationwide hotline (ⓣ023/997919) or Child Safe (ⓣ063/761096).

Post The post office is on Pokambor Av (daily 7am–5.30pm), where you can post parcels, collect poste restante mail (500 riel/piece) and make domestic and international calls.

Shipping agents DHL, 15a Sivatha Blvd, near the Central Market ⓣ063/964949, ⓦwww.dhl.com. They can make all the arrangements to get your purchases home in two days to UK and USA.

Supermarkets and shopping malls In addition to its markets (Psar Chas, Psar Leu and the Central Market) Siem Reap has several supermarkets, mini markets and a couple of malls. Angkor Trade Centre on Pokambor Av just north of Psar Chas has a supermarket, book stall, a few clothes stores and a branch of Swensen's. The best of Cambodia's supermarkets is the Phnom Penh chain, Lucky Market, which has a branch in Lucky Mall on Sivatha Blvd; for a mini-market the Star Mart, at Caltex petrol station on Airport Rd, is hard to beat.

Travel agents As well as arranging domestic and international travel, most of the travel agents can arrange for visa extensions, though it takes a couple of days as they have to send your passport to Phnom Penh. Angkor World Travel & Tours, 711 Wat Bo Road ⓣ063/966669; Neak Krorhorm Travel & Tours 3 Psar Chas ⓣ063/964924

The temples of Angkor

Designated a UNESCO World Heritage Site in 1992, the **TEMPLES OF ANGKOR** are scattered over some four hundred square kilometres of countryside between the Tonle Sap lake and the Kulen Mountains, although the most famous are clustered close to Siem Reap. Atmospherically surrounded by patches of dense forest and standing proudly above rice paddies, the temples do not feel like sterile museum pieces, but seem still to be part of everyday life – aspects of which continue much as depicted in temple bas-reliefs.

Angkor's sites are as diverse as the kings who built them, and each temple has its own distinct appeal. Steeped in myth and mystery, **Angkor Wat** is unmistakeable with its five magnificent corn-cob towers and vast complex of galleries. Also on everyone's itinerary is the walled city of **Angkor Thom**, whose much-photographed south gate, approached by a stunning causeway flanked by huge statues of gods and demons, is topped by massive faces looking out to the four cardinal directions. The faces are repeated in their hundreds at the **Bayon**, which lies at the heart of Angkor Thom and was the very last Angkorian temple to be built; figuring large among its claims to fame are two galleries of bas-reliefs. Two more must-sees are the "jungle temple", **Ta**

The cult of the god kings

The frenzy of building in the Angkor region was principally a result of the Khmer kings' desire to create **state-temples** to serve the **devaraja cult** (see p.328), which existed alongside the prevailing Hinduism. The **layout** of the majority of state-temples symbolizes the Hindu cosmos. A central **sanctuary tower** (or group of towers), housing the sacred image of the **devaraja**, would be raised on a platform, often in the form of a multi-level **pyramid** representing the mythical Mount Meru; surrounding this would be a series of concentric rectangular enclosures, created by walls and/or moats; in all but one instance (Angkor Wat), the temples were designed to be approached from the east.

As successive kings sought to outdo their predecessors, and as construction techniques improved, so the temples grew in complexity, making use of multiple sanctuaries, antechambers, galleries and elaborate **gopuras**, or entrance towers. Although practically all the temples were extensively carved with decorative motifs or detailed mythological scenes, the most magnificent carvings of all are the **bas-relief** panels at Angkor Wat and the Bayon. **Statues also abounded**, and the alcoves, antechambers and sanctuaries would have been crammed with images in wood, stone, bronze and even gold. There are few in situ these days; those that survived the years of abandonment, and avoided being stolen or destroyed, have been removed for safekeeping, mainly to Angkor Conservation (see box, p.181), though some prize specimens can be seen in the National Museum in Phnom Penh and the Angkor National Museum in Siem Reap. **For more on temple architecture and art**, see the *Temple architecture* colour section.

Conservation at Angkor

By the late nineteenth century, travellers and researchers from many countries, notably France, were arriving in Cambodia in search of its "lost" temples. The first major step towards a proper study of Angkor's legacy was the foundation in Vietnam in 1898 of the **École Française d'Extrême-Orient** (Ⓦwww.efeo.fr); their scholars mapped the temples for the first time, and created the body now known as **Angkor Conservation**, based 2km north of Siem Reap, which works on the restoration of temples.

Work at Angkor was carried out throughout the first half of the twentieth century, with only a brief pause during World War II. Particularly noteworthy among the researchers of the time were Henri Marchal and Maurice Glaize, the former remembered for his restoration in the early 1930s of Banteay Srei, the latter for restoring Banteay Samre, Bakong, Neak Pean and part of Preah Khan. It was during work on Banteay Srei that the restoration technique of **anastylosis** began to be employed in Cambodia, involving the temporary dismantling and analysis of intact parts of structures so that ruined sections could be reassembled faithfully. In 1960, Bernard-Philippe Groslier assumed control of Angkor Conservation, taking after his father George, who had previously held the post. He was able to commence work on the Baphuon before the monuments were again abandoned during the civil war and the Khmer Rouge years.

Contrary to common belief, the temples suffered little war damage, but looting undoubtedly occurred and the fabric of the temples continued to be at risk from encroaching vegetation. Things improved little during Vietnamese occupation in the 1980s, when only Indian conservators were allowed to work here; their work at Angkor Wat, where they used chemicals to clean the stone and cement to fill gaps, has been much criticized. By 1992, however, UNESCO had declared Angkor a **World Heritage Site**, and conservation projects to the tune of millions of dollars were put in place, sponsored primarily by Japan.

Since the 1990s conservation of the temples has been coordinated by **APSARA**, an NGO that also oversees the preservation of the cultural heritage of Siem Reap province. Their task is formidable: not only is looting a problem, particularly at remote temples with jungle cover and lack of sufficient guards, but the effects of growing visitor numbers, erosion and destabilizing of some temples, is devastating. Measures taken in an attempt to preserve the ruins include: banning over-flying of the temples; limiting access (the central sanctuary of Angkor Wat); creating set visitor routes (through the terraces at Angkor Thom); and cordoning off the bas-reliefs (at Angkor Wat).

Prohm, its ruins held in the vice-like grip of giant tree roots, whose appeal has actually been enhanced by the ravages of nature, and **Banteay Srei**, a unique micro-temple of intricately carved reddish stone.

The earliest surviving temples, at **Roluos**, east of Siem Reap, are more for the specialist, but a visit shows how the architecture evolved, with brick used almost throughout, in contrast with the later, more sophisticated temples where increasing use was made of sandstone, which could be carved and decorated. Roluos aside, there are some forty other sites accessible to the public.

Some history

The ancient Khmer wrote on specially treated palm trees or animal skins and none of their texts have survived. Consequently the history of Angkor (discussed in detail on p.311) had to be painstakingly pieced together through study of the temples and over a thousand inscribed steles – mostly written in Sanskrit – recovered across the empire. Even now, Angkorian history remains hypothetical to some degree, with the origins of many temples, the dates of their construction and even the names of kings uncertain.

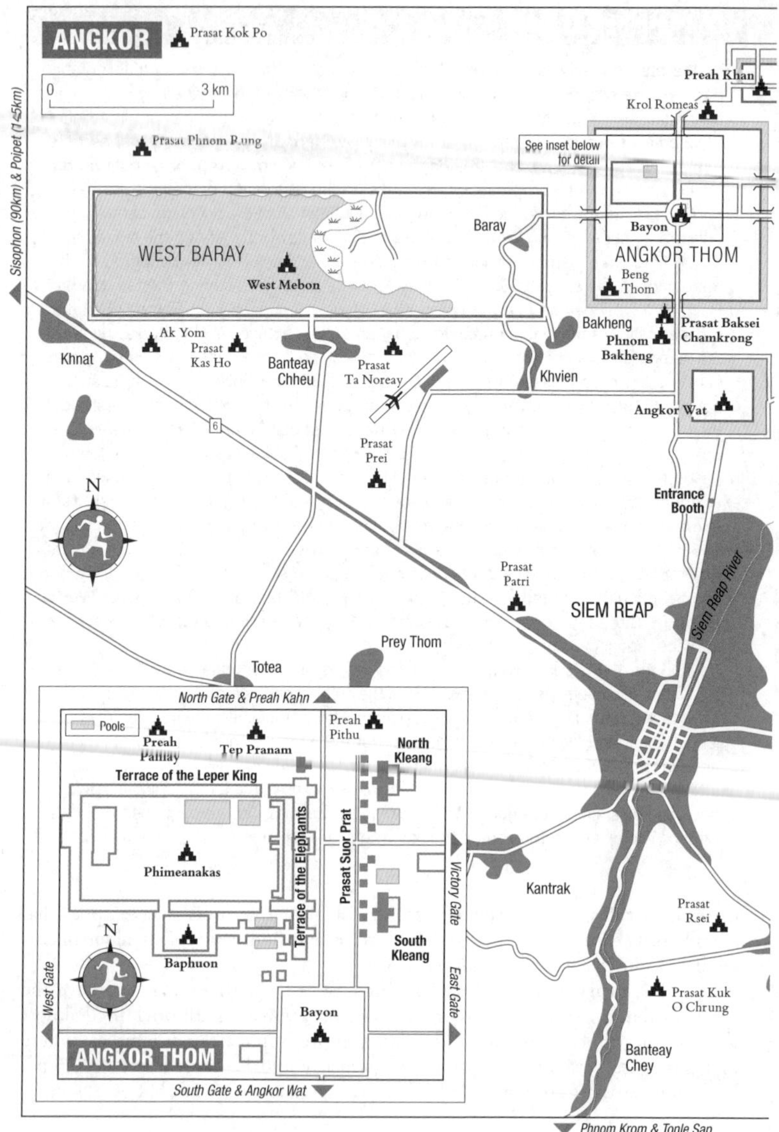

Angkor's **earliest monuments** date from 802, when Jayavarman II came north from Kompong Cham to set up court at Phnom Kulen. No further stone temples were built after the reign of **Jayavarman VII**, the greatest temple-builder of them all, came to an end in 1219; scholars theorize that either the area's resources were exhausted or the switch to Theravada Buddhism may have precluded their construction. After Jayavarman VII, the temples and palaces remained in use until they were sacked by the Thais in 1431; the following year, Ponhea Yat took his

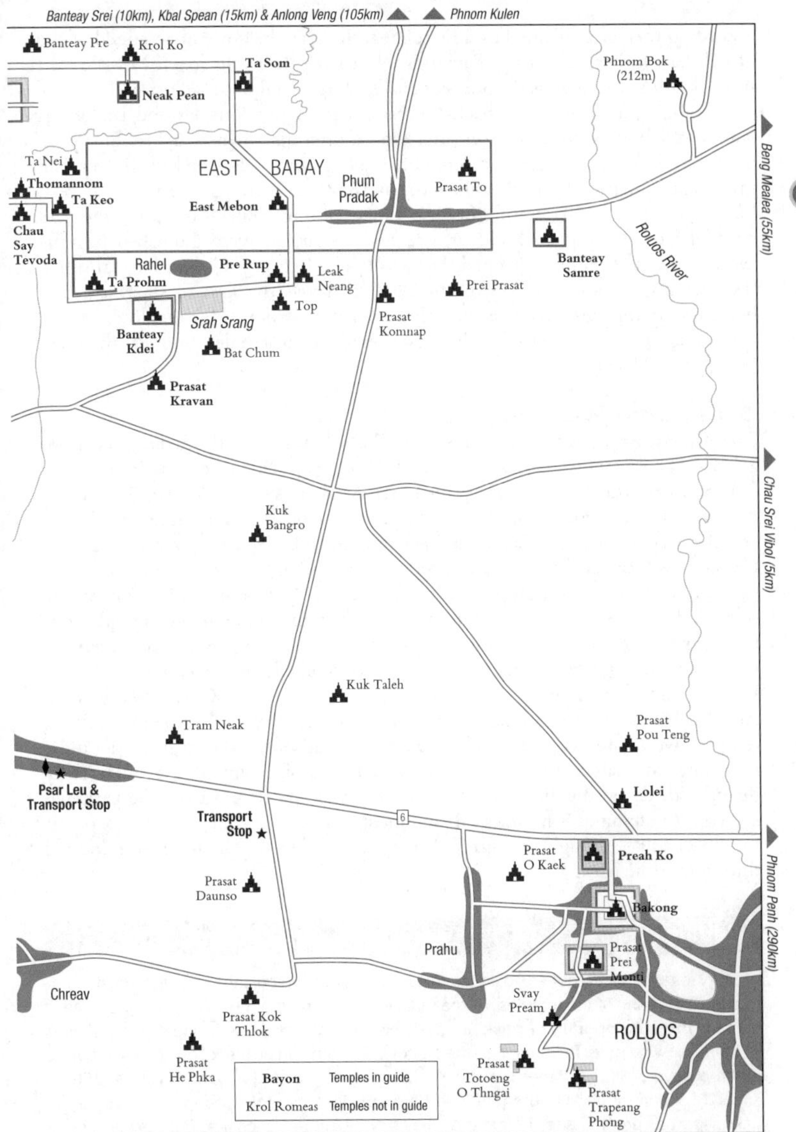

court south to Phnom Penh and left Angkor to the jungle. Though Angkor was never completely deserted, the local people who continued to worship at the temples were unable to maintain them.

Around 1570, **King Satha** was so enchanted when he rediscovered Angkor Thom deep in the jungle that he had the undergrowth cleared and brought his court there, though by 1594 he was back at Lovek. Another short-lived period of royal interest occurred in the middle of the seventeenth century when, according to a letter penned by a Dutch merchant to the governor-general of the Dutch East Indies, "the king [Barom Rachea VI] paid a visit to a lovely pleasant place known as Anckoor". Subsequently, despite tales of a lost city in the Cambodian jungle filtering back to the West via missionaries and traders, it wasn't until the nineteenth century that Cambodia opened up to European explorers. The first proper account of Angkor Wat, published by the French missionary Charles-Emile Bouillevaux in 1858, failed to arouse wide interest, but in 1864, the diaries of botanist and explorer Henri Mouhot, who had stumbled on Angkor by accident a few years earlier, were published posthumously, and the temples gripped the world. The Briton J. Thompson published the first photographs of Angkor in 1867, and was the first to suggest a link between temple architecture and the mythical Mount Meru. Close behind him came Doudart Lagrée, who discovered Beng Mealea and Preah Khan (Kompong Thom).

Organizing your visit

The Angkor Archaeological Park is **open daily from 5am to sunset**. Exceptions are Banteay Srei which closes at 5pm and Kbal Spean which closes at 3pm.

All visitors will at some point want to see Angkor Wat and Angkor Thom, but how you do this depends on time, as there are various possible routes around the temples – two classical trips are the **Petit** and **Grand Circuits** (seventeen kilometres and twenty-six kilometres respectively; see p.185). If you're short of time, you can just about cover Angkor Wat, the Bayon, Ta Prohm and Banteay Srei in one full day. Some visitors find it useful to see the temples in **chronological order** to understand better how they grew in complexity as new construction methods were tried, though inevitably this involves considerable backtracking: starting at Roluos, you'd have to head out to Bakheng and on to Prasat Kravan before doing Angkor Wat and then shooting out to Banteay Samre. If you plan to visit outlying temples we've not covered, you should **seek advice** from registered guides regarding the safety situation, as **some of the sites have not been fully de-mined**. Given the distances to be covered walking to and from the park and between the temples is impractical, and most visitors hire a moto, tuk-tuk or car for their visit – though the intrepid sometimes cycle. Public toilets are located throughout the park.

Getting in

Entry passes are required to enter the Angkor Archaeological Park, and must be shown at many of the temples. At the main entrance, on the Siem Reap–Angkor Wat road, **three categories of pass** are available: one day, this can be purchased after 5pm, allowing entry for sunset on the day of purchase and all the following day ($20); three days, valid for three days during the following week ($40); seven days ($60) valid for one month. Children under 12 are admitted free, but you must show their passport as proof of age; 12 and over they pay the full entrance fee. One-day passes only can be bought at the ticket office between the airport and Angkor Wat, at Roluos group and at Banteay Srei. Note that payment is by cash only, no cards are accepted; there is no need to provide a photo as these are now taken digitally at the ticket office. Most people find the three-day pass adequate, giving enough time to see all the temples in the central area and to visit the outlying temples at Roluos, Banteay Srei and Banteay Samre. **Separate tickets are required** to visit Phnom Kulen ($20), Koh Ker ($10; see p.225), and Beng Mealea ($5 see p.211); the fees are collected at those temples.

The classical circuits

The **Petit** (or Small) **Circuit** starts at Angkor Wat, heads north through the south gate of Angkor Thom to the Bayon, Baphuon (under restoration) and Phimeanakas and Terrace of Elephants, from where it heads east to Thomannom and Chau Say Tevoda, Ta Keo, Ta Prohm, Banteay Kdei and Srah Srang; if you've any energy left, take in Prasat Kravan on the way back to Angkor Wat.

Starting at Srah Srang, the **Grand Circuit** continues east, taking in the temples along the road looping around to Angkor Thom's northern gate – Pre Rup, East Mebon (from where you can extend the circuit to Banteay Samre), Ta Som, Neak Pean and Preah Khan.

Eating and drinking

There are **refreshment stalls** at the larger temples, including Angkor Wat, Terrace of the Leper King, Ta Prohm and Pre Rup. At Angkor Wat, small **restaurants** behind the souvenir stalls serve Khmer and Chinese food at prices only slightly higher than similar establishments in Siem Reap. Opposite the main entrance, the *Angkor Café* houses a branch of Siem Reap's popular *Blue Pumpkin* – good for bakery items, ice creams and fruit shakes. Acceptable Khmer fare can also be obtained at the restaurants on the road north of Srah Srang; the *Khmer Village* is reliable. Alternatively, bring a picnic with you from Siem Reap; many hotels now offer a picnic basket, or pick up goodies at one of the bakeries in town and find a nice spot to eat.

Souvenirs and trinkets

Inexpensive **souvenirs**, from bamboo trinkets to *kramas* are sold at stalls outside the most popular temples, and children at most temples hawk film, postcards, T-shirts and simple handicrafts made from rattan and bamboo. These children can be annoying, but they're restricted to where they can go these days so won't follow you around the temple; they usually live within the park area and so if possible just buy a few knick-knacks or postcards from them – they're just trying to make a living.

Angkor Wat

...the workmanship is so astonishing that the Cambodians themselves always refer to them as the work of angels rather than men...

Monsignor Jean-Baptiste Pallegoix, 1854

However many times you've seen it on film or in photographs, nothing prepares you for the majesty of **Angkor Wat**. Dominated by five majestic, corn-cob towers, this masterpiece of Khmer architecture, consecrated around 1150 to the Hindu god Vishnu, is thought to have taken around thirty years to complete. Stunning from a distance, as you approach its intricacy becomes apparent, with every nook and cranny filled with fine detail, each new feature surpassing the last. If time allows, it's worth visiting at different times of day to see how the colours of the stone change with the light.

Experts have long debated whether Angkor Wat was built for worship or for funerary purposes, because the site is approached from the west and the gallery of bas-reliefs is designed to be viewed anti-clockwise, both of which are associated

At the time of writing, parts of Angkor Wat (and some other temples) are undergoing restoration, and scaffold towers and tarpaulins may be in place.

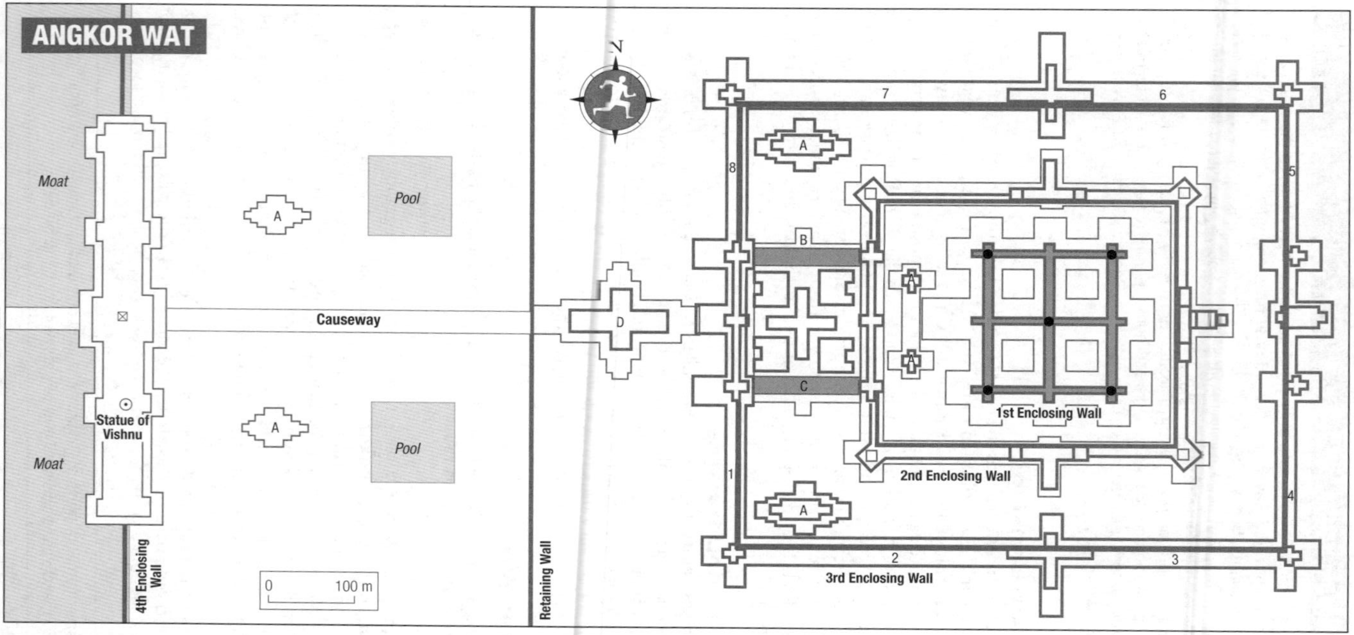

ANGKOR WAT

- ● Sanctuary Towers
- Galleries
- **A** Libraries
- **B** Chamber of Echoes
- **C** Gallery of a Thousand Buddhas
- **D** Terrace of Honour

BAS-RELIEFS

1. Kauravas and Pandavas
2. Suryavarman II battle scene
3. Heaven and Hell gallery
4. Churning of the Ocean of Milk
5. Vishnu and the asuras
6. Krishna and Bana
7. Gods and demons
8. Battle of Lanka

with death. Nowadays, it's generally accepted that it was used by the king for the worship of the devaraja during his lifetime, and became his mausoleum upon his death.

Moat and fourth enclosure

Entry to the complex is from the west, via an impressive laterite causeway built from massive blocks of stone. Paved with sandstone and edged by a crumbling naga balustrade with terraces guarded by lions, it crosses the 200-metre-wide **moat** to the west gopura of the **fourth enclosing wall**.

The **west gopura** stretches for nearly 230m and has three towers, plus entrances large enough to allow elephants to pass through. Inside the southern section of the gopura, invariably garlanded with offerings of flowers and enveloped in a fog of incense, is an eight-armed statue of **Vishnu**, over 3m tall. Looking out from the gopura, there's a panoramic view of the temple. The first of Angkor Wat's fabulous **apsaras**, born from the Churning of the Ocean of Milk (see box, p.188), are delicately carved into the sandstone on the eastern exterior of the gopura, their feet foreshortened and skewed to the side, possibly because of lack of space.

From the gopura, a second **causeway** leads to the temple, 350m long and even more impressive than the one across the moat. The buildings partway along are libraries, the one to the north already restored, the southern one still undergoing work.

In front of the temple is the cruciform-shaped **Terrace of Honour**, framed by the naga balustrade; apsara dances (see box, p.175) were once performed here and ceremonial processions received by the king. Beyond the terrace, a short flight of steps leads up to the third enclosing wall, whose western gopura is linked to a cruciform cloister and two galleries.

The third enclosure

Portraying events associated primarily with Vishnu, to whom the temple is dedicated, the famous Angkor Wat bas-reliefs, some 2m high on average, are carved into the wall of the magnificently colonnaded **gallery**, which runs around the perimeter of the temple, forming the **third enclosure**. This was as far into the complex as the citizens of Angkor were allowed to get, and the scenes depicted were meant to impress them with their king's prowess as well as contributing to their religious education.

The early sections of the bas-reliefs are delicately carved with minute attention to detail (in marked contrast to the poorly executed scenes added in the sixteenth century). In some areas you can still see evidence of the red and gold paint that once covered the reliefs, while other areas are black; one theory is that the pigments have been eroded and the stone polished by thousands of hands caressing the carvings over the years (nowadays a barrier stops you getting too close and signs ask you not to touch the reliefs).

Extending over 700m, the bas-reliefs are broken into sections by porches midway along each side, along with corner chambers. The account that follows assumes you progress around the gallery in an **anti-clockwise** direction, in keeping with the ancient funerary practices.

West gallery: south section

The battle between the cousins, the **Kauravas** (marching from the left) and the **Pandavas** (from the right), described in the *Mahabharata* is in full swing in the first section of the gallery. Fighting to the death at Mount Kurukshetra, the two families are respectively backed by the supernatural powers of Kama, son of the sun god Surya, and Arjuna. Along the bottom of the panel, the foot soldiers march towards the fray in the centre of the gallery; above them, the generals ride in horse-drawn chariots or on elephants. Amid thrilling hand-to-hand combat, the

Kaurava general, Bhisma, is shown shot through with arrows, while Arjuna can be seen on his chariot with Krishna serving as his charioteer.

Southwest corner

Despite erosion, some tales from the *Ramayana* (see box, p.94) and other Hindu legends can still be made out here. One panel shows Krishna protecting shepherds who have decided to worship him rather than Indra; against the storms sent by Indra, he holds up Mount Govardhana in one hand as a shelter. Another depicts the duel between the monkey gods Valin and Sugriva, in which Valin dies in the arms of his wife after he is pierced by an arrow from Rama; monkeys mourn Valin on the surrounding panels.

South gallery: west section

This gallery depicts a **battle scene** that runs west to east on two levels, beginning with a royal audience (upper level) and the palace ladies in procession (below). Further along, the Khmer commanders, mounted on elephants and shaded by parasols, muster the troops and march through the jungle. At the centre of the panel they surround Suryavarman II, who is of larger stature and has fifteen parasols around him. Beyond, the army – accompanied by musicians, standard-bearers and jesters – is joined by Cham mercenaries, identified by their moustaches and plumed headdresses. It is thought that the small niches along the wall were used as hiding places for golden artefacts, though some say the chunks of stone were removed by devotees who believed they possessed magical properties.

South gallery: east section

Called the **Heaven and Hell gallery**, this panel, carved on three levels and nearly 60m long, shows the many-armed god Yama mounted on a buffalo and judging the dead. At the start of this section, a path is shown on the top level along which people ascend to heaven, while a corresponding route at the bottom leads to hell, the two paths being separated by a frieze of garudas. The people in heaven can be seen living a life of leisure in palaces, whereas sinners are pushed through a trapdoor into the underworld to have terrible punishments inflicted on them – gluttons are cut in two, vandals have their bones broken and rice stealers have red-hot irons thrust through their abdomens.

East gallery: south section

This gallery contains the most famous of Angkor Wat's bas-reliefs, depicting the **Churning of the Ocean of Milk** (see box below). The story picks up when the churning is just about to yield results; in the central band of the panel, 92 bulbous-eyed *asuras* with crested headdresses are shown holding the head of Vasuki and pulling from the left, while on the right, 88 *devas*, with almond eyes and conical headdresses, hold the tail. To the top, thousands of divine apsaras dance along the

The Churning of the Ocean of Milk

A popular theme in Khmer art is the Churning of the Ocean of Milk, a **creation myth** from the Hindu epic, the *Bhagavata-Purana*, which is a description of the various incarnations of Vishnu. At the outset of this episode, the *devas* (gods) and *asuras* (demons) are lined up on opposite sides, trying to use Mount Mandara to churn the ocean in order to produce *amrita*, the elixir of immortality. They tug on the serpent Vasuki, who is coiled around the mountain, but to no effect. Vishnu arrives and instructs them to pull rhythmically, but the mountain begins to sink. Things get worse when Vasuki vomits a deadly venom, which threatens to destroy the *devas* and wall, and at the bottom, the ocean teems with finely detailed marine creatures. The chedi just outside the east gopura was placed here in the early eighteenth century when the temple was a Buddhist monastery; its history is recorded on a wall inscription within the gopura itself.

If you've had enough of the bas-reliefs or are running out of time, this is a good place to break off and enter the main temple; otherwise continue on through the remaining galleries.

East gallery: north section

The relief here was carved in the sixteenth century and the workmanship is rough and superficial. The scene records the *asuras* being defeated by Vishnu, who is shown with four heads and mounted on Garuda in the centre of the panel. The *asuras* approach from the south, their leaders riding chariots drawn by monsters; from the north, a group of warriors ride peacocks.

North gallery: east section

Also sixteenth century, the poorly rendered scenes here show the battle between **Krishna** and **Bana**, son of an *asura* who had come under Shiva's protection. Krishna, easily spotted with his eight arms and multiple heads, rides Garuda towards Bana, but is forced to halt by a fire surrounding a city wall, which Garuda quells with water from the Ganges. On the far west of the panel, a victorious Krishna is depicted on Mount Kailasa, where Shiva entreats him to spare Bana's life. Also along this stretch of wall can be found an image of the elephant-headed god, Ganesh, his only appearance in the entire temple.

North gallery: west section

Better executed than the previous two sections, the panel here shows 21 gods from the **Hindu pantheon** in a terrific melee between gods and demons. Some of the easier ones to spot are, from left to right, the multi-headed and -armed Skanda, god of war, riding a peacock; Indra standing on the elephant Airavata; Vishnu mounted on Garuda and fighting with all four arms; Yama's chariot pulled by buffalos; and Shiva pulling his bow, while Brahma rides the sacred goose, Hamsa.

Northwest corner

More scenes from the *Ramayana* are to be found here, notably a depiction of Vishnu reclining on the serpent, Anata; a bevy of apsaras float above him, while his wife, Lakshmi, sits near his feet; below, a procession of gods come to ask Vishnu to return to earth.

West gallery: north section

Turning the corner, you come to the superbly carved **Battle of Lanka**. In this action-packed sequence from the *Ramayana*, Rama is shown fighting the

asuras; Brahma asks Shiva to drink up the venom, which he does, but it burns his throat, which is blue thereafter. Vishnu meanwhile, in his incarnation as a tortoise, supports Mount Mandara, allowing the churning to continue for another thousand years, when the *amrita* is finally produced. Unfortunately, the elixir is seized by the *asuras*, but Vishnu again comes to the rescue as the apparition Maya and regains the cup of elixir. The churning also results in the manifestation of mythical beings, including the three-headed elephant, Airavata; the goddess of beauty, Lakshmi, who becomes Vishnu's wife; and the celestial dancers, the **apsaras**.

ten-headed, twenty-armed Ravana to free his wife, Sita, from captivity; bodies of the soldiers from the monkey army, Rama's allies, fall in all directions. The two adversaries are seen in the centre of the panel, Ravana in a chariot drawn by lions, Rama standing on the monkey king, Sugriva.

First level

Arriving back at the western gopura you can head east up into the **third enclosure** (which is also the first level of the temple pyramid), bare save for two libraries in the northwest and southwest corners. Within the cloister, if you look up, you'll spot a frieze of apsaras, while below are seated ascetics carved at the bases of the columns; many of the columns also bear Sanskrit and Khmer inscriptions. The **Gallery of Thousand Buddhas**, to the south, once housed a vast collection of Buddhas, collected here over recent centuries when Angkor Wat was a Buddhist monastery; those that weren't moved to Angkor Conservation in 1970 were eventually destroyed by the Khmer Rouge, though today a few modern images have taken their place. The chamber in the wall of the north gallery is the **Hall of Echoes**, where the sound reverberates if you stand with your back to the wall and thump your chest with your fist – as Cambodians do, thrice, to bring good fortune.

Second and third levels

The **second level** of the pyramid is enclosed by a gallery with windows to the courtyard within, into whose walls are carved a remarkable collection of over 1500 **apsaras**, each one unique. Elegantly dressed, these beautiful creatures display exotic hairstyles and enigmatic expressions; even their jewellery is lovingly carved. These are the earliest depictions in Angkorian art of apsaras in groups, some posed in twos or threes, arms linked and hands touching. Often there are a group of actors here dressed up as monkey gods, peacocks and so; for a dollar you can have your photograph taken with them using Angkor Wat as the background – a great souvenir for children.

During the time of Suryavarman II, only the high priest and the king were allowed to visit the **third level**, but now visitors can make the ascent. Bear in mind though that access to this level is difficult and from time to time, usually if there's been an accident, it may be closed.

Phnom Bakheng and Prasat Baksei Chamkrong

The first monument to be built in the Angkor area, the temple-mountain of **Phnom Bakheng** was built by Yasovarman I and dedicated in 907 at the heart of the first kingdom of Cambodia. The summit commands a magnificent view; west over the West Baray, Angkor Wat (to the southeast) and, further afield, south to the Tonle Sap lake and northeast to Phnom Kulen.

It was no simple task to convert the natural 67-metre-high hill into a symbolic representation of **Mount Meru**. Steps and terraces were hewn into the rock and then clad in sandstone, while a moat (originally 4km square) was dug around the hill in line with Hindu cosmology – part of it is still visible on the road in from Siem Reap, 600m before Angkor Wat. The temple pyramid, comprising five levels, has a total of 109 sanctuary towers: 44 around its base, twelve on each level, plus five principal towers at the top arranged, for the first time in Khmer architecture, in a

Sunset ascent

In the late afternoon, hundreds of tourists make the trek up the steep, badly eroded, rock-hewn steps of Phnom Bakheng to watch the sun set over Angkor Wat. If you don't want to walk, between 3 and 5pm elephants wait at the foot of the hill to ferry visitors up via a roundabout track ($20); downhill trips ($15) run between 5 and 6pm. The best time to see Phnom Bakheng itself though is in the early to mid-morning (which is not a bad time for the view either); it's likely you'll have the temple to yourself, with just a couple of grazing elephants for company, though you'll have to walk up under your own steam!

quincunx, to symbolize the five peaks of Mount Meru. The temple was consecrated to Shiva and the central tower would have contained a linga.

A few hundred metres north of Phnom Bakheng is the small, often ignored **Prasat Baksei Chamkrong**, the sole monument built by Harshavarman I. Consecrated to Shiva and his consort, the temple wasn't finished in the king's lifetime, and was re-consecrated by Rajendravarman I in 948. The simple temple comprises four square tiers of decreasing size, rising to a single brick sanctuary tower with decorated sandstone lintels and columns. A Sanskrit inscription on the door frame here records that the sanctuary contained a golden image of Paramenshavara, as Jayavarman II was known posthumously. If you want to head up to the top of the temple, the northern staircase is the best of a badly worn bunch.

Angkor Thom

The wall of the city is some five miles in circumference. It has five gates each with double portals... Outside the wall stretches a great moat, across which access to the city is given by massive causeways. Flanking the causeways on each side are fifty-four divinities resembling war-lords in stone, huge and terrifying...

Chou Ta-Kuan, visited 1296–97

Still recognizable from this description by the Chinese envoy Chou Ta-Kuan, who visited the Khmer court at the end of the thirteenth century, the great city of **Angkor Thom** (see inset map on p.182) covers an area of three square kilometres, enclosed by a wide moat and an eight-metre-high wall reinforced by a wide earth embankment (constructed by Jayavarman VII after the city had been sacked by the Cham in 1177). Numerous monuments are contained within the city. At the centre is the state-temple, the **Bayon**, one of the great sights of Angkor, dominated by huge faces looking out from its many towers, and boasting two enclosures of bas-reliefs.

North of the Bayon, Jayavarman VII had to squeeze his royal palace (which was built largely of wood, and thus has not survived) into a space between the **Baphuon** – the state-temple of Udayadityavarman II – and **Phimeanakas** – the tiny state-temple of Suryavarman I. In front of the palace he had two huge, gloriously carved **terraces** constructed, to be used as viewing platforms over the royal square and parade grounds.

The entry gates

A laterite wall 8m high, reinforced by a wide earth embankment, runs around the full perimeter of Angkor Thom's moat. The wall has a sanctuary tower at each corner and **five entry gates** – one per cardinal direction, plus an additional eastern portal, the Victory Gate. Actually elaborate gopuras, the gates each feature a tower topped by four huge faces of the benevolent Bodhisattva, Lokesvara, who looks out to each cardinal direction; these were in fact added at a later date.

The site is invariably approached from Angkor Wat through the 23-metre-high **south gate** and along a hundred-metre-long **stone causeway** flanked by 54 almond-eyed gods on one side, and 54 round eyed demons on the other. Though most of the heads here are replicas, the originals having been either stolen or removed for safety, you can see the genuine articles at the Angkor National Museum. Both gods and demons hold nine-headed nagas, which are said to protect the city's wealth. The base of the gateway itself is decorated with sculptures of **Indra** on a three-headed elephant; the elephant's trunks hold lotus blossoms which droop to the ground, cleverly forming columns that help support the rest of the sculpture.

The Bayon

...at the centre of the kingdom is a golden tower flanked by more than twenty stone towers and several hundred stone chambers."

Chou Ta-Kuan, visited 1296–97

From the south gate, the road runs 1.5km through the forest straight to the **Bayon**. A highlight of any visit is to arrive at the Bayon by **elephant** ($10–15); elephants wait at the stand by the southern causeway from 7.30am to 10.30am (in the afternoon they're at Phnom Bakheng). Arriving by car, tuk-tuk or moto, you'll be dropped at the main approach to the Bayon at the east, and your driver will go to the parking area near the Terrace of the Leper King about a kilometre to the north to wait for you while you visit the Bayon, Baphuon, Phimeanakas and the terraces; make sure to know exactly where he is waiting, as once you're there it's a mass of identical transport. Most people visit in the morning, when the light is at its best, but the light on the faces of the upper terrace can also be rewarding in the late afternoon and it's quieter then too.

Built in the late twelfth or early thirteenth century, the Bayon was intended to embrace all the religions of the kingdom, including the Islamic beliefs of the newly conquered Cham, but was consecrated as a Buddhist temple; when the state religion reverted to Hinduism, the Buddha in the central sanctuary was torn down and cast into the well beneath. As you approach from the south, all you can initially see down the avenue is a mass of ill-defined stone, dark and imposing. It's only after crossing the stone causeway that the intricacy of the Bayon's design becomes apparent, and you begin to make out the 37 towers with their massive faces of Lokesvara. It is said that there are more than two hundred in all; exactly why they are repeated so many times remains unclear.

Across the causeway, a few steps lead up to the **third enclosing wall**, a colonnaded gallery whose roof has long since collapsed. Its outer walls bear the first of the temple's **bas-reliefs**, deeper and less fine than those at Angkor Wat (and some are unfinished). Having viewed these, most people follow the passage from the middle of the south gallery to reach the bas-reliefs of the **second enclosing wall**, raised up about 1.5m above the level of the third enclosure. These carvings aren't in great condition, however, so if you're tired of studying yet more multi-armed gods you might as well look out just for those specimens we point out.

Both sets of bas-reliefs were intended to be viewed **clockwise**, starting from the **midpoint of the eastern wall**; this is how they are described below.

Third enclosing wall bas-reliefs: southern half

Heading south along the gallery from the east approach, you'll see a **military procession** depicted on three levels; bareheaded soldiers with short hair march

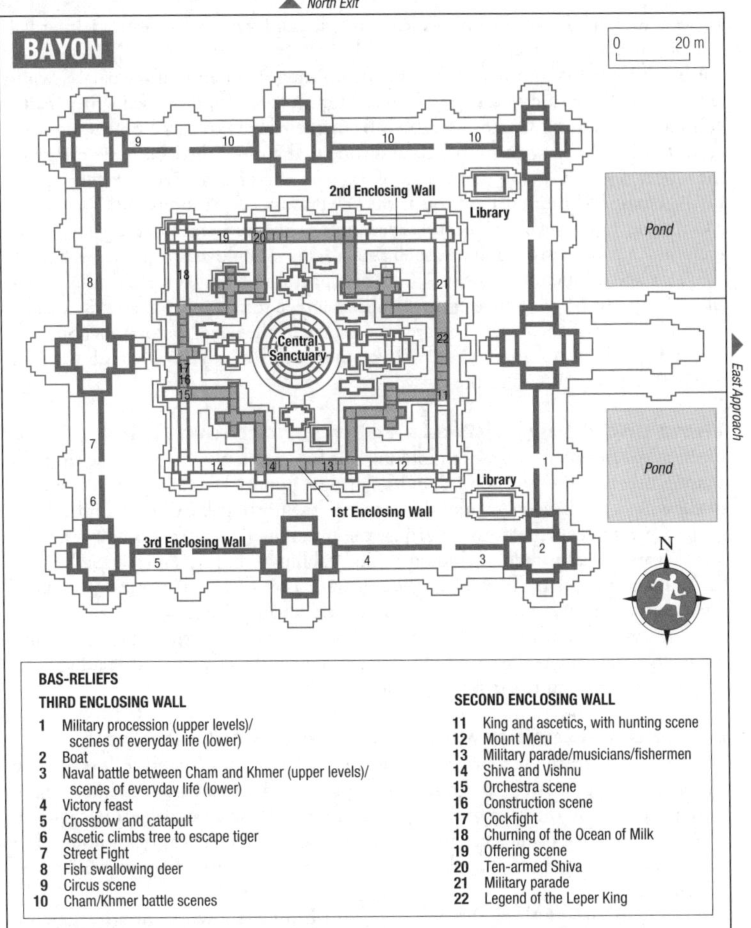

across the uppermost level, while the level just below depicts troops with goatee beards and elaborate hairstyles. Musicians and bareback cavalry accompany them, the commanders (with parasols) seated on elephants. Close to the next door to the courtyard are the army's camp followers, their covered carts just like those in use today. At the lowest level are some fascinating scenes of everyday domestic and rural life, many of them still as true now as when they were first carved.

The **southeast corner tower** is unfinished, but its carving of a boat is remarkable for continuing around a right angle. Turning the corner, you come to the **finest of the Bayon bas-reliefs**, depicting the 1177 **naval battle** between the Khmer and the Cham on the Tonle Sap lake. The victorious Khmer, led by Jayavarman VII, are shown with bare heads, whereas the Cham wear vaguely floral-looking hats. At the start, the king is seen seated in the palace directing preparations for battle, as fish swim through the trees – as in a rainy-season flood. Along the bottom are more carvings drawn from everyday life on the banks of the Tonle Sap: fishing baskets – just like those used now – hang from the ceiling, skewers of food are cooked over a charcoal fire and women are seen picking lice out of one another's hair.

A bit further along, princesses are shown amusing themselves at the palace, while around them wrestlers spar and a boar-fight takes place. Subsequently battle commences, and the Cham disembark from their boats to carry on the fight on land; the Khmers – with short hair and rope tied around their bodies – are given the appearance of giants, and are, of course, victorious. Back at the palace, **Jayavarman VII** himself looks on as the celebratory feast is prepared.

Only the lower level has been carved on the western side of the south wall, including a panel showing **arms**, such as a crossbow deployed from the back of an elephant and a catapult on wheels. The first portion of the western wall is unfinished; look out here for an **ascetic climbing a tree** to escape from a hungry tiger, near the centre of the panel. Towards the centre of the panel, before the gopura, a **street fight** is in progress: people shake their arms in anger, while above, two severed heads are shown to the crowd.

Third enclosing wall bas-reliefs: northern half

In the western gallery, it's worth looking out for a scene showing men with sticks chasing other men with round shields, passing a pond where a large fish is shown swallowing a small deer. Around the corner in the north gallery you'll find a light-hearted **circus** scene, featuring not just the usual jugglers, acrobats and wrestlers but also an animal parade, including rhinos, rabbits and deer. The section beyond the north gopura is badly eroded, though with a bit of effort you can just about make out the **fighting** between the Khmer and Cham resuming, with the Khmer running away towards the mountains. By the time you've turned the corner into the east gallery, the battle is in full swing, and even the elephants are taking part, one trying to rip out the tusk of another.

Second enclosing wall bas-reliefs: southern half

The bas-reliefs of the second enclosing wall are more difficult to follow as they are broken up by towers and antechambers into small panels. It is likely these were only seen by the king and his priests, unlike the scenes in the third gallery, which would have been accessible to the hoi polloi. Interestingly, although the Bayon was dedicated as a Buddhist temple, there are plenty of depictions here of **Hindu gods**.

In the vestibule south of the east gopura, a **hunt** is shown in progress, below which the king is shown tarrying in the palace and surrounded by ascetics. The wall is a bit crumbled as you turn the corner into the south gallery, but it's possible to make out **Mount Meru** rising out of the ocean – here denoted by the fish. Moving on, beyond the tower, warriors **parade** from left to right, while a band of musicians leaves the palace. Below, a dead child is being placed in a coffin; close by, a fisherman casts his net from his boat, while apsaras hover above. **Shiva and Vishnu** appear in numerous, mostly worn, scenes in the section west of the south gopura; towards the end of this section you'll see Shiva standing in a pool while ascetics and animals look on from the bank; in the same area people prostrate themselves around Vishnu, while a funeral is in progress.

In the west gallery, pop into the tower before the gopura and you'll find an **orchestra** depicted playing celestial music while the apsaras dance. Labourers hauling stones over rollers and lifting them into place can be seen in a curious **construction scene**, which oddly enough has had a depiction of Vishnu superimposed on it; you'll find this on the tiny section of gallery between the tower and the gopura. Just before the gopura is a harbour scene, where chess players get on with a game on board one of the boats, and a **cockfight** takes place on another.

Second enclosing wall bas-reliefs: northern half

The first few sections of carvings after the west gopura are in poor condition, so head straight to the section of gallery north of the tower, where there's yet another depiction of the story of the **Churning of the Ocean of Milk** (see p.188). In the centre of the panel, Vishnu, as the tortoise Kurma, holds up the mountain, while gods and demons can be made out hard at work churning. The reliefs around the corner in the north gallery are in better nick; in the first section servants are shown carrying **offerings** to a mountain sanctuary, while boats ferry in worshippers; look out for elephants and other wildlife in the mountains. Beyond the western tower, it's worth pausing to check out the pantheon of gods: a fine ten-armed **Shiva** is flanked by Vishnu on his right and Brahma on his left, and surrounded by apsaras.

Turning the corner, you're back in the east gallery, where there's a **military parade** featuring musicians accompanying cavalry, and a six-wheeled chariot drawn by Hamsa, the sacred goose and mount of Brahma. The final panel of note, in the gallery just before the gopura, pertains to the legend of the **Leper King**, in which the king contracts leprosy after being spattered with the venom of a serpent he fights; as women minister to the king, a cure is sought from ascetics.

The first enclosure and central sanctuary

Besides corner towers, the second enclosing wall appears to have a further three towers per side; these are actually part of the **first enclosing wall**, which takes the form of a toothed cross, the points of which merge into the second enclosing wall. The complexity of the construction is compounded in the first enclosure, where towers bearing four faces stand closely packed, at each angle of the cross and on the small sanctuaries.

Whichever route you take into the first enclosure, you'll be presented with a veritable forest of massive, four-faced towers, each face wearing an enigmatic expression with just a glimmer of a smile. Unusually in Khmer architecture, the low platform of the central sanctuary is more or less circular, with eight linked **meditation chambers** spaced around it.

Baphuon

The eleventh-century **Baphuon**, the state-temple of Udayadityavarman II, continues to undergo restoration and is closed to the public. Restoration began in 1959, was abandoned in 1971 because of war, and didn't restart until 1995; since then over $8m has been spent, although scarcely any progress seems to have been made since our last edition. It's worth at least taking in the approach from the east, via an impressive sandstone causeway (restored) 200m long and raised on three sets of stone posts, although the remains of the soaring temple-mountain bear little resemblance to the "tower of bronze" described by Chou Ta-Kuan. A cruciform gopura, topped by a lotus-petal motif, contains engaging square carvings depicting the animals of Chinese astrology. A path around the outside leads to a small display detailing the restoration work in progress.

Once comprising five tiers, the pyramid had galleries running round the full circumference on its first, second and third levels. The full length of the west side of the fourth level is taken up with a gigantic **reclining Buddha**, though in some lights it's hard to make out.

Phimeanakas

Suryavarman I constructed his small state-temple, **Phimeanakas**, within the grounds of his royal palace; it was the first palace to be built within fortifying walls. Subsequently used for many purposes, it was absorbed into Angkor Thom around two hundred years later. Phimeanakas is usually reached by a short northward trek from the Baphuon through the jungle.

This three-tier laterite temple is relatively simple, rectangular in shape, with damaged elephants at the corners of each level and lions flanking the stairs. The temple is designed to be approached from the east; the stairs up to the top are steep and narrow and don't allow you to step off onto the first two levels. Once at the top, you can walk around the surrounding gallery, at whose centre a single cross-shaped sanctuary tower is raised on a platform. Chou Ta-Kuan described it as a "tower of gold" and recorded that the sanctuary was said to be home to a **spirit** that took the form of a serpent by day and a beautiful lady after dark. The king was meant to visit her every night before seeing his wife or else disaster would follow. To the north of the temple are two paved bathing ponds, the smaller for women and the larger for men.

Terrace of the Elephants

East of Phimeanakas, the **Terrace of the Elephants** is named from the fabulous bas-relief frieze of near-life-sized elephants stretching some 300m. The elephants and their mahouts are shown in profile, mostly hunting, though some are depicted fighting with tigers. Having scrutinized the elephants, it's worth going up onto the terrace behind to get a view over the grounds and, while you're there, to check out the parade of waddling **geese** carved into a low wall atop the terrace at the northern end.

The palace of Jayavarman VII would have stood on the terrace, the edge of its grounds marked by a laterite wall, of which only a ruined gopura remains. The southern steps down from the terrace to the parade ground continue the theme of the frieze, decorated with three-headed elephants, their trunks delicately entwined around lotus buds; in a separate frieze around the terrace, **garudas** stand with wings outstretched as though they alone are supporting the walkway.

Recently the route through the terraces has been officiously signed with arrows, but there's no one to stop you going a different way if you want to.

Terrace of the Leper King

Adjoining the Terrace of the Elephants, the **Terrace of the Leper King** is believed by scholars to have been the site of royal cremations; appropriately, the headless statue on the terrace is that of Yama, god of the underworld, although the vandalized statue is in fact a reproduction. For many years, the statue was assumed to depict the Leper King, Jayavarman VII himself, who several legends say contracted the disease – although there is nothing to verify this.

The two walls here – one behind the other with a narrow gap between them – have been fully restored and boast elaborately bejewelled gods, goddesses and multi-headed nagas, up to seven tiers high. The inner wall is the original – it's assumed that the outer wall was built to allow the terrace above to be extended.

Tep Pranam and Preah Palilay

Tep Pranam, 100m north of the Terrace of the Leper King, dates from the ninth-century reign of Yasovarman I, but was added to over several centuries. Today, it's only worth visiting to see the six-metre-high seated Buddha, dating perhaps from the sixteenth century and reconstructed from the pieces found at the site. At **Preah Palilay**, set in a quiet wooded patch west of Tep Pranam, only the central sandstone sanctuary – dating from the first half of the twelfth century – remains in reasonable condition. It too has a large seated Buddha, of modern provenance.

Prasat Suor Prat and the Kleangs

Opposite the royal terraces, the twelve two-storey laterite-and-sandstone towers, each with doors on two sides and windows on three, are shrines known collectively as **Prasat Suor Prat**, "Towers of the Tightrope Walkers"; though their original purpose isn't known, it wasn't for supporting a tightrope. According to one legend they were places for resolving disputes – the parties and their families had to sit facing each other until one or other party became ill and so was deemed liable to pay reparations. They have recently been restored by Japanese conservators.

Behind Prasat Suor Prat are the **Kleangs** which comprise two enormous warehouse-like buildings, with 1.5m-thick walls, and open at both ends. The North Kleang is the older of the two and was erected towards the end of the tenth century, possibly by Jayavarman V or Jayaviravarman. The unfinished South Kleang is thought to have been constructed by Suryavarman I to balance the view from the royal palace.

You can leave Angkor Thom by taking the road between the Kleangs, which leads east to the **Victory Gate** and the Petit Circuit, or return to the Terrace of the Leper King and head north to the temples on the Grand Circuit.

Thomannon and Chau Say Tevoda

From the Victory Gate, it's only 500m to the tiny temples of **Thomannon** and **Chau Say Tevoda**, nestled in the jungle either side of the road, and another 200m further to a bridge, **Spean Thma**, built using carved sandstone from nearby temples. Once spanning the Siem Reap River, the bridge is now rather stranded, the river having shifted its course. If you step off the road you'll be able to spot the mismatched carvings visible on some of the stones, which were probably recycled from elsewhere when the bridge was rebuilt in the sixteenth century.

Thomannon

Consecrated to Vishnu, **Thomannon** was built by Suryavarman II in the early twelfth century, towards the end of his reign. Originally surrounded by a high laterite wall and moat, and approached from the east, the temple is nowadays approached from the road to the south, and you'll need to traverse the dry moat and clamber over a collapsed wall en route.

The sanctuary and gopuras were restored in 1935 and are in a good state. There are some decent **carvings** too. Vishnu is shown holding a foe by the hair on the north pediment of the elaborate eastern gopura, and elegant female divinities and fine leaf designs decorate the central sanctuary, reached via a reception hall to the east. The attractive western gopura is smaller than its eastern counterpart, with some tiny human figures decorating the door columns and a depiction of Vishnu on Garuda fighting demons above the door.

Chau Say Tevoda

The sister temple to Thomannon, **Chau Say Tevoda** also dates from the reign of Suryavarman II. More elaborate than its sibling across the road, but badly eroded, the temple was recently restored by Chinese conservators. The site was surrounded by a laterite wall – now mostly disappeared – with gopuras to the four directions, and designed to be approached from the east across a raised causeway. Much of the site is cordoned off, but it's worth looking at the octagonal columns of the raised causeway, and there are some stylish floral decorations on the long hall which connects the eastern gopura and the central sanctuary.

Ta Keo

At the western end of the East Baray reservoir, **Ta Keo**, the imposing state-temple of Jayavarman V, was begun around 975 but never finished; legend has it that construction was abandoned after the temple was struck by lightning, an unlucky omen. Entirely constructed of sandstone, Ta Keo is practically undecorated; some sources say that the particular sandstone used is exceptionally hard and too difficult to carve, although fine carving around the base of the pyramid seems to contradict that. Particularly stark in appearance, it is best visited in the early morning when the light is less harsh.

Almost the whole eastern side of the outer enclosure is taken up with two long halls to the north and south, their windows looking inward. In an innovative departure from earlier convention, a **gallery** runs the full perimeter of the inner enclosure, though oddly enough it has no entrance and thus seems to have been constructed for appearances only. The gallery's windows are decorated with balusters, but you'll only be able to look through those on the interior – those on the outside are blocked by a stone wall behind, though they're remarkably convincing from a distance.

From here, you can climb one of the steep stairways up the pyramid, over 21m from the ground. The five sanctuary towers are arranged in the usual quincunx pattern and are dedicated to Shiva. To the east, the view from the top is of rice fields and scrub, the East Baray now being dry.

Ta Prohm

Thanks to the decision to leave the jungle in place, **Ta Prohm** has become one of the most iconic, evocative and photographed of all the ruins. Enormous kapok trees grow from its terraces and walls, their massive roots clinging to the walls, framing doorways and prising apart giant stones. None of the 39 towers is intact and the partly collapsed, maze-like state of the temple makes it difficult to plan a route or work out its layout, which is in fact on a single level, with three closely spaced galleried enclosures in the central area. It doesn't matter if you get a bit disoriented, though, since part of the charm of a visit here is in leaving the well-trodden paths to clamber over collapsed masonry and duck through caved-in galleries. The temple attracts plenty of visitors, but it's usually quiet in the early morning, as mist rises off the algae-encrusted stones, or in the late afternoon, as the shadows lengthen.

Constructed by Jayavarman VII around 1186, Ta Prohm was a **Buddhist monastery** dedicated to Prajnaparamita, and would once have housed a statue of this deity in the image of the king's mother (inscriptions say that a further 260 holy images were installed in surrounding chambers and niches). As a working monastery it accommodated twelve thousand people, who lived and worked within its grounds, while a further eighty thousand were employed locally to service and maintain the complex. Additionally, the monastery supplied provisions and medicines to the 102 hospitals that Jayavarman instituted around the kingdom.

The site

The majority of visitors arrive **from Ta Keo** while on the Petit Circuit (see p.185), approaching from the west, but if you use the track off the road northwest of Banteay Kdei, you can enter from the east as was originally intended. From Ta Keo, the path meanders off the road and under towering trees for around 300m until it reaches a collapsed causeway which leads across the moat to the ruined western gopura, topped by the four massive faces of a Bodhisattva. Once through the gopura, you reach the three central enclosures, which take the form of **galleries**, by a paved causeway littered with broken statues and the remains of a naga balustrade. Moving quickly through the site, at the third enclosing wall, you can pause briefly to study the reasonably well-preserved gopura and roof of its colonnaded gallery.

Some of the most photographed **trees** in the world lie further in, scattered inside the second and first enclosures, particularly to the north and east. Few people can resist posing against the tree which crawls over the north side of the second enclosure's gallery – though you can no longer clamber on to it. It's easy to get so caught up in investigating the galleries and searching out new views of the trees that you actually miss seeing the central sanctuary, with collapsed towers at the corners. Remarkably, the carvings on the buildings are well preserved, almost as if nature has compensated for the overall destruction by preserving the details, which are well worth studying. The interior of the sanctuary is bare, but small holes in the walls indicate that it was once clad in wood or metal panels.

Banteay Kdei

Banteay Kdei (Citadel of the Cells), believed to have been constructed originally by Rajendravarman in the mid-tenth century, could be omitted in favour of the broadly similar Ta Prohm if you're short on time. Having been turned into a monastery by Jayavarman VII, the site remained in fairly continual use as one until the 1960s, and so has been relatively unravaged by nature. That said, the complex has seen some pretty major masonry collapses, which experts believe is due to a combination of the use of low-quality stone and poor building techniques.

You enter Banteay Kdei from the east, opposite Srah Srang, through a cruciform gopura topped with Lokesvara faces. The site was once linked to Srah Srang by a pavement lined with rest houses for pilgrims, the remains of whose paving stones can be seen by the pool. A 300-metre stroll through the forest leads to the remains of a laterite causeway across the moat, by which you reach the **Hall of the Dancing Girls**, named after its charming reliefs of apsaras on the columns.

Built of sandstone throughout, the central complex lacks a pyramid, as this was never a state-temple. The walls are intricately carved with elaborate leaf motifs, and niches below still contain delightful statues of female divinities; the Buddha images in the niches at the upper level were less fortunate, and have mostly been scratched out. The two galleries around the main sanctuary tower, linked to each other by corridors, are in fact the first and second enclosing walls.

Srah Srang and Prasat Kravan

East of Banteay Kdei is the royal bathing pool, **Srah Srang**; it was probably the work of Kavindramantha, an army general-cum-architect, who was also responsible for the building of the temples of East Mebon and Pre Rup. Excavated for Rajendravarman I, the pool once had simple earth embankments, and rules had to be issued to stop people allowing elephants to clamber over them to be bathed in the waters. Two hundred years later, Jayavarman VII had the banks lined with sandstone and built a regal terrace offering views over the water. The remains of a paved causeway edged with naga balustrades, which once linked the pools with

Banteay Kdei to the west, can also be seen here. Seeing the sun rise over its waters from the terrace is a special moment.

South of Banteay Kdei is the often ignored **Prasat Kravan**, the Cardamom Sanctuary, comprising a row of five brick-and-sandstone towers sitting on a low platform in a field. The structure has a delightful simplicity and a handful of remarkable reliefs, and remains in good condition thanks to restoration which largely made use of the original bricks. The sanctuary is known to have been consecrated around 921, during the reign of Harshavarman I.

The central tower, dedicated to Vishnu, is decorated with male guardians in niches on its exterior, but the main interest is in the brick reliefs of Vishnu inside. Here the god is depicted in several different guises: one shows him mounted on Garuda; another shows his dwarf incarnation – taking three steps to span the universe. A rather worn rendering of Vishnu with eight arms was probably once covered in stucco and painted. The northernmost tower is dedicated to Lakshmi, wife of Vishnu and goddess of good fortune; inside you'll find a skilfully carved relief of her, bare-breasted and wearing a pleated *sampot*, flanked by two kneeling worshippers and surrounded by swags of leaves and dangling pendant motifs.

Pre Rup

Back at Srah Srang, you can join the Grand Circuit by following the road east through paddy fields and scrub forest until you see the towers of **Pre Rup**, its name literally meaning "turning the body", a reference to a cremation ritual. Consecrated to Shiva around 962, this state-temple of Rajendravarman (son of Jayavarman IV – who built Koh Ker) was built primarily of laterite and brick, giving it a warmth lacking in many of the sandstone monuments.

An archetypal temple-mountain, Pre Rup is seen in its full majesty from the west, when it stands out against the rice fields. The ruined eastern gopura gives access to the second enclosure, its eastern side mostly taken up with two groups of **tall brick towers** – the pair to the north have space for a third tower which was never built. Long halls, now mostly ruined, line the first enclosure, giving it the appearance of having had a gallery, though in fact Pre Rup was the last temple to be built without one. Right in front of you as you enter this enclosure is a small stone cistern; long assumed to be associated with cremations, now it's agreed it was most probably the pedestal for a statue (of Nandin, the sacred bull associated with Shiva). The three levels of holes you'll spot in the brick libraries which flank the pathway leading to the enclosure were in fact for ventilation. An unusual feature in the northeast corner of the enclosure is a small, square, laterite building – open on all sides – which once housed a stele.

Stairways guarded by lions lead up all four sides of the **pyramid**, around whose lowest level stand twelve symmetrically placed small shrines. Two extra sets of stairs on the eastern side lead up to the top from the middle level, but these are impossible to get to as they're positioned right behind the small sanctuaries. **Female divinities** are featured in the carved reliefs on the western sanctuary towers, which once housed statues of Lakshmi and Uma, and include a female consort of Brahma on the southwest tower (here you'll spot remnants of the gritty, white, lime stucco that once coated the towers); **male carvings** adorn the central and eastern towers, once home to statues of Vishnu and Shiva. From the summit, you'll get a fine view across the forest canopy to the towers of Angkor Wat on the western horizon. The sole record of Jayavarman VI being at Angkor is an inscription on the south side of the southwest tower here.

Preah Khan

Preah Khan was built by Jayavarman VII on the site of an earlier palace, and came here to live here while he was restoring Angkor Thom after it was sacked by the Cham in 1177. The **sacred sword**, as the temple's name translates, is said to have been a weapon ceremonially passed by Jayavarman II to his heir, and Cambodians still believe that whoever possesses this sword has the right to the country's throne – many believe a replica of the sword is kept under lock and key at the Royal Palace in Phnom Penh.

The site functioned as both a **monastery** and a **university** for a considerable time; as the latter, it employed over a thousand teachers and 97,840 ancillary staff – inscriptions found here reveal that a daily delivery of ten tonnes of rice was made, enough to feed ten to fifteen thousand people. However, in 1191 Preah Khan was consecrated as an inter denominational temple, catering to worshippers of Buddha, Shiva and Vishnu, plus a further 282 gods, some made in the image of local dignitaries and national heroes; though the main deity was Lokesvara, made in the image of the king's father, and placed in the central – Buddhist – sanctuary.

Today, despite the temple's semi-collapsed state, the algae- and lichen-coated sandstone, surrounded by majestic jungle, lends it an almost enchanted appearance. Some experts attribute the ruinous state to faulty construction – the central area, closely packed with sanctuaries and passages, was extended on numerous occasions. Restoration is ongoing, by the World Monuments Fund, and the main passages are largely cleared of rubble, but some side passages and courtyards are cordoned off; one way to explore the jumble of ruins is to walk right through the centre at first, then dive off in different directions on the way back.

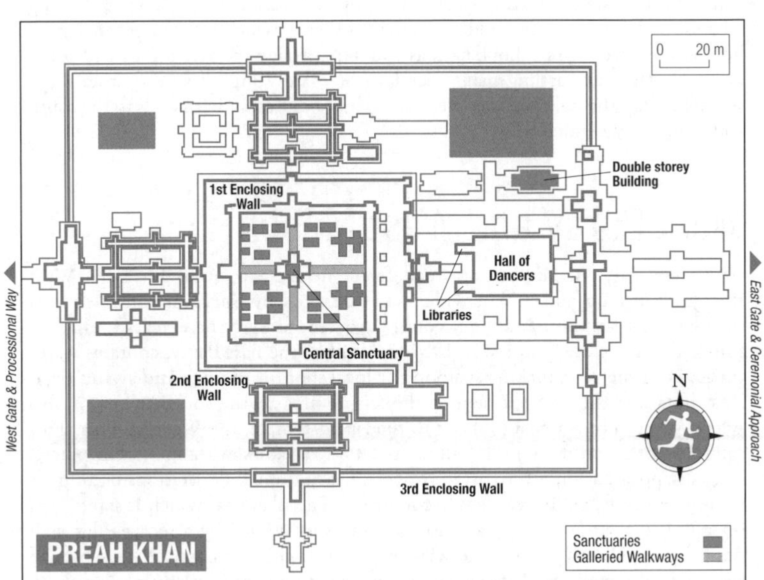

The site

Surrounded by four enclosing walls and a moat, with gopuras and causeways in each cardinal direction, Preah Khan is normally approached from the road to the west, along the Grand Circuit just north of Angkor Thom; but it can equally be approached from the east: ideally walk through (in either direction), arranging for your transport to meet you at the other side – we describe it west to east. Extending out here is the outermost enclosing wall, made of laterite and decorated with massive garudas spaced at fifty-metre intervals. From the road, it's a 500-metre stroll to the temple down the processional approach, lined with ceremonial lanterns; niches here once contained Buddha images, which were crudely cut out when the state religion reverted to Hinduism.

Entering the tranquil **third enclosure** you'll see a series of temple buildings which have been encroached upon by towering **kapok** trees. Even more appealing are the gorgeous **carvings** that grace the walls of the main temple buildings within the **first enclosure**, while floral motifs and bands of carved ornamentation enliven the pillars. Also dotted around here are more than twenty tiny sanctuaries which once contained the temple's holy images (Shiva or Vishnu) – more would have been housed in the alcoves of the surrounding gallery. To the south lie the sanctuaries of previous kings – when the temple was consecrated, the deity of Yasovarman II was given the central place, but it was later moved to make way for the demons of Jayavarman VII.

There should be no problems spotting the **central sanctuary**, which contains a dome-shaped **stupa**, added in the sixteenth century. More tricky to find in a collapsed section to the north are two sublime carvings of the sisters **Indradevi** and **Jayadevi**, who were both wives of Jayavarman – you'll need to ask your guide or the temple guards how to find them.

Further on, the eastern side of the second enclosure contains a number of structures, most notably a terrace, surrounded by columns and carved with dancing apsaras; and a two-storey building to the northeast, which it's thought may have housed the sacred sword. Look back as you step through the east gopura and you'll be confronted by startling giant garudas (there are 72 in all spaced around the walls) holding the tail of a naga. Beyond is a naga causeway with gods to the south and asuras to the north.

West Baray and West Mebon

Accessible only via the airport road from Siem Reap, Angkor's huge **West Baray**, 8km long and 2.2km wide, was excavated by Suryavarman I; experts calculate that six thousand men would have needed over three years to dig out this reservoir. It was restored in 1957 and, unlike the East Baray, contains water throughout the year, making it a popular local spot for **picnics and swimming**. Rest huts line the embankment at the leisure area to the south, which is also where you can hire a boat ($5) out to the island-temple, the **West Mebon**. This mid-eleventh-century temple, attributed to Udayadityavarman II, has practically disappeared; only the eastern towers, bearing small decorations of animals in square motifs, are in reasonable condition. The island on which it stands was once linked to the shore by a causeway, and surrounded by a rectangular wall with three pavilions per side and windows overlooking the baray. A huge bronze sculpture of a reclining **Vishnu** was recovered from here (it used to be on show in the National Museum in Phnom Penh), and would have been the main image in the central sanctuary.

Roluos Group

Off National Route 6, 12km east of Siem Reap, the group of temples now referred to as **Roluos** – after the nearby village of that name – is spread out over the former site of the royal city of **Hariharalaya**, and encompasses some of the earliest monuments of the Angkor period. Among those most easily visited are three brick-and-sandstone temples built by Indravarman I and his son, Yasovarman I, in the late ninth century, all featuring finely decorated columns and lintels. These are the **Bakong**, the first state-temple of the Angkor period; **Lolei**, which has particularly fine Sanskrit inscriptions; and **Preah Ko**, which preserves some elegant carvings despite its being one of the oldest of Angkor's temples.

Preah Ko

Preah Ko was built by Indravarman I in 879 to honour the spirits of his ancestors, as well as one of his predecessors, Jayavarman II. Nearly square in plan, the temple is entered from the east through the second enclosing wall (the third and outermost wall has pretty much disappeared) via a ruined laterite gopura with sandstone columns and over a crumbling terrace. Within the second enclosure, the most interesting building is the square brick structure with holes in the walls, which may have been a library or crematorium; look out for the **frieze of ascetics** seated in niches above the holes.

At the centre of the temple, on a low platform, stand two groups of brick-and-sandstone sanctuary **towers**. Sacred bulls – sadly now vandalized – guard each of the front three towers, which were dedicated to the king's paternal ancestors and bear carvings of male guardians; correspondingly, the three smaller rear towers, slightly offset on the platform, were dedicated to the maternal ancestors and have female guardians. Among the false doors, the west one of the centre rear tower is an oddity, being of plain brick, while all the others are of beautifully carved sandstone. While you're here, check out the leaf, floral and geometrical designs of the carvings on the octagonal door columns, which rank among the finest in Khmer art. The lintels are also splendidly decorated with garlands and several representations of Kala, a Hindu god of death. Remarkably, patches of stucco, which would have covered the whole temple, can still be seen.

Bakong

The **Bakong** is regarded as the first of the state-temples of the Angkor period, having been constructed by Indravarman I and consecrated to Shiva in 881. The central sanctuary is a sympathetic addition built some 250 years later, and remains in particularly good condition, having been restored in 1940 from original materials.

The temple has four enclosures but only three enclosing walls – the outermost enclosure, where you'll find the remains of 22 brick towers amid jungle and rice fields, is contained within a moat. Close to the parking area and **refreshment stalls** are the remains of a causeway and naga balustrade, all that's left within the third enclosure.

There's nothing of significance within the second enclosure, so head on to the ruined buildings of the **first enclosure**, where you'll find some sizeable square brick towers, the survivors of a set of eight. Their sandstone false doors display some fine carvings; on the northeast tower one door even has false carved handles. Also here are two square buildings with ventilation holes in their walls, probably crematoria.

The **pyramid** at the centre of the enclosure has five tiers, topped by a single sanctuary tower. Spaced out around the fourth tier are twelve small sandstone sanctuary towers, now empty, though they would once have housed linga.

Lolei

Now within the grounds of a modern pagoda, **Lolei** originally stood on an artificial island in the centre of the **Indratataka Baray**, though the reservoir is now drained and the temple looks out over paddy fields. The temple was dedicated to the parents and maternal grandparents of Yasovarman I and consecrated to Shiva, and originally consisted of four brick towers, though one has now collapsed and the others are crumbling. Lolei is worth a visit even so to see the well-preserved Sanskrit inscriptions in the doorways of the rear towers, detailing the work rotas of temple servants.

Banteay Samre

Remote from the popular sites, **Banteay Samre** lies east of **Phum Pradak**, a village 12km northeast of Siem Reap. No inscriptions have been found to date the temple, which was named after the Samres, a tribe who lived in the vicinity of Phnom Kulen. However, its style of architecture places its construction in the middle of the twelfth century, around the same time as Angkor Wat. It was superbly restored by Maurice Glaize in the 1940s.

Banteay Samre is unique among the Angkor temples in having **two moats** within the complex itself. The temple, enclosed by a high laterite wall with cruciform gopuras to each direction, is approached via a 200-metre-long paved causeway which was originally edged by a naga balustrade. Entering through the east gopura, you arrive in an open gallery whose rows of sandstone columns were once part of a roofed walkway which would have run the full perimeter of the enclosure. The paved sunken area ahead was once the first of the moats, forming the second enclosure. Tales from the *Ramayana* are depicted on various **carvings** here – the siege of Lanka is shown on the gopura pediments, the fight between Rama and Ravana on the east tower, and Rama carried by Hanuman on the north tower.

Crossing the moat, you're immediately within another cruciform gopura, with double vestibules to the north and south, the passages of which connect to a raised walkway that separates the two moats. Rising out of the inner moat like islands are the **central sanctuary**, connected to the walkway via a gopura to the east, and two **libraries**, which would only have been reachable by boat when the moats were filled.

Banteay Srei and Kbal Spean

Even if you're feeling pretty templed-out, you'll probably be captivated by **Banteay Srei**, 35km northeast of Siem Reap. Built of fine-grained rose-pink sandstone, it's the most elaborately decorated of all Angkor's monuments, its walls, false doors, lintels and exotic soaring pediments all richly embellished with floral motifs and *Ramayana* scenes. Comprising just a single level, it's positively diminutive compared with the region's state-temples. A little way further out from Siem Reap, at **Kbal Spean**, you can trek along the river to see fabulous scenes of Hindu gods and sacred linga carved into the river bed.

Banteay Srei (closes 5pm) is easily **reached** from Siem Reap on the new road from National Route 6 or by the old road which heads north from Pradak and passes through countryside and villages before reaching the temple. It's a further 10km to reach Kbal Spean (closes 3pm), and it's best to allow at least an hour and a half for the visit – it's around 45 minutes to climb the hill. **You need a valid Angkor pass to visit both sites; a one-day pass only can be purchased at**

Banteay Srei ($20). For **refreshments** there are restaurants at Pradak and on the new road near Banteay Srei, and food stalls at Banteay Srei and Kbal Spean. A new **visitor and interpretation centre** was opened at Banteay Srei in 2009, and things are now fairly organized with visitors being directed through the site in an attempt to prevent jams – unfortunately it doesn't work very well and it's as well to make sure you have plenty of time to make the best of this wonderful temple.

Banteay Srei

Banteay Srei was built not by a king, but by two local **dignitaries**, Yajnavaraha, who was a trusted guru to the king, and his brother. It was Rajendravarman who granted them the land and permission for a temple to be built, but although the sanctuary was consecrated in 967 to Shiva, it was not actually completed until the reign of Jayavarman V.

The temple **layout** is relatively simple, with three enclosing walls, an inner moat and a row of three sanctuary towers at the very centre. If the eastern gopura by which you enter the temple seems oddly stranded, that's because there was never an enclosing wall here – although the buildings just beyond the gopura are deemed to be in the "fourth" enclosure. The volume of tourists trooping past isn't conducive to lingering here, but it's worth taking a moment to scrutinize the very fine carving above the exterior of the east door, which depicts **Indra** – the sky god, ruling the easterly cardinal direction – squatting on the three-headed elephant Airavata.

From the gopura, a paved **processional way** leads 75m west to the main temple complex. Around the midway point, a pavilion to the north boasts a particularly detailed engraved pediment showing Vishnu in his incarnation as a man-lion. Just before you reach the gopura in the third enclosing wall, you'll find a carved pediment you can admire without craning your neck, as it's lying upright on the ground to the right of the doorway; it shows Sita swooning as she is abducted by Ravana. The gopura itself is one of the most dramatic at the site, with soaring finials and the carved scrolls of fine leaf decorations and floral motifs.

In the rainy season, you'll be treated to marvellous reflections of the temple when the moat within the third enclosure fills. The narrow second enclosure is jammed with six long galleries, each subdivided into rooms which might have been meditation halls.

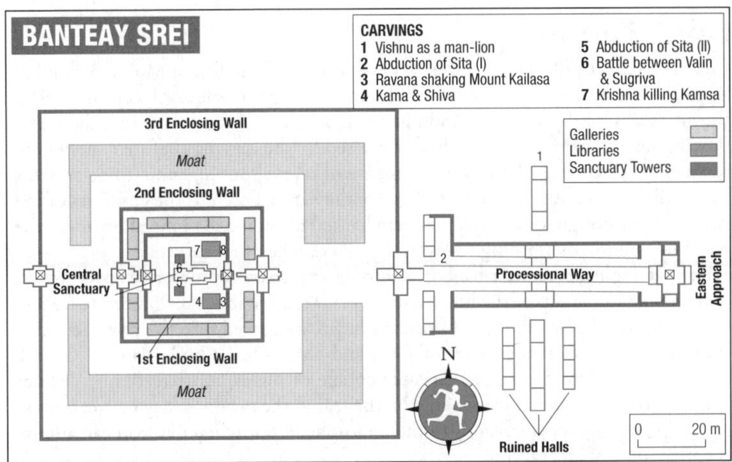

First enclosure

Virtually no surface within the first enclosure remains unadorned, and all seems perfect in every detail, the site having been **restored** in the 1930s. It's impossible to take in the sheer wealth of decoration here at first glance, so it's a good idea to wander around to get a general feel for the layout before returning to study the details methodically. Unfortunately, due to the large number of visitors and the minuscule size of the chambers, you're no longer allowed inside the sanctuary towers, and the platform on which they stand is roped off to protect the carvings.

The carvings on the **sanctuary towers** are almost fussy in their profusion; the niches around the central sanctuary shelter male **guardians**, while those on the other towers house serene female **divinities**, complete with elegant *sampots* and elaborate jewellery. Crouched near the temple steps are more guardians, mythical figures with animal heads and human bodies; not surprisingly, these are reproductions, the originals having been removed, like many of the best sculptures here, during the French colonial period (they remain at the Guimet museum of Asian art in Paris, despite attempts to have them returned to Cambodia). The *Ramayana* scenes carved on the lintels of the central tower are particularly fine, featuring another depiction of Sita being carried off by Ravana, to the west; and the fight between the monkey gods Valin and Sugriva, to the north. The multi-tiered roofs of the towers are decorated with tiny replicas of the temple towers – meant to be homes for the temple gods.

There are more fine carvings on the east pediment of the **south library**, where Ravana is shown shaking Mount Kailasa; Shiva sits on the mountain's summit with his wife Parvati, while the forest animals run away in fear. On the west pediment, Parvati can be seen asking for the aid of Kama, the god of love, after Shiva ignores her offering of a rosary; she finally wins Shiva's attention and his hand in marriage after Kama obligingly shoots him with an arrow. The **north library** is dedicated to Vishnu, and accordingly the carvings focus on him. The close parallel streaks on the east pediment represent rain pouring down on the forest, through which Krishna – Vishnu's human incarnation – and his brother make their way, surrounded by wild animals. Krishna is seen taking revenge on his cruel uncle, King Kamsa, on the west pediment – note how the palace is in uproar as Krishna seizes him by the hair and prepares to kill him.

Kbal Spean

In a mystical area of jungle in the western section of the Kulen Mountains, **Kbal Spean** was used by the Khmer as a hill retreat in the mid-eleventh century, when they carved sacred linga and Hindu gods into the bedrock of the river; the water flowing down the river would thus be blessed by the carvings before coursing on to Angkor. The scenes depicting Vishnu are of marvellous ingenuity, not only for their skilful execution but also for the way they are tailored to the contours of the river bed. Although looters have crudely hacked out some sections of bedrock, the scenes are almost as amazing today as they were when first carved.

The path follows the east bank of the river and has a couple of steep stretches; you'll come to the top of the hill, a natural bridge, after about forty minutes' walk, which is a good place to start. Upstream lingas are carved into the river bed, two reclining Vishnus and a carving of Uma and Shiva on the bull, Nandin. On the way down stop to admire the veritable cobble of lingas, more reclining Vishnus and associated pantheon. Depending on the season the carvings may be wet or dry; water splashing over them adds to the atmosphere, but when dry you can admire the ingenuity of the carvers.

Temple architecture

The ancient Khmer, Southeast Asia's most prodigious builders, left countless examples of their architecture scattered across the region. While their form is rooted in India, these temples and monuments have no Indian parallel. This is largely due to the uniquely Khmer cult known as devaraja, literally "god-king". Founded on the belief that Khmer kings were earthly incarnations of gods, the cult inspired dizzying heights of architectural megalomania as each successive king endeavoured to construct a temple that would eclipse the efforts of all his predecessors.

Angkor Wat from the air ▲

The sun rises behind Angkor Wat ▼

Bas-reliefs at Sambor Prei Kuk ▼

Better by design

While the mathematical equations that dictated the dimensions of Khmer temples are no longer understood, it is known that the ancient Khmer placed great stock in the auspiciousness of **precise measurements**. This can be discerned in the temple layout – most possess a severe symmetry.

A matter of life and death

The majority face **east** to catch the rays of the rising sun, symbolizing life. Angkor Wat, however, faces **west**, the direction of the setting sun – and death.

Scale models of the universe

Many Khmer temples are actually scale models of the **Hindu-Buddhist universe**, with moats and walls symbolizing the oceans and mountain ranges that encircled five-peaked Mount Meru, the home of the gods, portrayed in Khmer architecture by the central, spiked quincunx formation.

Khmer comic strips

Equally impressive are the "story-telling bas-reliefs" used to striking effect by the ancient Khmer. Illustrating historical events, mythology (such as the *Ramayana* and *Mahabharata*) and the exploits of kings, the **bas-reliefs** in sandstone cover over a thousand square metres of gallery walls in Angkor Wat alone. Depending on how they were executed, the bas-reliefs could be "read" from panel to panel like pages from a giant comic book. There was no truck with perspective: the importance of an image was illustrated by its size in relation to the images around it. The bas-reliefs at Angkor Wat depict grand images of the Hindu god Vishnu, his vehicle Garuda, and Vishnu's incarnations as Krishna, Rama and Kurma – evidence that Suryavarman II, the devaraja who had Angkor Wat commissioned, believed that he himself was an incarnation of Vishnu.

Bring on the dancing girls

To many modern visitors, the most easily admired images on Angkorian temples are the **apsaras**, celestial nymphs who seem to emerge, dancing, from the smooth sandstone walls. Angkor Wat has by far the most sensitively rendered collection of apsaras in the country, and it is readily apparent that the artisans who sculpted them spent much time ensuring that no two were alike – recent thinking is that they may even have been modelled on palace servants.

▲ Aspara at Angkor Wat

▼ Colossal stone faces at the Bayon

Inspiring Hollywood

Suryavarman II built Angkor Wat, ancient Cambodia's greatest architectural masterpiece, the silhouette of which graces the national flag. Yet it was ancient Cambodia's most prolific builder, Jayavarman VII, who produced its most enduring artistic motif: the four colossal stone faces that gaze with blissful detachment from the towers of the Bayon and the gates of Angkor Thom. The image of stone visages smiling enigmatically as the roots of mammoth banyan trees threaten to topple them into jumbled heaps has been used extensively by modern artists, including several **Hollywood film-makers**, to symbolize ancient civilizations lost to the ravages of time.

Sculpture detail at Banteay Srei ▲

Celestial dancer, with hands depicting a leaf ▼

Tamarind and termite mounds

The building materials used by the ancient Khmer changed over time. Early Angkor-period temples were constructed of **brick**. The most impressive brick temple at Angkor is Prasat Kravan, the interior of which has bas-reliefs carved right into the brick. A type of **stucco** made from such esoteric ingredients as pounded tamarind and the soft earth of termite mounds was used as a medium to sculpt ornamentation for the brick structures. **Laterite**, a porous stone that resembles lava rock, was used for foundations and walls. It was the use of **sandstone**, however, that set Khmer temples apart from those of the ancient Cham, Thai and Burmese, all of whom worked almost exclusively in brick and stucco. Soft, easily carveable sandstone allowed the talent of Khmer sculptors to reach its zenith.

An earthly paradise

While the architecture of the ancient Khmer inspires even in its ruined state, it is important to remember that only the parts of temples built of stone, brick and stucco have survived. What we do not see are the ornately carved pavilions of **golden teak** that housed those who inhabited the temples in their hey day: troupes of court dancers, minstrels, high priests and the god-kings themselves. Gone, too, are the **sheets of gilded copper** that covered unadorned stone walls and towers; the parasols, banners and tapestries of **delicate silk** that gave colour to dimly lit galleries and antechambers; and the scent of the finely woven **mats of aromatic grasses** that covered rough stone causeways.

The Tonle Sap lake

Temples aside, Siem Reap has another unique attraction in the fascinating **Tonle Sap**, the massive freshwater lake that dominates the map of Cambodia. The lake is at once a reservoir, flood-relief system, communications route, home and larder to the people who live on and around it; even Cambodians who live nowhere near depend on it as a rich food source.

At its lowest, in May, just before the rains, the lake covers an area of around 2500 square kilometres. Himalayan **meltwater** flows down the Mekong just as the monsoon rains arrive, causing the level of the river to rise so quickly that at Phnom Penh the pressure is sufficient to reverse the flow of the Tonle Sap River, which would normally drain the lake. As a result of this inflow, each year the lake inundates an area of over **ten thousand square kilometres**, making it the largest freshwater lake in Southeast Asia. The flow of water reverts to its usual direction in late October or early November, the receding waters leaving behind fertile mud for the planting of rice, and nutrients for the fry which have spawned amid the flooded trees. February sees a bumper fish catch, much of it going to satisfy the insatiable Cambodian appetite for *prohok*.

Fishing is big business on the Tonle Sap, and the government has awarded large concessions to wealthy businessmen at the expense of local fishermen, who have to either practise their trade illegally or rent a share from a concessionaire. The majority of these fishermen are part of the lake's huge itinerant population, mostly stateless ethnic Vietnamese, living in mobile **floating villages** on the lakeshore. The houses – which are utterly basic, with (unscreened) holes in the floor as toilets – are built on bamboo rafts and lashed together to keep them from drifting apart. Vietnamese villagers having been here for decades, they have not assimilated into Khmer society and are generally loathed by the Khmer – though they are not averse to exploiting their potential as tourist attractions.

The lake was designated a UNESCO Biosphere Reserve in 1997 – a status which reconciles sustainable use with conservation. One core area of the reserve, **Prek Toal**, is a sanctuary for a wide range of water birds, including three endangered species – spot-billed pelicans, greater adjutant storks, and white-winged ducks. Prek Toal lies on the northwest edge of the lake in the dry season and is easily reached from Siem Reap, though you'll have to take an organized tour (see p.179).

This lake may not always be here though; its fragile eco system is under threat, as upstream on the Mekong the Chinese continue with the controversial building of dams.

Phnom Krom

If you're heading to the lake, it's worth heading up the 137-metre hill, **Phnom Krom**, to the grounds of a modern pagoda on the summit, where there's a ruined tenth-century **temple** built by Yasovarman I. There are commanding **views** over the Tonle Sap from the top, particularly scenic at sunset. The three crumbling sandstone sanctuary towers, dedicated to Vishnu (north), Shiva (centre) and Brahma (south), stand in a row on a low platform; a few carvings can still be made out, with an apsara evident on the north face of the north tower and a hamsa (sacred bird) on the south tower. To reach the site, take the steep stairway that leads up from behind the petrol station in the village at the foot of the hill.

Floating villages near Siem Riep

A visit to the **floating villages** near Siem Reap is not the authentic ethnic experience that guides in town would have you believe; it is in fact a very organized and extremely voyeuristic affair, with all Siem Reap tour agents offering some sort of trip to the villages and dozens of boats ferrying visitors along the river. Just beyond Phnom Krom, at Chong Khneas, a new (privately run) toll station ($2) has set up business and you can't even get to the GECKO exhibition centre (Greater Environment Chong Khneas Office; daily 8.30am–5pm), an NGO whose main role is to improve the environmental awareness of the local fishing population, without paying the toll. Boats seating about a dozen people run from the toll booth every 15 to 30 minutes with a fixed price of $20 per person for a 90 minute trip. Naturally enough, villages visited by the boats have capitalized on the tourism – there's even a café now where many of the boats put in – so if you want to get out to the more genuine villages, you need to go further afield; consider going down to Kompong Phluk (about 40km from Siem Reap, south of Roluos Group) or to Kompong Khleang (about 80km southeast). Indeed, if you are travelling on through Cambodia, it's worth visiting the floating villages that are further off the beaten track (see p.135 & p.137). In the rainy season, when the lake floods up to the foot of Phnom Krom, you can get a feel of the floating villages just by walking along the causeway; here the houses are either on enormously tall stilts or are lashed to pontoons that rise with the flood waters.

Phnom Kulen

It was at **Phnom Kulen**, then known as Mahendrapura, that Jayavarman II had himself consecrated supreme ruler in 802 (a date that is regarded as marking the start of the Angkorian period), thereby instigating the cult of the devaraja (see p.328). Although ancient temples are scattered here and elsewhere in the Kulen Mountains, none of these can be visited due to the lack of roads and the danger of land mines. Instead, the main reason to visit Phnom Kulen, 50km north of Siem Reap, is to gawp at the massive **reclining Buddha** carved out of a huge rock in the sixteenth century, though once you're here you may find yourself more taken with the piety of the Buddhist devotees who come to worship at a chain of shrines.

You don't need an Angkor entry pass to visit Phnom Kulen, but foreign visitors are charged a hefty $20 to visit the site; this, coupled with the cost of hiring a vehicle ($20–50, depending what kind of vehicle and who you hire it from), will keep all but the most dedicated explorers from visiting.

The area was heavily mined by the Khmer Rouge and although HALO are working there now, it has yet to be fully cleared, so you shouldn't wander off to locations other than those described below unless you have an experienced local guide.

The hill

The entrance fee is paid at the foot of the hill, from where the road climbs steadily through forest to a sandstone plateau. On the left a track leads to a parking area from where you can walk down to the river where you may be able to make out some of the **linga** for which the river is famed, but as they're only 25cm square, they're hard to spot on the river bed if the waters are high or turbid. Near the bridge, another 500m along the road, more linga are carved in the river bed, but you'll need a guide to find the spot for you. It's a further 1km or so to the top of the hill – packed with stalls selling food, refreshments and Khmer medicine. A short climb brings you to a busy pagoda, Preah Ang Thom, which features a much-revered and rather impressive **reclining Buddha**, carved into a massive boulder. You'll need to remove your shoes at the bottom of the steps, and once at the top you'll have to squeeze in between Cambodians making offerings and having their photographs taken; from the rock there are good views over the surrounding Kulen Mountains. Around the base of the rock, a simple but impressive frieze of Buddha heads has been carved.

If you've come without a guide, the local children will take you to see the forest **shrines** behind the pagoda – in the hope that you'll come to buy food and refreshments from them before you leave. Alternatively, follow the locals, who come armed with huge bundles of incense to ensure they have enough to make offerings at all the shrines on the circuit. Nearly every boulder has a legend attached to it – one with holes that look like claw marks is said to be where Hanuman crash-landed. At the end of the track, Cambodians come to wash their faces in water from a **holy spring** which gushes from a boulder, believing this will give energy, good health and luck; old bottles are produced and filled to take home.

Beng Mealea

It isn't known exactly when or why the temple of **Beng Mealea**, 60km east of Siem Reap, was built, though experts, making deductions from its stylistic features, have placed its construction in the late eleventh or early twelfth century, possibly by Suryavarman II. The temple, known to have been Hindu, built on a single level and of impressive size, has yet to be restored, and gives a good idea of what the French archeologists found when they first arrived at Angkor. Less than seventy years ago, Glaize advocated combining a trip to Beng Mealea with a hunting party, noting that the area was rich in jungle wildlife, including "tigers, panthers and elephants, herds of oxen and wild buffalo"; though these days all you'll pass are rice paddies and scrub. Recently connected to Siem Reap by a reasonable road (which continues to Koh Ker; see p.225) a visit to both sites can be combined in a day-trip, heading to Koh Ker in the early morning and stopping off at Beng Mealea on the way back. Hiring a car and driver from Siem Reap will cost around $90–100 for the day (taking in both sites). Beng Mealea (entry $5) is still wonderfully unexplored, but although the site itself has been de-mined, you should take care not to stray too far into the undergrowth.

The locals claim that the temple, mostly hidden in scrub, was quite well preserved until the Khmer Rouge looted and destroyed much of it, though Glaize (see p.181) reported it being collapsed in 1944. Just over a kilometre square, with a formidable 45-metre-wide moat, the site was clearly of some consequence, and it has been posited that the temple was built as a precursor to Angkor Wat. All on a single level, the temple once featured three concentric galleries and a central sanctuary tower, though the main attraction of wandering the ruins is to glimpse apsaras peering out of niches amid the jumbled stones.

Anlong Veng

Some 140km north of Siem Reap near the Thai border, the hot and dusty town of **ANLONG VENG** is of interest solely as the former home and death place of Pol Pot. Accommodation is basic, food is bad, and there are no sights apart from the spot where Pol Pot's body was cremated after his death in 1998. Pol Pot didn't stay in the village itself but in a **hideout** up in the Dangkrek Mountains which takes about half an hour to reach by moto. Some say he died from a heart attack, but someone has also claimed to have witnessed him being murdered by his Khmer Rouge comrades; all that's known for certain is that Pol Pot was cremated on a pile of furniture and old tyres close to his house before anyone could verify the details. The sites on which the hut was located and where the hasty cremation took place are signed though there are only a few blackened rocks to see. Extraordinarily, the Khmer Rouge were benevolent to the people they lived among after their fall in 1979 and residents here are loyal to their memory. Bizarrely, Khmers come here in the belief that Pol Pot will reveal winning lottery numbers, heal the sick or provide auspicious luck in some other fashion from the grave.

Back in the village itself, the late Ta Mok, one of the most notorious Khmer Rouge cadres, left behind a house when he died in 2006 (signed "Ta Mok House") – turn left at the traffic circle and then right after a couple of hundred metres. He is well regarded locally for creating fishing ponds and endowing a local school, but better known in the world at large as "The Butcher" for having ordered the abduction of three Western backpackers from the Phnom Penh–Sihanoukville train in 1994. They were held for ransom but eventually killed when negotiations fell through. For years there were efforts to have Ta Mok stand trial for the murders, but like so many Khmer Rouge-era killers he died a natural death while Cambodia procrastinated.

Though it's unlikely that you would choose to stay over, there are plenty of **guesthouses** in town – though many of them double as brothels. *Monorom* (300m west of the traffic circle, ❶) is the newest guesthouse in town with clean, bright rooms and a restaurant. Another safe option is *Two Tears I* (❶), on the main road just south of the market; rooms downstairs are windowless and plain, the better ones are upstairs off a communal balcony. In addition to the market and the **restaurants** at each of the guesthouses, a pleasant place to eat or just have a drink is to the west of the traffic circle: no sign, but look for the heavy wood furniture. At the time of writing a new market was being constructed on the north side of the traffic circle.

Taxis to Anlong Veng (20,000 riel) leave from the NR6 near the transport stop in Siem Reap, or take a bus (GST and Paramount Angkor; 10,000 riel). You can also get to Anlong Veng from Thailand using either the border crossing point Chong Jom to **O'SMACH**, or the closer, Chong Sa Ngam to **Anlong Veng**. The most convenient way to travel between the border and Anlong Veng, or vice versa, is to take a place in a taxi; these run throughout the day in both directions taking around half an hour to make the thirty-kilometre trip (5000 riel). Both Cambodian and Thai visas are available on arrival at the border. In Anlong Veng you can hire a private taxi to go to Preah Vihear, an easy two-hour drive ($30 including waiting time).

Travel details

Buses

Siem Reap to: Anlong Veng (2 daily; 2hr); Battambang (1 daily; 3hr); Kompong Cham (2 daily; 3hr); Kompong Thom (more than 12 daily; 2hr); Phnom Penh (more than 12 daily; 6–8hr); Poipet (6 daily; 3hr); Sisophon (6 daily; 2hr).

Shared taxis and minibuses

Siem Reap to: Anlong Veng (1 daily; 2hr); Kompong Cham (6 daily; 2hr 30min); Kompong Thom (12 daily; 2hr); Phnom Penh (hourly; 5–6hr); Poipet (20 daily; 3hr); Sisophon (20 daily; 2hr).

Boats

Siem Reap to: Battambang (1 daily; 7–8hr); Phnom Penh (1 daily; 5–6hr).

Flights

Siem Reap to: Bangkok (5 daily; 1hr); Phnom Penh (6 daily; 45min).

Central Cambodia

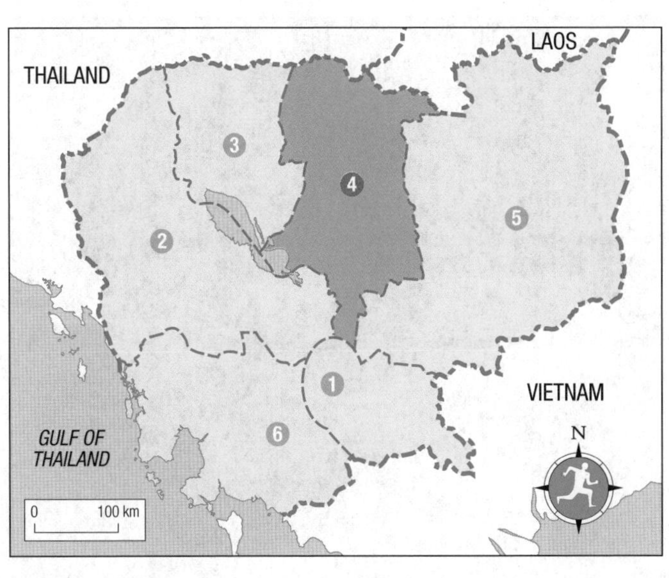

CHAPTER 4

Highlights

* **Phnom Suntuk** This bizarre hilltop pagoda is home to a massive rock-carved reclining Buddha. See p.218

* **Sambor Prei Kuk** Pre-Angkorian temples uniquely decorated with miniature flying palaces, believed to house the sacred spirits who protect the site. See p.221

* **Preah Khan** Once the largest temple in Cambodia, this complex still contains numerous ruined monuments hidden in the undergrowth. See p.223

* **Preah Vihear** Imposing temple poised in a spectacular position on a ridge above the Thai border. See p.226

▲ Reclining Buddha, Phnom Suntuk

4

Central Cambodia

The centre of Cambodia is a forgotten territory. Stretching north from Phnom Penh, through sparsely populated countryside right up to the Thai border, most of the soil is sandy and barren, and there's practically no way for people to eke out even a basic living. Amazingly, communities do get by somehow, farming tiny plots and scant, scattered rice paddies, and foraging in what remains of the forest. The only really dense vegetation in the region is in the **Boeng Peae Wildlife Reserve**, that National Route 64 passes through on its way north.

The region is hardly a popular tourist destination: all that most visitors see of it are the rice paddies that stretch either side of National Route 6, the major trunk road between the capital and Siem Reap, that cuts across the southern part of the area. But for those prepared to venture into obscure backwaters, central Cambodia has a few ancient temple sites worth visiting, although you'll have to brave the area's largely atrocious roads to reach most of them. The starting point is invariably **Kompong Thom**, the only town of any size hereabouts, and thus also your last taste of comfort for a few days if you're planning a trip north. Thankfully, it's no major expedition from here if you want to see either **Phnom Suntuk**, a revered though rather kitsch pagoda, or **Sambor Prei Kuk**, the country's most significant pre-Angkorian site, comprising three groups of well-preserved brick-built temples.

Beyond here, however, travelling gets harder – even reaching the massive ruined temple of **Preah Khan**, only 50km northwest as the crow flies, is a tough trip. You'll need to get right to the border to reach the area's jewel, **Preah Vihear**, perched magnificently high on a cliff in the Dangkrek Mountains. Built in the ninth century and added to by a succession of kings, it boasts superb, soaring pediments unlike anything else you'll see in Cambodia, and is well worth the effort

Disputed territory

As we went to press, fighting broke out between Cambodian and Thai military along the border at **Preah Vihear** temple. The flare-up was apparently caused by the Thais complaining about the Cambodian flag flying near the historic site. Disputes over the territory hereabouts go back a long way. Much to the chagrin of the Thais, Preah Vihear was awarded to Cambodia by an international court in 1962, a slight (as the Thais see it) that was exacerbated in 2008 when UNESCO awarded World Heritage status to the "Cambodian" temple. Currently the British Foreign Office is warning against all travel to the area and visitors are advised to check the situation before venturing to the border near Preah Vihear.

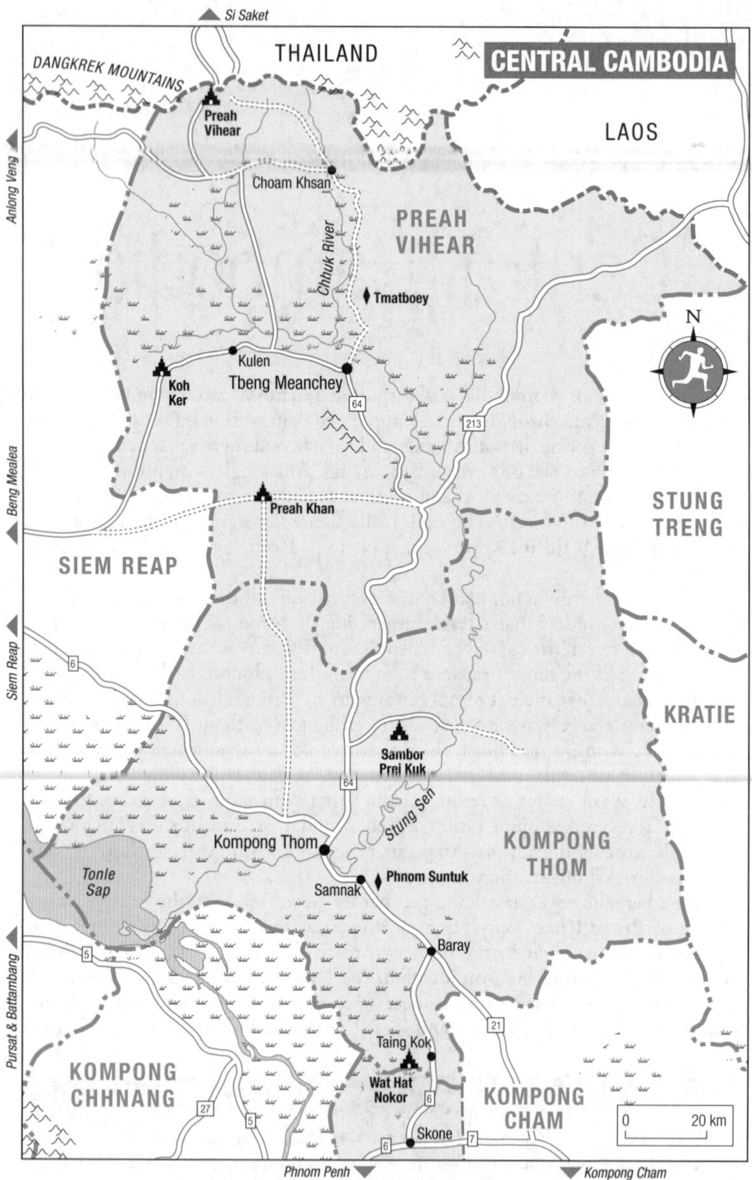

of getting to (though access is easier from Siem Reap). If you're feeling intrepid, consider a side-trip to the remote Angkorian capital of **Koh Ker**, roughly midway between Preah Khan and Preah Vihear.

Given the state of the roads exploring Cambodia's heartland is really only feasible in the **dry season** (Nov–May); when the rains come, every path and track turns to mud slurry, and deep fast-flowing rivers appear as if by magic, cutting off the main tracks and isolating such villages as there are. National Route 6 is the

only sealed road in this part of the country, and to travel north of Kompong Thom requires plenty of patience and a strong constitution, as National Route 64 to **Tbeng Meanchey** takes it out of vehicles and passengers alike. From here, other than the new road north to Preah Vihear, most of north-central Cambodia is inaccessible; travel is along rough forest tracks which are frequently blocked by broken bridges and streams.

Phnom Penh to Kompong Thom

Leaving Phnom Penh on National Route 6 the journey to Kompong Thom is relatively swift and painless. Once you leave the capital's urban sprawl, the scenery becomes quintessentially Cambodian – rice paddies and sugar palms punctuated with occasional diversions, such as blocks of laterite for use in construction for sale along the road.

The busy transit town of **Skone** is where Cambodians come to buy the local delicacy, *ah pieng* – hairy **tarantulas**, 5cm or more across. Hawkers swarm around vehicles, their trays piled high with the eight-legged monsters, which are caught in the jungles of Kompong Thom province by poking a stick in their burrows and hooking them out. Sold dry-roasted for a few hundred riel apiece, they taste a bit like crunchy fried prawns and are best tackled as though eating a crab: pull off the legs and you can suck the flesh which comes away with them, though be wary of the body, as it can be unappetizingly slushy and bitter. The critters also crop up around the country pickled in wine, a tonic especially favoured by pregnant women. Also much sought-after hereabouts, sold in bundles of five or ten for a few thousand riel, are **grolan**, bamboo tubes stuffed with sweet sticky rice cooked with black beans and coconut.

Wat Hat Nokor and Phnom Suntuk

If you want to break up your journey, you could check out two minor attractions off the road between Skone and Kompong Thom: **Wat Hat Nokor**, a small but enchanting eleventh-century temple around 20km north of Skone, and, close to Kompong Thom, **Phnom Suntuk**, a sacred hill with multiple pagodas and rock-face carvings. Travelling between the capital and Kompong Thom on private transport you could, at a pinch, visit both sites en route.

Wat Hat Nokor

Wat Hat Nokor is a small rural pagoda with tranquil, well-tended grounds surrounding a simple, charming laterite-and-sandstone eleventh-century **temple** built by Suryavarman I. The temple was never finished, and it's assumed that either the architect died or war intervened during its construction. A single gopura on the eastern side of the temple gives access to the courtyard enclosing a cruciform sanctuary, **Prasat Kuk Nokor**, which once contained a linga and niches housing statues of Shiva and his wives. The central section of the south wall has collapsed, but you can still see a chamber built into the wall, where the sick came to be cured using holy water blessed by flowing over the linga in the central sanctuary. The library in the southeast corner of the courtyard was formerly used as a prison by the Khmer Rouge. The *achar* has a visitors' book that he'll no doubt get you to sign, and it's polite to leave a donation.

The wat is about 2km west of the village of **TAING KOK**. Public transport will drop you either in the village or at the turning for the pagoda; motos are readily available at the turning for the journey to the temple (8000 riel including waiting time). If you're using public transport on to Kompong Thom, you'll need to flag down a taxi or minibus, best done from Taing Kok's small market.

Phnom Suntuk

Something akin to a Buddhist theme park, the 180m high **Phnom Suntuk** is most easily visited as a half-day trip by moto from Kompong Thom (20,000 riel including waiting time). Conspicuous in the flat countryside, the hill is accessed by a wide road, indicative of how busy it gets on Sundays and public holidays. A steep staircase of 809 steps wends its way up the scrub-covered hill, squeezing past massive boulders, with occasional rest-stops and gaudy shrines where you can pause for breath. Traditional **medicine vendors** display their wares on the steps, mainly tree bark and twigs to be boiled up in water to produce multipurpose tonics and cure-alls.

At the summit, the pagoda is a hotchpotch of garish statues and pavilions, mostly contemporary. Most alluring are the older Buddha images, many carved into the rock face around the hill, although no one can tell you when they were carved. Near the vihara, a large overhanging rock creates a natural shrine with several small Buddha carvings, and there are more small shrines tucked away in crevices behind the rocky hillside. To the west, a narrow stony path leads part of the way down the hill to a collection of rock carvings, including an impressive reclining Buddha. Back at the foot of the hill, you might want to pause to sink a glass of sugar-cane juice or fill up on Khmer fare at the veritable village of **food and drink stalls** here.

Heading back to Kompong Thom on NR6, you can stop off at the little village of Samnak where there are usually some small stone carvings to buy from local craftsmen (though small doesn't necessarily equate with light). Also in the village, is Santuk Silks – a silk enterprise run by Vietnam veteran, Bud Gibbons, where you can see silk worms munching on mulberry, watch spinners and weavers at work, and usually buy a scarf or two from the weavers.

Kompong Thom

KOMPONG THOM, 177km from Phnom Penh (and slightly closer to Siem Reap), straggles along National Route 6 and the Stung Sen River. The town used to be known as *kompong pos thom*, "place of the big snake", apparently because the locals used to take offerings to a large snake that lived in a cave on the river, though this may be yet another Cambodian myth as no one now has a clue where the cave is. Most visitors stop over just long enough to get to the temples at **Sambor Prei Kuk**, 30km northeast; a couple of hours is quite enough to have a look around the town itself.

Jackfruit-wood: drums

There's a rare opportunity to see **traditional drums** being produced at a workshop near Kompong Thom, look out for a small sign on the left 7km south of town on National Route 6. The small-waisted, vase-shaped *skor dae*, about 50cm tall, are carved here by hand from the heart of a jackfruit tree – the yellowish wood is valued for its resonant properties – and embellished with carved decorations; a dried snake skin is stretched across the head. The drums form part of the traditional *pinpeat* ensemble, a gamelan-style orchestra that plays at weddings and classical dance performances. Also made here are *skor sang na*, a kind of cylindrical drum, twice the height of *skor dae*, which are played slung over the shoulder during funeral processions. The welcoming family who own the workshop will encourage you to try your hand at drumming, and might give you an impromptu demonstration even if you don't buy anything.

Kompong Thom is also a possible jumping-off point for the remote **Preah Vihear**, two days' journey to the north, though access is now easier from Siem Reap via Anlong Veng (see p.212). Closer, but even more of an adventure to reach, is the massive Preah Khan – go now before the tour groups do.

The town's main landmarks are the tall *Arunras Hotel*, on the main road just south of the market, and the bridges across the Stung Sen, a concrete one for vehicles alongside an old metal one for pedestrians (though things don't necessarily work like that). The recently rebuilt **market** is fairly ordinary, but it's worth seeking out the **traditional medicine stalls**, which sell not only herbal products but the shrivelled gall bladders of bears, and dried snakes curled up like skeins of rope. Just south of here, you can check out the original lion statues from Sambor Prei Kuk, which are kept in the province's **Department of Arts and Culture** (Mon–Fri 8–10.30am & 2.30–5pm; $1), on the east side of the main dual carriageway through town. At the time of writing this was due to move to a new building on the riverfront just east of the bridges. Pleasant enough, especially if you've half an hour to kill, is the gaudy **Wat Kompong Thom**, on the main road about 500m north of the river. The wat is hard to miss, its compound crammed with exuberant pagoda buildings and stupas.

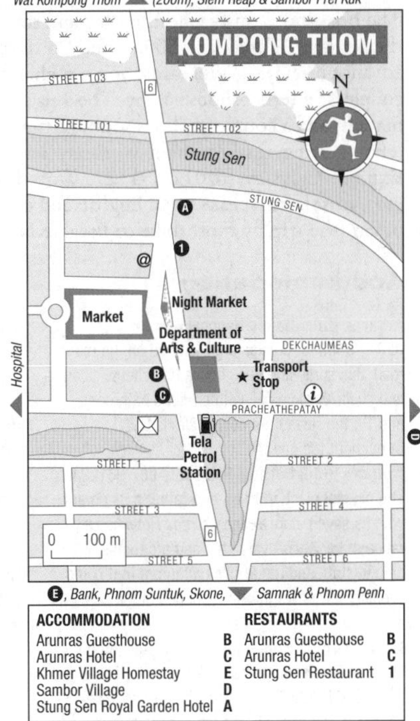

Practicalities

The town is centred around a stretch of dual carriageway on National Route 6 and the adjacent market. Buses from Phnom Penh and Kompong Cham will drop you on the main road opposite the *Arunras Hotel*; buses from Siem Reap stop outside the market. Arriving by shared taxi the **transport stop** is in the square, east of the main road, and north of Pracheathepatay. Taxis and minibuses to Phnom Penh go from the south side of the square; transport for Siem Reap ($5) and pick-ups to Tbeng Meanchey ($5 inside, 10,000 riel on the back) from the north. For the first stop on the journey to Preah Vihear, **Tbeng Meanchey** (pronounced "t-behng me-an-chay", though confusingly everyone refers to it as Preah Vihear, after the province of which it is capital), it's best to get to the transport stop early, as the journey by shared taxi (20,000 riel) or pick-up (20,000 riel for an inside seat, or 10,000 riel outside) can take over five hours. Things in Kompong Thom are fairly easily reached, but there are always motos around if you need one.

Kompong Thom's friendly **tourist office**, upstairs in a wooden building southeast of the transport stop, is a useful source of advice if you happen to find anyone there. For international **phone** calls, the Camintel office is inside the **post office** on the corner opposite the *Arunras Hotel*; for domestic calls, try the booths near the market.

The **hospital** is on Pracheathepatay and there are pharmacies on the street south of the market. Acleda Bank 500m south of the market will cash travellers' cheques and advance money on Visa cards; you can **change money** in the market and there are a couple of internet shops nearby. The Tela petrol station on the main road has a mini-market, and a couple of shops south of the market stock a few Western goodies.

For getting further afield you may want to check out the services of Cobra Explore Odyssey (Ⓣ012/691527, Ⓔguideimsokhom@yahoo.com); the proprietor, Imsokom, speaks great English and can arrange trips to all the sights by moto or car (the trip by motorbike to Preah Khan is about $50 return).

Accommodation

Arunras Guesthouse National Route 6 Ⓣ012/865935. Conveniently located on the main road, this sprawling guesthouse has cheap, clean and cheerful rooms all with en-suite bathrooms and TV; the restaurant downstairs is busy throughout the day. ❷

Arunras Hotel National Route 6 Ⓣ062/961294. The biggest place in town, and rather a landmark with its seven storeys, the *Arunras Hotel* has a range of very good-value fan and a/c rooms, helpful staff, and a massive restaurant that come evening spills over into the grounds of the post office. ❸

Khmer Village Homestay South of Kompong Thom at Baray village near the junction of NR6 and NR71 Ⓣ012/635718, Ⓦwww.khmerhomestay.com. Staying here affords the chance to get involved in village life; you can visit for just a day, or stay over for longer helping with projects in the community. ❸–❹

Sambor Village 1km east of town along the river Ⓣ062/961391, Ⓦwww.samborvillage.com. Delightful boutique hotel, surrounded by verdant gardens. The nineteen bungalows are individually decorated and all have a/c, hot water, TV and safety box; there's an inviting swimming pool, wi-fi, restaurant, bicycles and umbrellas (for the very sunny, or rainy, days). ❺

Stung Sen Royal Garden Hotel National Route 6 Ⓣ062/961228. Overlooking the river, this is looking a bit dated, though that said, rooms have TV, a/c and en-suite bathrooms with hot water, and if you've come by car there's secure parking. ❹

Eating and drinking

All Kompong Thom's **restaurants** serve Khmer and Chinese food. The restaurant in the *Arunras Guesthouse* is the most popular, with excellent, economical dishes available throughout the day. The restaurant at the *Arunras Hotel* is an unappealing box, but the food – all the usual Khmer dishes – is fine; it's best in the evening when it takes over the post office compound across the road. Just south of the *Stung Sen Royal Garden Hotel*, the huge *Stung Sen Restaurant* dishes up succulent sweet-and-sour fish and generous portions of stir-fried pork with vegetables, but it's really set up for groups and you can feel a bit lost here when you're alone. Inexpensive **food stalls** at the market open from early morning to mid-afternoon, and you can have your fill of fruit shakes and desserts at the **night market**, which sets up outside the east entrance to the market from late afternoon. If you're pining for cookies or cakes, there's a **bakery** on the main road just north of the market.

There's no **nightlife** to speak of in Kompong Thom, unless you enjoy listening to locals croaking through Cambodian tunes in seedy karaoke bars.

Sambor Prei Kuk and Preah Khan

Two major temple sites each lie within a day-trip of Kompong Thom. East off National Route 64, **Sambor Prei Kuk** is the site of a Chenla-era capital that once boasted hundreds of temples, although many of them have now been lost, perhaps smothered by the encroaching forest. Several temple groups have been cleared, and particularly fine brick carvings and decorated sandstone lintels and columns can be seen. Much further north, and more easily reached by cutting north from NR6, the temple enclosure of **Preah Khan** is the largest in Cambodia, its central sanctuary featuring the earliest example of four huge faces looking to the cardinal directions, a motif which later became a feature of many Cambodian temples.

Five kilometres north of Kompong Thom **National Route 64** veers off to the north; a wide dirt road, it can be slow going in the rainy season. After about 10km, turn east where the fifteen-kilometre side road to Sambor Prei Kuk is decent enough.

Unfortunately, there's no such thing as an easy trip to Preah Khan, around 70km to the northwest and actually in Preah Vihear province. It's best approached from NR6, turning north about 20km west from Kompong Thom. From the turning the dirt road is in quite good condition for 40km, but deteriorates to little more than a path, with endless opportunities to head off in the wrong direction. In the dry season, starting from Kompong Thom early in the morning and arriving back after dark, it's just possible to visit as a day-trip. In the rainy season it's virtually impassable.

Sambor Prei Kuk

The history of **Sambor Prei Kuk** goes back to the late sixth century, when Cambodia consisted of numerous small states; one of these was a kingdom on the Mekong ruled over by **Mahendravarman**, who extended his domain as far north as Khon Kaen in present-day Thailand. His brother **Bhavavarman** created his own kingdom by conquering lands in central Cambodia and territory as far north as Battambang, setting up his capital in the area of Sambor Prei Kuk. When Bhavavarman died in 598, the two kingdoms were merged under Mahendravarman, who retained Sambor Prei Kuk as his capital. From 610 to 628 the area was known as **Ishanapura** and was ruled by Mahendravarman's son **Ishanavarman**, who built the towers of the temple's south group, the earliest at the site. With his death, the kingdom gradually declined and split into smaller states, though Sambor Prei Kuk remained inhabited; it was from here that Rajendravarman I came to take the throne at Angkor in 944, after which references to it disappear from the records. The site was cleared in 1962, but restoration and research were suspended at the outbreak of civil war in 1970, and post-Khmer Rouge the threat of guerrilla attack meant that it remained inaccessible up until 1998. Today, it is looting rather than insurgency that the guards stationed here are supposedly trying to forestall.

The site is easily visited by **moto** from Kompong Thom ($10 round trip), the journey taking about 40min. The site is seldom busy; tour groups, arriving on day-trips from Phnom Penh, are usually on a tight schedule, and if you just wait awhile you'll have the place pretty much to yourself again. The admission charge is $3. There are **food stalls** near the ticket booth and a small shop.

The site

The temple divides into three main sections: the north and south groups, which date from the seventh century, and the centre group, a ninth-century addition. Separated from these by the access road are the ruined sanctuary tower of **Ashram Issey** and the single-towered **Prasat Bos Ram**, which has a lion's-head channel through which holy water flowed; it is now at ground level, but would originally have been more than a metre up the wall of the tower. The whole site is covered with the remains of towers, and carvings can be seen poking out from piles of earth or partly covered by undergrowth – exploring at random can throw up some real gems. If you've come with a driver, he may well know of new temples that have recently been uncovered.

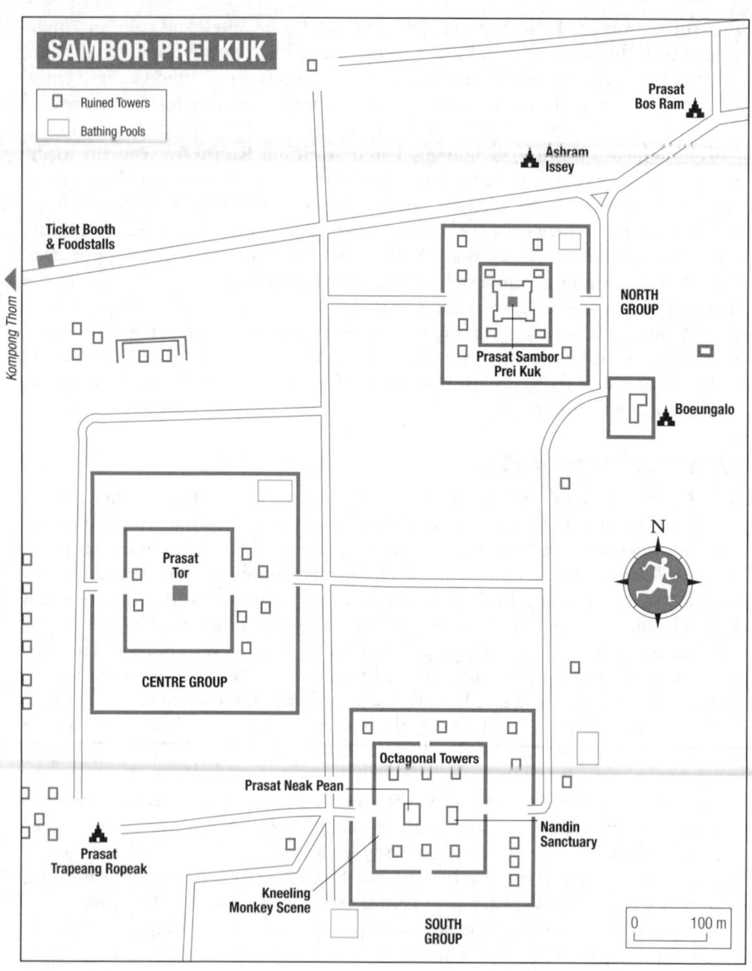

North group

The north group, sometimes called **Prasat Sambor Prei Kuk** after its central sanctuary tower, was extended and restored during the Angkorian era. Although the main approach is from the east, many people prefer to climb through the wall in the northeast corner, passing the bathing pool. The sanctuary towers are arranged in a quincunx. Carved into the brick on the southern side of the central tower is a **flying palace**, believed to be home to the local spirits who look after the temples (you can make out divinities on three levels of the palace). Several more of these palaces can be found in the south group.

Around the entrances you'll be able to make out the remains of decorated sandstone lintels and columns. The carvings on some of the other towers are in reasonably good condition – look out for cute winged horses and tiny human faces. Though there were once numerous other towers here, about all you'll be able to spot amid the ruins is the row of four on the west side. You'll also see a number of carved sandstone **pedestals** lying around the site, each about 1.5m square and designed to carry a linga; these were meant to be portable, allowing worship to take place away from the temples.

Centre group

Although only the main sanctuary tower, **Prasat Tor**, survives, it's a particularly photogenic structure, its entrance steps flanked by reproduction lions. The lintels to the south are well preserved, and you can still spot the intricate foliage designs for which the Chenla period (see p.310) is famed. Around 200m southwest of here, the crumbling **Prasat Trapeang Ropeak** retains elegant brick arches, and, at ground level, carved decorations, including flowers.

South group

Built as the state-temple of Ishanapura, the south group is known as **Prasat Neak Pean** after its central sanctuary tower. The main towers are located within two concentric enclosures; the ruined outer enclosing wall is of laterite, while the relatively intact inner wall is built of brick. The central section of the west side of the inner wall still bears elaborate **reliefs**, among them a lion fighting and a monkey kneeling as if making an offering. Also worth a look are the reasonably preserved carved **lintels** of the central sanctuary, originally linked to a nearby building which once housed a statue of Nandin. The image is long gone, however, and all that can be seen of the raised causeway that connected the two structures are a few pillars, though the building itself and some of the carvings around its central pedestal are well preserved. The **prasat** contains a damaged linga base that still shows the remains of delicate decoration. A number of unusual octagonal towers are located in the enclosure, their walls decorated with large, circular medallion-like carvings and more flying palaces.

Preah Khan

Little is known about the history of **Preah Khan**. To distinguish it from the temple of the same name at Angkor, it is sometimes suffixed with the province name "Kompong Thom" or the district name "Kompong Svay". To add to the confusion, locals call it Prasat Bakan. The earliest buildings are attributed to Suryavarman I, and it's believed that Jayavarman VII spent time here before moving to Angkor – the famous carved stone head of the king displayed in the National Museum in Phnom Penh was found on the site (see p.97). In the 1870s Louis Delaporte carried off the temple's prize sculptures (they're now in the Guimet Museum in Paris), while looters have also pillaged the temple in recent years, using pneumatic drills to remove statues – resulting in collapsed towers, crushed apsaras and the broken images which lie scattered on the ground.

Even so, the sprawling site – the largest temple compound of the Angkor period in the country – is rewarding, with four different temple groups and numerous prasats and buildings to be explored. A little confusingly, the three-kilometre-long **baray** to the east is partly contained within the outermost enclosing wall. East of the baray, a small ninth-century temple, **Prasat Preah Damrei**, is enclosed by its own laterite wall with its upper levels guarded by stone elephants, often draped in orange robes. The most noteworthy thing about the baray itself is what remains of **Prasat Preah Thkol**, a cruciform sanctuary on an (inaccessible) island in the centre. At the west end of the baray, 600m inside the enclosing wall, the elaborate eleventh-century **Prasat Preah Stung** boasts galleries, carvings of apsaras and a central sanctuary topped with four massive faces, the latter the hallmark of Jayavarman VII and found only in a few places outside Angkor.

West of here, at the heart of Preah Khan, the **main temple group** dates from the twelfth century and was most likely built by Suryavarman II. Its well-preserved causeway, not dissimilar to those at Angkor Thom, is decorated with a frieze of swans (peer over the edge just before the steps up to the gopura). Making your way through the complex, via the elaborate east gopura and two sandstone galleries, you'll come to the central sanctuary, where the Bayon-style, four-faced tower is, so far, untouched by looters.

There is **nowhere to buy food or drink**, and the ticket office is seldom manned (but it's $5 for foreigners if there's someone there).

Preah Vihear and Koh Ker

Overlooking both Cambodia and Thailand, the magnificent **Preah Vihear** takes maximum advantage of the Dangkrek escarpment to which it clings, successive temple enclosures taking you higher and higher until you reach the summit. Getting to the temple is somewhat easier than it used to be thanks to new roads from Tbeng Meanchey and Siem Reap, though it's still quite an expensive excursion (see p.178). There is currently no access from Thailand, as the border is closed.

Also accessible from Tbeng Meanchey, although more usually visited from Siem Reap, is **Koh Ker**, Cambodia's most remote Angkorian temple. Practically engulfed by jungle, it has been heavily looted and badly neglected, but plenty of monuments remain for the intrepid explorer, and its grandeur and majesty are still apparent.

Tbeng Meanchey

Though the journey is not without interest, it's a long, slow haul of 150km on National Route 64 from Kompong Thom to **TBENG MEANCHEY**. Passing by the **Boeng Peae Wildlife Reserve**, a (theoretically) protected area, gives some idea of the dense forest cover which used to blanket the country. The road is passable year-round, but it's not yet surfaced, so depending on the season the journey can take from four to eight hours. In fact, this is one of the few remaining trips in Cambodia where you may end up taking a pick-up as often they are the only vehicles able to negotiate the difficult road conditions. If so try to avoid travelling in the back, as it's easy to get thrown off when the vehicle pitches from side to side.

While in Tbeng Meanchey, it's worth visiting Weaves of Cambodia, a **silk-weaving co-operative** (250m east of the hospital; open mornings Mon–Sat; Ⓣ012/610719, Ⓦwww.weavesofcambodia.com). Originally a rehabilitation centre for local disabled people, it's now a prosperous concern, producing high-quality silk for overseas markets. Visitors are welcome to tour the sericulture chambers and the spinning and weaving workshops, and there's a selection of silk goods to buy.

Practicalities

From the traffic circle at the south end of town, Tbeng Meanchey sprawls northwards over 2km, with wide, straight dirt roads laid out on a simple grid. The main road leads in from the traffic circle, passing the hospital, while a second north–south road runs parallel to it to the west. These two roads are linked by a few east–west roads; the **transport stop** is located about 1km north and two blocks west of the traffic circle. From here you'll find the town's guesthouses and restaurants, 200m west in the area around the **market**.

All pick-ups and shared taxis arrive at and depart from the transport stop; transport to **Kompong Thom** leaves throughout the day. **Motos** congregate around the transport stop, and this is the best place to find someone who can speak a little English. For the trip to Koh Ker, Preah Khan or Preah Vihear (100km further north), be prepared for some hard bargaining as prices can be outrageous.

Acleda Bank, 200m south of the market, will change travellers' cheques, and you can **change money** at the market. Given that the town sees few tourists, the tourist office on the main road, 100m from the traffic circle on the left, is seldom open. It's probably best to forgo the outside world while you're here, international phone calls are impossible to make and internet access is limited, although you could try the internet shop 100m north of the traffic circle.

Accommodation and eating

All **accommodation** in town is pretty basic, and nowhere particularly stands out. Before taking a room, find out what hours the electricity is on, as it can be limited to the evening. The most convenient place to stay is the *27 May Guesthouse* (Ⓣ011/905472; ❶), which has simple en-suite rooms, some with air conditioning; it's located on the crossroads west of the transport stop, near the market. East of the transport stop on the other side of the road, the *Phnom Meas* (Ⓣ012/632017; ❷) has spartan rooms and bathrooms with squat toilets: some smallish, with TV and bath, others larger but windowless. Heading north from the market and then east at the next block the *Promtep Guest House* (Ⓣ011/747177; ❷) has decent-sized, but uninspiring rooms with fan or air conditioning and TV.

The town's only **restaurant** with an English-language menu is the *Dara Reas*, which may sound like a stomach complaint but actually serves up pretty good soups and stir-fries. It's rather inconveniently situated beside the Vishnu Circle about 200m west of the traffic circle and a kilometre south of the market. Across from the transport stop, a couple of restaurants do fried noodle and rice dishes, plus coffee. There are also some **food stalls** on the west side of the market.

Tmatboey

Tmatboey, one of only two nesting sites of the giant ibis in Asia, is 30km north of Tbeng Meanchey off the Preah Vihear road. Of major interest to twitchers, white-shouldered ibis, Greater Adjutants and Sarus cranes also frequent the area. The local community is actively involved with the ecotourism site which discourages hunting. Visits and homestays can be arranged through Sam Veasna Centre; see p.179 for more information.

Koh Ker

Located in rocky, scrub-covered terrain, **Koh Ker** ($10 for foreigners) was briefly capital of the Khmer Empire in the tenth century, when Jayavarman IV – who was already ruler of his own state here when he ascended the imperial throne – decided not to relocate to Angkor, but decreed instead that the court should come to him. Koh Ker is particularly renowned for its massive **statues**, which were the first in Khmer art to depict movement.

From Tbeng Meanchey it's a three-hour, 70km moto ride to Koh Ker, best tackled in the dry season (Nov–May). A few stalls along the way have food and drink, but there's little else. The area is still heavily **mined**, so stick to well-trodden paths and resist the temptation to dive off into undergrowth to explore on your own.

An alternative approach to Koh Ker (and the one most people choose) is on the recently **upgraded road from Siem Reap**, in parts surfaced, in parts graded. This road dates back to the time of Jayavarman IV, when Koh Ker was linked to

Angkor, and the temples of Beng Mealea and Banteay Samre were built along it; see p.211 and p.206. The road has been reopened by a private company, making it possible to visit Koh Ker as a day-trip from Siem Reap, perhaps stopping off at Beng Mealea on the way back; expect it to take around three hours in a Camray (hire cost around $90) and to pay a road toll of $5.

The site

The earliest structures here, Prasat Thom and Prasat Kraham, had already been built by the time Jayavarman IV ascended the throne. Entered from the east, **Prasat Thom** features three enclosures arrayed in a line, with the sanctuary at the centre of the final courtyard. The distinctive red-sandstone **Prasat Kraham** is part of the main gopura to the third enclosure, and has a full tower. A massive fragmented statue of Shiva was found here, with five heads and eight arms (the hands are displayed in the National Museum in Phnom Penh). Through the gopura is a wide moat, crossed by a causeway with naga balustrades, giving onto a narrow second enclosure, where long narrow buildings almost form a gallery. A final gopura through a sandstone wall leads into the first enclosure, where a terrace supports nine small sanctuaries in two rows, five in front and four behind; there are also the remains of twelve minor towers spread around the courtyard in various states of disrepair.

To the west, beyond Prasat Thom though unusually sharing a common wall, is the **Prang**, a 35-metre-high, seven-tiered sandstone pyramid; there's a stairway up its eastern side – though sometimes you may be stopped from climbing it. The Prang was meant to be Jayavarman IV's state-temple but was never completed; instead of a sanctuary tower, there's just a pedestal at the top, which would have supported a statue of Nandin. Just as high as the Prang is the man-made **hill** beyond, oddly known as **Pnoh Damrei Saw**, the Tomb of the White Elephant. More sanctuaries can be found east of the **Rohal**, a baray over 1km long hewn out of the rock at Jayavarman IV's instigation. In total there are believed to be around 86 temples in and around the site.

Preah Vihear

Constructed entirely of sandstone, Preah Vihear has an unusual layout for a Khmer temple, with four enclosures laid out in a row (rather than concentrically) linked by avenues and increasingly complex cruciform gopuras with elaborately carved pediments. It's worth looking behind you as you exit each gopura heading up (south), as some of the finest of the temple's decorated lintels are to be found on the south sides. From the summit, there are spectacular views along the jagged line of the Dangkrek Mountains and over the jungles of Cambodia, crisscrossed with tiny red tracks. Across in Thailand you can see the border marker posts in the scrub of no-man's-land and the massive road to the temple.

The Vulture Restaurant

In the depths of Preah Vihear province Chhep Protected Forest is home to three critically endangered species of vulture – red-headed, slender-billed and white-rumped. Trips can be arranged through the Sam Veasna Centre (see p.179), and involve camping overnight in the forest, followed by a morning of watching the vultures breakfast on a dead cow. The project is run by the Wildlife Conservation Society (Ⓦ www.wcs.org) and some of the fees collected go towards supporting livelihoods in the community.

Completely inaccessible for over two decades due to war and the presence of the Khmer Rouge, Preah Vihear was the scene of fighting as recently as 1995. Government troops were withdrawn due to concerns over damage to the complex, leaving the Khmer Rouge in control, but nevertheless bullet holes can still be seen on the outer walls of the temple's uppermost enclosure. The temple reopened to the public in 1998, but the hillside remains heavily **mined**, so don't stray from the well-trodden tracks.

Hugging the boundary between Cambodia and Thailand, Preah Vihear has been the subject of many **border disputes**. Things flared up in 1962, when the site was awarded to Cambodia by the International Court of Justice in The Hague; then in July 2001, Hun Sen sacked a senior tourism official for signing an agreement allowing the Thais to develop the site, and later that year the Thais closed access from their side, citing Cambodian lack of co operation on cross-border issues. The border reopened in 2003; but things got nasty again in 2008, when Preah Vihear was awarded UNESCO Heritage status. Since then there has been no access from Thailand. Razor wire has been installed along the border and the Cambodian army (complete with their families and myriad of weapons) have dug in. Before visiting, see the box on p.215) and check the current situation online.

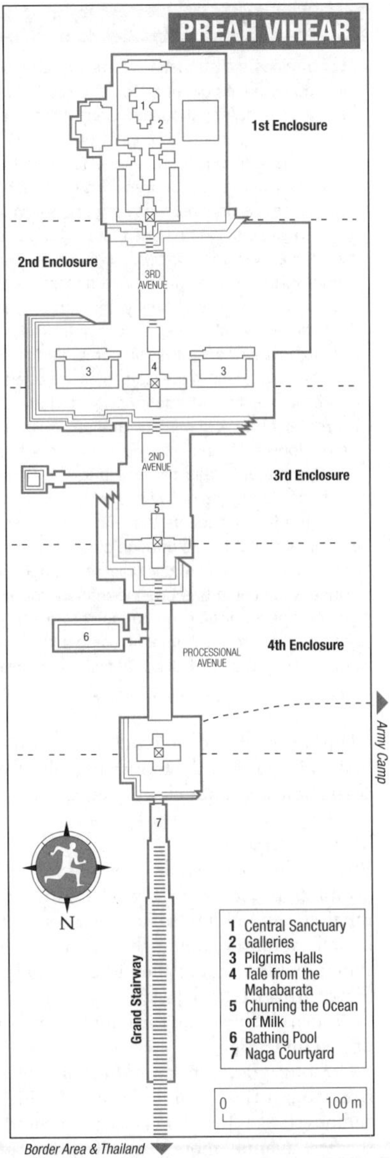

PREAH VIHEAR

1 Central Sanctuary
2 Galleries
3 Pilgrims Halls
4 Tale from the Mahabarata
5 Churning the Ocean of Milk
6 Bathing Pool
7 Naga Courtyard

Practicalities

The easiest way of getting to Preah Vihear is on one of the new roads, from Siem Reap (4hr via either Koh Ker or Anlong Veng, or from Tbeng Meanchey). At the foot of the hill you need to transfer to a local pick-up truck to ascend the hill (20,000 riel per person return); it's a ten–minute trip with fantastic views back over Cambodia. From the drop-off point at the top you walk further uphill to the temple; when you've finished your visit the pick-up will come to collect you. Due to the border issues, at the time of writing there is no entrance fee, but the soldiers welcome any gifts you care to bring (cigarettes are always appreciated, but no alcohol).

Cambodia's land-mine legacy

Land mines are supposed to maim rather than kill, but over a quarter of Cambodians injured by mines die of shock and blood-loss before reaching hospital. For those who survive – over forty thousand Cambodians have become **amputees** as a direct result of land-mine injuries – the impact of an injury on their families is financially devastating, emotional consequences aside. To meet the costs of treatment, their families usually have to sell what few possessions they have, reducing them to an extreme poverty from which they seldom recover. For **young female** mine victims, the stigma is often unbearable: being disabled means that they are frequently unable to find a husband and have to remain with their families, where they may be reduced to the status of slaves. The more fortunate amputees have access to a **prosthetics** workshop where, once their injury has healed sufficiently, they can receive a false limb. However, even if they are subsequently able to get a place at a skills or crafts training centre, there's no guarantee of employment once they've completed their training, and without the capital to set up on their own, land-mine victims all too often find their prospects little improved.

In Cambodia, international and domestic **NGOs** are undertaking the delicate, painstaking task of mine clearance. Trained crews of Cambodians (many of whom are the widows of land-mine victims) work hard to inform rural communities in heavily contaminated areas of the **dangers** of mines, which are more subtle than might appear: during the rainy season, mines which are buried too deep to go off can move towards the surface as the land floods, rendering previously "safe" territory risky.

The actual process of mine clearance is slow and expensive. As yet no mechanical system is available that is reliable enough to allow land to be declared as cleared. So, once a minefield has been identified, the site is sealed off and divided into lanes for trained **personnel**, lying on their stomachs, to **probe** systematically every centimetre of ground for buried objects, using a thin blade. The mines thus detected are carefully uncovered and destroyed, usually by blowing them up in situ.

During the day, drinks and some simple fare can be bought at the site or at the basic restaurants at the foot of the hill. If you get stuck there's a simple guesthouse with a few basic, but clean, rooms.

The temple

Preah Vihear was built over several dynasties from the ninth to the twelfth centuries, but most of the work is attributed to Suryavarman I. He enlarged an old religious centre founded here by a son of Jayavarman II, and installed one of three boundary linga defining the extent of his territory (the others were installed at Phnom Chisor and at the hitherto unidentified site of Ishanatirtha). Later, both Suryavarman II and Jayavarman VII made additions to the temple, which was dedicated to Shiva, and the temple was also referred to as Shikhareshavara, "a place of god under Shiva".

The long, grand, entrance **stairway** gives onto a courtyard – a little way downhill from your arrival point – decorated with naga balustrades. The **first gopura**, in a ruinous state, is raised on a platform ahead; from here you get a terrific view along the **first avenue**, more than 200m long and boasting a paved area of monumental proportions, lined with pillars that would have supported lanterns; the large **bathing pool** to the east, Srah Srang, is guarded by stone lions. At the end of the avenue, due to the angle of approach and the steepness of the steps, the only thing that can be seen of the well-preserved **second gopura** is the entrance door and the impressive triangular pediment, outlined against the sky. Above the exterior of the south door are two intricate and well-preserved carvings: the lintel shows Vishnu reclining, while the pediment shows a scene from the Churning of the Ocean of

Milk (see p.188). Here Vishnu in the guise of a tortoise supports the mountain – the churning stick – on his back; the serpent Vasuki is coiled around the stick acting as the rope, while gods and demons pull together. On the stick, Vishnu appears again as Krishna, keeping an eye on their progress.

Further uphill, beyond the 100m long **second avenue**, the double vestibules of the cruciform **third gopura** form an imposing entrance to the **third avenue**. It was at this level that royal rooms were located for use by the king when he visited the temple; two large buildings nearby were resting houses for pilgrims. The scene above the north door of the gopura is taken from the Hindu epic the *Mahabharata*, and depicts Shiva fighting with Arjuna, a member of the Pandavas family, one of two warring clans in the tale. The final avenue, leading to the **fourth gopura**, feels more like a courtyard as it is flanked by ruined buildings. The ground here is thick with collapsed masonry, some well-preserved carvings lurking in the undergrowth.

Through the gopura is the **main sanctuary**, much of which has collapsed leaving a jumbled heap of massive stones. Dark and austere, the enclosure has none of the vibrancy of the lower levels, but the air here is fragrant with burning incense. In its day, the temple was a pioneering project, and the vaulted galleries that surround the enclosure are some of the earliest examples in Angkorian architecture. Only the north gallery has windows facing out; the windows of the other galleries look in on the enclosure. You can climb through a hole in the western wall to get out onto the mountainside and enjoy the well-earned view.

Travel details

Buses

Kompong Thom to: Kompong Cham (2 daily; 2hr 30min); Phnom Penh (more than 12 daily; 4hr); Poipet (2 daily; 5hr); Siem Reap (more than 12 daily; 2hr).

Shared taxis and pick-up trucks

Kompong Thom to: Kompong Cham (6 daily; 2hr 30min); Phnom Penh (12 daily; 3hr); Siem Reap (12 daily; 2hr); Skone (12 daily; 1hr 30min); Tbeng Meanchey (3 daily; 3hr).

Tbeng Meanchey to: Kompong Thom (3 daily; 3hr).

The northeast

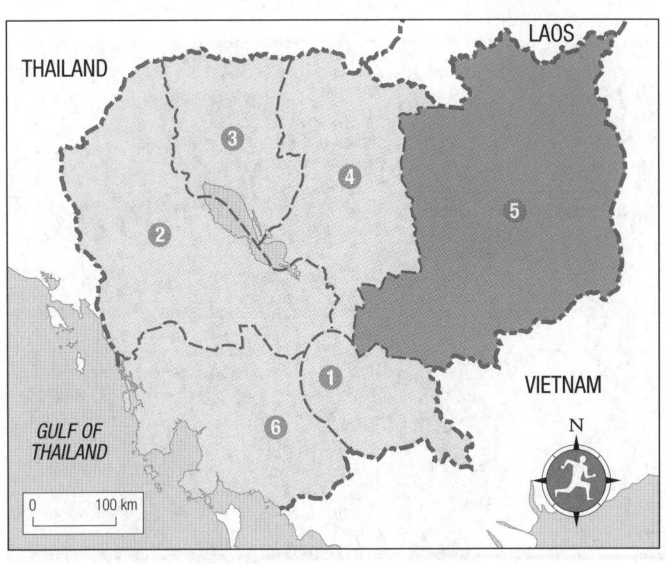

CHAPTER 5

Highlights

* **Irrawaddy dolphins** Spot the silver crowns of these rare creatures as they flit through the rapids at Kampie. See p.245

* **Banlung** A relaxed town emerging as a popular centre for exploring the natural attractions of Rattanakiri, with a bustling chunchiet market and excellent crafts. See p.252

* **Yeak Laom** Magical lake set in the crater of an extinct volcano surrounded by jungle. See p.257

* **Highland waterfalls** Blunging over 30m into a forested gorge remote Bou Sraa pluging over 30m into a forested gorge, may be Cambodia's best cascade, but the more accessible Chha Ong, near Banlung makes a picturesque alternative. See p.258

▲ Chha Ong Waterfall

5

The northeast

Flowing south from Laos, the Mekong River forges its way down through the rugged provinces of northern Cambodia, skirting islands and forming foaming rapids as it cascades over boulders. Further south the scrubby, wooded banks become softer, lined with the tiny vegetable plots of small farms. To the east lie the remote and forested highlands of the sparsely populated Rattanakiri and Mondulkiri provinces. Although the lower slopes of the highlands have been heavily logged, some jungle cover survives, providing a haven for wildlife. The highlands are also home to the country's **chunchiet** population (see box, p.236) who until recently were able to eke out a subsistence living, cultivating crops and foraging in the jungle. This centuries-old way of life is now threatened by the encroachment of the modern world and the loss of the forest on which they depend.

The gateway to the highlands is **Kompong Cham**, a quiet provincial capital that retains an air of faded gentility, easily reached by road from Phnom Penh; the province itself is home to several of Cambodia's Muslim Cham communities. To the north, the rubber plantations of Chup, originally planted in the 1920s, have recently been extended. The big draw at **Kratie**, another old colonial town on the Mekong, is the chance to see the rare Irrawaddy dolphins that inhabit the nearby rapids at Kampie. The most northerly town on Cambodia's stretch of the Mekong, **Stung Treng**, is a quiet backwater which gets hardly any visitors now that the road to the border bypasses the town. Though there's nothing by way of sights, it's close to other spots where you can see dolphins, and a good place to explore by bicycle. You might want to make a stopover on the way to or from the border crossing with Laos at Voen Kham.

For misty mountains, cool climate, a stunning volcanic lake and scattered chunchiet villages, travellers generally head to **Rattanakiri** province. Far fewer make it to **Mondulkiri** province. Until recently this province was isolated from the rest of the country and it still lacks much of the infrastructure; now that it's easily reached by a new road from Snuol, it will no doubt soon become quite developed along the lines of Rattanakiri. That said, in both these provinces, you have no choice but to slow down to the pace of life of rural Cambodia. The lack of decent roads, transport, and any other creature comforts outside the provincial capitals means that most tourists restrict themselves to making day-trips from **Banlung** (for Rattanakiri) and **Sen Monorom** (for Mondulkiri). Rattanakiri is

Note that Cambodians habitually refer to Banlung as Rattanakiri and Sen Monorom as Mondulkiri, as most provinces in Cambodia take their name from their provincial capital.

geared up to travellers now, with eco-lodges, a fledgling bar scene and busy trekking industry offering overnight treks into the Virachey National Park. From Sen Monorom you can make forays out to a number of spectacular waterfalls, go trekking or make an expedition by elephant into the jungle.

Kompong Cham and around

Situated on the west bank of the Mekong, the mellow town of **Kompong Cham** has little of the bustle that you'd expect of the biggest city in the northeast. Its small commercial port doesn't exactly hum with activity, and the riverfront, in the shadow of the massive Kizuna Bridge – thrown across the river in 2001 courtesy of the Japanese, is pretty quiet too since road improvements have led to the demise of most river transport. The place has a distinct charm though, and enough low-key attractions to occupy a day or two. Its few Western cafés and bars are packed in the evenings with tourists who are stopping over in town, on a slow journey through the country.

A few hours can be happily passed exploring the streets of the **colonial centre** and visiting **Wat Nokor**, known locally as Nokor Bachey, just outside the town, a modern pagoda built within an eleventh-century temple. In half a day you can follow the Mekong north to Phnom Hann Chey, a quirky hill-top pagoda with fabulous views of the river and some old prasats, while a day-trip will get you to the pre-Angkorian site of **Banteay Prei Nokor**, surrounded by a massive earth embankment, where a few ruined towers still stand, with a visit to the rubber plantation at Chup on the side. Pleasant **boat trips** can also be made to villages up and down the Mekong.

Arrival, transport and information

Buses run by Phnom Penh Sorya Transport Company arrive at the **bus depot** on Preah Bat Monivong Street, the boulevard northwest of the market. Buses from other companies stop at their various ticket offices around town, which tend to be on NR7 near the bridge. Shared taxis and mini buses to and from destinations to the north and northeast, including Sen Monorom, stop at Caltex petrol station on

Moving on from Kompong Cham

The staging-post for travel to the far northeast of the country, Kompong Cham lies on National Route 7, 144km from Phnom Penh; travel beyond Kompong Cham to the northeast is easy, with a good road looping north, via Snuol, to Kratie, Stung Treng and on to the Laos border. However, be aware that if you're heading to Rattanakiri, National Route 78 is still just graded dirt for all of its 133km to Banlung. Road improvements are underway, and the section from Banlung to the Vietnamese border is complete, but it'll be some time before the part from Banlung to NR7 is finished. From Snuol it's an easy couple of hours to get to Mondulkiri as, thanks to the Chinese, a new road has been cut through the highlands (though cynics might say it's only so they can reach their gold mines 50km north of Sen Monorom more easily). Transport for Kompong Thom, Siem Reap and Poipet runs regularly but leaves in the morning only.

By bus

Regular buses ply the excellent National Route 7 to **Phnom Penh** throughout the day and it's not normally a problem to get a seat if you just show up, though tickets can be bought in advance at the office on the boulevard west of the market (10,000 riel). There are three or four buses a day to Kratie (20,000 riel) and Stung Treng (25,000 riel), with some of them continuing to Banlung, but be prepared for a bumpy trip for a little while yet. Buses for Kompong Thom (18,000 riel) and Siem Reap (25,000 riel) leave the depot twice a day and there's just one bus a day through to Poipet (30,000 riel) in the early morning. For Sen Monorom you'll need to get a Rith Mony bus (though other operators may have started up by the time we are in print) from their ticket office on NR7 near the bridge.

By shared taxi and minibus

Transport for Phnom Penh (12,000 riel) leaves from the northeast side of the market throughout the day. For Kompong Thom (15,000 riel) and **Siem Reap** (30,000 riel), head for the transport stop at Psar Bung Kok, north of the post office. For destinations to the north and northeast, go to the transport stop at Caltex on the northwest side of the roundabout near the bridge. For Sen Monorom, you may need to take a taxi or minibus to Snuol and find a connection there. If you're heading for Vietnam, the border crossing at Trapeang Phlong (100km east of Kompong Cham) is open to foreigners (though you'll need to have your visa already); a place in a shared taxi is around 10,000 riel; transport runs to no particular frequency to Bavet via Prey Veng.

the roundabout just before the bridge; while those from Kompong Thom and Siem Reap arrive two blocks north of the post office. Other transport pulls up on the northeast side of the market. If you want to hire a **car with driver**, your hotel or guesthouse should be able to arrange it (about $40 per day). It's easy to get around town on foot, but if you want to hire a moto or tuk-tuk there are plenty around; going further afield expect to pay $5 for the return trip to Wat Nokor, and $15 to Phnom Hann Chey. To hire a motorbike or bicycle ask at *Lazy Mekong Daze*.

Northwest of the market, the **tourist office** is located in the government compound near the disused swimming pool. East of here across the road is the **Camintel** office,

The chunchiet

There are ethnic minority groups throughout Cambodia, Burma, Thailand, Laos, Vietnam and parts of southeastern China. In Cambodia they live primarily in remote highland villages and are usually known as the **chunchiet** (literally "nationality") or the **Khmer Loeu** ("upland Khmer"). It is estimated that the chunchiet make up just one percent of Cambodia's population, but in the provinces of Rattanakiri and Mondulkiri the chunchiet have always been the majority, though the balance is changing with an influx of Khmer from the rest of the country. Small communities of chunchiet also inhabit parts of Stung Treng and Kratie provinces, and a few live in the mountains of southwest Cambodia, near Koh Kong.

Darker-skinned than the Khmer and particularly small in stature, the chunchiet, along with the Khmer, are regarded as **indigenous** inhabitants of the country. There are more than thirty distinct chunchiet tribes, ranging from comparatively large groups like the Tampoun, Kreung-Brou, Jarai, Stieng and Phnong, all of which number in the thousands, to much smaller tribes, such as the Kavat, Lun, Peahr and Meul, which are believed to number fewer than a hundred each. Every group has its own distinct **language**, each with several dialects, which has historically made it hard for them to communicate with Khmers or even among themselves; additionally, none of the chunchiet tongues has a written form. Particular tribes can't usually be distinguished by their clothing, as traditional garments are now used only on ceremonial occasions (the rest of the time the women wear blouses and sarongs, the men T-shirts and trousers), though for the observant they do have subtly different features.

Traditional chunchiet **villages** vary in layout and design from tribe to tribe. The Kreung build their houses on the ground in a circle, leaving a communal open area in the centre, while the Tampoun build stilt houses in a row, and the Phnong, who form the major tribe in Mondulkiri, have houses with roofs that slope to within a metre of the ground. Unique to Tampoun villages are the tiny houses built for people of **marriageable age** to allow them to entertain and choose a partner away from public view; perched precariously on high stilts close to the family home, the houses for young men are taller and have both windows and balconies, while the young women's houses only have doors. There are several Tampoun villages in Rattanakiri.

Animism and **ancestor worship** are central to the chunchiet belief system, with rivers, lakes, rocks and trees regarded as sacred; the Jarai, for instance, place carved images near graves to protect the deceased and to keep them company. In general, however, little is known about chunchiet rituals and ceremonies, as even these days, strangers are normally excluded.

Crops were traditionally produced through **swidden agriculture**, in which plots, called **chamkar**s, were created by cutting down and burning patches of jungle near villages; new **chamkar**s would be cleared each year as others were left fallow for seven to ten years to regenerate. Generally, each **chamkar** produced only sufficient food to feed the family tending it, but any surplus would be either bartered or sold at market; their diet would also be supplemented by foraging in the forest, which also yields medicinal plants. The chunchiet are some of the poorest people in Cambodia:

where you can make domestic and international phone calls; the **post office** is a block southeast. **Internet** access ($1 per hr) is available at The World Centre, just southwest of the market and at other places around town; there's wi-fi at several cafés and bars which we mention in the text. The **police station** is a block back from the riverfront, near the market. Banks in town will cash **travellers' cheques** for the usual commission, and will advance cash on cards; there are ATMs at ANZ Royal and Canadia banks. As well as at the banks you can change money with the money changers in the market. There are plenty of **pharmacies** on the streets near the market; for medical emergencies the **hospital**, in the northwest of town, is the only place to go.

money has not played a major role, being used only to trade with outsiders, and any wealth they did hold was traditionally in the form of animals such as water buffalo or elephants. **Schooling** has only been introduced in the past decade, and life expectancy is low as a result of poverty, malnourishment, poor hygiene and limited access to **health care**.

Repeated attempts have been made to bring the chunchiet round to the Khmer way of life. The French recruited them to work in the rubber plantations and on road-building projects, while the Sihanouk government tried to restrict them to farming fixed plots. In the mid-1960s, government troops seeking the guerrilla **Khmer Rouge** – who had fled to the jungles of Rattanakiri – burnt down chunchiet villages. Bombed by the US in the early 1970s and continually harassed by Lon Nol soldiers, the chunchiet were ripe for recruitment by the Khmer Rouge, although experts now believe that those who did join the Khmer Rouge were siding with them against a common enemy rather than sharing their ideology.

Unfortunately, the traditional way of chunchiet life is nearly extinct. In theory, chunchiet lands are state-owned and cannot be sold to private Cambodians, but since 2001 tribal lands have been sold, sometimes by village headmen, to savvy Khmer who have cleared the land for farms. Much was made of this at the time with the press accusing the Khmer of duping the chunchiet. Latterly, the government has allowed economic land concessions (ELCs), which permit ground to be cleared for plantations. According to Cambodian law, ELCs can only be used to clear non-forested land, but regardless of this, vast swathes of forest have now been **cleared** to make way for plantations of rubber and cashew; according to a report by Global Witness (see p.[265]) this is a way of flouting the rules regarding illegal logging. The consequence for the chunchiet is that the forest on which they relied for their livelihood has been destroyed, making it impossible for them to continue with traditional ways of farming or foraging and appeals by the chunchiet for the return of their land has been to no avail.

Education too has brought changes; learning Khmer in school has increased the number of chunchiet able to communicate outside their own communities, while more contact with the outside world has increased the desire for televisions, motorbikes and a more "Khmer" way of life. Encouraged by the government to stay in one place, and thus benefit from schools and some improvement in health care, even the style of housing is changing and in Mondulkiri many Phnong villages have adopted the stilted, Khmer-style of dwelling. In the long term it's hard to see how they can survive as individual tribes.

That said, although many chunchiet villagers have become somewhat accustomed to foreign visitors, they still remain shy and modest – some may even see your presence as voyeuristic, so it's always better to visit in the company of a local guide who knows some of the villagers and their customs. It's also worth noting that the chunchiet do not like having their pictures taken and are highly embarrassed by shows of public affection and by exposed flesh (bare legs, arms and so on).

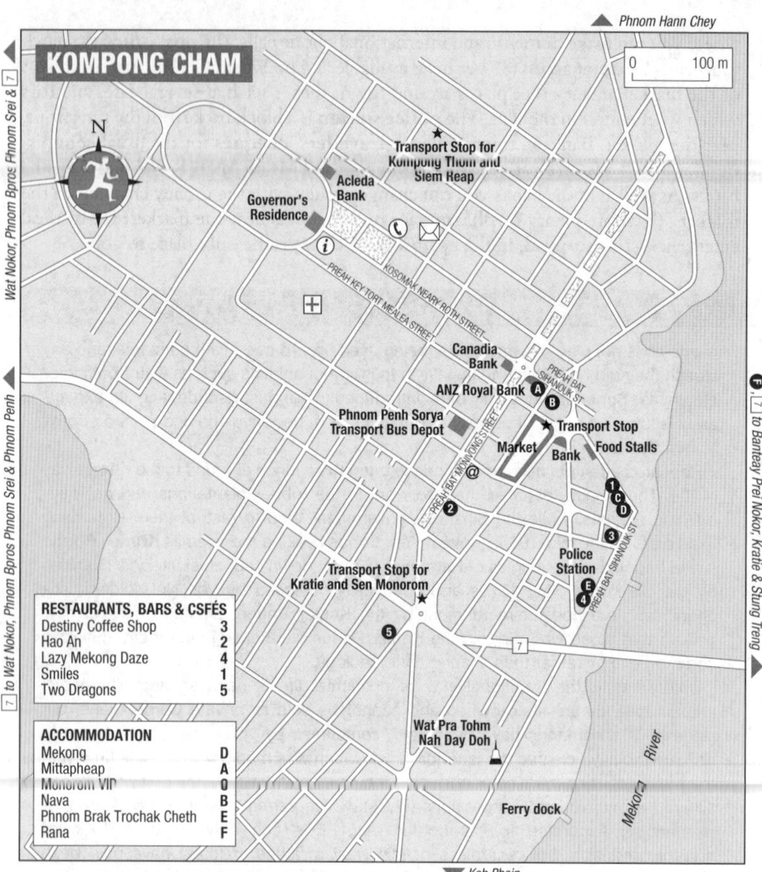

Accommodation

Kompong Cham has plenty of guesthouses and inexpensive hotels, and there's never a problem getting a room. The town's hotels are excellent value on the whole, offering spacious, bright accommodation at the same price as a small dingy room in some of the guesthouses.

Mekong On the riverfront ⓣ042/941536. The town's longest-established hotel has recently had a facelift. Popular with NGO workers, the rooms have been upgraded and bathrooms refitted, and there's even a lift. All rooms have hot water, a/c, TV and minibar; those at the front are the most expensive, with balconies giving great views over the Mekong. The café-cum-cocktail bar is a great addition; wi-fi. ❷

Mittapheap North of the market ⓣ042/941565. This small, friendly, modern hotel has rooms with TV and fridge; a/c available for a small premium. Good value. ❷

Monorom VIP On the riverfront ⓣ092/777102, ⓔinfo@monoromviphotel.com. The best rooms in this smart new hotel overlook the river and come with hot water, a/c, TV, fridge, bath and tea/coffee making facilities, though it has to be said that the soft furnishings are a little over the top with heavy swags, pelmets and drapes. Cheaper rooms have fewer frills and are at the back. It's worth paying extra for one at the front with a balcony. Wi-fi and lift. ❸

Nava 457 Preah Bat Sihanouk St ⓣ012/205615. This enduring guesthouse has smallish but comfortable rooms with TV and is easily identified by the external spiral staircase and plant-laden balcony. ❶

Phnom Brak Trochak Cheth On the riverfront ⓣ099/559418. Welcoming, family-run guesthouse in a great location. Clean, basic rooms, with fans; some also have TV, though most are windowless. Communal balcony with views of the river. ❶

Rana 7km towards Kratie on National Route 7 ⓣ012/686240, ⓦwww.ranahomestay.com, ⓔroksrey@yahoo.com. Booking by email is essential for stays in this Cambodian home. Coffee, tea and Western breakfast are included in the price but guest numbers are limited to five at a time. The aim is to give visitors a real insight into rural life in Cambodia with trips to local villages and a glimpse of life as it is for most Cambodians. ❸

The town and around

In the 1930s and 1940s, Kompong Cham was a prosperous trading centre for the rubber and tobacco trades and the most cosmopolitan town in Cambodia. Although nowadays it's all rather somnolent, evidence of its affluent past is still evident in wide, tree-lined streets flanked by shophouses. It's easy to while away a few hours meandering through the unhurried streets taking in the faded colonial architecture, particularly around the market. The riverside, though functional, is good for a late-afternoon stroll and a stop for *tuk krolok* (fruit shake) as you marvel at the towering bridge – known as *Spean Kizuna* after the company that built it – the first in Cambodia to span the Mekong. In the early evening locals come out to wander the riverfront and eat at the night-market stalls.

Following the Mekong south for about a kilometre brings you to the dry-season bamboo bridge to the river island of Koh Pbain. Just across the road, **Wat Pra Tohm Nah Day Doh** is well worth a wander, even though it's less than a hundred years old. In front of the complex is a huge standing Buddha, while the grounds are scattered with intriguing statues of people and animals, and a forest of miniature stupas. Across the river is the photogenic, newly painted pink **French lighthouse**; it's not open to the public. The town's **market**, a reasonably smart, single-level yellow building, doesn't get especially busy, which is just as well as the stalls are jammed so tight together inside, there's hardly a walkway between them. This is a good spot to pick up one of the cotton **kramas** made in Kompong Cham province, which are of good quality and thus in demand all over Cambodia; it's often possible to find colours or patterns that you won't get elsewhere in the country. Its food stalls are a good place to get a cheap coffee or an economical meal.

Wat Nokor

Two kilometres west of town on National Route 7, **Wat Nokor** is located in the grounds of a modern temple, just off the main road through an arched

River trips around Kompong Cham

There are several interesting places within the vicinity of Kompong Cham that can be reached by boat and make for a rewarding day out if there are a few of you to share the cost. There's the **Maha Leap Temple**, an old wooden building with gilded teak columns that was somehow spared by the Khmer Rouge; **Prei Chung Kran**, a village where silk is woven on traditional hand looms, located just upstream from Maha Leap Temple on the Tonle Tuok, about 20km south of Kompong Cham; and **Wat Hann Chey**, about 20km north of Kompong Cham, where there are fantastic river views from Chenla-era ruins and a modern temple. You can approach local boatmen directly to arrange these trips (expect to pay about $50 for a day's boat hire), or ask at **Lazy Mekong Daze** (see p.242). If you're travelling alone, most of these sites can also be reached (more cheaply) by moto or tuk-tuk.

gateway signed to Nokor Bachey Temple. The eleventh-century temple, surrounded by laterite walls (painted black during the Khmer Rouge occupation), is fairly well preserved, comprising a central sanctuary, over which a modern vihara has been built. Although purists may object to the gaudy modern walls and pillars of the new vihara, these quirky 1990s additions are a hit with Cambodians and ethnic Chinese. The latter closely identify with the temple's **legend**, which tells of a baby boy from Kompong Cham who was gobbled up by a large fish; the fish swam down the Mekong and on to the coast of China, where it was eventually caught and the child, still alive, discovered. The boy subsequently made his way back to Cambodia, bringing with him a retinue of Chinese, who all settled at Kompong Cham, which the locals say explains why so many Chinese live in the area, and possibly why there is a Chinese temple in the grounds.

Another modern building, just to the south of the temple complex, contains a **reclining Buddha**, decapitated during the Khmer Rouge era. The head was missing for years until a workman dreamt that it was buried close by; sure enough, the dream came true, and the head was soon dug up in the grounds and reunited with the body. Newlyweds use the temple as a backdrop for their photographs, and it's not unusual to find a group of women in the gopura helping a bride into each of her several wedding outfits.

Koh Pbain

Koh Pbain, a ten-kilometre-long island just southeast of town in the middle of the Mekong, is perfect for an out-of-town jaunt, especially by bicycle. Tiny tracks cross the island, fording small creeks and meandering through fields, and during the dry season the island is fringed with sandy beaches. Though you'll also see sesame and peanuts, the primary crop here is tobacco – the tall, thin, mud-walled buildings are drying-houses where the leaves are hung for several days before being packed into bamboo crates. The island has a number of **Cham villages**. The men work mainly as fishermen, while in the dry season the women weave *hol* silk and cotton *kramas*, using looms set up under the stilt-houses.

Outside the rainy season you can get to Koh Pbain across the sandbank about a kilometre south of town, via a bamboo toll bridge ($1 for foreigners with a bicycle); come the rains, you'll need to take the small ferry, just big enough for a couple of motos and a few passengers.

The Cham

Originating from **Champa**, a kingdom which extended from Hue to Phan Thiet on the coast of present-day Vietnam, the Cham are the largest minority ethnic group in Cambodia, numbering around 700,000, and thus accounting for about a third of the non-Khmer population. They also represent the largest minority religion, being Sunni Muslims who converted from Hinduism some time after the fourteenth century.

Historically, the Cham were frequently at war both with the Khmer, who bordered their kingdom to the west and south, and the Vietnamese, who occupied the territory to the north. In 1177, the Cham successfully raided Angkor, only to be defeated by the intervention of Jayavarman VII in a ferocious battle on the Tonle Sap – an event depicted in the bas-reliefs at the Bayon temple (see p.193). By the end of the seventeenth century, however, Champa had effectively ceased to exist, due to the gradual whittling away of their territory by the Vietnamese, and many Cham fled to Cambodia. The *traditional* Cham – who retain many of the old beliefs and rituals, but acknowledge non-Islamic gods – make up about two-thirds of Cambodia's Cham population. They

Phnom Bpros Phnom Srei

A popular outing among locals, **Phnom Bpros Phnom Srei** ("Man and Woman Hills"), as the two hills 8km west of town off National Route 7 are collectively known, can be tacked onto a visit to Wat Nokor ($7–8 return). The lower hill, **Phnom Bpros**, is topped by a collection of modern pagodas, the newest a grey cement structure with touches of ersatz Angkor Wat- and Banteay Srei-style decoration. It's possible to drive to the top of this hill, which is home to a colony of wild monkeys who hang around in the hope of being fed bananas, conveniently on sale at the refreshment stall.

At the foot of the hill, on the way to the second hill, is a collection of **stupas**, built by relatives of the thousands of victims murdered by the Khmer Rouge in the surrounding fields; most of the remains were removed to Phnom Penh in 2000. In an effort to protect the countryside all building in the vicinity has now been banned.

Phnom Srei is the higher of the two hills; leafy and less developed, it's reached by the track across fields past the stupas. From the base, a steep stairway goes straight to the top where, in addition to the view, you can take in the vihara's collection of Buddhas, the older ones dating from the colonial period. The statue of Nandin in front of the altar is much revered, and just asks to be stroked, which is what you'll see most visitors doing.

Back on National Route 7, at nearby Cheung Kok (turn west at Ampil Health Centre) a rural committee manages a small tourist enterprise, where it's possible to hire bicycles for tours of the paddy fields (Ⓣ011/855436, Ⓦamica-web.com).

Phnom Hann Chey

For stunning views of the Mekong, **Phnom Hann Chey**, 20km north of town on the west bank of the Mekong, is hard to beat ($15 return by tuk-tuk). Here you'll find a couple of Phnom Da-era brick-and-laterite prasats cheek by jowl with funky, giant concrete fruits, all in the grounds of a modern pagoda.

Eating and drinking

The town's **restaurants** provide a reasonable choice, with Khmer, Chinese and Western tastes catered for. Across the bridge a cluster of open-terraced restaurants have Khmer and Western food; some have live music and in the evenings you'll

settled around the Tonle Sap, along the central rivers, and in what is now Kompong Cham province. The *orthodox* Cham, who are more similar to Muslims in other Islamic countries, settled around Oudong, Kampot and Takeo. Establishing their own villages, they took up fishing, breeding water buffalo, silver-smithery and weaving, activities that the vast majority still practise today. Their villages can easily be identified by the presence of a mosque and Islamic school, and by the absence of pigs.

The Cham were not spared by the Khmer Rouge: easily picked out because of their Islamic dress and distinctive features (they seldom married outsiders) they were either massacred or persecuted – often by being forced to eat pork – and their mosques were destroyed. However, this has been the only ill-treatment they have experienced in Cambodia, where in spite of speaking their own language (Cham) and maintaining separate traditions, there are no racial tensions – even after a raid in 2003 on an Islamic school to the north of Phnom Penh resulted in three foreign teachers being expelled from the country for their links to the Saudi-backed terrorist group Jemah Islamiyah.

usually find them packed with local men. There are **noodle shops** and **food stalls** around the transport stop and market, while late in the afternoon stalls selling desserts and fruit shakes set up along the riverfront. There's no real **nightlife** in Kompong Cham, but *Lazy Mekong Daze*, the only Western-oriented **bar** in town at the time of writing, is a good place to catch up with other tourists.

Destiny Coffee Shop Just off the riverfront on Vithei Pasteur. This chic café is more Phnom Penh than Kompong Cham, and is the place if you're hankering for home-baked cakes or a slab of quiche with salad – this is also a training centre (free wi-fi).

Hao An Reliable and centrally located, the restaurant has a picture menu of tasty Khmer and Chinese fare, with particularly good fish dishes. At lunch times it's popular with folk on bus tours.

Lazy Mekong Daze On the riverfront. Great spot serving an excellent range of food throughout the day starting with breakfast – Western choices available. It's a great spot to hang out with a beer or cocktail as the sun sets while checking your email on the free wi-fi; later, if you can summon the energy, you can play pool.

Smiles On the riverfront. A trendy new café which is a training centre for orphans and vulnerable children. Western and Khmer fare from early morning until about 10pm. There's free wi-fi, comfy sofas and cheerful staff, but a lack of atmosphere.

Two Dragons Near the traffic circle for the bridge. This is a homely kind of place with a varied Khmer menu; the fried fish with coconut is good.

Kratie and around

Seventy kilometres north of Kompong Cham on the east bank of the Mekong, **KRATIE** (pronounced Kra-cheh) is especially lovely when the river is low and the town seems to be perched on a hill, from the top of which you can look out over the sandy beaches of **Koh Troung**, the large island across from the town. In the rainy season, it's another story, as the surrounding country is engulfed by water and the town virtually turns into an island.

Thanks to the **dolphins** upstream at nearby **Kampie**, Kratie has become a popular stopover on the backpacking circuit. The town itself is a pleasant enough spot to stay overnight, which is about all the majority of visitors do, generally arriving on the first bus in the late morning and spending the afternoon dolphin-spotting before making an escape the next day. A couple of pagodas to the north can easily be visited by moto if you allow yourself a little more time: en route to Kampie you'll pass the appealing hilltop pagoda at **Phnom Sambok**, while further north, about 30km from Kratie, **Sambor** is a quaint little village featuring an outsized pagoda.

Kratie escaped damage despite being occupied by the Khmer Rouge early in their campaign, and the town still has a distinctly French feel, the riverfront retaining some tatty but attractive colonial terraces. To the south of the town centre is a series of large colonial buildings (now housing government departments) and the gracious provincial governor's residence, where tame deer graze in the garden. Life in Kratie revolves around the river, and the riverfront is a good place to watch the comings and goings while you settle down with some sugar-cane juice at one of the stalls.

Practicalities

Getting to Kratie **by road**, although a roundabout journey via Snuol (4–5hr by bus from Phnom Penh; 20,000 riel), is a pleasant enough trip, passing through rubber plantations and skirting rolling fields of pepper, cashew and cash-crop cassava. **Shared taxis** arrive at and depart from the **transport stop** two blocks north of the market.

Buses operated by Phnom Penh Sorya Transport and Rith Mony pull up outside their respective offices, which are both on the riverfront. These companies run daily buses to and from Phnom Penh (25,000 riel), leaving through the morning and taking five hours. Heading north to Stung Treng, National Route 7 is in great shape, and the 140-kilometre journey (20,000 riel by bus) takes just two hours.

The town is easily negotiated on foot and all accommodation lies within 500m of the bus and the transport stops. There's a **tourist office** just off the riverfront 500m south of the town; you'll usually find someone there from 8 to 11am. Both Canadia and Acleda banks change travellers' cheques and have ATMs (Acleda accepts Visa only). Acleda Bank will **change dollars** to riel or you can go to the market. **Internet** access is universally 4000 riel per hour, though speeds are fairly slow. For Western goodies there are a couple of stores by the market or try the mini-market at Tela petrol station in the north of town.

Accommodation

There's a reasonable choice of **places to stay** in Kratie, although none of them are stunning.

Balcony On the riverfront north of the pagoda ⓣ016/604036, ⓦwww.balconyguesthouse.net. A great guesthouse with balcony restaurant and bar overlooking the river; capacious rooms come with hot water and fan; free internet for guests. ❷

Heng Oudom Street 10, near the market ⓣ072/971629. Clean, spacious and competitively priced hotel with a variety of fan and a/c rooms. ❶

Oudom Sambath On the riverfront ⓣ012/965944. The plushest place in town, this hotel has a choice of rooms: the more expensive ones are large, with fancy furnishings, a/c, hot water, TV and fridge, and there are also cheaper and good-value fan rooms. The bustling Khmer restaurant is worth trying even if you're not staying there. ❷–❸

Santepheap On the riverfront ⓣ072/971537. Well-appointed hotel rooms all with TV; more expensive ones have hot water, a/c and a river view. ❷

You Hong On the north side of the market ⓣ012/957003, ⓔyouhong_kratie@yahoo.com. Great budget guesthouse, with a range of clean and cheap rooms, restaurant, internet, book shop, bicycle and motorbike hire, and all traveller services. ❶

Eating and drinking

There's a reasonable selection of places to eat in Kratie but not much **nightlife**. Come the evening you can mix with other travellers at the *Red Sun Falling* or *You Hong*; sup on a fruit shake at a riverfront stall; or join the louche Cambodian crooners in the dingy, back street karaoke bars.

Heng Heng River Rd. The restaurant at the hotel of the same name is open from early morning to mid-evening and has an extensive menu (in English) with a good range of fish and Khmer and Chinese dishes, including pretty good sweet-and-sour vegetables.

Mekong Street 9, just off the River Rd. Khmer restaurant with a reasonable selection of acceptable dishes from an English-language menu.

Red Sun Falling River Rd, near junction with Street 8. This is the first place likely to catch your eye, a welcoming Western-run place that's open from 6.30am for breakfast until late (when the last person leaves). It has a menu of cheap dishes, a range of beers and cocktails and a cosy atmosphere.

Star Corner of Street 10 and Sihanouk. Guesthouse restaurant serving a fair Western breakfast, great shakes and traveller staples like pancakes and sandwiches.

You Hong Street 8, near the market. Economical travellers' restaurant with the usual Asian and Western dishes from around $2.

Around Kratie

You can see the dolphins at **Kampie** in half a day and still have time to visit the meditation centre of **Phnom Sambok** on the way back. With more time, it's possible to make the lovely journey along the river to **Sambor**, 40km north, a site of importance in pre-Angkor times – though nothing remains of the ancient buildings, and the attraction nowadays is the rural market and pagoda.

You'll have no trouble getting a **moto** for the trip to see the dolphins; count on around $8 return including waiting time. Alternatively you can hire a motorbike ($5 per day) or bicycle ($1.50 per day) from Ke Sok Heang shop opposite the post office or *You Hong* guesthouse and go exploring on your own. The fifteen-kilometre trip from Kratie to Kampie takes about forty minutes by moto on a reasonable road along a raised causeway – it's particularly enjoyable in the rainy season when it looks like a never-ending bridge. In Kratie the road is lined with towering tropical dipterocarp trees, all labelled with their botanical names (*Hopea odorata dipterocarpacea*), while a couple of kilometres out of town the highway runs between magnificent teak trees, some of them around a century old (and also tagged with their Latin name, *Tectona grandis*) – these are some of the biggest such trees you're likely to see in Cambodia, now that mature teak has almost completely disappeared from Asia due to illegal logging. The *kompong* houses in this area are particularly handsome, built from the local teak (identifiable by its silvery-grey

Mekong Discovery Trail Part 1

In addition to ideas given in our text, you may be able to pick up a leaflet about the Mekong Discovery Trail (Ⓦwww.mekongdiscoverytrail.com) – an initiative to get tourists off the beaten track – from the tourist office in either Kratie or in Stung Treng; but in case they've run out, we're giving details here.

Koh Trong Island Trail A 9km jaunt by bicycle or on foot around Koh Trong, the island in the Mekong. Take the ferry from the riverfront in Kratie, and once on the island turn north (right) and follow the dirt track around the island; at the extreme southern end there's a small floating village.

Kratie West to East Bank Trail A 44km round trip by bicycle or motorbike with the option to stay overnight at the wat at Sambor (Ⓣ011/768847). From Kratie head south to Peam Te village and turn right for the ferry crossing to the west bank; once across turn north (keeping the river on your right) and follow the dirt road to Vodthonak ferry to cross back to the east bank at Thun, about halfway between Kampie and Sambor. Either head north (left) to Sambor (a further 10km) or south (right) to return to Kratie (around 18km).

See also Mekong Discovery Trail Part 2, p.250.

Irrawaddy dolphins

Freshwater rivers, such as the **Irrawaddy** and **Mekong** in Southeast Asia, and the shallow tropical zones of the **Indian and Pacific oceans,** constitute the habitat of the **Irrawaddy dolphin** (*Orcaella brevirostris*). In the Mekong they now inhabit just a 190km stretch in the north of Cambodia, and can be spotted most easily at Kampie and north of Stung Treng near the Laos border, with occasional sightings elsewhere; in 2001, a pair were found just a few kilometres north of Phnom Penh.

Irrawaddy dolphins look more like porpoises than marine dolphins. The head is rounded, and the forehead protrudes slightly over a straight mouth; noticeably, unlike their seagoing cousins, they have no beak. Their dorsal fins are small and basically triangular, though slightly rounded. They vary from dark blue-grey to slate grey and pale grey, and are darker on the back than the belly.

Irrawaddy dolphins reach maturity at around 5 years of age, when they can measure up to 2.75m in length and weigh up to 200kg. More low-key in behaviour than the marine dolphin, they seldom leap out of the water, instead arching gracefully to expose their heads and backs for a moment before diving again. Family groups, or pods, usually consist of around six individuals, but larger groups are not unknown. In spite of good breeding rates, there is a high rate of calf mortality, which remains unexplained.

patina) and raised on tall stilts, with elaborate red-tiled roofs. Their front doors are level with the road, and you can't help but get glimpses of domestic life – people preparing food, washing clothes, and so on – as you pass by.

Kampie

Cambodians traditionally believe that the **Irrawaddy dolphins** (*psout*) that live around the Mekong rapids at **Kampie** are part human and part fish, and consequently they do their best to look after them. However, the dolphins' numbers have declined sharply due to the use of explosives and electric rods for fishing, and in 2004 the Irrawaddy dolphin was added to the IUCN Red List as a critically endangered species. They can be spotted throughout the year, but you'll get the clearest view in the dry season (Nov–May), when you can take advantage of the low water level to see their backs breaking the surface of the river. They are most active early morning and late afternoon, as this is when they tend to feed, although you'll still need to scan the water carefully to see their snouts or backs emerging a few inches above the murky waters of the Mekong, and photographing them is almost impossible. The site at Kampie is run as an ecotourism venture with fixed prices of $7–9 per person depending on the group size for an hour on the river, with some of the money going to the community. Once boats are out on the water the motor is cut and the boatman rows the craft to prevent disturbing these rare creatures. It's not, however, necessary to go out on a boat to see the dolphins. Just continue about a kilometre upstream, where from dry land, with a little patience, you will almost certainly see them playing near the river bank.

Phnom Sambok

Located in farmland roughly midway between Kratie and Kampie, the tranquil pagoda at **Phnom Sambok** is perfectly suited to its role as a meditation centre. The wooded slopes are dotted with small huts, which act as meditation cells for monks, while at the top the wat is fragrant with frangipani blossom. Murals inside the vihara depict moral fables in which gossips are threatened with having their tongues pulled out; adulterers with being impaled on a spiky tree; and those who cook live animals with being boiled live in a cauldron. Some of the murals show

Chinese and Japanese figures sporting bushy eyebrows and moustaches and wearing red shorts and turbans or bandannas, which is probably a hangover from the brief Japanese occupation during World War II. From the vihara balcony there are great views over the surrounding countryside to the river.

Sambor

Head north from Kampie and you come to the bridge where the Prek Patang joins the Mekong. As the water level drops in the Mekong every dry season, sandy islets are exposed and an impromptu resort (entry 2000 riel) springs up, complete with a wooden walkway linking the shore to the islands and picnic huts. The rapids between the islands are fierce, but there are sheltered places where you can swim.

About 8km north of the bridge, the road forks. The right branch is the continuation of the old National Route 7 to Stung Treng (it joins the new National Route 7 after about 10km), while the left follows the river to **SAMBOR**, a sprawling village with a couple of food stalls and a tiny market. Sambor is most notable for a modern pagoda, **Wat Tasar Moi Roi**, the Pagoda of One Hundred Columns, which was built in 1986 with the express intention of beating the number of columns at any other wat in the country. Other pagodas have now surpassed the figure of a hundred, but the locals point out that there are actually 116 columns, if you count both the round *and* the square ones. One of the columns originally belonged to a thatched temple that stood on the site and is believed to be 400 years old, and you may well be dragged along by a local to have a look. The vihara is also unusual in that it was built facing north rather than the normal east. The oldest stupa in the grounds is the gold one to the north, which claims to house the ashes of a princess and a royal family; clearer is the tale associated with the pagoda, depicted in a series of paintings in the pavilion near the vihara. The story tells how a lady turned herself into a crocodile for fun, and gave a monk a ride – unfortunately an evil fellow-crocodile tipped the monk off her back and gobbled him up. The woman was eventually caught, in her crocodile form, at Banlung and brought back to the pagoda as a trophy, or perhaps to warn other monks against cavorting with crocodiles.

About 500m behind Wat Tasar Moi Roi is the recently restored **Wat Preah Gouk**; now clad in concrete, you'll need to step inside to see the former glory of the old timber-framed pagoda. The magnificent tree in the courtyard is said by locals to be 700 years old, its trunk nearly 10m in circumference. The temple's roof was formerly decorated with golden finials and statues inlaid with precious stones until it was looted by the Khmer Rouge.

In the Mekong, just north of Sambor, the island of Koh Pdao is a community-based **ecotourism venture**; here you can do a homestay and experience local life on the island (from $35 per person for one and a half days; Ⓦwww.crdt.org.kh, Ⓔinfo@crdt.org.kh).

There is talk of the Mekong being dammed at Sambor for a hydropower station and the company concerned, China Southern Power Grid Company, are carrying out surveys.

Stung Treng and around

Situated on the Sekong River, 140km north of Kratie and about 200km west of Banlung, the welcoming town of **STUNG TRENG** is a bit of a backwater. Hopes that it was going to attract tourists heading to Laos have been somewhat dashed as the town is now largely skipped by traffic heading for the border on the excellent National Route 7 which flies across the swanky bridge a kilometre east of town. The town's only true sight is a rather mediocre temple, **Prasat Preah Ko**, but there

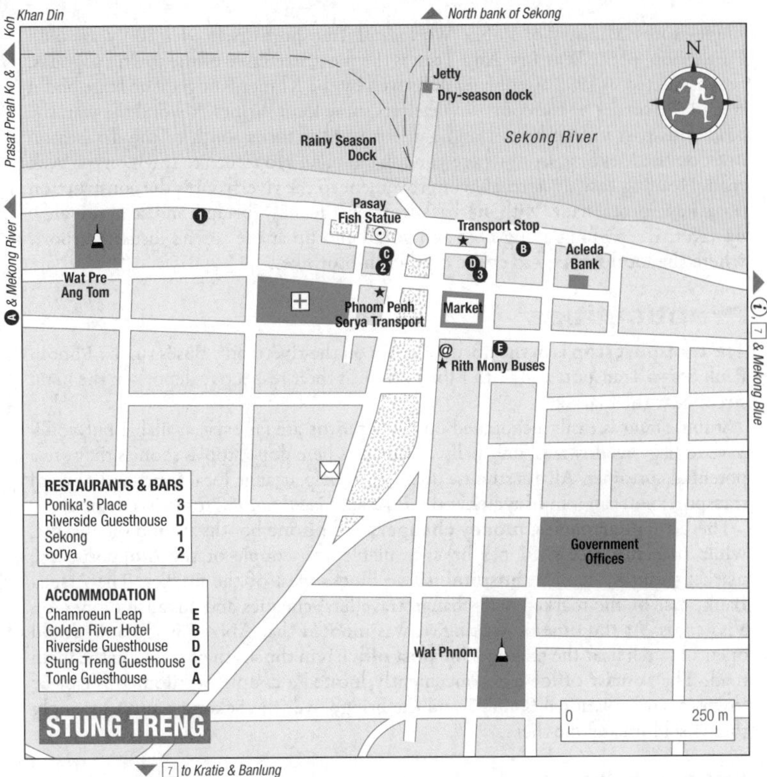

are various attractions in the countryside around, and guesthouse owners can arrange visits to a silk-weaving centre, fruit orchards, lakes, waterfalls and boat trips to remote villages. One of the best outings is a **Mekong trip** to the Lao border, with the chance to do some dolphin-spotting and have a look at the waterfalls that make the river impassable here.

The Town

Smack in the centre of town, Stung Treng's **market** features various products from Laos not available elsewhere in Cambodia, including textiles in plain colours with geometric borders, and wicker rice-steamers. A hardware stall along the main north–south alleyway stocks hand-rolled beeswax candles used for various religious ceremonies; resembling tapers, they're sold by length. Sizes include "finger-tip to armpit", "chin to belly button" and "circumference of the head". As well as the usual gold, a couple of jewellery stands sell silver, some produced in Laos. These days the market spills into the surrounding streets; in the mornings the chunchiet women come to town, selling produce and whatever herbs or roots they've foraged from the countryside.

A **statue** of a *pasay* fish can be found in the patch of gardens on the riverfront, celebrating a prized delicacy which is caught locally in June and July near Stung Treng; although the statue is about the size of a whale, the real fish is quite modest, weighing 1–1.5kg. Strolling west along the river road brings you to some of the town's oldest buildings, notably a bow-fronted Art Deco mansion next to the single-storey Ministry of Public Works and Transport (itself over 100 years old). Further on, petite **Wat Pre Ang Tom** is the most attractive of the town's pagodas, reconstructed in 1992 after being destroyed by the Khmer Rouge. The huge bodhi tree in the corner of the courtyard shelters some local shrines. Beyond the wat, the road runs past village houses and gardens until it turns south to the dry-season dock on the Mekong, from where you can cut inland to return to town on the back road. Heading east, an agreeable improvement to the riverfront is the construction of a new promenade with its backdrop of the new bridge and a good view up-river. Keep going along here and you'll end up at the town's disused airport, where the local guys go to cruise on their motorbikes.

Practicalities

The **transport stop** is in the north of town on the riverfront. Buses run by Phnom Penh Sorya Transport and Rith Mony arrive at their respective depots on the main street near the market.

Stung Treng is easily negotiated on foot; **motos** are (as ever) available but you'll have to flag one down as, unusually, the drivers here don't stop as soon as they see a potential customer. All guesthouse owners can help arrange local **tours** and onward transport; you can rent **bicycles** at the *Riverside Guesthouse* ($2 for half a day).

There are **pharmacies**, **money changers** and **phone** booths around the market, while **internet** access ($1 per hr) is available at a couple of shops opposite the market's south side. The **hospital** is two blocks west of the market. The Acleda Bank, east of the market, will change travellers' cheques and advance money on Visa cards. At the time of writing, it was mooted that ANZ Royal Bank would open a branch near the market. The **post office** is in the south of town on the main road. The **tourist office** is inconveniently located a couple of kilometres east of town towards National Route 7 and the bridge over the Sekong – unsurprisingly there's seldom anyone there.

Accommodation

Stung Treng has a range of accommodation which though not plush, is decent enough for a night or two.

Chamroeun Leap Southeast of the market ☎092/555058. Inexpensive guesthouse with clean and tidy rooms, all with TV; popular with Khmer business trade, the smiling staff are a great plus. ❶

Golden River Hotel Riverfront ☎012/980678. A new establishment overlooking the Sekong River; its rooms with all mod cons are the smartest in town – this is where visiting big-wigs stay. ❸

Moving on from Stung Treng

For Phnom Penh there are several buses a day (40,000 riel) leaving in the morning; these stop at Kratie (20,000 riel) and Kompong Cham (40,000 riel). Alternatively, shared taxis (50,000 riel) leave at around 7am from the transport stop. The buses from Phnom Penh (via Kompong Cham and Kratie) arrive around lunchtime, stopping briefly to pick up passengers for Banlung ($6). Shared taxis for Banlung leave in the morning and take about three hours (25,000 riel), if you want to take the full car ($25–30) they'll leave when it's convenient to you. Places on minibuses with 12–15 seats for all destinations can be booked through your hotel or guesthouse; they leave at around the same time as taxis but take a little longer to complete their journey. You'll pay a dollar or so more than booking direct, but it's generally more convenient as they'll collect you from your accommodation. Heading to the Lao border, you can go by minibus ($5) or shared taxi from the transport stop (around 15,000 riel).

Crossing to and from Laos

Provided you have a valid visa for Laos (called "Lao" in Khmer), you can cross the border (daily 7am–5pm) 57km north of Stung Treng at **Dong Kralor**. The road to the border **from Stung Treng** is now in excellent condition, with a new bridge spanning the Sekong, so there's really no reason to take an expensive boat. Minibuses can be booked through your guesthouse ($5) or you can take a shared taxi from the transport stop.

Entering Cambodia, visas are issued on arrival ($20, plus one photo). Onward transport on this side of the border is now straightforward with plenty of shared taxis (for Stung Treng, Kompong Cham and Phnom Penh) and one or two buses a day (though the bus companies haven't yet worked out that their first bus leaves before the border opens!). None the less, crossing first thing in the morning should mean you get away speedily and without hassle. Note though that if you are heading to Banlung you'll be put off at O'Bpong Mawn, in the middle of nowhere, to wait (usually several hours) for the connecting bus; a far better option is to get off in Stung Treng where you can at least get a meal while waiting for the bus from Phnom Penh to arrive at lunchtime. Alternatively ask around at the border for a direct **minibus** or **taxi**.

Riverside Guesthouse By the transport stop ⓣ012/439454. The best of the bright, clean rooms are at the front, though they're not for light sleepers as they overlook the transport stop; some have a/c for extra cost. Decent food, bar, book exchange, bicycle hire ($1.50 per day), motorbike ($7 per day) hire, boat trips ($15 per hour) and excursions. It's also a good place to meet up with other travellers if you want to share the price of boat hire. ❶

Stung Treng Guesthouse On the main road, across from the market ⓣ016/888177 or 012/430033. It looks more like a furniture showroom, as the heavy polished wooden furniture that's used in the rooms upstairs is on sale in the lobby; the large, bright, rooms come with TV and fan, or a/c and hot water if you pay more. ❷

Tonle Guesthouse 500m west of town on the riverfront ⓣ092/674990, ⓦwww.tourismforhelp.org, ⓔfieldco@tourismforherlp.org. In a traditional wooden house this guesthouse is a vocational centre for disadvantaged youths who train by enthusiastically looking after guests. Simply furnished, but comfy, rooms with fan only, open onto a communal, airy lounge; bathrooms are shared; meals are available but need to be pre-booked. ❷

Eating and nightlife

The **food stalls** on the west and south sides of the market do an excellent selection of cheap dishes and stay open into the evening, by which time the fruit-shake and dessert stalls have set up as well.

Ponika's Place Just northeast of the market. This trendy spot is a wonderful addition to the town's eating options; offering economical Khmer, Western, delicious Indian food (fish or chicken thali for $4) and desserts that include home-made ice cream and custard.

Riverside Guesthouse The restaurant here does a reasonable range of Western and Asian food throughout the day. By night it's really the only Western bar in town.

Sekong Riverfront 100m west of town. The popular restaurant at the *Sekong Hotel* serves up reasonable Khmer food and a few Western dishes.

Sorya On the main road, opposite the market. This Khmer restaurant turns out tasty food, although it's a bit pricey.

Around Stung Treng

There are several places worth visiting around town, some of which can be reached by bicycle or moto, others by boat. One easy-to-reach destination is the Mekong Blue **silk-weaving centre** (ⓦwww.mekongblue.com; closed Sun), run by the Stung Treng Women's Development Centre, 5km east of town along the river.

Mekong Discovery Trail Part 2

If you're lucky you can pick up a leaflet about the Mekong Discovery Trail (Ⓦwww.mekongdiscoverytrail.com) from the tourist office; but in case these have run out we're giving more information here. For Mekong Discovery Trail Part 1, see p.244.

Stung Treng North to Koh Khan Din and Sticky Rice (35km return). Best done by bicycle or motorbike, although you can take a local ferry to Koh Khan Din and walk back (14km). Take the ferry across the Sekong River and head north, at the school turn left until you reach the Mekong and turn right on the river road to Koh Khan Din. If you come by ferry follow this in reverse to head back to Stung Treng. If you're on a bike turn right at Koh Khan Din and after 2–3km you'll hit National Route 7, turn right and head back to Stung Treng. On the way back in the afternoon, you can watch sticky rice being produced at Hang Khou Ban village.

You can walk round the gallery, training centre and showroom, watch the weavers at work and support them by buying a stylish scarf or bag.

Riverside Guesthouse can arrange **boat trips**, either up the Mekong to the Lao border and back (about $80 including lunch) or along the narrower Sekong ($15 per hour). Heading up the Mekong **towards Laos** during the rainy season (June–Oct), you'll float past the treetops of drowned islands – an otherworldly sight. The thundering Khone Phrapheng falls created by a huge geological fault nearly 6km across block the route on into Laos. At Preah Rumkel (10km south of the border) you may glimpse the Irrawaddy dolphins; a homestay is possible here: contact Mlup Baitong (Ⓣ023/214409, Ⓦwww.mlup.org). The scenery along the **Sekong** is also enticing, and the wide sandbars that emerge in the dry season are great places to stop for a secluded swim.

Prasat Preah Ko

Across the Mekong from Stung Treng, the riverside settlement of **THALABARIWAT** is home to the ruined brick towers of **Prasat Preah Ko**, accessible by local ferry (1500 riel one way); the temple is 500m uphill from the village's market. Inscriptions found at Wat Tasar Moi Roi at Sambor (see p.246)

Illegal logging

Between 2000 and 2005 Cambodia lost nearly 30 percent of its tropical hardwood forest cover. Since then even more has been lost (though there are no reported figures) and if you're travelling through the provinces of **Pailin**, **Kompong Thom**, **Kratie**, **Rattanakiri** or **Mondulkiri** you'll now scarcely see any forest at all, with the situation not much better around Koh Kong. Most of the forest has been cleared to make way for plantations of rubber, cashew and cassava, and sadly, this has all been presided over by greedy and self-serving government officials, many of them close to the Prime Minister, Hun Sen.

From 1995 to 1999 multinational conglomerates were awarded logging concessions and used earth-moving equipment to extract massive hardwood trees from deep in the jungle, frequently destroying everything else in their path. This timber was generally shipped on to Thailand or Vietnam, to be turned into garden furniture and sold to Europe. The revenue from this should have swelled the treasury coffers, but instead, high-ranking officials, many military personnel, suddenly became very rich.

Though being lobbied by environmentalists, the Cambodian government lacked the resources and the will to enforce the terms of its logging licences and it wasn't until 1999, when the aid donors insisted on independent monitoring of logging as a suggest that the area was probably under the jurisdiction of a local ruler, and Prasat Preah Ko may have been built here to control river traffic. The stone statue of the sacred bull, Nandin, was once inlaid with gems, though these were stolen by Thai raiders; even stripped of its decoration, it is splendid, with a fine patina and a gentle expression. The statue is flanked by two shrines to an old man, Dah Jouh Juet. A unique annual **festival** is held here in late March or early April by the Jarai (see p.236), involving much loud drumming, men parading with fishing baskets over their heads and great quantities of wine being sprayed around.

Rattanakiri province

Bordering Laos and Vietnam in the far northeast corner of Cambodia, the province of **Rattanakiri** used to abound in lush jungle though these days you'll have to make a huge effort to see it as it's mostly been cleared to make way for plantations of rubber and cashew. But it's still an attractive province, worth the trip for its vistas of misty mountains, meandering rivers and gushing waterfalls. The town of **Banlung**, located pretty much in the centre of the province, is the only base for exploring the area, and with recent improvements in infrastructure has become a popular tourist destination. There are organized treks into the Virachey National Park, but for visiting sights close to Banlung such as Yeak Laom lake and local waterfalls, it's easy to rent a motorbike or hire a moto. Three or four days are enough to explore the area, though bear in mind if you're travelling from Phnom Penh or Siem Reap it'll take a day to get there and a day to get back, and many find the laidback atmosphere so attractive that they end up hanging around for a week or more. As befits a province whose name means "gemstone mountain", traditional gem-mining still persists here, a difficult and dangerous activity; miners drag soil to the surface from deep holes where it is painstakingly sifted for the gems you see in every Cambodian market.

One of the attractions closest to Banlung is **Yeak Laom**, a magical lake set in the crater of an extinct volcano, fringed with bamboo thickets and jungle. The northern part of the province is covered by the largest protected area in Cambodia, **Virachey**

condition of aid provision that the government reluctantly allowed a watchdog group, London-based Global Witness, to investigate the situation. But things were so bad that by 2003 Global Witness had been sacked by the Cambodian government who took exception to the frank reports that denounced it for poor management of the forests and associated corruption at the highest level. For a time the government seemed to be making some attempts to improve things; but no sooner were logging concessions terminated, than they were replaced by economic land concessions, which allowed for the wholesale clearance of forest and stripped the land bare.

Monitoring, although set as a condition of aid provision by the donors themselves – who include Asian Development Bank, World Bank and International Monetary Fund – has not been reinstated and no action has been taken by the donors to limit aid that is being poured into Cambodia at a rate of $1 billion per annum. Meanwhile, the Cambodian government has hawked the rights to the country's other natural resources, including oil, minerals and even sand (with buyers such as Total, Chevron and BHP Billiton). Unfortunately for Cambodians, there's no evidence that the money received for these rights has found its way into the treasury; instead it's more likely to be lining the pockets of the country's elite.

Gem mining in Rattanakiri

Gem mining is primitive and dangerous; miners dig a circular hole about a metre in diameter and as deep as 10m, without any internal supports or reinforcement, and with only candles for light. As the miner goes deeper, the earth is hauled to the surface in a wicker basket using a variety of low-tech winches made of bamboo and rope. A series of small steps are dug in the wall so that the miner can climb out. The main gemstone found in the area is semiprecious **zircon**, which looks like brown glass in its raw state but turns pale blue when heated. Also found in Rattanakiri are yellowish-green **peridot**, pale purple **amethyst**, clear **quartz** and shiny black **onyx**.

The sites where gems are mined in Rattanakiri province change regularly, so it's best to check in Banlung before setting out to look for them. Most activity currently centres around **Chum Rum Bai Srok**, in Bokeo district. There's not much to see – once you've seen one mining pit, you've seen them all – but the 35-kilometre trip from Banlung is interesting for the scenery, the awfulness of the track and for the sheer exhilaration of having made it. The gem-mining camp is difficult to find without a guide (around $15–20 per day; ask at your guesthouse) or a good command of Khmer. South of Ka Chhang, the road soon turns into a narrow churned-up track that winds up and down valleys and forks off left and right through encroaching jungle, until it deteriorates into an even narrower rutted path. If it starts to rain, the track can become impassable and visitors have had to spend the night in the site's blue-tarpaulin-covered shacks.

National Park, within which many endangered species are thought to shelter. Access to the park is difficult unless you go with an organized tour (see p.256), which you'll need to do to see any genuine jungle. On a day-trip from Banlung to **Voen Sai**, a small town on the edge of the park, it's possible to visit nearby Chinese, Lao and chunchiet villages. The journey from Banlung south to **Lumphat** is very different, the countryside consisting of rice fields, tiny streams and scrubby forest. Around here traditional gem-mining still persists.

Banlung

The small town of **BANLUNG** sprang to prominence in 1979, when it was chosen as the new provincial capital, replacing Voen Sai. Set out along wide red-dirt roads, it's reminiscent of a Wild West town in both looks and atmosphere, and although there are no particular sights of interest in town, you could enjoyably base yourself here for a few days while exploring the area and perhaps going on trek.

Arrival and information

There's no quick way to get to Banlung; since flights stopped in 2006 the only way is along National Route 78, a 150-kilometre stretch of (currently) dirt road, from O'Bpong Mawn (20km south of Stung Treng). The **transport stop** is next to the market, just south of the Independence Monument – in the centre of the traffic circle on the main road. The area between the market and the Independence Monument is the nearest the town gets to a centre and is home to an assortment of gem dealers, pharmacies, mobile phone shops and other amenities.

Staff at the town's **tourist office** (Mon–Fri 8–11am & 2–5pm), located behind the "Welcome to Rattanakiri Province" billboard near the overgrown airstrip, do their best to be helpful, and have a few leaflets. But your best bet for local advice remains the hotels and guesthouses; *Tree Top* and *Lake View Lodge* are particularly helpful.

Accommodation

With an increasing range of well-equipped hotels and guesthouses, Banlung has something to suit most people.

Kim Morakat ☎075/974121. This peach-coloured hotel on the main road near the Independence Monument has good-value clean, tidy rooms; bargain hard and you may get hot water thrown in. ❶

Lakeside Chheng Lok ☎097/6460789, Ⓔlakeside-chhenglokhotel@yahoo.com. Set in its own grounds overlooking the lake, this hotel has a block of budget rooms and more comfortable (and expensive) bungalows dotted around the garden with a view of the lake; free internet access. ❷–❹

Lake View Lodge ☎092/785259, Ⓦwww.lakeviewlodge-ratanakiri.com, ⒺLakeviewlodge.ratanakiri@gmail.com. On the outskirts of town near the lake, this friendly family-run guesthouse used to be the governor's residence. Rooms are simple, but large and airy; with a restaurant, wi-fi and free lifts to town. Dorm beds go for $1 per night. A great place to chill. ❶–❸

NorDen House By the Tribal Monument at Yaklom Lake ☎075/6900640, Ⓦwww.nordenhouseyaklom.com. Six pleasant fan-cooled bungalows and Swedish/Khmer restaurant-bar in peaceful gardens with free internet and solar-powered hot water. Electricity hasn't reached Yaklom Lake yet

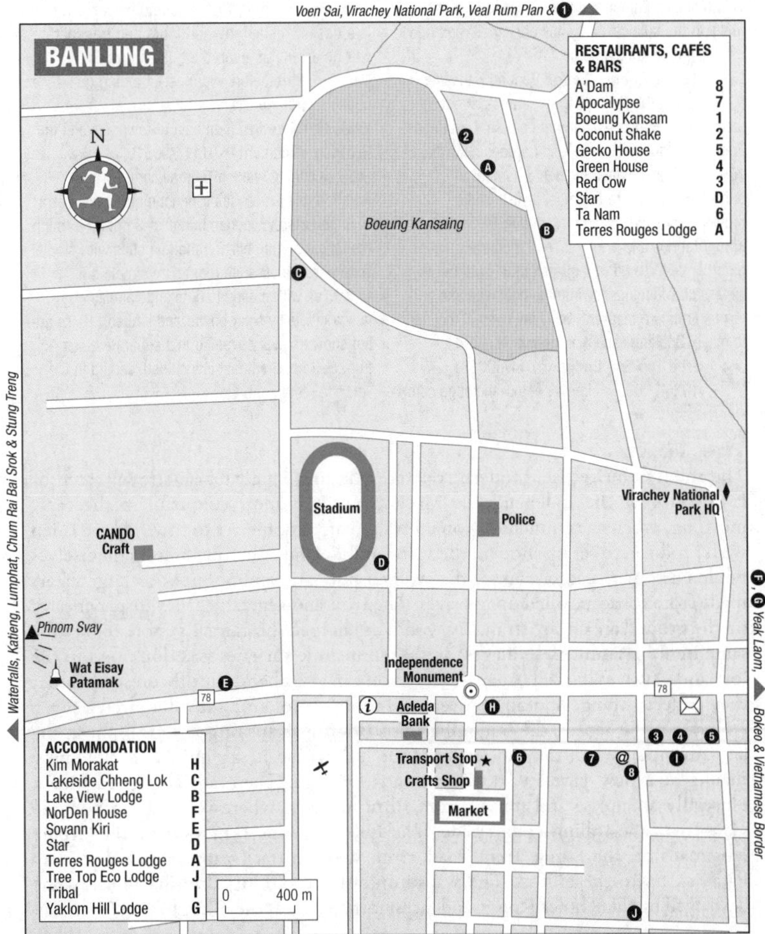

and from 6pm to 6am there's generator power only. 4

Sovann Kiri ⓣ012/654373, ⓦwww.sovannkiri_hotel.com. This vast palace of a place, set back from the road in pleasant gardens on the way into town, isn't as expensive as it looks, and great rooms can be had at a budget price. Rooms are bright and airy with plenty of polished wood, hot water, a/c and fridges; the cheaper rooms are in the motel-style annexe. Internet access, and an on-site restaurant which isn't always open. 2–3

Star 500m northwest of the Independence Monument ⓣ012/958322. Ostentatious, green-tiled hotel off NR78; its vast wood-panelled, en-suite rooms are a bit scruffy now and the bathrooms leaky, and while the communal balcony, courtyard seating and great restaurant-cum-bar, with Chinese, Khmer and Western food help to mitigate the failings, sadly this once well regarded establishment is past its best. 2–3

Terres Rouges Lodge Boeung Kansaing ⓣ075/974051, ⓦwww.ratanakiri-lodge.com, ⓔterresrouges@camnet.com.kh. Luxurious French-run guesthouse in lush gardens near the lake. The rooms, which include a number of bungalow suites, are the most stylish in the province, individually decorated with traditional Khmer fabrics and artefacts, and modern bathrooms. It's a bit of a stretch into town, but with superb surroundings, swimming pool, spa and a terrific French restaurant, you may not feel inclined to move. Booking essential, cash only. 5–7

Tree Top Eco Lodge ⓣ011/600381 & 102/490333, ⓔinfo@treetop-ecolodge.com. Clinging to the valley slopes a range of bungalows scattered across the hillside are reached by raised walkways. The cheapest have shared bathrooms, while the most expensive have a private hammock-strung balcony. Rooms are simply furnished, with natty use of natural materials – showers for example are pebbled with local rocks. Restaurant, bar, internet, excursions and other travellers' services, plus touches like refilling water bottles from a bulk supply. The kindly, switched-on, Mr T also owns *Riverside Guesthouse* in Stung Treng. 1–3

Tribal ⓣ017/858687, ⓔtribal_hotel@yahoo.com. 1km east of the town centre. The cheapest accommodation is a bed in the dormitory ($3 per night); the economy rooms are acceptable, but the most expensive are big and bright and come with a/c, hot water, TV, fridge and balcony. There is a decent restaurant, and tours and transport can be arranged; everything is controlled by Mrs Kim, Rattanakiri's longest-standing guest-house owner. 1–4

Yaklom Hill Lodge 6km east of town, beyond the Hill Tribe Monument ⓣ0111/790510, ⓦwww.yaklom.com, ⓔyaklom@gmail.com. For real isolation this Green Globe-benchmarked eco-resort of fifteen sturdy wooden bungalows dotted through the jungle fits the bill. Perched on stilts with ample verandas, the en-suite rooms are simple but stylish, all with mosquito nets and candles (electricity is by solar power and limited). There are hot showers every evening in a separate block from 6–9pm. Breakfast is included, served in the veranda restaurant. 4

The Town

The town's **market** is a modern concrete building on a rubbish-strewn patch of land south of the Independence Monument. It is most colourful in the early morning, when the chunchiet women walk many kilometres to town, *khapa* laden with produce, to set up shop on the surrounding land. Chatting among themselves while customers gather round, the women puff on bamboo pipes or large cigars made from tobacco rolled up in leaves. The fruit and vegetables they display neatly on the ground are cheap (strangely, you'll be charged substantially more to buy the same items in chunchiet villages) and often include varieties you don't find in the lowlands, such as big red bananas. Here you can also check out the forest food that they collect: strange-looking flowers and roots are sold for a few hundred riel.

North of the centre, the tranquil lake of **Boeung Kansaing** is a nice spot in the late afternoon when the sun sets over the hill behind it; it's quite accessible now thanks to a new paved walkway around the edge. There are also good views, especially at sunrise and sunset, from **Phnom Svay**, where you'll get panoramic vistas over the rolling countryside. The hill lies about 1km west of the airport crossroads off the Stung Treng road, from where a track runs behind Wat Eisay Patamak up to the hilltop. The wat's impressive **reclining Buddha** replaces one destroyed by the Khmer Rouge and faces north towards the misty hills of Voen Sai.

Shopping in Banlung

There's a good shop for **chunchiet crafts**, secured at a fair price by the proprietor, Sok Oeun, tucked in between the mobile phone shops just north of the market. Among the interesting buys here are **khapa,** the chunchiet's all-purpose, basketwork backpacks, woven from bamboo strips with plaited-rattan shoulder straps. The chunchiet produce them in the evenings after the day's work in the **chamkar**, and the finest take over a week to produce. Styles vary with the tribe: the Jarai put a strip of bamboo around the base, while the Tampoun weave intricate patterns and incorporate red-dyed rattan; the plain ones edged with black are Kreung. A large good-quality **khapa** will cost around $10–15 and can be put to decorative or even practical use, especially if your backpack is falling apart. While you're at it, you could go totally native and pick up a decent crossbow and set of arrows here for $7.

The chunchiet produce **textiles** of varying quality and style. Jarai cloth is loosely woven, generally in black with yellow and blue stripes, while the Kreung and Tampoun produce narrow, tightly woven lengths about 2m long for loincloths. Longer, wider lengths suitable for a wrap-around **sampot** are produced by the Tampoun; now that synthetic thread is used the colours are becoming quite vivid – though you can still find cloths in the traditional colours of black, cream and red. You may also come across dried **gourds (kloks)** which are used by the chunchiet for cooling water; carved with geometric patterns on the outside, they're remarkably tough and, being light, are easy to carry home.

CANDO Craft, 1km from town on a cul-de-sac southwest of the stadium (Ⓣ075/974189, Ⓔcandocraft@gmail.com), is an NGO working with the indigenous communities; it has a small shop where you can buy textiles, bags and woven mats.

Plenty of dealers in the centre sell cut and polished **gemstones**, which you can get made up into jewellery here or in the markets of Phnom Penh for $15–20; rings and pendants are also for sale. For uncut stones and large crystals, check out the gem galleries on the road to the market. The gemstones here are hardly world-class, but there's no evidence of fakes being passed off as genuine. Even so, it's not wise to pay a lot of money for a stone you like unless you have a trained eye (see p.252).

Eating, drinking and nightlife

Eating and drinking in Banlung is no longer the province of the guesthouses and new establishments are opening all the time.

A'Dam South of the road to *Tribal* guesthouse. Popular NGO haunt; the restaurant and bar are open for lunch until about 1.30pm and then for dinner from about 6pm til late; draft beer, good Khmer and Thai food for around $3 per dish, Western options available.

Apocalypse On the road to *Tribal* guesthouse, 500m from town. Also known as *Dutch Co & Co.* Though it opens for Western breakfasts, this is really a bar, ideal for an icy early-evening beer, or for a late-evening session while slouched on the sofa watching a DVD – *Apocalypse Now* (of course). No food.

Boeung Kansam Boeung Kansam, 5km north of Banlung. Nestled down by Banlung's lesser-known lake this Khmer restaurant is a great place for a lazy lunch, before hanging around in the hammocks until sundowners.

Coconut Shake Boeung Kansaing, beyond *Terres Rouges Lodge.* Shady Khmer restaurant in a pleasant spot with views across the lake; serves the usual staples, including *amok*, a mild Cambodian curry made with coconut milk (see p.39), and fruit shakes – though the coconut one isn't as good as you'd hope from the name.

Gecko House On the corner opposite *Tribal* guesthouse Ⓣ012/422228. In the mornings it's a café, by lunchtime a restaurant, before morphing into a bar late at night. Serving Thai, Khmer and European food, the chicken with ginger is excellent and the pizzas are crisp with lots of juicy toppings; happy-hour beers, cocktails, free wi-fi, takeaway and helpful staff.

Green House Opposite *Tribal* guesthouse. Khmer restaurant with a good local reputation; volcano beef and soups a speciality.

Red Cow Opposite *Tribal* guesthouse. Tasty Khmer food and nice ambience, though quite similar to *Green House* next door.

Star Good-value travellers' restaurant and bar serving economical, tasty food; though it's best when there's a crowd in and the owner, Mr Leng, is acting as host.

Ta Nam Just east of the transport stop. This reliable and friendly Khmer restaurant does great noodle soup and rice dishes; it doubles as a bakery so you can get coffee and cake from mid-morning to late afternoon.

Terres Rouges Lodge Boeung Kansaing ⓣ075/974051. Meltingly tender *coq au vin* is just one of the French classics at this classy restaurant; booking is essential and some dishes also need to be ordered ahead, but it's the place to go for a special meal by sultry lamplight. Cash only.

Listings

Banks Acleda Bank, a block northwest of the market, advances money on Visa cards only and cashes travellers' cheques for the usual commission; ATM.

Elephant rides Available in several out-of-town locations, typically Katieng (near the waterfalls) where $25 or so should get you an hour or two on a pachyderm's back. Unfortunately, the elephants are often overworked and it's sad to see them trudging around with tourists on their backs, but if it's one of your "must do's" then it's best arranged through your hotel or guesthouse.

Exchange Dollars can be changed at the market and Acleda Bank.

Hospital ⓣ012/528008. Medical services are limited to the basic hospital, north of town by the lake.

Internet There are internet shops dotted around town offering adequate access for $1 per hour. IT Centre Computer, on the road to *Tribal* guesthouse, is friendly and reliable, can burn photos to disc and so on.

Motorbike rental 100cc motorbikes can be rented from guesthouses or a couple of places on the main road near the Independence Monument for $5 a day; off-road bikes cost $10 a day. Rates are cheaper for long-term rentals.

Pharmacies There are plenty on the street running between Independence Monument and the market.

Phones The post office has facilities for international phone calls or use VoIP from the internet shops; domestic calls can be made at the cheap-rate booths near the market.

Police ⓣ012/308988. The police station is just north of the Independence Monument.

Post office On the main road 500m east of the Independence Monument (Mon–Fri 8–11am & 2–5pm).

Swimming Non-residents can use the pool at *Terres Rouges* for $5 per day.

Around Banlung

Road conditions vary dramatically in Rattanakiri; while the road to Yeak Laom lake, and on the Vietnam border is now surfaced, others remain in poor shape. If you're heading out alone it's worth telling someone at your hotel or guesthouse about your route, as punctures and breakdowns do happen. **Hiring a moto** in Banlung, though a little pricier than usual, at $15 per day, is worthwhile as the drivers not only know their way around the province, but are adept at negotiating the rough roads; many also speak some English and can give you a bit of local background too. **Four-wheel drives** with driver can be hired via guesthouses and hotels, where you can also ask about hiring a local guide. The only scheduled local transport is the bone-shaker of a **bus** that leaves Banlung market in the early morning for Voen Sai (2000 riel).

Trekking is the most popular activity in Rattanakiri; every guesthouse will be keen to sell you a trek and there seem to be tour operators on every corner. Treks usually involve a bamboo-raft ride down the river, a bit of a walk and an overnight in a hammock; inclusive rates are around $30 per person per day for two people or $20 per person for four. But on these you'll scarcely get into the forest. Far better are the **organized treks** arranged by the Eco tourism Information Office of the Virachey National Park Headquarters (office hours Mon–Fri 8.30–noon & 2.30–5pm; ⓣ075/974013, ⓦwww.viracheyecotourism.blogspot.com), located in the Ministry of Forest compound three blocks north of the post office, 2km from the centre. This is the only outfit that actually treks in the park area; regardless of what other operators may tell you they only trek in the outskirts. On offer is a range of treks from two to eight days; costs are inclusive of park entry fee, transport, food, indigenous guide and contributions to a community project. Their most popular trip is the O'Lapeung River Valley (three day/two night) trek, which includes walking on the Ho Chi Minh Trail, kayaking down the river and a homestay. Transport costs mean that treks can be very expensive for solo travellers (up to $150); getting a group together (maximum of eight) will reduce the cost dramatically (to around $60–70 per person for three days).

The best of the private operators are The Dutch Couple (contact them at *Apocalypse* ⓣ017/571682, ⓦwww.EcotourismCambodia.info); they help support the indigenous communities where they trek and claim not to use the same trails each time.

The problem, as ever, is that trekking can never be eco-friendly; contact with Westerners, and indeed with Khmers, and loss of their land is changing the way the chunchiet live forever.

Yeak Laom lake

Surrounded by unspoilt forest, the clear turquoise waters of **Yeak Laom lake** (daily dawn–dusk; 4000 riel), 800m across and up to 50m deep, are warm and inviting. There are wooden platforms for bathing, and the three-kilometre track around the lake perimeter makes for a tranquil little hike. The setting is mesmerizing: stands of bamboo rim the lake, lush ferns sprout from fallen trees, the reflections of clouds skim across the lake's surface, and in the late afternoon an ethereal mist can be seen rising off the water. It's no wonder that visitors often make several return trips.

The area is regarded as sacred by the Tampoun, who manage it for the benefit of their community, and chunchiet culture is showcased at the **Cultural and Environment Centre**, 300m anticlockwise round the lake from the entrance steps, which has different styles of *khapa*, textiles, ceramics and other everyday paraphernalia (although unfortunately the room is dimly lit). The small craft stall next door sells locally produced textiles, the money from sales going directly to the community.

To reach Yeak Laom, head east out of Banlung, turn south east at the Hill Tribe Monument; dropping down the hill you reach the lake after 1.5km. The round trip by **moto** costs around $5, including waiting time. Watch out for your stuff – there have been thefts from bags left on the bank while visitors are swimming.

If gardens are your thing, **Thida Phnom Resort** (1000 riel) is a formal garden set on the hillside just northeast of Yeak Laom lake – after the rains the hill is afire with blossom. A couple of lame, and fairly tame, Sarus cranes wander in and out of the shrubs and hedges, while chunchiet women do their weaving near-by; in a shed near the ticket booth an enormous tree root has been intricately carved with images of birds and beasts of the forest. To reach the gardens, which purport to be the biggest (and possibly only) in Cambodia, turn east just before entering Yeak Laom protected area; the turning to the gardens is about 500m up the road.

North to Voen Sai

On the pretty San River, **VOEN SAI**, 35km from Banlung, is the largest village in the vicinity of Virachey National Park; tourists come here to visit the nearby Chinese, Lao and Kreung villages, and it's easily reached by moto from Banlung.

As you head north out of Banlung past Boeung Kansaing, the road climbs steadily to the O Chum crossroads, about 10km from Banlung and signposted in English. The road east here goes to **Veal Rum Plan**, 4km away, an ancient **lava**

field of huge flat stones that could put many a Phnom Penh pavement to shame. Along the main road, the jungle has been cleared to make way for farms of pineapple, pepper, cashew and banana; sadly the chunchiet have been moved out of the forest to live in settlements.

On the outskirts of **Voen Sai** the **Virachey National Park** office is closed due to lack of funds. From here it's a couple of kilometres to the river and the centre of the village, where food and drink stalls and a couple of shops cluster together around the ferry to the far bank (2000 riel one way), on which there are some Chinese and Lao villages, notably different in appearance to others in the area. The Chinese village a couple of kilometres to the west has a tidy school and a general store; the main street is flanked by neat bright-blue houses planted firmly on the ground rather than on stilts. **Boats** can be hired at the river bank in Voen Sai for the trip east upstream to Kreung and Kraval villages (30min–1hr) and further on to a chunchiet cemetery (3hr); the trip all the way to the cemetery costs around $50 return.

The waterfalls

There are a few modest but picturesque **waterfalls** within easy reach of Banlung. The falls at **Chha Ong** (2000 riel) are the largest, the river flowing through lush jungle before plunging 30m into a gorge. The pool at the base is deep enough to swim in, and daring souls can climb onto a ledge behind the curtain of water. To reach the falls, head 2km west on National Route 78 to the signposted junction, then turn right (northwest) and continue 6km to the falls.

If you turn left (south) at the junction, the road runs through rubber plantations and past a rubber factory before heading downhill to a small bridge just beyond a line of food stalls and karaoke joints about 4km from the main road. Just before the bridge, a small path to the right leads into a bamboo-clad valley and down to the **Ka Chhang** falls, just 10m high, with a pool for taking a dip.

To get to **Katieng** falls, head back towards town and take the first narrow road on the left leading up a slope, then continue for about 4km until you reach a small river. Follow the path to the right on the opposite side of the river to reach the falls. Around here there's the opportunity for an **elephant ride** for about $10–15 per hour, but it's easier to make arrangements through your hotel or guesthouse. However, for a more authentic elephant-back excursion you're better off in Mondulkiri.

Lumphat

LUMPHAT is around 35km from Banlung, reached by heading west on the NR78 and taking a southbound turning after about 8km (the next one after the turning to the waterfalls – but it is safer to ask, as lots of new tracks are cropping up). Plans are being hatched to develop the Lumphat as a tourist resort, so there may be a signpost by the time we're in print. It's a scenic journey, the landscape varying from rice fields to scrubby forest until you arrive at the town and the Srepok River. Lumphat was the provincial capital during the Sihanouk era, and many maps still show the airport here, although it ceased to be the provincial capital in 1975 when the Khmer Rouge moved it to Voen Sai. Today, Lumphat remains a scattered village, with a few ruined concrete buildings the only testimony to its days as provincial capital. Patches of cratered wasteland bear the scars of B-52 bombing runs and rusty metal lies around in the undergrowth; if you want to see bomb craters, the best spot is on the edge of the village near the water tower. Though there are no land mines here, **unexploded ordnance** may still be a risk.

Mondulkiri province

Mountainous, sparsely populated **Mondulkiri** province sees fewer travellers in a year than Rattanakiri does in a month. Despite heavy logging, Mondulkiri still has impenetrable jungle and is home to rare and endangered wildlife, including water buffalo, Asian dogs, elephants and green peafowl. Besides its jungle scenery and cool climate (conducive to hiking), Mondulkiri's attraction lies in its isolation, although the only sights accessible to visitors are the compact provincial capital, **Sen Monorom**, and several gushing **waterfalls**, among them the mighty **Bou Sraa**. It's the place to come for an authentic elephant trek, and the chance to help out at an elephant care centre.

The main group of indigenous people of this impoverished province are the Phnong; not so long ago they made up nearly eighty percent of its population. In the 1990s they were joined by an influx of Khmer, who returned from the refugee camps in Thailand and could not afford to live in Cambodia's towns; the Khmer are still coming, though nowadays it's rich ones who are buying land cheaply then clearing it for farms and plantations. In recent years there have been a number of incidences of Vietnamese hill tribes (*montagnards*) fleeing here to avoid persecution at home; initially they were put in refugee camps set up by the UN, but most have now either been repatriated or have emigrated to the US. Most recently, easy access to the province has seen expats moving here, either seeking a reclusive haven or looking for a business opportunity.

Regrettably, Mondulkiri's unique, grassy rolling hillsides continue to be threatened; a few years ago bauxite was discovered by the Australian giant BHP Billiton, though fortunately they've decided that the reserves aren't worth bothering with (for the moment). Now, with the blessing of the Cambodian government, Chinese gold miners are quarrying about 51km northwest of Sen Monorom in Mimong.

Sen Monorom

SEN MONOROM is still little more than a large village with its houses spread sparsely over a couple of kilometres, culminating in a cluster of buildings around the

Getting to Mondulkiri

Getting to Mondulkiri is no longer a punishing experience; the road from Snuol was upgraded in 2010 making it possible to get from Phnom Penh to Sen Monorom in five hours by speedy taxi. Buses make the trip too, but take three hours longer, arriving in Sen Monorom sometime after 3pm. If you're travelling to Sen Monorom from Kratie **under no circumstance take a big bus** – you'll be put off at the road junction outside Snuol and have to wait for hours in the middle of nowhere for a connection; instead take one of the now-reliable minibuses that leave at about 8am (your guesthouse can book this for you, but let them know the day before) and you'll be in Sen Monorom around noon. Vehicles also run from **Kompong Cham** and **Snuol**, although getting a lift anywhere in between is difficult as it's hard to find a spare seat. After Snuol, the road heads east through **Snuol Wildlife Reserve** climbing steadily until it reaches the 900-metre-high plateau around 40km from Sen Monorom. Close to town, the landscape changes to rolling grass-covered hills – more reminiscent of England than Cambodia, and possibly the result of years of slash-and-burn cultivation – dotted with copses of pine, planted in the late 1960s at the king's behest.

Experienced **off-road bikers** may want to tackle the tracks between **Banlung** in Rattanakiri province from Sen Monorom; in the dry season (Nov–May) the journey can be done in a long day.

market in the centre of town. You can set off on foot in any direction and soon be in unspoilt and isolated countryside, though there are only a limited number of tracks.

Practicalities

Taxis and minibuses arrive and leave from the transport stop in the north of town, just uphill from the market; the driver will usually drop you off at a guesthouse of your choice. Buses run by Rith Mony and Ngi Lyheng stop at their respective depots on the main road.

The Acleda Bank, a couple of kilometres out of town towards Phnom Penh, changes travellers' cheques for the usual commission and advances money on Visa cards only; at present there is no ATM. It's rumoured that the bank may move closer to town in the near future – possibly to near the hospital. You can change dollars into riel at the market.

The tourist information office (Mon–Fri 8am–noon & 2–5pm) is at the top of the hill by the traffic circle; the post office is further north on the other side of the disused airstrip (which apparently has been sold to developers). If you get sick the only choice is the provincial hospital just out of the centre towards Phnom Penh; there are pharmacies around the market. Internet in town still isn't great, try *Green House* or the "no name" internet shop near *Phanyro Guesthouse* (both $1–2/hr).

At some point you're going to want to get out of town; regular and off-road motorbikes are available to rent at the guesthouses (around $10 per day, plus fuel), but road conditions vary dramatically so it's best to check before you commit yourself. By way of progress, there are newly installed road signs to help you find your way out of town at least; but if you're at all nervous it's best to hire a moto driver (around $25–30 per day). For treks in the area, and especially if you're keen to take the direct route to Banlung, contact Mony Hong at Mondulkiri Extreme (ⓣ085/586312, ⓔmony.hong@yahoo.com); trips are not cheap but you are assured of an authentic off-the-beaten track experience, with a licensed English-speaking guide, everything provided. Mony even bumped into celebrity chef Gordon Ramsey, on his latest cooking expedition in the middle of the jungle.

The Bunong Place (ⓦwww.bunongcentre.org), on the main road just south of the market, is a good place to pick up information on the chunchiet and buy souvenirs. The Bunong (Phnong) staff here can also arrange visits to the villages and elephant treks; they also hire out mountain bikes ($5 per day). Coffee lovers could consider buying Mondulkiri Coffee from the store near the market. At the time of writing a mini-market was opening up on the main road towards the traffic circle; this may be the place to pick up a Western goody or two.

Around Sen Monorom

The two lakes close to town are pleasant for an early morning or late afternoon stroll, while 2km northeast from town, is the sacred mountain, Phnom Dosh Kramom (known as Youk Srosh Phlom to the Phnong), a small hill with a meditation pagoda, from which there are splendid views. Keep going for a further 5km or so on the same road, then turn off right along a track and you'll come to oddly named Sea Forest (follow the signs); if you're lucky you'll have the area to yourself and be able to gaze wistfully into the misty distance where the majestic trees of the remaining jungle meet the sky. Look at it from upside down – legs astride with your head between them – and you can see why the forest got its name, for indeed it does seem that you're all at sea.

Elephant treks

Cambodia's highlands used to be home to 10,000 elephants, now there are just a few hundred with just 56 in domestic use in Mondulkiri. ELIE (Elephants Livelihood Initiative Environment) is an NGO working in Mondulkiri with the Phnong and their domestic elephants. The Elephant Valley Project, 10km northwest of Sen Monorom, is a haven, created in cooperation with local communities, where sick elephants are treated, mahouts trained and volunteers can stay in one of eight on-site bungalows. To help out with the care of elephants for the day will set you back $50, while volunteers on the week programme will have to fork out $100 per day all found; note too that on neither of these activities you get to ride the elephant. In fact ELIE actively discourages the riding of elephants, many of which are over-worked, malnourished and badly mistreated by their handlers – all issues that ELIE are working to improve. At the time of writing ELIE (ⓣ012/228219, ⓦwww.elie-cambodia.org, ⓔjackhighwood@yahoo.com) was due to open an office in town near the hospital where you can go in to ask about their work and to book a visit.

However, the reason that many visitors venture to Mondulkiri is to take an elephant ride through the jungle. Guesthouse or bar owners in Sen Monorom can help you arrange it, or contact The Bunong Place on the main road in town. Treks start either from the village of Phulung, about 8km north of town, or from Potang, 8km to the south; a half- or full day rolling around on an elephant costs $15/30, including transport to the village, a Phnong-speaking guide and lunch if you're out for the full day. Overnight camping treks are also possible, but for most the novelty wears off after a few hours of bumping about.

Accommodation

Considering it has only recently become accessible, Sen Monorom has a startling range of decent accommodation, none of it expensive, so your main consideration is probably going to be whether you want to stay in town (close to restaurants and the market), on the outskirts of town, or out in the country. This is the one place in Cambodia thats worth having the hot water and forgetting the air conditioning.

Arun Reah II ⓣ016/255999, ⓔarunreah mondulkiri@gmail.com. On the Phnom Penh road, about 2km from town, *Arun Reah* is the first place you'll come to on the way in from the south. Spread out over the hillside the most basic huts have a cold shower, balcony and fantastic views, while deluxe bungalows come with hot water and TV. There's a restaurant, internet access, free bicycles and motorbike hire. ❷–❸

Holiday ⓣ012/936606. A good budget option, this guesthouse has clean, tidy rooms in the centre of town, just down from the traffic circle. ❶

Long Vibol ⓣ012/944647, ⓔlongvibol12@yahoo.com. 1km from town towards Bou Sraa, *Long Vibol* has a selection of bungalows; the cheapest are no-frills, while the better ones have balconies, hot water and TV. It's appealing for its gardens, but quite a stretch to town; at weekends and public holidays it can get a bit rowdy. ❷–❸

Mondulkiri ⓣ012/777057, ⓦwww.mondulkiri-hotel.com. The plushest place around, this hotel is on the back road between the hospital and the wat. It has smart rooms, all with hot water, air conditioning, TV and mini bar; there's also a quite decent restaurant overlooking the river. ❸

Oeun Sakona ⓣ012/950680. In town, on the main road, just down from the market, this newish hotel has big, clean, airy rooms with hot water and TV, but not much ambience. ❷

Phanyro 500m from town, coming from Phnom Penh turn right opposite *Pich Kiri* ⓣ017/770867. Great little guesthouse with spacious, clean bungalows with hot water; it's often full when NGOs are in town. ❷

Pich Kiri On the uphill stretch on the way into town just east of the market ⓣ012/932102. Welcoming Madame Deu and her family oversee Sen Monorom's longest-running guesthouse; the cheapest rooms are slightly musty with fan and cold water only, while the best are in the classy new block and are larger, plusher and come with hot water. There's a great restaurant, leafy garden and seating to lounge away a few hours. ❷–❸

Sum Dy On the way into town near Acleda Bank ⓣ092/285721. Large bungalows on the road into town with views over the hillside; nicely furnished rooms have hot water, fans and balconies. The downside is that it's 1.5km to town and there's no restaurant or bar. ❷

Eating, drinking and nightlife

It used to be hard to get decent food in Mondulkiri, but things have changed and there are now choices to suit all pockets, from the cheap market stall to the great, though pricier, *Banana's*. Mondulkiri is also the one place in the country where avocados grow, and in season (April–June) you can buy basketfuls at a giveaway price. As ever, basic rice dishes and noodle soup can be had for breakfast at the market, but expect to pay around $1–2 though, as food here is a little more expensive than in other provinces. Sen Monorom goes to bed early, and nights can seem quite long; other than *Banana's*, your options are *The Green House* or one of the Vietnamese coffee shops north of the market.

Banana's 500m down the hill from the Oeun Sakona (noon–2pm & 6pm–till late). Tanja dishes up European delights with a Cambodian twist using local ingredients: schnitzels and meat balls are favourites, served up with vegetables or salads and often a slab of home-made bread. The food isn't cheap ($6–7) but servings are generous and you can ask for more bread; the house cake changes daily. Set in a mini-jungle by the river, this is a terrific place to hang out, drink a beer or cocktail or two and read something from the vast library of books – Elvis and DT, the house bulldogs, will keep you company.

Chom Nor Themei Off the main road 200m from Oeun Sakona. This is a popular place with a good (translated) menu and a few Western choices; their chicken or beef with Cambodian spices goes down well after a hard day on the hills, though they can seem to be more interested in serving Khmers than foreigners. Note that they expect to move to a new location on the main road towards the traffic circle.

Khmer Kitchen On the main road. Open throughout the day and popular with the NGO crowd. Sound Khmer/Chinese food for around $3 per dish.

The Green House On the main road near the market. This bar opens in the late afternoon serving beer, cocktails, shakes and a few simple meals; it's a good place to pick up local news and arrange trips. Its internet ($1 per hr) is as reliable as it gets in Sen Monorom.

Waterfalls around Sen Monorom

Immortalized in a song by the late, great Cambodian singer Sin Sisamot, **Bou Sraa** waterfall is a fabulous two-tiered cascade 35km from Sen Monorom, towards the Vietnamese border. The setting alone makes the falls worth visiting, the river dropping over 30m into a jungle gorge; though the road was improved by a private concern (toll $2) it's still not brilliant and in the rainy season can be tortuous – making it easy to see why the locals get around by elephant. Expect the journey to the falls to take an hour and a half or more.

Not nearly as dramatic as Bou Sraa, but easier to get to and reasonably pretty, are the three-tier **Romanea falls**: take the main road back towards Snuol for about 10km, and then fork left and left again. To get to either Bou Sraa or Romanea you'll need either to rent a motorbike from a guesthouse (around $10–15 a day) or hire a moto (about $30 a day); note though that the road to Romanea is unsurfaced and although at the time of writing in a reasonable state this can vary with a good rain storm.

It's possible to walk the 5km to the northwest of town to the ten-metre-high **Monorom waterfall** (also known as the Sihanouk falls). Along the way you'll pass the ruins of the (rarely used) royal residence, after which you should follow the left fork to the falls. You can swim in the pool at the base of the falls, even in the dry season.

Travel details

Shared taxis leave to no set schedule from early morning until mid-afternoon, though to and from Rattanakiri and Mondulkiri you'll generally be on the road by 8am. Note that the frequencies given below are only approximate, and the earlier in the day you get to the transport stop, the easier it is to get away. Under no circumstances take the big bus from Sen Monorom to Kratie (or vice versa) – you'll get put off at Snuol and have to wait hours for a connection; instead take a minibus that your guesthouse can arrange and you'll be in Kratie (or Sen Monorom) for lunch.

Buses

Banlung to: Kompong Cham (3 daily; 6hr); Kratie (3 daily; 4hr); Phnom Penh (daily; 8hr); Voen Sai (daily; 2–3hr).
Kompong Cham to: Banlung (daily; 6hr); Kompong Thom (3 daily; 2hr 30min); Kratie (4 daily; 3hr); Phnom Penh (11 daily; 2hr 30min); Poipet (daily; 7–8hr); Siem Reap (3 daily; 5hr); Stung Treng (3 daily; 5 hr).
Kratie to: Banlung (3 daily; 5hr); Kompong Cham (4 daily; 3hr); Phnom Penh (3 daily; 7hr); Stung Treng (3 daily; 2hr).
Sen Monorom to: Kompong Cham (2 daily; 4hr 30min); Phnom Penh (2 daily; 7 hr).
Stung Treng to: Kompong Cham (3 daily; 5hr); Kratie (3 daily; 2hr) Phnom Penh (3 daily; 8hr).
Voen Sai to: Banlung (daily; 2–3hr).

Shared taxis and minibuses

Banlung to: Kompong Cham (several daily; 6hr); Kratie (3 daily; 6hr); Phnom Penh (several daily; 8hr); Stung Treng (4 daily; 2hr 30min).
Kompong Cham to: Banlung (several daily; 8hr); Kompong Thom (6 daily; 2hr); Kratie (6 daily; 2hr 30min); Phnom Penh (20 daily; 2hr); Poipet (several daily; 7hr); Prey Veng (4 daily; 2hr); Sen Monorom (1–2 daily; 4hr); Siem Reap (6 daily; 4–5hr); Skone (20 daily; 30min).
Kratie to: Banlung (3 daily; 5hr); Kompong Cham (6 daily; 2hr 30min); Sen Monorom (daily; 4hr); Stung Treng (6 daily; 2hr).
Sen Monorom to: Kompong Cham (daily; 3hr); Kratie (daily; 4hr); Phnom Penh (daily; 5hr); Snuol (daily; 2hr).
Snuol to: Sen Monorom (daily; 2hr).
Stung Treng to: Banlung (4 daily; 4hr); Kratie (6 daily; 2hr); Phnom Penh (4 daily; 7hr).

6

Sihanoukville and the south

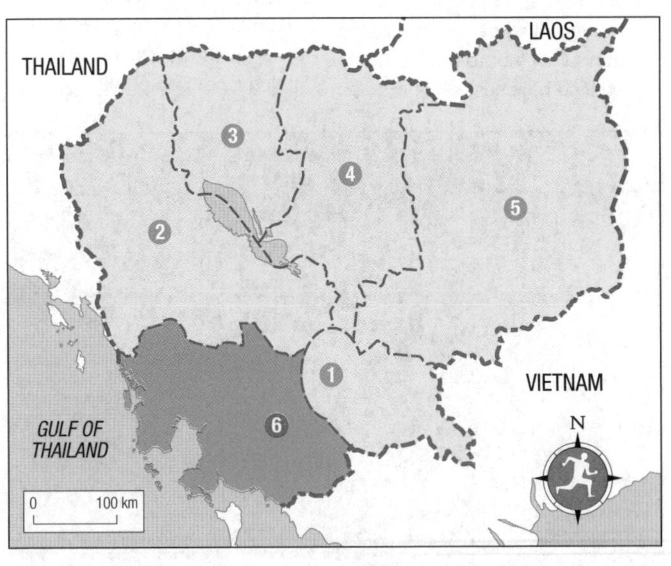

CHAPTER 6

Highlights

* **National parks** From the cool pine-studded hills and waterfalls of Kirirom to the stunning coastal scenery of Ream, the region's natural beauty is begging to be explored. See p.269

* **Sihanoukville** Cambodia's premier party town, mixing wild nightlife with a relaxed beach vibe. See p.272

* **Island hopping** Escape the mainland crowds for unrivalled peace and tranquillity, not to mention pristine beaches, on one of the south coast's palm-fringed islands. See p.284

* **Kampot** A charming riverside town with a rich colonial history that makes an ideal base for exploring the surrounding area's caves, waterfalls and islands. See p.292

* **Kep** Enjoy crab feasts at the beachside market or sip a sundowner in sumptuous luxury at this 1960s seaside resort now being restored to its former elegance. See p.298

▲ In the water at Sihanoukville

6

Sihanoukville and the south

It's a wonder that so few people visit Cambodia's southern provinces, given the ravishing contrasts created by a near-iridescent green quilt of rice paddies, the looming crags of the Cardamom and Elephant mountain ranges and a palm-fringed coastline stretching over 440km. The relative inaccessibility of much of the **southwest**, thanks to heavy forest cover, the presence of the mountains and the lack of roads, only add to its charm.

The central part of southern Cambodia – roughly comprising **Kampot** and **Takeo provinces** – is dotted with craggy karst formations that project starkly from the plains. This is one of the country's most productive agricultural regions: parts of Kampot province are like one vast market garden, producing durian, watermelon and coconuts, while in Takeo province rice paddies dominate. Salt and pepper are also key products. The former is extracted from the saltpans of the coast and plays an important part in the manufacture of the country's *prohok* (salted fermented fish paste); the latter is cultivated almost like hops, with regimented vines clinging to cords, and was once *the* condiment of the colonial occupiers – at the time, no Parisian table worth its salt was without Kampot pepper.

Most visitors come to the south to hit the beach at **Sihanoukville**, its white sands washed by warm, shallow waters. The town sits on a peninsula jutting into the Gulf of Thailand, its coastline scalloped with gently shelving, tree-fringed white-sand beaches, and misty islands looming enticingly out at sea. But don't expect atoll-like isolation: the town is attracting increasing numbers of party-animals keen to live it up in the clubs by night and in the beach bars that line **Ochheuteal Beach** by day. That said, a short moto ride along the coast in either direction uncovers stretches of less developed, peaceful beach, particularly during the week.

On the way to Sihanoukville, just two hours' drive south from the capital, you could stop off at **Kirirom National Park** to enjoy mountain scenery and experience a Cambodian **homestay**. Sihanoukville itself is the jumping-off point for another area of outstanding natural beauty, **Ream National Park**, with mangrove forest and fine sandy beaches. East of Sihanoukville, **Bokor National Park** may still be worth visiting for an eerie walk around the abandoned hill station amid its jungle-clad slopes, although private development is set to diminish some, if not all, of its unearthly appeal. It's most easily reached from the charming riverside town of **Kampot**, as is **Kep**, an increasingly popular seaside destination.

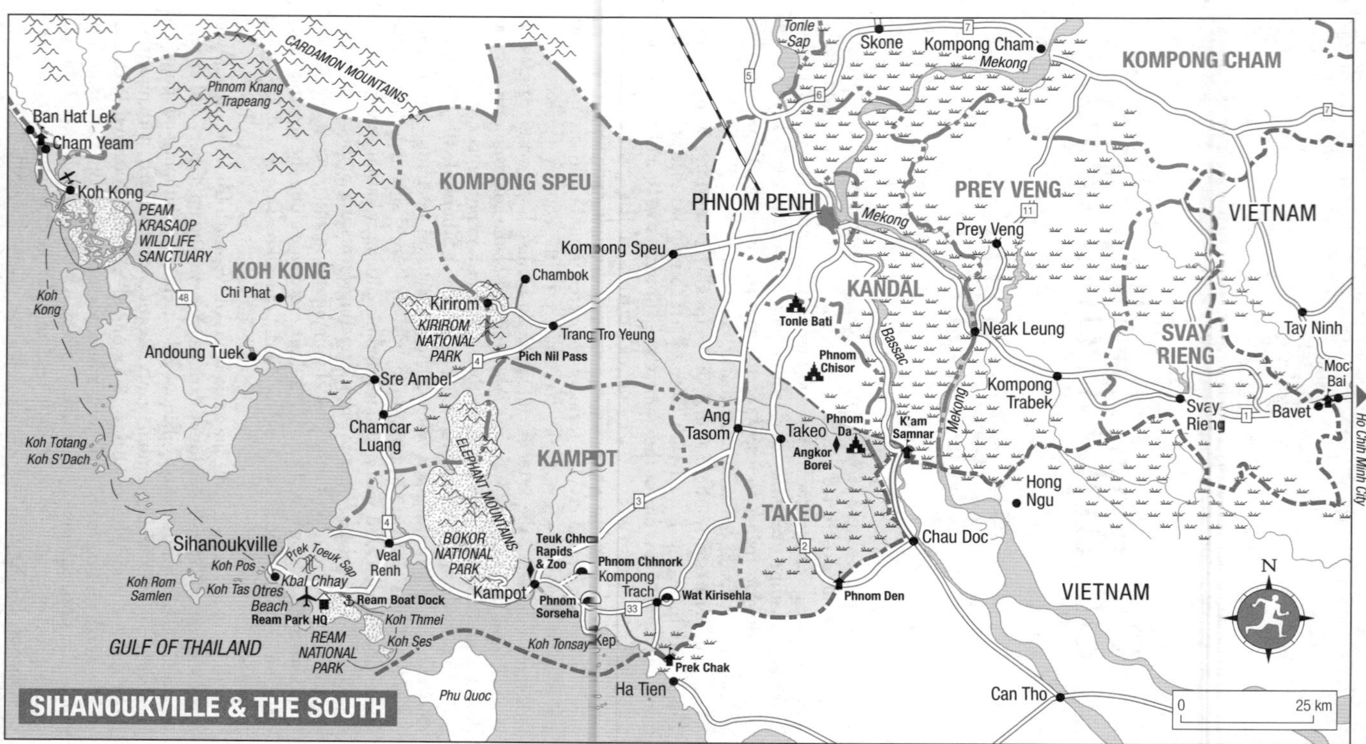
SIHANOUKVILLE & THE SOUTH
KOMPONG CHAM
VIETNAM
PREY VENG
SVAY RIENG
KANDAL
PHNOM PENH
TAKEO
KAMPOT
KOMPONG SPEU
KOH KONG
VIETNAM
GULF OF THAILAND
CARDAMON MOUNTAINS
ELEPHANT MOUNTAINS
Ho Chih Minh City
Tonle Sap
Skone
Kompong Cham
Mekong
Prey Veng
Tay Ninh
Moc Bai
Bavet
Svay Rieng
Neak Leung
Kompong Trabek
Hong Ngu
Chau Doc
Can Tho
K'am Samnar
Bassac
Tonle Bati
Phnom Chisor
Phnom Da
Angkor Borei
Takeo
Phnom Den
Ang Tasom
Wat Kirisehla
Prek Chak
Ha Tien
Kompong Trach
Phnom Chhnork
Kep
Koh Tonsay
Teuk Chhou Rapids & Zoo
Phnom Sorseha
Kampot
BOKOR NATIONAL PARK
Phu Quoc
Kompong Speu
Trang Tro Yeung
Pich Nil Pass
Chambok
Kirirom
KIRIROM NATIONAL PARK
Sre Ambel
Chamcar Luang
Veal Renh
Ream Boat Dock
Koh Thmei
Koh Ses
REAM NATIONAL PARK
Ream Park HQ
Prek Toeuk Sap
Kbal Chhay
Sihanoukville
Otres Beach
Koh Pos
Koh Tas
Koh Rom Samlen
Chi Phat
Andoung Tuek
Phnom Knang Trapeang
PEAM KRASAOP WILDLIFE SANCTUARY
Koh Kong
Cham Yeam
Ban Hat Lek
Koh Kong
Koh Totang
Koh S'Dach
N
0
25 km
1
2
3
4
5
6
7
11
33
48

East of here, you'll find the down-at-heel remains of the Funan-era city of **Angkor Borei**, home to a fascinating museum of early statuary and interesting records of the archeological digs of the ancient city scattered around the town; close by, the hilltop temple of **Phnom Da** is most easily visited by boat from **Takeo**, a shabby little town that still feels far removed from the tourist trail, despite its proximity to Phnom Penh.

Communications between the larger towns in the south are pretty good by Cambodian standards, with continual road works marking the progress. Travelling along **National Route 4**, one of the country's busiest roads, you can get from Phnom Penh to Sihanoukville in under five hours. From Phnom Penh, two other major roads lead south. The tarmac on **National Route 3** to Kampot was near completion at the time of writing, and dramatic improvements have been made to the route from Kep to Vietnam. **National Route 2** is also in the process of being asphalted as far as Phnom Den for the crossing to Vietnam. If you're arriving in this part of Cambodia **from Thailand**, it's possible to reach the capital using **National Route 48**, via the sleepy border town of **Koh Kong**, which not only links up with National Route 4, but makes a good base for exploring the surrounding natural attractions.

Phnom Penh to Sihanoukville

Leaving Phnom Penh, **National Route 4** makes its way through a typical Cambodian landscape of rice fields and sugar palms. South of Kompong Speu the views alter dramatically as the distant blue peaks of the Cardamom Mountains to the north and the Elephant Mountains to the south begin to loom on the horizon. A detour takes you to the pine-clad hills of **Kirirom National Park**, often ignored by travellers, but well worth the effort of reaching for its almost alpine scenery, crisp mountain air and **Chambok**, a community-based ecotourism site.

Kirirom National Park

The rolling hills of the **Kirirom National Park** are zigzagged with well-trodden trails and dotted with waterfalls, lakes and abundant wild plants. An important wildlife sanctuary, the park's slopes are home, despite illegal logging, to forests of *Pinus merkusii*, a pine tree not found anywhere else in Cambodia. Although poaching has taken its toll, species of deer, wild ox (gaur and banteng), elephant and leopard still inhabit the depths of the park. In a 1995 survey, tiger tracks were found, but the lack of subsequent sightings gives little hope that tigers survive here today.

In the 1940s a road was cut through the forest, and the development of a hill station began following a visit from King Norodom who named the area Kirirom, which means Happiness Mountain. Building the hill station was hard work, with construction perpetually hindered by the Khmer Issarak guerrilla troops who prowled the forests until the 1960s. The completed resort was abandoned during the Khmer Rouge years only to become accessible again as an attractive holiday destination, which included two royal residences, in 1996.

From the entrance, the road climbs steadily for 16km to a rolling forested **plateau**, where you'll find the majority of the park's attractions and its few facilities. About halfway up the hill, a signpost points down a narrow path to **Outasek waterfall**, a series of cascades just a short hike off the main road. There's always some water for splashing about in here, except during the very driest part of the year.

One of the first things you'll see when you arrive on the plateau is the *Kirirom Guesthouse*; a side road beyond here leads to a cluster of derelict buildings, including the newer of the two **royal residences**, a fairly well preserved white-ish

Cambodia's conservation muddle

With proper, sustainable management, Cambodia's **forests** could represent a valuable source of income for the country, not just in terms of providing timber, but also as a focus for eco tourism. Regrettably, the last few decades have seen forest cover in Cambodia decline dramatically, with the most recent survey by the UN Food and Agriculture Organization (FAO) suggesting it has decreased by nearly a third over a five-year period. Initially the forests were logged, mainly illegally for timber, but more recently they have been cleared in vast swathes to make way for plantations, such as rubber in Kompong Cham province, and more worryingly, for the illegal production of the drug MDMA, better known as Ecstasy, in the Cardamom Mountains.

In 2001, the Cambodian government (forced by the **World Bank**) began to take action to reduce some of the most glaring environmental abuses. However, the government soon fell out with **Global Witness** (Ⓦwww.globalwitness.org), the environmental watchdog appointed by the Bank to monitor Cambodia's forests, when its findings were not to its liking. Their most recent spat is a result of a damning report issued in June 2007 by Global Witness in which it named a number of high-ranking government officials as using the country's resources for personal gain; the government responded by calling for heads to roll at Global Witness. In the meantime, nearly a decade after a cessation in logging was announced, little has really happened and the country's natural resources continue to diminish at an alarming rate.

Cambodia's forests are home to a vast, diverse **wildlife** population, including globally threatened species like the tiger. Ironically, the improvements in infrastructure that followed the establishment of the country's national parks have sometimes made it easier for poachers to capture wild animals, which are either sold in local markets for the pot or used to produce medicines and charms. Until a government clampdown in 2001 it was possible to buy **game** taken from the park, particularly venison, along National Route 4 near Kirirom, while **restaurants** specializing in rare meats such as pangolin were easy to find in Phnom Penh. Nowadays, most of this appears to have stopped and you'll see anti-hunting posters along National Route 4 instead, though the message certainly isn't having much impact on the poachers, who continue to see the profits from hunting as too enticing to relinquish.

So, while Cambodia has made some of the right gestures, banning logging and outlawing trafficking in wildlife under the international CITES convention, it lacks the will to implement sound conservation policies. Most recently, concessions have been granted to international companies to explore for oil and gas offshore, and – after a nifty change in the law – for bauxite, gold and copper in a protected area of Mondulkiri.

Though it's easy to think that the government simply may not recognize the long-term implications of the present shambles, it's hard not to agree with the ecological organizations that exploiting the country's natural resources offers just too many tempting opportunities for personal profit. Resounding proof of this can be seen at Bokor National Park. For an alleged sum of $100 million, the Chinese conglomerate Sokha has acquired the mountain in its entirety on a 99-year lease. The company is in the process of building a vast luxury casino and hotel complex on the mountain's peak and has all but closed the park off to the public (see box, p.298).

For the foreseeable future, wildlife organizations working in Cambodia will continue to face a severe uphill struggle, producing useful surveys while generally being unable to affect government policy.

building with a red roof. A bit further on, the other, older royal residence, is also derelict, and you can scramble through the overgrown garden for views over the forest and out to a magical lake, **Sras Srorng**, which can be reached by heading downhill along a rough track from the palace. About 1km beyond the guesthouse is the **park office**; unsurprisingly, it has no information for visitors, although a nearby notice board has a useful map and shots of various park locations, as well as displaying photos of dead animals illegally caught here.

After another 500m or so you reach the only major road **junction** in the park, from where signs point towards various sights. The most appealing option (particularly in the rainy season) is the track north to a series of three **waterfalls**, I, II and III, numbered according to increasing size, and located roughly every 2km.

Practicalities

The park is just over 100km southwest of Phnom Penh; it can be reached by public transport, though with some difficulty, as it's a 26-kilometre trip from the turn-off from National Route 4 to the upland plateau and Chambok. Whether travelling from **Phnom Penh** (leaves from Psar Thmei; 12,000 riel) or **Sihanoukville** (14,000 riel) ask to alight at **Trang Tro Yeung** and then hire one of the moto drivers around the market to take you to the park (about $10 return). Make it clear where you wish to alight before you set off. Alternatively, it's easy to visit the park as a day-trip from either Phnom Penh or Sihanoukville by hiring a motorbike or a car and driver (around $60). The road to the top is sealed (if potholed), so access is possible all year round. It is, however, well worth staying a few days if you can. Kirirom just begs to be explored on foot, and you need have no worries about land mines, as the area has been cleared. The temperature up on the plateau averages 25°C by day, dropping by 5–10°C at night, making long trousers and warm clothing essential after dark. **Staying overnight**, especially on weekdays, allows you to fully appreciate the tranquil surroundings and pine-scented air. At weekends it tends to get overrun with trippers from the city, though few of these stay overnight.

To enter the park (daily 8am–5pm), you'll need to pay an **admission fee** ($5 per person for foreigners) at the small shack at the park entrance opposite the *Kirirom Hillside Resort*, which is 10km from the main road. If you're staying at the top for the night, you can arrange for your driver to return the next day to take you back to Trang Tro Yeung; otherwise you'll need to beg a lift with the accommodation's supply truck.

Chambok – community-based eco tourism

Just before the entrance to the national park, a sign indicates the road to the Chambok Eco tourism site (ⓣ012/500142 ⓔinfo@ccben.org, ⓦhttp://www.mlup.org/chambok/index.asp). This community-based project, begun in 2001, offers a rich and rewarding way in which to enjoy the forest while supporting the local inhabitants. The revenue generated by tourism is put back into the community, paying wages, funding forest patrols and training its members in nature awareness.

Activities include **guided treks** up to the nearby waterfalls, bat caves and the top of the mountain for some breathtaking views (price included in the $3 entrance fee), as well as entertaining rides in ox-drawn carts known as *rotei koh*, birdwatching, tree planting and **homestays** where you can get a taste of Cambodian life by staying with a family, who share their meals and their humble home with you for a few nights ($3 per person per night; meals $2.50 each). The families are wonderfully hospitable and kind, and you will be living as they do, so although they will have gone to great trouble to make your quarters spotlessly clean, be prepared for outdoor loos, minimal electricity and close proximity to farm animals.

Getting to Chambok requires a bit of effort if you are going it alone (see Kirirom "Practicalities"). Alternatively, the Chambok coordinators speak good English and will email you plenty of details on how to get there – they also have a list of Phnom Penh-based travel agents who can organize transport.

Accommodation and eating

The most economical way to stay in Kirirom is with a homestay in Chambok ($3 per person, per night; meals $2.50) while there are two more comfortable options within the national park, both with restaurants. The only other places to get food in the park are the **stalls** beyond the park office, which are open at lunchtime only.

Kirirom Guesthouse and Restaurant On top of the plateau ⓣ012/363459. Great location but basic facilities. Its five rooms are overpriced, though they have en-suite bathrooms (albeit with icy-cold water) while an in-house generator provides electricity from dusk until about 10pm. The restaurant serves steak and chips as well as tasty Khmer food, and there are wonderful views over the surrounding hills from the rooftop terrace. ❸

Kirirom Hillside Resort Just opposite the park entrance at the foot of the hill ⓣ016/590999, ⓦwww.kiriromresort.com. All mod-cons within a variety of smart bungalows scattered around landscaped gardens. Not everyone will find the dinosaur sculptures and piped birdsong in the restaurant to their taste, but the *Paradise* café is good for a sundowner, and the resort (admission $5) offers an impressive range of activities, from canoeing and fishing to tennis and horseriding, as well as a small zoo. ❺–❼

Kirirom to Sihanoukville

South of Kirirom, there are regular traffic jams on National Route 4 at the **Pich Nil** pass, where most Cambodian motorists break their journey to make offerings at the **shrine of Yeah Mao**, or Black Grandmother, who is believed to protect travellers and fishermen. The most popular version of the tale is that she perished in the waves after setting out to find her husband who had left to fight at sea. To pick out her shrine, follow the eye-watering haze of incense – a smoke-dimmed image of her can be found within it. The rows of spirit houses are recent additions and are a bit of a scam by local stallholders, but Khmer are often superstitious and most would prefer to make an offering rather than risk offending the spirits.

The traffic eases beyond the pass and the traditional agricultural landscape gives way to massive palm-oil plantations, until about 20km from the coast the road forks, with a side road leading to Sihanoukville's airport (currently closed) and Ream National Park (see p.286). Continuing along National Route 4, you get your first glimpse of the sea from the crest of a steep hill, closely followed by the modern, industrial buildings of Cambrew, Cambodia's national brewery, source of the ubiquitous Angkor beer. From here, it's just a few kilometres to the centre of Sihanoukville.

Sihanoukville and around

Cambodia's primary coastal party town, **SIHANOUKVILLE** occupies a hilly headland rising above island-speckled waters and six gently shelving white-sand beaches. The area is blessed with a pleasant climate all year round – cooling sea breezes in the hot season (March–May), comfortable heat in the cool season (Nov–Feb) and enough sun during the rainy season (June–Oct) to spend mornings on the beach. The town centre is a little way inland, and although the sprawling layout and architecture are workaday – plain concrete blocks connected by wide, undulating streets – the relaxed atmosphere is still what you'd expect of a seaside resort.

The main hub of activity is on and around **Ochheuteal Beach**, roughly 4km south of the town centre, off which you'll find the majority of the bars and guesthouses. Should you weary of the beaches, there are inland **waterfalls** to visit north of town, and the **Ream National Park**, 18 kilometres to the east, which includes

Moving on from Sihanoukville

Travelling from Sihanoukville to other parts of the south and the capital is straightforward.

By bus

Bus operators Phnom Penh Sorya Transport, Mekong Express, GST, Virak Buntham Express and others have offices at the transport hub by the market (Phnom Penh Sorya also has an office on Ekareach Street) from where they run efficient express buses to **Phnom Penh** ($5–6), with departures from early morning to early afternoon. You'll seldom have a problem getting a seat except on public holidays, when it's best to book in advance. There is one bus every morning to **Koh Kong** ($7) with Virak Buntham (Ⓣ016/754358) and Phnom Penh Sorya operates a daily bus to Kampot (16,000 riel). **Capitol Guesthouse** (Capitol Tours and Transport, Ekareach Street Ⓣ034/934042) runs its own coaches three times a day between Sihanoukville, Kampot and Phnom Penh (16,000 riel); *G'day Mate* runs a minibus (daily at 11am; $7) to Kampot.

By shared taxi and minibus

From the same transport hub, shared taxis and minibuses depart throughout the day for **Phnom Penh** and destinations en route (14,000 riel by shared taxi, 12,000 riel by minibus); for **Koh Kong**, there are intermittent shared taxis and pick-ups (35,000 riel for both, or 30,000 in the back of a pick-up); three leave for Kampot throughout the day (12,000 riel in a shared taxi, 10,000 riel by minibus).

a protected marine area enclosing a diverse landscape of rivers, mangrove forest, islands and farmland.

Arrival, information and city transport

All forms of public transport currently drop off in the northeastern corner of **Psar Leu**, within a couple of hundred metres of town-centre accommodation, as the old transport depot is being converted into a colossal international shopping mall (there are plans to build a new depot near the Independence Monument). The principal guesthouses send transport to meet buses and boats, and there are always motos on hand. Many of them get commission from guesthouses, so be firm if there's somewhere particular you want to stay. Following a fatal plane crash near Kampot in 2007, there are no flights to or from Sihanoukville's **airport** (off National Route 4, 23km from town).

Two booklets, *The Sihanoukville Visitors Guide* and *The Sihanoukville Advertiser*, keep abreast of new places to sleep, eat and drink. Both are available free in bars, restaurants and guesthouses; the latter has a volunteer section with information on opportunities to help out in town. A new **tourist office** (Mon–Fri 8–11am & 2–5pm) on Ochheuteal Beach is friendly enough, but, as ever, has no real information. The compact town centre is home to the town's **banks**, a Camintel office for overseas **phone** calls, places for **internet** access (for details, see p.283) and the town's market and supermarkets.

The main areas of interest are quite spread out, and as Sihanoukville is hilly, getting around on foot can be hard work. **Motos** and tuk-tuks are readily available around the centre and at Ochheuteal Beach, and motos hang around most other tourist spots. Expect to pay $1 from the market to the beaches or port by moto, more by tuk-tuk.

Renting a moto is a brilliant way to explore the coastline and escape the hordes, but tourists make easy pickings for patrolling policemen (see box, p.274).

On the road: how to survive the police

While there is no more exhilarating way to explore Sihanoukville's dispersed coastline than on the back of your own rented motorbike, you need to be on your guard for prowling policemen looking for a bribe. There is currently no legal infrastructure in place that requires tourists to hold a license but the police have come up with a few reasons to pull you over and take your money. There are some measures you can take to keep them at bay.

The first, and one that we would recommend regardless of police interference, is to wear a helmet; it's every man for himself on the road, so safety should be your number-one priority. Riding without a shirt on is enough to have you pulled over and, bizarrely, driving with your lights on in the day is unacceptable. This is allegedly because that privilege is reserved for travelling dignitaries, which the Western tourist is not considered to be.

Being stopped for any of these offences will result in you being asked to hand over a fistful of dollars (up to $100). However, in almost every case you can barter this down to one or two. If you know you haven't done anything wrong, insisting on handling the situation down at the station is a big deterrent as the police are not actually charging you with anything.

Accommodation

From $2 bunks to $200 suites, Sihanoukville caters to all budgets. Hotels and guesthouses can get incredibly busy during public holidays and festivals, when it's as well to **book** if you want to stay at a particular place, though you're unlikely to be completely stuck for anywhere to sleep. During peak season (Nov–March) and major holidays (particularly Khmer New Year), hotels may hike their prices up by 25–30 percent. It's worth trying to negotiate a discount if you plan to stay for a week or more, or if you arrive during the week, even during the peak season.

The beaches

Most people arriving in Sihanoukville head straight to the more developed beaches due south of the town centre, **Ochheuteal** and **Serendipity**, which is where you'll find the best range of budget and mid-range accommodation, not to mention Serendipity Beach Road, the main hub of bars, shops and restaurants. North along the coast brings you to **Sokha Beach** and **Independence Beach**, both of which are immaculate, but have been virtually requisitioned for the exclusive use of residents at their respective namesake resorts. Further north still, **Victory Beach** has one or two more secluded options, although the area has an insalubrious reputation after dark, meanwhile the three-kilometre **Otres Beach**, to the south of Ochheuteal, as yet remains mainly undeveloped with just some blissfully chilled out beach-bars, a couple of which have basic accommodation in bamboo shacks.

Serendipity Beach Road

Beach Road Hotel ⓣ017/827677, ⓦbeachroad-hotel.com. Despite its proximity to the wildest bars, and particularly its own popular sports bar, the rooms and pool area are impressively quiet and refined. Non-residents can lounge by the pool for $4. ❸–❹

Cool Banana ⓔcoolbananacambodia@yahoo.com. A great backpacker option with small bungalows behind the main restaurant and bar, and free movies and cheap popcorn in its home-made cinema. ❷

Le Jardin aux Hibiscus ⓣ012/219505, ⓦrega-guesthouse.com. Set around lovely, secluded gardens, the rooms are simple but attractive, in muted shades with some period furnishings, the more expensive coming with a/c and hot water. ❸–❹

MoHaChai ⓣ034/933586, ⓦmohachai.com. Options range from budget rooms for as little as $4 in the low season, to more comfortable rooms with private terraces. All rooms are well presented with private bathrooms, and the guesthouse prides itself on its lovely garden, affordable restaurant and top security. 2–4

Monkey Republic ⓣ012/490290, ⓦmonkey-republic.com. A real favourite with backpackers for its pretty blue bungalows and laid back vibe, while its bar is one of the most popular (and loudest) in town. 2

Reef Resort ⓣ034/934281 or 012/315338, ⓦreefresort.com.kh, ⓔrooms@reefresort.com.kh. This classy boutique hotel right in the thick of the action has fashionable rooms, with plenty of white linen and rattan furniture, set in blocks around the swimming pool. Breakfast included. The restaurant serves classic Mexican food, and there's a cocktail bar and pool table. 5

Serendipity Beach

Above Us Only Sky ⓣ089/822318, ⓦaboveusonlysky-cambodia.com. A relatively new addition to the bungalows on Serendipity, these are already a firm favourite for their spectacular, uninterrupted sea views and the excellent cocktail bar that sits at their base. Booking is essential to ensure one of the four tastefully decorated cabins, each with its own veranda. At the time of writing a small kitchen was being built to cater for breakfast and bar snacks. Prices vary dramatically depending on the season. 4–7

Cloud 9 ⓣ012/479365. At the furthest reaches of Serendipity, wooden bungalows sit dotted among the trees behind a beach-front restaurant-bar, justifiably famed for its delectable Thai green curry. 4–5

Coasters ⓣ034/933776, ⓦwww.cambodia-beach.com, ⓔcoasters@camintel.com. Rustic bungalows and some cheaper rooms, all nice and clean with hot water and mosquito nets, climbing the hillside overlooking the bay. Great communal area with library, a beach restaurant-bar serving both Western and Asian food, a high-speed internet café and shop, and a good stretch of private beach with free loungers for guests. Tours arranged, including overnight stays on Koh Russei (Bamboo Island; see p.285). 3–5

Ochheuteal Beach

Cambodian Resort 1 Kanda St ⓣ034/934657. A gleaming new addition to the accommodation options here, 200m from the beach. Each achingly smart room looks out over the lavish pool and bar area, and providing a service that meets western standards is taken very seriously. 6–9

Coolabah Hotel 14 Mithona St ⓣ017/678218, ⓦcoolabah-hotel.com. Sparkling new pool and spa, mouth-watering food and impeccable service – there are few that can match the Coolabah. 5

GST Guesthouse 14 Mithona St ⓣ016/210222. Run by the GST bus company, this sprawling backpacker joint is now one of three under the same name; GST2 is really just an extension of the original guesthouse and the GST3 (a little more expensive) can be found at the beach end of Serendipity Beach Rd. You'll usually find the footy on in the restaurant, which is a great place to meet fellow travellers on the party trail. Rooms are pretty good for the price and come with the standard choice of fan or a/c. 1–3

Hooha House 1 Kanda St ⓣ015/732000. A new, Western-run backpackers with great value rooms including wi-fi and hot water as standard and the draw of a free beer on arrival. Pool table and movies in the bar. 2

Markara 14 Mithona St ⓣ034/933448, ⓔmakarashv@camintel.com. At the more peaceful, south end of the beach, this guesthouse is always busy. The first floor restaurant serves acceptable food, and all tourist services are on offer, including motorbike rental. Security is excellent, as is the level of English spoken, but the walls are paper-thin. 2–3

Be aware

As Sihanoukville begins to flourish, so has petty crime. It is rarely serious, and mostly opportunistic, and certainly not something that should put you off visiting, but it's a good idea to make the most of hotel safety-deposit boxes and keep an eye on your belongings when on the beach.

Personal safety is another issue altogether; there have been several incidents of assault at **Weather Station Hill** at night, and drunken brawls are not uncommon, so it is safer to travel home by tuk-tuk rather than on foot or by moto, even around the main beaches.

Although none of this is anything to be paranoid about, it's as well to ask your guesthouse when you arrive if there have been any recent incidents. Ultimately, the fun happens in the well-lit parts of town, so it shouldn't be too hard to stick to them.

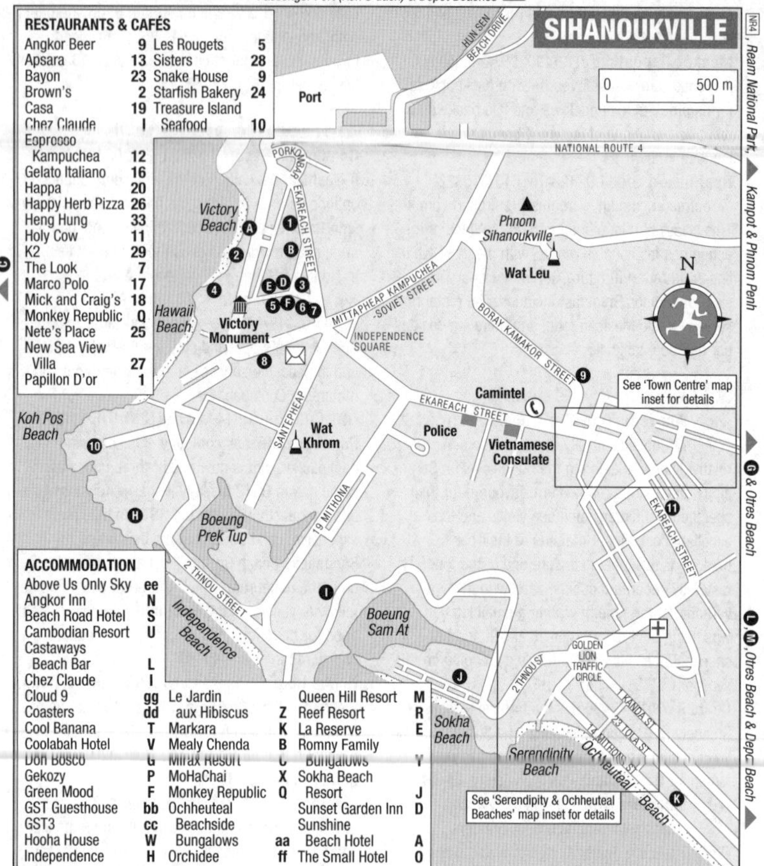

Ochheuteal Beachside Bungalows 14 Mithona St ⓣ016/953896. Lovely thatched a/c rooms with verandas and attached bathrooms (some have hot water) and an excellent restaurant. It's not exactly beachside, but only 70m away. ③

Orchidee 23 Tola St ⓣ034/933639 or 012/380300, ⓦwww.orchideeguesthouse.com. Colourful orchids hang everywhere in the shady courtyard of this hotel. Rooms are light and airy, with TV, a/c; bathrooms have hot water. There's a swimming pool, plus a quiet balcony sitting area. Popular with expats escaping from Phnom Penh, so worth booking at weekends and holidays. ③

Romny Family Bungalows 1 Kanda St ⓣ016/861459, ⓔromnytour@yahoo.com. Families are actively encouraged here. Accommodation is in tidy bungalows, new ones recently added, and there is a simple bar and restaurant. Staff are friendly and caring, and tours and onward travel can be arranged. If you want to cook for yourself they'll let you use the kitchen. 100m from the beach. ②–③

Independence and Sokha beaches

Chez Claude On the hill between Independence and Sokha beaches ⓣ012/824870, ⓔ012824870@mobitel.com.kh. En-suite accommodation in individually designed wooden bungalows on an extremely steep hill overlooking the bay, with private balconies looking out to sea. The hotel also has a French restaurant, and can arrange diving trips. ④

Independence Independence Beach ⓣ034/934300, ⓦindependencehotel.net. Sympathetically restored to its former glory, the

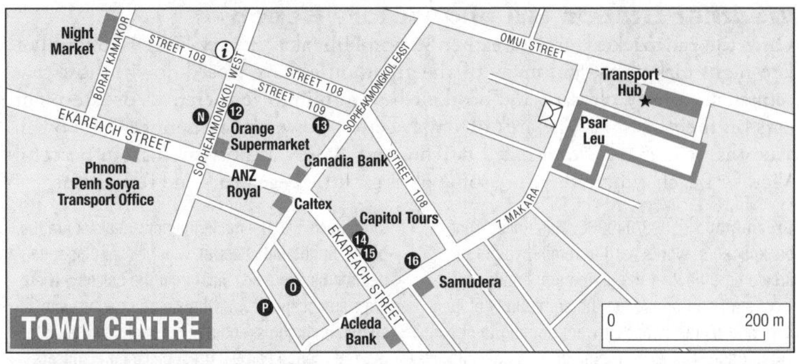

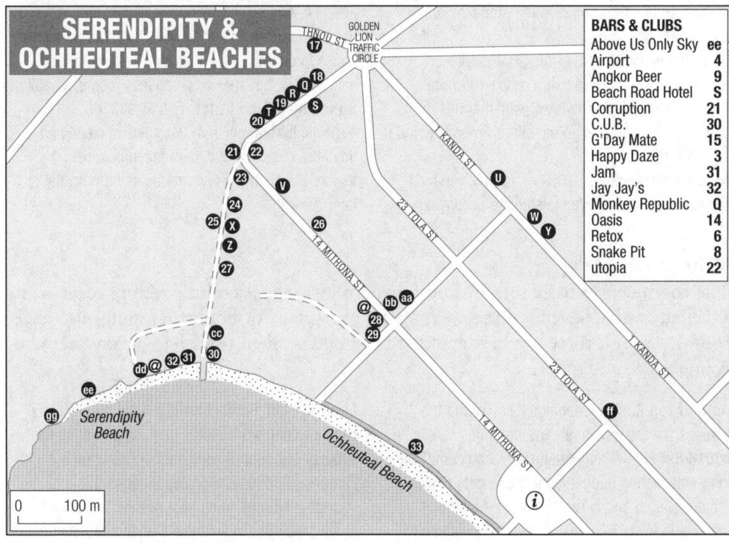

hotel towers impressively above the north end of Independence Beach. Known locally as *Bprahm-bpel Jawn* (Seven Storeys), the hotel was once a glamorous venue attracting celebrities such as Jacqueline Kennedy, after whom the finest suite is now named. At the onset of war, it was abandoned and from 1975 to 1979 housed high-ranking Khmer Rouge officials. Reputedly haunted, it's now a luxurious hotel and spa, with a private beach. 8–9

Sokha Beach Resort Sokha Beach ⓣ034/935999, ⓦwww.sokhahotels.com. This luxury hotel has nearly two hundred rooms in a huge complex occupying almost the whole of Sokha Beach. Rooms have all the amenities you'd expect and some have great views; there's also a swimming pool, spa, fitness centre, tennis courts, water sports equipment and a choice of restaurants and bars. Free shuttle to town and other beaches. 8

Otres Beach

Castaways Beach Bar ⓣ097/8611785, ⓦcastawaysbeachbar.com. All the accommodation on Otres comes in the form of basic wood bungalows; at the time of writing *Castaways* seemed to be the best kept, but all are very similar – what they lack in practically every form of amenity they make up for with their beautiful, completely chilled location and laidback atmosphere. 1

Queen Hill Resort ⓣ012/482418, ⓦwww.queenhillresortbungalows.com. Well-appointed bungalows, most with terrific views of the bays, perched on the northern headland at Otres Beach. Some have hot water and a/c. 2

Weather Station Hill and Victory Beach

Once the backpackers' area, Weather Station Hill (aka Victory Hill) is now full of late-night girlie bars, and many of the guesthouses have closed down; those that remain are pretty pleasant and do their best to minimize the effect of late-night bars on their visitors. The area by day is better, however, with more Cambodian vibe than the main Westernized beaches and is only a short walk from peaceful Victory Beach, where there are some pleasant little beach bars and restaurants.

Green Mood ⓣ098/949366. This Italian-run backpackers' works hard to remind you of the area's core beyond the girlie bars, employing local staff and promoting the community of local bars and restaurants that want nothing to do with prostitution. The clean rooms offer good value for money, as do their home-made stone-baked pizzas. ❶–❸

La Reserve ⓣ034/934429, ⓦlareserve-sihanoukville.com. Stylish, French-run hotel with glorious pool and views over the hillside and beyond. Also has an excellent French restaurant. ❺–❼

Mealy Chenda ⓣ034/933472, ⓔmealychenda@gmail.com. A massive guesthouse occupying three buildings. Rooms in the newest block are the best – bright and cheerful, with pleasant en-suite bathrooms and a sea view from the balcony. There are also cheaper, somewhat scruffy rooms, with shared bathrooms, and a number of dorm beds for $2. The rooftop bar is a great place for a sunset beer. ❶–❸

Sunset Garden Inn ⓣ012/761340. Lovely family house in charming gardens overlooking the bay with simple, but spacious, spotless rooms. ❶–❸

Sunshine Beach Hotel ⓣ034/933708, ⓔsoujuall@hanmail.net. Two rows of clean and tidy little cabins with decent amenities, set on Victory Beach just a few metres along from the bars. ❷–❹

Town centre

The town centre has a mix of budget and mid-range accommodation, some of it excellent value. Several of the area's sports bars (many of doubtful repute) also have rooms, though these are best avoided by single women travellers or anyone who wants peace and quiet.

Angkor Inn Sonbeakmongkol West, round the corner from the new mall development ⓣ016/896204, ⓔangkorinn99@yahoo.com. This long-established budget guesthouse gets plenty of repeat custom and is run by one of the kindest families in town. Rooms are plain but clean and cool; the quietest rooms are at the back. The inexpensive restaurant serves freshly prepared Asian food, with some Western options. ❷

Don Bosco 3km from town heading east from Psar Leu ⓣ034/933765, ⓦdonboscosihanoukville.org. This hotel provides its staff, all young adults from poor backgrounds, with the skills necessary to work in the tourist industry. Rooms are large, smart, bright and slightly more luxurious than you'd expect of the price range. Wins major points for its garden, swimming pool and attentive service from the students and teaching staff. Profits from the hotel are ploughed back into student training. Booking essential. ❹

Gekozy Two blocks southeast of Caltex off Ekareach St ⓣ012/495825, ⓦgeckozy-guesthouse.com. In an area of town still very much belonging to the local Cambodians, this French-run backpackers' ticks all the boxes with bright, well-equipped rooms and great communal hangout areas. ❷

The Small Hotel One block southeast of Caltex off Ekareach St ⓣ012/716385, ⓔthesmallhotel@yahoo.com. A small place with a big reputation, thanks in no small part to the Swedish–Khmer owners who are authorities on the local area and run the guesthouse brilliantly. Boasts an excellent library and a small restaurant famed for its meatballs. Rents motos; booking essential in high season. ❷–❹

The beaches

There's a great choice of beaches in and around Sihanoukville; indeed at a stretch you could visit a different beach every day for a week. **Ochheuteal** and **Serendipity** are incredibly popular and have toilets, showers, beach umbrellas and restaurants that put on fantastic nightly **barbecues** where you can choose the pick of the day's catch and watch them grill it for you, for only a few dollars. Other beaches, like **Sokha** and **Hawaii**, have been leased off to private developers. However, midweek at least on the public end of **Independence**, and **Otres** Beach, you can still find a little seclusion. On the downside, most of the beaches are pretty narrow, with barely enough space to lie stretched out at high tide.

For Khmer, a visit to Sihanoukville is an excuse for an eating and drinking binge, with a dip in the briny as a fringe benefit. Their conservative nature, coupled with a concern – verging on paranoia for the women – about maintaining whiteness, means that shade is everything. Accordingly, the most popular beaches have a plethora of beach parasols and deck chairs for rent at a nominal sum, and men, women and even the young take to the sea fully clothed. Consequently, many will stare in amazement at foreigners stripped off and baking in the blazing sun. For women, bikinis are just about acceptable, but going topless is a definite no-no.

You may find yourself almost bullied into buying **massages**, manicures and leg-hair threading from the women who patrol Ochheuteal Beach hour after hour, telling you that your nails are dreadful and must be tended to – men are targeted just as much as women and it takes nerves of steel not to buckle under their relentless attention. A $5 massage is not bad value for money, and usually turns out to be a rather relaxing experience, but buying bracelets and trinkets from the **children** that patrol the beaches only encourages them to stay out of school or work late into the evening when they should be in bed, so maintain a firm resolve if you can.

Ochheuteal Beach and Serendipity Beach

Ochheuteal, the town's longest and most popular beach, is a three-kilometre stretch of fine sand lined with casuarina trees, which you can just see poking out between the bars and restaurants that crowd the strand. The roads behind the beach have a great selection of hotels and guesthouses, while the sand itself is lined by identical beach bars, prevented from encroaching too far onto the beach by a new tiled pedestrian walkway. However, their respective beach umbrellas, deck chairs and tables still stretch to the water. Freshwater showers and toilets have been installed to cater for the pretty much 24-hour activity. During the day it's packed with Cambodian families and sun-soaking tourists; by night, the BBQs are fired up and the cocktails start flowing into the early hours.

At the north end of the beach, the area known as **Serendipity** is lined with bungalows that wind up the hill. There is no public sand here; the thin sliver is reserved for patrons of the bungalows. Fortunately most of the bungalows have bars at beach level that make great spots for a sundowner.

Thanks to the concrete foundations of the buildings, it looks like Serendipity will remain unaffected by the government's ruthless approach to property ownership in the town. Like the islands (see p.284) the beachfronts are also under attack from developers, with the Prime Minister Hun Sen himself in the process of completing a villa. The wooden shacks on Ochheuteal seemed safe at the time of writing, but for how long remains to be seen. Sadly, the dulcet tones of construction work fill the air even at the far reaches of these beaches.

Otres Beach and Depot Beach

A six-kilometre moto ride southeast from the town centre will bring you to **Otres Beach**, which boasts the best sand and is the best bet if you want to escape the vendors and crowds of the beaches in town, even if you won't escape the sounds of heavy machinery. In 2009, all the huts along the beach were unceremoniously shifted a kilometre to the west to make room for a holiday park that was still under construction at the time of writing. Although there's now less beach to stretch out along, and the sound of the waves barely masks those of the building site, this is still the best beach in town.

Some 3km north of town, beyond the express-boat dock and around the headland, **Depot Beach** is an untouched expanse of sand separated from the road by grass and scrub, and edged by trees conveniently spaced for slinging your hammock. On your way to the beach you'll pass a long, sprawling **fishing village** where stilt-houses are built out over the water and a small fleet of boats puts to sea in the late afternoon. The only people you are likely to see here are fishermen, though as the water is very shallow it's not much good for swimming.

Victory Beach to Independence Beach

West of the town, and the closest beach to Weather Station Hill, the dark-golden sands of **Victory Beach** are more relaxing than those of Ochheuteal, with a small row of beach bars along the northern tip and a major new landmark to the south – *Airplane* – a hangar housing a full-sized Antonov plane around which punters can eat, drink and dance the night away. You can even sit in the cockpit.

The rocky face of **Koh Pos** island used to be the only sight on the horizon to the south, but now you can watch the steady construction of a gargantuan bridge that will eventually connect it to the mainland at **Hawaii Beach**, just fifteen minutes' walk south of Victory Beach.

Named after a now-defunct restaurant, Hawaii Beach has become a construction site for a large luxury apartment complex; at the time of writing the northern half was a mass of concrete and cranes. The only accessible area for now is the tiny cove in front of the *Treasure Island Seafood Restaurant*.

You'll need to rejoin the road to reach **Independence Beach**. Over a kilometre long, it is rather narrow, and so best visited at low tide. At the northern end, and around the rocky headland, the beach is reserved for guests of the *Independence Hotel*.

Sokha Beach

Only 200m of the second best of Sihanoukville's beaches, **Sokha** is fully accessible to the public. The rest is reserved for residents of the *Sokha Beach Resort*. It is OK for foreigners (but not Cambodians) to walk along the full length of the beach, but if you want to crash out here you'll have to pay $5 per day Monday to Friday, $7 per day Saturday to Sunday and public holidays – which also includes use of the hotel swimming pool. Rocky headlands at both ends of the beach draw small fish and make for great snorkelling, and it's a wonderful place at sunset when the islands of Koh Tre and Koh Dah Ghiel are thrown into silhouette.

The Town

The **town centre** (also known as Downtown) has little of interest for most visitors; **Psar Leu** is perhaps its greatest attraction, a huge market that has been given a facelift after being devastated by a fire in 2008. It's a great place to meander, especially through the fish section where sea urchins, octopus, huge varicoloured crabs and mighty sea creatures with fierce eyes and bristling whiskers are on sale.

Sunset over Sihanoukville

The **sunsets** of Sihanoukville are some of the nicest in the country, and Independence, Hawaii and Sokha beaches have the best vantage points. At the fishing harbour on Hun Sen Beach Drive, you might get a classic photo of the small flotilla of fishing boats heading out to sea against the setting sun.

It is also the place to stock up on everything from fishing lines to fruit and vegetables before heading out on a trip to the islands.

Sihanoukville's modest sights are scattered around town and best visited by moto (or a rented motorbike if the ban on tourists hiring them is lifted). Furthest out, **Phnom Sihanoukville**, accessed by a track behind the Cambrew Brewery, is the highest point around, although at 132m it's hardly a mountain. The town also has a couple of pagodas: Wat Leu, on the summit of Phnom Sihanoukville, and **Wat Krom**, set on a boulder-strewn hillside off Santepheap Street, where a sanctuary commemorates **Yeah Mao**, of Pich Nil fame.

Eating

Don't leave town without savouring the local **seafood**, priced by the kilogram and cheaper than anywhere else in the country. If you prefer something informal, flop in a deck chair on the beach and order what you fancy from passing hawkers, and the fabulous (and fabulously cheap) evening seafood **barbecues** on Ochheuteal Beach. For a more formal meal, head for somewhere like *New Sea View Villa* or *Treasure Island Seafood* (see p.282).

For cheap eats in the centre, the **night market** opens up along Ekareach Street between Sopheakmongkol West and East in late afternoon, and there are dozens of street vendors around Psar Leu. You'll find a good range of **Western-oriented** places on the streets behind Ochheuteal and Serendipity, serving up everything from fish and chips to falafel; if you want to splash out, there are several restaurants serving delicious **French cuisine**.

Serendipity Beach Road

Bayon This little Khmer-run restaurant is a prime spot for watching street activity and serves up one of the finest fish coconut curries in town ($3).

Casa All comfy cushions and chairs, this little café-bar dishes up all manner of salads, burgers and pizzas for around $3. Chilled out during the day; livens up with the onset of happy hour from 5pm.

Happa Cosy place where you grill your own food on a teppanyaki hot-plate, to eat with a choice of tasty and tangy sauces. Tapas-size portions of fresh fish, meat and tofu at $3.50–4.50 per plate. Evenings only.

Mick and Craig's Look out for the special nights at this popular bar-restaurant; the Indian, Mexican and Italian nights, not to mention a slap-up Sunday roast, are as popular as the rooms in their excellent guesthouse. Daily 8am–2am.

Nete's Place Sweet new restaurant run by a Khmer family, with comfy satellite chairs and loungers, and excellent barbecued seafood dishes for $3 as well as the full range of typical Khmer cuisine.

New Sea View Villa ⓣ092/759753. Set in a beautiful, candle-lit courtyard, this is the perfect place to treat yourself without breaking the bank. The menu, largely fish with some European dishes, allows you to mix between more sophisticated fare such as the tequila-and-lime-marinated carpaccio starter of swordfish ($2.50) and an ample and perfectly grilled surf-and-turf ($6). Also runs a decent guesthouse (❸).

Starfish Bakery Run by disabled Khmer women who bake delicious Western breads, cakes, scones and other goodies to eat at tables in the shop that doubles up as a little boutique. Profits go to help needy people, particularly child beach vendors (ⓦwww.starfishcambodia.org). Daily 7am–6pm.

Ochheateal Beach

Happy Herb Pizza 14 Mithona St. Reliable pizzas, pasta dishes and salads from $4 in a branch of the popular Phnom Penh pizzeria.

Heng Hung Halfway along Ochheuteal Beach. By day this beach bar and restaurant looks like all the rest on the strip, but come sundown the barbecue is fired up and the place is packed; the seafood barbecue ($3) is superb value, perfectly accompanied by cocktails or a chilled beer as you recline in a satellite chair.

K2 10m inland from Ochheuteal Beach. Thatched restaurant with a terrific inexpensive Indian and Bengali menu from the same owners as the *Indian Curry Pot*.

Sisters 14 Mithona St, opposite GST. Devastatingly slow service, but if you are craving Western hangover cures, the toasted sandwiches and home-made chips ($2.50) really are worth the wait.

The road to Independence Beach

Chez Claude *Chez Claude* hotel, on the hill between Independence and Sokha beaches. Excellent, moderately priced French cuisine – the grills, succulent steaks and pork chops are particularly recommended, though there's not much for vegetarians. The terrace is an excellent place for a sunset drink, overlooking the peninsula, with views to the islands beyond.

Marco Polo Just west of the Golden Lions roundabout. Great stone-baked pizza and other typical Italian fare in big portions at this friendly restaurant, for around $5. Has a secluded garden out the back.

Treasure Island Seafood Independence headland. Head down the steps behind the decrepit *Koh Pos Hotel* to reach this idyllic, moderately priced, beachside Chinese restaurant, specializing in fish and seafood – the crab and shrimp dishes are delicious, and there's a lovely little beach to laze on afterwards. English-language menu available. Daily 10am–10pm.

Weather Station Hill and Victory Beach

Browns Victory Beach. The best of the little beach huts serving Khmer and Western staples for around $3, with a cheerful happy hour lasting well into the night.

Les Rougets At the top of the path leading down to Victory Beach. An excellent French restaurant with a loyal following, that also serves a few dishes from Laos from $4–10. Throws fantastic parties on national (and French) holidays; good, safe guesthouse above run by the same people.

Papillon D'or Weather Station Hill, Ekareach Street towards the port. Classy restaurant and bar attached to luxurious hotel (with a firm anti-prostitution policy) serving superb Belgian specialities by the pool.

Snake House Off Soviet St. International and Russian food is served up at this unique location, where you'll find rare and exotic snakes in glass cases around the shady garden and occasionally under the glass-topped tables (but not, fortunately, on the menu). For $2 you can visit its crocodile farm, while late at night the place morphs into a girlie bar with much reptilian cavorting. Daily 11am–11pm.

The Look Weather Station Hill. In shades of black, white and red, this restaurant has a friendly atmosphere with a hint of sophistication, specializing in Swiss dishes with an international wine list.

Town centre

Apsara Corner of Sopheakmongkol East and Street 109. Khmer and Chinese dishes, with a particular accent on seafood; busy from early morning until mid-evening. Foreigners get charged more than Cambodians ($5 a dish), but the food is worth it. English-language menu available.

Espresso Kampuchea Sopheakmongkol West. Small coffee shop serving all styles of coffee, along with beer, cocktails and a small range of desserts and cakes. Daily 10am–9.30pm.

Gelato Italiano Sopheakmongkol East. Ice-cream parlour serving delicious Italian-style ices (2000 riel) made by students at the *Don Bosco* hotel school; seasonal flavours, such as mango or jackfruit, are exceptional. Also has an outlet on Ochheuteal Beach.

Holy Cow Ekareach St. Inexpensive Khmer and Western food ($2–3) served in a traditional wooden house; laid-back atmosphere, eclectic music and *Cambodia Daily* on hand. 9.30am–8pm.

Drinking and nightlife

Sihanoukville has some of the best nightlife in the country. With such a high number of bars, and a new favourite popping up almost weekly, it's worth asking at the guesthouse or looking in the *Sihanoukville Visitors Guide* for the latest hangouts; at the time of writing *utopia* and *Monkey Republic* reigned supreme.

Serendipity Beach Road

Above Us Only Sky Serendipity Beach. Stunning sea views and the best cocktails in town, half-price happy hour 5–8pm.

Beach Road Hotel Serendipity Beach Road. A good place if you want to watch Western sports and have a few beers without being deafened or propositioned by girlies.

Corruption Perched precariously at the top of the Serendipity Beach Road T-junction, this tiny shack run by a man from Cheshire is a hit with backpackers. Long may it last.

C.U.B. On the beach at the bottom of Serendipity Beach Road. A small bar with a massive sound system and some American memorabilia on the walls.

Jam Serendipity Beach. Stalwart on the corner of Serendipity Beach and the pier, constantly vying with *Jay Jay's* for whose happy hour can run the longest. Open very late.

Jay Jay's Serendipity Beach. It's a miracle this place survives given the amount of free booze they hand out. Great full-, half- and black-moon parties.
Monkey Republic One of the most popular spots in the thick of the action on Serendipity Beach Road, with pool tables and plenty of drink deals on shooters, spirits and beers. Open late.
utopia Corner Serendipity Beach Rd/14 Mithona St. Possibly the busiest Western bar in town, with draught beer promotions from noon till 7pm, fire dancers round the pool and parties every night from 10pm onwards. Restaurant and bunk room (free).

Weather Station Hill and Victory Beach

Airport Victory Beach. This custom-built aircraft hangar houses a real-life Antonov plane for you to explore, although the area still doesn't attract many people, so parties generally die out by 1am.
Happy Daze Weather Station Hill. Anti-prostitution, pro-reggae, open late. A great bar with a laidback vibe.
Retox Weather Station Hill, opposite *Happy Daze*. Long happy-hour and a friendly welcome, with live jam sessions and a loyal expat following. Open late.
Snake Pit *Snake House*, southwest of Independence Monument. Exotic bar with two-metre screen and plenty of female (and reptilian) company. 8pm until late.

Town Centre

Angkor Beer Boray Kamakor St. Compact disco popular with young Khmer, the music a mix of Thai, Filipino and Indonesian, plus a few European numbers played extra loud. Nightly 8pm–2am.
G'day Mate Ekareach St. 24/7 expat bar and restaurant, with the usual Western and Asian dishes, plus pool table.
Oasis *Oasis Hotel*, Ekareach St. Bloke-ish bar with live sports screen, free pool, cheap draught beer, and Thai and Western food such as burgers and pizzas.

Listings

Airlines Contact a local travel agent for up-to-date information, At the time of writing, all flights suspended.
Banks ANZ Royal, Canadia and Union Commercial banks all have branches on Ekareach St, where you can change travellers' cheques and get cash advances on cards. Canadia Bank is the only one not to charge a $4 fee for withdrawals. ANZ Royal and Western Union both have ATMs at the Golden Lions end of Serendipity Beach Road. You can change dollars to riel at Acleda Bank, also on Ekareach St, or at the exchange booths and telephone shops in or around the market.
Books and newspapers Mr Heinz and Q & A, both on Ekareach St, and Casablanca Books, near the Golden Lions roundabout, have second-hand books to buy, sell or swap and a selection of new (well, photocopied) international titles. *Cambodia Daily* and the *Phnom Penh Post* is on sale at stands in front of Psar Leu.
Car hire Hotels, guesthouses and tour operators can help you hire a car and driver for the day. Alternatively, head to the transport stop and negotiate with the drivers directly.
Consulate The Vietnamese consulate is on Ekareach St, towards Independence Square ⓣ034/933724. Vietnamese visas issued on the same day for $45.
Cookery courses Traditional Khmer Cookery Classes (335 Ekareach St towards the Independence Monument ⓣ092/738615; $25 per day). Individual wok stations so you actually get to cook not just watch, and runs one-, two- and three-day courses on its airy rooftop. Cost includes soft drinks throughout the day, beer or wine with lunch and laminated recipe cards.
Hospital Sihanoukville Referral Hospital is on Ekareach St, towards the Golden Lions roundabout (ⓣ034/933111), and has limited facilities. International Peace Hospital on Ekareach St towards the Independence Monument (ⓣ012/794269) has a 24hr emergency service. Alternatively call International SOS Medical Clinic (Phnom Penh) (ⓣ023/216911).
Internet access Getting online is easy and costs between $1 and $1.50 per hour, with places all over town and around Ochheuteal Beach.
Massage and spas Seeing Hands 3 on Ekareach near the *Holy Cow* restaurant (ⓣ012/799016; $4/hr) gives massage by the blind and sight-impaired. More exclusive is the Jasmine Spa (*Sokha Beach Resort* ⓣ034/935999; from $50), where you can choose from a range of pampering massages and treatments.
Motorbike rental Most guesthouses rent out motos. It's no longer illegal for tourists to ride, but see box on p.274 for what to do if the police stop you.
Music Boom Boom Room and Rogue iPod on Serendipity Beach Road have a massive selection of tracks ($0.75 each) for iPod and MP3; their catalogues are in many of the bars and restaurants.

Phones You can make international calls at most of the internet shops. Ask at your guesthouse for domestic calls as there are no longer phone booths at the market.
Photography Almost all internet cafés have the capacity to burn digital photos to CD or DVD.
Police The main police station is on Ekareach St, 1km west of town towards Independence Square; there are tourist police (☎012/882071) stationed at Serendipity Beach and towards the middle of Ochheuteal Beach.
Post office The main post office is on Ekareach St near the Independence Monument and has all the usual services, including poste restante.
Shopping Western groceries, toiletries and wines can be bought at a number of supermarkets and minimarts around the town centre and on 14 Mithona St and Serendipity Beach Rd. These include Orange, corner Ekareach St and Sopheakmongkol West; Caltex, Ekareach St; and at Ocean Mart, Ekareach St near the Golden Lions. Boutiques selling beach and party attire and souvenirs line Serendipity Beach Road. On Ekareach, Khmer Artisans has a good selection of silk scarves, bags and clothes.
Swimming pools You can pay to use the swimming pool and other facilities as a day visitor at the *Beach Road Hotel* ($4) and at the *Sokha Beach Resort* ($5 per day Mon–Fri, $7 per day Sat, – Sun and public holidays).
Tennis There are floodlit tennis courts ($5 per hour) at *Sokha Beach Resort*.
Travel agents and tour operators The following can all arrange visas/extensions, boat tickets, bus tickets, car hire and local tours. Ana Internet and Travel (Serendipity Beach Road, next to *Beach Road Hotel*; ☎034/933929); Romny Family Travel & Tour Service (at *Romny Family Bungalows*, 1 Kanda St ☎016/861459). In addition to the above services, Sokun Travel & Tours, Serendipity Beach Road (☎034/933791), can also arrange international and domestic flights.

The islands of Sihanoukville

If you still haven't had your fill of beaches, then an outing to one of the **offshore islands** (a couple of which lie within Ream) could be just the thing, especially if you're planning on staying a couple of days. Cambodia's coastal waters are peppered with hundreds of tropical islands lapped by clear, balmy seas, many graced with **white-sand beaches**. Offering stretches of sand that

Diving

Much underrated, diving Cambodia's uncharted waters is a colourful experience, all the better for the lack of other divers. In places **visibility** reaches a staggering 30m, and, with a wealth of islands to choose from, operators can offer itineraries ranging from reefs encased in coral to an almost over-abundance of marine life, including barracuda, puffer fish, moray eels, giant mussels and parrot fish. Closest to Sihanoukville, **Koh Rong Samloem** is the most popular day-excursion; it is two hours out, allowing time for a couple of dives, a lazy lunch and a bit of beach-combing on its uninhabited sands between dives. Further afield, more experienced divers might prefer Koh Tang and Koh Prins (a 6–8hr boat ride away) which are dived on over night trips, with reefs, a wreck or two and good visibility in their deep waters.

The enthusiastic **Scuba Nation** (Serendipity Hill ☎012/604680, Ⓦwww.scubanation.com) is fully insured and the only five-star PADI centre in Cambodia; it offers a four-day Open Water course, day-trips ($75) and overnighters ($195) – including night dives – on their tailor-made boat. **Chez Claude** (between Sokha and Independence beaches, ☎012/840870) pioneered diving in Sihanoukville and runs superior trips for experienced divers. **Eco Dive** between Golden Lions and Serendipity Hill, (☎012/654104, Ⓦwww.ecoseadive.com) runs PADI courses, fun dives, day- and overnight trips, plus a three-day exploration of the waters around Koh Rong Samloem and Koh Tang. Getting further off the beaten track is now possible thanks to **Koh Kong Divers**, a professional and recommended English-run company that has started PADI courses and diving excursions in the coral-filled, crystalline waters of the **Koh S'dach archipelago**. The islands are a two-hour journey by express ferry (or 6hr night ride by fishing trawler) from Sihanoukville (see p.287 for details).

are infinitely more peaceful than those on the mainland, the spattering of **rustic accommodation** (or an outrageously luxurious hotel in one instance) makes the islands great places to get holed up in for a few days and drink in the idyllic surroundings.

There is trouble in paradise, however. Since 2006 the government has leased at least seven islands (though there are rumoured to be as many as 22) to international companies for the **development of luxury hotels and golf courses** instead of the fragile communities of wooden bungalows. So far, fourteen five-star resorts and a staggering **eighteen golf courses** have been mooted, and a Russian company, which has leased both Hawaii Beach and its off-island, Koh Pos (Snake Island), is in the process of building a **bridge** between the two. At the time of writing, the jutting piers of the bridge juxtaposed grimly against the crystalline waters below and the tumbling jungle flanking either side.

On the upside, these developments will provide much-needed **employment** for Cambodians, but it would seem that the downsides are greater, with the money spent by tourists going directly to the overseas corporations, and the resorts adding a further **drain on resources** such as water, which is already severely limited (in the summer months it's not unknown for Sihanoukville to run out of water for several weeks).

For now, a few stalwart bungalows and huts are weathering the developers' storm blowing through this southwestern corner of Cambodia, but time is of the essence if you want to visit the islands before their humble tranquillity is obliterated entirely.

Arrival and Information

The islands are very similar in their attractions: snorkelling, sunbathing, gentle walks and general lounging are positively encouraged and all of these improve the further you travel offshore (particularly the snorkelling and, subsequently, diving). **Koh Russei** (or Bamboo Island) is the most common destination due to its close proximity to the mainland, although, with a couple of beach bars and bungalows, it's not precisely a Robinson Crusoe experience. **Koh Tas** (an hour away by boat) has sandy, gently shelving beaches, great snorkelling and a good chance, if you take fishing tackle (check when you book if it's provided and if not buy it cheaply in the market), of hooking a fish for the barbecue. **Koh Rong Samloem**, two and a half hours beyond Koh Tas, has eight beaches and a rocky reef with good diving (see p.284); to the south, just off the coast, **Koh Khteah**, **Koh Chraloh** and **Koh Ta Kiev** offer reasonable **snorkelling**, with giant mussels to look out for in the waters north of Koh Ta Kiev. If you've got more time, you can get out to deeper waters, such as those around **Koh Tang** and **Koh Prins** five to eight hours from shore, or in the **Koh S'dach** archipelago (see box, p.287). Koh Tang's claim to fame is that it was the site of a major battle to free the *Mayaguez*, an American-owned container ship captured by the Khmer Rouge on May 13, 1975, in the early days of their regime. The US navy and air force launched a mission to liberate the ship but met heavy resistance, and Ream naval base and the industrial areas of Sihanoukville were bombed during the battle. Divers can try to check out two shipwrecks 40m down, northwest of Koh Prins.

You can either make your own arrangements with a local fisherman on Occheuteal Beach or take one of the organized excursions (from $10) with a Sihanoukville guesthouse such as *Coasters* or *Romny Family Bungalows*. If you choose to stay overnight on the island, it will cost you an extra few dollars to join a boat back the following day. All the bungalows have a restaurant of some description but it's a good idea to take your own water and a few basic provisions as electricity is unreliable and often turned off after 8pm.

Accommodation

EcoSea Bungalows Koh Russei ⓦecoseadive.com. Owned by the EcoSea Dive Center, these cabins each get an ocean view and the Dive Center can drop you off. Priority, however, goes to divers. The center tries to support the local community on the island, providing a doctor for several months with plans to do more. ❸

Jonty's Jungle Camp Koh Ta Kiev ⓣ092/502374, ⓦwww.jontysjunglecamp.com. The highlight of these super-chilled bungalows is the wonderful open-air restaurant. ❸

Koh Ru Koh Russei ⓔkoh_ru@yahoo.com. Super budget accommodation here, with bungalows for as little as $3. Restaurant is a great spot to enjoy the sunset. ❶–❸

Lazy Beach Koh Rong Samloem ⓦlazybeachcambodia.com. The extra money you spend goes a long way here, set along yards of sand so fine it squeaks, great communal areas, a decent restaurant and comfortable beds. Booking office on Serendipity Beach Road. ❹

Mirax Resort Koh Dek Koule, off Sihanoukville beyond Koh Pos ⓣ012/763805, ⓔinfo@miraxresort.com, ⓦwww.miraxresort.com. OTT tropical island retreat, with deluxe accommodation, restaurant, bar, infinity pool and spa. Activities include diving and power-snorkelling, and there's an electronic telescope for viewing the stunning night sky. ❾

M'pay Bay Koh Rong Samloem ⓦcambodianislands.com. Slightly smarter bungalows, each with an en-suite bathroom and comfortable veranda. Has full diving and snorkelling equipment. A good one for the eco-conscious; 25% goes to Marine Conservation Cambodia. ❸–❹

Day-trips from Sihanoukville

The top attraction outside town is the coastal **Ream National Park**, which covers a range of habitats and has fine scenery and plentiful wildlife. Closer to hand are the **Kbal Chhay waterfalls**, a series of cascades fed by the Prek Toeuk Sap; these are fairly impressive in the rainy season, though there's not much to see in the dry. To reach them, head out of Sihanoukville on National Route 4, turning left after about 10km at a sign for the falls, then continuing another 7km. A moto there and back costs around $8.

Ream National Park

Unique in Cambodia, **Ream National Park** (also known as the Preah Sihanouk National Park) covers 210 square kilometres of both terrestrial and marine habitat, including stunning coastal scenery, mangrove swamps, lowland evergreen forest and the islands of Koh Thmei and Koh Ses. At least 155 species of **bird** have been recorded in the park, and for resident and visiting waders, the mangrove-lined **Prek Toeuk Sap** River is an important habitat. Besides supporting a large population of fishing eagles, the river is also home to milky and adjutant storks, and kingfishers, which are regularly spotted on the river trips. The list of **mammals** includes deer, wild pig and fishing cats, though these are all elusive and you're more likely to see monkeys.

Practicalities

Most visitors to the park go on an all-day **trip** arranged through guesthouses and cafés, such as *Romny Family Bungalows*, or *Ana Tours* (about $20 per person, depending on numbers) in Sihanoukville; these include a boat trip down the Prek Toeuk Sap; a walk through the jungle either from or to Thmor Tom, a small village in the park; and swimming and picnicking at the stunningly beautiful white-sand **beach** of Koh Sam Pouch, followed by the return boat journey.

Alternatively, staff at the **park headquarters** also run boat trips on the river (about $35 for up to five people, plus $6 for each additional person), as well as organizing **guided walks** ($6 per person; around 2hr) along nearby nature trails. The headquarters (daily 7.30–11am & 2–5pm; ⓣ012/875096) is in a green wooden building just beyond the entrance to Kang Keng Airport, 23km from Sihanoukville – turn up early or phone the day before to book a boat and guide.

A moto from Sihanoukville will cost about $6; ask your moto driver to drop you at the bridge over the Prek Toeuk Sap, on National Route 4, 25km towards Phnom Penh, which is where the boats leave from. You'll need to take food, water and sun protection.

Koh S'dach and the outlying islands

Lying in clear blue waters roughly halfway between Sihanoukville and Koh Kong, just off the coast of Koh Kong province, the small rocky island of **Koh S'dach** (King's Island) gets its name from the legend surrounding the **royal spring** behind the port, which is said to have gushed forth miraculously when the king and his army were desperate for drinking water as they battled invaders here. Supporting a population of a couple of thousand, the island may not look too exciting at first glance, but has wonderful snorkelling and fishing (even quite close to shore, though you'll need your own equipment) and is a good base from which to explore outlying islands, which for the time being at least are completely undeveloped. It's also, by fishing village standards anyway, quite a prosperous little community due to the ice factory, which supports the fishing fleet.

The island is just a couple of kilometres long, and a kilometre wide. There's a rocky **beach** on its seaward side, reached by a path through the compound of the island's simple pagoda, **Wat Koy Koh**. The beach isn't brilliant, but vivid coral and shoals of fish found close to shore compensate. The island is a pleasant spot to mess about in boats and visit nearby islands, the closest of which is **Koh K'Maoit**, just 1km away, home to a small fishing community and with some sandy beaches. Alternatively, you can hop in one of the small, fibreglass boats that go across to the mainland (5min; $1), where there are also some fine, deserted beaches.

Practicalities

The Royal Kamera **express ferry** ($25) to Koh S'dach leaves Sihanoukville every other day at 1pm from the dock roughly 1km from the main port along Hun Sen Beach Drive. To get the overnight fishing boat, a journey not for the fainthearted, you need to head for the dock at 8pm on the days when the ferry hasn't run and wait for it to turn up (which can take up to 4hr). You will arrive on Koh S'dach at the end of a cramped five- to six- hour crossing but luckily the guesthouse owner also runs the dock and has an office at the far end of it. Few people speak English.

To get to neighbouring islands or go fishing, you'll need to **hire a boat**; agree a programme with the boatman beforehand and expect to pay upwards of $30 per day. Alternatively, the **Koh Kong Divers** (ⓣ017/502784, ⓦkohkongdivers.com) have a base on neighbouring **Koh Totang** island from where they run snorkelling and diving trips and charter, and are currently the only PADI-certified dive outfit in the area.

The *Koh S'dach Guesthouse* (ⓣ011/983806; no English spoken; ❷–❸), signposted when you get off the boat, has a range of accommodation, the cheapest of which is in clean bungalows with spectacularly uncomfortable mattresses compensated for by their proximity to the waves. There is a decent but pricey restaurant here too and a smaller hut from which you can order a hearty breakfast. For isolated luxury, the newly completed *Belinda's* (ⓣ017/517517, ⓦwww.belindabeach.com; ❼) takes up the end of the peninsula with its air-conditioned bungalows, infinity pool and breathtaking views of the mainland across azure seas. It has a decent French restaurant and a bar.

The only other places to **eat** are near the ferry along the market road. The grocery shop is well stocked with water, drinks, biscuits and general products, but expect to pay slightly more than you would on the mainland.

Koh Totang

This tiny island, 2km off Koh S'dach, has a population of seven that almost doubles during the dry season when the delightful Swiss owners of *Nomad's Land* bungalows (Ⓣ011/916171, Ⓔnomadslandcambodia@hotmail.com; essential to call in advance ❶–❸) come back from Europe to open up shop. The six rustic bungalows fit in gently with their glorious natural surroundings and are accompanied by shared outdoor showers and compost lavatories. Welcome to the world of Robinson Crusoe – there's good snorkelling and diving from the beach and the vibe couldn't be more laidback; meals are shared (usually in the form of a buffet; $6) around the large table in the communal area.

Koh Kong and around

The reason most people come to Koh Kong is for the **border crossing** with Thailand at Cham Yeam. It's a shame, however, that so few people hang around to enjoy the simple pleasures of the area – stunning virgin forests, pristine beaches, hidden waterfalls and white water rapids. At present limited access means that you're somewhat restricted in the amount of exploration you can do, though there's some indication that this may change, as a couple of Western-run establishments are now offering treks into the mountains and boat trips to Koh Kong island.

The town and around

Koh Kong used to be a prosperous little logging town, though it's now lapsed into a quiet backwater, with an easy familiarity. Laid out on a simple grid on the east bank of the river, the town consists mostly of wooden houses whose style owes more to neighbouring Thailand – only a few are built on stilts in Cambodian style, and there's no colonial architecture at all.

The sights within town, such as they are, are all low-key. Locals will point you to the unexciting **Red House**, built for Norodom Sihanouk, who never visited it; it's a pleasant enough walk 1km north from the centre, along the river. A pleasant jaunt can be made across the river to **Resort 2000**, a weekend haunt for locals, where there are thatched huts, refreshment stalls and jet skis for hire. To get there, hire a motorbike or moto (about 40 baht) and look for a dirt road branching left about 1.5km beyond the bridge, from where it's another 2km to the beach.

A couple of small companies offer excursions to explore **waterfalls** upstream or the **beaches** on nearby **Koh Kong island**, which is a surprisingly large and attractive

Moving on from Koh Kong

Shared taxis (50,000 riel) and minibuses (30,000 riel) leave from the transport stop at the market to Sihanoukville and Phnom Penh. National Route 48 is in great shape and it's a scenic trip as it winds through the foothills of the Cardamom Mountains – though it's a shame so much jungle has had to be cleared in the process. A bus runs every morning from the transport stop 2km west of town beyond the disused warehouse to Sihanoukville ($7; 4hr). Taxis for the border at Cham Yeam also leave from here, so it's easier to get a moto for the 20-minute trip.

Border scams

Watch out for this scam at the border – the attempt to charge 1000 baht (around $30) or more for a Cambodian visa, with the excuse that "this is a land crossing, it's different". No it isn't! A Cambodian visa is $20 regardless of where or how you enter the country. If this happens to you demand a receipt; record the time, date and the name of the border official and report it, as soon as you get the opportunity, to the Ministry of Tourism (ⓣ023/212837, ⓔinfo@mot.gov.kh) and the Immigration Department (ⓣ012/581558, ⓔvisa_online.com.kh.

place, with pristine stretches of sand on its seaward side. The boat ride there takes about an hour.

Upriver from Koh Kong, it takes five minutes to reach a **pagoda** overlooking the river on the west bank, where rock paintings portray scenes of torture in hell, mixed up with what appear to be scenes of Khmer Rouge atrocities – the latter presumably painted quite recently, as this was Khmer Rouge territory until around 1997. As you journey further upstream, the imposing backdrop of the Cardamom Mountains comes into view. After about fifty minutes you'll reach a stretch of river between towering cliffs, where you can stop to take in a pounding waterfall and a stretch of rapids.

Practicalities

Arriving by **road** (the only way to arrive, as the new road from Sihanoukville has replaced the boat) you'll be dropped at the transport stop beside the market in the southeast of town, 500m from the river. From here it is a 1km moto ride into town ($1). Motos will also do the 12km trip to the **border crossing** at Cham Yeam (daily 7am–8pm) for about $3. Minibuses (30,000 riel) and shared taxis (50,000 riel) run to Koh Kong direct **from Phnom Penh**, bypassing Sihanoukville. Shared taxis and minibuses to Sihanoukville run from the market (50,000 riel and 30,000 riel respectively).

Baht, riel and dollars are all accepted in town, though baht is the favoured **currency**. Dollars can be exchanged at stalls in and around the market, or at the Acleda Bank just north of the market. The **hospital** is 500m north of the market, but you may be better off going across the border to the one at Trat. The **post office** is further north along the same road. International **phone** calls can be made from some shops near the market; they are routed through Thailand, and so are usually cheaper than calling from Sihanoukville. There are several **internet** cafés along the high street ($1 per hour).

If you want to **explore** the surrounding area, Koh Kong Divers (office at the *Waterfront Restaurant and Bar* ⓣ017/502784, ⓦkohkongdivers.com) operates a range of first-rate excursions from day-trips up river to secluded waterfalls or the pristine beaches of Koh Kong island, to week-long trips further afield, to the Koh S'dach archipelago where the diving is excellent and still virgin in many places. They can arrange overnight stays on Koh Totang (see p.288).

Accommodation

Most accommodation is within walking distance of the jetty, though there are plenty of motos around if you need one.

4 Rivers Ecolodge Tatai village, 22km out of town on the road to Phnom Penh ⓣ023/217374, ⓦecolodgesasia.en. Nothing quite like this exists elsewhere in Cambodia; luxury abounds to the point of decadence in floating tents containing four-poster beds, DVD players and all other mod cons, while trying to neutralize its carbon footprint with sustainable building materials and solar electricity, among other measures. The resort benefits from a magnificent location on the river and offers river- and land- based tours, including trips up to the thundering Tatai rapids. ❼

The Dugout High Street, 20 yards north of the roundabout ⓣ016/650325, ⓦkoh-kong-cambodia.com. After a recent refurb, this hotel is doing a great trade with clean, smart rooms, bicycle hire and a swimming pool. Management can book bus and tour tickets for you. ❸

Koh Kong City On the riverfront, just north of the boat dock ⓣ035/936777, ⓔkkcthotel@netkhmer.com. Posh, new hotel with business-class rooms and a riverside restaurant-bar. ❸

Koh Kong Guesthouse Opposite the old boat dock ⓣ099/800200. Rooms in this cheerful family-run establishment are small and a bit dark, but kept clean and fresh. The upstairs restaurant and bar is a popular place for economical and tasty Asian and Western food, including an unforgettable *pad Thai*. ❶

Koh Kong International Resort Club 12km from town at Cham Yeam ⓣ016/700970. Massive, luxury hotel and casino complex at the border, with a choice of deluxe rooms and bungalow suites, in tropical gardens running down to an attractive beach. ❺

Oasis 2km north of town ⓣ016/331556, ⓦoasisresort.netkhmer.com. The resort has five simple, but roomy, family bungalows with adequate amenities in a garden. There is also a swimming pool (non-residents can use it for $3), restaurant and great views to the mountains. ❸

Otto's Signposted 50m down a small road from the old boat dock ⓣ012/924249. Located in a traditional stilt-house, this is the original backpacker guesthouse and still the cheapest in town. Rooms are small and rather dingy with shared bathrooms, but there's a good inexpensive restaurant and bar. ❶

The Rainbow Lodge Tatai Koh Kong, 25km towards Sre Ambel ⓣ099/744321, ⓔtherainbowlodge@netkhmer.com, ⓦrainbowlodgecambodia.com. Newly opened eco-lodge of seven stilted bungalows set in verdant scrubland with river views; eco-initiatives include solar power and rainwater collection. Prices are fully inclusive of breakfast, lunch and three-course dinners (menu choices available). Can organize treks to the Cardamom Mountains and boat trip to the waterfalls. Book by email as there's no phone; cash payment only. ❺

Eating

Baan Peakmai Three blocks to the north of the market. This restaurant has a covered terrace around a garden and serves good Khmer, Thai and Western food, including many vegetarian dishes, all at reasonable prices.

Café Laurent Just north of the old boat dock. A sumptuous restaurant on stilts over the river with an extensive menu of Khmer, Thai and Western dishes.

Fat Sam's High Street. The expansive Welsh owner, Sam, is well known and liked around town, not just for the hearty English breakfasts ($5) his restaurant serves. Popular with expats; has a pool table.

Waterfront Bar and Restaurant. Opposite the old boat dock. By day, a laidback café serving big pizzas ($5) and noodle dishes; by night a lively bar, popular with locals, expats and visitors alike.

Around Koh Kong

Natural beauty and biodiversity abound across the Koh Kong province, a holy grail for nature lovers that stretches down as far as the northern tip of Sihanoukville. The magestic **Cardamom mountain range**, over 1800m at its highest elevation, is still home to some of the rarest species on the planet including the Asian elephant, the clouded leopard and the Indochinese tiger (although there have been no official sightings of the latter since the 1990s). Meanwhile, the Irrawaddy dolphin is often seen playing in the saline waters of the extensive mangrove network along the coast, explorable in the **Peam Krasaop Wildlife Sanctuary**. Further south, the remote village of **Chi Phat**, a shining example of the success of community-based ecotourism projects, makes a wonderful base for discovering the mountains.

Peam Krasaop Wildlife Sanctuary (PKWS)

Koh Kong has the country's largest area of mangrove forest, forming a vast and intricate network of "islands" which are the foundations of a rich and varied saltwater ecosystem. An enjoyable excursion from Koh Kong is a visit to the **Peam Krasaop Wildlife Sanctuary (PKWS)**, a 250-square-kilometre area of stunning mangrove forest that was designated as part of Cambodia's system of Protected Areas in 1997 in an attempt to nurture and sustain one of the province's greatest natural attributes. Ten thousand people, mainly fishermen, live in floating hamlets within the protected area and make their livings off the abundant marine life.

Recently, however, unlicensed Thai and Cambodian boats have been found fishing along the coast and are threatening the supply. This has led to the fishermen turning to illegal fishing methods, such as cyanide and grenades, in the hope of increasing their yield. The Participatory Management of Mangrove Resources (PMMR) is working closely with the local communities in PKWS to improve awareness of the surrounding habitat and reintroduce more sustainable fishing methods. Your visit could provide much needed financial and social support for their efforts.

Arriving early in the morning from Koh Kong you may be rewarded with a sighting of the rare Irrawaddy dolphin and you will be unlucky not to spot monkeys and an array of birdlife whether you are exploring by boat or on foot. The Sanctuary (5000 riel; 6.30am–6pm) is easily accessible from Koh Kong via moto ($3). Tours can also be arranged by Koh Kong Divers and the main guesthouses in Koh Kong if you want to visit by boat ($10/person).

Chi Phat

Another of Cambodia's Community-Based Ecotourism projects, Chi Phat is a remote riverside village nestled in the southern valleys of the Cardomom Mountains, accessible only by long-tail boat from Andoung Toeuk some 20km away, up the Preak Piphot River. Andoung Toeuk is roughly two hours and thirty minutes from Koh Kong along the N48 (4hr from Phnom Penh).

Thanks to its inaccessibility, Chi Phat is still a good hike off the tourist trail and provides an excellent opportunity to immerse yourself in the natural environment and local culture. **Homestays** make up part of the range of accommodation available here, alongside a few basic guesthouses.

An overnight stay is enough to get a flavour of what Chi Phat is about, although a week is more appropriate if you want to explore the huge network of **jungle trails**, either on foot or **mountain bike**, to waterfalls in secluded clearings, bat caves and ancient burial sites ($6–10 a day). Gentler ways to enjoy the surroundings are sunrise **birdwatching** excursions (the silver oriole, the yellow-bellied warbler and great hornbill are some of the highlights) and peaceful river cruises in traditional rowing boats.

To get to Chi Phat, the **bus** from Koh Kong passes Andoung Toeuk on its way to Sihanoukville every morning. Similarly, the early bus from Phnom Penh to Koh Kong also drops off here, as does the Sihanoukville–Koh Kong bus. All these buses should arrive in time for you to catch the **public boat** upriver to Chi Phat (midday; $2.50; 2hr 30min) although it is easy to charter motorboats of varying sizes, which cost significantly more. Watch out for **rogue motorboat owners**, who are conning tourists by saying there's no public boat. This is not the case, although if you miss the one at midday, it's a 24-hour wait for the next one.

Accommodation can be booked with the on-site CBET Visitor Centre, or in advance via Ⓔ chiphatbooking@gmail.com. There are twelve guesthouses ($5) and five homestays ($3) at present in Chi Phat, all of which are humble but very well tended. The small CBET **restaurant** ($2.50 breakfast, $3.50 dinner) serves substantial, nourishing meals made from local produce – notably fried lobster and shrimp, *Bampong kdam ning Bangkang* – and you can buy cheap noodle dishes for less than $1 at the market.

Kampot and around

Charming, compact **KAMPOT TOWN** enjoys one of the nicest settings in Cambodia, situated on the north bank of the Teuk Chhou River, with a panoramic view of the forested Bokor hill slopes. Once a hustling trading port, Kampot still boasts a large Chinese population, their single-storey houses, built without stilts, contrasting with the Khmer stilt-houses and colonial shophouses that grace the town's streets.

Kampot has become a popular destination for weekending Khmer and expats from Phnom Penh, as well as for foreign tourists: the surrounding province is one of Cambodia's most picturesque, the landscape ranging from the cloud-topped mountains of the **Bokor National Park** to salt-flats and misty, uninhabited offshore islands. Kampot is ideally located for visiting a wealth of nature-based attractions in the area and is en route to the tiny seaside resort of **Kep**.

Arrival, transport and information

Built on a grid system, the town is bordered on the west by the Teuk Chhou River (aka Kampong Bay River), spanned in the south by a rustic old bridge for local

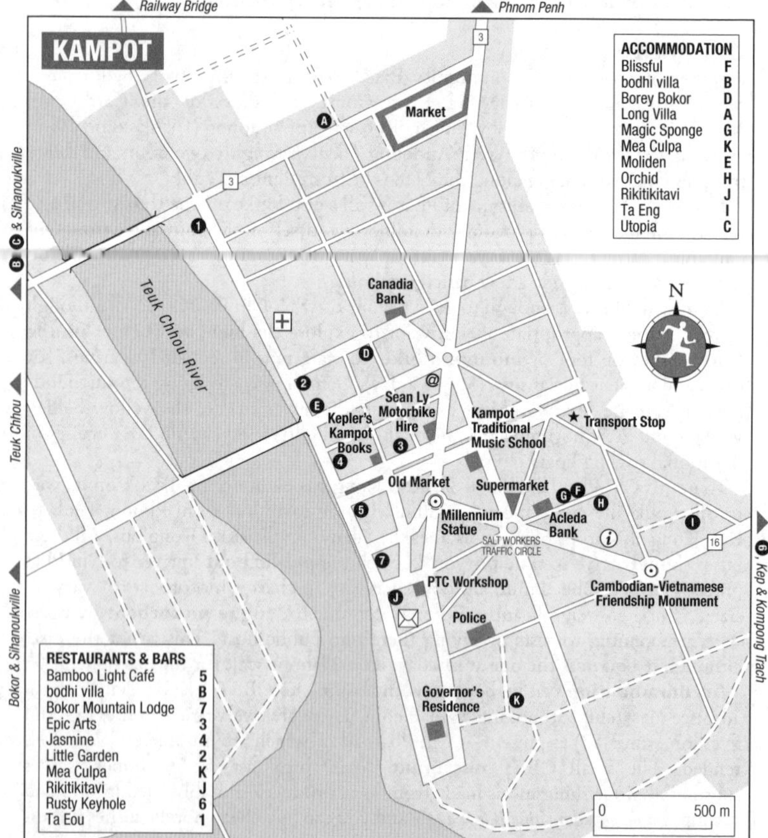

The Chinese in Cambodia

There has been a **Chinese presence** in Cambodia since the very earliest times – indeed accounts written by Chinese traders and envoys from the third century onwards have played a major part in chronicling the country's history – but it was only after the fifteenth century that the Chinese began to settle in significant numbers. Marrying into rich Khmer families and assuming positions as tax collectors, bankers, gold dealers and restaurateurs, ethnic Chinese soon established themselves as arguably the most influential minority in the country.

A flood of new immigrants arrived as a result of China's economic crisis in the 1930s. In the main, the Chinese community continued to prosper until the 1970s, when they were **persecuted** first by the Lon Nol government – which resented their success – and then by the Khmer Rouge – who wanted them eliminated. Things became more complicated in 1979 when the Vietnamese liberation of Cambodia was followed by a short-lived Chinese invasion of Vietnam. This resulted in many Cambodian Chinese fleeing to Thailand; those Chinese who remained were subsequently permitted to resume limited business activities, but it wasn't until after the 1993 elections that they were properly able to reassert their influence on business – which they did wholeheartedly, capitalizing on their access to investment capital through their extensive overseas networks. Nowadays, the number of Chinese-owned businesses is clear to see from the Chinese signage on streets in any Cambodian town.

Cambodia's Chinese have managed to retain their own culture and language (most are **bilingual**) while at the same time integrating very well into Cambodian society. It is not easy to pick them out, though in towns such as Voen Sai and Kampot they are more visible by virtue of maintaining their own Chinese-language **schools**. Indeed, although Chinese New Year is not an official holiday, it assumes a festive importance in Phnom Penh akin to the Khmer New Year, with energetic dragon dances performed in the streets.

traffic, while to the north a modern concrete bridge carries National Route 3. The town centre is a roundabout at which roads converge from all directions. Arriving by **road** from Phnom Penh, you can either get dropped by the market, north of the centre on the main road or 700m further on at the **transport stop**, which is also where taxis, pick-ups and the bus from Sihanoukville arrive.

Kampot can be easily explored on foot; the lack of traffic and the pleasant climate make it a relaxing place to wander around. The owners of all the main guesthouses can arrange sight-seeing trips, including visits to Bokor, the surrounding countryside and boat trips upriver or to the islands. **Renting a motorbike** is also a great way to explore the surrounding area on your own ($4–7 a day); most guesthouses have their own for hire, or will be able to help with this. The **tourist office** is 1km from the main roundabout on the Kep road.

Accommodation

There's a pleasant selection of **places to stay** in Kampot, including some of the cheapest backpacker accommodation in the south. Whatever your budget, you shouldn't have a problem finding a decent room.

Blissful On a quiet side-street about 1km south of the roundabout ⓣ012/513024, ⓔblissfulguesthouse@yahoo.com. Western-run place with very competitive rates (dorm beds go for $2). Rooms are well kept and all beds have mosquito nets. Free welcome beer on arrival. ❶

bodhi villa 1.5km out of town across the river towards Teuk Chhou ⓣ012/728884, ⓔbodhivilla@mac.com. This is in the running to be the best backpacker guesthouse in Cambodia. Set in a veritable jungle of garden on the river it features a recording studio that's free for any muso with as much passion for music as the Australian owner, Hugh. From a $2 mattress and mosquito net on the balcony to comfortable open-fronted bungalows there's accommodation for all budgets – try and stick around for one of the owner's Friday-night live music sessions; they take some beating, as does the heavenly beef *lok lak* on the menu. ❶–❸

Borey Bokor One block north of the main road to the bridge ⓣ016/960700. Reliable, if unexciting, pleasant modern hotel with decent, roomy accommodation with hot showers, TV, fridge and a/c. ❸

Long Villa Southwest of the market towards the new bridge ⓣ012/210820. Clean and simple rooms with their own bathrooms start at just $2 in this family-run guesthouse. In a cheerful courtyard, it provides all travellers' services, plus there's a blackboard of Cambodian phrases in the restaurant to help you with your language skills. ❶–❸

Magic Sponge Just south of *Blissful* ⓣ017/946428, ⓦwww.magicspongecambodia.com. New backpacker guesthouse with a party attitude and bright, cheap and clean rooms and dorms in a refurbished villa with a mini-golf course in the grounds. Their cocktails currently come a close second to those at *bodhi villa*. ❶–❷

Mea Culpa A block back from the river, behind the governor's house. Clean and comfortable, new guesthouse with bright bedrooms and all mod-cons including cable TV and fridges. It's a little pricey, however, considering that breakfast is not included. [illegible]–[illegible]

Moliden Opposite the old road bridge ⓣ012/820779, ⓦmolidenguesthouse.wordpress.com. New and rather swanky guesthouse built in polished wood, with smart a/c rooms, firm mattresses and a lively bar/restaurant below. Excellently located on the waterfront. ❹

Orchid Across the road from the Acleda Bank ⓣ033/932634, ⓔorchidguesthousekampot@yahoo.com. Charming bungalows with their own tiny balconies in a garden. Restaurant, tours and pleasant owners combine to make this a good choice. ❷–❹

Rikitikitavi On the riverfront south of the old bridge ⓣ012/235102, ⓦwww.rikitikitavi-kampot.com. Booking is essential here to secure one of the six comfortable and stylish rooms. The 1st-floor bar is a fabulous spot to watch the sunset. ❹

Ta Eng 36 Street 726 ⓣ012/330058. This long-established guesthouse is a little way out of the centre, but it gets a lot of repeat custom for the kindness of the family who run it. Rooms are large and clean, and there's a dorm ($3 per person), plus a small outside restaurant and sitting area. ❷

Utopia 8km from Kampot ⓣ012/1724681. Surrounded by orchards this out-of-the way guesthouse is perched on the river bank opposite Teuk Chhou Zoo. With just a few well-appointed rooms, booking is essential, especially at weekends when it fills up with expats from Phnom Penh. Restaurant, bar and watersports – the owner will teach you to row standing up Khmer-style, if you're interested. [illegible]–[illegible]

The Town

Kampot, with its sunkissed riverfront lined with splendid trees and old colonial houses, is a pleasant little town to wander around, even though there are no sights as such. To the southwest of the central roundabout is the colourful **French quarter**, where shophouses line the streets through to the river and flowers planted in cans, pots and just about any other available container give the place an almost Mediterranean atmosphere. Getting to the riverfront with a camera for the **sunset** as the night fishermen head out to sea in their brightly coloured boats is a must. The elongated old market – abandoned some years ago when a new market building was constructed and stallholders forced to move – was being restored at the time of writing. An altruistic expat has designs on it as a community sports centre, but whether this gets the go-ahead or not remains to be seen. Further along are the government offices, imposing prison (said to house at least two Westerners at any one time), post office and, at the end of the road, the Governor's Residence, which has been restored to its original opulent grandeur.

Another pleasant stroll is to follow the river from the old road bridge to the disused railway bridge in the north. At the railway bridge you can cross the river on the rusty, pockmarked walkway, and return to town along the other bank.

While in town you could drop in at **Kampot Traditional Music School** (see p.296), where you can see students practising traditional dance and music. Alternatively, visit the Provincial Training Centre Kampot (PTC Kampot), in a compound behind the post office, which trains women from the province in weaving. The theory is that they can learn a trade, which will give them a sustainable income, but in practice once they leave, there simply isn't enough demand for their products. You can help by buying a silk length, a cotton scarf or *krama* at the workshop, which comes complete with a label bearing the weaver's name and photograph.

Eating, drinking and nightlife

Kampot has plenty of **eating** options. In addition to the restaurants listed below, there are the usual rice and noodle shops around the market, by the transport stop and along the road from the roundabout to the old bridge. In the evening, stalls selling fruit shakes and desserts set up west of the roundabout on the road to the old bridge. **Nightlife** in Kampot is low-key, with a couple of Western bars along with the ubiquitous karaoke places, the most popular of which are across the river near the old road bridge.

Bamboo Light Café South of the old bridge on the riverfront. Sri Lankan/Indian restaurant with plenty of choices at very reasonable prices, and vegetarian options too.
bodhi villa 2km north of the new road bridge, on the opposite river bank to the town. Even if you don't stay here, the journey out of town is worth it for the delicious food, ranging from Cambodian and Thai to Western classics. The Friday-night parties are the talk of the town.
Bokor Mountain Lodge Terrific riverfront location for a pre-dinner cocktail or post-dinner brandy, with an impressive menu comprising New Zealand lamb and Pacific dory.
Epic Arts Just northeast of the old market ⓦwww.epicarts.org.uk. Run by a group of deaf people, this tiny café serves home-made cakes, teas and coffee. Instructions in the menu help you sign your order.
Jasmine On the riverfront, one block north of the old market. A foodie's heaven, where you can dine on excellent Asian–French dishes such as crab with Kampot pepper, for around $5 a dish. Specials change daily depending on market availability. If you only eat at one posh place in Cambodia, make it here.
Little Garden Bar North of the bridge on the riverfront. Pleasant, welcoming place in a quiet garden. Drinks and snacks are better than the full meals.
Mea Culpa A block back from the river, behind the Governor's Residence. This newly opened guesthouse is a little pricey, but the food in the open-air restaurant is truly excellent. The stone-baked pizzas (from $6) are delicious, as is the mouth-watering array of ingredients in the "build your own" sandwiches – perfect to take away if you're off on an excursion.
Rusty Keyhole Signposted off the road to Kep, 1km out of town. This welcoming bar and restaurant has kept its loyal customers despite moving out of town. Surrounded by fields and palm trees, it's a lovely spot to relax over a beer or two while your spare ribs are barbecued; one portion will fill two.
Ta Eou East bank of the river ⓣ012/820832. This breezy restaurant protrudes over the river on stilts, with fine views up to Bokor and inexpensive, tasty Khmer and Chinese dishes, including superb grilled shrimps and steamed crabs, and excellent fried fish with coconut cream. English-language menu.

Listings

Banks and exchange To change travellers' cheques and get cash advances on Visa and MasterCard, go to the Canadia Bank a block northwest of the traffic circle. There are money changers in the market and in shops round the traffic circle; there's an Acleda Bank near the *Blissful* guesthouse.
Books Kepler's Kampot Books near the old market has a great selection of second hand and photocopied books, with a good range on Cambodia; the *Blissful* guesthouse has a book exchange and sells some second hand books too.
Buses Phnom Penh Sorya Transport and Hua Lian have adjacent booking desks at the restaurant opposite the transport stop; both run buses (16,000 riel; 5hr) to Phnom Penh via Kep. The former also runs a daily bus (2.30pm; 3hr; $3) to Sihanoukville via Kep. A private fourteen-seater minibus leaves *Bokor Mountain Lodge* daily at 2pm (1.5hr; $7) for Sihanoukville. It is run by the bar, *G'Day Mate*, in Sihanoukville, but you're under no obligation to take one of their rooms.

Car and motorbike rental Cars with driver can be hired through hotels and guesthouses for around $50 per day. Motorbikes are available for rent at many of the guesthouses as well as Sean Ly, on the street that runs to the west of the *Phnom Khieu Hotel*; a 100cc runabout costs $3 per day, a smart 250cc off-road bike is $10.
Cultural performances Kampot Traditional Music School, on the edge of the park southeast of the old market, gives lessons in traditional and folk music and dance to orphaned and disabled children. Visitors are welcome (free, but a donation is appreciated) and a timetable is displayed outside.
Hospital On the riverfront, between the new and old bridges.
Internet Plenty of internet access around town ($1.50 per hr); brilliant high-speed internet at Kepler's Kampot Books.
Massage Seeing Hands Massage, near *Bokor Mountain Lodge* on the riverfront ($4 per hr).
Phones There are booths around the market for domestic calls; international calls can be made from the internet shops.
Post office On the riverfront, south of the old bridge.
Shopping Metaheap supermarket is on the northern side of the salt workers' traffic circle. Dorsu, opposite the old market, sells pretty dresses, *kramar*s and other attractive accessories. The clothes are made by local women as part of a social-enterprise system with an impressive ethical focus, well worth supporting.
Volunteering If you're interested in volunteering around Kampot, contact Dorsu (Ⓣ012/960225, Ⓔdorsucambodia@gmail.com), or Barbara or Norman at *Little Garden Bar*. *Little Garden Bar* runs Tin Lid Kids, which provides treats such as trips to the zoo for the street children who collect cans.

Around Kampot

There are some great excursions to go on in the surrounding area. The biggest tourist draw in these parts was once **Bokor National Park**, but this extraordinary deserted hill station has fallen into the hands of developers (see box below). Now the main attractions are some **wild rapids**, a zoo and a smattering of **temple caves** as well as trips to the pepper plantations and along the river. Kampot's proximity to Kep and **Rabbit Island** also make either one a possible day-trip (although we recommend spending a bit longer in both).

Bokor National Park

The story of Bokor National Park is a fascinating but sad one. Wandering through the crumbling, chilling remnants of the 1920s **French colonial hill station**, often swathed in thick fog, has been the area's most popular attraction for the past decade, but in 2007 Hun Sen's government effectively sold the mountain in its entirety to the Sokimex Group (owner of the Sokha Resorts and Sokimex Oil among others) for US$100m. The Chinese conglomerate now owns a 99-year lease and has begun an extravagant development project that will see the refurbishment of the dilapidated hill station (which was also the scene of a dramatic showdown between the Khmer Rouge and the Vietnamese in 1979) and the construction of a towering casino complex comprising hotels, golf courses and water parks. The plans extend to the coast, where a major port is being built with a view to landing cruise ships there then helicoptering guests to the plateau.

The first foundations have been laid and a new 32-kilometre road carving a thick ribbon of tarmac into the steep hillside is almost finished. The whole mountain was closed off to visitors while the road was being built and now there is a charge to use it. It is impossible to visit without going through local tour operators who have been forced to up their prices to accommodate the toll. At $20, the day out no longer offers value for money. Depending on the developer's rate of progress and their attitude towards them, the tours may soon be a thing of the past anyway.

Teuk Chhou Zoo and rapids

Set among gardens and fruit plantations at the foot of the Elephant Mountains on the west bank of the Teuk Chhou River, 12km northeast of Kampot, the **Teuk Chhou Zoo** (daily 7am–5.30pm; $5) is home to a wide range of fauna, including tigers, a pair of playful young elephants, lemurs and gibbons. The zoo is privately managed and spreads over a wide area, permeated by incongruous piped music. As in most zoos, the animals look none too happy, belying the almost unintelligible praises of the zoo's founders on a board at the entrance.

Just a couple of hundred metres further upstream from the zoo, the river becomes particularly scenic, racing down the valley and bubbling over the rocks in a series of gurgling **rapids**. There's a fee ($1 per day for foreigners) to go further, which gives you access to the rapids and car park, where you'll find plenty of food stalls and places to hire inflated inner tubes. Paths lead down to the river, where you can paddle or, if you're a good swimmer and the water isn't in full spate, plunge in for a swim – but be careful at all times, as the current is deceptively strong and the water incredibly cold. The north bank of the river gets really busy at weekends and it's worth paying 3000 riel to cross the chain-link bridge to the other side where you'll find plenty of quieter bathing spots, although the rapids may be at risk, as a massive, new hydroelectric power station is being built by the Chinese 3km upstream and locals are concerned that this will change the water flow. You can reach the zoo and rapids in twenty minutes from Kampot by hiring a moto for a half-day ($4).

Caves around Kampot

East of Kampot, looming up from flat rice paddies, the rugged limestone outcrops of **Phnom Chhnork** and **Phnom Sorseha** have some caves to scramble through. Although you could visit both these sites in a morning, to give yourself time to travel between them and explore properly, you'd do as well to allow a couple of hours each. Note that there are no facilities in the caves and it is a good idea to wear stout shoes and take a torch.

Phnom Chhnork (foreigners' fee of 4000 riel) is closest to Kampot; turn left off the road to Kep about 5km from town, signposted through a portico, and then head out along a well-made but unsurfaced road to the hill (about 4km in total). The entrance to the hill is through a wat, where you can leave your motorbike with a local boy for a few hundred riel. From here it's a kilometre-or-so's walk through fields of well-tended vegetable plots to the foot of the hill. Intrepid explorers can explore a couple of pokey holes at the foot of the hill before venturing up the rickety steps, passing a collection of pagoda buildings, to the main caves. If you look carefully, through the gloom you will see a brick-built **pre-Angkor prasat**; the rock seems to be trying to claim the ruin, which is slowly being coated with limestone as water drips from the roof. Child guides don't have much information but for a dollar or so they are very helpful for negotiating the paths within the caves.

Back at the main road, the dirt-track turning for **Phnom Sorseha** is further on towards Kep, on the left about 14km out of Kampot and signposted in blue and white through another grand portico; the track stops after 1km at the foot of the hill; steps within the grounds of the pagoda here lead up to the caves. From the top it has a great view over the province to the Vietnamese island of Phu Quoc, and more caves to explore.

Turn left at the top of the steps and follow the rocky path for 50m to reach **Ruhng Dhumrey Saw** (White Elephant Cave). Just inside the entrance is a seated

Buddha statue, from where rickety steps head down into the cave proper; here you can see the large cream-and-grey rock formation, vaguely resembling an elephant's head, which gives the cave its name. Back at the main steps, take the path to the right, which leads after about 150m to the far side of the hill and **Leahng Bpodjioh** (Bat Cave), filled with the ear-splitting sound of squeaking bats. The stench of ammonia is overpowering, and watch you don't get guano in the eye if you look up. The cave is smaller and darker than Ruhng Dhumrey Saw, although a few shafts of light penetrate the gloom, highlighting the tree roots that poke down spookily from the roof of the chamber. Back outside, you may be lucky enough to see the monkeys that live in the woods on the hillside, while from the top of the hill there's a good view over the rice paddies along the coast.

Hiring a moto to take you to both caves will cost $8–10; renting your own motorbike costs $4–6.

Kep and around

KEP was already an affluent seaside resort back in the 1960s, when Sihanoukville was just a fishing village, though subsequent events were unkind to the town. Despite being eclipsed by Sihanoukville, Kep is now making a spirited comeback as a day-trip destination from Phnom Penh, though not for its beach, which is narrow, black and pebbly. Instead, Cambodians come for its food – particularly the crab. Foreigners too are arriving in ever-increasing numbers, attracted by its mellow atmosphere and excellent accommodation options. Currently, apart from just kicking back and relaxing, the main attractions here are the trips to offshore islands and beautiful surrounding countryside. These can be organized through any of the guesthouses or hotels.

Traces of the town's sombre past remain, however. The region is dotted with the gutted shells of colonial villas – tragic evidence of the Khmer Rouge's wanton lust for destruction. Until recently, most of these were smothered by the prolific tropical vegetation and home to squatters; now some have been restored and it's likely that more will follow, although the difficulty of establishing ownership means this'll be a relatively slow process.

East of Kep, the coast runs to the **Vietnamese border**, and the newly opened crossing at Prek Chak (for Ha Tien and Phu Quoc).

Arrival and Information

Kep is 25km from Kampot (10,000 riel by moto) and three hours from Phnom Penh ($4) along a fantastic new tarmac road. There's a **tourist office** on the beachfront near the showers in Kep Thmei, though it has little to offer. It's here that the **buses** from Sihanoukville, Kampot and Phnom Penh drop off and where you'll find a string of small **tour operators**, an **internet** cafe (seldom in service – communications are still rather archaic in these parts) and plenty of motos to take you to your guesthouse. Of the tour operators here, the most reliable is Moly Tours (ⓣ097/7520906, ⓔmolytourkep@yahoo.com) who sell tickets to the country ($4–15 depending on group size), Rabbit Island ($7; see box, p.301) and snorkelling trips to Koh Poh ($25) as well as Phu Quoc and the Vietnam border.

Opposite the transport stop, a circular precinct contains a couple of hotels, some local stores and several of the ubiquitous huts furnished in mats and hammocks that Cambodians love to rent out for a day's relaxing.

From here to the famous **crab market**, the one-way system dictates that you head north away from the beach and take the first left at the roundabout. The

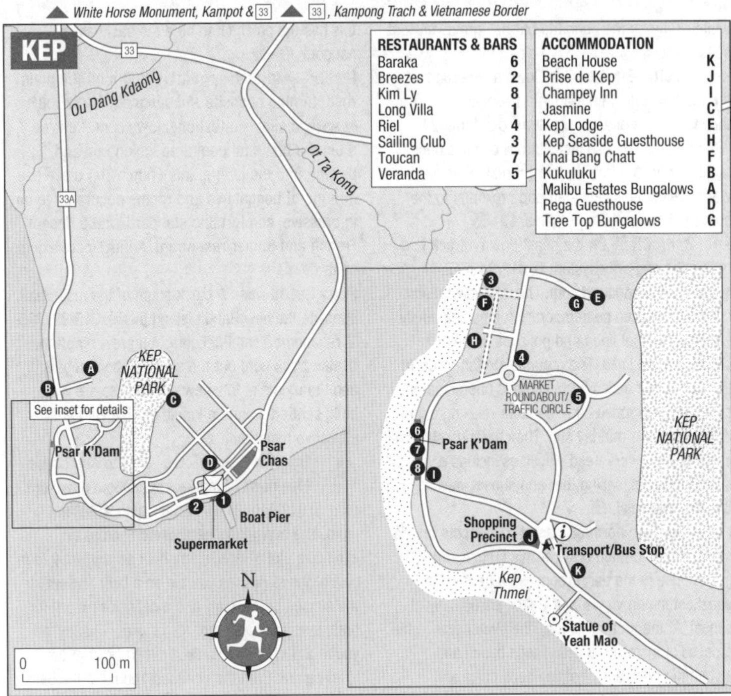

market is flanked to the south by dozens of **seafood restaurants** that form the bulk of Kep's low-key nightlife. There are no banks or **ATMs**, but you can change dollars to riel at the market and *Kep Lodge* can do cashback on credit cards for a small charge; the **post office** is on the way to Psar Chas opposite the new pier.

Accommodation

Accommodation in Kep ranges from stunning converted villas to rustic guesthouses; the very best are sumptuous and stylish. While the cheaper places are clean, they may have electricity for only part of the day.

Beach House In the centre of Kep near the beach ⓣ012/240090, ⓦwww.TheBeachHouseKep.com. Smart, modern rooms with sea views and all amenities at a new hotel on the hillside in the centre of Kep; swimming pool, spa and terrace café. ❺

Brise de Kep Opposite the transport stop in the shopping precinct ⓣ012/301017 or 011/937117. Decent, spacious rooms put together with attention to detail, professional and enthusiastic ownership and a very good 1st-floor restaurant. Well located by shops, the beach and the transport stop. ❷–❸

Jasmine ⓣ097/791 7635, ⓦjasminevalley.com. There simply aren't enough superlatives to describe this eco-lodge, tucked away in Jasmine Valley at the base of Kep National Park with views into dense forest on one side (with the chance of spotting nesting Great Hornbills) and the ocean on the other. The range of mud-brick bungalows, some built at dizzying heights, are tastefully decorated with personal touches and the establishment is on the road to total self-sufficiency, with fruit and vegetables growing in the elaborate gardens and fish in the ponds; they even brew their own starfruit cider. A spectacular guesthouse. ❹–❺

Kep Lodge 1km north of market roundabout, signposted on the right with *Treetop Bungalows*. ⓣ092/435330, ⓦwww.keplodge.com. These hillside bungalows are decorated with original watercolours on the walls and each is named after the plant that grows in its own patch of garden; enjoy fresh produce from the garden restaurant while sitting by the pool; the bar has great views at sunset. ❸

Kep Seaside Guesthouse Down a side road on the right off the main road into town, just before the start of the one-way system ⓣ012/684241. What this guesthouse lacks in obvious aesthetics (angular and concrete in form) it makes up for in a warm welcome, lovely staff and proximity to the crab market. Rents motorbikes. ❶–❷

Knai Bang Chatt On the coast down a track just before the one-way system ⓣ012/349742, ⓦwww.knaibangchatt.com. This exclusive resort comprises eleven contemporary rooms beautifully furnished in cool linen and polished stone with clean, modern lines. The grounds stretch down to the sea where a slender beach has been created – complete with muslin day-beds for relaxing out of the glare of the midday sun. The charming staff will cater to your every need. Facilities include a swimming pool, sailing, bar and sunset views. Booking essential. ❾

Kukuluku 2km north of market roundabout on the main road. The main draw of this French-run guesthouse is the dorm room ($5 a bed) which boasts stunning views over Bokor, particularly at sunset. At the time of writing, the owner was in the process of installing a man-made beach and swimming pool, and hosting pool, darts and petanque competitions. When the work is finished, this has the potential to be a top backpacker hangout. ❶–❹

Malibu Estates Bungalows 500m off the main road, turning opposite *Kukuluku* ⓣ016/379086, ⓦwww.malibuestatesbungalows.com. Centred around a beautiful pool area looking up and beyond into the jungle, this French-run place has a range of bungalows and rooms decorated to an impressive, comfortable standard with a decent French and Khmer restaurant. An idyllic, relaxing spot. ❺–❼

Rega Guesthouse A block south of the main road, opposite the new Rabbit Island pier ⓣ012/897205, ⓔregahome@camintel.com. You are a bit off the beaten track here but the staff can book motos, and the rooms at this new guesthouse are well built, centred around a jungle garden with an attractive restaurant. ❷

Tree Top Bungalows Next to *Kep Lodge*, 1km north of market roundabout down dirt road ⓣ012/515191, ⓔkhmertreetop@hotmail.com. The bungalows here stretch across an extensive plot of land, some built so high *they form* part of the skyline as you sip on a beer and watch the sunset. Lovely staff and a delicious muesli for breakfast. They also rent motorbikes – handy, as you're a decent stretch up a dirt track from the town centre. Even the cheapest rooms at the back are a great deal at $6. ❷–❹

The town and around

Kep is a sprawling sort of place. The road for Kep branches away from National Route 33 at the prominent White Horse Monument, from where it's five or six kilometres to the right turn to **Psar K'Dam**, the **crab market**; from here the road runs along the seafront for a kilometre or so, to the beach at **Kep Thmei**, where the narrow and pebbly beach broadens out fractionally. It gets crowded at weekends with day-trippers from the capital, so plan your visit for a weekday if you're looking for peace and quiet. If you carry on along the seafront, at the end of Kep Thmei you'll come to a massive white statue of a naked woman, **Yeah Mao**, of Pich Nil fame (see p.272), looking out to sea for her husband. Between here to Psar Chas, the tiny market at the east end of town, and the new pier, you can still see villas which were deliberately wrecked by the Khmer Rouge and left to be swallowed up by the jungle. You'll also see plenty of ostentatious government buildings, a vast mansion on the hill belonging to a government minister and another near *Breezes* restaurant, known as the **Queen's Palace**, that King Norodom Sihanouk built but never stayed in. Nothing has been done as yet to repair the damage caused by the Khmer Rouge and for $1 you can climb the bullet-strewn stairway to the ruined balconies on the first floor that look through the trees to Rabbit Island.

Trips to the offshore islands are well worth making. Closest is **Koh Tonsay** (Rabbit Island), with three good beaches (see box, p.301). Further out, **Koh Poh** (Coral Island) has clean white-sand beaches, turquoise water, coral reefs and great snorkelling. The huge island that dominates the horizon is **Phu Quoc**, in Vietnamese waters; some Cambodians still call it Koh Kut, from the times when it

Rabbit Island

The beaches in Kep aren't up to much; slim stretches of dark sand that don't lend themselves to lounging. Luckily, **Koh Tonsay** has the answer. Rabbit Island, as it is better known, is a 40-minute journey from the mainland and is, for now at least, an undeveloped paradise of pale sand, clear waters, lofty palms and a few very basic bungalows. Just 8km in circumference, you can find stretches of beach around the south western side that remove you even further from the sparse crowds that turn up on the island's shore every day in search of some desert island action. It makes a great day out, but by far the best time to be here is at 4.15pm when the final day-tripper boat has disappeared behind the peninsula, in the direction of the mainland, and you are left behind with a few other shipwrecked souls, a cold beer and the sun heading gently for the horizon.

Four or five small businesses run basic bungalows for between $5–7, the best at the time of writing being those at the western end of the beach.

The boat journey over here should cost you no more than $7. Some operators will offer you lunch, guided walks and snorkelling for a few dollars more, but this is not recommended as too many travellers tell tales of errant guides and rumbling stomachs. The snorkelling isn't up to much anyway and it's best to do the exploring yourself – there's a rocky path that circumnavigates the island – or better yet, just find yourself an empty strip of sand and while away a day in paradise.

belonged to Cambodia. **Boats** can be arranged to Koh Tonsay and Koh Poh through the town's guesthouses, or you can charter long-tailed boats on the beach – ask at the food stalls or at the new pier towards Psar Chas. The two-hour trip to Koh Poh costs $40, though it shouldn't be considered in stormy weather.

On the hill behind Kep, you can get quite away from it all and enjoy fantastic views over the province and bay, by following a track through the jungle (access is behind *Veranda Natural Resort*); the hike to the mountain top will take about an hour and a half, or you can go around the mountain in two to three hours.

Eating and drinking

There's nothing doing in Kep after about 11pm, but there are some excellent restaurants; **crab** is the local speciality. Unfortunately for budget travellers, there's not much in the way of cheap eats - the **market** is a good place to pick up barbecued seafood, and there is a **supermarket** by the Rabbit Island pier.

Baraka Northern end of crab-market strip. *Baraka* offers some respite from seafood with good pizza (from $5) and other western fare in a nicely decorated restaurant overlooking Bokor; turns into a decent little bar later in the evening.

Breezes ⓣ12251454. Along the coast road towards the Rabbit Island pier, signposted after the Provincial Hall. The final word in taste and elegance, jazz plays lightly in the background as you immerse yourself in fine dining. The menu includes oysters, a rare treat in these parts, and the owner is happy to offer a free lift back to your guesthouse at the end of dinner ($15–20), as the restaurant is quite a way out of the town centre, and it would be a shame not to sample something from the excellent wine list.

Kim Ly Southern end of crab-market strip. The most famous of the seafood restaurants along the water here, packed every night. The crab with Kampot pepper ($6.50) is particularly good. Its reputation precedes it, but most of the restaurants here are of a similar quality.

Long Villa Next to the Rabbit Island pier. This cheerful Khmer-run restaurant is the cheapest in town, serving eggs for breakfast from $1 with views over to Rabbit Island.

Riel Just north of the market roundabout. 6pm until late-ish. Has regular live music and dancing, plus a discount if you pay in riel.

Sailing Club Next to *Knai Bang Chatt*. The best place to enjoy a sunset happy-hour cocktail, the *Sailing Club* has a stunning location gently lapped by the waves. The food (largely seafood) is expensive but good value for the price and size. By day, you can rent Hobie cats or waterski with a boat captain from here.

Toucan In the centre of the crab-market strip. Pool table, classic rock and cheap beers, this is the closest Kep gets to a party bar. Open late-ish.

Veranda *Kep Mountain Hillside Resort* ⓣ033/399035, ⓦveranda-resort.com. The restaurant at this smart resort is a must-visit, even if you just pop in for a beer (meals from $5–12); the views from this height over wild jungle fauna, dilapidated colonial villas and beyond across the sea to Bokor will stay with you for years to come. The hotel itself is very fine, with rooms going from between $70–120.

Kompong Trach and Wat Kirisehla

East of Kep, amid stunning karst landscapes, lies the friendly town of **KOMPONG TRACH**. The main reason to head out here is to visit **Wat Kirisehla**, 5km outside town, which is home to a reclining Buddha set in a substantial natural cavity in the limestone hills.

An excellent **resort** in this area is the *Vine Retreat* (ⓣ016/984156, ⓦthevineretreat.com; ❹–❺), which doubles up as an organic farm with breathtaking views of the countryside stretching as far as the Gulf of Thailand. It's a 5km hike off 33 between Kep and Phnom Penh, call the resort for directions.

Once in Kompong Trach, to reach the wat take the turning north off the main road, about 100m east of the market; the road passes the hospital before leaving town and heading off into the rice fields, where you'll soon see a large craggy hill ahead. En route to the temple you will most likely be approached by smiling children offering to give you a guided tour. Ask them how much and they'll say "up to you", but $1 is really the minimum. They don't have any real knowledge of the history, but the good ones have torches and can show you such dubious relics as the blood of Buddha on the cave floor. Exploring alone, it's a good idea to take your own torch as the 100m-long tunnel to the centre of the hill is rather dark. Many of the formations in the cave have names; look out for the **elephant** at the entrance and a **tortoise** just beyond it. The centre of the hill is an almost circular cavity around 50m in diameter, ringed by high cliffs whose walls are eroded into caves. The large **reclining Buddha** here is a recent replacement for one destroyed by the Khmer Rouge, who holed up here for years without being rumbled.

Kompong Trach is on National Route 33, 30km east of Kampot and 15km from Kep. The road has recently been upgraded, making the journey relatively painless. You can get **food and drink** at the market and a couple of restaurants, all of which are opposite the main pagoda in the middle of town.

Takeo and around

Much of **Takeo province** disappears in an annual inundation by the waters of the Mekong and Bassac rivers, leaving **Takeo Town** isolated on the shore of a vast inland sea, and outlying villages transformed into islands. As the waters recede, an ancient network of canals, which once linked the area to the trading port of Oc Eo (now a ruined site across the border in Vietnam), is revealed. These continue to be vital to local communication and trade, and getting around the area is still easiest by boat – indeed, for much of the year there is no alternative.

Takeo makes a good base from which to visit the only **Funanese** sites so far identified in Cambodia, **Angkor Borei** and the nearby **Phnom Da**, which can be combined on a boat trip from Takeo; an informative museum at Angkor Borei displays artefacts and statues unearthed at both sites. Since Takeo is only two hours from Phnom Penh, it's possible to visit these sights on a day-trip.

Takeo

A key port on the trading route with Vietnam, **TAKEO** (pronounced *ta-kow*) consists of two separate hives of activity: to the south, a dusty (or muddy, depending on the season) market and transport stop on National Route 2 – which has little to recommend it unless you want to visit one of the karaoke parlours – and to the north, a more interesting area around the lake, canal and port. The **lakeside**, southwest of the canal, has been given a face-lift and there is now a park with views over the marshy, lily-covered lake, which makes a pleasant spot for an early morning or sunset stroll.

Taking up a beautiful spot in the middle of the lake, the home of former Khmer Rouge chief of staff, **Ta Mok**, has since been turned into a police training facility. Evidently paranoid about his inhumane crimes coming back to haunt him in later life (gruesome enough to have him nicknamed "The Butcher"), Ta Mok had the house built here in 1976. Although you can't enter the building, it is worth wandering across the bridge to stroll in the grounds.

You could also while away a little time at the port watching large wooden boats arriving from Vietnam laden with cheap terracotta tiles destined for Phnom Penh; the vessels are easily identified by the protective all-seeing eye painted on their bows. A crumbling square behind the waterfront is evidence of Takeo's colonial past, and there's a small market here, **Psar Nat**, which is busy in the early morning and late afternoon with local farmers and fisher-folk. The town's shophouses are sadly neglected, but still retain a discernible sense of French style.

Practicalities

Takeo is straightforward to reach by bus or shared taxi on National Route 2 from Phnom Penh (8000 riel); if you're arriving from the south you can get a shared taxi from Kampot (10,000 riel). Wherever you're arriving from, you'll enter the town on National Route 2. Shortly afterwards, the road forks; the left branch takes you past the lake and out to the port, while the right fork (National Route 2) continues 1km to the Independence Monument traffic roundabout and then a further 1km to the market and nearby **transport stop**. Here you'll be able to get onward transport for the 30km trip to Phnom Den (for Tinh Bien in Vietnam border open daily 7am–8pm, Vietnamese visas not available). **Boats** to Angkor Borei and Phnom Da can be hired at the waterfront. Set back a couple of blocks from the boat jetty is the **tourist office** (Mon–Fri 7–11am & 2.30–5.30pm; ⓣ032/931323). **Money changers** can be found at the market, and there's an Acleda Bank by the Independence Monument, though there's nowhere in town to cash travellers' cheques. There are several **internet cafés** ($1 per hr) around town.

There's no outstanding **accommodation** in Takeo, but the friendly *Mittapheap Guesthouse* (ⓣ032/931205; ❷–❸), set back from the road off the Independence Monument roundabout, has acceptable rooms, some with air conditioning and hot water, and it's the place of choice for NGOs and business visitors to town; although there's no restaurant, it's close to inexpensive food stalls. Near the lakeside *Boeng Takeo Guesthouse* (ⓣ032/931306; ❷–❸) has reasonable en-suite rooms with cable TV, fan or air conditioning and balcony. On the canal near the boat dock *Phnom Da* has good rooms (ⓣ016/826083; ❶–❷); you'll probably get invited to join in a game of dominoes or cards. They also have a boat for rent ($30 for one person, $35 for two or more people). A block back from the canal, overlooking Psar Nat, the *Angkor Borei Guesthouse* (ⓣ032/931340; ❶–❷) has basic en-suite fan rooms with TV.

Eating options in Takeo are limited, although the few restaurants along the lakeside promenade produce some very elegant seafood dishes; a local freshwater **lobster** soup will set you back about $10 with rice, but will do for two. The road from the market to the Independence Monument has a number of restaurants, and the **market** itself is a safe bet for breakfast, with stalls selling sweet doughnuts, fried bananas, bread and coffee. On stilts over the canal just south of the boat jetty, the *Thmor Sor Restaurant* has a menu in English and a wide range of Khmer dishes.

Angkor Borei and Phnom Da

Twenty-five kilometres from Takeo lies the pre-Angkorian site of **Angkor Borei**. The site can be reached year-round by boat, an interesting journey through wetlands which are home to a variety of water birds, with all types of boats coming and going. The fine local **museum** is the main reason to come here, but you may well want to explore the excavated Funan-era archeological sites here and at **Phnom Da** (though be warned that these are closed in the rainy season).

The easiest way to get to Angkor Borei and Phnom Da is by **hiring a boat** in Takeo (about $30). These have powerful outboard motors and seat six to eight people, making the trip to Angkor Borei in forty minutes (the onward leg to Phnom Da takes fifteen minutes), either across open water between June and January (approximately), or by canal and river the rest of the year. There are also occasional **boat taxis** to Angkor Borei (4000 riel per person one way), but you'll probably face a long wait both to go and to come back. You should allow a full day if you want to do justice to both sites, though a half-day excursion is sufficient to get a feel for them.

Angkor Borei

The pleasantly leafy town of **ANGKOR BOREI** sits on the banks of the Prek Angkor, a tributary of the Bassac. The town is well known to scholars as the site where the earliest-known example of written Khmer was discovered, and archeological excavations here have identified many features of the town that once stood on the site, including a moat 22m wide, a section of high brick wall and numerous extensive water tanks. Unfortunately, there is now little to see apart from the finds in the museum.

Boats pull up on the riverside near the bridge, just downstream from which, on the same side of the river, a white colonial building surrounded by a large garden houses Angkor Borei's well-managed **museum** (daily 7–11.30am & 2–5.30pm; $2), with a diverse collection of ceramics, beads, stone statues, carved pediments from the Funanese era and a photographic exhibition of the excavations. Some stylish sculptures of Vishnu and Shiva line the walls, but the eight-armed Vishnu surrounded by an arc is a reproduction. One of the highlights is a pediment removed from Phnom Da showing Vishnu reclining on a dragon. Aerial photos show clearly the extent of the old settlement and identify many of the features being excavated.

Phnom Da

Ironically for a site that has given its name to a style of sculpture, the remains of the temple of **Phnom Da** are now rather bare, as everything of value has been removed to the museums in Phnom Penh and Angkor Borei for safekeeping. The ruins remain pretty imposing, however, constructed on top of two forty-metre-high mounds built to protect the temple from rising waters. Experts differ on the temple's vintage, some believing that it was built in the early sixth century by Rudravarman, others that it dates from a later period, perhaps the seventh century.

Boats moor at the small village at the foot of Phnom Da, where local children will offer to show you up meandering paths to the top of the hill, passing at least three of the site's five caves on the way. On the higher of the two mounds the ancient **Prasat Phnom Da** ($2) comprises a single laterite tower, visible from way off and dominating the landscape. The tower's four doorways boast ornate sandstone columns and pediments of carved naga heads, though all but the eastern entrance are false.

On the lower hill, to the west, is a unique Hindu temple, **Ashram Maha Russei**, dedicated to Vishnu and built of grey laterite. Dating from the seventh century, the structure is a temple in miniature, the enclosing walls so close together that there's barely room to squeeze between them. On the outside, a spout can still be seen poking through the wall, through which water that had been blessed by flowing over the temple's linga would once have poured.

Travel details

Shared taxis and **pick-up trucks** leave to no set schedule from early morning until early afternoon (roughly 6am–2pm); you may have to wait for them to fill up before they leave. Note that the frequencies given below are only approximate, and the earlier in the day you get to the transport stop, the easier it is to find transport.

Buses

Kampot to: Sihanoukville (daily; 2hr 30min).
Kep to: Phnom Penh (2 daily; 3hr).
Sihanoukville to: Kampot (daily; 2hr 30min); Phnom Penh (6 daily; 3hr 30min).
Takeo to: Phnom Penh (4 daily; 2hr).

Shared taxis, minibuses and pick-up trucks

Kampot to: Phnom Penh (12 daily; 3hr); Sihanoukville (10 daily; 2hr 30min); Takeo (8–12 daily; 2hr).
Kep to: Phnom Penh (8 daily; 3hr).
Koh Kong to: Phnom Penh (several daily; 6hr); Sihanoukville (4 daily; 4hr).
Sihanoukville to: Kampot (10 daily; 2hr 30min); Koh Kong (4 daily; 4hr); Phnom Penh (20 daily; 3hr 30min).
Takeo to: Kampot (8–12 daily; 2hr); Phnom Penh (12 daily; 2hr 30min).

Contexts

Contexts

History

The study of Cambodia's history is hampered by a lack of records. During the time of Angkor, the texts that filled temple libraries were written on **tanned skins** or **palm leaves**, but unfortunately these were not copied by successive generations and none has survived; inscribed stone steles at temple sites usually recorded only aspects of temple life, and even this information ceased to be compiled with the demise of Angkor. But the steles, coupled with accounts by Chinese traders and envoys, have at least allowed historians to piece together something of Cambodia's story up until the late thirteenth century.

Though foreign traders and Western missionaries in Cambodia wrote various accounts after the sixteenth century, these leave substantial periods unaccounted for; more recently, the French documented their protectorate in some detail, but these records were largely destroyed by the Khmer Rouge. What is known of Cambodia's history is thus something of a hotchpotch, and though much has been deduced, even more remains obscure and will probably continue to be unknown.

Beginnings

The **earliest settlements** so far uncovered in Cambodia date from 6800 BC and were situated along the coast, where the risk of annual flooding was minor and there was a ready supply of food. Hunter-gatherers were living in the caves at Leang Spean, northwest of Battambang, by 4300 BC; they cultivated dry-season rice and produced ceramics, which are uncannily similar in shape and decoration to those in use today. **Neolithic** settlements uncovered at **Samrong Sen**, in central Cambodia, indicate that by 2000 BC animals had been domesticated and slash-and-burn agriculture developed. Five hundred years later, Cambodia entered the **Bronze Age** when the art of smelting copper and tin was mastered, the ores probably originating from present-day Thailand. By 500 BC, a prosperous **Iron Age** civilization was in full swing; farming implements and weapons were produced, and skills for working with ceramics, metal and glass were being refined. The population slowly divided: highland dwellers continued growing only rainy-season rice, while lowland settlers farmed the river valleys and coastal strips, where they learned to make use of the floods, conserving water for dry-season irrigation and prospering from the fertile soils deposited.

Funan

Around the first century AD warring tribes forced traders to seek alternatives to the established overland trading routes between China and India. Sailing along the coast, they landed at Oc Eo, in the state of **Funan**, on the Gulf of Thailand (now in Vietnam) – an area populated by the **Khmer**, a dark-skinned, curly-haired tribe who had migrated from the north along the Mekong, and from whom Cambodians today trace their origins.

Funan is first mentioned in Chinese chronicles of the third century, and scholars believe the name may have originated from the Chinese transliteration of the word *bnam*, an old Khmer word for "mountain". It's known from Chinese accounts that the Funanese were an affluent, Indian-influenced society, living in wooden stilt-houses thatched with palm, speaking Khmer but writing in Sanskrit. Using engineering skills learnt from Indian traders, they dug canals and developed the inland port of Angkor Borei; drainage and irrigation channels were cut to allow wet-rice cultivation and provide fresh water. The Funanese ruthlessly exploited their advantageous situation: ships had to pay dues to travel up the canals to the wharf, to berth and to take on fresh water. Huge warehouses were built to store the high-value cargoes – animal hides, rhinoceros horn, spices and gold.

Accompanying the Indian traders were Brahmans, Hindu priests, who converted many Funanese to Hinduism. Rich Funanese gained merit by financing temples, while the poor earned theirs by contributing the labour to build them. By the fifth century, shrines had been built on Funan hilltops and the king had begun to add the suffix – *varman* to his name, meaning "protector".

Funan was partly the architect of its own downfall when, in the late fifth or early sixth century, assuming its position to be unassailable, it increased already steep shipping tariffs. New ports along the coast began to compete, feuds sprang up, and the state fragmented and declined. One of the last mentions of Funan is in the Chinese chronicles of 539, when it is reported that King Rudravarman I sent the Chinese emperor a live rhinoceros.

Chenla

In the late sixth century, **Chenla**, previously a northern dependency of Funan, gained its independence. Details of the Chenla period are particularly sparse, and such information as there is comes from Chinese sources; some scholars suggest that the word "Chenla" may have been the name by which the Chinese referred to parts of present-day Cambodia, though there is no clear picture of the extent to which Chenla and Cambodia might have overlapped. Early Chenla temples, constructed of wood and brick, were on a modest scale and few have survived **Sambor Prei Kuk** is one of the best preserved.

By the seventh century, all references to Funan had ceased. Around this time **Bhavavarman I** founded a capital at Sambor Prei Kuk, in Kompong Thom province. He was succeeded by **Ishanavarman I** (reigned 610–625), who founded Ishanapura (named in accordance with the Indian-derived custom of naming a capital by suffixing the king's name with *pura* – the Sanskrit word for town), whose state-temple became the largest in Southeast Asia. Although already elderly when he became king, Ishanavarman seems to have succeeded in annexing many smaller states. He was succeeded by his son, **Bhavavarman II**, about whom nothing is known.

The capital tended to change location with each new king. **Jayavarman I** (great-grandson of Ishanavarman; reigned 635–681) ruled over an area extending at least from Battambang to Prey Veng. Although many sanctuaries were consecrated during his reign, none can be specifically attributed to him, and his capital has so far not been identified. Inscriptions indicate that he was an able soldier who succeeded in extending his territory, though he was ultimately killed by invaders, probably from Java, after which the succession passed first to his son-in-law and then to his daughter, **Jayadevi**. She was one of only a handful of queens in the whole of Cambodian history, in spite of the fact that women were regarded as equals and inheritance of property, slaves and lands passed through the female line.

By the eighth century, Chenla had **divided** into two states, Land (or Upper) Chenla and Water (or Lower) Chenla. In the late eighth century, **Jayavarman II** mysteriously appeared on the scene, supposedly arriving from Java; an inscription dating from the eleventh century, now in the National Museum in Bangkok, records that "he spent time at court in Java". In 795, he declared himself ruler of a kingdom called Kambujadesa and, after moving his court no less than five times, in 802 he settled at **Phnom Kulen**, northeast of Siem Reap.

The Khmer Empire

Jayavarman II's arrival at Phnom Kulen marked a northward shift of power to the region that would later be known as **Angkor** and become the capital of the **Khmer Empire**. It is from this date, therefore, that the **Angkorian period** is deemed to have begun, although it was some years before temples that are now considered Angkorian were built.

Until the eleventh century Khmer kings followed the **Hindu** religion, and temple-building was considered one of their most important duties. Temples were considered akin to a palace for the god to whom they were dedicated (most were consecrated to Shiva), and with whom the king was believed to merge on his death. Consequently, temples built by one king were seldom used by the next; instead the subsequent king would begin his own building programme in a new location – which accounts for the constantly shifting capitals of the Angkorian period. These enormous building works invariably used vast resources, both in terms of labour and materials. Some temples were not completed before the death of the king – in which case a later king would finish the construction for his own use.

The little that is known about the reign of Jayavarman II (ruled at Angkor 802–850) derives from inscriptions made two centuries later, when he was held in high regard, though no records have been uncovered to substantiate this reputation. Arguably the most notable thing about his reign is that Jayavarman II founded the **devaraja** cult (see "Religion and beliefs", p.328) that would persist for over five hundred years. Jayavarman II subsequently moved his court from Phnom Kulen to Hariharalaya, present-day Roluos, where he died. He was succeeded by his son, **Jayavarman III** (850–877).

The empire in the ascendant

Indravarman I (877–889) established a pattern of three-fold building work that most subsequent Angkorian kings would emulate. First, he honoured the water gods by creating the Indratataka baray at Roluos; secondly, he built a temple to his ancestors at Preah Ko; thirdly, he erected the Baking, a temple-mountain which was also his state-temple housing his devaraja deity.

Indravarman was succeeded by his son, **Yasovarman I** (889–900). He had to fight his brothers to assume the throne, and his reign seems to have carried on in a military vein. After completing the temple of Lolei at Roluos he moved northwest, where he constructed the first state-temple in the Angkor area proper, on the hill of Phnom Bakheng. He followed this by excavating the massive East Baray, over 7km long and almost 2km wide. Yasovarman was succeeded by his two sons, **Harshavarman I** (900–922), who built only the small temple of Baksei Chamkrong, and **Ishanavarman II** (922–927) who was responsible for Prasat Kravan at Angkor, and Prasat Neing Kmau near Takeo. Their uncle, **Jayavarman IV** (928–941), became the only Angkorian king to rule from a distance. He ascended the Angkorian throne when he was already ruling his own state from Koh Ker, some 150km east of Angkor.

After the death of Jayavarman IV, his son **Harshavarman II** (941–944) gained the throne, though he lasted just a short time before he was ousted by his cousin, **Rajendravarman I** (944–968). To appease the gods of his ancestors, he had the temple of Baksei Chamkrong decorated and rededicated, and went on to build two massive temple-mountains, the East Mebon in the middle of the East Baray, and his state-temple, Pre Rup. He also granted land to his guru, Yajnavaraha, to build a temple, the beautiful citadel of Banteay Srei. He waged war against the Cham, who populated the state of **Champa** on the coast of Vietnam, and annexed neighbouring states, making them provinces of the Khmer Empire.

When Rajendravarman I died, his son **Jayavarman V** (968–1001) was just 10, and officials had to rule on his behalf. At some time he was successful in extending his territory into what is now northeast Thailand. Many inscriptions relating to the period survive, some of which are decrees about the temples, while many others concern land disputes over which the king had to adjudicate – gruesome punishments were meted out to those he deemed guilty, including having their nose, lips or ears cut off. One unfortunate woman was sentenced to have her head crushed with a rock.

In 1002, two rivals, Jayaviravarman (1002–10) and Suryavarman I were both proclaimed king. **Jayaviravarman** resumed work on Ta Keo, the state-temple begun by Jayavarman V, but it was never completed as it was hit by lightning and the evil omens this signified could not be expunged. Jayaviravarman also built the North Kleang and a fortifying wall to the northeast of Angkor Thom before he was overthrown by **Suryavarman I** (1011–50), during whose long reign further territory was added to the kingdom, with provinces as far away as Lopburi in present-day Thailand paying allegiance to him. Suryavarman I left a substantial legacy: at Angkor, his palace was the first to be surrounded with defensive walls; a number of religious settlements, including Phnom Chisor and Preah Vihear, were founded; and he built a massive reservoir, the West Baray, still impressive today.

His successor, **Udayadityavarman II** (1050–66), had his work cut out warding off rival claimants to the throne, but he still found time to build the Baphuon, which lay at the heart of his capital, in the vicinity of Angkor Thom. The only thing known of his brother, **Harshavarman III** (1066–80), is that in 1076, according to Chinese annals, he was ordered by the Chinese emperor (who considered the Cambodians and Cham to be under his rule) to join with the Cham to fight against the Vietnamese. His successor, **Jayavarman VI** (1080–1107), was not the natural heir, coming from a remote line of the royal family, but enjoyed a peaceful reign, and was content to make additions to existing temples rather than build new ones, although he may have had a hand in the construction of the impressive temple of Phimai, near Nakhon Ratchasima in Thailand.

Angkor at its height

Dharanindravarman I (1107–13), the brother of Jayavarman VI, was soon overthrown by his nephew, **Suryavarman II** (1113–50), possibly the best known of Angkor's kings, thanks to his state-temple, Angkor Wat. A few minor ups and downs apart, his reign marked the beginning of a golden period for Angkor; the empire was at its height, stretching from Champa in the east to Pagan (in present-day Burma) in the west, and from the north of Thailand south into the Malay peninsula. Both diplomat and warrior, he restored relationships with China (with whom trade had ceased in the eighth century) and fought a great battle against the Vietnamese. In forcing the Cham to join in on his side, he succeeded in alienating them, before completely destroying the relationship by installing a king of his own choosing on their throne.

Uncertainty surrounds his supposed successor, **Dharanindravarman II** (1150–60); some scholars doubt that he actually ascended the throne, suggesting that he merely ruled over an independent kingdom in the area. He was the **first Buddhist king** of the Khmer, but did not attempt to convert his subjects. He is credited with building Preah Palilay and (with less certainty) the addition of Buddhist carvings to Banteay Samre and Beng Mealea. After him came **Yashovarman II** (1160–65); he built no new monuments, but continued work on those of his predecessors, including restoration at Roluos. He was overthrown in 1165 by **Tribhuvanadityavarman** (1165–77), who was killed during the Cham invasion of 1177, during which Angkor Thom was sacked and a Cham prince, Jaya-Indravarman IV, was briefly put on the Khmer throne.

It was **Jayavarman VII**, son of Dharanindravarman II, who restored the status quo, leading his troops to war with the Cham and winning a huge naval battle against them on the Tonle Sap – his success is commemorated in the bas-reliefs of the Bayon. Once Angkor was regained from the Cham and Champa annexed, he set about re-establishing the kingdom's institutions; by 1181 he had rebuilt Angkor Thom and reunited the country sufficiently to have himself consecrated devaraja. As well as managing his vast empire, which rivalled that of Suryavarman II, the king was a prolific temple-builder, completing Ta Som, Preah Khan, Banteay Chhmar and Neak Pean, as well as a state-temple, the Bayon, consecrated to Mahayana Buddhism. Under his direction, Angkor Thom gained not only its fortifying wall but also extravagant causeways flanked by gods and demons; furthermore, Banteay Kdei and Srah Srang were restored, and the irrigation system improved. The enormous Terrace of Elephants and the Terrace of the Leper King also owe their existence to his reign. An inscription made in 1186 at the newly consecrated Ta Prohm records some of his good works, noting that 102 hospitals and 121 "houses of fire" – rest houses for travellers – had been built across the country.

The decline of Angkor

After Jayavarman VII's death the Khmer Empire began to fragment; it's likely that Jayavarman VII's massive building programme, which heavily depleted the kingdom's resources, was partly responsible for its decline. Little is known about the following two kings, **Indravarman II** (1219–43) and **Jayavarman VIII** (1243–95); the Mongols arrived in Southeast Asia during the latter's reign, and he seems to have been prudent enough to send tribute to Kublai Khan. A zealous Hindu, Jayavarman VIII was also responsible for destroying many of Cambodia's Buddhist images.

Legend tells that Jayavarman's beloved daughter took the sacred sword, Preah Khan, and gave it to her husband, causing Jayavarman VIII to abdicate. The tale is mentioned in the writings of the Chinese envoy Chou Ta-Kuan, who spent a year at Angkor in 1296 and left a colourful account of the court, its buildings and ceremonial pomp. But in spite of Chou's glowing account, Angkor was already weakening. The kingdom was dramatically reduced in size by the middle of the thirteenth century, by which time the Thais had ousted the Khmer from Sukhothai, and Lopburi had claimed independence. By the early fourteenth century, the Cham had also reclaimed their independence, leaving what was left of the Khmer kingdom exposed and unable to summon much resistance to Thai invasions.

When the Thais next sacked Angkor in 1432, **King Ponhea Yat** left Angkor, and taking his court with him, set up a new capital in **Phnom Penh**, where he created a number of Buddhist monasteries which still exist today.

Lovek and Oudong

Some evidence exists in Thai records that the capital may have returned briefly to Angkor around 1467, but by the early sixteenth century, **Ang Chan** (1505 or 1516–56) had set up court at **Lovek**. While the Thais were busy fending off advances from invading Burmese, Ang Chan gathered an army and made a successful attack on the Thais, managing to regain control of towns such as Pursat and Battambang, which had been lost when Angkor was abandoned.

The **sixteenth century** saw the arrival of the first **Western** missionaries and explorers in Cambodia; though the former were utterly unsuccessful in gaining converts, some of the latter became influential within the Khmer establishment, such as the Spanish adventurers Blas Ruiz and Diego Veloso, whose knowledge of firearms would eventually earn them marriages with Cambodian princesses and provincial governorships under **King Satha** (1575–94). Accounts of the time, by Spanish and Portuguese colonials from the Philippines and Malacca respectively, report multicultural trading settlements at Lovek and Phnom Penh, with quarters for the Chinese, Arabs, Japanese, Spanish and Portuguese; the area around these two towns was the most prosperous in the country, trading in gold, animal skins and ivory, silk and precious stones.

However, the Khmer court continued to face threats from the **Thais**, forcing King Satha to ask the Spanish in the Philippines for help. This aid never materialized, however, and Satha fled to Laos (where he subsequently died) while Lovek was sacked by the Thais in 1594. The succession subsequently passed rapidly to a number of kings, including **Chey Chettha**, who took the throne and established his capital at **Oudong**, between Lovek and Phnom Penh, where it would remain for some two hundred years.

Towards the end of the seventeenth century, the **Vietnamese** began to move south into Champa and, before long, into the Mekong delta. Cambodia was now squeezed between two powerful neighbours, and over the next century the royal family aggravated matters by splitting into pro-Vietnamese and pro-Thai factions, the crown changing hands frequently. The populace, without a strong king to look to, paid scant regard to what was said in Oudong, which further aggravated the king's inability to resist invasions.

Events took a turn for the worse in 1767 when a Thai prince sought refuge in Cambodia, intending to set up a government in exile. This incensed the Thai general, Taksin, who launched an invasion, destroyed Phnom Penh and assumed control of Cambodia for several decades. The Thais put a 7-year-old prince, **Ang Eng** (1779–97), on the throne under a Thai regent, and then reinforced their influence by taking him to Bangkok, where he stayed for four years. On his return, he installed himself at Oudong, where he died in 1797, leaving four sons and a lineage that lasts to this day.

The run-up to the French protectorate

Worsening to-ing and fro-ing between the Thais and Vietnamese ultimately led to the Cambodians appealing to France for protection. Ang Eng's eldest son and heir, **Chan**, was only 6 at the time of his father's death and didn't assume the throne for nine years. Meanwhile, the Thais annexed the province of Battambang, which then stretched as far as Siem Reap. It remained under Thai rule until 1907. By the time he was crowned, Chan (1806–34) had become fervently anti-Thai and soon asked the Vietnamese for help; the Vietnamese promptly annexed the whole of the Mekong delta and also took control of Cambodia. In 1812, Chan relocated the court to Phnom Penh, from where he proceeded to send secret emissaries to Bangkok, trying to keep them sweet by assuring them of his continued allegiance.

The Thai king, Rama III, decided in the early 1830s to re-exert his influence on Cambodia and, seizing upon the opportunity provided by the death of the Vietnamese viceroy in 1832, sent in an army to oust the Vietnamese – who had already left by the time Thai troops arrived, taking Chan with them. The Thais sought to install as king one of Chan's two brothers who had been living in exile in Bangkok, but later abandoned the idea, unable to gain any popular support for either. The Vietnamese, keeping Chan under close supervision, returned to Phnom Penh a couple of years later; he died shortly afterwards, leaving no male heir. They duly installed Chan's second daughter, **Mei**, as queen (1835–41) thinking she would be malleable, and set about imposing Vietnamese culture and customs on the Cambodians. Their disregard for Theravada Buddhism and their attempts to enforce the use of the Vietnamese language sowed deep resentment, and anti-Vietnamese riots flared repeatedly from 1836. Losing their patience, the Vietnamese blamed Queen Mei for their own failure to install a disciplined Vietnamese-style administration, and arrested her in 1840; though the Cambodians had not much liked being forced to accept a Vietnamese-appointed queen, they now resented her detention and rioted yet again. Thai troops poised on the border marched in and forced the Vietnamese out, and despite sporadic skirmishes the Vietnamese never regained control. They withdrew from Cambodia in 1847, and the following year, Chan's brother, **Duang** (1848–59), was crowned king at Oudong with full Buddhist ceremony, the reinstatement of which, after years of Vietnamese disapproval, contributed to the Khmer's sense of national identity.

Meanwhile, the **French** had arrived in Southeast Asia, but were rebuffed in their attempt to establish trading arrangements with Vietnam. On the pretext that French missionaries were being persecuted, they invaded the Mekong delta, annexing the southern provinces of Vietnam. In Cambodia, Duang feared another Vietnamese invasion and asked the French for help; they eventually sent a diplomatic mission but it was turned back before it could reach him at Oudong and Duang died before any discussions could be held, leaving it to his successor, **Norodom** (1859–1904), to agree a treaty with the French in 1863.

The French protectorate

Norodom's **treaty** with France afforded Cambodia French protection in exchange for wide-ranging mineral and timber rights, along with freedom for the French to preach Christianity and to move around the country. Having signed the treaty, however, Norodom continued the double-dealing of his predecessors and was secretly reassuring the Thais of his loyalty to Bangkok. On discovering this, the French lost their trust in Norodom and, in due course, their confidence in his ability to govern at all. With riots flaring in the provinces against Norodom and his allegiance to France, the French decided it was time to exert more control themselves, and began to press for a new treaty that would allow them to install administrative **residents** in all provincial centres and take over the day-to-day running of the country. Rebellion sprang up across the nation, which the French, even with the assistance of Vietnamese troops, had difficulty in quelling. By the time the treaty was signed in 1886, the French had eroded much of Norodom's power and were collecting all taxes; two years later they had residents installed in ten provincial towns.

Towards the end of the century Norodom, already an **opium addict** (a habit fed by the French) became ill, and the French *résident supérieur* was granted permission from Paris to assume executive authority. By the time Norodom died in 1904, France was ruling Cambodia. His compliant half-brother **Sisowath** was installed on the throne in Phnom Penh (1904–27), the French having passed over Monivong, Norodom's son and natural heir; a mere figurehead, Sisowath had little impact on affairs during his reign.

By the early part of the twentieth century, the French were thoroughly disillusioned with the Cambodians, whom they regarded as indolent and corrupt. Consequently, they did little to develop Cambodia's human resources (the most tangible legacy of their ninety-year rule is arguably the country's communications network, including over 5000km of roads and a railway line from Phnom Penh and Battambang to the Thai border). Instead, the French filled key clerical positions with Vietnamese, who also ran many of the small businesses and took jobs as labourers; meanwhile, the ethnic Chinese, who had been established in Cambodia for centuries, continued their lucrative trades as bankers and merchants.

This neglect of the Khmer, and the crippling taxes which the French levied on Cambodia, bred resentment to which the French, in their complacency, remained oblivious. They were shocked when revolts against taxation broke out in 1916, and doubly horrified when Felix Bardez – the French resident in Kompong Chhnang – was **beaten to death** by locals in 1925 while investigating resistance to tax payments in a provincial village.

World War II

The **Japanese invasion** of Southeast Asia in 1941–42 brought little change to the status quo in Indochina, where the Japanese allowed the (now Vichy) French to continue administering the day-to-day running of the country. The Thais, who were allies of the Japanese and who sensed a degree of vulnerability in the French position, took the opportunity to launch attacks across the border into Cambodia, with the aim of recovering the provinces of Battambang and Siem Reap which they had reluctantly given up to Cambodia earlier in the century. The French roundly defeated the Thai navy, however, forcing the Japanese to save Thai face by compelling the French administration to hand over the provinces for a nominal sum. **King Sisowath Monivong** blamed the French for this loss of territory and refused to deal with them ever again – in fact he died shortly afterwards. The Japanese actually allowed the next king to be chosen by the French who, seeking a compliant successor, passed over Monivong's son in favour of his youthful and inexperienced grandson, **Norodom Sihanouk**, who was duly crowned in September 1941.

Despite their hands-off approach in Indochina, the Japanese were supportive of anti-colonial feeling, partly to gain support for their own presence. The effect of these sentiments would become manifest after the Japanese surrender in August 1945, by which time they had dissolved the French administration.

Towards independence

Though the French had reinstated their officials by the end of 1945, the prewar status quo was never quite restored. The Thai government were funding anti-Japanese and anti-French causes, and anti-royalist Cambodian groups in exile began to gather along the Thai border. A year later these factions had banded together to form the essentially left-wing **Khmer Issarak**, a band of fledgling idealists which grew into a powerful armed guerrilla movement that waged something approaching a war of independence against the French; between 1947 and 1950, the Khmer Issarak actually controlled fifty percent of the country.

The seeds of the movement had been sown back in the 1930s with the opening of Cambodia's first high school, the **Lycée Sisowath** in Phnom Penh, whose students soon began to question the standing of educated Khmer in a country where Vietnamese dominated the middle levels of the administration. When the first Khmer-language **newspaper**, *Nagara Vatta*, was launched (Khmer had hitherto been used only for the publication of religious texts), it was aimed at these newly educated Cambodians, propounding Khmer nationalist views and objecting to the influence of the Vietnamese and Chinese on Cambodian society. The editors were allied to the *sangka* (the Buddhist clergy), led by Phnom Penh's

Institut Bouddhique, the backbone of Buddhism in Cambodia, which had taken responsibility for most education until the opening of the *lycée*.

When Sihanouk requested Cambodia's independence late in 1945, the French (afraid of losing their grip on Indochina) reluctantly agreed to allow elections and the formation of a National Assembly, but refused to contemplate granting complete independence. Thus, for the first time in Cambodian history, political parties were formed, **elections** held (in 1946) and a new government formed. The election was resoundingly won by the democratic (and anti-royalist) party, Krom Pracheathipodei, which adopted a constitution along the lines of that of republican France; Sihanouk, although he retained his throne, was left virtually powerless. Late in 1949, Cambodia was granted **partial independence**, though the French continued to control the judiciary, customs and excise and foreign policy, and retained the right to maintain military bases in the country.

Frustrated by his lack of political power and the residual French grip on the country, in June 1952 Sihanouk staged a **coup**, dismissing the cabinet, suspending the constitution and appointing himself prime minister; in the early months of 1953 he declared martial law and dissolved the National Assembly. Sihanouk then took the first of what was to become a habitual series of trips abroad "for his health" – in reality to lobby the French in Paris to withdraw and grant Cambodia full independence. With France fighting a losing battle in Vietnam against the communist Viet Minh, the French government eventually did an about-face; on **November 9, 1953**, Cambodia duly celebrated full independence.

The Sihanouk era

Cambodians were ecstatic at achieving full independence, and Sihanouk was feted as a national hero. The following year, accords were signed in Geneva laying down the terms of French withdrawal from Indochina, including among its key points the disbanding of the Khmer Issarak, **neutrality** on the part of Cambodia and the **partition of Vietnam** at the seventeenth parallel into what would become communist North Vietnam and the non-communist South Vietnam.

Early on, it was clear that Sihanouk, though politically adept, would change sides at the drop of a hat to achieve his ends, driven by an unassailable belief that, having won independence for Cambodia, he should be the one to run it. He needed the adulation of his public and took to making trips to the countryside, where he made lengthy orations and attracted polite attention thanks to an ingrained respect for the monarchy. These outings stoked his huge ego and made him believe that his "children", as he referred to the people, supported his policies. However, for subsistence farmers, who formed the majority of the population, independence had brought no benefits; they still had to work overlong hours in the rice fields and suffer the effects of flood and drought.

When Sihanouk's efforts to manipulate the constitution to gain power for the monarchy failed, he surprised everyone by **abdicating** in 1955 in favour of his father Norodom Suramarit, taking once again the title of prince. Gambling on the continuation of massive popular support for himself in the wake of the independence struggle, he set up his own political party, **Sangkum Reastr Niyum**, the Popular Socialist Community (Sangkum for short). The party managed to win all the seats in the National Assembly in the heavily rigged 1955 elections, during which opposition candidates and electors were intimidated by the military on the king's orders, ballot papers tampered with and ballot boxes lost. Sihanouk's tactics ensured that Sangkum remained unchallenged at the next elections two years later.

The monarchy was effectively dissolved in 1960 when King Suramarit died, whereupon Sihanouk became head of state.

Sihanouk was both hard-working and creative – he even found time to produce a number of films which drew upon traditional Cambodian cultures and values – but his conceited attitude and bullying approach made him difficult to work with. Many right-wing intellectuals, whom the prince perceived as competition, mysteriously disappeared; meanwhile he toyed with socialism and often favoured the left. At the same time, in the schools and colleges left-wing teachers such as **Saloth Sar** (later known as Pol Pot) and **Ieng Sary** (so-called Brother Number Three in the Khmer Rouge hierarchy) had become senior communist party figures by the early 1960s and were recruiting members; another future senior figure in the Khmer Rouge, **Khieu Samphan**, meanwhile hid his communist leanings and joined Sangkum.

In 1963, in yet another of Sihanouk's policy shifts, a government purge of known communists saw Saloth Sar flee Phnom Penh to take up the life of a full-time revolutionary. Along with many others in the Cambodian communist movement, he spent time in Vietnam and China, where he was trained and groomed by communist forces.

The slide towards war

In the late 1950s, with the knowledge of the United States, plots had been hatched against Sihanouk by a paramilitary, right-wing, anti-Sihanouk group, the **Khmer Serei** (led by a former editor of *Nagara Vatta*), who were recruited and supported by the Thai and South Vietnamese governments. Although these events compounded his distrust of the pro-American Thais and South Vietnamese, the prince continued to court the US and accept American military aid – while at the same time forming an alliance with China, who wanted to prevent US dominance in the area. But in another abrupt change of direction, in mid-1963 Sihanouk accused the US of supplying arms to the Khmer Serei, and later that year ordered all US aid stopped. The same year, Sihanouk nationalized banking, insurance and all import-export trade.

The economy was soon destabilized by the combination of Sihanouk's policies and the spillover into Cambodia of the conflict between North and South Vietnam. Sihanouk had to perform a delicate **balancing act** to preserve some semblance of neutrality and avoid Cambodia being drawn into the Vietnamese conflict. In 1963, he broke off relations with South Vietnam, which was receiving financial and military support from the US, though US planes were not prevented from overflying Cambodia in the mid-1960s, on their way to bomb North Vietnam. Meanwhile Sihanouk had been unable to prevent North Vietnam sending men and arms via Cambodian territory to the communist **Viet Cong** guerrillas in South Vietnam, leaving him little option but to sign a secret agreement with the North Vietnamese in 1966, allowing them safe passage.

The prince made a serious political error, though, when in 1966 he was involved with arrangements for a prestigious visit from Charles de Gaulle and neglected to pay sufficient attention to preparations for the elections; as a result, the National Assembly for the first time included members not handpicked by the prince, who were to prove a focal point for opposition to him a few years later. Meanwhile, in the northeast of the country, the CPK (Communist Party of Kampuchea) – or the **Khmer Rouge**, as Sihanouk dubbed them – comprising Cambodian communists who had been sheltering in North Vietnam, began a campaign of insurgency. Ironically, the Khmer Rouge probably owe their eventual victory to the United States, who launched a vast covert bombing programme, code-named **Operation Menu**, over supposedly neutral Cambodia, aimed at destroying communist bases and supply lines in the southern provinces of Cambodia along the border with Vietnam. All in all, over half a million tonnes of ordnance were dropped on the country in three thousand raids between March 1969 and January 1973, which had the effect of forcing communist Vietnamese deeper into Cambodian territory and thus alienating provincial Cambodians, causing them to side with the CPK.

Lon Nol takes charge

Elected prime minister in 1966, **General Lon Nol** had been regarded as Sihanouk's man, but began to shift his position in response to unrest among a military upset by a lack of equipment and supplies, and a middle class dissatisfied with the prince's economic policies. Plots continued to be hatched against Sihanouk, and in 1970, while he was out of the country, **Lon Nol** headed a coup, removing the prince as chief of state, abolishing the monarchy and renaming the country the **Khmer Republic**. Sihanouk broadcast an impassioned plea from Beijing, begging his supporters to fight Lon Nol, but the Chinese persuaded him to join with the communists whom he had forced into exile in 1963 to form an alternative government.

At home, details of Sihanouk's secret treaty with the North Vietnamese surfaced, and the elimination of their supply trail from Cambodian soil became a national preoccupation. Thousands of Cambodians joined the army to help, but they were poorly trained and ill-equipped (despite renewed US financial support, which served only to feed widespread corruption). In the event, the Cambodians were no match for the battle-hardened Vietnamese, and after tens of thousands of Cambodians died in fighting, Lon Nol called a halt to the offensive in 1971.

The **Khmer Rouge** meanwhile were battling towards Phnom Penh. In 1970 they already controlled an estimated twenty percent of Cambodia, primarily in the northeast and northwest; by the end of 1972, all but Phnom Penh and a few provincial capitals were under their control. Although heavy American bombing brought a momentary halt to their advance in 1973, they pushed steadily forward; refugees fled to Phnom Penh ahead of their advance, bringing with them tales of whole villages being slaughtered. The stories were dismissed by the capital's inhabitants as unfounded, and all blame was laid at the door of the Vietnamese. By early 1975, Phnom Penh was surrounded, access to the rest of Cambodia was cut off and the US was flying in supplies to the besieged city. The corruption of the Khmer Republic and constant war took their toll on the people, and when the communists walked into Phnom Penh on April 17, 1975 they were greeted with relief. Two weeks later, on April 30, the last Americans withdrew from Saigon, just ahead of North Vietnamese forces, and US military involvement in Indochina came to an end.

It's believed that **over 300,000 Cambodians** were killed as a result of the four years of fighting against the Vietnamese and the Khmer Rouge, coupled with indiscriminate bombing by the US. Sihanouk's worst fears had been realized, but this was nothing compared to what was to come.

The Khmer Rouge era

The Khmer Rouge had its roots in the Khmer People's Revolutionary Party (**KPRP**), formed in the early 1950s. As well as appealing to anti-monarchist elements, the KPRP attracted young Cambodians who had been exposed to communist ideals while studying in France. Three of these rose to powerful positions in the Khmer Rouge: Saloth Sar – later known as **Pol Pot** – who rose to

Pol Pot

The contemptible Pot was a lovely child.

Loth Suong, Pol Pot's older brother

The factors which turned Pol Pot from a sweet-natured child into a paranoid mass-murderer will probably never be fully understood. He was born **Saloth Sar** in 1928 at Prek Sbaur, near Kompong Thom, where his father was a prosperous farmer. Sent to live with his brother, Loth Suong, in Phnom Penh, at the age of 6, he had a relatively privileged upbringing – the family was well connected through a cousin, who was a ballet dancer at the royal court. Educationally Saloth Sar was unremarkable, and it was probably thanks to the influence of his cousin rather than through innate aptitude that he was chosen to attend the newly opened Collège Norodom Sihanouk in Kompong Cham in 1942 – Sar subsequently left the college without passing a single exam. Going on to study at the Lycée Sisowath in Phnom Penh his academic performance must, at some point, have improved, since in 1949 he was among a hundred students chosen to study in France.

In Paris, Sar joined the French Communist Party (along with his friends Ieng Sary and Khieu Samphan) and was exposed to radical new ideas; he also met Khieu Ponnery, a highly educated Cambodian woman who was to become his first wife. Returning to Cambodia in 1952, Saloth Sar joined the Vietnamese-run Indochina Communist Party and set about campaigning for the socialist cause in Cambodia. Imperceptibly, he began veiling himself in secrecy, isolating himself from his family, keeping a low profile and beginning to use an alias, "Pol". An ardent member of the newly created **Cambodian Communist Party**, he appeared content to work in the lower ranks of the party, giving seminars and recruiting for the cause through his job as a teacher. Those who met him at this time remarked that he was a kind-hearted and mild-mannered – albeit enigmatic – figure. Without ever seeming to promote himself, he rose steadily through the party ranks, from lowly assistant to Party Secretary.

By 1963, Sihanouk's support for the socialists had turned to persecution, and Saloth Sar, along with other key party members, was forced to flee the capital and seek refuge on the border with Vietnam. Moving frequently, the Cambodian communists were supported first by their North Vietnamese comrades, and later by the Chinese – whom "Pol" visited on several occasions and held in great esteem for the "success" of their Cultural Revolution. Isolated in the northeast by the escalating Vietnam War, "Pol" had ample time to develop his own plan for a better state, run on Marxist–Leninist principles. Living simply in the jungle he developed great admiration for the peasant's life, and by the time the revolutionaries – now dubbed the **Khmer Rouge** – had gained control of Cambodia in 1975, he was probably reasonably certain of his formula for returning to a basic agrarian society and the implementation of his (ultimately disastrous) "Four Year Plan".

the exalted rank of "Brother Number One" within the Khmer Rouge; his contemporary, Ieng Sary, who eventually became foreign minister; and Khieu Samphan, the future party chairman.

When the Khmer Rouge arrived in Phnom Penh, they set out to achieve their ideal: a nation of **peasants** working in an agrarian society where family, wealth and status were irrelevant. Family groups were broken up, money was abolished and everyday life – down to the smallest detail – was dictated by **Angkar**, the secretive revolutionary organization behind the Khmer Rouge. Within hours of entering Phnom Penh, the Khmer Rouge had begun to clear the city; within a week the capital was deserted. In other towns around Cambodia (now renamed **Democratic Kampuchea**) the scenario was repeated, and practically the whole population of the country was

Ever secretive, the Khmer Rouge leaders, rather than expose themselves as individuals, now hid behind a collective name, the mysterious **"Angkar"** – the central committee of the "Organization", as the leaders now referred to the party. This committee comprised thirteen members (eleven men and two women), its unchallenged head being Pol Pot, as Saloth Sar was by now known (it isn't known why he chose this pseudonym, which has no meaning in Cambodian). He was also known as "Brother Pol" and, after his appointment as prime minister of Democratic Kampuchea (1976), as **Brother Number One**. Other leading members of Angkar were Pol Pot's long-standing comrade and second in command, Nuon Chea (Brother Number Two); and Pol Pot's friends from his student days, Ieng Sary (Brother Number Three) and Khieu Samphan, the party frontman.

Increasingly suspicious, the cadre were convinced that they were surrounded by traitors; it was Pol Pot, though, who had direct responsibility for **purging** the party of "enemies", personally authorizing the torture and murder of around 20,000 comrades and their families at the Toul Sleng torture prison (interrogation at Toul Sleng was reserved for those who were close to the leadership – in fact most were loyal party members). While it's not clear whether Pol Pot directly ordered the interrogations and killings, it is certain that he was fully aware of, and probably supported, them. Whether or not he ever felt any remorse isn't known, but he certainly refused to acknowledge any responsibility – instead, when the atrocities were exposed by liberating Vietnamese forces in 1979, he accused the Vietnamese of being the perpetrators. Choosing to flee rather than face the Vietnamese army, he escaped to Thailand. He never doubted that the path he had chosen for Cambodia was the right one, believing instead that he had been betrayed by those whom he had trusted.

Sentenced to death by a Cambodian tribunal in absentia, Pol Pot lay low and remained at liberty in Thailand. In the mid-1980s, Khieu Ponnery went insane; Pol Pot divorced her in 1987 and married again, fathering his only child, a daughter called Malee. At some point, probably around 1993, Pol Pot crossed back into northern Cambodia where, surrounded by loyal supporters in the relative security of a Khmer Rouge enclave in the vicinity of Anlong Veng, he organized guerrilla attacks against the newly elected Cambodian government. Meanwhile, Ieng Sary, who had been waging a disruptive guerrilla war against the government from Pailin, defected in 1996. This must have come as a blow to Pol Pot, and signalled the end of the Khmer Rouge. Just a year later, an increasingly paranoid Pol Pot ordered the murder of his long-standing friend, Sun Sen and his family; for this murder he was tried by his own people and sentenced to life imprisonment. Eleven months later he was dead – apparently in his sleep from natural causes – his body was cremated a few days later on a pile of rubbish and old tyres. Bizarrely, Pol Pot has something of a cult status among Cambodians, and the site of his cremation near Anlong Veng is now a tourist attraction.

displaced. **Forced labour** was deployed in the fields or on specific building projects supervised by party cadres. The regime under which people worked was harsh and nutrition inadequate; hundreds of thousands perished in the fields, dying of simple illnesses and starvation. Almost immediately after seizing power, the Khmer Rouge began a programme of **mass execution**, though the twisted logic that lay behind this has never been made clear. Senior military commanders were among the first to die, but before long it was the turn of monks, the elite, the educated, those who spoke a foreign language, even those who wore glasses.

Prince Sihanouk, his wife and family had returned to Phnom Penh from exile in Beijing in mid-1975; they lived out the rest of the Khmer Rouge years under virtual house arrest.

As time went on, the regime became increasingly paranoid and began to look inward, murdering its own cadres. It's estimated that between one and two million people, around twenty percent of the population, died under the Khmer Rouge. Those who could escape fled to refugee camps in Thailand or across the border to Vietnam, but the majority had no option but to endure the three years, eight months and twenty days – as any older Cambodian will still say today – of Khmer Rouge rule, and to which they still refer as *sa'mai a-pot*, the Pol Pot era.

The Khmer Rouge's eventual **downfall** was orchestrated by their original mentors, the Vietnamese. Frequent border skirmishes initiated by the Khmer Rouge irritated the Vietnamese, who sent troops into Cambodia in 1977, though this incursion lasted just a few months. The final straw for the Vietnamese came when the Khmer Rouge massacred Vietnamese villagers along the border in early 1978. This caused Vietnam to begin supporting anti-Khmer Rouge factions, a shift that led to the formation of the Khmer National United Front for National Salvation, or **KNUFNS**. On December 22, 1978, a Vietnamese invasion force of more than 100,000 entered Cambodia, and just seventeen days later they had taken Phnom Penh. The leaders of the Khmer Rouge made their escape just ahead of the invading forces, Pol Pot by helicopter to Thailand, the rest crowded onto the train north to Battambang. Following their leaders, Khmer Rouge troops and villagers loyal to them retreated to the jungles along the northwest border.

The Vietnamese era

Although opinions about the **Vietnamese era** are divided between those who call them liberators and those who call them occupiers, no one disputes that they were widely welcomed, their arrival saving countless Cambodian lives. The Vietnamese found the country starving and devastated, the infrastructure shattered. Cambodia now became the **People's Republic of Kampuchea (PRK)**, as the Vietnamese formed an interim government in Phnom Penh made up of members of the KNUFNS; the president was Heng Samrin, an ex-Khmer Rouge divisional commander, and its foreign minister another ex-Khmer Rouge member, **Hun Sen**, who had fled to Vietnam in 1977.

Under the PRK, markets, schools, freedom of movement and private farming were re-established immediately, and by the following year, the use of money and religious practice on a limited scale were reintroduced. Nevertheless, the formation of the PRK caused many educated Cambodians, who had no intention of suffering more communist rule, to flee to Thailand, where they swelled the already bursting refugee camps; by 1981, 630,000 refugees had descended on Thailand (many of them Khmer Rouge) and a further 150,000 were living in Vietnam.

Although coverage of Cambodia's plight brought limited aid from the West, the havoc wrought by the Khmer Rouge was in general disregarded by the major powers, who deemed Cambodia to be occupied under the Vietnamese and consequently **ostracized** the PRK (the USSR and India were notable exceptions). Safe in Thailand, Pol Pot was supported by the Thai, Chinese and US governments, all ardently against the communist Vietnamese, as the prime minister of the legitimate government. As news of the atrocities committed by the Khmer Rouge surfaced, his supporters preferred to continue to punish Vietnam; bizarrely, the Thais and Chinese fed, clothed, trained and even rearmed Khmer Rouge soldiers, while UN agencies were allowed to look after Khmer Rouge in their camps, but were prevented from helping the decimated population of Cambodia.

As a counterweight to the PRK, the **Coalition Government of Democratic Kampuchea (CGDK)** was created as a government-in-exile in Thailand in 1982. It comprised Prince Sihanouk, persuaded to join by the Chinese, and his FUNCINPEC party; Son Sann, a previous prime minister of Cambodia and leader of the Khmer People's National Liberation Front (KPNLF); and members of the Khmer Rouge. Although the CGDK shared a common aim to rid Cambodia of the Vietnamese, they had no mechanism for achieving it. The Khmer Rouge had the superior military forces and sent frequent sorties across the border into Cambodia where they were repelled by the Vietnamese and PRK. After particularly harsh fighting in 1983–85, the PRK went on a mine-laying spree along the border with Thailand in an attempt to prevent these forays – the start of the land-mine scourge which still plagues Cambodia today.

The Vietnamese withdrawal and its aftermath

Vietnam had never considered the occupation of Cambodia to be a long-term goal, and while in charge had trained the Cambodian army in preparation for its own withdrawal. With the crisis in Eastern Europe building up, the USSR drastically reduced aid to the PRK government, making the occupation too expensive for the Vietnamese to sustain, and by the end of September 1989 they had withdrawn completely; shortly afterwards, the PRK government renamed the country the **State of Cambodia (SOC)**. Meanwhile, the government had altered the constitution to institute Buddhism as the state religion and allowed people the right to own, trade and inherit property. This was all very well, but the country was virtually bankrupt; practically no aid was being received, electricity and fuel were in short supply, and even basic needs such as health care couldn't be provided. Corruption, although not on the scale of earlier regimes, was still rife: the nouveaux riches built spacious villas, drove smart cars and ate out in restaurants, while the majority of Cambodians could barely afford rice. On the borders, a black economy thrived, with gems and timber flowing out, and consumer goods – which commanded a premium price on the home market – coming in.

Meanwhile, the Khmer Rouge was stepping up guerrilla activities, capturing Pailin in 1989. During 1990 they consolidated their position along the Thai border and regularly encroached further into Cambodia, destroying bridges, mining roads and raiding villages; by the end of that year they controlled the jungle areas to the northwest and southwest, going so far as to threaten Sihanoukville and Kampot. In the middle of that year, however, first the US, then China, changed their stance and **withdrew support** from the Khmer Rouge, which was to prove something of a turning point: a ceasefire was declared in July 1991, and in October a conference was held in **Paris** to discuss the future of the country.

To the millennium

Thirteen years of war should have come to an end with the Paris conference, at which a number of agreements were reached. The central idea was to establish an interim coalition government for Cambodia, the **Supreme National Council**, to be made up of representatives of the three factions of the CGDK and the SOC, pending United Nations-supervised elections; to this end, factional groups would disarm and 300,000 refugees be repatriated from Thailand. But the Khmer Rouge had other ideas and, still supported by Thailand, continued to create insurgency around the country, unsettling an already shaky peace.

UNTAC

The United Nations Transitional Authority in Cambodia, **UNTAC**, was created to stabilize the country and supervise the promised elections, though its forces didn't arrive in Cambodia until March 1992, and even then they were deployed slowly, allowing the Khmer Rouge to expand the area under its control. Refusing to lay down arms or be monitored, the Khmer Rouge continued with disruptive attacks, mining roads and railways, intimidating villagers and murdering over one hundred ethnic Vietnamese over two years; they also refused to stand in the elections. The return of refugees proceeded relatively peacefully, at least.

Costing $2 billion, the UNTAC mission (numbering 22,000 military and civilian staff) was, at the time, the most expensive operation ever launched by the UN, though it's debatable just how successful it really was. The international forces (from around a dozen countries, including Indonesia, India, Ghana, Uruguay, Pakistan and Bangladesh) were ill-prepared for their role as peacekeepers – many were only trained for combat – and had little concept of what was required of them or what to expect of Cambodia. Often criticized for insensitivity, many of the UNTAC forces – unaccustomed to the high salaries they were being paid – led high-rolling lifestyles, paying well over the odds for even basic services. At the time, business boomed, only to collapse when UNTAC withdrew; a fledgling tourist industry started up (albeit limited by the guerrilla tactics of the Khmer Rouge); and prostitution mushroomed – UNTAC did not test staff for HIV and, rightly or wrongly, is widely blamed for the AIDS epidemic now affecting Cambodia. Today, Cambodians' feelings about UNTAC remain decidedly ambivalent. The naysayers argue that it failed to restore peace and indeed created more problems than it solved, and that the subsequent elections were far from fair. The alternative view, just as widespread, is that without UNTAC the country might well have fallen again to the extremism of the Khmer Rouge.

The return of constitutional monarchy

The elections of July 1993, although marred by intimidation and political killings, were a resounding success with the electorate, with a turnout of nearly ninety percent. However, even though the **FUNCINPEC** party – headed by Sihanouk's son **Prince Ranariddh** – emerged with a majority, the interim government, led by Hun Sen, refused to cede the authority they had held since 1979. In the event, a government was formed which had two prime ministers, Prince Ranariddh and Hun Sen. A **constitutional monarchy** was reinstated, and Prince Sihanouk persuaded to resume the throne that he had abdicated in 1955, without being given any direct say in government.

Political infighting soon led to the government being dominated by the Cambodian People's Party (**CPP**) of Hun Sen, which had retained control of police, defence and provincial governments, and Prince Ranariddh became little more than a figurehead. The tensions between the two prime ministers grew until July 1997, when fighting broke out on the streets of Phnom Penh, resulting in many deaths, and Prince Ranariddh, who had just left the country, was ousted by Hun Sen. Foreseeing a bloody struggle, many foreign workers fled the country and investors hurriedly pulled out, leaving projects half-completed, bills unpaid and thousands out of work; the Asian financial crisis of the time only exacerbated matters.

The **1998 elections** were the first to be self-administered post-Khmer Rouge. In addition to the CPP and FUNCINPEC, the elections were contested by **Sam Rainsy Party**, a breakaway association of ex-FUNCINPEC members (for all the proliferation of parties, there remains little real ideological difference between them, although FUNCINPEC is generally regarded as royalist, the CPP as "communist", and Sam Rainsy as "democratic"). Even though the run-up to the polls was tense, with widespread intimidation of candidates and voters, the election itself was peaceful; scrutineers pronounced it "not perfect", but sufficiently free and fair, in spite of allegations of ballot rigging. The CPP won the majority of the seats in the Assembly, but failed to achieve the required two-thirds of the vote to form a government, and a tense few months ensued until another coalition was formed, with Hun Sen as prime minister and Prince Ranariddh as speaker of parliament.

The end of the Khmer Rouge

Outlawed in 1994, the Khmer Rouge started to suffer **defections** to the government almost immediately. Nevertheless, they retained control of the north and northwest of the country, where their leaders remained in hiding, amassing immense wealth from the proceeds of illegal logging and gem mining. Their guerrillas continued to stage random attacks, kidnapping and murdering foreigners and Cambodians, while their presence prevented access to many parts of Cambodia and deterred tourists and investors alike.

The ultimate demise of the Khmer Rouge came a step closer in 1996, when after striking a deal of immunity from prosecution, **Ieng Sary**, erstwhile Brother Number Three, and two thousand of his troops defected to the government side, leaving a last rebel enclave, led by Ta Mok and Pol Pot, isolated in the north around Anlong Veng and Preah Vihear. An internal feud led to Pol Pot being tried by a court of his comrades in July 1997 for the apparent attempted murder of a cadre. Some nine months later he was dead, though it remains unclear if this was due to natural causes or whether he was murdered; whatever the truth, he was hastily cremated in Anlong Veng. Late in 1998, **Khieu Samphan**, who had been the public face of the Khmer Rouge and president of Democratic Kampuchea, and **Nuon Chea**, Brother Number Two, gave themselves up to the authorities. Anlong Veng was effectively returned to Cambodian jurisdiction the following year. **Ta Mok**, "The Butcher", was arrested attempting to cross to Thailand in March 1999, and finally, in May the same year, Kang Kek Leu, alias **Duch**, the notorious commandant of Toul Sleng torture prison, was tracked down and arrested.

The new millennium

Modern Cambodia faces many challenges, and progress is slow at best. In spite of being supported by hundreds of millions of dollars of aid per annum, the country's infrastructure is slow to improve, in no small part due to entrenched corruption. While some city-folk may have seen a modest improvement in their standard of living, for the majority of Cambodians, whose homes lack clean water and electricity, there has been no change; health care remains inadequate and land mines and unexploded ordnance continue to be a problem. Aid donors, fed up with deep-rooted corruption, repeatedly try to get tough, but their warnings are consistently ignored and things carry on pretty much as before.

Essentially an agricultural nation, Cambodia has never had much of a manufacturing base, although investors tempted by a plentiful supply of cheap labour have set up garment and shoe factories in Phnom Penh, Sihanoukville and Bavet. It was thought Cambodia's prospects for trade would improve with its entry to **ASEAN** (the Association of Southeast Asian Nations) in 1999, but so far the benefits don't seem to cover the $5m annual membership fee.

The Khmer Rouge on trial

After considerable procrastination the Cambodian government reluctantly put in place the laws for a tribunal against the Khmer Rouge to go ahead in 2001. Late in 2004, and only thanks to considerable donor aid, the "Extraordinary Chambers of the Courts of Cambodia for the Prosecution of Crimes Committed during the Period of Democratic Kampuchea" (ECCC) was instituted. Judges – both Cambodian and international – were recruited and trained, Khmer Rouge leaders rounded up and the trials proper eventually commenced in 2008.

So far though, only born-again-Christian **Duch** – now 67 and known as Kaing Guek Eav – has been tried. Arrested in July 2007, his trial commenced in March 2009; he was finally found guilty and sentenced to 35 years (commuted to 19 years) in prison in July 2010 for crimes against humanity and war crimes – an appeal is pending. Given the protracted nature of the tribunal proceedings, and that this is only the first – ironically Case 001 – of the trials, it's going to be some time yet before any more, or indeed any, Khmer Rouge members are brought to account.

However, four further, aged cadre have now been indicted: Nuon Chea, **Brother Number Two**, arrested in September 2007, continues to protest his ignorance of Khmer Rouge atrocities; **Ieng Sary**, Pol Pot's brother-in-law, now 86, and his wife, **Ieng Thirith**, the minister of social affairs for Democratic Kampuchea, were arrested in 2007 from the comfort of their Phnom Penh home; **Khieu Samphan**, the public face of the Khmer Rouge, likewise arrested in 2007, is in ill health. All four are expected to come to trial in mid-2011 – if they live that long. **Ta Mok** (see p.000) died in 2006 before he could be arrested.

Whether the Cambodians want the tribunal, however, remains a matter of debate. For many it offers a chance to ask "Why?" and to effect closure on tragic events; while others, in spite of having lost family and friends to the Khmer Rouge, don't want to resurrect bad memories and fear it'll leave even more questions unanswered.

The country's first-ever **local elections** were held in February 2002, against a background of political intimidation and the murder of several candidates. The result was a landslide victory for the CPP. The fact that the polls were held at all, however, was an achievement of sorts, as was the fact that fewer people died than during any previous election. **National elections**, held the following year, were acknowledged as having been the most successful to date. Although they were won, unsurprisingly, by the CPP, opposition parties were well represented, with Sam Rainsy Party (SRP) – the nearest the country has to a liberal party – and FUNCINPEC polling enough votes between them to stop the CPP forming a government. The resulting stalemate lasted the best part of a year, and it wasn't until June 2004 that Hun Sen and Prince Ranariddh agreed to form a coalition.

The new king

In October 2004, just days before his eighty-second birthday, Cambodia's long-reigning king, Norodom Sihanouk, surprised the country by abdicating, something he had threatened to do on many occasions previously. Writing to Prince Ranariddh (who had announced several years before that he did not want to be considered as an heir) from Beijing, the former king cited ill-health and advancing age as the reasons for stepping down, and left it to his son to break the news to the government and media. Royal succession is not hereditary in Cambodia: the constitution merely states that a new monarch must be over 30 years old, a member of the royal family and descended from one of three previous kings, but gives no clear method for making a choice, which was left to the hurriedly assembled Throne Council – comprising six members of the government and two Buddhist leaders. Selecting the sole surviving son (four others had died during the Khmer Rouge era) of Norodom Sihanouk and his wife, Monineath, **Norodom Sihamoni** (who had earlier been "suggested" by Sihanouk himself), seems to have been uncontroversial. A former ballet dancer, the 51-year-old Sihamoni has been a UNESCO ambassador and has lived mostly in France; he returned to Cambodia in mid-October 2004 just days ahead of the coronation, pledging to do all he could for the country.

In the years since his coronation King Sihamoni has kept a relatively low profile. That said, he has regular, and reportedly outspoken, meetings with the government, and though it's not reported often in the press, he pays regular visits to towns and villages around the country and seems to be held generally in kind regard. Meanwhile, the self-named King Father, Norodom Sihanouk, continues to be in ill-health, although this isn't bad enough to stop him writing regular bulletins on his website and issuing letters to the media when he disagrees with something.

Parties and politics

National elections were held again in 2008, and although contested by eleven political parties only two achieved enough votes to hold any influence in government. As expected, Hun Sen's CPP retained power, increasing the number of seats it has in parliament by taking almost 60 percent of the vote. Much to his disgust, and to calls of "rigging", Sam Rainsy's party was the runner-up – taking just under 22 percent of the vote – most would say it did as well as could be expected. Observers suggest that the elections were free ('ish) and that there was less violence than in any of the previous elections. So for the time being, that is the next five years, Hun Sen remains in control of the government and the country.

Religion and beliefs

Buddhism influences practically every aspect of Cambodian life, as is evident from the daily gifts of food made to barefoot, saffron-robed monks, and the almost obsessive dedication to preparing for offering days and major festivals, when pagodas take on a carnival air. However, it was **Hinduism** which predominated among the Khmer from the first century until the decline of the Khmer Empire in the early fourteenth century; consequently, much temple art and architecture is influenced by the Hindu cosmology.

Islam is the most widespread of Cambodia's minority faiths, being practised by the Cham community. **Christianity**, introduced by various missionary groups, has failed to make much impact. **Buddhism** in Cambodia is noticeably less dogmatic and formal than in Thailand or Burma, and the age-old traditions of paying respects to **spirits** and deceased **ancestors** survive, so woven into the fabric of Cambodian life that at times there is no clear line between them and local Buddhist practice.

Hinduism's historical role

Hinduism was introduced to the area by the Brahman priests who accompanied Indian traders to Funan around the first century, and was adopted by the majority of the pre-Angkorian and Angkorian kings. Even today, **Hindu influences** play an important cultural role in Cambodia: two Hindu epics, the *Ramayana* and (to a lesser extent) the *Mahabharata*, form the basis for classical dance and shadow-puppet performances and a subject for contemporary artists.

The Hindu creed is diverse, encompassing a belief in **reincarnation**, the notion of **karma** (the idea that deeds in one life can influence status in subsequent reincarnations), a colourful **cosmology** – including a vast pantheon of gods – and the building of temples. The three principal deities are **Brahma**, the creator and lord of all gods; **Vishnu**, the benevolent preserver who regulates fate and has ten avatars (incarnations); and **Shiva**, the destroyer, who is responsible for both death and rebirth. Shiva was especially worshipped in the form of a **linga**, a phallic-shaped stone pillar. Frequently these linga were carved in three sections, the square base representing Brahma, the octagonal middle corresponding to Vishnu, and the circular top symbolizing Shiva. Just as linga were frequently a melding of the triad of gods, so the **Harihara**, a popular deity of the pre-Angkorian era, melded the characteristics of both Shiva (on the right-hand side of Harihara images) and Vishnu (on the left).

In the ninth century, Cambodian Hinduism was pervaded by the **devaraja cult** introduced by King Jayavarman II. The idea was that, on ascending the throne, the king created an image (consecrated to Shiva or Vishnu) that was installed in the main sanctuary of the king's state-temple. On his death the king was believed to become one with the god and to be able to protect his kingdom from beyond the grave.

Buddhism

Buddhism has its origins in India, developing out of Hinduism around the sixth century BC, when the teachings of prince-turned-ascetic, **Siddhartha Gautama**, became popular. Born to a royal family in Lumbini, in present-day Nepal, around 560 BC, Gautama was protected from the sufferings of the outside world and knew nothing other than the comfortable life of the court, where he married and fathered a son. When he reached the age of 29, however, curiosity caused him to venture out of the palace, where he variously encountered an old man, a sick person, a funeral procession and a monk begging for alms. Horrified by what he had seen, Gautama undertook to give up his life as a prince, leaving the palace and taking up the simple life to see if he could discover a way to end suffering. Having sought out different religious instructors to no avail, he eventually adopted a programme of self-denial, fasting almost to the point of death, until he finally understood that this austerity only perpetuated the suffering he was trying to resolve. On three successive nights, while meditating under a bodhi tree, he received revelations leading to his **enlightenment**: on the first night he saw his former lives pass before him; on the second night he understood the cycle of life, death and rebirth; on the third night the four holy truths of suffering were shown to him. Rather than passing straight to **nirvana** – a state free of suffering – as was his right as one who had attained Buddhahood, he remained on earth to spread the **dharma**, the doctrine of the **Middle Way**, encompassing the four noble truths (see below) and avoiding both the extremes of self-indulgence and self-denial. He preached his first sermon at Sarnath, near Varanasi in northern India; his converts were sent out to pass on the teachings; and for the rest of his life, the Buddha travelled India, teaching and begging for food.

Schools

Soon after the Buddha's death at the age of 80, his followers met to agree a consensus on his teachings, which were passed on by word of mouth. By the time another meeting of this type was called a hundred years later, variations had crept in (indeed Buddhist teachings weren't to be written down until around 100 BC), leading to a schism: two schools of Buddhism developed, Theravada and Mahasanghika, the latter giving rise to **Mahayana Buddhism**. Mahayana Buddhism propounds that some individuals who have attained enlightenment remain on earth in order to help others; known as **Bodhisattvas**, "beings of wisdom", they are worshipped in their own right as compassionate deities. An example is Lokesvara, whose image appears at Angkor in the four-faced gateways of the Bayon. Crucial to Mahayana Buddhism is the notion that nirvana is accessible to everyone, not confined to just a few ascetics.

In contrast, **Theravada Buddhism** does not encompass the notion of the Bodhisattva, and has it that enlightenment can only be attained by following a lengthy path of meditation, making nirvana practically unattainable even for monks, let alone lay people. Ancient Theravada Buddhist texts tell that seven Buddhas have already been to earth, the most important of whom was Gautama, with one left to come, though later texts say that nearly thirty Buddhas would appear (but only one per historic period). Among Buddhist countries, it is only in Burma, Cambodia, Laos, Sri Lanka and Thailand that Theravada Buddhism dominates.

Doctrine

The objective of Buddhist teachings is to release the individual from the cycle of birth, death and rebirth. Each life is affected by the actions of the previous life, and it is possible to be reborn at a higher or lower status depending on earlier actions. By right thoughts and deeds, individuals accrue **karma**, or merit, in this life towards the next world and the next reincarnation.

At the heart of Buddhist teachings are the **Four Noble Truths**, revealed to the Buddha under the bodhi tree. The first is that all of human life is suffering. The second deems that suffering results from desire – the need for possessions, company, food, even for rebirth – or is born of ignorance – doing the right things, but in the wrong way. The third reveals that suffering can cease, and that once it is removed, the cycle of reincarnation is broken and the ultimate goal of nirvana nearly achieved.

The fourth truth is the path to the removal of suffering, namely the **Eightfold Path** (also called the Middle Way), comprising right knowledge (an understanding of the Four Noble Truths); right attitude (a quiet mind free from desire, envy and greed); right speech (truthful, thoughtful and wise words); right action (good moral conduct); right occupation (one's way of life must not harm others); right effort (good actions develop good thoughts and deeds); right mindfulness (carefully considered actions, speech and mental attitude); and right composure (concentration and focus). The Eightfold Path fosters morality, spirituality and insight without either austerity or indulgence; much store is set by meditation, putting away the ups and downs of everyday life to achieve a calm, level mind, relinquishing the desire for status and wealth and ultimately achieving peace.

Buddhism in Cambodia

In Cambodia, Mahayana Buddhism survived side by side with Hinduism from the days of Funan, both creeds having been brought by Indian traders. It was not, however, widely adopted until the twelfth century when, under Jayavarman VII, it briefly replaced Hinduism as the state religion. With the passing of Jayavarman VII, Hinduism experienced a brief resurgence in the early thirteenth century, but thereafter it was Theravada Buddhism that gripped the population, though the reasons for the change are unclear. This decisive switch to Buddhism resulted in the cessation of temple construction, in whose stead **monasteries** were founded; the pagodas founded by King Ponhea Yat in Phnom Penh in the middle of the fifteenth century are the oldest surviving Buddhist places of worship in Cambodia today. Monasteries provided schooling, housed collections of texts and acted as guardians of the national religion, language and moral code; it also fell to them to provide other social services such as care for the elderly and sick.

In 1975, the Khmer Rouge banned all religion, destroying or desecrating pagodas, texts and statues, and persecuting Buddhist monks; fewer than 3000 out of an estimated 65,000 monks survived the regime. Buddhism was tolerated, if not encouraged, during the Vietnamese occupation, and reinstated as the national religion in 1989, when the reconstruction of pagodas commenced. Today, Buddhism is practised by some 95 percent of the country's population.

Wats

The typical rendering of **wat** into English as "pagoda" can be confusing, as a wat is essentially a monastery. Cambodians are under no pressure to go to the wat, but will pop in on offering days and as and when they feel the need; in fact they also visit as something of a leisure activity, even picnicking within the grounds.

A wat is enclosed by walls with entrances on each side; at its heart is the **vihara**, the main sanctuary, which contains the most important Buddha images. The walls of the vihara are generally painted with colourful scenes from the life of the Buddha, many of which will have been donated by rich Cambodians to earn merit for the next life; many are personalized to reflect the donor or the times. The vihara is used solely by the monks for their religious ceremonies, and is often kept locked. A separate hall is the main centre of the pagoda's activity; here meals and religious classes are taken and ceremonies for the laity performed. Scenes from the

Jataka, a collection of tales of the previous lives of the Buddha, are frequently to be found painted on the walls; most commonly depicted are those tales dealing with the Buddhist perfections – generosity, virtue, renunciation, wisdom, energy, patience, truthfulness, resolution, kindness and even temper.

Also commonly found within pagodas are **crematoria**, reflecting the prevalence of cremation rather than burial, and **chedi** containing the ashes of the deceased. The small huts that are often dotted around the pagoda compound may be used as places for meditation, though more often they are quarters for nuns and for elderly folk.

At the **altar**, Buddhists pay their respects to (rather than worship) the Buddha: palms are placed together in front of the chin and either they are raised to the forehead while bowing slightly, or the forehead is touched to the floor; either action is carried three times. It is also usual to light three sticks of incense and place them in a holder near the altar or by the main door; if asking for divine assistance, lotus buds are placed in vases near the altar. It is customary for worshippers to leave a donation of a few thousand riel.

For information on suitable dress and other points of **etiquette** when visiting a temple, see p.54.

The Sangha

Monks play an important role in Cambodian life, and it's not uncommon for Cambodian men to enter the **Sangha**, or monkhood, for a period in their lives, often between the ages of 13 and 15 or upon the death of a parent (in the not so distant past this was seen as a right of passage, making men fit for marriage and raising a family). This ordination can be for quite short periods, perhaps a couple of months, or reflecting modern times, even just a day. Novices are ordained in the rainy season, when their heads are shaved and they receive their saffron robes, comprising the *sampot ngout*, the undergarment; a *sbang*, covering the lower body; a *hang sac*, a garment with many pockets worn over one shoulder; and the *chipor*, a shawl that covers the upper body and is thrown across the shoulders (inside the pagoda, the right shoulder is left uncovered). Women are never ordained but can become lay nuns, undertaking various tasks around the pagoda, including looking after the senior monks and maintaining the altar; often this is a way for older women and widows with no family to be looked after in their twilight years.

Besides practising meditation and chanting, monks have to follow 227 precepts, and undertake daily study of Buddhist scriptures and philosophy. Life in the pagoda is governed by ten basic injunctions, including not eating after noon, abstaining from alcohol and sexual relations, not partaking of entertainment (television is thus not permitted, though, in Cambodia at least, having a mobile phone and using a computer seem to be allowed), not wearing personal adornments or sleeping on a luxurious bed.

The most evident aspect of the monkhood in Cambodia is the daily need to go out into the community to ask for **alms**. Begging monks go barefoot, signifying the simplicity of their lives (the donor should also be barefoot when giving alms). Donations of money go to support the pagoda or to pay for transport, while food is collected in the monks' bowls or bags, to be shared among all the monks at the pagoda. In return, the donors receive a simple blessing from the monk, helping them to gain merit for the next life.

Though monks themselves are not allowed to marry, they are often asked to bless couples who are to be married, and they also officiate at funerals, presiding over the cremation of the body and storage of the ashes at the pagoda. Monks also play a major role in the private religious ceremonies that many Cambodians undertake, for reasons ranging from alleviation of bad luck to acquiring merit for the next life. These events can involve anything from a blessing at the pagoda, with elaborate offerings and chanting monks, to making a small offering of fruit or the purchase and release of a small bird from a cage.

Islam and Christianity

Islam arrived with the **Cham**, who fled to Cambodia from Vietnam around the beginning of the eighteenth century; today, the Cham (see p.240) account for some three percent of the population. The most striking thing about Islam in Cambodia is the mixing of the precepts of the faith (the monotheistic worship of Allah, the requirement to pray five times a day and make the pilgrimage to Mecca, and so on) with elements of traditional animist worship – some Cambodian Muslims use charms to ward off evil spirits or consult sorcerers for magical cures.

The Cham suffered badly at the hands of the Khmer Rouge; mosques were destroyed or desecrated, and forty thousand Muslims murdered in Kompong Cham alone. After the Khmer Rouge, the Cham were able to resume their religious practices, rebuilding their own mosques, each with its own *hakim* or leader, and imam, responsible for communal prayers; the number of followers now exceeds that pre-1975. The country's **main mosque**, built with Saudi money in 1994, is in the Boeung Kak area of Phnom Penh and has space for five hundred worshippers.

In spite of the efforts of missionaries and a lengthy period under the Catholic influence of the French, **Christianity** is followed by less than one percent of the population. Phnom Penh once had a Catholic cathedral but it was razed to the ground by the Khmer Rouge. Over a hundred Christian NGO and missionary groups operate in Cambodia today, providing services in the fields of education (in particular English-language lessons), health care and rural development. A few years ago however the government curtailed their freedom, and now groups have to seek approval before building churches and are banned from proselytizing as a result of reports of children being coerced with sweets and gifts into becoming Christian.

Animism, ancestor worship and superstitions

According to **animist** belief, all things in nature have an associated spirit; trees, rocks, streams and so forth may be deemed sacred for either their beauty or their supposed magical or medicinal properties. To keep these spirits happy, and to request good luck or give thanks, particularly before the rice harvest, offerings of incense, fruit, flowers and water are made at **spirit houses**, found all over Cambodia; trees and boulders, private houses and businesses sport anything from a simple wooden tray with a tin can for the burning of incense, to an elaborate, gaudily painted concrete affair resembling a doll's-house version of a pagoda.

Respect for the **ancestors** is important to most Cambodians. In **chunchiet** culture small wooden funerary figurines are placed on graves to protect the dead. **Buddhists** celebrate their ancestors in the three-day festival of **Bonn Pchum Ben**, in September or October, when offerings are taken to as many as seven pagodas and picnics are shared by the family around the chedi. The homes of ethnic **Chinese** often have two spirit houses, one dedicated to the house spirit, the other to the ancestors; incense should be burnt daily to assure good fortune.

Cambodians are highly **superstitious**, regularly consulting fortune-tellers, astrologists and psychics, and even making use of sacred **tattoos** for self-protection. Fortune-tellers are often found at the pagoda, where they give readings from numbered sticks drawn at random or a book of fortunes. Astrologers are key to arranging a marriage and are normally consulted early on to ensure that couples are compatible and to determine the best day for a wedding. The Cambodians also practise a form of *feng shui*, and practitioners are consulted particularly to assess land before purchase and advise on the removal of trees and construction of property.

Books

Until fairly recently books about Cambodia fell into two categories: dry, factual tomes about the temples of Angkor, and harrowing Khmer Rouge-era autobiographies. Coverage of culture and the rest of Cambodia's history was relatively sparse, and novels hardly existed. Now, however, there's an ample choice of contemporary books, but it's still worth seeking out older titles if you are interested in the country's pre- Khmer Rouge history. Out-of-print titles or those with overseas publishers can most easily be tracked down over the internet – Ⓦwww.amazon.com and the publishers own websites are good starting places. Note that if you are buying books in Cambodia, apart from in reputable bookshops and hotels, most will be photocopies, albeit tidily bound and sometimes even in colour.

In the reviews below, if a book's **publisher** is the same worldwide, the publisher is simply stated after the title; otherwise the publishers in the UK and the US are given in that order, or indicated by "UK" or "US" if the book is published in only one of the two countries. For books published outside these two countries, we also give the city of publication. Where a Kindle version is available it is stated in the review. Titles marked ✱ are particularly recommended.

Travel and general

Liz Anderson *Red Lights and Green Lizards* (Green Print). Moving account of early 1990s Cambodia through the eyes of a British doctor, who volunteered in the riverside brothels of Phnom Penh and set up the city's first-ever clinic for prostitutes.

Ghillie Basan *The Food and Cooking of Cambodia* (Southwater). Illustrated cookery book of authentic Cambodian recipes. Although many of the dishes aren't what people eat at home, or even things you'll find on typical restaurant menus, it has a good selection of easy-to-follow recipes and plenty of mouth watering photographs.

François Bizot *The Gate* (Vintage). Gripping first-person account of being kidnapped by the Khmer Rouge for three months in 1971; the author's release was attributable to the rapport he built up with the notorious Duch, who was recently convicted of war crimes.

✱ **Robert Casey** *Four Faces of Siva* (Kessinger Publishing, US). Eminently readable 1920s travelogue, in which the author weaves fact and fantasy into his personal discovery of Cambodia's hidden cities. The compelling description of the author's foolhardy trek to explore the remote Preah Khan in Kompong Thom province is still valid today.

✱ **Karen J. Coates** *Cambodia Now: Life in the Wake of War* (McFarland & Company Inc, US). Smashing collection of insightful, anecdotal tales from the time the author spent in Cambodia as a journalist on the *Cambodia Daily*. She sensitively portrays the lives of the ordinary people of Cambodia, probes the events that affect them and depicts how they survive in often distressing circumstances.

Adam Fifield *A Blessing Over Ashes* (HarperCollins, US). The author's candid account of growing up in 1980s America with Soeuth, his adopted Cambodian brother, seen from both sides of the cultural gap. Especially touching is the visit to Cambodia, where Soeuth discovers that his Khmer family is still alive.

Amit Gilboa *Off the Rails in Phnom Penh* (Graham Brash (Pte) Ltd, Singapore). Self-styled, voyeuristic "guns, girls and ganja" foray into the seedy side of Phnom Penh in the mid-1990s.

Geoffrey Gorer *Bali and Angkor: A 1930s Pleasure Trip Looking at Life and Death* (o/p). The acidic, condescending comments on everything from transport to temples make it hard to see why Gorer bothered to visit Angkor at all, but his off-the-wall interpretations of the rationale behind Khmer art certainly make for an alternative view to the accepted texts.

Gillian Green *Traditional Textiles of Cambodia: Cultural Threads and Material Heritage* (River Books, Bangkok). Full-colour study of Cambodian textiles; comprehensively researched and containing a wealth of information on why and how textiles are produced.

Christopher J. Koch *Highways to a War* (Vintage). This novel embraces the war in both Cambodia and Vietnam; the conflict is given a human touch through the experiences of its intrepid, war-photographer hero.

Bree Lafreniere *Music through the Dark* (University of Hawaii Press, US). Musician Daran Kravanh only survived imprisonment by the Khmer Rouge because the cadre took a liking to his music, often calling him to play his accordion after a day toiling in the fields.

Norman Lewis *A Dragon Apparent: Travels in Cambodia, Laos and Vietnam* (Eland Publishing, UK). Though light on Cambodia content, what there is gives a fascinating, all-too-rare glimpse of the country around the time of independence; best of all are the observations of the people and everyday events.

Carol Livingstone *Gecko Tails: Journey Through Cambodia* (o/p). A lighthearted account of the life of a would-be foreign correspondent during Cambodia's free-rolling UNTAC era; a bit of politics, some history and a lot of human interest wrapped up in a sensitively told yarn.

Jeff Long *The Reckoning* (Simon & Schuster). Novel with a supernatural bent: a missing-in-action team search the Cambodian countryside for lost comrades; while deep in the jungle a deserted temple gradually gives up the secrets of a disappeared GI patrol, but not without wreaking revenge on those who dare to venture there. Kindle version available.

Longteine De Monteiro and Katherine Neustadt *The Elephant Walk Cookbook: Cambodian Cuisine from the Nationally Acclaimed Restaurant* (Houghton Mifflin, US). Comprehensive cookbook from the restaurant of the same name in Boston; many of the recipes recorded here were all but lost to Cambodians when the Khmer Rouge decimated the population.

Henri Mouhot *Travels in Siam, Cambodia, Laos and Annam* (White Lotus Co, Bangkok). The first Cambodian travelogue, Mouhot's diary contains a fascinating account of the "discovery" of Angkor Wat in 1856, and was responsible for sparking off Cambodia-fever in nineteenth-century Europe.

Haing S. Ngor and Roger Warner *Survival in the Killing Fields* (Robinson Publishing, US). Harrowing account by a doctor who survived torture by the Khmer Rouge, but was unable to save his wife, who died in childbirth. Fleeing Cambodia, the author eventually reached America, where he won an Oscar for his role as Dith Pran in the film *The Killing Fields*. He was murdered in 1996 by muggers.

U Sam Oeur *Crossing Three Wildernesses* (Coffee House Press, US). Poet, scholar, engineer and politician, Oeur's memoir recounts not only his enthralling life story, but is packed with details of everyday Cambodian life, historic fact and political intrigue.

Toni Samantha Phim and Ashley Thompson *Dance in Cambodia* (Oxford University Press). This compact guide crams in information on the history and styles of Cambodian dance, along with a pictorial glossary of traditional musical instruments.

Colin Poole and Eleanor Briggs *Tonle Sap: Heart of Cambodia's Natural Heritage* (River Books, Bangkok). Superb photographic record of life, people and nature on the Tonle Sap lake.

Geoff Ryman *The King's Last Song* (HarperCollins). Page-turner of a novel about the discovery of an ancient diary etched in gold. The story cleverly interweaves the intrigue of the twelfth-century Angkorian court with the lives of its present-day heroes, an ex-Khmer Rouge soldier and a young moto driver. Kindle version available.

Lucretia Stewart *Tiger Balm: Travels in Laos, Vietnam and Cambodia* (Chatto & Windus; o/p). A sizeable chunk of this book is taken up with a visit to the poverty-stricken and oppressed Cambodia of 1989, when only the bravest of travellers ventured there; a good read for the characters the author meets along the way.

Jon Swain *River of Time* (Vintage). Part love affair with Indochina and part eyewitness account of the fall of Phnom Penh, written by a respected war correspondent. Kindle version available.

Loung Ung *First They Killed My Father* (HarperCollins, US). The author pulls no punches in this heart-rending personal narrative of the destruction of her family under the Khmer Rouge regime.

Connor Wall and Hans Kemp *Carrying Cambodia* (Visionary World Ltd, Hong Kong). Delightful photographs of Cambodia's transport system in all its amusing and colourful guises.

History and politics

David Chandler *A History of Cambodia* (Westview, US). Now in its fourth edition, this is a readable, concise history of Cambodia from prehistoric times to the early twenty-first century by a pre-eminent author on Cambodia.

David Chandler *Voices from S-21* (University of California Press, US). This thought-provoking book delves into archive material from the interrogation and torture centre at Toul Sleng to attempt an explanation of why such atrocities happened – often neither captive nor interrogator knew what crime had supposedly been committed. Kindle version available.

Chou Ta-Kuan *The Customs of Cambodia* (Siam Book Society, Bangkok). The sole surviving record of thirteenth-century Cambodia, written by a visiting Chinese envoy, with graphic accounts of the customs of the time, the buildings and ceremonies at court.

Ian Harris *Cambodian Buddhism: History and Practice* (University of Hawaii Press, US). At last, a readable, if slightly dry, account of the history and practice of Buddhism in Cambodia to the present day.

Eva Mysliwiec *Punishing the Poor: The International Isolation of Kampuchea* (Oxfam; o/p). Dated, but valuable chronicle of how the West ostracized Cambodia after the Vietnamese invasion.

Vann Nath *A Cambodian Prison Portrait: One Year in the Khmer Rouge's S-21* (White Lotus, Bangkok). A survivor's account of Toul Sleng; Nath, a trained artist, has since used his skills to create a pictorial document of the appalling practices once visited on inmates in the Toul Sleng Genocide Museum.

William Shawcross *Sideshow: Kissinger, Nixon and the Destruction of Cambodia* (Cooper Square Press, US). Starting with a single mission to destroy a North Vietnamese command base believed to be located in Cambodia, this book traces the unfolding of the United States' horrendous clandestine bombing campaign against the country and its subsequent cover-up – compulsive reading.

John Tully *A Short History of Cambodia: From Empire to Survival* (Allen & Unwin). Straightforward – though not as short as the title suggests – history of Cambodia. Kindle version available.

Angkor

George Cœdes *Angkor, An Introduction* (o/p). This old faithful offers useful background to the temples in a slightly rambling vein.

Bruno Dagens *Angkor, Heart of an Asian Empire* (Thames & Hudson; o/p). The story of the rediscovery of Angkor Wat and the explorers who brought the magnificent temple to the attention of the Western world, illustrated with old photographs and detailed sketches.

Maurice Glaize *The Monuments of the Angkor Group* (o/p). Classic guide to the temples originally published in 1944, with detailed maps and photographs; read it online or download in full from ⓦwww.theangkorguide.com.

Claude Jacques and Michael Freeman *Ancient Angkor* (River Books, Bangkok). Superbly illustrated guide to the monuments of Angkor. Ideal for those who don't want to spend every moment at the temples gazing though their own camera lens.

Claude Jacques and Michael Freeman *Angkor: Cities and Temples* (River Books, Bangkok). Stunning coffee-table volume featuring fabulous photographs and evocative descriptions of the temples.

Steve McCurry *Sanctuary: The Temples of Angkor* (Phaidon Press). Magical images of the temples from this renowned photographer; paperback edition available.

Christopher Pym *The Ancient Civilization of Angkor* (o/p). Fascinating wander through the life and times of the ancient Khmer, exploring everything from how kingfishers were caught to the techniques used to move massive stone blocks for the building of temples.

Dawn Rooney and Peter Danford *Angkor: Cambodia's Wondrous Khmer Temples* (Odyssey). Easy-to-use guide, with good background information and plans for each of the principal temples; now in its fifth edition.

Vittorio Roveda *Sacred Angkor: The Carved Reliefs of Angkor Wat* (River Books, Bangkok). Perfect for temple buffs, this is a detailed study of the reliefs, offering alternative suggestions for their interpretation.

Biography

David Chandler *Brother Number One: A Political Biography of Pol Pot* (Westview Press, US). The original work on Pol Pot, this meticulously researched book reconstructs the life of this reclusive subject. The rather scant actual information about him is bolstered by juicy details about other Khmer Rouge leaders.

Nic Dunlop *The Lost Executioner: A Story of the Khmer Rouge* (Bloomsbury Publishing). Duch, the infamous commandant of the Khmer Rouge torture prison S-21, was found living in a remote area of Cambodia. This easy-to-read book reveals details of his life and ponders the rise of the Khmer Rouge, comparing their philosophy to those of Stalin and the French Revolution. Kindle version available.

Harish C. Mehta and Julie B. Mehta *Hun Sen, Strongman of Cambodia* (Graham Brash (Pte) Ltd, Singapore). Based on interviews with Hun Sen himself, his family and colleagues, this provides a frank portrait of the man, though the authors have undoubtedly chosen their words carefully.

Milton Osborne *Sihanouk, Prince of Light, Prince of Darkness* (University of Hawaii Press). No-nonsense behind-the-scenes look at the contradictory King-Father. He comes across as a likeable, all-too-human character, if often petulant and egotistical.

Philip Short *Pol Pot: The History of a Nightmare* (John Murray). Although rather lengthy, the author draws on such first-hand accounts as there are for this in-depth analysis of Pol Pot and the circumstances that allowed the Khmer Rouge to come to power.

Language

Language

Khmer

Belonging to the Austro-Asiatic family of languages, **Khmer** is the national language of Cambodia, and is also spoken in the Mekong delta and pockets of northeast Thailand, as well as forming the basis of the language used at the Thai royal court. Many Khmer words have their origins in two old Indian languages – Sanskrit (which was introduced along with Hinduism during the Funan era) and Pali – while Malay, Chinese, Vietnamese, Thai, French and English have all added to the language's development.

Although in the major towns and tourist centres English is increasingly spoken (particularly by the younger generation who learn it at school and often take private lessons to develop this sought-after skill), learning even a few words of Khmer will go a long way to endearing you to Cambodians; off the beaten track you'll find it especially helpful to know some basic Khmer phrases. Fortunately, Khmer is a relatively easy language to get to grips with, being **non-tonal** and relatively simple in its grammar. Sentences follow the subject–verb–object pattern of English, although adjectives are added after the noun as in French. Khmer verbs don't conjugate, and tenses are indicated by the addition before the verb of a word indicating the timeframe; *nung*, for instance, indicates an action taking place in the future. Articles – "a", "an" and "the" in English – and plurals aren't used in Khmer (quantity is indicated by stating the number or using general terms for "some" or "many").

If you are trying out your language skills, the Cambodians will do their best to understand you and will patiently repeat words for you to copy. Understanding what is being said to you is another issue; **regional dialects** present a challenge, as many words are quite different from the formally correct words in Phnom Penh. Another problem is that Cambodians often abbreviate their sentences, missing out many words, chopping them short and changing words and phrases around.

Khmer **script** is an artistic mix of loops and swirls, comprising **33 consonants** and **23 vowels**; the vowels are written above and below the consonants and to either side. Capital forms of the letters exist, but are seldom used. In writing, words run left to right with no spaces in between; sentences end with a little symbol that looks a bit like the numeral "7", playing the role of a full stop or period.

A variety of self-study Khmer **courses** are available. Multilingual Books (Ⓦwww.multilingualbooks.com) and The Ultimate Language Course (Ⓦwww.theultimatelanguagecourse.com) both sell basic courses on CD-ROM with supporting books, some MP3 format and downloads available. *Talk Now!* is aimed at travellers, while *Cambodian Basic Course* and *FSI Khmer Basic Course* are courses for those wishing to delve deeper; both are good, though pricey.

Also available on CD with supporting book is the long-standing *Colloquial Cambodian* (Routledge) – check on Amazon (Ⓦwww.amazon.co.uk or Ⓦwww.amazon.com). In Phnom Penh, at Psar Thmei and Psar Toul Tom Poung, you can purchase the excellent *Seam & Blake's English–Khmer* pocket dictionary ($3–4), which lists words in Khmer script and in Roman transliteration. At the same outlets, you can also pick up the *United Nations English–Khmer Phrase Book*, though the phonetics leave something to be desired.

An **iPhone app**, with a 15-minute Khmer language lesson and fifty introductory phrases, is available at Ⓦjournals.worldnomads.com/language-guides and is also available as an MP3 player download. It's also worth checking out Ⓦwww.youtube.com: search under "learn Khmer", where there are a number of useful video clips.

Pronunciation

Some sounds in Khmer have no English equivalent and require a little time and practice to master, the best way being to listen to and imitate native speakers. Cambodians use intonation for emphasis, but while you're learning Khmer it's best to keep your speech somewhat monotonous in order to avoid causing misunderstanding.

Transliteration of Khmer into the Roman alphabet is not straightforward, and differences in approach account for many of the variations on maps and restaurant menus. The rudiments of a system were developed during the French protectorate, though this is rarely employed nowadays.

Consonants

Most consonants in our transliteration scheme are pronounced as they would be in English, though note that consecutive consonants are pronounced individually. The following combinations should also be noted:

bp sharp sound, between the English "b" and "p".

dt sharp sound between the English "d" and "t".

gk guttural sound between the English "g" and "k".

ng as in si**ng**; often found at the beginning of words.

ny as in ca**ny**on.

Vowels

a as in **a**go.

aa as in b**a**r.

ai as in t**ie**.

ao or **ou** as in c**ow**.

ay as in p**ay**.

e as in l**e**t.

ea as in **ear**.

ee as in s**ee**.

eu is similar to the French fl**eu**r.

i as in f**i**n.

o as in l**o**ng.

oa as in m**oa**n.

ohs as in p**o**t (the hs is practically silent).

oo as in sh**oo**t.

OO as in l**oo**k.

ow as in t**oe**.

oy as in t**oy**.

u as in f**u**n.

Useful words and phrases

The polite **form of address** for men is "*loak*", for women "*loak srei*"; in a formal situation Cambodians will often introduce themselves with one of these two terms, then give their full name with the family name first. Although you will be asked your name a lot as you travel around, Cambodians do not really use names in everyday situations, preferring to use a range of respectful forms of address. These terms can be either polite or familiar depending on the situation, and are used even when meeting someone for the first time. The choice of term depends not only on whether the person being spoken to is male or female, but also on whether they are older or younger than the speaker. An older person is often (both politely and familiarly) addressed as either *yeah* or *dah* (grandmother or grandfather), or *ming* or *boh* (auntie or uncle), depending on just how much older they are than the speaker. When speaking to someone younger, *kmoouy bprohs* or *kmoouy srei* (nephew or niece) can be used, or more familiarly, *bpohn bprohs* or *bpohn srei* (younger brother or sister). Take your lead from the Cambodians and listen to how they address you or other people.

Greetings and civilities

hello (formal/informal)	chum ree-eu-bp soo-a/soo-a s'day
welcome	swah-ghOOm
how are you?	nee'ak sok sa bai gee-ar dtey?
I'm well/fine	k'nyom sok sa bai
goodbye (formal/informal)	chum ree-eu-bp lear/lear haowee
see you later	chewubp kynear t'ngai keraowee
please	som
if you please	unchurn
thank you	or-kOOn
excuse me/sorry	som dtohs

Basic terms and phrases

yes (spoken by a male/female)	baht/jahs
no	dtay
large or big	tom
little or small	toight
come/go	mow/dhow
to have (also used for "there is/are")	mee-un
sleep	gayn
take	daea
what is your…?	nee'ak…ai?
name	ch-moo-ah
nationality	jon-jee-ut
where do you come from?	nee'ak mau bpe pro-teh nar?
I am from…	k'nyom mau bpe pro-teh…
Britain	onglais
Ireland	ear-lond
US	amei-rik
Canada	kana-daa
Australia	orstra-lee
New Zealand	nyew seelend
are you married?	nee'ak riep-ghar hauwee roo now?
how many children do you have?	nee'ak mee-un gk'cone bpon maan nee'ak?
I don't have any children	k'nyom ot towan mee-un
I have one child/two children	k'nyom mee-un gk'cone moi/bpee
where are you staying?	nee'ak s'nak now ai nar?
can you speak English/Cambodian?	nee'ak jehs nit-yaiy pia-sar onglai/k'mair roo dtay?
I know (can speak) a little	k'nyom jehs tick-tick
I don't understand	k'nyom s'dabp men baan/k'nyom ot yull
how old are you?	a'yup bpon-maan chnam?
not yet	ot toe-un
I don't know	k'nyom ot dung
there aren't…/we don't have…	ot mee-un…
none left/finished	ohs haowee
it can't be done	ot baarn
no problem	ot banyaha
just a minute/please wait a minute	som jam bon tick

Getting around

where are you going? (also used as a general greeting)	dtow nar?
I am going to a/an/the…	k'nyom dtow…
I want to go to a/an/the…	k'nyom chong dtow…
where is the…?	…now ai nar?
airport	jom nort yoo-un hohs/drang yoo-unhohs
bus station	seta-nee laan kerong
taxi stand	seta-nee laan dtak-see
train station	seta-nee roteh pleung
jetty	gkumpong bpai
bank	t'nee-a-geer

embassy (Thai/Lao/ Vietnamese)	sa-tarn-toot (tai/lao/ vietnam)
guesthouse	pteah sumnat
hotel	sontdakee-a/owhtel
market	psar
money changer	gonlaing dt'loi
museum	sarat montee
pharmacy	farmasee
police station	bpohs bpoli
post office	bprey-sa-nee
restaurant	porjarnee-a tarn/ restoran
shop	harng
go straight	dtow dtrong
please stop here	som choap tee neeh
(turn) left/right	(bot) ch'wayng/s'dam
north	dteu khang jeung
east	dteu khang kea-et
south	dteu khang tb'ohng
west	dteu khang leh'j
bus	laan tom
cyclo	see-klo
minibus	laan dubp-bpee gonlaing
motorbike taxi	motodubp/moto
pick up	laan noo oan/laan ch'noo-ul laan gk'bah
taxi	dtak-see
express boat	karnowt lou-en
slow boat	karnowt
small boat	dtook
where do I buy a ticket?	k'nyom trouw ting sambort now ai nar?
how much to go to…?	dtow…bpon maan?
will you go for…?	dtow…baan tday?
…per person	…moi nee'ak
does this…go to?	laan neeh mee-an dtow…dtay?
when does the… depart?	…neeh je-ny dtow maung bpon maan?
how long does it take to get to…?	doll…o'h bpon maan maung?
is the…far away?	…che-ngai dtay?
it's (not) a long way	(ot) che-ngai
how much to hire…	ch'noo-el teeyeng
outright?	oughs…nee'ak yor bpon maan?
don't pick up any other passengers	kgom to-tooel nee'ak dhum-now tee-et dtoh
do you agree to the price?	dumlai neeh baan dtay?
is this seat vacant?	gonlaing neeh dohs dtey roo dtay?
it's vacant	dohs dtey
it's taken	mee-un nee'ak
what's wrong with the vehicle?	laan neeh koit dtay?
I need to stop to go to the toilet	k'nyom som choap bot cheung

Accommodation

do you have any rooms?	nee'ak mee-un bontobp roo dtay?
do you have a single room	bontobp sum-rab moi nee-ak
room with two beds with…	bontobp graiy bpee mee-un…
air conditioning	maa-sin dtro-chey-at
bathroom	bontobp dtuek
fan	dong harl
hot water	dtuek g'daow
toilet	bong-kgun
window	bong-ooit
how much is it per night?	moi yoobp bpon-maan?
can I see the room?	som merl baan dtay?
can you discount the price?	johs bon-tick baan dtay?
can I have…?	k'nyom som…?
a blanket	bphooey
a mosquito net	moohng
a telephone	toora-saap
the room key	souw bontobp leik
toilet paper	gro-dahs
a towel	gkon-saing
how many nights will you stay?	nee'ak s'nak now tee neeh bpon maan yoobp?
can you clean the room?	som sum-art bontobp neeh baan dtay?
can I move to another room?	k'nyom som doa bon-tobp?

this room is…	bontobp neeh…
full of mosquitos	mee-un moohs che-raan
too noisy	telong payk
do you have a laundry service?	mee-un bauk cao-aow?
do you have a bicycle/motorbike for rent?	mee-un kong/moto sum-rabp ch'ooel?

Shopping and changing money

where do they sell…?	gay mee-un loo-uk …now ai nar?
do you have…?	nee'ak mee-un…?
candles	dtien
cigarettes	baar-rai
clothes	cao-aow
medicine	t'nam
mosquito coils	took dot
silk	soort
soap	saa-boo
souvenirs	kgar-dow/soo-ven-neer
toothpaste	t'nam doh t'meny
washing powder	saa-bo bowk cao-aow
what do you call this?	neeh how awaiy?
how much does it cost?	telai bpon maan?
very expensive!	telai nahs
what is your best price?	dait bpon maan?
can you go down a bit?	johs bon tick baan dtay?
I only have riel/dollars	k'nyom mee-un dtai riel/dol-lar
I want to change money	k'nyom chong dow loi

Emergencies and health matters

help!	choo-ee
thief	jowl
my passport has been stolen	brum-dain/pa'hport rebohs k'nyom gai lou'it
I have lost my…	k'nyom bat lik-khet ch'long…
my pack/suitcase is missing	gkar-borb/val-lee trauv bat
there's been an accident	mee-un kroo-ah t'nak
please take me to hospital	som june k'nyom dtow mon-tee pey-et
please call an ambulance	som hao laan pay-et
I am not well	k'nyom men se-rooel kloo-un dtay
I need a doctor	k'nyom trauv ghar gkroo pay-et
I have…	k'nyom mee-un…
a fever	gkrun
diarrhoea	rey'ak
pain	choohs
where is the toilet?	mee-un bong-khun now ai nar?
are there any land mines here?	gon-laing neeh mee-un min dtay?
I'm lost	k'nyom vung-veing plaow

Numbers

zero	sohn
one	moi
two	bpee
three	bpai
four	bpoun
five	bphrahm
six	bphrahm-moi
seven	bphrahm-bpee/bpel
eight	bphrahm-bpai
nine	bphrahm-bpoun
ten	dhop
eleven, twelve, etc	dhop-moi, dhop-bpee
twenty	m'pay
twenty-one, twenty-two, etc	m'pay-moi, m'pay-bpee
thirty	sam-sep
forty	si-sep
fifty	hahs-sep
sixty	hohk-sep
seventy	jet-sep
eighty	bpaet-sep
ninety	cow-sep
one hundred, two hundred, etc	moi-roi, bpee-roi…
one hundred and one	moi-roi moi

one thousand, two thousand, etc	moi-bpouhn, bpee-bpouhn…
ten thousand	moi-meun
one hundred thousand	dhop-meun
one million	moi-leuhn
first, second, etc	dte-moi, dte-bpee

Times and dates

The time is generally expressed by stating the word for hour, then the hour itself, then the number of minutes past the hour and the word minute; thus 5.05 is rendered *maung bprahm, bprahm nee-ar tee*. Morning, afternoon or night are added to confirm the right time. In business the 24-hour clock is usually used, and months are referred to by number – thus October is *kai dhop*.

what's the time?	maung bpon maan?
hour	maung
minute	nee-ar tee
morning	bpel p'ruk
noon	t'ngai terong
afternoon	bpel rohsiel
evening	bpel l'ngeit
night	bpel yob
day	t'ngai
today	t'ngai neeh
tomorrow	t'ngai sa-all
yesterday	m'sell-mine
Monday	t'ngai jarn
Tuesday	t'ngai ong-keeya
Wednesday	t'ngai bot
Thursday	t'ngai brou-hohs
Friday	t'ngai sok
Saturday	t'ngai sou
Sunday	t'ngai ah-tet
last/next/this…	…mun/k'raowee/neeh
week	ah tet
month	kai
year	chnam
now	ailouw neeh
later	bpel k'raowee
not yet	ot t'w-an
just now	a-bany mainy
already	hauwee

A food and drink glossary

As most Khmer dishes are ordered simply by stating what type of food you want to eat and how you'd like it prepared (thus stir-fried pork with ginger is *sait jerook cha khyay*), we've listed Khmer terms for various ingredients and standard cooking methods; a few specific dishes are also listed by name. To specify that a particular ingredient should *not* be added to your food, prefix the item in question with *ot dak* (without) – thus if you don't want sugar in your drink, say *ot dak skar*.

Cooking methods and general terms

…cha	stir-fried…
…cha knyay	stir-fried…with ginger
…jew aim	sweet-and-sour…
…ang	grilled…
…dot	roasted…
ma-horb	food (prepared)
nOOm-bpang	bread
pong mowan pong (hen's)/ dteer (duck's)	egg
be jaing/msow sobp	monosodium glutamate (MSG)
m'rik	pepper
um-beul	salt
skar	sugar
bong ai'm	dessert
k'nyom poo ahs	I'm vegetarian
k'nyom nyam bai t'ngai neih l'ngeit	I'd like to eat in the evening (to order meals in advance where restaurants would normally be shut by late afternoon)
ot bpah'aim	not sweet (useful when ordering drinks)

Meat, poultry and fish

sait gow	beef
sait mowan	chicken
g'dam	crab
sait dteer	duck
trei	fish
kongaib	frog
ot yoh kroeng knong	offal, intestine or gizzard
sait jerook	pork
trei muk	squid

Vegetables (bon lai)

tro-ab	aubergine/eggplant
sun dike	beans
sun dike bon dohs	bean sprouts
spei	cabbage
mteahs plouwk	capsicum
karot	carrot
pgar katnar	cauliflower
mteahs	chilli
draw sok	cucumber
k'tum	garlic
gee	herbs
sal-lat	lettuce
trokooen	morning glory
pset	mushroom
k'tum barang	onion
sundike day	peanuts
dumlong barang	potato
bpowrt sngaow	sweet corn
bpenh pohs	tomato

Soups (sumlar/sop), stews (kor) and curries (ka-ree)

amok trei	mild fish curry cooked in banana leaves
kaar	stew made with pig's trotters
sop chhnang day	fondue-like dish, cooked in a clay pot at the table
sumlar mjew gruoeng	slightly spicy soup made with beef, deer or chicken, along with lemon grass, turmeric and galangal
sumlar mjew vietnam	Vietnamese sour soup, usually based on fish (it can be made with chicken), complemented by pineapple, tomato and lotus flower stems, sometimes with added egg
sumlar ngam ngouw	lemon chicken soup
sumlar sngaow jerooet	clear chicken or fish soup
sumlar troyoung jayk sait mowan	chicken with banana-flower soup (variations use fish or duck in place of chicken)

Noodles (mee) and rice (bai) dishes

bai sait mowan/ sait jeruk	rice topped with fried chicken/pork
borbor	rice porridge
borbor sawr	unseasoned rice porridge
geautieuv	rice noodles
geautieuv sop (sait...)	rice noodle in soup (with...meat)
loat chat	fried macaroni-like noodle
mee ganychop	instant noodles made up from a packet
mee kilo	yellow noodles
nom bany jowk	flat white noodle served cold with a curry sauce

Some common meat and vegetable dishes

cha bon lai cropmok	fried mixed vegetables
cha katnar chia moi pset	fried pak choy with mushrooms
chhnang phnom pleung	thin slices of beef barbecued at the table over a charcoal burner
dumlong barang gee-yan	French fries
jay yior	spring rolls
mowan dort	baked chicken

Fruit (pelai cher)

pelai bporm	apples
pelai burr	avocado
jayk	banana
tee-ab swut	custard apple
pelai sroegar ne-yak	dragon fruit
tooren	durian
dum pay-yang bai jew	grape
troubike	guava
kroit chhmar	lime
meeyan	longan
koulen	lychee
svai	mango
morkgoot	mangosteen
kroit pursat	orange
lehong	papaya
pelai seyree	pear
manoahs	pineapple
kroit telong	pomelo
sow maow	rambutan
le-mot	sapodilla
tee-ab barang	soursop
umpbel	tamarind
ohluck	watermelon

Snacks (jum neigh arehar) and cakes (noam)

banh chhaev	savoury pancake stuffed with bean sprouts, pork and shrimp
bok lehong/som tam	papaya salad
chook	lotus seed
grolan	sticky rice in bamboo
jayk ang	grilled bananas
jeruik	pickles
nam bpaow	dumplings
noam downg dot	coconut cake
noam eclair	éclair
noam ensaum jayk	sticky rice cakes with banana
noam gachiey	chive burger
noam gdam	croissant (literally, crab cake)
noam pang patey	sandwich made with pâté
noam pong teeya/ noam barang	cupcake
noam srooey	cookie
pong dteer braiy	"thousand-year egg", a duck's egg preserved in salt
pong dteer gowne	duck's egg containing unhatched duckling
prohok	fermented fish paste
sait kreyuam	dried meat slices

Drinks (pay-sejeyat)

sraa bier	beer
dorbp	bottle
kumpong	can
coca	Coca-Cola
ka-fei	coffee
kafei kmaow (tuk kork)	black (iced) coffee
kafei tuk duh gow (tuk kork)	white (iced) coffee
tuk sot	drinking water
tuk krolok	fruit shake
tuk kork	ice
tuk dhowng	juice of green coconut
tuk duh	milk
tuk sun dike	soya milk
tuk krolok dak kropmok	mixed fruit shake
tuk umpow	sugar-cane juice
tuk tnaowt jew	sugar-palm beer
siro	syrup
dtai	tea
dtai gdouw kroit chhmar	hot lemon tea
dtai tuk kork kroit chhmar	iced tea with lemon
dtai grolab	strong local tea

Glossary

Abacus Upper, flat part of the capital of a column.

Achar Learned lay-person at a pagoda.

APSARA Authority for the Protection and Management of Angkor and the Region of Siem Reap.

Apsara Celestial dancer of Hindu mythology, born of the Churning of the Ocean of Milk.

ASEAN Association of Southeast Asian Nations.

Asura Demon (from Hindu mythology).

Avatar Incarnation of a Hindu deity.

Banteay Citadel or fortified enclosure.

Barang Slang term meaning French, and often applied to foreigners in general.

Baray Reservoir.

Bodhisattva One who has attained enlightenment but forgoes nirvana to remain on earth and help others.

Brahma Hindu god, often referred to as the Creator.

Brahman Hindu priest.

Buddha One who has achieved enlightenment.

Chedi Structure in which cremated ashes are interred; also called a stupa.

Chunchiet Generic term for the minority hill-tribe groups.

CITES Convention on International Trade in Endangered Species of Wild Fauna and Flora.

CPP Cambodian People's Party.

Cyclo Three-wheeled bicycle rickshaw.

Deva God.

Devaraja Literally "god who would be king"; the Khmer king, according to the devaraja cult, would fuse with a deity upon his death.

FUNCINPEC Front Uni National pour un Cambodge Indépendant, Neutre, Pacifique et Coopératif – the royalist political party.

Garuda Mythical creature associated with Vishnu, having the body of a man with the head and feet of a bird.

Gopura Entry pavilion, gatehouse to the sacred area of a temple.

Harihara God created from the union of Shiva and Vishnu.

Heng Cambodian mythical bird.

Hol Method of weaving and a pattern of silk fabric.

Indochina Cambodia, Laos and Vietnam.

Jataka Tales recounting the past lives of the Buddha.

Kala Mythical creature with bulbous eyes, claws and no lower jaw.

Khapa Chunchiet basket with shoulder straps, worn on the back.

Khmer The principal indigenous people of Cambodia – the term is often used interchangeably with Cambodian – and also the name of their language.

Koh Island.

Kompong Village on a river or lake.

Krama Cambodian checked scarf.

Krishna The eighth incarnation of Vishnu.

Lakshmi Wife of Vishnu, and the goddess of good fortune and beauty.

Laterite Soft, porous rock that hardens in the sun to a hard, resilient stone.

Leahng Cave.

Linga Phallic-shaped stone representing Shiva.

Lokesvara One of the Bodhisattvas, often called "the compassionate".

Mahabharata Hindu epic dealing with the rivalry between the Kaurava and Pandava families.

Makara Mythical sea monster with the body of a crocodile and the trunk of an elephant.

Mount Meru Mountain home of the gods, at the centre of the universe in Hindu cosmology.

Mudra Traditional Buddhist poses, widely depicted in Buddhist art, and also in Cambodian classical dancing.

Naga Sacred multi-headed snake, seen as a protector and often depicted along staircases or across causeways.

Nandin Sacred bull, and mount of Shiva.

NGO Non-governmental organization engaged in relief or campaigning work.

Nirvana A state in which desire ends and the cycle of birth, death and rebirth is broken.

NRP Norodom Ranariddh Party.

Pagoda Cambodian wat.

Pediment Section above the lintel of a doorway.

Phnom Mountain or hill.

Phum Village.

Pilaster Shallow rectangular column attached to a wall.

Prasat Sanctuary tower.

Preah A title of spiritual respect, used for gods and holy men; also means "sacred".

Psar Market.

Quincunx Arrangement of five objects with one at the centre and the others at each corner of a rectangle – like the five dots on the face of a die. Used to describe the placing of sanctuary towers in Cambodian architecture.

Rahu Demon with a monster's head and no body, usually depicted swallowing the sun and moon.

Rama Seventh avatar of Vishnu, hero of the *Ramayana*.

Ramayana Hindu epic tale describing the battle between Rama (an incarnation of Vishnu) and the demon Ravana.

Reamker Cambodian version of the *Ramayana*.

Sampot Wraparound skirt; by extension, a length of fabric sufficient to make a skirt.

Shiva One of the three principal Hindu gods, often referred to as the Destroyer.

Sita Wife of Rama, who was kidnapped in the *Ramayana*.

Spean Bridge.

SRP Sam Rainsy Party.

State-temple Principal temple built to house the god with whom the devaraja king was associated; a temple-mountain.

Stele Upright stone block inscribed with writing.

Stucco A type of plaster made with lime, and used for decoration, particularly of brick buildings.

Stung Medium-sized river, smaller than a *tonle*.

Stupa See *chedi*.

Temple In the context of Cambodia, an ancient building or collection of buildings, built by kings to honour ancestors, or to house the devaraja god.

Temple-mountain Temple constructed as a representation of Mount Meru.

Tonle Major river.

Toul Low mound.

Tuk-tuk Motorbike-drawn passenger carriage.

Tympanum Recessed section of a pediment, bound by the cornices.

UNESCO United Nations Educational, Scientific and Cultural Organization.

UNTAC United Nations Transitional Authority for Cambodia.

UXO Unexploded ordnance.

Vihara Main sanctuary of a wat.

Vishnu One of three principal Hindu gods, the Preserver.

Wat Buddhist monastery and associated religious buildings; often translated into English as "pagoda".

Yaksha Male spirit, depicted with bulging eyes, fangs and a leer; serves as a temple guardian.

Yama God of the Underworld.

Yeak Giant.

Travel store

FAIR FARES from NORTH SOUTH TRAVEL

Our great-value air fares cover the world, from Abuja to Zanzibar and from Zurich to Anchorage. North South Travel is a fund-raising travel agency, owned by the NST Development Trust.

ALL our profits go to development organisations.

Call 01245 608 291 (or +44 1245 608 291 if outside UK) to speak to a friendly advisor. Your money is safe (ATOL 5401).
For more information, visit northsouthtravel.co.uk.
Free Rough Guide of your choice for every booking over £500.

EVERY FLIGHT A FIGHT AGAINST POVERTY

Visit us online

www.roughguides.com

Information on over 25,000 destinations around the world

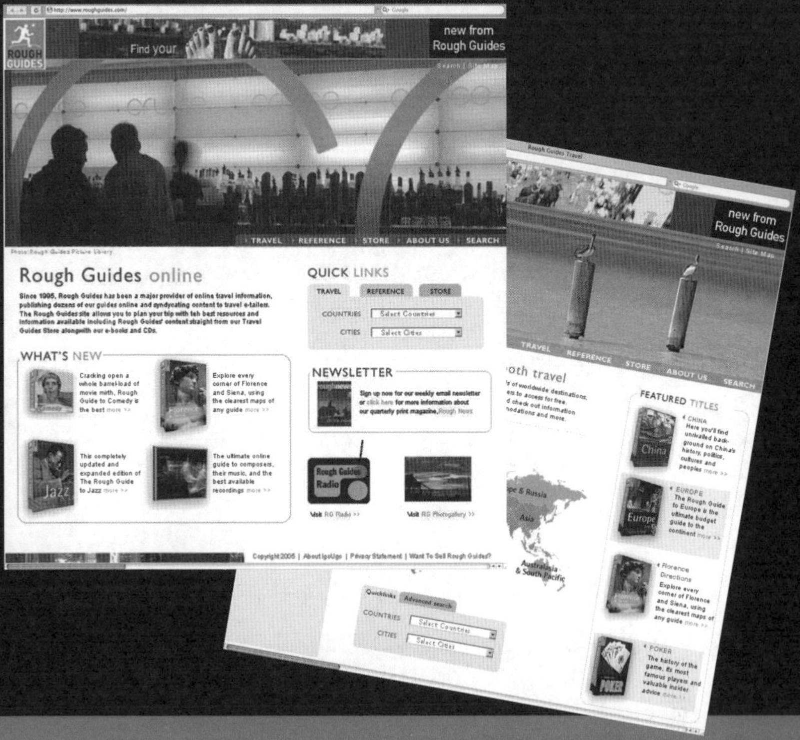

- **Read** Rough Guides' trusted travel info
- **Access** exclusive articles from Rough Guides authors
- **Update** yourself on new books, maps, CDs and other products
- **Enter** our competitions and win travel prizes
- **Share** ideas, journals, photos & travel advice with other users
- **Earn** points every time you contribute to the Rough Guide community and get rewards

BROADEN YOUR HORIZONS

NOTES

NOTES

NOTES

Small print and
Index

A Rough Guide to Rough Guides

Published in 1982, the first Rough Guide – to Greece – was a student scheme that became a publishing phenomenon. Mark Ellingham, a recent graduate in English from Bristol University, had been travelling in Greece the previous summer and couldn't find the right guidebook. With a small group of friends he wrote his own guide, combining a highly contemporary, journalistic style with a thoroughly practical approach to travellers' needs.

The immediate success of the book spawned a series that rapidly covered dozens of destinations. And, in addition to impecunious backpackers, Rough Guides soon acquired a much broader and older readership that relished the guides' wit and inquisitiveness as much as their enthusiastic, critical approach and value-for-money ethos.

These days, Rough Guides include recommendations from shoestring to luxury and cover more than 200 destinations around the globe, including almost every country in the Americas and Europe, more than half of Africa and most of Asia and Australasia. Our ever-growing team of authors and photographers is spread all over the world, particularly in Europe, the US and Australia.

In the early 1990s, Rough Guides branched out of travel, with the publication of Rough Guides to World Music, Classical Music and the Internet. All three have become benchmark titles in their fields, spearheading the publication of a wide range of books under the Rough Guide name.

Including the travel series, Rough Guides now number more than 350 titles, covering: phrasebooks, waterproof maps, music guides from Opera to Heavy Metal, reference works as diverse as Conspiracy Theories and Shakespeare, and popular culture books from iPods to Poker. Rough Guides also produce a series of more than 120 World Music CDs in partnership with World Music Network.

Visit www.roughguides.com to see our latest publications.

Rough Guide credits

Text editor: Ros Belford
Layout: Ajay Verma
Cartography: Deshpal Dabas
Picture editor: Harriet Mills
Production: Rebecca Short
Proofreader: Diana Margolis
Cover design: Daniel May, Sarah Cummins
Photographer: Tim Draper
Editorial: London Andy Turner, Keith Drew, Edward Aves, Alice Park, Lucy White, Jo Kirby, James Smart, Natasha Foges, James Rice, Emma Beatson, Emma Gibbs, Kathryn Lane, Monica Woods, Mani Ramaswamy, Harry Wilson, Lucy Cowie, Alison Roberts, Lara Kavanagh, Eleanor Aldridge, Ian Blenkinsop, Charlotte Melville, Joe Staines, Matthew Milton, Tracy Hopkins; **Delhi** Madhavi Singh, Jalpreen Kaur Chhatwal, Dipika Dasgupta
Design & Pictures: London Scott Stickland, Dan May, Diana Jarvis, Mark Thomas, Nicole Newman, Rhiannon Furbear; **Delhi** Umesh Aggarwal, Jessica Subramanian, Ankur Guha, Pradeep Thapliyal, Sachin Tanwar, Anita Singh, Nikhil Agarwal, Sachin Gupta
Production: Liz Cherry, Louise Minihane, Erika Pepe
Cartography: London Ed Wright, Katie Lloyd-Jones; **Delhi** Rajesh Chhibber, Ashutosh Bharti, Rajesh Mishra, Animesh Pathak, Jasbir Sandhu, Swati Handoo, Lokamata Sahu
Marketing, Publicity & roughguides.com: Liz Statham
Digital Travel Publisher: Peter Buckley
Reference Director: Andrew Lockett
Operations Coordinator: Becky Doyle
Operations Assistant: Johanna Wurm
Publishing Director (Travel): Clare Currie
Commercial Manager: Gino Magnotta
Managing Director: John Duhigg

ROUGH GUIDES

SMALL PRINT

Publishing information

This fourth edition published August 2011 by

Rough Guides Ltd,
80 Strand, London WC2R 0RL
11, Community Centre, Panchsheel Park, New Delhi 110017, India

Distributed by the Penguin Group

Penguin Books Ltd,
80 Strand, London WC2R 0RL

Penguin Group (USA)
375 Hudson Street, NY 10014, USA

Penguin Group (Australia)
250 Camberwell Road, Camberwell, Victoria 3124, Australia

Penguin Group (NZ)
67 Apollo Drive, Mairangi Bay, Auckland 1310, New Zealand

Rough Guides is represented in Canada by Tourmaline Editions Inc. 662 King Street West, Suite 304, Toronto, Ontario M5V 1M7

Cover concept by Peter Dyer.

Typeset in Bembo and Helvetica to an original design by Henry Iles.

Printed in Singapore

© Beverley Palmer, 2011
Maps © Rough Guides
No part of this book may be reproduced in any form without permission from the publisher except for the quotation of brief passages in reviews.

368pp includes index

A catalogue record for this book is available from the British Library

ISBN: 978-1-84836-889-7

The publishers and authors have done their best to ensure the accuracy and currency of all the information in **The Rough Guide to Cambodia**, however, they can accept no responsibility for any loss, injury, or inconvenience sustained by any traveller as a result of information or advice contained in the guide.

11 12 13 14 8 7 6 5 4 3 2

Help us update

We've gone to a lot of effort to ensure that the fourth edition of **The Rough Guide to Cambodia** is accurate and up-to-date. However, things change – places get "discovered", opening hours are notoriously fickle, restaurants and rooms raise prices or lower standards. If you feel we've got it wrong or left something out, we'd like to know, and if you can remember the address, the price, the hours, the phone number, so much the better.

Please send your comments with the subject line "**Rough Guide Cambodia Update**" to mail @uk.roughguides.com. We'll credit all contributions and send a copy of the next edition (or any other Rough Guide if you prefer) for the very best emails.

Find more travel information, connect with fellow travellers and book your trip on www .roughguides.com

Acknowledgements

Beverley Thanks to all my friends in Cambodia, but especially to Ray Warner, Seng Luna, Lee Hong, Venerable Yos Hut Khemacaro, Pho Socheat, Hun Chantha, Phean Sopheak, Tanja Kishner, Dave Perks, Warren Garber and Nick Butler for all their help, kindness, and friendship. Also to my "guides", moto and tuk-tuk drivers Ta (Preah Vihear), Mony Hong (Mondulkiri), Dollar (Battambang), Tiara (Siem Reap), Ben (Kratie), Channy (Kompong Chhnang), Chork (Kompong Cham), Im Sokhom (Kompong Thom), Heit (Banlung) and others, who were without exception, patient and tenacious always making sure that I arrived safely even over difficult terrain; also to Sary and Mary for their dedication to horses in Siem Reap. To my editor, Ros Belford, for her support and inspiration. And, of course, to the people of Cambodia for their friendliness and unending cheerfulness. This Edition is dedicated to my cousin, Paula Brinkley (1965–2008) whose love of Cambodia and its people endures.

Charlie Would like to thank James Vervoort, Maggie Quinn, Mao Phhoung, Hun Chan Tha, Seang Sensary and Peter Foster for their input in during the research trip, making it as smooth and fantastic an experience as it possibly could have been; to Rong who became a trusted companion in the hot days spent exploring the environs of Phnom Penh; and finally to Ros the editor who, despite a catalogue of accidents and incidents, has remained ever-upbeat and a pleasure to work with.

Readers' letters

Thanks to all the readers who have taken the time to write in with comments and suggestions (and apologies if we've inadvertently omitted or misspelt anyone's name):

Ben Hanna , Brigitte Michalski , Petra Hoyer, Will Peskett, Allan and Margaret Rickmann, Katie Burrell. And the otherwise anonymous David.

Photo credits

All photos by Tim Draper © Rough Guides, except the following:

Introduction

p.1 Monks at Phnom Penh Independence Monument © John Miles/Getty

p.6 Buddhist worshippers praying at Wat Phnom © Pascal Deloche/Corbis

p.7 Woman collects sugar palm in a pan © Mak Remissa/epa/Corbis

p.8 Fishing boats on Ochheuteal Beach, Sihanoukville © imagebroker.net/SuperStock

Things not to miss

04 Sambor Prei Kuk, Prasat Yeai Pouen © A.A. Johnson/Photolibrary.com

05 Beach at Ream National Park © Imagebroker RF/Photolibrary.com

12 Tourists riding elephant at Bayon Temple, Angkor Thom © Jose Fuste Raga/Corbis

15 Kbal Chhay Waterfall near Sihanoukville © Nicholas Pitt/Alamy

19 Budddha from Tuol Ta Hoy, National Museum of Phnom Penh © Luca Tettoni/Corbis

20 Irrawaddy dolphin, Kratie province © Chor Sokunthea/X01072/Reuters/Corbis

Temple architecture colour section

Angkor Wat, stone sculpture at south gate, sunset © Chris Noble/Getty

Aerial view of Angkor Wat © Jose Fuste Raga/Corbis

Sunrise at Angkor Wat © Miles Ertman/Corbis

Festivals and ceremonies colour section

Cambodians celebrate the Khmer New Year © Mark Remissa/epa/Corbis

Prayers and offerings for Bonn Pchum Ben © Chor Sokunthea/X01072/Reuters/Corbis

Royal Ploughing Ceremony in Phnom Penh © Chor Sokunthea/X01072/Reuters/Corbis

Elderly woman with betel-stained lips, Angkor Wat © Nicole Newman

Index

Map entries are in colour.

T

U

V

W

Y

Z

INDEX

Map symbols

maps are listed in the full index using coloured text

International boundary
Provincial boundary
Chapter division boundary
Road
Unpaved road
Path
Railway
Ferry route
Waterway
Bridge
Peak
Mountains
Cave
Waterfall
International airport
Domestic airport
Transport stop
Point of interest
Border crossing
Mountain lodge
Ferry/boat stop

@ Internet access
Ruins
Gate/gopura
Statue
Monument
Information office
Telephone
Hospital
Post office
Fuel station
Pagoda
Khmer temple
Chinese pagoda
Church
Building
Market
Stadium
Park
Beach
Swamp/seasonally flooded area

o now we've told you about the things not to miss, the best places to stay, the top restaurants, the liveliest bars and the most spectacular sights, it only seems fair to tell you about the best travel insurance around

WorldNomads.com

keep travelling safely

Recommended by Rough Guides

www.roughguides.com
MAKE THE MOST OF YOUR TIME ON EARTH